LOVE AND REVOLUTION

LOVE AND

REVOLUTION

My Journey through an Epoch

MAX EASTMAN

RANDOM HOUSE   NEW YORK

The chapter entitled "With Trotsky in Prinkipo" was originally published
in Great Companions, Copyright © 1942, 1959 by Max Eastman and reprinted with permission of the publishers, Farrar, Straus and Company.
"I Didn't Raise My Boy To Be a Soldier," words by Alfred Bryan—music
by Al Piantadosi, Copyright © 1915; copyright renewal 1943, Leo Feist,
Inc., New York, New York. Used by permission copyright proprietor.
The poems on pp. xiii, 99, 131, 224, 282, 304, 485, 552, 579 were
originally published in Poems of Five Decades, by Max Eastman, Copyright © 1942, 1954 by Max Eastman. Reprinted by permission of
Harper & Row, Publishers.

Second Printing

Library of Congress Catalog Card Number: 62–12729

Contents

PART TWO
1922—1927

Contents

PART THREE

1927—1941

Contents

(*Note: Illustrations follow page 368*)

Foreword

This book is the continuation of a previous memoir which I called
Enjoyment of Living, and which carried my life story up to the eve of
the Russian revolution and of America's entrance into the First World
War. In order to make this book readable by itself, I have had to repeat a few things from the last pages of that one.

In writing of my early years, I tried so hard to tell the intimate
truth that a number of critics, and even some of my friends, thought I
was bruising or punishing myself. (The idea of a disciplinary relation
between an Ego and a Superego was in fashion among the Freudians
at the moment.) As a fact, my sole wish was to push aside such motives
altogether, and write about myself and my behavior with the same
rigorous effort of objectivity with which I have written about poetry
and art and laughter and Marxism, the communist police state, and a
good many other subjects. Selves are to me one of the most interesting
of subjects, and my own is the only self I have known with entire
intimacy. I hope those who have no interest in selves will realize that
this book is not written for them.

Peter Quennell said in a recent essay: "The writer who composes an
autobiography should be inspired by a burning devotion to the truth.
He must write because—regardless of personal pride, even of dignity
and social decency—he finds that he cannot resist the impulse. . . ."
For me devotion to the truth can hardly be described as "burning"—it is
too lifelong and detailed a passion for that—but otherwise this describes
in exact terms the effort I made in that book, and am making here.

In the process I have found modesty quite as hard to overcome as pride. A certain mood of defiance comes to your help when you have to tell how weak and foolish you were, or quote some distinguished critic who told the world your prose was turgid and your poems sentimental. But when you have done something of which you are proud, or have received such praise as I have once or twice from men who were highly esteemed, although it belongs just as vitally to an honest record of your life, it is *bad taste* to recall it. Perhaps that is what Quennell was thinking of when he mentioned "social decency" as one of the standards to be ignored in telling the truth about your life. You do have to say things that are in bad taste—things, sometimes, that propriety would confine to a Kinsey report.

I said so many of these Kinseyish Things in my previous memoir that often at night, when it was nearing completion, I would lie awake in a sweat through dread of its publication. What sustained me and kept my purpose firm I hardly know. It was not natural stubbornness or tenacity of will. I was never sure until it went to press that I would not remove the indiscreet passages from my book. Somehow I could not bring myself to gut the thing. For me it existed as a work of art in and by its resolute and reckless inward-looking truthfulness.

The effort in this book has not cost me quite so much. But I would like the reader to know that both pride and modesty have had to be pushed aside in setting down the truth about these twenty-three years of my life. Scott Fitzgerald wrote in one of his notebooks: "Max Eastman —like all people with a swaying walk, he seems to have some secret." I believe I am less burdened with secrets—at least I will be after I publish this book—than any other of Scott's friends. (But then also I don't have a swaying walk.)

I must ask the reader to remember that the word "revolution" as used in Part One does not mean the setting up of a one-party police state such as now exists in Russia. This outcome of the October revolution was not foreseen or dreamed of, by any of us on the old *Masses* and *Liberator*. If communism triumphs in America, it will certainly claim us as its forerunners, but the claim will be in a deep sense false. We were firm in the belief that "a seizure of power by the proletariat" would bring about "the enfranchisement of the proletariat and therewith all society," as Marx had promised. To us, in short, the word "revolution" still meant liberation. It meant an untrammeled, bold approach to the old utopian goal of all social rebels, a "Society of the Free and Equal."

Instead of a dedication, I will place here a poem I wrote long ago, but which will convey the mood in which I have undertaken this difficult task.

INVOCATION

Truth, be more precious to me than the eyes
Of happy love; burn hotter in my throat
Than passion; and possess me like my pride;
More sweet than freedom, more desired than joy,
More sacred than the serving of a friend.

PART ONE

1917–1922

Chapter 1

MY ACHIEVEMENT OF LOVE

I was happy as only the immortals are supposed to be in the years approaching our entrance into the First World War. So happy that I found solemnly written in a notebook of those days: "My life began in January 1917."

In order to make this understandable, I must give some little account of my early inhibitions. Although lucky in home and circumstance, I was a neurotic child. I was a prey to sleepwalking dreams and midnight fears, and was abnormally timid. My nightmares, frequently repeated, were visions of some undefined awfulness groping toward me, descending upon me, threatening to envelop me; in later years this awfulness assumed the form of a woman, still too undelineated to be called a hag, but dreadful in a softly implacable way. After these nightmares I would be found roaming the house, fast asleep with my eyes open. Even in the daytime I was morbidly—I would almost say, pathologically—shy. I suppose my grown-up boldness of opinion might be roughly described as an overcorrection of this clutching demon of self-consciousness that would jell my limbs and make me speechless in social situations. Combined with a rabidly puritanical upbringing, it so inhibited me in my physical relations with girls that I was deprived, in its proper season, of the joys of adolescence.

My marriage set me free belatedly in this respect, but it did not make me happy in spirit. The girl I married, Ida Rauh, was gifted and graceful, thoughtfully witty, ambitious of freedom, which a moderate income enabled her to enjoy, and very good to look at. But something in me having irresistible power rejected my commitment to her as soon as it became overt. That happens often, I tried to think, and told myself that a fruitful everyday companionship would hush it down or silence it. But our companionship was not fruitful. Through some accident of her temperament or mine, Ida damped in me the creative verve and zest for being by which I live. I delighted in her witty and intellectual charms, her rare dramatic and artistic talents. I enjoyed and admired her, but I was not enhanced by her love—not lifted up to myself and set forward on what I might become.

We were married in 1911, and in the spring and summer of 1916, while still living with her and our three-year-old son in a Greenwich Village apartment, I was seeking a feeling of my independent self in solitude. I had rented a separate room which I called my study, and was spending most of my energetic hours away from home.

Greenwich Village, I pause to say, was a visibly distinct region then, a region of low houses, transformed bakeries and livery stables, and streets that meandered around until they ran at times almost into themselves. It contained alleys; it contained nooks and crannies. Studios sat in back and you had to go through a tunnel under the street front to reach them. We were living in one of these in-back studios on Thirteenth Street just west of Seventh Avenue when my son Daniel was born. The diminutive red brick house in front was occupied by two charming and sophisticated old maids, Helen Marot, Ida's best friend, and Caroline Pratt, who founded the City and Country School. The cement-lined tunnel under their house was not wide enough to extend your elbows in, but there was room in the back yard for a game of catch, had there been anybody to play catch with.

My memory goes back to the time when people first began to talk of "the Village" and call themselves "Villagers." I never used the term, and I disliked it. I disliked group-consciousness of any kind. I disliked belonging. I still wanted to live as an individual and nowhere but in the universe. Moreover when I became a socialist, a fighter, supposedly, with the working class for a universal "Big Change," I was on principle opposed to the anarchist flavor in the cult of Bohemianism. I was conscious of this—rather priggishly conscious of it, I fear, for after all I *was* a Villager, I did live in the Village. I enjoyed its free-and-easy mode of life. It was, in fact, the mode of life that I hoped, when we got rid of classes and class rule, would become universal.

At the time I am writing of, when I was drifting from matrimony into what I called solitude, we had moved, Ida and I and the baby and the baby's nurse, into a third floor at 118 Waverly Place, just west of Washington Square. My "separate" study was a small partitioned-off piece of a dusty attic on West Tenth Street. To reach it, I had to walk along the stately north side of the Square, around Mrs. Philip

Lydig's handsome red brick mansion on the corner of Fifth Avenue—where, by the way, in a memorable moment I exchanged a few words with Sarah Bernhardt and looked into her tragically beautiful eyes—then three blocks along the tranquil south end of Fifth Avenue, with Mark Twain's house and the old black-brick Brevoort Hotel opposite.

Besides renting that separate nook on Tenth Street, I had in the same year, 1916, bought with my own money—and my father's—a tiny house and barn at the crest of Mount Airy Road in Croton-on-the-Hudson. The house had four small rooms, one of which I turned into a bathroom, and it had an uncovered porch from which you could look down through forest trees to the river. Beside the porch, and overarching it almost like a roof, was an Osage orange tree some twenty feet high, the only one I ever saw in our part of the world. I got Philip Schnell, Croton's good-natured carpenter, whose benignly keen smile was as satisfying as the work he did, to make me a long oak dining table, heavy enough to live the year round outdoors on that roofless porch. When weather permitted, the porch was the dining room, and the catbirds would come and eat butter out of the dish in front of us. Philip told me my house was the second oldest in Croton, and showed me how strangely it was built, with yellow clapboards outside and papered plaster walls inside, but between them a concealed solid wall of brick. For further isolation, I had him fix me up a little study in the barn. And below the Osage orange tree I carved out from my rough acre of sloping land an excellent tennis court—a little short for professionals, but with plenty of room for a hot game by first-class amateurs.

Ida would come up to Croton sometimes with the baby, and even helped me to plant things in the run-down flower beds, but she knew in her heart how deeply the whole thing was mine. My zeal for the tennis court told her that, for she had no interest whatever in play. In October of 1916 I was saying to my typewriter:

> The flowers we planted in the tender spring,
> And through the summer watched their blossoming,
> Died with our love in autumn's thoughtful weather,
> Died and dropped downward altogether.

I was spending more and more of my time there alone with that typewriter—and with a few neighbors (for Mount Airy Road was already assuming the traits of a rural Greenwich Village). My house had once been a cider mill and it backed up for the convenience of the apples straight into the road up the hill. "He was a friend to man, and he lived in a little house by the side of the road," I used to say, conceiving myself to be something very different from what I am. It was a romantic conception borrowed from a classic source; and that at least was characteristic. For I tend to elude the distinction between classic and romantic. To myself, at least, I seem to contain them both in a state of warring equilibrium.

During that year, I was very much overplaying the romantic. I was dwelling in dreams of young love as steadily as I had during my junior year in college. I was undergoing a second adolescence. I remember passing one day on Thirty-fourth Street a dark-eyed girl of the Leonardo type walking rapidly eastward, carrying over her head a gaily painted Japanese parasol. I was coming down Madison Avenue as she approached, and I stopped still because the unconventionality of the act pleased me, and because she was so beautiful. She was by far the most beautiful being I had ever seen—so I sincerely thought. And I turned mechanically as she passed and walked beside her, believing she must look up and give me a chance, or a genuine impulse, to say something. But she quickened her pace and kept her eyes down, and I dropped back. All that evening I was tormented with sadness because I had lost in a vast city the most beautiful girl I would ever have the luck to see.

In the same shy, baffled, boyish way I yearned over the beautiful girls I saw on the stage. For weeks I was in love with three, at least, of Isadora Duncan's pupils, but especially with Lisa, whose lithe golden beauty in motion was as perfect an embodiment of music in its lightly melodious forms as Isadora was of all music. Isadora and her five pupils dancing to a great orchestra combined art with nature, restraint with abandon, in the very proportions that bring me the feeling of perfection. But I cannot pretend that my emotion about the half-naked bodies of those girls, so simple in their little Greek tunics, so dedicated to nature that their hair hung free, their feet were bare, and their armpits unshaven, was what is called purely aesthetic. I was passionately desirous of them. I was sure, moreover, that with the opportunity to choose, I could find a true-love friend in one of them. Irma, Anna, Lisa—it would be one of those three, and probably Lisa.

But when I went one day to their studio and actually met them, I could not think of a thing to say. They spoke English imperfectly then, and Ida was there, and Mabel Dodge, who always embarrassed me, and a crowd of radicals—the antiwar party. I only murmured a word of congratulation to Lisa and passed on to the high priestess, toward whom my adoration was indeed purely aesthetic. That evening I was sad again with a sense of frustration. If I could only meet a girl like Lisa alone by accident, everything, I was very sure, would turn out well. But I did not possess even in this second and adult adolescence the audacity to scheme up such an accident, still less to go to the girl, propelled frankly by the principle of causation, and ask if we might have a cup of tea together, or even perhaps a drink.

So I would drop back from these obsessing dreams to the home life with Ida, and to my now surprisingly comfortable affection for our baby, as one returns to sobriety after a debauch. With a great muster of resolution, I would be "realistic"—until some new vision of nubile beauty would tempt and torment me back into the mood of romance.

The most startling of these visions appeared, without forewarning, at the *Masses* ball, which was held in Tammany Hall, of all places, on December 15, 1916. Fate, in preparing its path, made firm in Ida's heart a whimsical decision not to go. Those balls were gay and tumultuous affairs put on for money-raising purposes by our business manager. They were a reflection, within the frame of American morals, of the "Quat'z Arts" balls in Paris. All bars against "Greenwich Villageism" were let down and many curious visitors came from uptown to see them. Among the curious on this occasion was the popular novelist, John Fox, Jr., author of a wildly best seller, *The Trail of the Lonesome Pine*. He brought with him to the ball a young actress named Florence Deshon who had just won acclaim in the movies— playing the lead in a film version of *Jaffery*, a popular novel by William J. Locke. Here once again—and this time it was not just a romantic notion of mine but a general opinion—was as beautiful a girl as I would ever have the luck to see. Her hair and eyes were dark brown, her features keenly chiseled, her coloring rich yet delicate, and she wore the ghost of a pout. There was the merest suggestion of something wantonly sulky in her beauty.

We danced together while John Fox sat at a table sipping highballs and looking on in what I chose to regard as a fatherly manner. We talked fervently as we danced, and our minds flowed together like two streams from the same source rejoining. She was twenty-one, and was in exactly that state of obstreperous revolt against artificial limitations which I had expressed in my junior and senior essays at college. Even in my wish to transcend patriotism she outran me in our conversation, describing with happy laughter how she had almost caused a riot in a theater by refusing to stand up when they played "The Star-Spangled Banner."

"What do I care about a flag? I'm living in the world, not a country!" she exclaimed. And there was no zealotry in the exclamation, just a joyous overflowing of bounds.

I walked rather dizzily home in the dawn from that *Masses* ball. I went to sleep believing that I had miraculously found what all young men forever vainly dream of, the girl who is at once ravishingly beautiful and admirable to what lies deepest in their minds and spirits. At noon, when I awoke in my home, I realized that this could hardly be true. To prove it was not true, I remembered a certain unmanageable excess and impetuosity in her judgments which troubled what is classic in my nature. No one person could really fulfill the ideals of another. Besides, she was John Fox's girl, and here was I, the husband of a faithful wife, father and dutiful teller of bunny-rabbit stories to a three-year-old baby. I kept the telephone number she gave me and the address—111 East Thirty-fourth Street—where she lived with her mother. I kept them very carefully, but I lacked the force of character to use them. Shyness, the dread of disillusionment, the inhibiting weight of Ida's emotions, my sense of guilt—I could not make a habit of drifting away and then coming back to her—these things all held me in a tight circle which I called "reality." There was no place in it, obviously, for pure romance.

Nevertheless, it so happened that during that same month, for reasons unconnected with romance either in dream or reality, my home life became so filled with anger that on the day after Christmas I summoned the courage to walk out—just walk down the stairs and abandon married life, as I thought, forever. I gave up my study and moved with a small bundle of clothing into a room offered to me by my close friend, Eugen Boissevain, a vacant room in his apartment at 12 East Eighth Street. There I came down with a fever, a mixture of influenza with homesickness, which made my bare lonely room look for a time like the end of the world. But my convalescence was rapid, and I was soon brave enough to go up to Croton to my little house by the side of the road, and enter with classic reality into that lonely life as a friend-to-man which had been my romantic dream. I considered myself set free from love and dedicated to a hermit's life—with occasional interludes—for many years to come. I would marry my art, my science, my evangel of liberty. That would be enough.

Just out of fidelity, however, to an underlying dogma that life must be adventurously lived, I did, in a mood of Calvinistic self-discipline, push myself into a telephone booth and ring the number that Florence Deshon had given me a month before at the *Masses* ball. By that act, my dedication was disrupted, my romantic dream of a classic life exploded, the whole temper and tenor of my living changed.

Florence had, besides that mixture of the sculpturesque and wayward which made her beauty so startling, a richly melodious voice. Her laughter was a riotous tumble of jewelly tone qualities poured out like colors in a kaleidoscope. I don't know what she said, or I, but she filled the whole telephone booth, and filled me, with mirthful excitement. We agreed to meet for dinner the next day, and I came from the telephone in a state of credulous wonder. Could it be true then, after all, my midnight dream of finding a girl utterly beautiful, and yet possessing the qualities of mind and feeling I adore? Could the whole dance-elated invention have been true! Of that large proposition I was convinced by the tones of her voice in the telephone and her few words deftly and joyously spoken.

For journeys to Croton, I had bought a disintegrating Model T Ford car in which I could, with a noise like Gettysburg and a similar recklessness of human life, go forty miles an hour—almost as fast as a railroad train! It was not the vehicle in which John Fox would have called for a movie star, and I was arrogantly aware of that as I drove over to 111 East Thirty-fourth Street—past the corner where I had been turned around and pulled mutely along like an iron filing by the girl with the Japanese parasol. That girl had been a wish; this one was a reality, and I was on the way in my actual self to see her. Perhaps only those tormented as I am by an irrepressible romanticism combined with an obdurate allegiance to fact will understand what was happening to me. I was *believing* that reality might conceivably live up to a dream. I was facing it out with the Ascending Moon. I was giving nature a chance to be divine.

I pushed the bell believing, but when the buzzer gave a loud roar, my belief faltered and I went up the two tight little flights of stairs with businesslike steps. Florence herself opened the door. She had on a slim dress of heavy black silk that clung softly to her body. She wore no jewelry. Her incomparable colors and precisely carved features, and the lustrous dark waves natural to her hair, were beyond adorning. I drew a breath that I think was almost a gasp when I saw her, she was so startling in her beauty, and so simple.

She introduced me to a bright-eyed Hungarian mother, whom she called Caroline and treated more like a child than a mother. I made aimless conversation with Caroline, while Florence put on a hat and coat in an adjoining room. Then we went down the two flights of stairs together and climbed into my old Ford car, admiring its good points with a like laughter and wondering with a like mixture of whim and honest perplexity where it was going to take us.

There is no reason why I should recite these simple details of our coming together, except that their simplicity was a fact of importance to my emotions. Once again, and even more explicitly than at the *Masses* ball, we seemed to have poured from a common source. We seemed to be, underneath the thrill of our strangeness, surprisingly alike. She was not, at least, rich or poor, humbled by her social position or proud of it, and neither was I.

The old Ford took us across town to Mouquin's famous restaurant that stood opposite a dance hall called the Haymarket on Sixth Avenue at Twenty-ninth Street. The Haymarket was the sole place in New York where one could, without fear of police interference, make a date with a prostitute. This mysteriously unique fact made that street corner a little like Montmartre in Paris, and Mouquin's restaurant, although perfectly respectable, partook of the French atmosphere. It occupied an old-fashioned wooden clapboard house, dull yellow and rambling as no house in New York rambles any longer. You climbed the porch stairs to get in, and dined in any one of three or four once stately living rooms. It wasn't very expensive either—not too expensive for me to entertain Florence with a "Jack Rose" cocktail, a four-course French dinner, a bottle of wine, and enough brandy to keep us talking about ourselves, and finding out with continuing astonishment how much akin we were, for three or four hours. As though this miracle of impetuous communion, adjoined to her unutterable beauty, were not enough to unsettle all the points of my compass, luck had to add to it one last touch of divinely contrived romance.

She had been expressing petulantly, almost in the language of my college essay "O Mores!", her scorn of men's slavery to custom, and to illustrate their sheeplike conformity, she said:

"You can't do any little thing to please your own taste in this town without starting a riot. I once got a present of a little Japanese silk parasol. It was becoming to me, and I thought it would be fun to carry it. Do you know I never got farther than Fifth Avenue—I had to turn back home, it caused such a commotion!"

We could not part when the restaurant closed. I had told her about the house in Croton. It was waiting. And the car was waiting to take us there. We slept side-by-side in the corner bed by the big moonlit window, a very tranquil tenderness filling our hearts. Florence was extremely chaste and reticent in her instincts, and I was still diffident and unexpert in the art of unfamiliar love. But in this relation, too, which seemed to me the farthest that magic could reach, we were mysteriously not unfamiliar. The night gave to our bodily union the same instinctive simplicity, that quality of the destined, the awaited, which had marked the flowing together of our minds. The sense of having come from the same source, of finding ourselves in each other, the flame of "very ownness" burning in both our hearts, dissolved all the little problems of reticence and self-consciousness. In each of us, for the first time, the ideal rapture and the physical achievement of love were so blended as to be indistinguishable.

Chapter 2

MY SELF AND THE OLD MASSES

If the reader is more interested in love than politics—and I am far from disagreeing—I must ask his indulgence for a chapter or two, since I have set out to tell the whole story of my journey through an epoch of war and revolution. And I have to confess that I was passionately, not to say licentiously, addicted to revolutionary politics. I must first explain then, who and where, in a political sense, I was.

If there was anything in my childhood to account for my leaning toward revolution, it lay rather in the good than the bad luck of my birth. I grew up in a family where kindness and fair-dealing and sound logic prevailed to such a degree that, when I got out into the public world, it looked excessively unjust, irrational, a subject for indignation and extreme action.

My father and mother were both Congregational ministers. My mother was famous enough so that her name appeared in *Who's Who In America*, but her eloquence was attained without loss of what a fellow minister called "the fine flavor of womanliness." And she did not dominate my father, who was loved for his force and courage as well as his devotion to the parish in Elmira where they served as joint pastors. It was Mark Twain's wife's parish, and they shared between them the melancholy honor of officiating at the funerals of that great American and of his wife and his best-loved daughter.

My brother and sister were older and more robust than I; they seemed more *momentous* and saved me from thinking I was a big thing. My father, although dedicated to preaching the gospel, had a more instinctive passion for farming. The happiest day of his life was when his health broke down and he had to abandon the pulpit and get out on the soil. In consequence my boyhood was spent outdoors on a stock farm instead of indoors in a parsonage. My early life was benign, and but for the long summer days I had to spend cultivating corn or hoeing potatoes, I was free. I loved farm work; I loved all kinds of farm work. But I didn't like to do it. I preferred to watch other people do it. This caused a rather sharp difference between me and my father, but it all came right in the end. I persuaded him that I was a student—an ingenious name I invented for my disinclination toward physical labor —and he finally decided that my case was hopeless.

At Mercersburg Academy, which I entered in 1898, I really was a student—quite a fanatical one. The principal wrote my father that I had attained the highest marks ever on record in the school—a great help to me in the corn-hoeing argument. But I soon got over that infatuation, my greed to excel being extensive rather than intensive. I had shown in prep school what I could do in the scholarship line, and on reaching college I decided to abandon that and go in for "living life." This meant conviviality, drinking, dreaming, roaming the hills, swimming, diving, skiing, writing poetry, writing stories and essays, falling in love, taking a taste of Broadway, spending a summer bumming my way through the Wild West with a friend. It meant everything but poring over books. Not until my senior year, 1904–05, did I begin seriously to put Williams College to the use it was made for. In that year I managed to catch up with the Phi Beta Kappas, squeezing into this noble company at the very tail of the list, and I won prizes enough to pay my debts and get out of town without any very complicated trouble.

I began during the following year to take writing seriously—so seriously that I did not want to make it a profession. Instead of deciding to write for my living, I decided that I never would do that, and with negligible exceptions I stuck to that resolution for thirty-five years. My first ambitious essay, "Patriotism, A Primitive Ideal," published in the *International Journal of Ethics*, netted me twenty-five dollars. "The Ignominy of Being Good" in the *Atlantic*, and "The Poet's Mind" in the *North American Review*, were a little better rewarded financially, but not much. The big reward was an invitation from John Dewey to come up to Columbia and teach logic, or more exactly The Principles of Science, to a class of sophomores. I knew little or nothing about logic or the principles of science, and I honestly think Dewey was more interested in educating me than the sophomores. He had better success with this, at any rate, for while the sophomores came and went, I stayed on at Columbia four years, studying quite hard, and learning enough to pass the requirements for a Ph.D. in philosophy, with psychology and political science on the side. I did not take the degree because I do not like such ornaments, but I carefully preserved the paper which says I can have it any time I want to go up and get it. Again I was satisfied, so far as my vanity went, to show what I could do.

The remarkable and very American fact is that in all those years of study, which included James Harvey Robinson's famous course in The Intellectual History of Western Europe, I never once heard of the Marxian doctrine of class struggle. I learned about it after I left Columbia and was living in Greenwich Village, supporting myself as a lecturer on various subjects, mostly woman suffrage. My teacher about the class struggle was Ida Rauh, the girl I subsequently married.

"You don't think the people who own the earth are going to give it up voluntarily, do you?" she exclaimed. "That's utopian socialism. Marx's idea is that the working class, acting in its own economic interest, will take over the industries and socialize them. After that you'll have a society without classes, a real society, and real reform and education can begin."

She summarized it as clearly and forcefully as that.

"Ida, that's a perfectly wonderful idea!" I said.

"Of course! And it's an international idea too. The class division cuts across national boundaries and puts an end to patriotic wars. Marx would have been a great statesman if he had never thought of anything but the slogan: 'Workers of the world, unite!' "

That was a turning point in my mental life. From childhood I had despised valuations based on wealth, social position, race, color, caste, or class. I took very seriously the American ideals of freedom for all, justice and equal opportunity for all. They were axioms of my emotional nature. The Christian ideal of sympathy for all was an axiom. So was the Greek ideal of reason. Patriotism is unreasonable, as the Stoics observed. It is also a limitation of human sympathy. And my essay against patriotism revealed the reckless extremes to which such abstract ideals could carry me.

This need for extremism, a need to line up fiercely with the ideal against the real, seems natural enough. Indeed Nature, if anyone, is to blame. She should not have produced these highly sensitized nervous systems called human in a world so tough-grained, if she did not expect a certain proportion of them to show exaggerated reactions against the whole thing. In the past, religions have usually taken care of these reactions, but in our day religious beliefs are losing their hold. In my ministerial parents they were not continually firm. Even my maternal grandmother was plagued by moods of skepticism. "Filled with doubt and unbelief," she exclaimed in a letter to my mother. "I can only cry to God have mercy on me a sinner." In me, unbelief was a simple and tranquil state of mind which involved no rebellion and induced no pain. But I suppose the absence of any supernatural attachment was a cause, or a determining condition, of my devout zeal for pure, clear and unqualified ideals.

Together with this gravitation toward ideals, I was afflicted, so to speak, with an equally impetuous liking for hard facts. I was dubious about the extent to which my ideals would ever be realized. I distrusted evangelists, and had a high sales resistance against utopias. I used to look around in church on a Sunday morning when the too beautiful gospel of Jesus was being proclaimed. I would say over to myself the names and professions of the pillars of the church: Gridley the hardware dealer; Thompson who ran a big dry-goods store; Langdon the coal merchant; Bement of the lumber yards. Good men, all of them, the best in town. But how many hours, or rather minutes, of the week did any of them spend in carrying out the precepts of this beautiful gospel? What would be the ratio between those minutes and the hours they spent in a respectably egotistical pursuit of personal gain? Such thoughts held me back from any program of reform which rested upon education or evangelism. I could have replied as Mark Twain did when an Elmira nephew asked him what he thought about socialism: "I can't even hope for it. I know too much about human nature."

It was this clash of impetuosities, the thirst of extreme ideals and the argumentative clinging to facts, which led me to seize so joyfully upon Marx's idea of progress through class struggle. It was not a conversion, a dedication, a profound emotional experience such as Upton Sinclair and other socialists have described. There was no great change in my state of feeling. A suggestion that seemed practical had been proposed to my mind, that was all—a solution of the problem of how to move toward an ideally free and just society when human beings, by and large, are more interested in their own advancement than in freedom and justice. This man Marx seemed to offer a scheme for attaining the ideal based on the very facts which make it otherwise unattainable. Instead of trying to change human nature, I said to myself, he takes human nature as it is, and with that as a driving force tries to change the conditions that make it work badly. Far from glorying in a "conversion," I was loath even to call my new-found equilibrium socialism. I called it "hard-headed idealism." And to what I accepted of the Marxian philosophy I gave the name "matter-of-fact interpretation of history."

Just the same, I wanted to do something about it. I wanted to "make my contribution to the movement." Thus in the late August of 1912, when I received a communication scrawled with a paint brush on a

Drawn by Art Young

ART YOUNG, MAX EASTMAN
The Masses   April 1916

torn-off piece of drawing paper, "You are elected editor of *The Masses* —no pay," I was not indifferent to it. The *Masses* was a socialist magazine owned co-operatively by a group of artists and writers including John Sloan, Art Young, Maurice Becker, Louis Untermeyer, Mary Heaton Vorse, Ellis O. Jones and others. It was a "yellow" socialist paper, more interested in consumers' co-operatives than in the class struggle. But that was due to an editorial shepherd named Piet Vlag, who had run out of money and abandoned his little flock of collaborators some months before they sent me the above charming scrap of paper. They were inviting me to raise money and run the business as well as edit the magazine, and it was easy to infer, from the nature of artists and the climate of opinion then prevailing in Greenwich Village, that anyone who took on the job could change the editorial policy from "reformist" to "revolutionary" with a turn of the hand.

I have described in my earlier book the process by which I became involved in the position of editor, manager, money-raiser, and political policy guide, for that extraordinary magazine. It was a process of drift rather than decision, and was due to the amazing fertility, force, wit and imaginative daring of the group who gathered to produce it. Its pages still glow with the light of a dawning epoch of revolution. The times demanded that it be kept going, and I had not the strength to resist the times. I deceived myself that I could run the magazine with my left hand, or in the afternoons, while dedicating my mornings and my major energies to more permanent forms of literature.

Its producers, most of them well known then, and many subsequently famous, met monthly in various studios to read manuscripts and vote on pictures and drink beer and talk. They would talk all night long if necessary—about the next issue, about the defects of capitalist society and what the working class was going to do to it, about life and laughter and art. This naturally did not produce a magazine; the "co-operation" lay in the fact that they received no pay for their drawings and writings. But it produced a mood and a social situation which enabled Floyd Dell and me (Floyd was my superbly gifted associate editor) to bring out a magazine which drew a great deal of attention, pro and con, in the years leading up to the First World War. Sherwood Anderson remarked in one of his published letters:

> The "old *Masses*" was of tremendous significance to everybody when it appeared. It was bolder and freer than anything we had ever had. I can remember with what eagerness I used to watch for its appearance out in Chicago.

John Dos Passos wrote:

> The old *Masses* was the only magazine I ever had any use for.

George Santayana, on the other hand, sent me a deprecatory letter that I tried (not quite successfully, I remember) to dismiss as stodgy:

> I am not sure whether *The Masses* represents one of the classes —the most numerous—or rather a few independent and excep- tional individuals. In either case it would not represent the princi-

pal values which life in our times can possess. Consciousness must not quarrel with its instruments: and as its instruments in other ages have been religious or family institutions, so today they are nations and corporations and scientific bodies—and the press, too, no doubt: and if you cultivate ill will and bitterness—as you do— towards the best things that are possible for us in these times— gallantry, disillusion, courage to face the real world, and heartiness in enjoying what is to be enjoyed in it—you are wasting your only true opportunities. You are also closing your heart to the only sweet and voluminous human sympathies which you could have shared: you are spoiling life for others and for yourselves in the very ignorant and factious pursuit of some inopportune ideal. . . . I know as well as anyone what it is to tread the wine press alone: but why should a man who suffers from injustice be himself unjust? If you are incapable of loving what other people love, why should you hate it and hate them? It is an illusory revenge, by which nobody can gain anything.

Well, he did not understand the doctrine of progress through class struggle! We were cocksure enough to believe we could teach him about that. And if our cocksureness seems today less wise than his lack of understanding, please don't put it down to mere youthful folly. We were living in times innocent of world war, of fascism, nazism, so-vietism, the *Führerprinzip*, the totalitarian state. Nothing we were talking about had ever been tried. We thought of political democracy with its basic rights and freedoms as good things permanently secured. Planting ourselves on that firm basis, we proposed to climb higher through another struggle to industrial or "real" democracy. It was not vengeful hatred but scientific procedure!

The *Masses* was not ill-humored and bitter, it was lusty and gay. I doubt if socialism was ever advocated in a more life-affirming spirit. We did shock the American mores with some gloomy-grim and cruel writing, and with saber-toothed cartoons that set a new style in both art and satire. And we spoke our minds with unprecedented candor on both sex and religion. A communication from Paul H. Douglas, now a United States Senator but then a graduate student at Harvard, illustrates the recoil of many who favored our opinions but rejected our attitude to life. His letter printed in the *Masses* for November 1916 reads in part:

As one who thoroughly believes in the mission of the Socialist press, I wish to protest. . . . Like you, I believe the profit system to be vicious, but I do not see how the co-operative commonwealth is being furthered by the nastiness that you encourage.

Do not fall into the mistake of labeling as prudes all those who object to your methods. We are simply those who do not believe that the proper way to attract a man's attention is to pander to his passions. . . .

Even our natural ally, Bernard Shaw, saw fit to "sermonize" us against "putting things in just because they are heterodox" which we would not put in if they were orthodox. "In the last few numbers you were admitting vulgar and ignorant stuff just because it was blasphemous, and coarse and carnal work because it was scandalous. . . ."

I replied to him:

When we read the first page of your letter we imagined our correspondent as a very liberal Unitarian prelate who enjoyed shocking with his intelligence the good ladies of a New England congregation, and was a little jealous of our liberty to shock him. . . . We are perfectly naïve in our sophistication. We publish what we find excellent to our own tastes and moral judgment with a really pastoral unconcern about the opinionated public. . . . I know we never published anything that was vulgar or coarse *to our taste*, because we are not any of us vulgar or coarse. I don't say the same thing about your word carnal. . . . You ought to try to be a little more carnal. A brain like yours is almost as terrible, the way it burns up everything, as a medieval soul. . . .

To support us against these protests from the heartlands of puritanism, came a letter from Romain Rolland, in Paris, reading:

Liberty, lucidity, valor, humor, are rare virtues, still more rarely found in combination in these days of aberration. . . . They make the high value of *The Masses*. I congratulate you, and I congratulate your collaborators, both artists and writers, on the rude and good fight you are putting up.

We were coarse enough at least to play a role in creating what has been called the "Ash-can School" of art. Indeed George Bellows' revolting lithograph in the old *Masses* of two bums picking scraps out

of a refuse can was the *ne plus ultra* of that school. Stuart Davis'
picture of two drabs from Jersey City, for which John Sloan invented
the caption, "Gee Mag, think of us being on a magazine cover!"
epitomized its motivation. And besides being coarse, we were subtle
enough to introduce the one-line caption for which the *New Yorker*
commonly receives the credit.

Drawn by Robert Minor

"YOUR HONOR, THIS WOMAN GAVE BIRTH
TO A NAKED CHILD!"
The Masses   September 1915

"My dear, I'll be economically independent if I have to borrow
every cent!"

"Oh papa, that poor little birdie hasn't got any cage!"

"Your honor, this woman gave birth to a naked child!"

"Why a fella says to me only yistiddy, he says, 'This ain't war
it's murder.'"

That was our style in captions. And we were distinguished from all
magazines dedicated to an ideal by the fact that we did not perpetually

harp on it—or rather, bugle and drum and trombone on it—until only those fanatically committed could stand the noise. We talked of other things. And we weren't hating anybody or cultivating "ill will and bitterness!" You don't have to be a misanthrope to take vicious swipes at an old world when a bright new one sits firm in your hopes. I don't know how many of us really believed, or how firmly, in the Marxian paradise where the "wage system" would disappear, liberty and organization lie down together like the lion and the lamb, and everybody, not only the exploiting classes, enjoy the "best things that are possible to us." But that was the general idea. That gave us courage not only to face the real world, but to portray its evils in unmitigated colors, and lambaste it.

So far as editorials and political policy were concerned, there was no pretense at co-operation. These were entirely in my hands—too much so for my good, I think now, for I find my editorials less compact and more unconvincingly emotional than under adept criticism they might have become. Notwithstanding its supposedly scientific framework, there was plenty of romantic rapture in my revolutionism. It looked more like hurrah than hypothesis a good deal of the time. To be sure, I left the concept of revolution abstractly defined: the conquest of power by a new class. I did not envisage the overthrow of the United States Government, and both for the law and my conscience's sake, I avoided "advocating violence." There is violence now in the class struggle, I wrote, and the question how much more there will be depends largely on how many of the super-class idealists take the revolutionary side. A lot of them did take the revolutionary side as a result of our propaganda in the *Masses*. And although we had not a notion of that armed assault of the proletariat on the state and the pillars of society which extreme-left Marxists in Continental Europe projected, we went as far in that direction as any Anglo-Saxon organ of socialism had. We were, as Walt Whitman's Horace Traubel said, a "red paint signal post" on the road that led—how little we guessed—to the Russian Bolshevik Revolution.

Chapter 3

STOPPING A WORLD WAR

Like all my radical friends, I had mistaken for final reality the comparative paradise that prevailed in America at the turn of the century. Notwithstanding Ludlow Massacres and bomb warfare in the structural steel industry, it was a protected little historic moment of peace and progress we grew up in. We were children reared in a kindergarten, and now the real thing was coming. History was resuming its bloody course.

Europe's plunge into war did not immediately make this felt in America; the awful truth was slow to sink home. To us of the *Masses* it was little but a confirming footnote. "We told you Capitalism was rotten, and now you see for yourself," was our first reaction. As the year 1916 elapsed, however, antiwar and antimilitarism took increasing precedence among the things we stood for in the *Masses*. Our "Preparedness Number" featured an article by John Reed, "At the Throat of the Republic," attacking Colonel Roosevelt and Elihu Root—and incidentally Assistant Secretary of the Navy Franklin Roosevelt—as "unscrupulous patriots."

"The country is rapidly being scared into an heroic mood," he wrote. "The workingman will do well to realise that his enemy is not Germany, nor Japan; his enemy is that 2% of the people of the United States who own 60% of the national wealth, and are now planning to make a soldier out of him to defend their loot. We advocate that the workingman prepare himself against that enemy. This is our Preparedness."

It was a kind of preparedness that would lead us into a big fight before we got through, but John Reed as a pacifist was only too eager for a fight. He was a big man with jovial animosities and powerful muscles. He picked up our safe one day in the little office over on

Greenwich Avenue, and put it down outside on the sidewalk, "just to give you boys something to do." We had to call the Fire Department to get it back. I remember his presence as a rather unsettling phenomenon. He had a habit of looking away when he was talking to you, not looking in any particular direction but everywhere, as though he were afraid he might miss something. You couldn't get away from him, the office was too small and he was too big and too loaded with energetic ideas. But also, somehow—this at least was my experience—you couldn't get *at* him. He was a little abstract, or abstracted, or impetuously just *passing through*, like a storm or an earthquake. I described him in an essay-portrait as having a face like a potato, and Alfred Rosmer, the French syndicalist who knew him in Moscow, while remarking on the exact truth of this description, added that Jack's aspect was at the same time noble and inspiring. On this paradox we agreed completely.

Milk-blooded people with a near-sighted morality, consisting principally of fear and decorum, when they see a young man so full of power and poetry that he sets out really to live, are apt to call him "wild" and "crazy" and "irresponsible." That is the way they talked about Reed when he left Harvard, but he refuted them abundantly. Starting off with brilliant perceptions and phrases in his head like the colors of burning driftwood, he gradually added to these native and so often misleading gifts the habit of verification and industrious understanding. He did not live, alas, to reap all the fruits of that understanding.

Another "wild" man in that Preparedness number was the fighting Irishman, Jim Larkin, a syndicalist rebel with big shoulders, a big nose and a black forelock, unhappy unless he was being arrested, or threatened with arrest, for advising the workers to prepare themselves with rifles for the General Strike. His contribution sang praises to James Connolly and the premature Irish rebellion: "the most glorious thing that has happened during this carnival of blood-lust in Europe." Our views on Preparedness were further expressed by Cornelia Barns with a drawing illustrating the news item: "An alarmed patriotess has appealed to the Boston auxiliary of the National Security League to register automobiles for the purpose of carrying the virgins inland in case of invasion." Some of the virgins were making frantic efforts to fall off the vehicle. Cornelia possessed an instinct for the comic in pictorial art that few American artists have ever surpassed. She was a gentle brown-eyed girl with soft hair sleeked down around a comely and quiet face. She had no ambition or aggression in her nature, and came through the open door of the *Masses* like a child into a playroom, moved only by her liking for what she saw there. When its door closed she disappeared from fame as quietly as she had entered upon it—I don't know why.

A more historic contributor to that Preparedness number was Boardman Robinson, then and perhaps permanently regarded as one of America's great artists. "His masterly drawings had the breathlike delicacy as well as the power of the old Masters," in the judgment of a fellow artist, Reginald Marsh. Surprising as it may seem, he actually introduced into America the idea, as old as Daumier, that cartoons should have the values of art as well as of meaning. He was a big, burly, bluff, sea-captain sort of a character, with dancing blue eyes under bushy red brows, a red beard, and a boisterous way of "blowing in" as though out of a storm, instead of merely entering, a place of habitation. Inside his big ulsterlike personality, the lines of his character were finely drawn: he was delicate, chivalrous, touchy, and romantic. His genius lay in the uniqueness of his vision of reality and the power with which he reproduced its special properties. Everybody called him Mike, and I guess it must have been in memory of Michelangelo, whose fury and rapture his powerful and meaningful drawings did recall. When Mike blew in with a picture of a white-clad, saintly Jesus standing against a stone wall facing the rifles of a brutish firing squad—"The Deserter"—I felt that our Preparedness number deserved a place in the history of art.* To finish it off, Robert Minor drew for the back cover a prodigiously muscular but headless giant bared for the Army Examiner: "At last a perfect soldier!" In an editorial, I spoke as though ready to barricade my house and shoot it out with the State of New York if Governor Whitman's proposal to draft men into the National Guard were adopted.

The passion against war is almost as rabid as the military passion; it gangs men up and stampedes their minds in a similar way. I belonged heart and soul to the antiwar party; I was a swashbuckler in the cause of peace. It seemed to me that all I loved in my country, all that I thought of as "American," would be lost if the spirit of militarism got a foot-

* In the book of Mike's life and drawings composed by Albert Christ-Janer and published by the University of Chicago Press, it is stated that the finest examples of the mature phase of his drawings are to be found in the *Masses* and the *Liberator*, but only one or two of the most "innocuous" of these drawings are reproduced. His mighty assault on the evils and hypocrisies of war, and of what we called Capitalism, are only to be found in the bound volumes of these magazines.

hold on these shores. I was fighting off an invader—giving no quarter, taking no prisoners.

This fervor against war not only pushed aside, but somewhat toned down our proletarian revolutionism, or mixed it in a rather opaque

Drawn by Robert Minor

ARMY MEDICAL EXAMINER: "AT LAST A PERFECT SOLDIER!"
The Masses   July 1916

solution with "bourgeois pacifism." A two-months' visit to Europe in 1915 had a sobering effect upon me especially. I realized that war, from being an exploit in glory, had become a mere business of slaughter, dull as well as dreadful. I said this in an editorial entitled, "The Uninteresting War," and attempted to express in a poem my horror of its violation of life's values.

Since our first issue I had flown a banner over my editorial page reading "Knowledge and Revolution." By "revolution," I explained, I did not mean anything "necessarily attended with bloodshed," but in the same breath I likened my slogan to one from Mazzini: "Insurrection and education to be adopted simultaneously." This equivocation had always bothered me a little, and on my return from Europe I hauled down that very red banner. At least I hauled down the noun and ran up the adjective. "Revolutionary Progress" was my slogan now, and I explained that it meant any measure which narrows the gulf between the owning and the working class. This ruled out the Progressives, who never proposed a redistribution of wealth, yet allowed me to insist more vigorously than the "yellow socialists" did on class pressure as the instrument of democratic progress. But it marked a reining-in of my literary sky-horses, a climbing down toward myself in the real world. I was calling to mind now the mangled bodies and manic hatreds implied by that lyric word *violence*, so dear to humdrum petty-bourgeois dreamers like Georges Sorel—so little different on the tongue from *violets*.

A similar thing happened, I think, to a good many American socialists. The reality of armed conflict in Europe dampened the proletarian-revolutionary part of their credo, and stepped up to a high pitch the antimilitary part. Even Bill Haywood and the hard-fisted rebels of the IWW were more interested in keeping the American capitalists out of the war than in overthrowing them. I was theoretical enough to remark in an editorial that I was not against all war, but only this particular one: "It was, and is, altogether possible that a situation should arise in which a national war must be fought to a finish for the liberation of the world." But this did not prevent me from collaborating with Boardman Robinson and George Bellows and Art Young in thinking up Christian pacifist cartoons, or from joining a forlorn little group of peace-lovers in a last-minute effort to stop the war with paid advertising.

My sister Crystal was the initiator and magnetizing director of that effort. She was beautiful and socially disarming, and yet inwardly a "mighty girl," as we named her in the bosom of the family. She was mighty enough, it now seems, to have played perhaps a critical role in shaping the course of North American history. For she organized and directed—and in fact to all intents and purposes, she *was*—The American Union Against Militarism. And the historian, Arthur S. Link, in his *Woodrow Wilson and the Progressive Era*, gives that organization credit for deterring Wilson from his irate determination, in June 1916, to take steps that "would have meant a war that would

THIS man subjected himself to imprisonment and probably to being shot or hanged

THE prisoner used language tending to discourage men from enlisting in the United States Army

IT is proven and indeed admitted that among his incendiary statements were—

THOU shalt not kill

and

BLESSED are the peacemakers

Drawn by George Bellows   *The Masses*   July 1917

end only in the occupation of every square mile of Mexico by American soldiers!" A clash between Mexican forces and an American detachment at Carrizal which resulted in the death of twelve Americans and the capture of twenty-three, had been reported to General Pershing and to Wilson as a treacherous ambush on the part of the Mexicans. An American Captain Morey told the truth, which was that the American detachment had charged the Mexican troops, believing they would run away, and they instead had fought gallantly with fatal results on both sides.

Says Arthur Link:

Captain Morey's report, which proved that the Americans had been the aggressors at Carrizal, was published in the newspapers on June 26. It was taken up by the American Union Against Militarism, a pacifist organization, which printed it and a fervent plea against war, in full-page advertisements in all the metropolitan newspapers. As a result, Wilson was immediately overwhelmed with a flood of telegrams, letters, petitions; and from the replies he made to the appeals for peace, it is evident that he was shaken and deeply moved. Not slowly, but almost at once, good sense returned to official circles in Washington.

I quote this, not only as a tribute to my sister, but to make a little less fantastic her effort, by similar means, to stop Woodrow Wilson from going to war against Germany. She had got together a considerable sum of antiwar money from rich members of her American Union, but there was not time now to put the whole organization behind each step to be taken. Somebody must raise a cry every few days, and for this purpose she formed a little publicity battalion to which I belonged.

A press clipping dated February 6, 1917, reads:

Amos R. E. Pinchot, Randolph S. Bourne, Max Eastman, Paul U. Kellogg, and Winthrop D. Lane, independently of any organization, have opened at 70 Fifth Avenue an emergency office, and have asked all persons who believe, as they do, that the United States should not be forced into war, to join the movement to prevent this.

Randolph Bourne was the most stalwart of these publicists, a hunchback with twisted face and ears, a bulblike body on spindly legs, and yet hands with which he could play Brahms melodies on the piano with such delicacy as brought tears both of joy and pity to one's eyes. He had a powerful mind, philosophic erudition, a commanding prose style, and the courage of a giant. As a member of the staff of *Seven Arts* magazine, he stood against the war hysteria with sound and strong arguments, implacably, and to his own social and financial ruin. Paul Kellogg was a leader among social workers, editor of *Charities and the Commons*, which became, still under his editorship, the *Survey*, and then the *Survey Graphic*. He was a devoted friend of Crystal's, pale-skinned and with a kindly twisted smile that chimed with the mood of our meetings. For we all knew well enough how feeble we were. Winthrop D. Lane was known too, though not so well known, among social workers—a criminologist by profession. Amos Pinchot (my very dear friend and financial supervisor on the business end of the *Masses*) gave the prestige of an old American name to our little group. Its triple-column fourteen-point manifestoes "To the people of Chicago," "To the people of New York," "To the people of . . ." everywhere that Crystal's fund could reach, sounds pathetically intelligent now.

> The President and Congress ought to use every expedient of diplomacy and economic pressure to bring the belligerents into conference. . . . Our glory and our virtue lie in our having with independent and magnanimous courage, withheld our hand from the quarrel of the world, and stood firmly for the ideals of friendship and civilized understanding. . . .
>
> Petition your President and your Congressmen to employ every resource of intelligence and resolution and patience, and all the time they may require. . . .

We were trying to stem Niagara with a placard, but there was sense in what was printed on it. In 1937 George Gallup took a nation-wide poll on the question: "Do you think it was a mistake for the United States to enter the [First] World War?" Seventy percent of those questioned voted *yes*. I agreed with them then, and though I supported our entrance into the Second World War, I have never changed my mind about the First.

I spoke my mind fully at a giant mass meeting in Detroit three days before we entered the war. The meeting was organized by Kathleen Hendrie, a wealthy woman whose husband, George T. Hendrie, although more interested in horses than social reform, backed her with unflinching affection in every unpopular cause she took up. Beautiful and animated, with intelligent laughter in warm brown eyes, she was a cherishing mother of progress in many fields, and had regarded me as an ally ever since the days of my speeches on woman suffrage. It would be hard to exaggerate the size and success of that meeting. An immense hall was jammed with people and I was saying what they all wanted to hear—what far more than half the nation, in my opinion, wanted to hear. To quote the *Detroit News*:

> Men and women thronged the stairway and the corridor and even the sidewalk outside, thrilling with what intoxication could be derived from the cheering. The program was a succession of applause punctuated with intellectual inserts by Mr. Eastman.

My final "insert" was this:

> You ought to prevent the declaration of this war if you possibly can, and if you can't you ought to stay out of it and save your strength to renew the sad struggle for liberty when it ends.

As those words indicate, I was steering under full sail into a storm. In proportion, as Wilson's wrath against Germany boiled up, and the war threat spread out like a steam cloud from the White House, our magazine became again more revolutionary than pacifist—or rather its pacifism became revolutionary. As early as January 1917, I voiced a sentiment which, although I had never heard of Lenin, foretold that I would not be repelled by his extreme formula: "Turn the imperialist war into a civil war!"

> We are not advocates of violence, but as between two current misfortunes, we much prefer domestic to international violence. For in domestic violence it usually happens that some definite benefit is being fought for, and not infrequently the fighting holds a possibility of gaining the benefit; whereas in international wars the fighting usually arises at the bidding of blind tribal instincts, wholly maladjusted to the present real world, and even where concrete ends are aimed at, they are habitually lost in a welter of patriotic emotions before the war ends.

Although so guarded about violence, there was enough dynamite in that sentiment, uttered only three months before we entered the war, to keep me busy for two years trying to stay out of jail.

Chapter 4

HEAD-ON AGAINST WAR AND AGAINST WILSON

My relation to Woodrow Wilson and his policies differed widely from that of the orthodox socialists. To me socialism was never a philosophy of life, much less a religion, but an experiment that ought to be tried. I poked fun at the Marxian idea that a proletarian revolution is inevitable, and waged war on those who thought it would solve all social problems if it came. I dismissed Marx's philosophic system as "a rationalization of his wish," and declared: "We must alter and remodel what he wrote, and make of it, and of what else our recent science offers, a doctrine that shall clearly have the nature of hypothesis." *

I doubt if anybody outside my family noticed this formidable pronouncement, and I cannot pretend that it controlled my emotions or tempered my speech as an agitator. I developed, in spite of it, an art of making wild statements in a cool scholarly manner that was successfully inflammatory. But it did enable me to back up with intellectual self-confidence that pluralistic and practical view of the problems of society which European Marxists regard as naïvely American, but which is in reality more adult than their total immersion in a politically motivated philosophy of the universe.

One of my heretical opinions concerned the subject of war and peace. According to the socialist scripture, wars were caused by capitalist rivalries and would cease when the workers of the world overthrew capitalism. I judged that wars were due primarily to the bellicose and herd instincts of the human animal, and would cease only when the herds were merged in a world-wide federation. More than that, I agreed with Norman Angell that modern war had become bad business, and inferred from this that such a federation would probably be formed by

* The *Masses*, September 1916.

the capitalists before we got around to our proletarian revolution. This put me in a special relation to Woodrow Wilson and his policies which had important consequences in my life.

I had had a friendly relation with Wilson dating back to 1912, when we addressed together a banquet of the Chamber of Commerce in Syracuse, New York. We sat side by side through an eight-course dinner and talked searchingly about everything under the sun, starting with woman suffrage. Knowing that I had spoken in favor of it, he asked me earnestly and with a flattering deference for "instruction" on the subject. His own contribution was the familiar question: "In demanding their rights, aren't women proposing to neglect their duties?" I reminded him that this had been said, and always would be, of any group who demanded their rights, and with that start made him quite a speech. I pride myself that our conversation led him some way along toward his belated decision to support the Nineteenth Amendment. It led at any rate to a friendly feeling between us, which survived until the summer of 1916 when I turned up at the White House with a group of liberals protesting against increased military appropriations. Recalling our conversation at the banquet, Wilson greeted me with special warmth. He was not impressed by our arguments, but impressed us rather with his gift of suave and perfect diction—I can hardly call it eloquence—and almost embarrassed us with his outspokenness. I can still see him holding out his fingers as though clinging to a handful of sand, and saying: "You cannot do anything with these Latin Americans, they slip right through your fingers." He called us "we," and imparted to us his private and exciting plan to stay out of the war in Europe until both sides were exhausted and then step in with a proposal of peace and an association of nations to prevent future wars. This was a radical proposal in those days and fell in pat with my own anti-Marxist views on the war problem. For that reason—much to the disgust of the dogmatic pundits of the Socialist Party—I spoke up for Wilson in the November elections. Neither his personality, which seemed a little off-on-a-mountain to me, nor the slogan "He kept us out of war," would have swerved me that far from my "revolutionary" course. But that he had a plan—the very plan I had been advocating—for ending war altogether, swung me strongly to his side. When in January 1917, he made his famous "peace without victory" speech, I was enraptured.

"The histories of all the nations will hold a venerated record of that address," I wrote in the *Masses*. "Peace without victory, and the

United States not involved in the quarrel, but standing with all her impartial power for international union—that is the highest hope and purpose for us and for the world."

Three months later Wilson threw the whole thing over, and entered the fight, heart, soul and ideology, on the side of the Allies. To us of the antiwar party this looked treacherous and capricious, and his biographers still wrestle over the causes of it. We did not know that the slogan "He kept us out of war" had been launched by his campaign managers, and that he had tried to call it back.* But even if we had, the change from *Peace Without Victory and a League of Nations* to *War for Democracy and No Mention of Peace Terms*, was too much for us. It shattered the pattern of perception with which we were making a hero of Wilson, or reshuffled it with all his weak points in the focus.

In an editorial on his speech of April 2, 1917, demanding the declaration of war against Germany, I paid an ironical tribute to his "talent for mobilizing noble ideas in behalf of whatever he has decided to do." His speech began, I pointed out, by citing the *defense of our national rights* as both cause and justification of our entering the war, but ended, with serene indifference to logic, by representing us as having joined a *crusade for democracy*. I asked that this seeking out of "ideological forms" under which we were to fight be replaced by a concrete statement of the purposes for which we were fighting. I recalled the President's statement three months before: "The singularity of the present war is that its origin and objects have never been disclosed. They have obscure European roots which we do not know how to trace." And I asked him, before conscripting American citizens to fight in a war whose roots are unknown and objects undisclosed, to state at least what his own objects were. This still seems to me a valid criticism of Wilson's character and his course—a criticism amazingly

* The incident is described by George Creel, Wilson's Director of Information, in his autobiography, *Rebel at Large*, p. 155. Creel's testimony is supplemented by Gilson Gardner's account of the "Sunrise Conference" in the spring of 1916 at which Wilson tried to persuade the Speaker of the House, the Democratic Floor Leader, and the Chairman of the House Foreign Affairs Committee that the time had come for the United States to get into the war. These revelations suggest that the President was more war-minded throughout the whole period in question than he allowed his pacifist friends to believe. Gardner's story appeared in *McNaught's Magazine*, was reprinted by Harry Elmer Barnes in *The Genesis of the World War*, and retold by Gardner in *Lusty Scripps*, pp. 194–96.

reinforced by the disclosure in Colonel House's memoirs that the President never learned of the secret treaties signed by his allies until he arrived in Paris to attend the peace conference.

The *Masses* was not alone, of course, in attacking Wilson's war policy. We had the whole Socialist Party and the IWW with us, the pacifists, many of the humanitarian uplifters, most of the Quakers and deep-feeling Christian ministers, the Irish, the "hyphenated Americans," the old-fashioned patriots still faithful to George Washington's Farewell Address, and millions of plain folks whose hearts were in it when they sang a song that swept the country in those days:

> I didn't raise my boy to be a soldier,
> I brought him up to be my pride and joy. . . .

Better for us, if we *had* been alone in opposing the war policy. For this immense opposition, this nation-wide conflict of passionate opinion, created a state of mind in which laws were unable to protect the liberties or lives of the citizens. In nations as well as individuals, hysteria is caused by inner conflict, and the United States on entering the First World War suffered a violent attack of this disease. No other such event in our history is comparable to the nation-wide witch hunt of those mad days.

In spite of a ruling by the Attorney General that "the constitutional right of free speech, free assembly, and petition exist in wartime as in peacetime," nearly two thousand men and women were jailed for their opinions during the First World War, their sentences running as high as thirty years. The Espionage Act, signed by Wilson one month after our entrance into the war, although it contained no press censorship clause, and was ostensibly designed to protect the nation against foreign agents, established three new crimes which made it dangerous to criticize the war policy and impossible to voice the faintest objection to conscription. A subsequent amendment known as the Sedition Act, defined as seditious, and made punishable, all disloyal language and attacks on the government, the army, the navy, or the cause of the United States in the war. Under this act it became a crime to write a "disloyal" letter, or an antiwar article which might reach a training camp, or express antiwar sentiments to an audience which included men of draft age, or where the expression might be heard by shipbuilders or munition-makers. Postmaster General Burleson suppressed an issue of the *Nation* because it criticized the labor leader Samuel Gompers; he barred other periodicals for attacking the British

Empire, for stating that French culture was materialistic, and for reprinting Jefferson's opinion that Ireland should be a republic. A movie producer got a ten-year jail sentence for producing a picture called *The Spirit of '76*, which dealt exclusively with the Revolutionary War, but showed scenes unflattering to the British army. Rose Pastor Stokes was sentenced to ten years in the penitentiary for stating in a letter to a newspaper editor: "I am for the people and the government is for the profiteers." A man named Wallace was sentenced to twenty years for saying that "when a soldier went away he was a hero and when he came back he was a bum." D. T. Blodgett got the same sentence for circulating a pamphlet urging the voters of Iowa not to re-elect a congressman who had voted for conscription. Twenty-seven South Dakota farmers were convicted for sending a petition to the governor objecting to the draft quota for their county and calling the war a capitalists' war. It became a crime to advocate heavier taxation instead of bond issues, to criticize the Allies, to say that a referendum should have preceded the war, or hold that war was contrary to Christ's teaching. German music was banned, German editors and orchestra leaders were mobbed, German fried potatoes were swept from the table or renamed. A rabid organization of private citizens named The American Protective League acted as an auxiliary of the Department of Justice. Its membership and that of similar organizations ran into the hundreds of thousands. One such organization carried a full-page advertisement in newspapers from coast to coast, guaranteeing to make every man a spy-hunter on payment of a fee of one dollar.

This elemental hysteria was whipped up by public officials and prominent citizens as well as the press. The country was advised to mob, whip, shoot and kill all dissenters. An ex-governor of Maryland offered his services to the Baltimore police to prevent the famous German director, Karl Muck, from conducting a symphony in that city: "I would gladly lead the mob to prevent this insult to my country and my flag," he cried. A well-known New York clergyman declared publicly: "I would hang everyone who lifts his voice against America entering the war."

The Reverend Herbert S. Bigelow, a noted liberal preacher of Toledo, who spoke *for* the war but *against* hating the Germans, was kidnapped and horsewhipped "in the name of the women and children of Belgium." My friend Fred Boyd was beaten up in Rector's restaurant in New York City for not standing up when the national anthem was played. Women in charge of the Emergency Peace Federation headquarters in Washington were ordered by militiamen to close the office and "beat it" or they would be "raided and raped." Six farmers in Texas were horsewhipped because they would not subscribe to the Red Cross. Gus Lindin, a Socialist of Duluth, was tarred and feathered by the "Knights of Liberty." Elmer White of Yerington, Nevada, was beaten with an iron cat-o'-nine-tails for alleged disloyal remarks. George Maynard of Medford, Oregon, a member of the International Bible Students' Association, had an iron cross painted on his chest and was driven out of town. Robert Prager, accused of pro-Germanism, was lynched in Collinsville, Illinois; the mob leaders were tried and acquitted. Meetings of the People's Council, the Socialist Party, the IWW, the Nonpartisan League, the International Bible Students' Association, were attacked and broken up by mobs from one end of the country to the other. Out of an estimated forty-five hundred to five thousand persons prosecuted in cases involving freedom of speech, press or assemblage, not one was proved to be a spy, or to be acting for a foreign government.*

The cause of all this was, in my opinion, that the majority of the population was opposed to our entering the war. They had to be dragged or dragooned in. Even the editors of the *New Republic*, ecstatically pro-war, admitted that the war policy had been imposed by a minority whom they called "the intellectuals" upon "a reluctant or unwilling majority." In the light of these facts, Wilson's bland announcement that his so-called "selective draft" was "in no sense a conscription of the unwilling, but selection from a nation that had volunteered in mass," struck me as adding insolence to injury. Of all infringements of the rights won by Anglo-Saxon common men in their great history, military conscription then seemed to me the most ominous. It changed the whole form and aspect of American life, and made the freedoms I was hoping for almost unthinkable.

"For my part," I wrote, "I do not recognize the right of a government to draft me to a war whose purpose I do not believe in. But to draft me to a war whose purposes it will not so much as communicate to my ear seems an act of tyranny discordant with the memory even of the decent kings."

---

* I have refreshed my memory of these facts from paragraphs in the old *Masses*, from Lucille B. Milner's article "Freedom of Speech in Wartime" in the *New Republic*, November 25, 1940, and from Dwight Macdonald's profile of Roger Baldwin in the *New Yorker*, July 11, 1953. For accuracy's sake I have adopted certain important sentences from these articles verbatim.

Nor was I content to make this declaration on my own account. I wanted others to make it, and I said so without thought of discretion.

We wish to persuade those who love liberty and democracy enough to give their energy or their money or their lives for it, to withhold the gift from this war, and save it to use in the sad renewal of the real struggle for liberty that will come after it. We want them to resist the war-fever and the patriotic delirium, the sentimental vanity, the sentimental hatred, the solemn hypocrisies of idealists, resist the ceremonious installations of petty tyranny in every department of our lives, resist conscription if they have the courage, and at whatever cost to their social complacence *save themselves* for a struggle of human liberty against oppression that will *be* what it says it is.

These defiances were reinforced in our June and July numbers with two antiwar cartoons by Boardman Robinson: a picture of Uncle Sam in chains and handcuffs, "All ready to fight for liberty," and one of Jesus Christ being dragged in on a rope by an idiotic recruiting officer named Billy Sunday: "I got him! He's plumb dippy over going to war!"

George Bellows contributed another Jesus, in stripes now, with ball and chain and a crown of thorns: "The prisoner used language tending to discourage men from enlisting in the United States army: 'Thou shalt not kill—Blessed are the peacemakers.' "

A "Heavenly Discourse" by Charles Erskine Scott Wood ridiculed both the war and the Christian theology. A review by Floyd Dell of Trotter's *The Instincts of the Herd in Peace and War* pointed up these irreverences. A message from Bertrand Russell, in jail in England for conscientious objection, urged others to be as loyal to themselves. An editorial in the June number endorsed the cry of the Socialist Party in its St. Louis platform: "We brand the declaration of war by our government as a crime against the people of the United States and against the nations of the world." John Reed contributed antiwar blasts, including an announcement of our solidarity with the "council of Workingmen's and Soldiers' Delegates" in Petrograd. My contributions totaled six pages, an all-time high for me as an editor. It was a number to rejoice the heart of both pacifists and revolutionists, and even wrung a cry of praise from the old wheel horse of the Socialist Party's officialdom, Algernon Lee: "I don't believe there has ever been a number of any magazine in America that could equal this."

We were heading upstream in a stampede, and ought to have

realized it, for that book of Trotter's explained how feebly reason functions when gregarious animals like man go on the rampage. My whole argument for international union had been based on that instinct psychology. But we were full of our political opinions and our "constitutional rights," not realizing that laws are little stronger than grass blades in such a stampede.

Chapter 5

AGAIN ABOUT LOVE

I must here explain that I am a very scattered person. Although ardently enlisted in the antiwar campaign, I was far from focused on it. My life was brimful and running over with other things to dwell on and do. Besides continuously editing a magazine, I was intermittently writing poems—twenty out of the thirty-odd written during this period I subsequently thought worth preserving. I was preparing for publication a volume of poems already written, with a study of the contrast between Poe and Walt Whitman by way of preface. I was earning half of my living lecturing. And I was at work on what I then regarded as the prime ambition of my life, to offer a scientific explanation of humor, and have the humor there to be enjoyed as well as understood.

All these things I was doing, or trying to do, at once. And at the same time I was plunging into the turbulent currents of a first love. I must have begun actual writing on *The Sense of Humor* just when I was falling in love with Florence, for I adorned the first chapter with a miserably unsuccessful attempt to describe her laughter. I tried it again just now and failed. It must suffice to say that I never in my life saw and heard anything more beautiful, more joy-conveying, than Florence when she laughed. I was of course diabolically jealous, and tried with half-hearted nobleness not to be. "My heart is sick," I confided to my notebook.

> My heart is sick because of all the eyes
> That look upon you drinkingly.
> They almost touch you with their fever look!
> O keep your beauty like a mystic gem
> Clear-surfaced—give no fibre grain of hold
> To those prehensile amorous bold eyes.

But in a second stanza I became magnanimous enough to allow her to be looked at by them all.

To her I wrote:

I feel only the utter loveliness of your being, you to whom I give and commit all that I am. Your love is around me. I am warm. I am not fearful or distrustful. Tonight I dare believe that nature made her most beautiful miracle for me, and that time really contained such an hour. . . . I want you to know this and so I let myself go into the sweet music of saying it.

I will try to refrain from quoting too much of that sweet music in this book. Love letters are *too* sweet except for those who write and receive them. I later described her, with temperate accuracy, as "beautiful and strong and kind and full of rebellion." And I wrote: "I love you proudly because you are so noble always, and you are so mettlesome, and your intelligence is so keen—ever a swift and careless blade."

Those qualities were visible in her features, and they had given her, without any great gift for acting, a certain success in the theater as well as the movies. She was playing in a Belasco production during that winter of 1917, and was away some weeks in Boston and Washington. I was away sometimes too, fighting an oratorical battle against the approaching war. Thus our love was nourished upon its two most powerful stimulants, togetherness and separation. This lent a kind of festival joy to our getting into bed together—sometimes late at night in my room at 12 East Eighth Street, or after driving up in the old Ford for a week-end in the little house at Croton.

One of the constraints against which Florence rebelled volubly at that age was the institution of marriage, and as I have always resented this interference of the state in my emotional life, our thoughts of the future never clashed. We both only wanted to be free and wanted each other, and these were the two easiest things at the moment for us to have.

Eugen was so preoccupied with the import business he had established downtown that I rarely saw him except late at night when he would stagger home and crawl into bed. Ida, after our parting, had gone into such a state that our physician, Dr. Herman Lorber, advised me not to try to see either her or the baby "for a few years at least." The rumors of her hostility, and its two-sided exacerbation in some letters we exchanged, had so alienated me that, although I felt waves of

sadness about the baby, who was appealingly beautiful, I was not sorry
to take the doctor's advice. As it turned out, owing to Ida's removal to
New Mexico and my long absence from the country, I did not see my
gifted child again for twelve years. We are good friends now; he has
overpassed me by actually taking his Ph.D. in psychology at Columbia; and he has forgiven me, I think, for being such an inadequate
parent.

Chapter 6

TWO SOURCES OF STRENGTH

Florence shared completely my mood of rebellion against what we considered the putting over of a foreign war on the American people. We were as fluently at one politically as physically during that spring and summer of 1917. We did not exactly "live together." Though Florence spent a great deal of her free time with me in the little house at Croton, she was still always a visitor there, and resolutely so. A thin and diminishing old maid from down the hill would come up daily to do the cooking and housekeeping for us. Her name was Miss Mary Smith and she was insanely neat and clean, so insanely that she ended her life in an asylum, but we got the benefit of the early phases of her psychosis. Florence felt no glimmer of the wish to "make a home" for a man, and I liked that. But I was unprepared for the extremes in the opposite direction to which she might go. One day when I was absorbed in writing, she went into the kitchen to get a lunch for us both. Coming to a blockage in my thoughts, I got up from my desk and strolled out of the house and up the road a little way, wrestling with an idea. When I came back in about fifteen minutes, she had put out the oil stove, leaving the food half-cooked, and was in the doorway in a black rage.

"What do you think I am, a servant?" she said. "Do you think I came up here to cook for you while you stroll around the countryside?"

I was too filled with astonishment to feel any other emotion—unless it was admiration of her beauty, which in fury excelled that of the fiercest maenad. I managed, after a while, to convince her that no question of status was involved, that we merely happened to be doing different things. But the task was not easy. She was only twenty-one years old, intemperately proud, and convinced she could carry the world by storm. She told me, when her anger subsided, that she had once slapped a policeman in the face because she did not like the way he ordered her not to cross the street in the vicinity of a fire. He must also have thought her fury beautiful for he did not arrest her. But although she had that proud, impetuous and fiery-tempered heart, her mind was not dimmed by it. She was too intelligent to be rancorous or narrow-hearted or ignoble as people rich in pride so often are. She was kindly, thoughtful, magnanimous, a person upon whose nobility you could, in the long run, absolutely depend.

The question how much you care about your loved one's happiness, whether almost as much as your own or more, is always an important one. Equality, or some level of similarity, in this trait is almost essential to a happy union. In me, although I am a fairly selfish person in many ways, a habit of considerateness had been highly developed since childhood. That tender-hearted, mutually responsible, loving-kindly family in which I grew up had been like a nest. Florence's father had been cold and hard, her mother a selfish infant. She had yearned from her early years to get away from home. This caused the principal discord in our relation. It made her careless of what the things she did might mean to me, and it made me babyishly expect her to be careful. She would make appointments to meet me in town at a particular place and time, and arrive without apology as much as two hours late. I remember once in the lobby of the Brevoort Hotel, where she might easily have telephoned, she came four hours late to a rendezvous. I, to be sure, was not there when she came, but I was not anywhere else either. I was suspended in space—incapable of thought, action, or realization, until the pain, worry, and misery of those hours were lifted. I tried hard, or thought I tried, to learn to be as casual as she, but not so hard as she tried to learn to be thoughtful. And to a remarkable extent she succeeded.

She grew gloriously in the years of our love—not only, or even predominantly, through association with me, although she went earnestly to work reading and studying the things I thought she ought to know. Even more important in her development was the group of people like her, or like what she was born to be, into which she entered as my companion. Shyly at first, and with hesitations, she became good friends with my sister Crystal and her husband, Walter Fuller, with Ruth Pickering, Amos Pinchot, Floyd Dell, John Reed, Boardman Robinson, Marie Jenney Howe, Doris Stevens, Dudley Field Malone. Any list of names is inadequate, but all my friends, personal, political and literary, loved this wonder-child I had discovered who was so simple in her dress and movements, so quick-minded, so unconscious of her astounding beauty. They provided a medium in which she grew and blossomed, and which soon became her native habitat.

Although love has seemed to me the most precious and momentous of the fruits of being—only when in love are we fully conscious of our being—it has never played a deciding role in what I did or created. I am not aware that I ever found what is called "inspiration" in a woman. Joy, rapture, self-abandon, yes, and wings of exaltation, but not the motive that carried me forward on my own course. I say this because I want also to say that I was strengthened and tranquillized beyond measure by the astonishing discovery that I could give myself in love. I was "surprised with an inward comfort," to borrow a phrase from William Penn. And that combination of ecstasies with inner equilibrium no doubt made me extra brash and belligerent in my antiwar and antigovernmental utterances. A speech I made on July 18 at a Free Press Conference called to denounce the lawless censorship being exercised by the Post Office, shows how cocky I was feeling.

The worst thing I can say for this situation is that it actually surprises me. I spent the whole winter trying to think up the worst possible consequences of our going to war, and advertise them in the public press, but I never succeeded in thinking up anything half so bad as this. I used to say that there was nothing very peculiar about Prussia except that she was organized for war, and that if we organized for war we would turn into another Prussia. But I thought it might take us a little time to do it. I didn't know we had so much imperial talent already in office. The suppression of the Socialist press has actually been more rapid and efficient in this republic than it was in the German Empire after the declaration of war. And as for our celebrated Anglo-Saxon tradition of free speech—it is the memory of a myth. You can't even collect your thoughts without getting arrested for unlawful assemblage. They give you ninety days for quoting the Declaration of Independence, six months for quoting the Bible, and pretty soon somebody is going to get a life sentence for quoting Woodrow Wilson in the wrong connection. . . .

If we cannot rescue from the military bureaucracy this one basic right to express our opinion both of the foreign policy of the United States and of the laws that have been passed by Congress, we might as well move into the cyclone cellars and start writing the memoirs of the republic. . . .

It was a sassy speech—one of those speeches where you are so cocksure of your opinions that you spend your effort trying to express them cleverly instead of proving them true. Nevertheless, it made a hit with my fierce-eyed old professor of psychology, J. McKeen Cattell, a world-famous scientist, editor and author, president of all sorts of international societies, member of the Legion of Honor. He made up for having scared me half to death at my *viva voce* examination for a Ph.D. by almost embracing me for that speech.

It was a motley crowd who stood up for the right to speak and think in that crisis—some eminent, some forceful but unknown, some inconsequential but excited. They were held together mainly by the Civil Liberties Committee, an organization that grew out of my sister's American Union Against Militarism, and which she surrendered into the hands of a militant social worker and conscientious objector who turned up from St. Louis loaded with charm and energy, Roger Baldwin.

Aside from that "inner comfort" I spoke of, what made me so cocksure those days was the astounding news coming out of Russia. I do not mean the overthrow of the Tsar and setting up of a parliamentary government, though that too was a matter for joy. What lifted me off the earth intellectually was the formation, side-by-side with that government, of a council or "soviet" of workers' and soldiers' deputies, which on many questions spoke with more authority than the government. I described this unheard-of phenomenon as "like an A.F. of L. convention with a majority of IWW's," and observed with delight how, although the "representatives of the people" were sitting in the same building, these representatives of the working class were edging gradually into all the vital functions of government. To me this was a confirmation of the whole class theory of society as I had learned it from Karl Marx. I did not realize how large a part believers in that theory had played in organizing the Soviet. I thought of it as a "natural phenomenon," so to speak. The long-heralded emancipation of the workers by the workers themselves, I believed, was on the road.

"What makes us rub our eyes at Russia," I wrote, "is the way our own theories are proving true. Nothing else could give us this crazy feeling of surprise."

It is indeed a dizzying thing to have an idea one has been loving in a

kind of Platonic super-world fly down and alight casually, still shining
and exact, right here on earth. And not only that one idea flew down,

Drawn by John Sloan

PUTTING THE BEST FOOT FORWARD
The Masses   June 1915

but seemingly the whole flock of them. The entire esoteric terminology
of the Marxian theory, heretofore locked up in the library of the Rand
School or employed to enliven in foreign accent the esoteric delibera-

tions of East Side debating societies, suddenly appeared on the front pages of the metropolitan press. "Class struggle," "expropriation of the capitalist," "international solidarity," "transition period," "dictatorship of the proletariat," "resistance of the bourgeoisie" (that last word we didn't even know how to spell in America) were key concepts now in front-page dispatches. And some of our experts in current history had trouble getting the hang of the new language. One hard-working foreign correspondent managed to translate a motto hanging upon the façade of the Imperial Palace in Petrograd: "Proletarians of every country, join yourselves together!" And he was moved to admire the skill with which this significant watchword had been "evolved from the brains of ignorant Slavic peasants."

Upon me this all had the effect of a revelation. "The facts have already confirmed our hypothesis. . . ." I cried in the August *Masses*.* "A working-class will yet own the tools with which it works, and an industrial parliament will yet govern the cooperative affairs of men."

Besides reinforcing in this way my general belief, the Petrograd Soviet reinforced my demand that Wilson inform us with what aims he had entered the war. Under pressure from the Soviet, the Provisional Government proposed to all the warring nations an immediate conference to discuss terms of peace, and the Soviet issued a call to the people of these nations to compel their governments to accept:

> You must not allow the voice of the Russian Provisional Government to remain isolated. You must force your governments to proclaim resolutely the program of peace without annexations or indemnities and the right of the people to settle their own destinies.

This chimed with our views to perfection, and for the few brief months that the *Masses* survived, determined its basic policy.

> We join our voice to that of the great Council of democracy in demanding of our government *an immediate offer* to discuss terms of peace.

* In this remark about our "hypothesis" there is little left, I fear, but the form of scientific thinking. Still it is important, if you wish to follow my political history, to grasp the significance of that form. The Russian socialists who created and directed the soviet were Marxian fundamentalists. They believed one and all that they were the agents of an evolving universe, whose "inner law" had been discovered by Karl Marx, and which was carrying through these revolutionary events with iron necessity. To me, no matter how unscientifically I tumbled over myself to believe it was confirmed, the idea of achieving socialism through working-class revolution was a working hypothesis, and the action taken upon it continued to be an experiment.

Again, however, we were not alone, but backed by immense throngs of people. Indeed the response of American radicals and pacifists to that plea of the Petrograd Soviet was clamorous enough to alarm the authorities, both political and military. A small but distinguished group of stalwarts summoned a People's Council to meet in New York on August 4, and "sit until the war ends." It was attended by delegates from thirty local councils and 378 affiliated organizations representing 1,200,000 Americans. Preceding it, a giant mass meeting was held in Madison Square Garden, a packed meeting addressed by all the principal antiwar agitators whom patriotism had not brought to heel with the declaration of war. William Jennings Bryan gave us the glad hand in private—a sweet, rather sad-hearted man, he seemed to me, floating so comfortably on the stream of sonorous words his mouth poured out that thought seemed unnecessary. Publicly, however, he would not associate with any who were not ready to die for their country, right or wrong.

Rabbi Judah L. Magnes, subsequently so prominent in Israel, was the chairman of the meeting. I can hear his voice wailing sublimely among the rafters of that gigantic building as I imagine Jeremiah's wailed, and remember thinking what a letdown mine would be. Mine was sufficiently resounding, however, to have left an echo in Dos Passos' novel *U.S.A.*, and provocative enough to make up for anything it lacked in sublimity. It ended in these words:

> There is nothing pro-German in what I have said, and nothing pro-Irish either. I dislike the German Empire and I dislike the British Empire too, and I don't want to fight for either one of them. I want to fight in the struggle for democracy. I will be able to recognize it without any elaborate explanations. I will recognize it by the fact that it won't be necessary to conscript the working people in order to get them to fight in it.

As the conscription law, adopted three months before, was just going into effect, that jibe, greeted with prolonged applause by twenty thousand people, set in motion a train of events which came within an ace of costing me my life, and afterward my liberty.

Chapter 7

ESCAPE WITH MY LIFE

I well remember the benign day in August 1917, the luncheon dishes shining in the sun on my little porch at Croton, Florence sitting opposite, and a dreadful letter lying among the dishes. It was the inevitable result of my speech, an invitation to tour the country for the People's Council. All expenses would be paid, except the expenditure of quietude and nervous strength and love's happiness and—to me quite indispensable—freedom from fear. The task was not only dangerous and hard, but also, as my thinking brain kept telling me, futile. More pointedly and unanswerably, however, it was a challenge to my courage. It was a challenge to back up all the bold revolutionary things I had been saying in the *Masses* for the last five years. I have an overriding guilt complex, most unfortunate in a literary man, about being a mere spouter of words. I had to deliver the goods now. I had to go. There was no way out. . . .

The schedule was arranged by Lella Fay Secor, a slim milky-skinned golden-red-haired girl with hard force but a smile like a Correggio madonna. Where did she come from? Why was she there? The whole People's Council, like most things supposedly deriving from "the people," was operated by less than a dozen of these unusual beings who combined tenderness with toughness in the proportions proper to put up a fight against fighting. Rebecca Shelley, similarly slim and comely and always mixed up in my mind with Lella; Hollingsworth Wood, a big-chested, kind, strong-hearted Quaker; Scott Nearing, a fanatic of the socialist gospel; Norman Thomas, ex-minister and head of the Fellowship of Reconciliation (an organization born in England); my sister Crystal, with her American Union Against Militarism; Margaret Lane of the Woman's Peace Party; Louis Lochner, an able and yet naïve idealist who had engineered the Ford Peace Ship and is now a noted journalist. These and a handful more really did the work, and the four girls with Louis Lochner, the executive secretary, did most of it. I had hung around the headquarters once or twice, watched them do it and admired them, but that was the extent of my consecration. Now I was going forth to battle just as if I were a brave man and a saint.

Something that almost deserves the name of psychosis is the physical pain that stabs me at the moment of parting from someone I love— especially if I am mounting a vehicle or taking a train. It was at its sharpest on that morning when Florence and I drove down to the station, I to enlist in a forlorn war against public hysteria, she to take a later train back to her proper home in New York. I could hardly find the strength to climb the little steps that led to my prison in the train. Once the parting was over, and her lovely image in the white fluttering dress had dwindled into the distance, a more adult dread and sadness took the place of that infantile pain. It was a heavy sadness, and as the event would prove, a very reasonable dread.

Trains were, indeed, prison houses in those days—the day coaches at least, and emissaries of the People's Council did not ride in parlor cars. I don't know who invented car windows that could be raised—although it took a burglar's jimmy to raise them—just high enough so that a broad red bar of imitation mahogany stood exactly opposite your face, so you could neither breathe the air nor observe the landscape. It took many years to develop cross-country trains into the streamlined, smooth-gliding, comfortable, and convenient living quarters that they are today. It took less excusably long to enlarge the windows and allow the bumped and trundled passengers to enjoy at least an unobstructed look at the scenes they were so uncomfortably passing through. I enlarge upon this because I am going to be very tired, physically as well as spiritually, before I get home from this safari into a country going wild, and I want to make the causes of my weariness clear.

At first the oratorical part of it was easy and auspicious. My first speech was in the same big hall in Detroit where I had been so successful in April. Indeed I have always been a success in Detroit, a sort of circus attraction, ever since March 1916 when I was denounced in screaming headlines by the minister of the First Presbyterian Church as an obscene blasphemer, and defended with similar publicity by the Unitarian minister as an exemplary Christian. I had more friends there among the radicals than anywhere else, and I knew there was more danger of a fight in the audience than an attack upon me. There was, as it happened, no disturbance at all. The entire audience, so far as I could judge, was enthusiastically in favor of the "Russian peace terms," and of a conference of the warring nations to discuss them. Even the policemen who lined the walls of the auditorium as an inner hard shell, slapped me on the back and mock-arrested me as I left the building.*

"Nobody likes this war very well," I wrote to Florence from Detroit. And from Chicago, where I spoke in the open air, "The people (whoever they are) are against the war." In St. Louis I reported speaking in the opera house to a veritable mob who "stood up and yelled" their applause, and "got everybody laughing so hard at the war (so the local comrades reported) that the Secret Service men sent there to arrest me hadn't the strength left to do it."

Notwithstanding these successes I was in a painful tension. I don't enjoy defiance. It doesn't exhilarate me to have Secret Service men in the wings and a special detail of policemen out in front, whether to protect or arrest me. In the happiest circumstances I suffer acutely from stage fright, and in all circumstances I have a pathological horror of even the friendliest contact with what is called "the Law." Therefore I was doing here just everything that is hardest for me to do. I was sleepless and half sick. I couldn't hold my legs still when I lay down in bed. "I keep toying with the idea of telegraphing Miss Secor that I'm dying, or that I've joined the army, or that I can't find South Dakota . . ." I wrote to my sister.

To Florence I wrote: "My sweet love, our dreams, so wild and yet so tender, so quietly excited, are the wonder of every hour." And I wrote other things as little restrained, but added: "Now I must never write to you this way again, because it is contrary to all the wisdom of how to make a girl love you."

She answered: "Do not think, my beloved, there are ways and means of making me love you. It is just yourself that I love. I think of you all the time."

How often those words have been written: "I think of you all the time!" And how true they can be, no matter how mathematically impossible!

In Kansas City I was met by a wondrously gentle friend named

---

* I owed a similar debt to President Van Hise of the University of Wisconsin who, at the beginning of an earlier lecture tour, refused to let me speak on the campus. The students hired a hall off the edge of it, and came in a noisy throng to hear me. The incident was broadcast by the Associated Press, and brought me eager audiences throughout the country.

Henry Faxon, who lived with his vivid Irish wife in a big farmhouse four miles out in the country. I dined with them, and they suggested I leave my bags at the hotel and sleep in their guest room. It was a lovely room opening on a fenced-in lawn, with silvered trees and oval bushes casting shadows in the moonlight. I felt peaceful at last. But when I tried to get into bed. . . . Well, there are beds you can't get *into*. You can get *on* them if you have a mind to, just as you can get on the slab of granite that is laid across a Viking's tomb. I really was frightened when I hit that slab of rock. I *had* to sleep. I was fagged out. After speaking next day in Kansas City, I had to travel fourteen hours through the desert for a speech in Parkston, South Dakota. Only neurotics and spoiled children will sympathize, I suppose, but I lay there tense with anxiety and almost in tears for two hours and a half. Then I heard the drone of a trolley car in the distance. I got up and dressed—all but my shoes—sneaked out of the room, shut the door noiselessly behind me, and crept down the staircase and out onto the lawn. I was halfway to the gate, still tiptoeing, when Nero, the police dog who had been so friendly by daylight, took after me with a roaring mouth. I had the presence of mind not to throw my shoes until I had imparted enough momentum to them so that they flew over the gate, and were there when I landed head-first on the other side. I caught the last trolley into town, and crawled into a paid-to-be-friendly bed at 2 A.M.

Waking at ten the next morning, I called my hostess on the telephone.

"Why, Max, where in the world are you?" she said. "We're still tiptoeing around the house so as not to disturb your slumbers. Did Henry wake you going after the rooster?"

"What rooster do you refer to?" I asked dreamily.

"Max, Henry got up before dawn and climbed the tree outside your room to catch our brown Leghorn rooster so he wouldn't wake you up crowing!"

Twenty years later I lectured on poetry in Kansas City, and Henry and Lavinia Faxon were in my audience. She whispered to him:

"Max looks so tired I'd like to take him home and put him to bed."

Henry said: "We tried that once!"

I believe it was the nearest he ever came to making a complaint about anything.

Parkston was one of a thousand small square towns that line the railroads out there like rows of boxes. They had wheeled a shaky tribune into the public square, laid planks over barrels for a grandstand, and played "The Star-Spangled Banner" to summon the public. Again an immense crowd came, larger than the whole population of the town.

"The people here," I wrote home once more, "are almost all of them against the war."

I quote these remarks because I think they have some historic interest. We were then five months into a war for which Wilson declared the people had "volunteered in mass." However, the pro-war party, the fighting patriots, were gathering force. The people were going to wage a war whether they wanted to or not, and they weren't going to lead off by holding meetings about peace. That fact was brought home to me in Fargo, North Dakota, a newly sprung-up, neat, rather toylike city, but one in which soldiers were quartered and military training was in progress. The valiant young boy who had planned my Fargo meeting greeted me with the news that every hall in town had been closed against it. He had announced that I would speak in a vacant lot at a certain street corner, but a military drill had promptly been announced for the same street corner at the same hour. The rifles carried in that drill, my hotel proprietor confided, would be loaded. He added that he would shoot me himself if I tried to speak from the porch of his hotel.

These were good and sufficient reasons to back down, and if I hadn't been born scared, that is what I should have done. But timid people are often driven by an impulse to pretend they have courage, which makes them more foolhardy than the brave. A Unitarian minister offered his chapel over on the edge of town. The house of my dinner hostess, Mrs. Weible, was near by, and my young sponsor proposed to drive through the streets with a megaphone announcing the place and hour of the meeting. I brushed aside the warnings of more prudent minds and said: "Sure, I'll speak!"

A company of soldiers, I learned later, was given a night's leave to break up my meeting. There were two hundred people jamming the chapel when I got there, and hundreds waiting outside to see what would happen. There was no chairman. I walked quietly down the aisle, ascended the three steps to the platform, and began my speech in a very calm voice. I had talked about five minutes when a gang of six soldiers burst through the crowd surrounding the door. They crashed in like a football team, almost knocking a woman down in the process. Every head turned toward the commotion, and I paused.

"There are seats up here on the platform," I said, "if you can't find any back there."

The six came noisily down the aisle, cold-eyed, coarse, low in the brow, big in the torso—at least, so they looked to me—and sat down sprawlingly in the chairs on the platform. Their purpose was obvious, but they were nonplussed by my courteous attitude and their conspicuous position. I told them I would go back a few sentences so they could get the drift of my argument. Turning my back halfway to the audience, I addressed them directly. They tried to act as though they were not listening, but they were. If I had possessed the full equipment of an orator, the gift of molding a timely speech impromptu, and had not taken my eyes from theirs, I might have come off the victor in spite of their intentions. But I said exactly what I had learned by heart to say. And I made the further mistake, when I had fully compelled their attention, of turning again toward the audience.

As soon as my back was turned, all six of them began to yell. It was something they had come there to do, and now was the time to do it. I managed to call for a rising vote on whether I should be allowed to speak or not. The audience rose in a mass when I said, "Those in favor"; eleven got up when I said, "Those opposed." It gave some pause to the soldiers, but they were soon shouting again.

While this was happening, a middle-aged woman came up from the audience and stood silently beside me on the platform. I think she saved my life. Other soldiers came pouring in the door and up the aisle. One of them started turning out the lights. A soprano voice shrieked, "For God's sake, don't do that, there are women and children here!" The lights went on again. In four minutes about twenty men in uniform had gathered behind me, and were crowding closer as my voice died in the noise.

"All the ladies will please leave the building," one of them shouted.

Even then I was less possessed by fear than by the dread of showing it. I turned about coolly and examined the soldiers, then peered around among the audience as though making up my mind to take some action. That again caused a lull, though I had no idea what action to take. A. C. Townley, the old agitator-organizer of the farmers' Nonpartisan League—a big man in North Dakota in those days, for the League had 300,000 members—was sitting a few rows from the front. Three or four of the League men were with him, one of them a brawny old IWW who had come to see me in the hotel. I stepped down and put my hand on that big man's shoulder as though he were my best friend.

"What would you advise me to do?" I asked.

"You'd better give it up," he answered.

Townley said: "If I had been in your place, I would have paid them some compliment and then gone on and made a speech about something else."

"I *can't* do that," I said.

Then he quickly looked up at the soldiers and said: "Come around here behind me."

The woman who had stood silently beside me was arguing with the soldiers now, amusing them with her indignation. Another woman joined her and while the argument continued the first woman ran down and begged me for everybody's sake to leave the building. These words released my intelligence, for I was standing there locked fast by the notion that I must be brave at the risk of death. The soldiers began singing "The Star-Spangled Banner," and shouting "Get up!" As everybody rose, I moved with extreme leisure in the direction of a large side chapel which opened from the main hall. I had to go up two steps to reach it, and one of the soldiers, seeing me, shouted: "Mr. Eastman retires—now everybody leave the hall in orderly fashion." This sounded like an accusation of cowardice and brought me straight back to the top of those two steps. But my two defending angels again drew the battle front in their direction, and there was still another stanza of "The Star-Spangled Banner." I resumed my slow exit, and passing Mrs. Weible, who was standing in an aisle talking to a friend, I whispered, "I'm going—I want you with me." I had emerged from my concern with heroics now, and decided to try to save my life. In her company I moved in so seemingly casual a manner to the door that the gang there did not recognize me. We walked slowly through them, through the crowd outside, and up the street to her house two or three blocks away before any soldier grasped the fact that I had left the hall.

On entering the house, I sank into a chair in total exhaustion, while she began locking doors and pulling down shades as though expecting a siege. The telephone rang. It was A. C. Townley calling from a booth nearby.

"If Eastman is in your house, hide him and deny it if anybody calls."

"What do you mean? How far would they go?"

"I mean just what you're thinking. That's how far they will go if they catch him."

They had in fact surrounded my hotel, guarding all exits, stopping everyone who entered and openly promising a "necktie party" to those who inquired.

Mrs. Weible repeated the conversation, and asked if she hadn't better get her automobile and drive me out of town. I said, "Yes," and was surprised at the odd metallic sound of my voice. Fear had won out now over pride. I was a hunted animal—hunted by a pack of my own species.

Her car was parked in front of the house. She slipped out to bring it around into a rear street. Mr. Weible meanwhile went upstairs and came down with two loaded revolvers. He muffled me in a topcoat and felt hat, and we sneaked down through a weedy garden and climbed into the car. I lay in the bottom of the car as we passed through the lighted streets. When Mrs. Weible asked me a question, my answer was a convulsion of the throat muscles. I was faint. I was chilly. I was sick. I was in love with that gun. We drove twenty miles down the track to Sabin, where I boarded the night train for Minneapolis.

I had been expecting a message from Florence in Minneapolis, though not with much confidence. She had tried hard to get a word to me at the points agreed upon, for she knew what an ordeal this campaign was—"the hardest thing I ever did," I wrote—but the trick was new to her, and I did not always receive the letters. It had been so in Fargo, and the experiences I have described were preceded by a seizure of lonely woefulness that was no help in the matter of being brave. I did find a letter in Minneapolis on the morning after my escape, but it was brief and far from comforting:

> I really can not write today. I feel too unhappy. I hope everything
> will go all right in Minnesota. Everybody in other countries is
> crying for a leader. In America I think you are the leader.

I am not a leader; the only trait of a leader I possess is that I cannot be led. I never felt more keenly aware of it than on that morning after my frightened display of courage in Fargo. So I found no satisfaction in the tribute, only distress at the mysterious bad news in her letter. What was she unhappy about? Was I the cause of it? Was she falling out of love with me? Was the world coming to an end? I thought her cryptic statement inconsiderate to the point of cruelty, and wondered how I could contrive to exist as the lover of a girl who cared so little for the effect of her words upon my feelings. Remembering this painful thought now, I judge that it came from the egocentric and too cherished baby in me. It came from the fact that Florence was robust and I frail. I had the sense, at least, to say nothing about it in my answer. There was one more speech on my schedule—in some town back westward again. Every cell in my body wanted to go in the other direction, but I managed to hold them all together, lead them onto a train, herd them into a little baseball park, and make them stay there while I made that final speech.

It was the last flicker of my faith that the People's Council was "the main hope of democracy in this crisis," as I had described it in the *Masses*. I saw it to be an untimely and impractical gesture. The nation was going to war, and those who stood in the way would be crushed. We of the peace party must step aside and conserve our forces until the first rapture was past and the dead began to be counted. I said this at a meeting of the Council in Chicago on my way home. It shocked a good many fervent evangelists, but I think it also released a good deal of nervous tension and permitted some highly overwrought people to go home and get a good night's sleep.

When I got home to Croton I found Florence waiting in a golden blouse to meet me—it really seemed of pure though filmy gold like those the angels wear—and with celestial gladness in her eyes. I also found— marked "*Undelivered*"—the letter I had so woefully missed in Fargo. It read:

My dearest I love you so much. I do not feel I will ever love anyone but you, you are everything in the world I want.

Chapter 8

UNNATURAL DEATH OF THE MASSES

It is customary, I suppose, when a country goes to war with a divided will for the war party to crack down on the peace party and smash it by fair means or foul. Laws are stretched for the purpose, and where they won't stretch, they are broken. I had not read enough history to know this; I had to learn it by experience. That near-lynching in Fargo taught me quite a little of it. The North Dakota papers carried the whole story next morning, and William Langer, Attorney General of the State *— to whom I had given a mark of 100 in Logic at Columbia in time past—telegraphed me in Minneapolis an invitation to come back. He said that the governor would call out the Home Guard if necessary to protect my right to speak. Since it was Company B of the Home Guard that had raided my meeting, I thought it best to regard Bill's telegram as a poem rather than a promulgation of state policy.

Meantime another series of events was teaching me that wartime necessity knows no law. In Washington, the Attorney General of the United States, the Solicitor of the Post Office Department, and the Judge Advocate General of the Army held a conference on the *Masses* and decided that it must be put out of business. This was a rather ticklish job, for the *Masses* had influential friends and backers, among them E. W. Scripps, the great newspaper magnate, and Samuel Untermyer, one of the nation's most astute and formidable lawyers. It was so ticklish that I think it was regarded as an unusually amusing sport, rather more like big-game shooting than duck-hunting, by those who engineered it. But I was in too serious a mood to realize this at the time. The attack began on July 5, 1917, with a letter from the Postmaster of New York City informing us that our August number

* He died, a United States Senator, in the summer of 1960.

was "unmailable under the Act of June 15, 1917." This was that same "Espionage Act," which penalized words as distinct from actions—the first federal law to do that since the notorious Alien and Sedition Laws of 1798—and which made unmailable any matter violating the Act. I knew nothing of all this; I knew only that the rights of free speech, press and assemblage were guaranteed by the Constitution and were not revocable in wartime. I appealed for help to Senator La Follette's old law partner, Gilbert E. Roe, who had come to our help in 1913 when Art Young and I were indicted for criminal libel at the instigation of the Associated Press.

Roe "filed a bill of equity" asking the federal court to enjoin the Postmaster from excluding the *Masses* from the mails. The bill was made returnable before Judge Learned Hand, the most distinguished liberal jurist in New York—also the one most gifted with a sense of humor. Argument on the motion for an injunction lasted the whole day of July 21. The Post Office Department was represented by an Assistant U. S. Attorney, who explained that the Department construed the Espionage Act as giving it power to exclude from the mails anything which might interfere with the successful conduct of the war. Four cartoons and four passages of text were cited as violations of the law. The cartoons were: a drawing by H. J. Glintenkamp of the Liberty Bell falling to pieces along the old cracks; a cartoon, also by Glintenkamp, entitled "Conscription"—two naked young men, "Labor" and "Youth," chained to a cannon, and a naked woman, "Democracy," lashed to its wheel; a double page by Boardman Robinson, "Making the World Safe for Capitalism," showing Elihu Root preparing a noose for the Petrograd Soviet (satirizing the famous "Root Mission," which had been sent to Russia in a forlorn attempt to keep her in the war); a cartoon by Art Young representing a group of big businessmen studying "War Plans" with Congress at the door hat-in-hand: "Excuse me, gentlemen, where do I come in?" "Run along now!—we got through with you when you declared war for us." The texts objected to included a paragraph of mine about the anarchists, Emma Goldman and Alexander Berkman, then under indictment for advising young men who did not believe in the war to refuse to register for the draft: "Whatever you think of the practicability of such a protest, you must, with their friends, pay tribute of admiration to their courage and devotion"; an unsigned article upholding the rights of nonreligious conscientious objectors; and an editorial of mine entitled "A Question."

I wonder if the number is few . . . who feel inclined to bow
their heads to those who are going to jail under the whip of the
State, because they will not do what they do not believe in doing.
Perhaps there are enough of us, if we make ourselves heard in
voice and letter, to modify this ritual of contempt in the daily
press, and induce the American government to undertake the imprisonment of heroic young men with a certain sorrowful dignity
that will be new in the world.

Judge Hand, in a weighty and for the moment "historic" decision,
sustained the contention of the *Masses* at all points. The interpretation
by the authorities of the Espionage Act, he declared, was not valid, nor
were the specific provisions of the law violated by the magazine. (Not
one of us, of course, had ever read or noticed the provisions of the law.)
The cited cartoons and editorials, he said, "fall within the scope of that
right to criticise, either by temperate reasoning or by immoderate and
indecent invective, which is normally the privilege of the individual in
countries dependent upon the free expression of opinion as the ultimate
source of authority." The expression of such opinion might militate
against the success of the war, but Congress had not seen fit to exclude
it from the mails, and only Congress has the power to do so. The
pictures and text might tend to promote disaffection with the war, but
they could not be thought to counsel insubordination in the military or
naval forces "without a violation of their meaning quite beyond any
tolerance of understanding." The conscription cartoon might "breed
such animosity toward the Draft as will promote resistance and
strengthen the determination of those disposed to be recalcitrant," but
it did not tell people it was their duty or to their interest to resist the
law. The texts expressed "High admiration for those who have held
and are holding out for their convictions even to the extent of resisting the law," but the expression of such admiration is not a violation of the Espionage Act.

Judge Hand also remarked—and years after he called my attention
to this with a grin—that if the magazine *had* violated the law, the
proper procedure was to indict the editors. That passed unnoticed by
us, however, and for a day we felt triumphant. It was the day on which
the officers of the government most enjoyed their sport. For while
Judge Hand was affixing his signature to an order requiring the
Postmaster to transmit our August number—or at least before the ink
was dry—and while we were going gaily ahead with the September

number, all eyes were suddenly turned, of all places, to Windsor, Vermont. From that center of juridical culture came two pieces of news wrapped up in one: the New York Postmaster had appealed Judge Hand's decision to a higher court, and in approximately the same instant a Tory judge up there had signed an order staying the execution of Judge Hand's order until the appeal could be heard. That would be sometime in October, when the August *Masses* was no longer salable.

A stay of execution on an injunction is a legal procedure, but one long in disuse. Both the bench and the bar generally have realized that intolerable confusion would arise if one judge were in the habit of staying an injunction granted by another. Judge Hough himself, the obliging Vermonter, began his decision with the remark that "no other instance of application to a Judge of the Appellate Court to stay an appealed order of this nature is known to me." Nevertheless, he decided to hold up our August issue until its value was lost in order to find out whether it should be held up or not.

That was only one half of the government's joke, however. When we presented the next issue for mailing, we were invited to Washington to show cause why our mailing privilege should not be revoked on the ground that we were irregular in publication and therefore not "a newspaper or periodical within the meaning of the law." We went to Washington and showed cause: namely, that we had not mailed it regularly for the sole reason that the Post Office had secured this stay of execution, permitting them to forbid us to mail it *pending an appeal which should determine whether they have the right to forbid us to mail it or not.* This did not seem sufficient "cause," and our mailing privilege was revoked because we had not mailed the August issue!

We went back to Vermont and appealed to Judge Hough to revoke his order on the ground that a use not intended was being made of it. He dismissed this vital fact as "technically immaterial," but permitted himself to remark that the act of the Postmaster General in revoking our mailing privilege on the ground of an omission for which the postmaster himself was responsible seemed to him "a rather poor joke." We had the comfort of this literary criticism.

However poor the joke, it was enjoyed with good-natured laughter in Washington. I know this because my friend E. W. Scripps took me to see the Postmaster General, a slick, large-faced, ruddy, unwhiskered Texas politician named Albert Sidney Burleson, hoping to dissuade him from destroying so valuable a property. Burleson had written to Scripps after the 1916 campaign: "I want you to know that I know that it was the Scripps papers that determined the election." Therefore I could hardly have been more weightily introduced.

"Why, we *love* Max Eastman!" was Burleson's first word to my influential friend. It became a byword among my confreres. And after that same "we"—by which he meant the Wilson Administration—had tried twice to send me to jail for twenty years it acquired quite a wealth of meaning.

At that date, however, Wilson was still friendly to me, and he made a very teacherlike contribution to my education about civil rights in wartime. On August 24, 1917, it must be remembered, after five months of war and preparation for war, Wilson did finally "make a concrete factual statement of the purpose for which we were fighting." His letter to the Pope was in large measure, whether consciously or not, a concession of the things that the People's Council (and the *Masses*) had been demanding. In that historic letter he declared his readiness to enter into peace negotiations with a government responsible to the German people; he acceded, in almost their own words, to the Russian peace terms; and he made clear his dissent from the imperialistic ambitions of his Allies. I acknowledged this in a full-page editorial hastily inserted in the October issue of the *Masses*, an act for which I was roundly denounced by the zealots of revolutionism, but which was precisely consistent with the position I had taken. "This removes a little of the insult at least," I said, "from the injury of conscription. . . . There is hope in this letter of permanent just peace and international federation for the world."

At the same time I wrote the President a letter, describing what had happened to me in Fargo at the hands of soldiers and officers in his command, and what happened to my magazine at the hands of his Post Office Department and Department of Justice. I asked him if there was not "grave danger to our civil liberties" if such things were perpetrated under the plea of wartime necessity. He made my letter the occasion for a declaration on this subject which he gave to the press, and which was front-page news throughout the country. It seemed to me, as an answer to my letter, to exemplify that flight into abstractions which was the principal infirmity of his mind, but I was not above learning something from it about war.

My dear Mr. Eastman:

I thank you very warmly for your generous appreciation of my reply to the Pope, and I wish that I could agree with those parts of your letter which concern the other matters we were discussing when you were down here. I think that a time of war must be regarded as wholly exceptional and that it is legitimate to regard things which would in ordinary circumstances be innocent as very dangerous to the public welfare, but the line is manifestly exceedingly hard to draw and I cannot say that I have any confidence that I know how to draw it. I can only say that a line must be drawn and that we are trying, it may be clumsily but genuinely, to draw it without fear or favor or prejudice.

Cordially and sincerely yours,
WOODROW WILSON

We managed to publish an October *Masses*, and one marked November–December, selling them only on the newsstands. But that was the end. The last number contained a letter from John Reed in Halifax on his way to Russia to report the revolution. Jack was our most brilliantly rambunctious editor and the nation's great war correspondent, and I had raised two thousand dollars from a New York socialite named Mrs. McCullough, a friend of Eugen Boissevain, to send him on this trip. His exclusive articles were to be financially the "making" of the *Masses*. Fate had different ends in view. Mrs. McCullough, whoever and wherever she may be, is responsible for a famous classic: *Ten Days That Shook the World*, but the *Masses* did not live to see that book. Its dying words, however—printed in big type on the back cover of the last issue—remain as true a prophecy as ever was penned:

> John Reed is in Petrograd. . . . His story of the first proletarian Revolution will be an event in the world's literature.

Chapter 9

A REST FROM EDITORSHIP

We closed up the *Masses* office in November 1917, on the very date, almost, of the Bolshevik revolution in Russia. It was as though we had achieved the revolution and could now take a rest!

At any rate we did take a rest, and for me it was a joyful one. There was no conflict in my heart between love and revolution; thanks to Florence's rebel temper, the two preoccupations were in perfect harmony. But there was not *time* for both of them! Editing a revolutionary magazine in October 1917 was a full-time job. So was being in love. Not that Florence was a demanding person. Quite the contrary—she was brimful of her own ambition. It was love, as it behaves in my heart, that was demanding. "He loved the girls he made love to, too much," is a line spoken by the young priest of Baal in my poem, "Lot's Wife." I was thinking of myself when I wrote it. And if that was true of "making love," it was a thousandfold true of being changed by love into a new being cherishing as one's own the joys of another.

Florence's ambition was a joy because it seemed so sure of fulfillment. It was not, moreover, a mere wish to shine and startle, but a noble desire to rise out of the plight of mediocrity into which she had been born. Her father, a tall, cold-tempered man, had calmly packed his bag and moved out one day, leaving his beautiful daughter and ineffectual child of a wife to get along in a dingy flat on the poor side of Second Avenue without his company. Instead of continuing her education as she would have loved to, Florence had to leave high school and support her mother. Her clearly delineated beauty made the task rather easy just then because photographs were in great vogue among advertisers—photographs of good-looking girls especially. All I had to do if I wanted a picture of Florence was run through the advertising pages of the magazines. From photographer's model to chorus girl was a short step, and from there to acting a bit part on the stage or in the movies was another—and so on up as high as one could go. To make the ascent easier, Florence invented the name Deshon, which she accented on the last syllable, thinking it sounded rather French. At least it sounded better than her patronymic, Danks.

Soon after we met, she moved down from those two meager Thirty-fourth Street rooms where I had called for her to an apartment on West Ninth Street a little way from Fifth Avenue. This gave her mother a sense of respectability, and it brought Florence closer to her friends in Greenwich Village, though it was a little too far on the respectable side to be in and of the Village. Her ambition, though so passionate, was not narrow. It was not mere stardom that she wanted—much less social status, which she scorned—but to belong to what I can only call the natural aristocracy, the people who love ideas with an intellectual passion, and love life, and live it in a restlessly aspiring, rather than a carefully conforming, way.

This phase of her ambition was in great part achieved, I think, by the warm and happy eagerness with which my friends, and the friends of the old *Masses*, welcomed and received her into their midst. (I see I am saying that my friends and the friends of the old *Masses were* the natural aristocracy, or a substantial part of it, and I am afraid I will have to let that stand.)

When one of your friends separates from his wife and starts floating around detached and lonely, you wait with rather breathless hopefulness to see what girl he is going to latch on to. I suppose my friends were in this condition after I parted from Ida, and it must have been a large relief to have me turn up with a natural phenomenon like Florence. (I am not referring only to her beauty now.) We were all close together down there in the Greenwich Village region; we were most of us neighbors on Mount Airy Road in Croton, too, for Crystal and Walter, Boardman Robinson, Floyd Dell, Jack Reed, and "Doris and Dudley," had bought houses up there. We played charades and gave impromptu theatricals; some of us played tennis on my court; we dined and took long walks; we swam in a small brown lake. I was for once steadily and firmly happy, having achieved the sustained emotion which I had dreamed of since boyhood, but long ago dismissed as beyond my reach. Thus to me as well as to Florence, this turn of events was a fulfillment of ambition as well as a happy love. Her great success in *Jaffery*, though regarded by the profession as a "hit," did not immediately bear fruit in other movie contracts. She was still earning her living with secondary parts in the theater, still waiting for the great moment when she would sign a contract with Fox, or Vitagraph, or Samuel Goldwyn. But it was a tranquil waiting. She had achieved one part of her ambition—to be among her peers. The more spectacular and flashy part could take its time.

One of the charms of people who don't know much, if they have bold minds, is that they do not know what knowledge is. They are not buffaloed by it. Florence never hesitated to dash into an argument or exchange earnest opinions with learned authorities upon the most complicated subjects. One of the eminent men of those days—and still as eminent in my esteem—was Norman Angell, author of *The Great Illusion*, a book which first proved with icy logic that modern war, aside from being barbarous, is bad business, and that victory in modern war is a disaster.* He came up to see me once in Croton, and we dined— quite a group of us—on my little roofless porch under the Osage orange tree. He is a small man, smaller than Florence, and of a palish color, with pale hair and eyes, although the clarity of those eyes is beautiful to see, and his brow also is impressively beautiful. But Florence, never having read his book, seemed a little like a down-swooping bird of bright plumage when she undertook to abolish one of his statements with a few hasty remarks. They were not foolish remarks exactly, but her innocence of the depth of the subject, and of his learning, was a little embarrassing—except to Sir Norman himself, who seemed delighted to defend himself from so lovely and irrelevant an attack.

Another famous man we once assembled a dinner party for was

* It was a prodigiously famous book. Published in 1909, it spread through the world as though a dam had burst. Inside of eighteen months it was translated into French, German, Italian, Spanish, Dutch, Norwegian, Danish, Swedish, Russian, Polish, Finnish, Czech, Arabic, Turkish, Japanese. Cabinet meetings were held about it. In England the German ambassador made it the subject of a special pronouncement. The king presented copies to his ministers, Norman Angell societies were formed. Norman Angellism seemed actually to be going to prevent the impending war. Moreover his *effort* to prevent it by demonstrating its impracticality was as clear as a Sahara sky. No one outside a lunatic asylum, you would think, could have misread his message. And yet a vast majority of those who have heard about him or his famous book—70 or 80 percent of them, he estimates in his autobiography—believe that he told people not to worry, war has grown so expensive that it can't happen again! I was shocked to see this wide-spread perversion—an hysterical expression of a universal wish, I suppose— reiterated and elaborated upon by Barbara Tuchman in her otherwise scholarly book, *The Guns of August*.

Thorstein Veblen, a hero of mine since postgraduate days when I undertook to write a popularization of his *Theory of the Leisure Class*. I was also deeply influenced in my youth by a paper he wrote on animistic belief as against emerging scientific knowledge.* My sister had brought him east to attend some symposium she was holding in Amos Pinchot's house on the folly of going to war against Germany, his *Imperial Germany and the Industrial Revolution* being one of the key sources for arguments on that subject. Veblen looked like a Lapland papoose, and he sat at our table as mum as though made of wood. We could not get a word out of him. We tried him on Imperial Germany; we tried him on the Instinct of Workmanship; we tried him on the Leisure Class; I tried him on Animism versus Science; but aside from recalling that I had written him a postcard on that subject ten years before, he would hardly so much as grunt in response. We might as well have invited a donkey to dinner. There were eight of us at the table, all alertly intellectual, or hoping to be, and eager to get some profound thoughts out of him. About halfway through the meal, when we had given up in despair and were holding a learned discussion among ourselves, Florence, who sat next to him, remarked in a confidential half-whisper: "This meat is a little too well done for my taste—what do you think?" He turned in his chair, gave her one look of very masculine appreciation, and launched into a two-sided conversation on his tastes and hers, his distastes and hers, which covered pretty near the whole range of life's experience, and lasted through the rest of the dinner. Subsequently, in Amos Pinchot's drawing room, my sister introduced him with encomiums to a company of highbrows, and aside from a polite bow and a "Thank you," he never said a word.

We laughed a long time at that incident, which epitomizes the enlivening fun it was to have this young, gay, and theatrical creature, with her bold mind and beauty, her magnetism and her inimitable laughter, so near by and so glad to be among us. I was proud to have found her. I dare to say that she felt proud of me too, for however disreputable my opinions were, they bore no tinge of that mediocrity which she was so zealous to rise out of. To be in love and be proud of each other is an intoxicating mixture of emotions. I cannot wish the reader any headier joy.

Thus you need not picture me as buried in gloom over the death of

* "The Evolution of the Scientific Point of View," *University of California Chronicle*, Vol X, No. 41 (1908).

the *Masses*. For me at least the closing up of that little red brick office over on Greenwich Avenue, giving away the office furniture and selling the empty safe—well, there was pathos in it, but I was glad to be free. My sin of wanting to experience everything was bad enough—wanting to *do* everything was too much. I would settle down now and really become a writer.

Chapter 10

HISTORIC NECESSITY OF THE LIBERATOR

It must have been History that defeated my noble purpose to become a writer. History was unwilling to let the *Masses* die intestate in the very months when its revolutionary prophecies were being fulfilled. There had to be an heir; there had to be a magazine to talk understandingly about what was happening in Russia. Leaving History in its home on the shelf, however, the actual cause of the emergence of the *Liberator* was personal and accidental.

My brilliantly executive sister, her Union Against Militarism having expended its last breath in those prewar outcries I quoted, happened to be looking for a job. And it occurred to me that I could realize all my conflicting ambitions, including a show of resoluteness and "devotion to the cause," by getting her to join me as co-editor and manager and money-raiser. Crystal was as steady of purpose as I am of opinion, and she would not be troubled as I was by a constant wish to be doing something else. I never wanted to run a magazine, and I kept pretending I wasn't running it, but just presiding over its parturition. With Crystal to raise the money and conduct the business, I could make this fantastical pretense come true. I could live my creative life, and yet also preserve this glamorous institution which had grown up in my hands of its own spontaneous will rather than because I had any intention to produce it.

Crystal met my suggestion with some of the eagerness she used to feel for the games we played in the cherry tree at the Old Farm or out on the barn roof at West Bloomfield—also with some hesitations arising from the same source. Psychologically, it was not good for her, or for me either—it was a mistake. But Jack Reed's cablegram arriving from Petrograd in the midst of our discussion settled the question:

THIS MORNING I WAS AT THE SCENE OF THE DISPERSAL OF
THE JUNKERS DEFENDING THE WINTER PALACE BY THE SOVIET
TROOPS IN THE AFTERNOON I WAS PRESENT AT THE OPENING
OF THE ALL-RUSSIAN ASSEMBLY OF SOVIETS IN THE EVENING
I WITNESSED THE ASSAULT ON THE WINTER PALACE ENTERING
WITH THE FIRST BOLSHEVIK TROOPS

The priceless news story those words promised belonged to *me*. Jack
had given me exclusive rights, and we had drawn up a rough code so
that he could send confidential additions or corrections by cable. He was
widely regarded as the most brilliant correspondent in the United
States, and he was certainly the only one who could get the inside
story—the Bolshevik story—of the October revolution. His articles
were worth thousands of dollars, and I was in fact offered thousands for
them. With that asset, and the subscription list, and the fame—and yet
more, the infamy—of the old *Masses*, and its brilliant staff of contributing editors, the opportunity to start a magazine was irresistible.

The *Liberator* would differ in three principal ways from the *Masses*.
Of necessity it would be less rambunctious. Some things we felt deeply
must be left unspoken; on others we would have to temper our speech to
the taste of the Postmaster General. Aesthetically that was too bad. A
good many friends—Margaret Sanger among them, I remember—
expressed the hope that we would "go down with our colors flying."

I explained to her my feeling that we ought to sacrifice the glory of
such a going-down for a chance to serve, in whatever less beautiful way,
the new society coming into being in Russia. She wrote again assenting
to my view, and I was happy because of my admiration for her.

A second, and to me most vital difference, was that my freedom to
lead a creative life apart from the magazine was embodied in the
organization of the staff. My sister, Crystal, who as joint editor really
ran the magazine, received the salary she had been accustomed to,
something like ninety dollars a week. Floyd Dell, as I remember it,
received something like seventy-five dollars; and I, to justify and
encourage my truancy, drew only sixty dollars.

Floyd disputes this recollection, and thinks it is ridiculous to imagine
an editor receiving less pay than an associate editor.

If I had had knowledge of such an astounding fact [he writes
me], it would have made an indelible impression on my memory.
If you were to report it now, it would not be believed. "No," the
cognoscenti would say, shaking their heads, "no, no—Mahatma

Gandhi, perhaps—St. Francis of Assisi, yes—but Max Eastman —no."

It sounds convincing, but he follows it with an argument which, while flattering to my ego, is so far beside the point as to strengthen my faith in my own recollection:

> The picture you sketch of yourself (to account for your fantastic story of paying yourself less than me)—the picture of yourself as a lazy fellow, is not strictly accurate. You certainly did give an impression of laziness, but I think it was a pose that you took for your own pleasure—you liked to think of yourself as lazy. But it was a fiction. You were a very hard worker. You were dilatory, but you wrote a great deal for the magazine, you edited my own writings very carefully (and often improved them with some brilliant phrases), you read every word that was printed in the magazine, you made all the important decisions, and, after I had made up the magazine, you came at the last minute to the office or the printer's and took it all apart and put it together again to suit yourself. To anyone who knew about your editorial activities, there would be no question of your earning your salary as editor.

I do not, as a matter of fact, picture myself as lazy, nor do I agree with those who think I am. It happens that my organism, like that of the crocodile, feels at ease in a horizontal position, and I always assume one when space, time, and the social amenities permit. But my reason for an unusual manipulation of salaries was just the opposite of laziness, it was ambition. I was *doing something else* all the time, and wanting to do it more than I wanted to edit a magazine.

For instance, it was during the very year we started the *Liberator* that Alfred Knopf brought out my second volume of poetry, which I called by the unrevolutionary title *Colors of Life*. Knopf, who had already published my *Journalism Versus Art*, was the super-aesthetic avant-garde publisher of those days, though I must say he did not look the part. Indeed, if he will pardon my saying so, Alfred looked to me more like a Caribbean pirate than a connoisseur of literary art. But he and his wife Blanche brought a fresh vein of cosmopolitan culture and sophisticated good taste into the business of book publishing in the United States, and I was on a full vacation from revolutionary editorship while preparing a sheaf of poems for him. Alfred liked my idea of publishing poems in small volumes that would fit into a side pocket—it was part of a pleasing delusion that somebody was going to read them—and he made an exquisite little blue gift book out of *Colors of Life*.

There was another big difference between the *Masses* and the *Liberator*: in the latter we abandoned the pretense of being a co-operative. Crystal and I owned the *Liberator*, fifty-one shares of it, and we raised enough money so that we could pay solid sums for contributions. It was a little nervy, perhaps, to switch into our hands the loyalties of what had been a jointly owned enterprise. But no profit, of course, was contemplated, and, nervy or not, it worked. The *Liberator* was a better magazine than the *Masses*, and instead of dwindling, the group surrounding it grew larger and attracted new talents of high distinction.

We did not continue on the *Liberator* the old utopian custom of "*Masses* meetings," at which the whole crowd, and even casual outsiders, would "vote" on the pictures and writings submitted. Those votes, of course, except for a pretty strenuous veto exercised by the artists, were far from decisive. But they were hilarious fun, and of immense educational value to the editor. A good deal of that fun and education survived in the more unregulated gatherings in the *Liberator* office and the studios of its contributing editors.

As printed alphabetically in the first number, the list of contributing editors, largely brought over from the *Masses*, reads as follows: Cornelia Barns, Howard Brubaker, Hugo Gellert, Arturo Giovannitti, Charles T. Hallinan, Helen Keller, Ellen La Motte, Robert Minor, John Reed, Boardman Robinson, Louis Untermeyer, Charles W. Wood, Art Young.*

To these eminences we added after a few months: Maurice Sterne, whose lustrous drawings lent both fame and beauty to the magazine; K. R. Chamberlain and Clive Weed, artist-cartoonists of the school of Boardman Robinson; Eugene Debs; and for a time Alexander Trachtenberg, who revived English Walling's page of international socialist news comment. Joseph Freeman was a poet-friend whose belated election to the staff seems now to have been an accident. An even closer friend was Claude McKay, the Negro poet, who for a time replaced

---

* Ellen La Motte was merely a name on our masthead placed there because she had written *The Backwash of War*, a little book we all admired, describing her experiences as a nurse in a French military field hospital in 1915. She was a passerby. And so, essentially, was Charlie Hallinan, a keen-minded, genial Irishman, a dear friend of my sister, who served us more—as Irishmen are apt to— by talking about us than contributing.

Floyd Dell as my associate editor. At a New Year's party in 1921, we
elected Michael Gold and William Gropper to the staff—two opposite

Drawn by Stuart Davis

"WE'VE GOT OTHER THINGS TO DO, HAVEN'T WE, MARY,
BESIDES INTERFERE IN POLITICS!"
The Masses   November 1915

poles of a magnet: Gropper as instinctively comic an artist as ever
touched pen to paper, and Gold almost equally gifted with pathos and
tears.

Such was our masthead. But it told only half the story. There lingered in the background, very near by and steady with contributions, such artists as Adolph Dehn, Eugene Higgins, H. J. Glintenkamp, Arthur B. Davies. Homeric John Sloan never came back after the "Greenwich Village revolt" of 1916, nor Glenn Coleman, but Maurice Becker and Stuart Davis began after a while to turn up with a picture or two. John Barber, whose languidly delicate drawings of coarse and vigorous people had enriched the pages of the *Masses*, continued to give them to the *Liberator*. He subsequently, while continuing to be a painter, was elected president of Harcum Junior College—the one time in history, I believe, when an artist, and certainly a revolutionary artist, ever became a college president.

It seems a casual collection of names now, but my account of those years will be but half understood if the charm and brilliance and ragged-edged individuality, the inexhaustible ferocity and laughter, of those companions in candid creativeness are forgotten. They made the magazine both an adventure and a crusade, a model of the combination of fervor and fun. One of the principal emotions of my life as an editor—it came second only to anxiety about the funds—was surprise. I never got used to the fact that time and the idea, all by themselves, had rounded up such a gang of creative talents as fell to on the job of making our two magazines good. I never went out in search of those talents, and neither did Floyd. They just emerged out of the rosy fog of hope with which the true motions of history were shrouded from us in those days.

Although last in the alphabet, Art Young was among the first in the order of talents. Aside from his rough-hewn and clumsily delicate drawings, his fame as a cartoonist and comic artist was one of our chief assets. He was famous enough to have been chosen to write the article on cartoons in the fourteenth edition of the *Encyclopaedia Britannica*, and they used one of his cartoons from the old *Masses* to illustrate the article:

"Ay gorry, I'm tired!"
"There you go, you're tired. Here I be standin' over a hot stove all day, and you workin' in a nice cool sewer!"

It was a joke, yes, but also—in Art's mind at least—a reminder of the lot of the underprivileged, a socialist reminder. "Oh Mamma, look at the stars—thick as bedbugs!" was another such reminder. Art loved humor as he loved graphic art—for its own sake, but he loved them best when he could weave a little socialism into the mixture. He was slow-brained and his humor was of the gradually-dawning-on-you, not the flashing kind. But he was a past master of the art of the caption. You could never improve by a syllable the words he placed under a picture.

He lived week-ends in a little farmhouse in Bethel, Connecticut, but most of the time he was to be found at 21 East Seventeenth Street, in the middle of a bleak, long block of furnished rooms and minor business places. His studio was a big top-floor room, barren of beauty and lacking a single comfortable chair to sit on. He shared it with a commercial artist by the name, I think, of Howard Smith. It took a little courage to go up there, for when you arrived at his door, panting after a run up three creaking flights of stairs, Art's greeting would be both gruff and sluggish—it would be ferocious. He found it necessary, being too full of human love and kindness, to make you think you were intruding on the meditations of some hibernating bear or year-round sleeplessly misanthropic Schopenhauer. In a profile I wrote for the *New Yorker*, I noted that Art actually looked a little "like a cigar-end-chewing Schopenhauer or Hendrik Ibsen, notwithstanding his kind mouth and mild blue eye."

Some of my life's best hours were spent in a hard-bottomed Morris chair in that bleak studio, conspiring with Art how most graphically to overthrow the capitalist system, or at least assassinate the socialists who had gone over to the war. One of our most vicious perpetrations was a double-page landscape scene entitled "Not Biting." It portrayed a tired and troubled fisherman labeled "The Press," fishing in "the Sea of Labor." For bait he was using a canful of worms called "Renegade Socialists." The small head of each worm was a recognizable caricature of one of the prominent Socialists who were opposing the Bolsheviks: William English Walling, Frank Bohn, A. M. Simons, Charles Edward Russell, J. G. Phelps Stokes. John Spargo was hanging on the fishline with a hook through his body. "The Sea of Labor" was calm, and the fisherman was anxiously examining his worms. Art and I worked out that much of it together, but when he brought it around to the office, I found he had placed in the background one of his big-bellied gluttons labeled "Capitalism." Capitalism, peering over a boulder, was shouting; "Spit on the Bait!"

An editor as famous then—or at least as notorious—as Art Young was Arturo Giovannitti, a poet of power and a writer of exciting prose. Although seventeen years old when he arrived from Italy, Arturo had a larger English vocabulary than any of the rest of us, and wielded it with compelling force. He first swam into my ken as an IWW orator-agitator on trial for murder in Lawrence, Massachusetts, where he and Joe Ettor had led a long, fierce strike of the textile workers. While sitting in prison he wrote a free-verse poem called "The Walker," which through some caprice of sympathy, Ellery Sedgwick published in the solidly conservative *Atlantic Monthly*. It was an account of the poet's thoughts about human life and history as he heard above him at night the footsteps of another prisoner pacing back and forth, four steps, "between the stone wall and the iron gate." The poem made a country-wide sensation and did much, I think, to secure the acquittal of the two men, who had been viciously framed.

While admiring the flood of emotion carried by the formless lines of this free-verse poem, I was more delighted to read a metrical and adroitly rhymed sonnet that Giovannitti addressed in the courtroom to his fellow defendant, Joe Ettor. "The Prisoners' Bench," he called it.

> Passed here, all wrecks of the tempestuous mains
> Of life have washed away the tide of time;
> Rages of bodies and souls, furies and pains,
> Horror and passions awful, yet sublime.
> All passed here to their doom. Nothing remains
> Of all the tasteless dregs of sin and crime
> But stains of tears, and stains of blood and stains
> Of the inn's vomit and the brothel's grime.
> And now we too must sit here, Joe. Don't dust
> These boards on which our wretched brothers fell;
> They're still clean—there's no reason for disgust.
> For the fat millionaire's revolting stench
> Is not here, nor the preacher's saintly smell—
> And the judge—he never sat upon this bench.

The phrase "Ettor and Giovannitti" was almost as common as "Lenin and Trotsky" on the lips of American radicals in those days; and the fact that one of them, a "labor agitator" grossly defiant of existing respectabilities and powers, should also turn out to be a poet in the classic style, chimed to perfection with the mood of the *Masses* and *Liberator*. As a mere matter of logic, Arturo became, upon his liberation, a member of the staff. He contributed both poetry and prose of excellent quality, and once for a short time tried to earn a small salary as a kind of promotion expert—a bright scheme of mine which his total irresponsibility brought to nothing. In March 1914, Frederick Bursch of the Hillacre Bookshop published a volume of his poems called *Arrows in the Gale*—most appropriately, for they flew a little way and then dropped to earth. Inscribed on the front page of my copy, I find these words: "To Max, who made me a better revolutionist and something of a poet, Arturo Giovannitti." This was written in 1929, and we were still political as well as personal friends then, but subsequently Arturo disappeared into a world where I never saw him. His gifts deserted him, or rather he deserted his gifts, and did little else that I ever heard of except to die an obscure death in 1960.

We owed to Giovannitti the revered name of Helen Keller on our masthead. Her only other contribution was the gleam of true, courageous and unaffected joy in living that shone out of her gray-blue eyes, lonely though they were among her senses. Her face was round; she was a round-limbed girl, perpetually young in her bearing, as though her limitations had made it easy instead of hard to grow older. The feelings were young which brought her name to our masthead. They were expressed in an introduction she wrote for her friend Arturo's book of poems:

No one has ever given me a good reason why we should obey unjust laws. . . . When a government depends for "law and order" upon the militia and the police, its mission in the world is nearly finished. We believe, at least we hope, that our capitalist government is near its end. We wish to hasten its end. . . . I am sure this book will go on its way thrilling to new courage those who fight for freedom. It will move some to think and keep them glad that they have thought.

The first number of the *Liberator* was dated March 1918. My sister and I had raised thirty thousand dollars to launch it. We had no second-class mailing privilege, but we had the first installment of John Reed's great story of the Bolshevik revolution. And we had unbounded dream-hopes of a new world coming to birth. I led off with an editorial describing the measures of confiscation adopted by Lenin's government in Russia, and his dissolution of the Constituent Assembly in favor of an "industrial parliament," as "without doubt the most momentous event in the history of peoples." That these events were no accident or mystery, but the orderly and accurate enactment of ideas born in the mind of Karl Marx over sixty years before, gave hope, I declared, "that intelligence may play its part in every event."

Never in all history before could one so joyfully and confidently enter upon the enterprise of publishing and propagating ideas.

. . . We issue the *Liberator* into a world whose possibilities of freedom and life for all are now certainly immeasurable.

These rapturous sentences were not out of key with the mood of bold-minded idealists the world over in those tumultuous days. The waves even swept as high as the top of the Bethlehem Steel Company, where Charles M. Schwab told his associates: "Call it socialism, social revolution, bolshevism, or what you will, it is a leveling process, and means that the workman without property who labors with his hands is going to be the man who will dominate the world."

That birth-number of the *Liberator* was like rain from heaven to a host of thirsting minds. John Reed's fourteen-column inside story of the October revolution ended with the words:

Lenin and Trotsky send through me to the revolutionary proletariat of the world the following message: "Comrades! Greetings from the first proletariat republic of the world. We call you to arms for the international Socialist revolution."

Our circulation doubled that of the *Masses* in the first month, and it rose to sixty thousand at its peak. We were a bugler in the forefront of a new march of freedom over the earth. So we all thought. And to provide a link with our heroic past, the aged widow of William Lloyd Garrison, still living in Boston, wrote with her subscription: "We are glad to see the old name revived in such a good cause."

Chapter 11

SHADOWS ACROSS MY PATH

Crystal was a great one for thinking up new schemes for the happier, and more economical, living of life. Not "conduct of life"—that would sound too ethical. She wanted to save money and have fun. And one of her schemes for that winter of 1918–19 had been to gather a few congenial friends, rent a house in Greenwich Village, hire a house-keeping cook, and live somewhat—though carefully not too much—like a family. She found the house on Washington Place, just east of Sheridan Square. It stood in a little row of red brick houses, all on the same level, with five steps going up to a white doorway with a brass knocker. Perhaps the doors were not all white and did not have brass knockers, but they should have. It was a once-genteel and still quiet street. Ours was a venerable house with slim white pillars in front, and all the beautiful old doors and woodwork left untouched. It cost us $179.17 a month. Sheridan Square itself was quiet and genteel then by comparison with what it is now, a mere accidental crisscrossing of five different travelways, none of which except Seventh Avenue seemed to know quite where it was going—Fourth Street, Christopher Street, Grove Street, and our unobtrusive Washington Place. All of New York was so much quieter, so much less packed with people and cars, in those days, that words falter when one tries to say what any portion of it was like. The part I am trying to describe now, the habitat of our housekeeping experiment, as I dream my way back to it, was more like residential London than present-day New York.

Besides the comely and convenient house, Crystal collected a delight-ful halfway family to live in it. My long-ago child neighbor, Ruth Pickering—star of the chapter "Half Way to Ruth" in my *Enjoyment of Living*—took the big front room on the first floor. She subsequently married Amos Pinchot and moved up to Park Avenue, and was indeed close to that transformation now. Amos, one of the real princes of this world, if it has any, was quite often a guest at our table.

Eugen Boissevain, also a character in my earlier memoir, took the second floor. I described him as "handsome and muscular and bold, boisterous in conversation, noisy in laughter, yet redeemed by a strain of something feminine that most men except the creative geniuses lack." It pleased him to bask in a reflected glory as the husband, first of Inez Milholland, then of Edna Millay, but there was something not less than glorious in his own gallant response to the challenge life offers. He had gone into the importing business at the beginning of the First World War, bringing to this country the trade of the Dutch East Indies barred from Europe by the German blockade. In three years he had a twelve-story building downtown with his name carved in granite on the lintel, and was shore commander of a whole fleet of merchant ships. But business was to him a laughable adventure, and his tales of the deals he was putting over, told with Gargantuan laughter at the self-importance of the business class, were a source of delight and instruction to us all. He had a way of blurting out the very truth on subjects that others were skirting around. Even his own egotism he would describe with a laugh instead of concealing it as the rest of us do. I remember his telling us one morning that he had dreamed he was walking on the water with Jesus Christ. "Now look!" he was saying to the Lord: "You're not doing it right—just watch the way I put my foot down!"

I lived above him on the top floor in two rooms with slanty ceilings, and Florence, although still ostensibly living with her mother on Ninth Street, stayed much of the time in those rooms.

By an odd evolvement Crystal, the prime mover in this companionable creation, lived some way down the street and she and her husband only took their dinners with us. We ate those dinners in a large room in the basement, a dim room in the daytime, but with the evening lights turned on, its white walls decorated with drawings borrowed from the *Masses* artists, it was as gay as a gambling den.

Crystal would sit at one end of the table, a sort of general manager and Queen Mother, although she was far younger and more beautiful than those words sound—"the most beautiful white woman I ever met," in the words of the Negro poet, Claude McKay. Her husband Walter Fuller sat at the opposite end, a rather small man in rimless glasses, who looked at first glance like an "organizational" bank clerk, but turned out to be brimming with irreverently humane irony and wit.

Sinclair Lewis, introducing him as his "new best friend," described Walter as "one of the most charming people I know." His compatriot, Llewelyn Powys, said of him more poetically: "Mr. Walter Fuller had a heart of pure gold. He possessed the kind of goodness that it is difficult for an American businessman to appreciate, the goodness of a clod of earth out of which a plant of clover is growing, the goodness of a soft-crusted cottage-loaf baked in a village oven." *

I sat at Crystal's right, and Florence next to me, Ruth and Eugen on the other side—Eugen always full of laughter and Ruth emitting a soft cool radiance because she was loved and in love. We were, on the whole, as happy as Crystal predicted—as economical too, though we each paid extra for guests and guests had a way of getting in pretty often. The place had atmosphere, and that was beginning to command a high price in Greenwich Village. Air after all is cheap, but not atmosphere.

I spoke of Ruth's radiance and the gay walls. We were all radiant, and the scene always gay, as it lives in my memory—until one day a surprising shadow passed across it. I remember the shadow, no doubt, as darker than it was, because it was lengthened for me. It was the first dark streak across my love.

We had hired gentle elderly black Geneva, slow-footed but not shuffling, to cook and take care of us. One day, in passing a roast of lamb at the table, Geneva omitted Florence for some accidental reason, and when Florence called this to her attention, instead of coming back, answered curtly: "Just you wait till I get around."

It surprised us all, and it made Florence angry. She said nothing then, but vented her rage the next morning by refusing to greet Geneva, or respond to her attempt at an explanation. Those bright lips of hers congealed in a sulky curve which made them look more than ever as though carved in marble. She was implacable; she was a child; and our happy family seemed doomed to be blighted by a feud. I tried to make her see that it was unlovely—it was neither democratic nor aristo-cratic—to behave so to a servant. I begged her to speak a friendly word to Geneva, but she was stubborn as an untrained colt. My effort only turned her anger against me. She did not come for dinners or to sleep in our rooms for several days. Geneva meanwhile was deeply distressed, and the whole picniclike dining company subdued to a rather embar-rassed gloom. I wrote Florence a letter which shows how obstinate her recoil had been.

* *The Verdict of Bridlegoose*, pp. 104–05.

Florence, my dearest, I think you must misunderstand me completely, or you couldn't be angry at me because of the request I made, or my sadness that you refused to grant it. I do not deny that Geneva spoke in a bad and maddening way to you. I do not take her part against you. I only ask you to recognize that you have never expressed your feelings to her, nor given her a chance to explain or apologize. I only want you to be generous to one who is subordinate and so much less fortunate than you. . . . You used to love my gentleness and aspire to it a little, as I aspire to your impetuous strength. You are growing away from me now, resenting me and so easily pushing me out on the edge of your world. I am bewildered that I should be the object of your anger.

She was just then leaving for Washington to act in the opening of a Belasco play, and she sent me a note by messenger:

Dearest, I am ashamed of the way I have been acting, please forgive me. I feel unhappy, and unable to rise above it, so I thought I would go away for a few days. I shall be thinking of you all the time, dearest.

Her next note came in the envelope of the National Office of the Woman's Party (the "Suffragettes") in Washington: "Beloved, I miss you. I'm sorry I went away."

Both she and Geneva behaved like aristocrats when she did come back, and our dining room was again made young and luminous by her presence.

A second shadow fell across my path—more like a tree trunk, this one—while I was in the Midwest on another lecture tour. The lectures had been contracted for the previous winter, and fortunately for my neck the subjects were literary, not political. Even so I was far from feeling safe. "I have just been talking to Crystal," Florence wrote, "and she thinks you ought to be very careful, carry a revolver and go with a lot of people." As always, my most popular offering was a "humor lecture," in which I made people laugh and explained to them why they were laughing. It's a delicate trick and has to be performed with verve and precision. I was standing in the wings of a lecture hall in Oak Park, Illinois, preparing my mood for this feat, when a young man rushed up and handed me a telegram. Just as the chairman was announcing the delightful experience the audience was about to receive at my hands, I read these sickening words:

YOU DELL REED YOUNG GLINTENKAMP MERRILL ROGERS AND
JOSEPHINE BELL INDICTED UNDER THE ESPIONAGE ACT STOP
BAIL HAS BEEN POSTED AND A DEFENSE COMMITTEE IS BEING
FORMED STOP EVERYTHING WILL BE TAKEN CARE OF STOP
DON'T WORRY

I quote this from memory, but my memory of the last two words is perfect. For a long time I saved a press clipping describing the success of that lecture as a testimony of my prowess, for I delivered it with a vacuum where my solar plexus is supposed to be. The feeling is more like a dream-horror of embarrassment than like physical fear. I wouldn't so much mind going to jail if they would let me go down privately and crawl in. It is being *put in*, being seized by so alien a thing as a government and *put* anywhere—perhaps only on trial—that has this qualmy effect on my vital organs. I remained, at any rate, in what I call my *trepidatious* condition the better part of all that winter. It is a condition in which you are not trembling but feel as though you were.

It was April and the second number of the *Liberator* was already on the stands when our trial for sins committed in the *Masses* finally took place. Our Defense Committee, with Amos Pinchot as chairman, had raised enough money to employ Morris Hillquit, the political leader of the Socialist Party, as chief counsel. And my friend and Croton neighbor, Dudley Field Malone, the Democratic Party's brilliant Irish orator, volunteered to act as assistant counsel. They were a formidable pair. Hillquit, although of small stature and handicapped by a foreign accent, was a man of astute intelligence and great personal force. Had socialism prospered in this country as it did in Europe, he would have been famous. As it was, he had alarmed the administration by winning, in the November 1917 election, a tremendous vote for mayor of New York on an antiwar platform. Dudley Malone, besides being the idol of every policeman and the adored buddy of every Democratic politician in town, had been Woodrow Wilson's loved disciple only a few years before. Wilson had made him Collector of the Port of New York—a token of friendship, I have been told, rather than a job. But he had fallen in love with Doris Stevens, a militant suffragette, at the very moment when she was engaged in getting arrested and locked up in jail for picketing the White House. Outraged by this violation of the principles of civil liberty and political chivalry, Dudley resigned his position and broke off his very close and very valuable friendship with the head of the nation. A like romantic recklessness led him to take on the defense of the *Masses* editors, lending his charm and the aura of his popularity to a cause that seemed pretty sure to be lost. For by the time we came to trial the hysteria I have described had reached its height. No single case like ours throughout the country had resulted in an acquittal or even a temperate weighing of evidence by the jury. Federal Judge Charles W. Amidon, of the District of North Dakota, sub-sequently described the situation in the courts:

> For the first six months after June 15, 1917, I tried war cases before jurymen who were candid, sober, intelligent businessmen, whom I had known for thirty years, and who under ordinary cir-cumstances would have had the highest respect for my declarations of law, but during that period they looked back into my eyes with the savagery of wild animals, saying by their manner, "Away with this twiddling, let us get at him."

It was a little like being herded into the stockyards to be put on trial for what amounted to treason in those ominous days. But New York was a little less out of its head than the rest of the country, and New York was full of our influential friends. We were not without hope.

For me New York was full of happy love. Indeed I experienced little flickers of a wish that I were not just at that moment so celestially happy. I wanted to be brave and "stand by my guns" on the witness stand, but to exchange my life's one unqualified experience of joy for a term of even a year in prison—and the possible sentence was twenty—was hard to contemplate in the stony mood proper to a martyr.

Chapter 12

THE FIRST MASSES TRIAL

We filed into the mahogany-lined chamber in the old Post Office Building opposite City Hall at ten-thirty in the morning of April 15, 1918—all of us except Jack Reed, who had learned of his indictment in Petrograd too late to make his way back, and H. J. Glintenkamp, who had waded the Rio Grande and joined the "Soviet of Slackers" in Mexico. It was at the height of the Hindenburg drive, an anxious moment for America and her allies, and the windows of the courtroom looked down on a Liberty Bond booth where patriotic airs were played by a brass band every few hours. To offset this we had two advantages. First there was not a drop or recollection of German or Austrian blood in our veins; we were all, absolutely and from way back, American, and we looked it. Second, the court was presided over by Augustus N. Hand, a judge who could have upheld in a hurricane the dignity of the law. He was less genial and less patriarchal than his cousin, Learned Hand, but he had a like unshakeable integrity.*

He was to meet the surprise of his life at our trial, and confront a problem of judicial behavior that probably never challenged a jurist before or since. The court had hardly seated itself and the stately proceedings begun, when that band outside the window struck up "The Star-Spangled Banner." As though lifted by an automatic spring, our natty little business manager, Merrill Rogers, sprang to his feet and stood rigid as a soldier on parade, five-feet-two-inches of unalloyed patriotism. If a rooster had suddenly flapped his wings and crowed in

---

* In accepting Augustus Hand's resignation from active duty at the age of eighty-nine on June 30, 1953, President Eisenhower wrote: "Your great contribution to American jurisprudence is a part of history and will continue to serve as an inspiration, not only to those who must now take up your burdens, but also to generations yet to come."

his court, Judge Hand would hardly have been more surprised. So firmly and portentously seated up there in his black robe, he gazed down at this tiny phenomenon in total bewilderment. Finally he heaved himself out of his chair, and the whole courtroom, packed with distinguished friends, enemies and onlookers—for this was a *cause célèbre*—got up and stood in reverent attention until the air was played through. To his dismay, it was played again in about twenty minutes. Merrill leapt to attention once more, and the courtroom solemnly followed. When after a few hours it happened a third time, a few smiles began to peep through the curtain of decorum, and the judge peered down at Merrill with something more than curiosity. After the fourth performance he summoned the audacity to say: "Well, I think we shall have to dispense with this ceremony from now on."

By the majority of onlookers who had come to this trial to see a show, Merrill's act was regarded as a great joke. And it was, of course, subsequently attributed to me. I've never heard the last of this cleverly impudent trick I played on a judge who was trying me for treason. To me it was, in simple truth, an appalling disaster. My flag was still the red flag, and I was not in the habit of standing up for "The Star-Spangled Banner." To begin my trial that way was to begin by backing down, and I was possessed to an almost morbid degree by an anxiety *not to back down*. We had been indicted for "conspiring to cause mutiny and refusal of duty in the military and naval forces," and "obstruct the recruiting and enlistment service" of the United States. To call the *Masses*, and above all its editorial meetings and general mode of parturition, a conspiracy, was about the most cockeyed fantasy the war psychosis produced. I had no wish, and no intention if I could help it, to spend twenty years in jail for a crime I did not commit; but to avoid this without betraying my convictions was, in the existing hysteria, an extremely delicate operation. I was planning to devote my most discriminating efforts to it, and this witty stunt of Merrill's scotched my plans completely. If I rose, I would be subscribing to that "Religion of Patriotism" which I had analyzed and rejected in a recent essay in the *Masses;* if I refused to rise, with the whole court standing, I might as well withdraw my plea of "not guilty" and hand myself over to the sergeant-at-arms. I did get up, of course—reluctantly, and, no doubt with a very solemn expression, for my thoughts as I stood there were concerned with the relative merits of different ways of murdering Merrill Rogers.

To atone for my sin, I resolved to tell the court just what I thought of patriotism before the trial ended. There was plenty of opportunity, for I was on the stand almost three days, Morris Hillquit and I giving the jury an education in the principles of international socialism that was more like a postgraduate course at college than a trial. During the progress of it I managed, upon some thin pretext, to drag out my book *Understanding Germany*, published two years before, and read this passage from the preface:

> I can truthfully say up to the present moment that I am not a national patriot. My altruism, when it operates, is too generous to wish to love a group with any boundary lines around it; and my egotism is too arrant to identify itself with anything but itself. It seems to me, moreover, a kind of betrayal of the ideals of intelligence for a man to accept the accident of his birth and take his vision of the universe from the little valley where fortune dropped him. The man without a country is the only one who is able to think clearly and love truth no matter what occasions arise, and he is the man whose elevation I envy.

Hillquit was puzzled at my reading this to the jury, and I did not explain it. My oration on graduating from college had been about Giordano Bruno; I had pondered much on the problems of martyrdom and recantation. I was only trying to stand firm.

But I was trying at the same time to stay out of jail, and these motives came into another and more disastrous conflict later on. That was during my cross-examination at the hands of the prosecuting attorney, Earl Barnes, a bald-headed hawk-faced clothes-pole of a man, with a perpetual tight little smile under his nose. He would dangle a paper in his hand, something he had found in my impounded correspondence, and approach me with a question. The game was to get me to say something he could disprove with that paper. One of these papers was a telegram I had sent in April to a couple of boys in New Orleans who asked me whether I thought that conscription, if adopted in America, would be resisted. My reckless answer had been: "I don't know, but I hope so." Barnes asked me whether I had ever expressed to any individual a hope that a conscription law would be resisted in the United States. I had no memory of that telegram, but I had the good sense to answer: "I was angry enough to say something like that when the idea was first proposed."

In such ways I outwitted him in this tense and too exciting game. And I was more concerned with winning the game than being honest when he threw up to me a deprecatory remark I had made in some impounded letter about such patriotic rituals as standing up for the national anthem.

"Will you tell us if the sentiments therein expressed, which I have just read to you, are still your sentiments?"

He had me in a trap now, and thanks to Merrill Rogers a hard one to get out of. The jury had seen me stand up when the national anthem was played, and now he was going to prove to them that I had risen merely to fool them about my feelings. The truth was more subtle that that: I had refrained from *refusing to stand up* in order to avoid *expressing my feelings!* But that was too fine a point for a jury. There was no escape there. In the split second allowed me for thinking, I could find but one way out of the trap.

"No, they are not, Mr. Barnes," I said. "My sentiments have changed a good deal. I think that when the boys begin to go over to Europe, and fight to the strains of that anthem, you feel very different about it. You noticed when it was played out there in the street the other day, I did stand up. Will you let me tell you exactly how I felt?"

"Go ahead."

"I felt very sad; I felt very solemn, very sorrowful, because I thought of those boys over there dying by the thousands, perhaps destined to die by the millions, with courage and even laughter on their lips, because they are dying for liberty. And I thought how terrible a thing it is that while they are dying over there, while the country is gradually coming to a feeling of the solemnity and seriousness of that thing, the Department of Justice should be compelling men of your distinguished ability, and others like you all over the country, to waste their time persecuting upright American citizens, when they might be hunting up the spies of the enemy, and the profiteers and friends of Prussianism in this country, and prosecuting them. That was my thought while the hymn was being played."

It was good fencing, and it left Mr. Barnes without a word to say. But it was far from the inner truth—far also from my determination not to back down. Unfortunately, however, those words appealed to Floyd Dell as the high point of the trial both morally and politically. Floyd was never so much concerned with "being a revolutionist" as I, and he had not only ceased to oppose the war, but had gone in for it heart and soul. "My own standing up when the band played," he wrote me afterward, "was as genuine a response to emotional stimulus as any kiss I ever gave a girl." And so in preparing an account of the trial for the June

Liberator, Floyd picked out for eulogistic quotation this very reply of mine, which I regretted as not altogether honest.

"Max Eastman said what was in all our hearts," he wrote.

I had been tempted to edit the passage a little when I saw the proofs of his article. I could at least put quotation marks around that phrase "dying for liberty," which had been so much better attuned to the Liberty Loan drive going on under the windows than to my rather complicated opinions about the war. But I wanted to do that too much! I had spoken the words, and that organic puritanism, which accounts for so much that is both good and bad in man's behavior, insisted that I take the consequences.

The consequences were bitter indeed. Only one who has called himself a revolutionist can know how bitter. My words gave a weapon to my political enemies that they brandished in public, and privately plunged into my breast, whenever an occasion arose. They pictured me for the purpose as a "flaming revolutionist," who "went star-spangled banner" when brought to trial—a rather simplified pen drawing both of my nature and my sin. I took what comfort I could from Morris Hillquit's description of the trial, and I am going to quote it here, though I must remind my reader-confessor that Morris was not, and had never called himself, a "revolutionary socialist." He was regarded, in the camp of the revolution, as the symbol and sum-total of "compromise," "reformism," "opportunism," the institutional selling-out of the straight Marxian program of class war. The consolation to be drawn from his words was therefore limited. Indeed the most rabid of my detractors would consider Hillquit's praise an additional disgrace. Here at any rate is what he said:

I am used to courtrooms. I have seen a great many cases tried. I believe never in the history of American jurisprudence was there a case of this character tried in an American court.

It did not seem a trial. It had the appearance of a university for uneducated, unenlightened American citizens in the jury box and outside of it. They were instructed upon the rights of American citizens to think for themselves on all vital questions, including the questions of war and peace and conscription.

And I want to say to you, standing before you here tonight as one of the attorneys for these defendants, I am proud of my clients. You never know the value of a man or woman until such time as you see them on the witness stand in a case in which their liberty is at stake. I had known Max Eastman before; I had known Floyd Dell somewhat. I had known Art Young well—but I had not known any of them.

When we had Max Eastman on the stand for two consecutive days, when he was grilled by the prosecution upon every article of his belief, and when, quietly, honestly, and courageously, at the same time with compelling force, he drove home every argument he had made in the *Masses* or in public speeches during those troublous days after we entered the war, when he advocated his right, our right, to think and to speak—and when finally he became so convincing that even half of those jurors, hostile as they were, were won over, and the crowd in the courtroom that had come to scoff remained, as it were, to pray, then I could see that trials of this kind, if continued long enough, if they force their way into the papers, will be about the only medium of education for the American public.

Notwithstanding these reassuring words, my wound of self-reproach was still inwardly tender in 1925 when Genevieve Taggard, a girl whose poetry I had loved and godfathered—and herself too, for a time—plunged a small knife into it. She made an anthology called *May Days* of the poetry that had appeared in the *Masses* and *Liberator*, a beautiful memento of those magazines and of the bright hopeful times in which they flourished. But when I opened it, I was slapped in the face—and Floyd too by implication—with a preface in which we appeared as traitors to our faith. Quoting my unhappily astute rejoinder about standing up for the flag, which Floyd had published with such enthusiastic endorsement, she wrote: "His followers felt . . . that a revolutionary leader does not purchase immunity from jail by repudiating his revolutionary opinions." To Floyd it mattered little, for he had no trouble in his heart; he dismissed it as "bad manners." But it caused me both pain and resentment.

Genevieve was a born fanatic, or if not so born, rendered so by the hardships of her early life. The memory of these hardships made her fierce in her devotion to the revolution, and as the revolution degenerated into an unscrupulous police state, still fierce in her devotion to that—incapable of fresh judgment, unable to flex her mind. An ironical fact is that in this new totalitarian communism to which she gave her allegiance, a skilled repudiation of one's principles when brought to trial has become a virtue. The party's evangelists are now formally instructed to lie their way out of such predicaments without scruple of truth or honor.* Thus in Genevieve's camp both my remorse and her reproach have become quixotic. There is nothing left, under the red flag, of the world of values in which the emotional conflict described in this chapter arose.

* This change is discussed with authority in Theodore Draper's excellent book, *The Roots of American Communism*, p. 313.

Chapter 13

A HUNG JURY

If our trial was like a university course, much of the credit is due to Morris Hillquit's masterly conduct of it. I doubt if any other man in the country could have defended our legal position with such astute force, yet at the same time opened before the court for each one of us the true contents of his mind. He had to choose the jury from a group of veniremen, a majority of whom confessed a prejudice against socialists and pacifists, though twelve thought they could rise above it. That took two days, and then the prosecution took another day proving that we published a magazine and that it contained the reading matter and cartoons in question. No proof was offered that we had endeavored to do anything with the magazine besides publish it, or even that we had *conspired* to publish it. Hillquit moved to dismiss the indictment on this ground. He remarked that one of the defendants, Josephine Bell, author of a poem in the August issue, had never even seen the other defendants until she met them in the courtroom. The judge asked to see the poem, which was a piece of super-free verse beginning:

> Emma Goldman and Alexander Berkman
> Are in prison,
> Although the night is tremblingly beautiful
> And the sound of water climbs down the rocks. . . .

After studying it thoughtfully, he said: "Do you call this a poem?"

"It is so described in the indictment, your Honor," Hillquit replied.

"The indictment against Miss Josephine Bell is dismissed," the Judge said with something between a sigh and a smile.

He also dismissed that half of the indictment which accused us of conspiring to cause mutiny and refusal of duty in the armed forces, leaving only the charge of conspiring to obstruct the draft. The fact that we were associates in the same magazine was *"prima facie evidence"* of conspiracy, he thought. Whether it was conclusive evidence he would permit the jury to decide. Thus we were left at the mercy of those twelve men, all but three of whom, if I remember rightly, had confessed to a prejudice against our opinions.

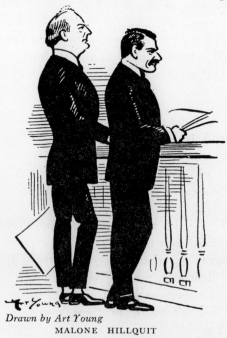

Drawn by Art Young
MALONE   HILLQUIT

THE DEFENDERS
The Liberator   June 1918

Our defense was, first, that there had been no plan or agreement of any kind to publish the items in question; it being summertime, there had not even been a *Masses* meeting. Second, no evidence was introduced to prove that any of us had intended to obstruct the draft, or do anything at all but exercise our lawful right to express opinions. To prove the lawfulness of our intent, Merrill Rogers testified that he had gone down to Washington to consult Wilson's Director of Information, George Creel, generally regarded as an unofficial wartime censor, as to the legality of a certain advertisement that had been offered to us. He also testified that I had ordered him, after the Espionage Act was passed, to withdraw from circulation the issue containing my indiscreet editorial about resisting conscription. In rebuttal the prosecution subpoenaed George Creel himself, who added to our celebrity by coming up from Washington to testify. The prosecutor had not noticed, perhaps, that our June number, one of those on which we were indicted, contained this paragraph:

> One of our most esteemed contributors, George Creel, has been appointed Chairman of the Board of Censorship for the war. Once George Creel wrote an article on "Rockefeller Law," which was censored by all his employers, including the most radical popular magazine in the United States. He brought it to us. We published it. Our readers will remember. So will George Creel, we hope.

Apparently George did remember, for his testimony differed so little from what Merrill had said that it made no real point for the prosecution. Moreover he paused to shake hands with me on the way out, saying in an audible whisper, "I hope I didn't do you boys any harm," a friendly gesture which meant more to the jury than his testimony.

It was, as Hillquit said, a most unusual trial. Floyd Dell, who had already been inducted into the army, had to explain that he was by profession a soldier, a rather incongruous trade for so slight and pale-skinned and delicate a poet—a sort of Shelley or John Keats in appearance. Floyd expressed his views with an engaging freedom which he explained afterward in these words—so different from anything I could say:

> Since I am engaged in telling how it feels to be tried, I may as well confess that I took it with pleasure. I had always secretly felt that my opinions were of a certain importance. It appeared that the government agreed with me. And a government does not do things by halves; it had provided a spacious room, and a special and carefully elected audience of twelve men, who were under sworn obligation to sit and listen to me. Under such circumstances it was naturally a pleasure to tell the government what I thought about war, militarism, conscientious objectors and related subjects. Moreover I found in cross-examination the distinct amusement of a primitive sort of a game of wits. . . .

The real hero of that first *Masses* trial, to my thinking, was our much-loved cracker-barrel humorist, Art Young. Rotund, gentle, se-

verely dignified, and yet with comedy in every tone of his voice, he would
have impressed a Torquemada, it seemed to me, with the absurdity of
sending us to jail for conspiracy. Art was an absolute pacifist, against
war anywhere and all the time, and quite ready to go to jail if this
position was a crime. He had drawn a picture called "Having Their
Fling," in which a capitalist, an editor, a politician, and a Christian
minister are dancing a war dance while the devil in a balcony directs the
orchestra. He was rather bewildered when the prosecutor asked him
what he meant by that picture.

"Meant?" he said. "What do you mean by meant? You have the
picture in front of you."

"What did you intend to do when you drew this picture, Mr.
Young?"

"Intend to do? I intended to draw a picture."

"For what purpose?"

"Why, to make people think—to make them laugh—to express my
feelings. It isn't fair to ask an artist to go into the metaphysics of his
art."

"Had you intended to obstruct recruiting and enlistment by such
pictures?"

"There isn't anything in there about recruiting and enlistment, is
there? I don't believe in war, that's all, and I said so."

With that out of his system, Art began to smile. He had been
drawing pictures most of the time during the trial, and one of them had
been a caricature of Mr. Barnes which the jury had laughingly passed
around among themselves during a recess. Art alluded to this, and said:
"I suppose some of the jurors may think I drew that picture in order to
discourage *you* from enlisting, Mr. Barnes."

For me that was the high point of the trial. After his ordeal was over,
Art went back to his seat and fell into a tranquil slumber. Our assistant
counsel, Dudley Malone, leaned hastily over my shoulder and whispered: "For heaven's sake, wake Art up before he starts snoring. Give
him a pencil, and tell him to stay awake until he gets to jail."

Art woke up with a start, and a look of surprise at finding himself on
trial for conspiracy that stays in my mind as a sound comment on the
whole proceeding. He took his pencil and drew a picture called "Art
Young on Trial for His Life," which became quite a collector's item in
subsequent years.

Our attorneys in their summings up lifted the argument to a very
high plane indeed—too high for an average jury in those brutishly

impassioned days. Dudley delivered a moving discourse on a text from Thomas Erskine, the English jurist who defended Tom Paine in 1792: "His opinions indeed were adverse to our system, but I maintain that opinion is free and that conduct alone is amenable to the law."

"I hope you will take that," Dudley said, "as the crux idea in this case in formulating your judgment—that opinion in a democracy like

Drawn by Art Young   ROTHWELL   COBB   BARNES

THE PROSECUTORS
The Liberator   June 1918

ours, must be free, freely spoken, freely written. Only conduct is amenable to law."

And Morris Hillquit, among much else that was impressive, said a memorable thing:

> Constitutional rights are not a gift. They are a conquest by this nation, as they were a conquest by the English nation. They can never be taken away, and if taken away, and if given back after the war, they will never again have the same potent vivifying force as expressing the democratic soul of a nation. They will be a gift to be given, to be taken. . . .

The chief prosecutor, Earl Barnes, while sincerely convinced that we should go to jail, seemed in some deeper part of his nature reluctant to send us there. As Floyd wrote afterward:

> He was not what one would call an eloquent speaker; and yet, strangely enough, a note of real eloquence came into his voice whenever he referred to us not as defendants in the abstract but as persons. . . . He went out of his way to pay us compliments which seemed utterly sincere. Especially he seemed genuinely troubled at having to ask the jury to convict Art Young.

To illustrate this, Floyd copied from the court record a passage of his summing up, arranging it in the form of a free verse poem.

A TRIBUTE

These men
    Are men of extraordinary intelligence.
Eastman is one of the brainiest men of our
    time—
A college professor, a writer of remarkable
    poetry, a brilliant orator, and a keen analyst
    of social conditions.
Rogers is a graduate of Harvard University
    and a hustling
Man of business.
Dell,
A trained journalist, a writer of
Exquisite English,
Keenly ironical, bitingly sarcastic.
Young, a cartoonist of national reputation,
A friend of Congressmen, and the Washington
    representative of one of our
Great magazines. . . .
Take Arthur Young.
I could cry
When I think of the position
In which this undoubtedly fine personal character
Finds himself today.
For the situation that he is in
I know your hearts went out to him,
Today.
But gentlemen,

We cannot let those feelings of sympathy,
Feelings of affection,
Of love almost,
That we might have for a man like Art Young—
We cannot let those feelings interfere
With our solemn duty at this time
To examine the evidence against Mr. Young
And to give a verdict on that evidence
And on that evidence alone.

The trial lasted nine days, and the jury stayed out from five forty-five on Thursday until the following Saturday at noon. Every once in a while they would come back for further instructions, looking more and more beaten and disheveled. "Hot, weary, angry, sad, limp and exhausted," was Floyd's description of them. The most dignified among them, juror number two, had evidently been crying. Only one remained fresh and gay in his bearing throughout. He was number twelve, the last man chosen—square-shouldered, blue-eyed, young and powerful, a factory manager from the Bronx. Art Young said he had "brawn and a jaw, like a good sputtering light in a lantern." Each time they filed in, this last man in the back row would glance down at me and laugh.

A strange thing happened on Friday evening while we were strolling in the corridors of the courthouse waiting for a verdict. We saw in the unlighted windows of the Woolworth Building opposite an imperfect reflection of the jury room. The jurors seemed surprisingly animated, one after the other getting up and shouting, one of them waving in the air what seemed to be a magazine; and we saw this twelfth juror, Henry C. Fredericks by name, stand up and take off his coat. We learned afterward that he alone had firmly made up his mind we should not be sent to jail for a crime we had not committed. He won two other jurors to his side, one of them the man who had come back with tear-stains on his cheeks. The rest berated him and yelled at him, and finally, learning that he was of Austrian descent, threatened to lynch him as a pro-German when they got him outside of the courthouse.

He said: "Why wait till you get outside? I'll take you on right here, either one at a time or all in a bunch, as you prefer."

That was when he took off his coat. The District Attorney, who told me this, added:

"If I had noticed that man's jaw, I would never have let him on the jury."

Art Young and Floyd and I went up to the Bronx afterward to call on Henry Fredericks, but he was away from home. I wrote him a sonnet which gave rest to my turbulent emotions about that first *Masses* trial.

TO THE TWELFTH JUROR

When I looked hard in those blue eyes, my son,
And saw no mercy and no melting there,
No heat of conscience, and no pious care
For points in virtue to be lost or won,
But just like the cool barrel of a gun,
A level gentle look into the air,
Too humorous for faith, too brave for prayer,
I knew that in twelve chances I had one.
And when you looked up laughing at the judge,
While his *good* jurors, locked up sixty hours,
Confessed in sweat they could not make you budge,
I did not feel like calling all the Powers
To righteous witness justice had been done—
I felt that to be with you would be fun.

Chapter 14

THE DIFFICULTY OF BEING A LOVER

I suppose I am a rather "sexy" person—and I judge it is true of the whole tribe of lanky, dark ministers and deacons from whom I derive. Although bent, most of them, on religious sublimation, I think *lecherous* is not too strong a term for the natural instincts they wrestled to hold in check. The term has been applied to me more than once and not without reason. Perhaps I can best summarize the facts by saying that I experienced no glimmer of surprise or disbelief when Dr. Kinsey published his book of statistics about *Sexual Behavior in the Human Male.*

I make these remarks by way of preface to an avowal of the blissful singleness of my devotion to Florence throughout the whole period I am describing. For the first time in my life I experienced no carnal or romantic yearning toward the shapely breasts and delicately upward curving calves of the summer-clad girls that would pass me on the street. Night and day I was absorbed in my great love. I was, in fact and to my amazement, monogamous. Indeed I was so completely lifted into heaven by Florence's body and spirit, that I feared for my own terrestrial selfhood, for my ambitions. Together with this fear of losing myself, I began also to experience a fear of losing her. I thought I saw evidences that she was drifting away from me. One of these evidences was her anger against me in the incident involving our cook, Geneva. But there were other angers and, I thought, other evidences. A list of these evidences, and the solemn counsels that I addressed to myself in consequence, concludes: "My problem is how to recover my self-reliant romantic nomad love of the world and of being, without losing the sustained attachment of my love for her."

The signs of coolness that I saw in Florence seem to have been but a phase in the naturally hesitant growth of her love—in her, too, a revolt perhaps against its expanding empire in her spirit. A strange thing about lovers' quarrels is that you can never remember what they were about. Even Tolstoy, in his *Family Happiness*, has a hard time inventing—or remembering, for it must be memory—the concrete details of those first scenes of anger in a couple once too blissfully in love. If Tolstoy could not do it, I need not try. Apart from the details, however, I think a disposition toward abstract reflection when concrete feeling is called for, often sets the scene for an explosion of wrath against me. While a companion is engaged in expressing emotions, she finds me passionately concerned with defining the facts. It must be a maddening trait.

I do remember one scene in which, besides crying out wildly against me, Florence actually struck me with her fists. Some letter was lying near us which I did not want her to see—perhaps from Mary or Sara Bard Field, or some special friend of Ida's, advising me about my conduct toward her, a problem in those days. I can't remember the letter. But I remember that, thinking she was going to pick it up, instead of telling her quietly that I did not want her to read it, I made an impulsive, almost hysterical grab for it. It was a feverishly foolish gesture, since the last thing in the world Florence could do would be to read a private letter of mine without permission. I suppose I remember this particular example because the shame of it was mine—but that was not always so.

I am not sure it was possible to solve the problem so accurately formulated in my self-reminder: "To recover my nomad love of the world and of being, without losing my love for her." It would necessitate my becoming classic rather than romantic in love, and that was hard for me to do. I have a penchant for loving women such as one is supposed to have for writing poems, and I give myself to it; I am absorbed into it as into a song. A recoil, a self-recovery, would seem almost inevitable. Especially so in this love for Florence, because her own selfhood was so strong and shining. She had all the poise and self-reliance and sure volition that I lack. I do not mean that she was bossy, or inflexible, or cocksure, or unteachable, or unsympathizing— none of these words apply. She could be like a little girl, and was so always toward my superior knowledge. But she had more momentum than I have, more self-reliance. She stood more firmly on her own feet. I wrote her what I called a "Praiseful Complaint" about this:

> How can you pass so proudly from my face,
> With all the tendrils of your passion furled,
> So adequate and animal in grace,

> As one whose mate is only all the world?
> I never taste the sweet exceeding thought
> That you might love me, though I loved you not.

But I wanted her to be like that, salient and separate, a being that I could—not humbly perhaps, but self-forgetfully—admire. This gave to her career, or her absorption in it, an unusual importance in my apprehension of her. It was not the glamour of Broadway or of Hollywood that mattered to me. As a revolutionary poet I was immune to all that. Indeed it is plausible—psychoanalytically, at least—that a career in the Christian ministry would have served as well or even better! It is a fact, at any rate, that her ambition was as important to me as it was to her, and its being a theatrical ambition was incidental.

To her it was inevitable. Of her performance in *Jaffery*, a discriminating critic had written: "Miss Deshon's impersonation has subtlety as well as dramatic vigor, and shows an unerring sense of drama. I do not know why she is not a star. Not only has she beauty and distinction, but a tremendous fund of emotionalism never at fault in its manifestations."

She came near, indeed, to being "a star." But she was too impetuous and too thinking a person to please the kind of producers and directors that had charge of the movies in those days. And she was proud; she was incapable of ingratiation toward people whom she did not respect. She was, besides, an ardent feminist. Her only poem during those early years was addressed to Susan B. Anthony, an incongruous object of hero worship for a fashion model and chorus girl on her way to becoming a movie star.

> I think of the tug boats on the river
> Steaming, strong and self-reliant
> Alongside the great white ship,
> Coaxing, encouraging,
> Until the beautiful timid maiden
> Feels her strength,
> And goes sailing
> All over the strong seas alone.

I am sorry I have to use the word feminist, or any word ending in *ist*, because Florence was no reformer. But the fact that her bent was to sail over the strong seas alone, and that I have a weakness for women who can do that, is essential to the portrayal of our relation.

I turn from that portrayal now to the equally subtle question of my relation to the Bolshevik revolution.

Chapter 15

THE DIFFICULTY OF BEING BOLSHEVIK

During the spring and summer of 1918 when the *Liberator* was lifting up, a little cautiously, the fallen red banner of the *Masses*, Woodrow Wilson himself was moving steadily to the left. With the best will in the world to be revolutionary, we could do little but endorse his pronouncements. His Letter to the Pope, his Fourteen Points, his message of good luck to the "republic of labor unions" in Russia, his refusal (as yet) to let the Japanese invade Siberia, his warning to the Allied Powers that their treatment of Bolshevik Russia would be the "acid test" of their "good will . . . intelligence and unselfish sympathy": these moves were immensely impressive to us. They were impressive also to the Bolshevik leaders in Moscow. It was at this time, indeed, and for Woodrow Wilson, that the Russian War Commissar, Leon Trotsky, invented the now famous notion of "fellow traveler." In an interview on March 5, 1918, Trotsky said:

America and Russia may have different aims, but if we have common stations on the same route, I see no reason why we cannot travel together in the same car, each having the right to alight when it is so desired.

This notion was developed and the term "fellow traveler" (*popuchik*) formally launched on its career in 1923, in Trotsky's *Literature and Revolution*. But I noted this earlier source because it fell in so pat with the political line I was taking in the *Liberator*. Together with his firm words on foreign policy, Wilson warned the leaders of his party not to let our soldiers come home to the "economic serfdom to which some of them had been accustomed." He also issued an executive order on conscientious objectors which I found quite shockingly and delightfully almost Christian. These things won me again strongly to his side. I did not go so far as Upton Sinclair, who proposed that the Socialist Party call a convention and formally declare its support of the President. But I endorsed the "sagacious opportunism" of Trotsky's figure of speech, and described the fluidity of Wilson's thinking as a "boon to us who believe in industrial and ultimate freedom and democracy." I was still regretting we had entered the war, but I felt that Wilson might find a fruitful way out of it.

As all the indicted *Masses'* editors were supporting these views in the *Liberator*, it seemed a crazy foolishness to prosecute us all over again. We thought it certain that the President, if diplomatically approached, would instruct the Attorney General to drop the case. Moreover, Lincoln Steffens, who prided himself on the diplomatic approach, kindly offered his services in this direction. Steffens, having renounced his effort to inject Christian forbearance into the struggle between labor and capital, was now devoting his skill as a persuader, and his prestige as a muckraker, to helping along everything that savored of revolution. He got me down to Washington and as near to the throne of grace as the office of the Solicitor General, John W. Davis—afterward Democratic candidate for President. Davis received me sternly but graciously, agreed that it was extravagant to push the prosecution, but made no promise. He knew, I guess, how stubborn the President was and how sulky against those who opposed him—especially if they had once been friends. But Steffens also got me an appointment with Wilson's alter ego, Colonel House, and sent me traveling out to his summer dwelling, a tiny cottage behind the trees in Beverly Farms, near Boston. My memory of this pilgrimage is dim—I suppose because I was a little ashamed of it—but I dined and spent the evening tête-à-tête with this shallowly shrewd, chameleonlike character who had so great an influence on the President. House was a professional smoother, a natural-born yesman, and that is what made him so useful to his aloof and socially fastidious master. I put these talents to a considerable strain because I felt obliged, in asking a favor of a "capitalist" government, to explain my revolutionary convictions with candor. So I gave the Colonel an extended lecture on class struggle as the method of progress toward universal freedom. He thought it was a fine idea, and I couldn't restrain him from falling in with it heart and soul, dragging Wilson in too. In the effort to disamalgamate us, I made some disparaging remark about Lord Balfour—the British Conservative who was then heading a mission to the United States.

"Oh, you needn't worry," the little man said. "I know him well. He's one of us!"

Naturally since we were all revolutionary good fellows, it would be folly for one to prosecute the other, and he would report our pleasant conversation to the President. A most enjoyable evening, a good dinner, and we parted the best of friends. But the net result was that when the Attorney General moved for a retrial, I knew it was the President himself, and no minor official, who had made the decision.

In the midst of this rather conciliatory phase of my revolutionism, John Reed arrived home from his great experience in Russia. He had come underground all the way across the world to stand trial with us, resisting both the laughs and the logic of Leon Trotsky, who thought such punctilious conduct amusingly un-Marxian. Jack never subscribed any more than I did to the religion of immoralism that the Bolsheviks inherited from Marx and Nechayer.* His sense of honor and good fellowship demanded that he come home, and he came. He rented an upstairs room on Sheridan Square around the corner from where I lived, and went to work daylong and nightlong on his great story of the October insurrection. I would meet him sometimes on the street sneaking out to get a sandwich, unkempt and in furtive haste, for no convivial friends must find out where he was.

"I've got a great name for it, Max," he confided one morning. "Ten Days That Shook the World!' " To his surprise and dismay—and later my own—I was not at all sure it was good.

Jack was an incarnation, more than any of the rest of us, of the spirit of the old *Masses*—gay and jocular and daring. He had a reckless equilibrium in walking life's tightropes that abashed me a little, and made me feel secondary, as though he were my more muscular big brother who knew all about living and was equal to it, whereas I was still trying to grow up.

We went swimming together once in the shallow foul mud of the Hudson, south of Croton Point, and while I held my head high above the water, feeling squeamish and eager to go back, Jack plunged in and out, doing his famous dolphin dive, as though these were the waters of life and not the sewage of Peekskill. The waters of life are, I am afraid, a good deal more like the sewage of Peekskill than the poets have told us, and that was the way Jack plunged into them—and through

* This heritage is described in "The Religion of Immoralism," Chapter VII of my book, *Reflections on the Failure of Socialism*.

them—reminding me of the phrase from Spenser that Keats loved to roll on his tongue, "the sea-shouldering whale."

Intellectually it was the other way around. Jack was still trying to grow up and I was, if anything, overconfident of my brains and judgment. I had explained to him about the theory of the class struggle, but he steadied me in the prosecution of it. And thus although our affection remained—except once—unspoken, we were very equal friends.

It was in 1916 when he went to Johns Hopkins to have an infected kidney removed that I wrote to him, expressing my admiration and concern. I told him I could not say "be of good courage," for he was made of courage, and he was too much the very spirit of life to die. I will place his answer here, since it is one of the things of which I am proud.

Dear Old Max—

I am very much touched and humiliated by your lovely note. Believe me, I feel that I should like to be the man you are—and I've always felt that.

Being in the one position for fifteen days, I cannot do more than just scribble this.

But it carries very deep and admiring affection.

I'm almost well now.

Love,
Reed

I recall this now because Jack's mood when he got back from Moscow had, inwardly, a damping effect on my zeal for the revolution. He wrote wonderful things about the seizure of power, the Red army, the Soviet system, revealing a mental industry and a grasp of complex facts that surprised us all. But he had lost much of his gaiety. It seemed to me that a person who had seen the victory of the working classes ought to have joy in his eyes. Instead Jack came home in a state of tension that was almost somber.

He had given himself, and been given by Lenin and Trotsky, the duty of organizing a genuinely American Bolshevik movement and he went about it without elation. This fact was more eloquent than his words. I remember it was my first marginal glimpse of a disappointment that would be fifteen years swimming to the center of my thoughts. America, with its scorn of cloudy ideologies, its loyalty to fact and philosophical respect for laughter, is intellectually, in so far as it *is* intellectual, a very advanced country. It is hard for an American to go back into medieval Russia, with its cults of mystical belief—especially hard, perhaps, when the belief in question is pure wishful metaphysics imported from Germany. It is like racing a car backward for a well-educated American to compete with a Marxian fundamentalist. That is what Jack had to do in order to fulfill his task of creating a Bolshevik party in the United States. He had also to lay aside the arrows of light with which Apollo had endowed him. "This class struggle plays hell with your poetry," he said to me one day.

To prove my mettle, I joined him in addressing a subversive street meeting down on the East Side, concluding my speech with "Long live the Soviet Government of the United States!" He gave me a glance of gratitude when I sat down. He knew it was a token performance on my part; I had no intention of joining him in his career as a "professional revolutionist." But it meant a good deal to him. He was in a rather lonely position, for almost all the active Bolsheviks in America at that time were foreign-born.

On the other hand, Jack was disturbed by the pro-Wilson tone of my editorials in the *Liberator*. The whole magazine must have seemed to him, fresh from an insurrection, rather lacking in belligerence. In the May number I remarked that "the hypothesis of international working-class revolution against war was tried out by Lenin and Trotsky, and it failed." I followed this in the July number with a proposal that the American Socialists lay aside their antiwar platform, and "join the British Labour Party and the Socialists of France, Italy and Belgium in endorsing President Wilson's war-aims." The St. Louis antiwar platform, I said, "bears no relation to a world in which there exists a Soviet Republic in danger of annihilation. . . . It bears no relation to a war in which the peace terms proposed by that republic have been embodied in the organized war program of our country. Our business now is to draft a platform for the congressional elections—a platform that will make clear that we stand for the revolutionizing of all industry along the lines outlined in the abstract by the British Labour Party, and being put to the test of extreme experience by the ruling proletariat of Russia."

That was not certainly a "Bolshevik" editorial, but no American, not even Jack Reed, knew then exactly what a Bolshevik was. Louis Fraina's volume, *The Proletarian Revolution in Russia*, containing key translations from Lenin and Trotsky, was still on the press. Lenin's "Letter to American Workingmen" had not arrived. His slogan, "Turn the imperialist war into a civil war!" was as far from our thoughts as the moons of Jupiter. Even Bill Haywood and Bob Minor, reddest of the red, had come over to the war party after Germany marched into the land of our dreams. Jack read my July editorial in manuscript, and gave a hasty assent to it, but I suppose he had a hard time defending it among his colleagues. His attempts to be an organizer had to begin largely among the Socialists of the Slavic Federations, most of whom, having been Menshevik enough before, became super-Bolshevik from the day Lenin seized the power. To them my salaam to the British Labour Party's new program of gradual socialism was "Menshevik"—which indeed it was—and that was the unpardonable sin. They further assumed, and I think a good many others did, that I had abandoned the revolution and gone over to Wilson, bag and baggage. Jack must have found this embarrassing, for the *Liberator* was his organ as well as mine.

Jack's home was in Croton, a little white house a half mile up the road from mine, and he came over one night after dinner, and walked up and down the room in his abstracted manner while Florence was clearing the table and I was puttering with some papers in my desk. He seemed to be neither coming to see us nor going away. Finally he said:

"Max, I think I've got to resign from the magazine."

It struck me like a gunshot. All the old doubts of my adequacy for the role of revolutionist rushed to my mind, the tears to my eyes.

"Well, it's your fault!" I said—always the first words on the lips of a guilty child. "I showed you my editorial. . . ."

Here my voice faltered, and I sprang up and walked out of the house. He had no chance to reply, if indeed he fully understood what I was saying. When I had composed my feelings out in my study in the barn, I came back very mature and calm, and joined in the conversation he was having with Florence. He sat around with us a long time, reluctant to go, knowing that he had hurt me—and he was a gentle person—and moreover undoubtedly wanting to discuss the whole situation and the policy of the magazine. But I would not revert to the subject—why, I can hardly tell. I suppose it was pride that sealed my lips—it was troubled feelings about my unmartyrlike role in the recent trial. He gave up hope finally of the conversation he wanted, said, "Well, so long!" paused once more in the doorway, and strolled up the road to his little white house. It was some days before I got his letter of resignation, which I published with my answer in the issue of September 1918. We continued to be good friends and neighbors, closer indeed than before, but neither of us ever mentioned these two rather formal letters.

Dear Max:

I'm going to have to resign as one of the contributing editors of the *Liberator*. I've thought about it a long time, and I make this decision not without emotion, remembering our long work together on the *Masses*.

But I feel I must take my name off the editorial page. The reason is, I cannot in these times bring myself to share editorial responsibility for a magazine which exists upon the sufferance of Mr. Burleson.*

Of course, this does not mean that I want to stop contributing to the *Liberator*. And in the happy day when we can again call a spade a spade without tying bunting on it, you will find me, as you have in the past,

Yours for the Profound Social Change,
John Reed

Dear Jack:

I haven't a word of protest—only a deep feeling of regret.

In your absence we all weighed the matter and decided it was our duty to the social revolution to keep this instrument we have created alive toward a time of great usefulness. You will help us with your writing and reporting, and that is all we ask.

Personally I envy you the power to cast loose when not only a good deal of the dramatic beauty, but also the glamour of abstract moral principle, is gone out of the venture, and it remains for us merely the most effective and therefore the right thing to do.

Yours as ever,
Max Eastman

An odd thing about those two letters is that my position was a good deal more "Bolshevik" than Reed's, which was rather on the anarchist or "Left Social Revolutionary" side. Lenin judged everything by the standard of purposive practicality, and in particular he always insisted that a revolutionary party must have *both* a legal and an illegal organ. Any good Bolshevik could serve on either one. I did not know that then, however, and neither, I suppose, did John Reed.

* The Postmaster General.

At any rate, this story has a happy ending, for Jack substantially withdrew his resignation by contributing to the *Liberator* more often, and more editorially, than before, identifying himself completely with the magazine in its two brilliant years of battle for the Soviets. At the time of his sad visit, I was already writing the essay on Lenin as "A Statesman of a New Order" which appeared in the same issue of the magazine with his letter of resignation. Had he seen that manuscript, or had I possessed the sense and simplicity to speak of it, he would never have resigned.

Chapter 16

AN ENEMY INSIDE MYSELF

I had barely recovered from the blow to my public pride of Jack Reed's resignation, when a far more grievous thing happened in my private life. It was, as I look back, the most tragic blow I ever received—almost gruesomely tragic because struck by some potency inside myself. I cannot explain it, but only describe the circumstances in which, of a sudden, it was delivered against me.

For some reason—no better to be defined than the *luck* that plays so deadly or exalting a role in all theatrical life—Florence's career ran, during the spring and summer of 1918, into a dead calm. In June we moved joyfully together into the little house in Croton, and, being idle, she did—in spite of herself—become almost a wife. She "settled down" into my house, and seemed content to stay there. This was quite reasonable, for there was no use running after theatrical engagements in midsummer, and I had no conscious thoughts, or even feelings, about it except the natural, and sometimes rather triumphant, pleasure of a lover in being able to offer a home to his love. The exhilaration and the tender joy of our days together, our walks through the wakening woods, or over the hill roads to the great dam, and in the midst of those days the sudden thought, quickening my pulse, that the nights also were mine, made me believe in love in a way that I would once have called old-fashioned. The present was thrilling, the future was full of events and adventures for us both: "Till death do us part," if those words had been spoken, would not have been discordant with my thoughts and feelings during the early summer of 1918.

But my self had a dreadful surprise in store for me. One morning in late August Florence was lying down reading on a couch under the window in our central room while I was working at a desk in the smaller room beyond. I got up and as I walked through the room where

111

she lay, as suddenly as a cramp seizes one's muscles, I was seized by the wish that she was not there. It was a wish to escape, to break from a chain, to be free of a commitment, to be myself again in my own house. Although this present love was so much greater, and the comparison pains me, the recoil was, I have to admit, similar to what had happened to me in 1911 when I awoke and found myself on an ocean liner, married, and committed to a journey abroad with Ida Rauh. And as then there came, together with the recoil, as an intrinsic part of it, the *certain knowledge* that I could never return to my unqualified joy in her again. It was the end forever of my one experience of "the Absolute."

I did not say any of this to Florence. I never told her about that sudden dreadful moment. I regarded it as the reappearance of a neurotic disease with which I am afflicted, a thing to be ashamed of and to conceal. Moreover, it had no place in the reasoned procedure of my life. My friends loved Florence as much as they loved me; they loved us together. She was the same beautiful and noble being as before; she had lost none of the qualities I adored. Both ideal wisdom and plain common sense rejected this intrusion from alien depths in my nature. And so I went right on, or tried to go on, as though nothing had happened.

I was an adept in the art of kept-up lovingness. I had practiced it as a husband for five years—not, I am sure, with convincing success, but well enough to get along. If there was a change now in my external behavior, it probably took the form of increased devotedness. But Florence most certainly sensed the subtle, underlying, unmaneuverable change in my feelings. I still loved and still adoringly admired her. We embraced with the same passion. But always a something within me like a semaphore rose up on the road to my total rapture, a warning that the switch was closed.

Chapter 17

A LIFT FROM EUGENE DEBS

There was a darkness over all my days now, a darkness from my own thoughts, and it was not lightened by the impending doom of a new prosecution for crime with a possible sentence of twenty years in prison. Out in Cleveland, Ohio, Eugene Debs, the standard-bearer of American socialism, was to go on trial in early September for the same crime of opposing the war. I went out there, both as a reporter and to get a little training for my own ordeal. I wanted also to renew an acquaintance which, except for an occasional exchange of letters, had been too brief. Indeed I think Debs and I had hardly spoken together except on one morning when he came unexpectedly up to the office of the old *Masses*, the little narrow upstairs office at 2 West Fifteenth Street. By good luck I happened to be there, but besides me none of the "crowd" except Stuart Davis, the least political-minded of our contributing editors. Stuart was prowling around looking for the originals of some of those powerful slum-amorous drawings of his. He stopped prowling when Debs came in, but listened in complete silence to our no doubt extremely political conversation. I had the idea that Davis was probably bored to death, a foolish idea, for he is keenly sensitive, and Debs was an electrical phenomenon that made the air in a room spark and crackle no matter what he was talking about. When he had grasped our hands and gone, Stuart drew a big breath as though he had been through some kind of shock treatment, and gasped: "My God, that man is *alive!*"

More than ever Debs was alive during that trial in Cleveland, and my experience of him, both in the courtroom and in the gatherings of friends in his hotel room in the evenings, gave me a lift out of the gloom. Debs had made his antiwar speech in Canton the previous June, and when I slipped into the courtroom, a pretty young man in a

pin-stripe suit and a bow tie was reading a transcript of it to the jury.
The young man was a trifle embarrassed to find so much wit and
eloquence and so little treason in his mouth.

The jury was composed of old men, rather tired and hard-looking.
Their average age was seventy years, their average wealth over fifty
thousand dollars—a lot of money in those days. But they had worked
for it; they looked worn and wearied out of all sympathy with a struggle
they had individually surmounted. Debs expressed their aspect to
perfection in one of our meetings after the court adjourned:

"There is something pathetic about dressed-up faces. If they had
been in rags it would have been all right."

To which he added a remark which shows how much more Christian
evangelism than Marxism there was in the American blend of socialism:

"What a contrast to turn toward the back of the courtroom and find
a little group of beautiful Socialists, with stars for eyes—you can
always tell them!"

Debs was a poet, and more gifted of poetry in private speech than in
public oratory. He was the sweetest strong man I ever saw. There is
both fighting and love in American socialism, and Debs knew how to
fight. But that was not his genius. His genius was for love, the ancient
real love, the miracle love that really identifies itself with the needs and
wishes of others. That gave him more power than was possessed by
many who were better versed in the subtleties of politics and oratory.
And he had another gift, the very one that Stuart Davis perceived. Every
instant and incident of life was keen and sacred to him. He handled his
body—and his mind too—all the time, as though it were a delicate
instrument. His tongue would dwell upon a *the* or an *and* with a kind
of earnest affection for the humble that threw the whole rhythm of his
sentences out of the conventional mold, and made each one seem a
special creation of the moment. He was tall and bald and long of finger
like a New Hampshire farmer, and yet as vivid, intense and exuberant
with amiability as the French—a kind of French Yankee.

I can see him sitting there before his judges, with detached emotion
but precise intellectual attention, his brow high, high wrinkles, William
Lloyd Garrison spectacles—something saintlike, infinitely uncompromising about him, infinitely undisturbed. . . .

I brought home with me a sample of what he had to listen to, an
hour long assault from a clumsy-thumbed hulk of a prosecutor with a
round jowl and a pointed nose.

Now I'll tell you in a nutshell the situation of this man an' all those he assumes to represent [he began]. I knew a farmer out here who had a barn an' the barn caught fire, an' he had a flock of sheep in the barn an' he got 'em out in the yard all right, but there was one old ewe [he pronounced it "yo"] at the head of the flock, an' she bolted around the barn and went back by another door, and the whole flock followed her. And then he got them out again on that side, and this old yo, she bolted round an' come in again on this side. An' that's the way it goes. And if this old yo [pointing to Debs] wants to go to the penitentiary I've got no objection, but I object to his taking a whole flock of the people with him. Congress has pledged the resources of the United States to win this war, and the resources of the United States are the body of Eugene Debs just as much as the cattle and crops. Just because he's got a smattering of history, enabling him to lead after him a rabble o' half bakes like that conglomeration over there in Russia, where the American boys have had to go over there to preserve for the Russians their rights against these Bolsheviki—why—why—I tell you these doctrines lead to nothing but trouble and distraction. He says that if Kate Richards O'Hare's guilty, he's guilty—if Rose Pastor Stokes is guilty he's guilty. Here's what Rose said [grabbing a paper] and you've heard the record that she got ten years for this job. . . . And here's what Debs says about the Stokes woman. Let's see now what Debs says about Rosie. Here's what Debs says about Rosie. . . . Why, they ought to be tried for treason, the whole outfit. If it had been any other country in the world but the United States they'd have faced a firing squad long ago.

So it flowed out of his mouth for an hour. I credited the district attorney with at least three of the six hours that the jury had to stay out recovering from the emotional impact of the scene they had witnessed. It would have been easy enough to convict Debs, for the wartime hysteria was still raging in the Middle West, and he made no attempt to deny that he had said what he was quoted as saying. But after that ungainly, greasy wolf with a high whine through his teeth had poured raw insults around the room until everyone present, from the judge to the stiff little bailiff, was mortified, and his own more clever assistant squirmed in his chair with embarrassment, it became difficult for the most patriotic jury to do its duty.

When the prosecution rested, Debs looked up at his chief attorney, Seymour Stedman, and Stedman looked over at the prosecutor.

"Let's see—you rest?" he said. "*We rest.*"

A kind of numb surprise possessed the court. Nothing was said for a while. The prosecutor was disappointed. He was to be deprived of his good sport of bulldozing witnesses for the defense. Finally the judge declared a recess of ten minutes, and everybody with a good seat settled to wait.

"Mr. Debs will conduct his own defense," Stedman said when the court assembled again, and he went over to the press table and sat down. The other attorneys sat down. Everybody waited, watching intently, as though for lightning. But Debs got up very deliberately, gathering some papers, and he looked in the eyes of his judge a full minute, while the room grew very still, before he began, courteously and quietly, but with that intense magnetic precision of his, to discuss the only question that engaged his fervent interest—the question whether or not what he had said in his speech at Canton was true.

For the first time in my life I appear before a jury in a court of law to answer to an indictment for crime. I am not a lawyer. I know little about court procedure, about the rules of evidence or legal practice. I know only that you gentlemen are to hear the evidence brought against me, that the Court is to instruct you in the law, and that you are then to determine by your verdict whether I shall be branded with criminal guilt and be consigned, perhaps, to the end of my life in a felon's cell.

Gentlemen, I do not fear to face you in this hour of accusation, nor do I shrink from the consequences of my utterances or my acts. Standing before you, charged as I am with crime, I can yet look the Court in the face, I can look you in the face, I can look the world in the face, for in my conscience, in my soul, there is festering no accusation of guilt.

I wish to admit the truth of all that has been testified to in this proceeding. I have no disposition to deny anything that is true. I would not, if I could, escape the results of an adverse verdict. I would not retract a word that I have uttered that I believe to be true to save myself from going to the penitentiary for the rest of my days.

It was dark when Debs began speaking, though only two o'clock in the afternoon, and as he continued it grew steadily darker, the light of the chandeliers prevailing, and the windows looking black as at nighttime with gathering thunderclouds. His utterance became more clear and piercing against that impending shadow, and it made the simplicity of his faith seem almost like a portent in that time of terrible and dark events. It was as though love and the very essence of light were inspired to lead the world straight on into the black heart of storm and destruction. . . .

On the following evening the jury, hardened up at last to their unwelcome task, tottered back to their seats. Cyrus H. Stoner, aged fifty-eight years, the youngest man among them, rose in a courtroom as silent, and as little illumined with hope, as the tomb.

"We find the defendant guilty, your honor."

Debs was sentenced to ten years in a federal prison, and received the news as calmly as one would receive a call to supper. I had remarked to him, in one of our conversations, that the trial did not seem to be much of a strain on him, and I remembered his answer:

"No, it doesn't rest on my mind much. If I'm sent to jail it can't be for a very long time. It's different with you. If you go, it may be an important part of your life. That's why my heart has been with you boys all these months."

The thought was not exactly a cheering one for me, and yet the fellow-feeling in it, the sense of being in such company—of having so noble an accomplice in my crime—was strengthening to my resolve to speak the whole truth and stand firmly by it in the ordeal that was coming.

On my way home to my half-happy love, I could at least comfort myself with the reflection: This time I won't feel too sublimely joyful to face with composure the prospect of a term in prison.

Chapter 18

ANOTHER HUNG JURY

The second *Masses* trial took place at the beginning of October 1918, just a month after Debs was condemned. As a dramatic performance, it was enhanced by the presence of John Reed among the defendants. Like our first trial, it somewhat resembled a course at a university—only now there wasn't any teacher. Hillquit was busy on another case, and Dudley Field Malone, whose witty and eloquent tongue had done so much to humanize Judge Hand's courtroom, called me up two days before the trial to say he had joined the navy and was off to Washington. Seymour Stedman, the attorney for Debs and for Socialists in general, came on by express train from Chicago. But he had no time to prepare his case, and moreover, came down with a fever the first day in court. A postponement was out of the question—we were a public nuisance as well as a crime wave now—and so we went ahead with little or no defense. A young law graduate named Charles Recht gave us what legal advice was indispensable, and Stedman, when present, would stagger from his seat occasionally, sweating with fever, and offer an objection for the record. Most of the time he was not there at all, and we just walked up to the witness stand, took the oath, and recited our lesson much as Hillquit had taught us to.

I think we had all quietly made up our minds we were going to jail this time, and the conclusion was not weakened when one of the talesmen, to an inquiry whether he had any prejudice against socialism, answered: "I don't know what it is, but I'm opposed to it." Another, a pompous, heavy-set, gold-watch-chained gentleman, when asked his business, replied conclusively: "Wall Street." A study of the new judge, Martin Manton, confirmed us in our mood of tranquil pessimism. He was hard, brisk, and mean-looking, unpossessed of dignity, and always in a hurry as though he had larger interests elsewhere.

"Let's get along with it! Let's get along with it!" would be his answer to Charles Recht's timid attempts to protect our rights.

He listened with alert interest, however, while Floyd Dell explained again, in his precise and slightly nervous manner, why he had opposed the war, and exactly what changes in the President's policy had brought him to support it. He listened as attentively while Art Young, solemn as a bloodhound and yet funny underneath, confessed his absolute pacifism and explained once more why cartoons can't be explained; and while John Reed recited to the jury, or rather to the upper half of a high window in the wall opposite the jury, his experiences as a war correspondent in Mexico, and then Europe, and all the general horror of the conflict over profits that had brought him to socialism and to Russia. He was very boyish and high-voiced and inept and uneasy in his clothes, but all the more likable and believable because of it. Some people, you look in their eyes and you say, "This man is honest and kind," and you feel that no further question need be asked. Jack had such eyes.

There was an ease and directness, and also an element of humor, in this lawyerless, if not lawless, mode of conducting a trial. It tended to mellow the jurors, no matter how dreadful they thought our crime was. Earl Barnes was again the prosecutor, and was again impeded in working up the anger that prosecuting attorneys are paid to deliver by his personal liking for us. Manton's brisk and unjudicial manner—he was unjudicial enough to accept enormous bribes later on, and spend the best years of his life in jail—still further helped to generate the atmosphere of a schoolroom.

On our side I, being the editor, was naturally the captain or head usher, and it fell to me to make the summing up. I took voluminous notes, and arranged the whole thing in careful order in my mind. In fact I spent the most of seven nights arranging it. I spent them alone in our bedroom under the slanty ceiling, for Florence was away on the road with a play. I was glad she was away. Even at the apex of love's curve I would have been glad, for I had to be alone. No one could help me learn my lines. I had to *be* the Attorney for the Defense, not just play the part.

Clarence Darrow remarked in his memoirs that when defending himself against the charge of bribing a juror in the MacNamara trial, "I felt as much at ease and as indifferent over my fate as I would have standing comfortably at a harmless fireside surrounded by loving friends." He belonged to a different species from me. I was keyed up to a degree that made eating painful and sleep impossible. My heart would pound unbelievably all night long, and I would go over the points of my summing up until they had a hard shine to them and fitted my mind like a well-worn suit of clothes.

The judge had ruled against our attempt to bring in testimony as to what was happening in Russia, but I assumed the right, as relevant to our intent, to state *our opinion about what was happening in Russia,* and he did not stop me. This permitted an exposition of the entire socialist philosophy, and incidental to that, a defense of the party's St. Louis resolution condemning the entrance of the United States into the war. I stated that during the past winter when Germany was invading Russia, I had felt a doubt as to the wisdom of that resolution, but I now thought the Socialists were right as well as courageous. On the subject of conscription I quoted Daniel Webster, not omitting to mention that he was a member of the Eastman family, and not hesitating to pour all the force I inherited from two generations of preachers into his resounding eloquence.

My speech, issued as a pamphlet, was sold in large quantities by the *Liberator.* I will quote, as relevant to the ideological part of this travelogue, what I said about the socialist theory after explaining it to the jury.

> And so I ask you that, whatever your own judgment of the truth or wisdom of our faith may be, you will respect it as one of the heroic ideas and ardent beliefs of humanity's history. It is a faith which possesses more adherents all over the surface of the earth who acknowledge its name and subscribe to its principles, than any other faith ever had, except those private and mysterious ones that we call religious. It is either the most beautiful and courageous mistake that hundreds of millions of mankind ever made, or else it is really the truth that will lead us out of our misery, and anxiety, and poverty, and war, and strife and hatred between classes, into a free and happy world. In either case it deserves your respect.

It was the only long extemporaneous speech I ever made—I mean not written out and learned by heart—and I was intemperately proud of its success. Judge Manton adjourned us for lunch just after the above peroration, and when we came back the walls of the courtroom were lined with official-looking people, some of them in uniform. As we entered the door, Jack Reed murmured: "My God, are they getting ready to take us to jail already?"

It looked that way. But just before I got up to resume my argument, Jack leaned back in his chair and whispered: "All of those people have come from other parts of the building to hear the rest of your speech."

It was an intimately honest speech, and for that reason, I think, brought me unusually warm words of praise. The most unexpected came next day in a letter from one of the prosecuting attorneys: "As an address of a man accused of a crime, it will probably live as one of the great addresses of modern times." The most treasured came from Eugene Debs in Atlanta penitentiary: "Your speech before the court was a masterpiece, and will stand as a classic in the literature of the revolution." Floyd Dell, in his famous little book, *Love in Greenwich Village*, made me famous too with these words: "Max Eastman was the acting editor: Tall, handsome, sleek, and in repose as lazy looking as a hound-dog lying on the hearth, he exhibited an immense energy on the platform; he was one of the two real orators I have heard in my lifetime—and his best speech, I think, was made at the *Masses* trial, when what were left of its editors were solemnly prosecuted for making jokes about the war for democracy."

But what most strengthened my heart was John Reed's account of the trial, written for the next issue of the *Liberator* at Floyd's request. Jack, I believe, was regretting his resignation from the editorial staff—for a reason the next chapter will explain—and he described my conduct at the trial in terms that modesty forbids, but candor perhaps— in view of their importance to my troubled self-esteem—will justify my quoting.

The one great factor in our victory was Max Eastman's three-hour summing up. Standing there, with the attitude and attributes of intellectual eminence, young, good-looking, he was the typical champion of ideals—ideals which he made to seem the ideals of every real American. I had attempted to bring in the case of the Russian Soviet Republic, to combat the insinuations of Mr. Barnes that the Bolsheviki were German agents and that we supported them in their corruption. With suspicious reluctance the Court ruled all that evidence out. But Max boldly took up the Russian question, and made it part of our defense. The jury was held tense by his eloquence; the Judge listened with all his energy. In the courtroom there was utter silence. After it was all over the District Attorney himself congratulated Max, and it is rumored that Marshal McCarthy began to preach socialism to his deputies.

Stedman revived sufficiently to make a brief address to the jury, appealing dextrously to the one thing we had a ray of hope in, their good-humored common sense. He was, as Reed said, "the kind of man men listen to." Both Stedman and I predicted what the prosecuting attorney would say in his summing up, and he confirmed our prediction so exactly that it made him seem a little like a long-legged parrot. He concluded with the tragic tale of a friend of his who had died in the trenches in Europe so that the world might be made free.

"Somewhere in France," he cried, "he lies dead, and he died for you and he died for me. He died for Max Eastman. He died for John Reed. He died for Merrill Rogers. His voice is but one of a thousand silent voices that demand that these men be punished. . . ."

Art Young, who had been quietly sleeping at the counsel table, awoke at this point. He listened for a moment with growing perplexity, then leaned across the table and said in a loud whisper: "Didn't he die for me too?"

Judge Manton's charge to the jury was eminently just, and in the general state of opinion surprisingly liberal. He declared that anyone in the United States could say that the war was not a "war of democracy," that it was an imperialist war, that the government of the United States was hypocritical—in sum, he reminded the jury that even under the Espionage Act, every American had the right to criticize his government and oppose its policies, so long as he did not intend to discourage enlistment and recruiting or cause mutiny and disobedience in the armed forces. As my argument had, in form, been addressed wholly to the question of intent, this was almost a punctuation of what I had said.

Thanks to the absence of lawyers, this second trial lasted only five days. The jury retired late Friday afternoon, and on Saturday brought in the result of their deliberations; again a hopeless disagreement, but this time eight for acquittal and only four for conviction. It was a heavy score against the government, the only setback they received, so far as I can remember, in all these "espionage cases." Apparently it dammed the overflow of that abounding love which, according to Burleson, the administration felt toward me, for the case was dropped and our impounded correspondence promptly sent back.

One always speculates as to what is in the mind of the various jurors, whether their vote is going to be determined to any degree by the evidence presented. I was particularly curious about a bland, sandy, slickly brushed juror, who sat in the front row expressionless and almost motionless throughout the trial. He came up to me as the others filed out, extended his hand and said: "Mr. Eastman, I am familiar with your book on poetry and I was on your side from the beginning."

A few days after the trial, another crisis arose in my life as an antiwar Socialist. I received on October 15 a notice from my local draft board that I had been placed in Class I, and that I must appear for physical examination at 4 P.M. on November 2, 1918. "Failure to do so is a misdemeanor punishable by one year in prison . . . or immediate induction into military service." The draft board occupied the office at 59 Washington Square of Vincent Pepe, the rotund, glinty-eyed Italian real estate agent for all Greenwich Village—a man as affable as he was unpersuadable on questions of life and death like a delay in the payment of one's rent. (He did, though, once make a contribution toward the survival of Margaret Anderson's *Little Review*.) Pepe's name was signed to the card ordering me to appear.

After meditating awhile and summoning up the courage, I mailed this letter:

Local Board 153, New York City
Dear Sirs:

Before I appear for physical examination, I should like to give you this account of my state of mind. I do not believe in international wars, and I do not recognize the right of a government to conscript the bodies of its citizens for service upon foreign soil. I think it is an abandonment of those principles of human liberty upon which the American republic was founded. In the name of those principles, therefore, I must decline to serve.

I am aware that the Conscription law takes no account of such principles, although they are more sacred and of more value to the country than any religious scruple, or membership in any antimilitary sect, could possibly be. Therefore I do not expect any deferred classification upon the ground of this statement. I hand it to you merely because I wish to have the record clear from the beginning.

Yours sincerely,

On the morning of November 1, I received a notification that I had been reclassified in Class IV and that I need not appear. I met Vincent

Pepe on the street one day after the war ended, and he said: "That was an interesting letter you wrote to the draft board. I placed it, just as a kind of curiosity, in the bottom drawer of my desk."

I have been a lucky devil all through life, but this has won me so much enmity that I sometimes think a little bad luck would have smoothed the way.

Chapter 19

THE IMPACT OF LENIN

Up to this point, I think you could hardly describe me as a wild or fiery radical. At least it is not true that I was "so red my shadow turned the grass on Union Square to crimson," as the *United Mine Workers' Journal* once remarked. Jack Reed's resignation from the *Liberator* is strong evidence to the contrary. Now, however, a thing happened which did add reckless force to my revolutionism. It was my reading of Lenin's *Program Address to the Soviets*, published by the Rand School with the misleading title, *The Soviets at Work*. It is the same pamphlet that, picked up on a newsstand seven years later, brought Whittaker Chambers into the Communist movement, and set going a famous series of events.*

In order to explain the impact upon me of Lenin's pamphlet, I must amplify a little what I said in Chapter 4 about my attitude to socialist ideas. To me socialism was not a doctrinal belief, but a working hypothesis. I did not think Marx explained the world or told us where history was going; I thought he proposed a method of procedure by which we might make history go, in certain defined respects, in a particular direction. To me the procedure was experimental, and the ideas were subject to correction. This distinguished me in vital ways from the general run of "believers" in socialism.

Since it was a method rather than a doctrine I believed in, and class struggle was the heart of the method, my belief placed me, from the beginning, in the militant or revolutionary wing of the movement. I actually had more to do—as orator and editor—with strikes led by the Industrial Workers of the World than electoral campaigns conducted by the Socialist Party. I have described in the previous memoir my Sabbath day speech to the striking silk-workers in Paterson, New Jersey, the momentous meeting with their leaders, Bill Haywood, Carlo

* See *Witness* by Whittaker Chambers, p. 194.

Tresca, Elizabeth Gurley Flynn. It was my first real taste, you might say, of the revolution I was talking about. The IWW was the only genuinely *proletarian* revolutionary organization that ever existed in America—one of the few that ever existed anywhere. Under Bill Haywood's leadership it was engaged in "direct" as against "political" action when I became a Socialist. Bill was expelled from the party in 1912 for "advocating sabotage and violence." I was on his side, and my first political utterance was a defense of the IWW and an attack on Article VI of the party constitution under which he had been expelled.

However, there was no place in the IWW for mere intellectuals—you had to be a "fellow worker"—and I felt honor-bound to take some public stand for my principles. The Socialist Party had at that time, in addition to its program and constitution, a little pink slip to be signed by prospective members pledging their loyalty to the class struggle. I don't know how that happened, for the party was largely captained by reformers and humanitarian settlement workers of the type of John Spargo and the millionaire J. G. Phelps Stokes. Eugene Debs, the party figurehead, had started in as a militant labor leader, but retired and became a lecturer as a result of his conversion to Marxism—a rather undynamic Marxism! However, that little pink slip went to the heart of my method, and I signed up (on February 14, 1912), not feeling that I had found a home, but that I had cut off avenues to success that might conflict with my loyalty to my ideals. With one inconsequential exception, to be mentioned later, that is the only time I ever joined a party.

The slip I signed was probably not pink; that is a comment my memory makes on it. But the party was—or rather it was all the colors of the spectrum, and I was very conscious of being at the red end. I was more steadily conscious, however, of my doctrinal heresy—my wish to substitute experimental method for the bigotry of the Marxian religion. I waged a one-man war on "dogma" that was quite as distasteful to the Reds as to the Pinks and Yellows. Indeed I attacked the dogmatism of the Socialists almost as often and violently as the tyranny of the capitalists. My idea of a revolution conducted in the spirit of experimental science, conducted by completely flexible, and I even called them "liberal," minds, enabled me to exercise independent judgment upon many questions that for the true believers were "covered" by their faith in economic evolution.

For instance, I declined to believe that the problem of women's rights would settle itself automatically under social ownership of the means of production. That article of the Socialist credo I regarded as a hoax. I took the same view of the problem of population control—man's primary problem, I believed, and still believe—and this also put me in conflict with the Economic Interpretation of Everything that Troubles You. I also resisted the temptation to subordinate moral standards to the temporary exigencies of the class struggle, and I wrote editorials on the folly and illogic of class hate.

These heresies will illustrate the free judgment permitted me by my special brand of socialist belief. I was not trying to escape from the tough-minded revolutionism, but from the bigotry, the theological finality, the mystic priest-begetting over-allness of the Marxian theory. I was taking the phrase "scientific socialism" seriously, using the word "science" in the British and Latin sense, not in the sense of the German *Wissenschaft*, least of all as that word was employed by the mystical materialist, Karl Marx. I never formulated this view except in scattered editorials, an unpublished lecture called "What Socialism Really Is," and three chapters of an unborn *magnum opus* entitled *Towards Liberty, the Method of Progress.** Few even of the steady readers of my editorials realized that I had any such independent philosophic viewpoint. You would not naturally expect one in a magazine of art, poetry, and satire such as I edited. I was certainly left alone with it. I never had a follower, never a "disciple," in my life.

In Lenin's *Program Address to the Soviets*, I felt the living presence of that practical-minded and free-minded engineer of revolution for which I had been waiting. From beginning to end its language was that of astute, flexible, undoctrinaire, unbigoted, supremely purposive, and I judged experimental, intelligence. It had an impact on my political thinking that no other printed words ever had. I still think—although the sense it conveys of an all-powerful will and intelligence consecrated to the highest ideals is tinged with bitter pathos now—that this document marks one of the high points reached by human mind and character. That an inveterate lifelong rebel, who could lead a mob in overthrowing a state and seizing an empire, could on the next day turn his mind to the patient, fine, laboriously affirmative social and psychological task of replacing it with a new and nobler civilization, seemed wonderful to me then, and it seems hardly less so now. I have no

* The three chapters were published in the *Masses* in the summer of 1916.

patience with those who equate Lenin with Stalin. Lenin committed crimes enough in his passionate infatuation with the Marxian religion. "He had the courage to believe that the evil he did would not live after him." * He derived this disastrous courage from his faith. He was absolutely sure that his master, Marx, and his God, the dialectic universe, if he never betrayed them, would not in the long run let him down. And the evil he did never went beyond what might have been

Drawn by Robert Minor

CLEMENCEAU: "BUT WHERE WILL YOU GET THE TROOPS?"
LENIN: "I'LL USE YOURS."
The Liberator   February 1920

judged expedient if this pseudo-scientific religion had been science. Stalin's regime was a brutish burlesque both of the religion and the practice based upon it.

I did not know that Lenin was a "true believer" in this religion then. None of his other works were translated, and I saw no trace in his pamphlet of any inferences from philosophic dogma. I thought he had a scientific mind.

* I quote from George Backer in *The Deadly Parallel, Stalin and Ivan the Terrible.*

Thus in the *Liberator* for September 1918—the same issue that contained Reed's letter of resignation—I published the first of two articles entitled "A Statesman of the New Order," in which I greeted Lenin with unqualified and, I fear, adulatory endorsement.

"He has the habit," I wrote, "of defining a problem before he enters it, and he enters it with the trained equilibrium of one who knows the true relation between facts and ideas in scientific thinking—and one who knows what to do with his emotions while thought proceeds. . . . Unlike most scholars, most idealists, and above all perhaps, unlike most Marxian Socialists, he knows how to think in a concrete situation."

I did make one criticism of Lenin's position, but it only testified to my trust in the scope and freedom of his mind. I said that in his discussion of means for increasing the productivity of labor, I missed a reference to the means of decreasing the production of people. Aside from that, my two articles were a paean of intellectual praise. I was completely swept along by his careful pointing out, amid the hard bitter fights and anxieties of the struggle for production and power, the path to a realization of the extremest humane dream of socialism.

People who cite the utopianisms in Lenin's *State and Revolution*, written just before the seizure of power, and imagine they were the tricks of a demagogue, or remark cynically that he forgot them as soon as the power was in his hands, should read a little of this fervent address to the soviets in the spring of 1918. It contains the remark quoted against him that "the dictatorship of individuals has frequently in the history of revolutionary movements served as an expression and means of realization of the dictatorship of revolutionary classes." A dangerous remark, but in this case at least Lenin was not using it to recommend individual dictatorship as a form of government. He was using it to persuade the workers who had joined him in the joys of a revolution to *go to work* now that the revolution was over, and to recognize that modern machine industry demands unity of effort, and unity demands "absolute submission to the will of the Soviet Director, of the dictator, *during work*." (Lenin's italics.)

This submission to authority during work, he insisted, must be offset by an absolute and continual control by the masses of those in whom the authority is vested. It must be offset also by meetings of the workers in which they will gradually learn to discipline themselves. "This meeting-holding," he exclaimed, "is ridiculed, and even wrathfully hissed at by the bourgeoisie, the Mensheviks, etc., who see only chaos, senseless bustle, and outbursts of petty-bourgeois egotism. But without this 'meeting-holding' the oppressed masses will never pass from discipline enforced by the exploiters to a conscious and voluntary discipline."

Yes, Lenin really expected a millennium to grow out of the chaos and bustle of these workers' meetings. And already in this early speech he was pitting himself against the "petty-bourgeois tendency to turn certain members of the soviets into parliamentarians or into bureaucrats. . . . This should be combatted by attracting *all* members of the soviets into practical participation in the management. Our aim is to attract *every* member of the *poor* classes into practical participation in the management, and the different steps leading toward this end (the more diverse the better), should be carefully registered, studied, systematized, verified on broader experience, and legalized. It is our object to obtain the *free* performance of state obligations by *every* toiler after he is through with his eight hour 'lesson' of productive work. This transition will secure the definite realization of socialism."

That much will show the magic this pamphlet exercised upon minds that wanted socialism to be real as well as revolutionary. But I must quote one more paragraph in order to reveal the quality in Lenin's thinking which made me think I had found in him my ideal of a modern engineer of revolution.

It is not enough to be a revolutionist and an adherent of socialism, or in general a Communist. One must be able to find at any moment the particular link in the chain of development which must be grasped with all strength in order to hold the whole chain and assure the passage to the next link. And the order of the links, their form, their connections, their distinction from one another in the historical chain of events, is not as simple and obvious as in an ordinary chain which is made by a blacksmith.

Lenin did excel all Marxists, and it seems to me most consecrated men of any faith, in combining inflexibility of purpose with fluidity of plan. And he was selfless enough to do this without moral confusion. I was so moved by this discovery that I tried to express in poetry as well as prose the kind of force and equilibrium that such a mind must possess. My sonnet to Lenin, published in the *Liberator* for November 1918, was written while he lay stricken, perhaps fatally, by the bullet of a member of the opposing party of "Socialist Revolutionaries"—an extreme idealist too, but of the old dogmatic type which I believed he had superseded.

Men that have stood like mountains in the flood
Of change that runs like ruin through the earth,
When murder takes the sanctity of birth,
When food is fire and harvest-treasure blood,
Men that like fixed eternal stars have stood,
Their faith clear-shining sadly, and their mind
Unmaddened by the madness of their kind—
They were the godlike, they the great and good.
With light, and mountain steadiness, and power,
And faith like theirs in this all-fluid hour,
You to the dreadful depth of change descend,
And with its motion, moving it, you blend
Your conquering purpose as blue rivers roll
Through all the ocean's waters toward the pole.

I did not want to use the word "faith" in this sonnet; it was forced on me by a rhythmic necessity. But the rhythm was wiser than I, for I was mistaken in thinking Lenin's judgment was free or his attitude scientific. It was only *within* the dialectic faith that he was free; and it was only with the support of a mystical belief that history and the universe were on his side, that he kept his purpose firm.

This is clear to me now in the simile quoted above about the "chain" of historic development. The chain is already stretched there, you see, across or through a chaos of events, and it is obviously fastened securely at the forward end, for we are traveling along it hand-over-hand. I remember, when I first read the pamphlet, imputing this imperfection to a lack of liveliness in Lenin's imagination. "His images are not so clear as his logic," I said to myself. But I was wrong; Lenin's images were always clear. The central essence of his thought, and of his will also, is revealed in that simile of the chain. He was a fanatic of the Marxian religion. Though he excelled Karl Marx both in mental clarity and moral character, he never wrote or uttered one word in criticism of the Marxian scriptures. A superstitious belief that the chain of historic events was attached with iron necessity to an earthly paradise, and that he was responsible only for getting a firm hold on the next link, was the inward cause both of his success and his failure, his noble devotion and its dreadful result.

This steadfast superstition enabled him, while events sufficiently conformed to it, to defeat his parliamentary rivals and create out of the soviets a new form of government supposed to introduce the genuine self-rule of the toiling masses. But it also permitted him, when the events got out of hand, to curb them with a party dictatorship which made a farce of his new government. The "Council of People's Commissars," so loudly proclaimed as the sovereign body in the early days, was never actually distinct from the Politburo of the party, and even its name was soon forgotten. The *notion* of soviet government was a valid inference from Marxian theory; the *fact* of one-party dictatorship was both result and proof of its untruth.

Never, I think, was the superiority of science to superstition made more manifest. If Lenin had known that his gigantic effort in Russia was an experiment, he might have seen instantly and constantly made clear to his followers when, at which points, and in what degree, it was failing. But he was unable to entertain such a conception. His mind contained no avenues opening upon it. His brain was encased, as firmly as by his skull, in this primitive superstition which had put itself over on radical minds for a hundred years as the last word in social science. He could only hold fast to the power of the party, believing it to be the "next link," and waiting with agony of impatience for the movement of events to overtake him. He died in this attitude, and I think very near to the day of despair.

But I was long in finding this out, and I am afraid it has carried me rather far from the particular chain of events I am supposed to be retracing here. Let us come back, then, to the unqualified delight my mind experienced in finding this political genius possessed, seemingly, of the very traits and place in history I had wished for and predicted. I was firmly convinced now that in Marxism, remodeled as a method of experimental procedure, we had a science of social action which, when applied by a great engineer, might actually transform the world in the direction of man's otherwise utopian dreams.

Chapter 20

CLOSE TO CONSECRATION

Ever since prep school, my disposition to study and think has been mitigated by the wish to be a "regular guy." I had a veritable horror of being despised as a highbrow. This had much to do with my success as editor of the *Masses* and the *Liberator*. After a thoughtful essay like my "Statesman of a New Order," or like the chapter you have just finished—if you did finish it—I would play up a fanciful or frolicsome drawing, or sprinkle a few pages with things merely lovely or mirthful in poetry or prose. One of my most reliable aides in these maneuvers was Hugo Gellert. He was a Hungarian, slight of frame and with a sad-faced smile. His gift—or at least the gift he gave most often to the *Liberator*—was to draw delicate, fairy-tale pictures like illustrations for *A Child's Garden of Verses*. He was addicted to sprightly, naked little boys and girls hunting rabbits and gazelles with a bow and arrow, or sucking their breakfast from the teats of a complaisant goat. No other magazine ever published so many pictures of goats. But they were gay, heart-lifting goats. Hugo had fancy. And fancy in its pure form is a rare thing in our concrete-pavement civilization. His gift, although slender-seeming, was priceless to me, not only as a relief from heavy thinking, but because it helped me to approach my ideal of a universal magazine, one that should get away from the monotonous hammer-tone of propaganda. But Hugo had in him, beneath this light foam of fancy, a raging anger at the world. After helping so deftly to keep the *Liberator* from being fanatical, he became something of a fanatic himself. To serve the Communist Party gods, he employed his genius in drawing illustrations for the ponderous abstractions of *Das Kapital*. That required fancy too, I must say, but I can hardly agree with those who think it was a putting away of childish things. For many years he also drew pictures for the *New Yorker*, illustrating their profiles of celebrities with ironical portraits that seemed to have more kinship with the old *Liberator* goats.

Another genial mainstay in combining mirth with socialism was Howard Brubaker. Ernest Poole describes him in his memoirs as "a little man with a chuckle that nobody ever forgot and a smile that went from ear to ear." That much of his person I too remember, but little more, for, although he contributed a column of jocose paragraphs to every issue of the *Masses* and the *Liberator* for the whole ten years of their existence, I never saw him but about three times in my life. He had belonged to a socialistic writer-reformer group that centered around the University Settlement: Leroy Scott, Walter Weyl, Robert Hunter, William English Walling, Ernest Poole, Arthur Bullard, Frances Perkins. It was Frances' husband, Paul Wilson, who suggested that Howard would make us a good contributing editor. From the standpoint of the editor's anxieties, he made one of the best in the whole history of journalism. His column of astutely-grinning paragraphs would arrive with the regularity of a railroad clock just twenty-four hours before the deadline. Subsequently he made for many years a similar, though slightly less explosive, contribution to the *New Yorker*, and that too, I am told, with the same punctuality. Never before were good jokes cracked so exactly on time. And they were not only on time, but timely.

> Rev. Charles A. Eaton says his head is bowed in shame over the appointment of George D. Herron, a Socialist, to meet with the Russians. In the distressing years ahead Dr. Eaton's head will be bowed so constantly that he will look like a doughnut.
>
> Prof. John Graham Brooks says that labor will bungle horribly in its new policy of mixing in world politics. Obviously the bungling should be left to the professional bunglers.

While speaking of mirth, I must contribute my mite to the mounting celebrity of Louis Untermeyer. Since the *Liberator* days, Louis has been so ubiquitous on the literary scene that few great poets are better known. He is an excellent poet himself, too, and was among the gayest and most life-giving friends of the *Liberator* and the *Masses*. His wit and the perpetually amused expression he wore behind old-fashioned rimless glasses, were a priceless asset in our literary gatherings. He was also one of the few contributing editors who made it their eager business to contribute.

A similarly mirthful member of our staff, and more in need of memorializing, was Charles W. Wood. He had only to dip his pen in the ink in order to turn out a jovially funny dramatic criticism, or a comically rhymed verse. But in order to perform these feats he had to dip his pen in the ink several times, and he found this an almost excruciating effort. Like that of many humorists, Charley's look was sad; and it was also a little sick, for he drank too much beer to do him any good.

While holding to this policy of gaiety, or universality, in the magazine, I came pretty close in my own heart, after my discovery of Lenin, to the mood of consecration. I was, at least, from the winter of 1919, a fixed and fervent evangelist of revolutionary socialism—or, as it began to be named, communism. I was thirty-five years old, but my mood approached that of a young convert. The surprise of having my abstractly reasoned beliefs come concretely true was, indeed, for a person of my skeptical temper, as exciting as a conversion.

My "bolshevization" had been helped along when Woodrow Wilson decided, in August 1918, to join his European Allies in their military intervention in Soviet Russia. The austere talking-to he had given them about the "acid test" was forgotten now; his good-will message to the "republic of labor unions" was forgotten. "Economic Serfdom," the rights of conscientious objectors,* peace without annexations or indemnities—all the lofty abstractions were floating away. It was the second time he had taken a bold stand in the abstract and backed concretely, and very suavely, down.

Moreover on the very day when he declared that "everything for which America fought has been accomplished," and "it will now be our fortunate duty to assist by example . . . in the establishment of just democracy throughout the world," his Attorney General Palmer announced that the censorship of information and opinion under the wartime espionage law, instead of being relaxed, would be tightened throughout the period of settlement. It would be hard to find in the history of freedom a cruder violation of "just democracy" than that censorship as the federal police proceeded to nail it down over the country. No mention of these "Palmer Raids"—nor indeed of the wartime witch hunt which I described in an earlier chapter—is usually made when Woodrow Wilson is eulogized as a champion of democratic freedom. He was sick now, to be sure, but even so, such an extreme

* His indifference to violations of his executive order on this subject was obdurate.

measure of oppression could hardly have been adopted without his express consent. It reveals again the ease with which his mind could soar among abstractions with hardly a glance down at the concrete facts, hardly a flutter of the wings.

In an article in our February number, I lined up as a token display of the "New Tyranny" these sixteen headlines from one issue of the *New York Times:*

ROUND UP OF REDS

100 Taken in and near Buffalo
Raids in 17 Connecticut Towns
Fifteen Taken in Bridgeport
Seize 150 Radicals in Nashua
65 Arrested in Manchester
Seize 30 Russians in Boston
Seize Eight at Lawrence
Nine Arrests Made at Holyoke
Worcester's Total Exceeds 50
Take Thirty at Lowell
Twenty-one Arrested in Haverhill
Springfield Rounds Up 65
Several Arrests in Rhode Island
Round Up 18 at Baltimore
Oakland Raid Nets 15
Louisville's Bag Is Twenty

It is now established that Attorney General Palmer obtained warrants for the arrest of six thousand "dangerous aliens," and that on January 2, 1920, his agents swept down on thirty-three cities and netted a bag of twenty-five hundred "suspected radicals." (I quote from Daniel Bell in *Socialism and American Life*, Volume I, page 330.) A total of four thousand persons were arrested, one thousand ordered deported. Roving bands of vigilantes and ex-servicemen raided with impunity foreign-language clubs, IWW headquarters, and other radical meeting places, beating up as well as arresting anyone found there. Even the Rand School for Social Science, so academic in its socialism that we called it stodgy, was fined three thousand dollars for publishing a pamphlet disrespectful of the war. An effort was made to close it by injunction, to annul its charter and wipe it from the earth. The witch hunt got so bad that a group of lawyers headed by our most distinguished jurist, Charles Evans Hughes, issued a report declaring that "perhaps to an extent unparalleled in our history, the essentials of liberty are being disregarded. . . . We know of violations of personal rights which savor of the worst practices of tyranny."

Why our *Liberator* office was not raided we never could guess, unless it was that Wilson failed so miserably in his two previous efforts to put us in jail. We were most inconveniently and awfully American.

My point here is that this manifestation of "capitalist tyranny" by the genteel prophet of the New Freedom strengthened me in the belief that only those who identify themselves with the struggle of the working class have a reliable interest in building a free and just society. At the same time, the honest efforts of the Bolsheviks to build such a society in Russia were so fabulously lied about in the American press, pulpit, barroom, and drawing room, in Congress and on the lecture platform, that truth itself seemed to be crying for help. I think over half the country actually believed that "Lenin and Trotsky" had decreed the "nationalization of women"—whatever that might mean—and that this was the essence of the new and monstrous thing called "bolshevism." As late as April 1919 we were publishing an article by Louise Bryant refuting this meaningless myth. A hint of the madness that possessed ignorant minds may be seen in the fact that so well-educated a man as Walter Lippmann, left-liberal and ex-socialist, described "going Bolshevik" as *repudiating all authority and obligation.* Summoning his most oracular intonation, Walter defined Bolshevism in the *New Republic* as "a complete dissolution of centralized organization into local atoms of self-government." (!)

To us who knew the facts and counted Lenin and Trotsky as our comrades, the challenge was tantamount to a command. We had no choice but to plunge in and fight the battle of opinion on their side.

At every meeting we hold and in every paper we publish it is our duty as socialists of the United States to stand up and say that the whole story of Russian affairs as it has been fed into the minds of the American people is a conspiracy and a lie. With all the sincerity of our hearts, and our most sober and deliberate judgment concurring, we believe, and we continue to believe, that there is growing into maturity in that country the most just and wise and humane and democratic government that ever existed in the world.

So I wrote in the *Liberator* for January 1919, and the task outlined there absorbed my best energies for the next two and a half years. They were the years of bloody civil war in Russia. Our co-believers were fighting on seven fronts against the White Guards backed by armies from the great capitalist nations of the world. We of the *Liberator* fought for them from behind the American lines with all the force of wit, poetry, philosophy, art, beauty, and laughter we had in us, and we fought well. Even critics in the capitalist camp acknowledged the radiance of the torch we carried for Soviet Russia. To those on our side, we were a well of drink in a desert. The IWW having been smashed by wholesale arrests, and the left socialist press put out of business, the *Liberator* was alone on the newsstands in reporting Russian developments with theoretic understanding. It was alone, almost, in the Western world. I was told later by Antonio Gramsci, then secretary of the Italian Communist Party, that even in Italy the first inkling of what was really going on in Russia came through a translation from the *Liberator* of my essay on Lenin. So tight and bristling was the blockade around the Bolsheviks.

My old inferiority complex about not being in or of the proletarian movement was assuaged in those days. One night, by mysterious appointment over the telephone, an unknown Bolshevik named Nuorteva brought upstairs to my sun-yellow room at 123 Washington Place a worn and battered copy of Lenin's "Letter to American Workingmen," for publication in the *Liberator*.* Bill Haywood, uncompromising rebel who scorned even the Socialist Party as counterrevolutionary, contributed articles and announcements to the *Liberator*. So did William Z. Foster, the slim Irish-American syndicalist who headed the great steel strike of 1919. Robert Smillie, the beloved head of the miners' federation of Great Britain, cabled through the *Liberator* his "Greetings to you, my comrades of all ranks of American labor." A similar message "to the American workers" was sent through the *Liberator* by William Gallacher of the embattled workers of the Clyde. Tom Mann, the old antimilitary rebel, *enfant terrible* of the British labor movement, sent us his "love of comrades" across the seas. Alexander Berkman, deported anarchist, published his "Log of the Transport Buford" in the *Liberator*. Bela Kun, while holding his brief power in Hungary, sent a greeting to the American workers through the *Liberator*, and he sent another after his downfall.

* I learned long after that it had been brought over from Stockholm by Carl Sandburg, and that it was worn and battered because it had been through the print shop of the *Revolutionary Age*, a proletarian Marxist paper published in Boston by Louis Fraina. But my impression then was that it had traveled in the shoe soles of some "Baltic sailor" arriving underground from Moscow.

To grasp the import of this, you must realize that the *Liberator* was also publishing contributions from such significant American writers as Edna St. Vincent Millay, William Carlos Williams, Elinor Wylie, E. E. Cummings, John Dos Passos, Ernest Hemingway, Louise Bogan, Robert Hillyer, Elmer Rice, S. N. Behrman, Edmund Wilson, Sherwood Anderson, Vachel Lindsay, Amy Lowell, Heywood Broun. . . . The list is very long.*

Strange things happened to people who read the old *Masses* and the *Liberator*—to Roger Baldwin, for instance, the incorrigibly executive secretary of the Civil Liberties Union. Imagine this go-getting do-gooder composing meditative love lyrics to a tree that glanced in at his window! It was a window, to be sure, in a New Jersey prison cell where he was confined as a conscientious objector; there wasn't much else for him to do or to go-get. But I still give our magazines the main credit for this astonishing metamorphosis. Another poet-contributor of surprising talent was Francis Biddle, who became Franklin Roosevelt's attorney general. His wife, Katherine Chapin, is a poet unalloyed, and a gifted one, but only the *Liberator*, I am sure, could have evoked poetry from a potential attorney general.

I wish I were a more gregarious person than I am, an affable habitué of cafés, bars, clubs, taverns, expresso joints, and other places where properly constituted artistic and literary Bohemians get together and drink and talk all night long—usually under a ceiling so low that the din excludes cogitation. Drink as I might, I couldn't talk all night to save my neck. Some stimulus that gregarious animals are supposed to derive, and ought to derive, from the mere fact of being together was omitted from my constitution. I mourn about this now because, reading over the list of those eminent artists and writers whose early works I published, I wish I had personal memories of more of them. I never saw William Carlos Williams; I never saw Amy Lowell; I never saw Rolfe Humphries. Until last summer I never saw S. N. Behrman, though I admired his story, "Hickey and Mother Goose," which we published in 1920, and have admired him ever since. I never saw Elinor Wylie, although she came down to the office one day, all in high colors and quite dazzling, according to Claude McKay, who was sitting at my desk. His color must have startled her too, for according to his story she

* An alphabetical list of artists and writers who appeared in the old *Masses* and *Liberator* will be found in Daniel Aaron's excellent book, *Writers on the Left*, p. 403. "A kind of who's who of artistic and literary Americans for the next two or more decades," Aaron calls it.

had expected to offer her poem to me. Another contributing genius that I never saw in those days was my subsequent dear friend E. E. Cummings, though I can boast that we published some of his poems four years before *The Enormous Room* made him famous—among them "Maison," one of his loveliest and most wraithlike lyrics.

I did for one moment see Djuna Barnes, and I can see her still, writhing into our office, slim and sinuous and tempting, newly arrived from the West with a sheaf of drawings under her arm. Sly and inscrutable, she seemed, and, like her prose style, always intending mischief.

Carl Sandburg stayed a few days with John Reed in Croton, and I saw him poking among the weeds in the garden one morning as I strolled up the road. Although I had published some of his best poems, I repressed—or some infantile diffidence within me repressed—an impulse to turn in the gate and say hello. So I can't describe an illuminating conversation with Carl Sandburg in Jack Reed's garden. I content myself with remarking that he anticipated Hemingway in substituting what I call straight talk for the elegance and spun-out lacy niceties of so much poetic literature. American poetry was still inclined to surround the downright facts of life with pretty tunes and pictures when Carl started writing his very often almost prose poems. You remember the man who surrounded his goldfish bowl with picture postcards so the goldfish could think they were going somewhere? Poetry was a little like that. And Carl was one of those who decided that it ought to quit kidding us—it ought to talk real even at the risk of sounding like prose. It was a happy day when we could publish one of these outbursts of unwashed reality in the *Masses* or the *Liberator*. Too many of our poet contributors were on the delicate side.

Sherwood Anderson is another famous contributor that I no more than shook hands with in those days. His stories came to us through Floyd Dell, who has written recently a charming little essay, "On Being Sherwood Anderson's Spiritual Father." I knew Sherwood later, and I see him very plainly now when I think of him, more plainly than some friends who were closer to me. It is a tribute, I think, to his genial smile and easygoing, tramplike physical posture. He was imperturbably genial—not held fast in any mold of attitude or opinion. He was always asking questions where others make assertions. Opinions didn't go with his riverlike nature. Even when he held opinions he did not hold them very tight. He just kept rolling along. I think it was highly characteristic of him that when he moved to Marion, Virginia, he bought and became the editor of two newspapers—one Democrat and one Republican. It didn't matter.

I do remember a dinner with Sherwood, though it happened years after, probably in the late thirties, for Tom Wolfe was there. We were guests in one of those little square houses on Washington Mews that used to be barns. Our conversation lasted far into the night, so far that all I can remember of it is Sherwood's frankly stating that he was never wholly at ease—never quite himself—except with women. Tom Wolfe, towering above him, bubbling with eloquence like "Mount Ida of the many springs," took a violently contrary position. Unless memory deceives me, I was inclined to agree with Sherwood.

John Dos Passos I never saw at all in those *Liberator* days. I only remember my sister's bringing me a manuscript called *Two Soldiers*, telling me she got it "from a funny Portuguese boy." It would not have helped much if I had seen him, for Dos is so shy that he seems cold as an empty cellar with the door locked when you meet him. Those flames of passion and sky-licking imageries that illumine his novels are damped down so they don't even smoke in social intercourse.

Another contributor that rejoiced our hearts from time to time without ever turning up in person was "Edmund Wilson, Jr., Princeton, New Jersey." Bunny has won himself a seat as a "critic" now—at the very top of the reviewing stand, and it's a hard place to climb out of—but for me he was, and persists in being, a storyteller, a humorist, a writer of biting satires both in poetry and prose.

A notable person I did see in the days of the old *Masses* was lanky, clumsy, tousle-haired, warm-eyed George S. Kaufman. He must have been at least twenty-four or twenty-five, but as I remember him he looked like a schoolboy. He had brought with him a sheet of paper with five or six jokes typed on it—not as contributions to the magazine, he explained, but in order to get my advice. Did I think they showed enough promise to justify his going in for a career as a comic writer? I did not honestly think they were very good. I was not impelled, at least, to ask if we might have one for the magazine. But I liked him; I liked his shy and humble attitude; perhaps I was flattered by his approaching me as a judge of wit and humor. At any rate I told him to go ahead. When he did go ahead, and became a famous playwright, director, producer, participator in any and every theatrical enterprise designed to generate laughter, I remembered that interview with ever renewed surprise. I spoke to him once about his having come to see me, and he remembered it, but we couldn't either of us remember—or pretended we couldn't—why he had come.

I have boasted of the eminent writers we brought into confluence with militant labor; I must boast also of the artists. Besides our contributing art editors and co-operating friends, we published drawings and lithographs by George Bellows, Robert Henri, Randall Davy, Al Frueh, Mahonri Young, Abraham Walkowitz, J. J. Lankes, George Grosz, Wanda Gag, Arnold Blanche, Ilonka Karasz, Jo Davidson, Morris Cantor. Even Pablo Picasso showed up in the *Liberator*.

It is sometimes said, or implied, that the graphic art in the old *Masses* and *Liberator* was superior to the literary text. This is a natural result of the visual prominence of pictures, and of the fact that we gave them—*for the first time in an American magazine*—adequate space. But I don't think it is true. Examined at leisure, even today when the news value of so much of the prose is lost, the art and literature in the magazines make a single impression. To me it is a quite startling impression of surviving life and vigor.

Chapter 21

BOLD ORATORY AND BAFFLED LOVE

I spoke of my talent for "kept-up lovingness"—a terrible thing, although not quite so bad as the words sound. Love is, except in its period of rapture, a quantitative phenomenon, and one may exaggerate the quantity a little without total hypocrisy. It was only the *absoluteness* of my love, the pure ecstasy, that had been snatched from me in the inner landslide of that fatal moment I have described. I had descended from heaven, yes; but that was a private matter. I might with honesty withhold from my beloved the fact that I was back here on the old unsatisfactory earth.

Even this, however, I could not very long or completely succeed in doing. Florence was too perceptive, and my urge toward candor was too strong. I still wanted to be united with her, as a sinner does with his God, in knowing and living the truth. A talk between us about the change in my feelings was inevitable. . . .

It was, when it came, a sort of maundering semiconfession on my part, a midnight speech about selfhood propelled into the darkness while she lay silent beside me. Her answer was reassuringly calm and matter-of-fact. She wanted me to regain my self if I felt that it was getting lost. I must not think that love, in her conception of it, involved a merging of personalities, or even a pledge of sexual fidelity.

"The highest kind of relationship is one in which the lovers both feel free to have other experiences of love."

That is what she said. But she was not telling the whole truth of her feeling any more than I had of mine.

Six months earlier, she had aroused my apprehension by suggesting that I might love someone else and it wouldn't make much difference. Now the same thing gave me, together with my sadness, a feeling of relief.

In that state of mind I set forth, in the early winter of 1919, on a "Hands Off Russia!" speaking tour across the country. My speeches were bold, and in the madness of the Palmer Raids it was bold to make the trip at all. But in my private self I felt baffled rather than bold. I had aspired toward something sublime and through some irremediable flaw in my nature, some frailty of the poet in me, had failed to attain it.

The number of thinking people who were willing, in those days, to stand up for "Lenin and Trotsky," and give free play to the great experiment in Russia, was as noticeable as the obtuse hostility of the unthinking public. I got a full taste of these contrasting attitudes in the course of my tour. In Cleveland, where my sister and co-editor accompanied me, the Labor Temple in which our meeting took place was surrounded by a gang called "vigilantes"—American fascists in embryo—with the purpose of kidnapping us after the meeting. With the connivance of our trade-union friends we spent two hours locked in a tiny closet where they stored their banners. In searching the building, the gangsters came to our hiding place and rattled the doorknob, but the thump of my heartbeats was drowned by the drawling voice of the union secretary: "Aw, that's just a closet where we keep the insignia, I musta left the key home." I listened to Crystal's heartbeats and they were steadier than mine.

In Chicago, by contrast, the famous Woman's Club received my speech with warm applause, and a collection taken up for the *Liberator* yielded almost two thousand dollars. And for another contrast, I read in the *Chicago Tribune* this account of a speech by Theodore Roosevelt, Jr., to the American Legion:

> You will always find us ready to stand for the ideals of this country handed down by our fathers and tempered by Europe's fire. First, last, and always we are 100 per cent Americans. Bolshevists, the I.W.W. and red flag Socialists I see as criminals, to be treated as such. Don't argue or temporize with criminals. Go to bat and meet 'em head on.

I proceeded west with a feeling that the American Legion had been advised by its most conspicuous leader to assault and if necessary murder me and several million like me for our opinions.

In Spokane, Washington, where I was graciously entertained in the home of a cultivated and well-known literary critic named Helen Bullis, and where I made exactly the same speech I had to the Woman's Club in Chicago, the event was reported in the local press as follows:

Credit for a shrewd move should be given Commissioner Tilsley, Chief of Police Weir, and other authorities in their handling of the public appearance of Max Eastman in Spokane Friday night. Eastman's effort to "start something" for the red radicals was given free rein and fell flat. Allowed to go his full limit in his wild ranting against American ideals of democracy, our Russian policy, President Wilson's brand of liberalism and the anti-anarchist activities of the government, his utterances served to show all reasonable people of Spokane that the Eastman brand of extreme radicalism is really nothing more than a kind of mild insanity, evidenced chiefly in an overflowing of rash words. An able move, Tilsley, and well played.

There were, in fact, no grounds on which to interfere with my meetings, and the attendance was so vast that a lawless move on the part of the police would have been foolhardy. Those meetings were the first big rent in the blanket of silence that Wilson's sedition acts had imposed upon the unregenerate radicals. They were a gathering of clans for the renewal of the old struggle. They were, also, in most towns, the first unqualified public declaration of the real aims and ideals of that mysterious "Bolshevik government," against which all the great nations of the world were waging war. The sedition acts, to be sure, were still officially in force; the Palmer Raids were in full swing; Wilson's queer stubbornness against those who had opposed him was having its effect. I felt sometimes, seeing the police lined up around the hall I was to speak in, more like an invading army than a man on a lecture tour. But the recoil against this wartime tyranny was beginning; the reaction was setting in. In Butte I spoke in a hall controlled and jammed to the doors by striking miners. In Seattle I addressed a "mob" of proletarian thousands in the public square, for the city was in the midst of its famous General Strike—the only one this country ever saw. In Denver, where I spoke in a theater, an unknown friend of the *Liberator* handed me a thousand dollars in bank notes when we shook hands in the wings. In San Francisco my meeting, which packed the old skating rink, was literally beamed on by the police. . . .

A strange thing happened there, of purely personal interest. Just before starting on that trip I had had an attack of influenza, and to bolster my strength Dr. Lorber had provided me with a large bottle of tonic containing strychnine and iron. Strychnine in large enough quantities locks your muscles like tetanus, and I took large swigs out of that bottle whenever I felt the need of a little bracing-up. There were no loudspeakers those days, and in that skating rink I needed all my strength. So I slipped into the coat room before going on and took two big swigs out of that large bottle. When I got up to speak, one of my ankles refused to bend. I had not the faintest idea what had happened to me; I learned it from the doctor afterward. Assuming that I had a cerebral hemorrhage and would probably drop dead in the first sentence, I made the sentence extra loud. This sent the blood coursing through my veins, the spasm passed, and nobody ever suspected I had been at death's door.

In the Los Angeles Opera House, a square-shouldered, businesslike, energetic member of the audience came up after my speech with congratulations and a genial handshake. It was Bob Wagner, author of *Filmfolk* and editor of a little local semisocialistic paper. He greeted me with the startling news:

"Charlie Chaplin is in the wings and would like to meet you."

It was a breath-taking announcement. Charlie Chaplin was then the most famous man in the world, not excepting President Wilson, Lloyd George, General Foch, not excepting anybody—the most famous, and the most mysteriously inaccessible. I remember his exact words in praise of my speech, and since I have quoted the contrary opinion of the Spokane editor, perhaps I will be allowed to repeat them. "You have what I consider the essence of all art—even of mine, if I may call myself an artist—restraint."

We had supper together that night in a downstairs tavern near the opera house, and the next day I visited him at his studio, which was a little island of architectural beauty and trim landscaping among the dreary and half-built barnlike structures in which most of the moving pictures of those days were made. Externally, it was a row of English houses running along one side of La Brea Avenue, each house differing from the other but all suggesting a street scene from a novel by Thackeray or Thomas Hardy. Inside—when you had found which house was the entrance—the scene was of a neatly kept front yard, a trimmed bit of lawn, some shrubs and lemon trees, a swimming pool. Charlie called a cameraman and we had a moving portrait taken, a laughing portrait, for in want of anything else to do we picked lemons off one of those trees and ate them as though they were apples. As we strolled out of the studio into a large and parklike space of grass behind it, I saw some green apples lying under a tree. Another tree in front of us, a tall evergreen, was lifting a high thin candle to the sky. I am always tempted to throw things at a mark like that.

"You see that treetop?" I said.

And by the rarest luck of my life I clipped the candle with a green apple. Charlie looked at me with an expression of admiring astonishment. It put me in a different class from that of a socialist orator with restraint. Moreover I had restraint enough not to throw another apple.

Hollywood was a romantic little village then with one old-fashioned hotel, and the five days I spent there were a blessed interlude in my too tensely belligerent tour. Surprisingly, many of the current celebrities seemed to be on my side. I remember with particular warmth the friendliness and rare, clear-eyed beauty of Blanche Sweet, famous in those days, and, justly so, for she was a fine actress among some rather sorry compeers. David Wark Griffith, whose battle scenes in *The Birth of a Nation*, and whose creation of long dramatic pictures, close-ups, fade-outs, and flashbacks were opening an epoch in film history, was also on my side. He was a lank, tall, sporty, eagle-faced type, British-seeming if not British, and too easeful to put me at my ease, but I liked him when he said:

"You are a braver man than I am, I would say the same things you do if I had the courage. I served in the war and made a famous war film, but I don't really believe in wars. I think they're always wrong on both sides."

I reported this proudly in a letter to Florence, for I was in *her* world now. I told her I had suggested to Griffith that he make a motion-picture history of the class struggle, and promised to send him a copy of *The Ancient Lowly* and the *Communist Manifesto!* But I had also to report that Cecil De Mille gave me an embarrassing snub, turning on his heel deliberately when introduced to me. "He's a screaming patriot," I explained. A similar patriotism was evinced by the newspapers of Los Angeles—as also by the police. There must have been fifty of those blue-coated athletes surrounding the opera house or lining its walls during my speech, and they were not smiling. The contrast with San Francisco was startling, but the acoustics were better and, not being afflicted with lockjaw, I made a better speech.

I had taken along on that trip a friend of the revolution named Isaac McBride, an old IWW agitator, a bellicose rebel against things in general, brilliant and handsome and defiantly dressed in a black string tie. His function was to raise money after I finished my speeches. His way of doing this was to attack and browbeat the audience from the standpoint of the suffering and hungry workers for whom they ought to be glad of an opportunity to redeem themselves by shelling out all they had in their pocketbooks and wallets. I calculated that his soapbox harangues cut down by about one half the amount I might have raised for the *Liberator* if he had not come along. But he was good company; he reinforced the impulse which had pushed me out on this new oratorical raid on public opinion. I don't think he liked my speeches any better than I liked his, but we laughed together, and I was not lonesome. In consequence, my letters to Florence were briefer and fewer and more poised than they would otherwise have been. They troubled her heart. She loved and wanted me still, but she had not recovered, she never would recover, from the wound I inflicted with my blunted dagger of semiconfession just before I left home—that speech about "selfhood" preached into the midnight while she lay so still beside me. "I am afraid to write a love letter to you, you seem so full of business," she wrote.

And just at that time, she experienced a sharp personal disappointment. She turned down an offer of a good part in a play because she had two movie offers that she liked better, but after the part in the play was filled, the movie offers fell through. That was a wound to her inordinate ambition—to that feeling of the glory of being herself which was an intrinsic part of her love for me, and which my adoration nourished. This and my *poised* letters, whatever they may have said—for during those months she destroyed them all—turned her troubledness into a reckless gloom.

Our love was in peril, and it was nothing more divine than the dates on the calendar that saved it. On leaving Hollywood, I stopped in the California hills at Grass Valley, where my adventurous college friend, Sid Wood, was mining silver. I had planned in New York to visit him, and given Florence the dates and the address, hoping she would write to me there. She did write, and what she wrote would have shattered the frame of my emotional life, if I had received it. But it came too late. I had gone to San Francisco, and these succinct lines announcing the end of the world went back to her unopened:

"Max dear, what will you think of me? I have run away from you. Your letter pains me, and I see your face before me, sad and pained because you do not miss me. Do not be sad."

To be more specific—and more true to my life's confusion—it was not the dates on the calendar that caused this failure of communication, but a beautiful Russian girl whom I had met the night I made my speech in San Francisco. Vera was beautiful in a mysterious and tragic way, with smouldering blue eyes under a storm of dark hair, and she was troubled as I was by problems of love. She had been troubled all her life by these problems. At fourteen she had stabbed and killed with a carving knife a man who tried to rape her, and had left Russia because of the sinister clouds that pursued her in consequence. I had heard of her beauty and intelligence, for she had been the cherished friend of my colleague on the *Liberator*, Robert Minor. She came up and introduced herself after my speech, and we left the hall together. The next day we took a stroll on a hillside that sloped toward the sea. When we parted I promised to stop longer on my way home from Los Angeles and renew our friendship. It was to keep that promise that I left Grass Valley before receiving Florence's fateful letter.

We lived a lifetime of five days together, Vera and I, not in San Francisco, but in the surrounding region, sleeping in small rural hotels, roaming by the sea, exploring the giant forests and tumbled hills of Marin county. No self-deceiving dreams were involved; we both knew that our destinies lay elsewhere. But those days and nights are one of the purest and most untarnished of my memories of brief love. I can still call back the emotion of infinitude—readers who can be as romantic as I can will know what I mean—which filled me when I waved good-bye to her from the rear platform of the train east. I have saved her letter describing a similar emotion—a song, almost, of praise to those who can "live in the moment and breathe infinity with it."

When I reached Chicago, I found a thick letter awaiting me from Florence. The letter was a confirmation of what she had written to Grass Valley, only more final because based on her feelings, not mine. It was a veritable death sentence upon our love. But the clerk who handed me the letter held in his other hand a telegram which had that moment arrived. I opened the telegram first, and read:

> I DO NOT WANT YOU TO READ THE LETTER I WROTE YOU
> PLEASE BRING IT BACK TO ME

Since I did not read that letter until years later, it does not properly belong to this one-sided story I am so glibly telling. But it gives at least a glimpse of her side.

> Max dear, I have turned away from you because you no longer mean happiness to me. My heart is hurt so deeply I only

want to run away. I went to your house in the country and tried to warm myself, but your house has become like other houses, it did not warm me. I went to your room in New York, but I could not stay there. Sometimes when I am walking on the street I almost fall when I think of that terrible night you leapt at me suspicious that I would read a private letter you had received. How could you ever feel that way toward me?

Please forgive me for the cruel way I acted then. I am so ashamed of it. You are too lovely and sweet, too light and sunny, for anyone to treat so harshly as I did. Please, please try to forgive that. I didn't seem to know what to do. I guess I am not grown up.

I do miss you so much. You are wonderful and courageous to go across the country speaking at a time like this. Your tender letter from Grass Valley could not pass into my mind. It is too full of the truth which you tried so hard to tell me before you left.

It had been a long warm letter that I finally wrote from the train out of Hollywood, arriving just in time, that gave her the impulse—not usual with her—to call back what she had said. My letter told her I longed to clasp her like a child in my arms and "take care of her"; it promised that we would be happy together "no matter what comes."

I fear I will offend the authorities on conjugal bliss, but I believe that my five days of brief true love with Vera on the shores of another ocean, had increased the life-expectancy of our more deeply rooted love. We were excitedly happy now when we came together. It was like clasping all April and May in my arms when we met at the station. She had a part in a play that Belasco was putting on, the best possible stimulus to my kind of love, and a measure of food for her proud spirit too. She was to be away on the road for a month, and our letters during that month were full of young, gay, passionate longing for each other. We really began our romance all over again when she came back in June, fixing up the little house with very far-looking joy. Although still mysteriously held back from the mood of the romantic absolute which for eighteen months had made a heaven of my earth, I was learning in a more classic way to be in love. And Florence was just a little—the little that is possible in a wild colt without breaking its spirit—subdued. The ghost of a pout that lived in her lips meant only amorous passion now, not anger any more—never again, it seemed to me, anger.

Chapter 22

A SNAG FOR WOODROW WILSON

In that same June of 1919 when love's turmoil so happily subsided, I took a political plunge which cost me a different kind of sleeplessness. To explain it, I must go back and quote a small slice from a bellicose speech I made to a mass meeting at Harlem Casino celebrating the first anniversary of the October revolution.

> I understand they maintain at the District Attorney's office that it is unlawful to denounce the invasion of Russia by Woodrow Wilson. I maintain that it is unlawful for Woodrow Wilson to invade Russia. Just before I came here I was regaling myself with that delightful old romance, the Constitution of the United States, and I noticed that the Constitution locates the power to declare war in the representatives of the people. It nowhere delegates to the executive branch of the government the right to ship citizens out of the country, and half way round the earth, to wage war on a foreign power *without* a declaration of war by the representatives of the people. . . . President Wilson is waging his own private war on Russia, in direct violation of the spirit, and even of the letter, of the United States Constitution.

Now, a year and a half later, I was sitting in the *Liberator* office one day (it was the front half of a third-story loft at 34 Union Square East) when the telephone rang, and a tremulous voice said: "I have some important documents that I want to convey to you personally, but I do not want to come up to your office. Could you meet me on a street corner?"

I said: "Sure, I'll come down to the corner of Sixteenth Street in just a minute."

I found a slim young man in a soldier's uniform standing very straight by the edge of the curb. His features were firm, but he trembled and drops appeared on his brow as he drew a package of letters from his pocket and handed them to me.

"These are dynamite," he said. "I found them in the wastebasket when they were cleaning up one day after a meeting of the Big Four at Versailles."

I glanced through the letters. They were from Under-Secretary Polk to the Secretary of State, Robert Lansing, who was with Wilson in Paris at the Peace Conference, and they warned the President in very pointed terms of the opposition in Congress and in the country to his military intervention in Russia.

"I hope you will know what to do with them," he said, and added, "I needn't tell you what will happen to me"—and he glanced at his uniform—"if anybody finds out where you got them."

He gave me his name and explained that he was a member of the Military Intelligence at Versailles. I promised to guard the secret, and to make the best use I could of the letters. We parted rather hastily, for he was apprehensive, and for me his heroism was painful to see. It was also pretty good evidence that the documents were genuine.

I was scheduled to speak on June 20 in Madison Square Garden at a mass meeting called to protest against American intervention in the Russian civil war, and specifically against a raid by federal police on a sort of unrecognized "embassy" set up in New York by the Soviet Government with a mild-faced mechanical engineer named Martens as "ambassador." It was a red revolutionary meeting addressed in a tone of imminent insurrection by all the leaders of incipient American communism: Charles E. Ruthenberg, Rose Pastor Stokes, Dennis E. Batt, Ben Gitlow, A. A. Stoklitsky (who spoke in Russian), and the formidable Irish Rebel, Jim Larkin. My own remarks included, according to the *New York Times*, the promise of a dictatorship of the proletariat in the United States, to be gained without any help from outside. "All we ask of the Russian Soviet Republic is that it should continue to exist." But my assertion that Woodrow Wilson was waging a private war against that republic, and offering in proof of it a decoded letter from the acting chief of the State Department, naturally eclipsed everything else in the news. The revolution was, I think for the first time, on the front page of every great newspaper in the country. REDS IN GARDEN URGE REVOLUTION AND SOVIETS HERE was the headline in the *Times*, then "Eastman Attacking President, Reads Alleged Secret Message from Polk to Lansing," "Federal Agents Say They Will Question Him Today." The text of the letter then followed—still on the front page.

green & cipher
Washington
Jan. 24, 1919

Ammission
Paris
391. Jan. 24. 3 P.M. Very confidential

For the Secretary of State: Referring to my answer to 376, Jan. 21, regarding Siberian Railway plans, I take the liberty of calling your attention to the political situation here. Critical spirit today is being clearly manifested in regard to Russia.

1. By attack on War Trade Board Russian Bureau.

2. By attacks on personal conduct of Ambassador Francis. La Guardia apparently got his information from Consul Winship, now at Welland, and Lieut. Commander Crolley, formerly at St. Petersburg, and now Naval Attaché at Madrid.

3. By Senator Johnson's continually attacking Administration policy of keeping troops in Russia and Siberia.

There is no question but the Republicans are trying to force an extra session and leading Democrats seem to feel that the extra session should be considered inevitable. If successful, Republicans, resenting control of various committees, will make attacks on every phase of policy of administration in Russia.

We are committed now to a proposition for the operation of the Siberian Railway, and I wish to lay stress on the fact that money must be supplied in large sums in order to carry through this plan. In view of the attitude of Congress on the food bill I should give up the possibility of seeking money through appropriation. The Russian Ambassador has no funds and has already exhausted sums set aside for maintaining Siberian Railway corps.

I am taking the liberty of stating the case so that the President or yourself may have all the facts before you before he commits himself to supplying money for this purpose from his private fund. I have not consulted Japanese Ambassador, and for this reason would like to have your views as soon as possible.

POLK

On the following day the papers contained an acknowledgment by the State Department that such a "very confidential green cipher" cablegram had been sent on the date specified, an expression of anxiety lest other confidential messages passing between the State Department and the Peace Commission in Paris had fallen into the hands of unauthorized persons, and as to whether those persons possessed the cipher enabling them to translate still other secret messages. To protect themselves, they added, of course, that the translation was inaccurate "in a number of important particulars," but no particulars were specified. In an editorial the *Times* said:

> Though there is no sufficient law against the organization of revolution . . . there is enough law to take care of the present brood if only it is firmly enforced without first looking to see who is going to be hurt. For instance, confidential communications from the Acting Secretary of State to his superior officer are not supposed to be acquired by mysterious agents of disorder and read before 6,000 shouting Reds at Madison Square Garden. When that happens, somebody ought to suffer. The incident is disquieting because nobody can tell how many other such communications may have been stolen, or whether this very thing did not go on during the war.

The same paper contained a headlined account of police raids on an office of the IWW, and on the Rand School for Social Science, a notice that Lenin had been denounced as The Anti-Christ, and a dispatch from Washington that Polk was initiating an investigation of my unlawful possession of a confidential message belonging to the government. Such was my reading matter on that pleasant June week-end of 1919, and the New York *Journal* topped it:

"It is not yet known how Max Eastman, a notorious anarchist, frequently arrested in connection with bomb outrages, obtained the message."

It was my turn to sweat now. I could not honorably account for my possession of the letter, and that seemed to leave me as guilty as though I had stolen it myself. To escape telephone calls from the press, I went to the house of my friend and neighbor, Dudley Field Malone. After I had told him the story, he said:

"You have other documents of the same kind?"

"Yes, though not so damagingly explicit. The one I read was the worst."

"I'll tell you what to do," he said. "Just issue to the press the statement that you have more of these letters which you haven't made public. That'll stop them."

So I called my friends in the United Press and gave them a carefully worded statement, which I quote as it appeared in the *New York World* on June 23:

MAX EASTMAN GLAD
CABLE IS VERIFIED

Says State Department Acknowledgment
of Its Authenticity Reassures Him

Max Eastman issued this statement yesterday regarding the cablegram to Secretary Lansing made public by him at a recent meeting:

"I am glad the State Department has acknowledged the authenticity of the cablegram I quoted from Frank Polk to Lansing. I felt sure of its authenticity, although my only proof was the internal evidence contained in other similar documents sent to me anonymously along with it. I should not like to publish them all merely in order to establish the authenticity of this one.

"I have no desire to expose the private plans of the President and his political advisers except as they contain matters that every man and woman in the United States has a right to know. President Wilson has been and still is waging a war against Soviet Russia without a declaration of war and without an appropriation of funds for that purpose by the representatives of the people.

"This is a flagrant violation of the Constitution and there is no reason to suppose that the person who sent me these documents is anything more than a patriotic citizen who believes in constitutional government. None of them contains anything relating to the war that had been declared by Congress against Germany and Austria."

I slept little for a few nights, but more tranquilly as the days passed and no further peep came from Washington. I hated to waste the other letters, so I took them down finally to Oswald Garrison Villard, who published them in the *Nation*, saying that such letters seemed to be "turning up mysteriously" on the desks of anti-interventionist editors. When a short time later Woodrow Wilson withdrew the American troops from Siberia and northern Russia, Mr. Villard told me that he thought my exposure of Polk's letter to Lansing had brought it about. I should have liked to convey his opinion to the brave man who brought me the letters, but he had disappeared out of my life.

Speaking of our office in a loft on Union Square reminded me that the great literary phenomenon, Frank Harris—half genius and half mountebank—had an office in that same loft. It was a long railroad-car of a place, and Frank moved into the rear end of it with *Pearson's Magazine*, an institution which he had bought in its death agonies, hoping to make a sporting gentleman's living out of it. The job was a desperate one, but he thought he could do it by being socialistic enough. He invited me to dinner one Saturday evening and earnestly proposed that we join together and get out a really tremendous magazine. "Two of the best editors in the world, why should we struggle along separately?" Frank was a brilliant and resounding talker, especially on the subject of his own great history as an editor—a true history, by the way—and I joined heartily in the evening's conversation. Indeed I expressed only one doubt.

"I don't know how a revolutionary magazine could pay two editors," I murmured. "I would want a salary of at least twenty-five hundred a year."

"Twenty-five hundred!" he boomed. "Twelve *thousand!* Max, you have still to learn to *live!* We're going to get out the greatest magazine ever published."

Not long after that, Frank printed in *Pearson's* a story called "Lenin the Aristocrat," in which Lenin's life in Switzerland was described in terms that made him out a dude, a prig and a sissy. It made me mad, and I said so in the next month's *Liberator*. "A slander against Lenin," I said, "is an offense to all revolutionists. Frank Harris is not a scientific socialist, but he is enough a man of the world to know that this exceeding prig and little political Oscar Wilde portrayed in his May issue as 'Lenin the Aristocrat' could not by any caprice of destiny have become the leader of a proletarian revolution."

Harris attributed his information to a man who said he had worked with Lenin in Switzerland. Lenin, according to this source, insisted on using Lily of the Valley perfume, changed his silk underwear every few hours, wore thousand-dollar pearls in his necktie, despised the smell of the masses, and spent most of his time flirting with Junker girls from

Berlin. In short, he possessed all the attributes of a smooth, rich,
fatuous, egotistical, highborn snob with personal magnetism. "The
picture," I wrote, "is so elaborately akin to the idea which certain
infants and infantile hot-house spinsters and side-board ninny-whoops
have of the nature of a 'great man' that I almost think it is a sincere
creation. I think Frank Harris interviewed a man who really does think
he worked with Lenin, and if the interview had lasted a little longer he
would probably have admitted that he *is* Lenin."

I was agitated enough to go up to the Soviet Bureau and get this
report from a man who really did work with Lenin in Switzerland:

> Lenin had no income. He lived, as Trotsky did in New York, on
> the small earnings of revolutionary writings and lectures. It was
> his principle never to sell anything to capitalist papers and he never
> did. When the German socialist leader, Bebel, favored giving
> higher pay to editors than to other party workers, Lenin—an
> editor—opposed it. He lived in a simple house with his wife—also a
> veteran of the revolution—to whom he was devoted. He worked at
> a plain uncovered table sitting in an ordinary kitchen chair, and
> was accessible to anybody who wanted his advice. Indeed he would
> leave home and go any distance to explain a point—no matter how
> trivial—to any group that was working for the revolution. Unlike
> Plekhanov who dressed as a rich man, Lenin wore the clothes of
> a workingman. He liked soft collars and usually worked with his
> collar unbuttoned and no necktie (and no $1,000 pearl in his neck-
> tie!). And like all men of great concentration he was "absent-
> minded," and did not always notice when his coat was torn or
> minus a couple of buttons.

So I presented—with fair accuracy, as it turned out—the facts about
Lenin's private life in Switzerland, and I concluded:

> My informant has known Lenin for fifteen years, but he admits
> that he doesn't know as much about Lenin's underwear as Frank
> Harris does.

Frank, of course, was in a rage, and he blasted me the best he could
in the next number of *Pearson's*. He did it skilfully—and with, I fear, a
trifle of justification, for my allusion to his friend Oscar Wilde, followed
by that crack about the underwear, was mischievous, to say the least.
Frank was as far from a homosexual as nature could go, though he did

like to dress up in loud suits and splashy vests and exceedingly white spats. After this editorial episode, he would omit the "Good morning" when we passed on the way to our offices, making me an ironically stately bow—if a small man so dressed and wearing a curled-up mustache can be stately—staring past me like a statue and never speaking a word.

Chapter 23

BACKING THE THIRD INTERNATIONAL

In that momentous June of 1919, Florence's great day came—a munificent contract, and with it a slip of paper in the great producer's handwriting:

Dear Miss Deshaunt
    You are to start for our studio not later than August first, 1919, and you are to begin work not later than August 8th, 1919.
                                                    Samuel Goldwyn

Everyone who knew Florence felt certain that this was the beginning of a quick rise to fame. It meant opulence too, and Florence offered to find a house for us to live in together if I should come to Hollywood. I was nearing the last chapters of *The Sense of Humor*, and I promised to break loose from the *Liberator* long enough to finish it there. On July 9 she boarded the train that was to carry her to glory, and I redoubled my efforts, which were perennial, to organize the magazine in such a way that it would run without too much attention from me.

It was not easy just then, because Crystal was in Europe, and I had maneuvered myself into a position of some political importance. After being confirmed—to use a churchly expression—by Lenin and the October revolution, I lost my squeamishness about adhering to the faith. I no longer hesitated to call myself "Socialist," or even, with mental reservations, "Marxist." Although I never attended a meeting of my "local" so far as I can remember, I was writing and speaking in these years 1917–19 as a member of the American Socialist Party. I took an earnest part in the debate on the party platform for the 1918 elections, and we published the platform in full in the *Liberator*. We also published a key article by the party leader Morris Hillquit, who was then still able to speak of Soviet Russia as "the vanguard of democracy and social progress . . . from top to bottom in the hands of the people, the working class, the peasants." Clive Weed's drawing of Eugene Debs was our cover design for May 1919, and we gave a whole page to Debs' announcement:

FROM THE CROWN OF MY HEAD TO THE SOLES OF MY FEET I AM BOLSHEVIK AND PROUD OF IT. THE DAY OF THE PEOPLE HAS COME!

Both Debs and Hillquit receded from these positions as the purpose of Lenin to split the world's socialists into hard and soft began to grow clear. The division was more complex than those words imply. The hards were those not only sympathetic to the October revolution in Russia, but ready to agitate and conspire toward a similar seizure of power in their own countries. The softs were those who, while glad of what happened in Russia, were unwilling to take the role of idealistic traitors to their own governments. It was, in effect, a sharpening of the old distinction among socialists between revolutionary and reformist. But those words "hard" and "soft" had actually been employed to distinguish Lenin's followers from his opponents in the famous Congress of 1903 before the terms Bolshevik and Menshevik (majority and minority man) replaced them. The distinction was akin to that between hard-headed and soft-headed idealism, which I had made much of in trying to modernize the Marxian philosophy. Naturally I took the "hard" side, and I made its superiority plausible with a sermon based more on the Bible than on Karl Marx.

The children of this world are wiser in their generation than the children of light was my text. "Up to now," I preached, "they have always been able to *bunco* the children of light. And this is because the latter, besides having tender hearts, have permitted themselves to have tender minds. Being in love with an ideal, they have permitted themselves to idealize the real, to soften and falsify it, and falsify the path also which might lead from it toward their ideal. They have had no taste for the hard mood of practical action. . . . But the children of light are getting wise. And that is the real ground and meaning of the prodigious 'menace' of Bolshevism. . . . The communist movement is a prodigious menace because it reveals at every word and turning the mood of aggressive and calculating achievement linked up with the most beautiful and most extreme of all the aspirations of the human spirit. . . ."

In that mood of reckless elation, I took my stand with the Bolsheviks against the Mensheviks, the Communists against the "democratic" socialists—against those who believed that a revolution in property ownership could be brought about by voting at elections.

"Just as the waters of the Mediterranean flow back into the Atlantic underneath the great current that sweeps in at Gibraltar, so the principles of Bolshevism pass under the armies of her enemies that seem all-powerful, and though they conquer they do not advance."

Thus I exulted in the defeat of the Allied and American armies invading Russia.

The issue came to a crisis during that year 1919, for the radical world was swept by an upsurge of joy in the October revolution and faith in its future that was torrential. The year began with the "Spartacide" revolt in Germany, a leftwing insurrection which, though it failed, revived the hope that all Europe, and then the world, would ultimately "go Bolshevik." Then on the night of March 21, Bela Kun, a zealous Bolshevik, became premier of Hungary, and began the determined conversion of that nation into a Soviet Republic. It was far from a "seizure of power" by the proletariat, or even by a proletariat party; the power was handed to Kun on a silver platter by the bewildered liberal, Count Karolyi. But we found it easy to forget that. Crystal went to Hungary and was the first American to carry greetings to the new government.

In her speech (translated by one of the People's Commissars and published in a party paper), she declared it "the most beautiful moment of her life when she could address the central council of the Hungarian Soviet Republic," and predicted that "the victory of the Russian proletariat, which has come over to Hungary, will spread to all the other countries of the world."

This was a traveling fire of opinion among leftward-leaning liberals the world over just then. Even Bernard Shaw told Robert Wolf, who interviewed him for the *Liberator:* "A Bolshevik as far as I can tell is nothing but a socialist who wants to do something about it. To the best of my knowledge I am a Bolshevik myself." Maxim Gorky, who had opposed Lenin in October, now appeared on our first page with a manifesto urging all men to follow "the torch of the Russian revolution which throws its light over the whole world" and is "held firmly in the hand of Lenin." I have mentioned Robert Smillie's cable to the *Liberator* in the name of the British miners; it was an appeal "to the workers of America to realize that until the whole wealth produced by labour . . . is secured for the common enjoyment of those who produce it, there can not, and there ought not to be, any rest from agitation toward this end." C. T. Cramp of the National Union of Railwaymen of Great Britain and Ireland sent us a similar cable, assuring "our comrades of the American railroads" that "liberty really means more to us than bread." Robert Williams of the National Transport Workers was more specific: "We in Great Britain, despite our conservative outlook, have fashioned an industrial organization which is probably the most potent ever created—the Triple Alliance. We 300,000 transport workers have allied ourselves with 500,000 railroad workers and 800,000 miners. . . . We believe it our duty to use every instrument in our power to challenge the institution of capitalism." Of course those cables were Crystal's doing, and her idea, but none the less they were part of a wave that was passing across the world. Here at home, Eugene Debs joined our staff of contributing editors, and on his way to prison in Atlanta sent us this message: "Now is the time for all of us to be true to the best there is in us; to resolve to do and dare for the cause. . . . As for myself my position is immovable. I stand by every word of the Canton speech."

Lenin threw something of a bomb into this literary and labor-union excitement by assembling in Moscow in March 1919 the first congress of a new International to be called Communist instead of Socialist. It was the third time since 1864, when Marx first conceived the idea of a workers' International, that such an organization had been formed; and the word *Third* as against *Second* thus acquired all the flavor of Hard against Soft. It wasn't, of course, much of a congress; the "delegates" were mostly hand-picked from among revolutionary pilgrims already in Moscow. But the program, reflecting the brilliant and erudite minds of men like Radek, Bukharin, Zinoviev, Trotsky, and Lenin himself, was immensely impressive, and compelled excited radicals all over the world to take a firm stand for or against the revolutionary seizure of power.

I met the challenge in an eight-page essay containing some very sober reflections, and also some of the most intemperate utterances of my editorial career.* Asserting that the Marxian theory had "survived every test and observation throughout this great and bewildering spasm of history," I called this "the one thing that has ever happened in the political sciences comparable to the confirmation of the hypotheses of Copernicus and Kepler and Newton in the physical sciences." And I excoriated the socialists of Great Britain (the Independent Labour Party) for holding fast to the principles of *political* as against economic

* "The New International" in the *Liberator* for July 1919.

democracy, in language that makes me wonder now what had become of that part of me which really is a little bit hard—my sense of fact.

"Democracy," "liberty," "suffrage," "responsible government," "free speech," "the right of assembly," "the people"—these words from their platform I dismissed with intolerant scorn. "In other words," I shouted (if ever an essay did shout), "let us cling firmly to all those plausible ideologies and moralistic disguises of the rule of capital which brought us into this universal ruin and bloody death and savage degeneration of mankind, and by that means we will get out of it again—methodically. It is a disgrace that a body of men and women supposedly trained to understand the economic forces that lie beneath these impotent forms and formulas, controlling our destinies, should listen to such bland irrelevant chatter after all these years of enforced hatred and compulsory imperialistic murder and crime."

Although so near to becoming a fanatic in my horror at the war and my joy in the distant glimpses of Lenin's mind, I was too canny to join his American party—too self-regarding, perhaps. I could not join it without turning the *Liberator* over to its strict yet amateurish control. That would have been death to the *Liberator*. I could not join it without becoming one of its disciplined leaders, a "professional revolutionist." That would have been death to my poetic and meditational ambitions. These were reasons enough for doing what it fitted my nature to do—elude the tentacles of membership altogether.

I attended as an observer the Socialist Convention in Chicago in August 1919, at which the split caused by Lenin occurred and American communism was born. Art Young went with me, and illustrated my report of the explosion with comical portraits and caricatures that immortalized it. The party exploded into three, not two, fragments: one, the old "rightwing" Socialist Party; two, the native American "Communist Labor Party" organized by John Reed and Ben Gitlow; and three, the "Communist Party" created, bossed by, and consisting of the Slavic Federations, which had had a certain autonomy in the old party. These Russian immigrants gave America its first taste of a convention completely prepared in advance by a caucus of leaders, the delegates being accorded the privilege of making speeches before adopting a platform that was presented to them precooked and predigested by the ruling clique. This seems to be a quite general Russian conception of democracy in operation and not a whole-cloth innovation of the Bolsheviks.

Besides reporting the event in the *Liberator*, I took my stand with the Communist Labor Party, and delivered my judgment on the relative merits of the two leftwing fragments in the tone of an engineer of revolution saying the last word on a problem of social dynamics. My imagination works in a practical way on political questions, and it so takes possession of me that I forget I am not a man of action in the front line of the battle. My pontifical tone must have exasperated some of the real workers for communism, for such a separation of theory from practice, besides being morally unlovely, is criminally un-Marxian. It was tolerated, I suppose, because the movement was inchoate, and the *Liberator* was so useful to the cause.

"The Communist Labor Party," I pontificated, "has a certain atmosphere of reality, a sense of work to be done, a freedom from theological dogma on the one hand and machine politics on the other, which is new in American socialism and hopeful. A strong movement of the rank and file of revolutionists to the Communist Labor Party would weaken, convince, or drive out its uncertain minority, and at the same time leave the foreign Federations where the attitude of their leaders naturally places them, in a separate or autonomous Slavic Party of Communism."

No such strong movement of the rank and file occurred. Within four months both parties were driven underground; the "uncertain minority" in the CLP was repelled by the threat of arrest; the too Slavic control in the CP was considerably reduced by jailings and deportations. From around twenty-five thousand, the total membership came down to eight or ten thousand. Attempts to unite these small groups or factions were inevitable; and they were many and complicated. Their story is told with bewildering exactitude by Theodore Draper in his *Roots of American Communism*. It must suffice here to say that under a more tolerant regime in Washington, question of nationality became replaced, or blended in subtle ways, with the question whether a communist party in America should come into the open and observe the forms of law, or should remain illegal as the Russian parties had.

In 1921 the dominant leaders, both American and Russian-American, decided to form a legal mass party and call it the Workers' Party. And in Moscow in 1922, under the influence of Lenin and Trotsky, it was finally decided that "a legal party is possible in America," and that the American comrades should "devote their main efforts to work in the legal field." The decision was qualified, however, by a suggestion that the American comrades might hold in reserve an "illegal apparatus."

The result, and I can hardly doubt the true meaning, of this decision was that America would have an ostensibly legal party, but this would be steered and controlled by an underground group of hardened Bolsheviks. That, at least, is what happened. And Moscow took care to have its own secret representative in that underground group.

While taking that strong stand for the Third International and the Communist Labor Party, I was not moved to do anything about it. I did not even take out a membership in the party. I behaved as though my interest in values that are timeless—like scientific truth and poetry —exempted me from active participation even in the most momentous battles that were being fought to a finish in the time in which I lived.

All I can say in my defense is that I kept up no deception, but quite shamelessly acknowledged it. In the very month when the Third International was coming to birth in Moscow, I published in the *Liberator*— at Knopf's expense, I trust—a flamboyant advertisement of my politically innocuous book of poems, *Colors of Life*.

They'd never intern him for this book.—*The New York Tribune*

Whatever may happen to Max Eastman as a political agitator, his reputation as a poet is secure.—*The Chicago Herald*

No matter what they say about your *ologies* and *sophies*, it is a poet that you are first and last.—Arturo Giovannitti

Besides a general neglect of the contemporary struggle toward liberty, the book contained, by way of preface, an explicit declaration of poetic independence:

Life is older than liberty. It is greater than revolution. It burns in both camps. And life is what I love. And though I love it for all men and women, and so inevitably stand in the ranks of revolution against the cruel system of these times, I love it also for myself. And its essence—the essence of life—is variety and specific depth. It can not be found in monotonous consecration to a single principle. Therefore I have feared and avoided this consecration, which earnest friends for some reason always expect me to exemplify. . . .

That, I suppose, served notice on the militants that, however much help I might give—and I gave some help in that same month with a satirical dialogue in which Lenin psychoanalyzed Wilson—I was not to be counted on for disciplined service to the cause.

I must have dreamed once in a while that I might, in spite of my poetic and meditative temper, enlist for action in the struggle. I find, at least, this piece of self-admonishment in a notebook of those days:

> You must go into the blood of the battle with doubt;
> Truth lies not in the ash when time burns out.

Or was I perhaps only planning to write a poem on the conflict between the truth-lover and the man-of-action? That seems more likely —and I was not even man-of-action enough to write the poem.

I received some reproaches—one, I remember, from Carl Haessler, a consecrated militant—for my cowardice in not joining the organized movement. I also received some encomiums for my courage in maintaining an independent position. I was indeed pursuing the safer course, and I had to fall back for self-esteem on Plato's definition of courage as doing the intelligent thing regardless both of safety and danger.

My position, at any rate, was unique, and would have been impossible in later years. I was not what is now called a "fellow traveler." The phrase used to mean a man of independent judgment whose aims coincide with those of the party for a time. They can "travel" together until or unless their routes diverge. Under Stalinization the phrase came to mean one who, without joining the party, surrenders his independent judgment and "toes the party line." In the old sense, I might perhaps have been described as a fellow traveler, but one with the privilege of riding in the engine. At least I remember being confidentially consulted several times by leaders of the party. On one occasion I actually took a hand in shaping party policy on some question that I cannot quite remember. The organizing convention of the new Workers' Party had met in the Star Casino in New York and had adopted a platform drawn up for it by the underground machine that controlled the proceedings. One of their leaders, Jay Lovestone, a tall, watery-blue-eyed, innocent-looking but flinty-minded militant, brought it around to me after it was adopted, and asked me to edit it from the standpoint of good English.

"It's terribly written," he said. "We can't let it go out like that."

He laid it on my desk and I went to work on it while he stood aside, chatting with his companions. Pretty soon I said, pointing to a not unimportant item:

"This seems to me not only badly expressed, but politically foolish."

He read it over my shoulder.

"Oh, go ahead, fix the thing up," he said.

Chapter 24

A FLIGHT FROM EDITORSHIP

It took me all summer to fulfill or evade enough duties in New York so that I could join Florence in Hollywood as I had promised. That Chicago convention intervened first, and then a service to my priceless companion, Art Young, who was going home to a great event in his life. He was starting a magazine of his own—a small, lively and merrily biting publication called *Good Morning*. I thought this was a mistake; Art was too big to edit a Little Magazine, and too impractical to manage one. But his popularity and the expanding empire of his adoring friends tempted him into this waste of genius. They were tendering him a banquet on *Good Morning*'s birthday, October 1, and I was duty-bound, the committee told me, to make a speech at the banquet. I *was* so bound, though by a necessity that probably did not occur to them, that of retaining Art's loyalty and the indispensable inflow of his contributions to the *Liberator*. We must not seem to be rivals. A certain light-hearted banter in my remarks at the banquet may have had that purpose. At any rate they were successful. Though swamped in editorial labors of his own, Art never ceased to conspire with me in overthrowing capitalism on the pages of the *Liberator*.

An accidental meeting with Art Young at a dinner in honor of Jack London had been the primary cause of my being captured and dragged in to the editorship of the *Masses*, and there was some real feeling under my playful remarks. "Instead of tendering hypocritical congratulations to my friend," I said, "I am going to confess frankly that I came here to assist in his downfall. I happen to know that in helping him to become an editor we are destroying all that was free and beautiful in his soul, and I do it in a spirit of revenge. For this same Art Young is the man who corrupted my young life and dragged me to the editorial chair before my time. I was an unformed lad, full of promise, hope, ambition, with an infinite capacity for poetry and sin, and thanks to his adroit manipulations, I am now filled up with such things as patience, responsibility, faithfulness, punctuality, accuracy, honesty-in-moderation, and all those other rigidities which distinguish editors from living men. I am glad to see this tempter caught in his own toils, and I hope you will all contribute right loyally to the cause."

Another thing that delayed my departure for Hollywood was the great strike on Broadway, the fight of the actors against the managers for the right to organize in the Actors' Equity. That was one of the highest licks of the revolutionary flame so rapidly engirdling the earth, and I thought the *Liberator* ought to have a part in it. I also thought it was fun to watch celebrities like Ethel Barrymore and Ed Wynn and Walter Hampden turning themselves into soapbox orators. A particularly wonderful thing to see in action was the big famous joyous comedienne, Marie Dressler. In principle she was all for universal Christian peace and brotherhood.

"We must try to bring labor and capital together," she urged upon me in private. "We must allay this terrible *unrest* that is going all through the country and all over the world."

But that same night she pulled out the entire chorus of the Hippodrome, and after they had marched across the stage of a theater hired by the actors amid peals of thunder from the audience, Marie got up and shook her fist out over the orchestra.

"I'm in this fight to win!" she shouted. "And I can tell you, and I can tell those managers, that I'll stick through till justice is done to these people or every last ounce of fighting strength I have is exhausted!"

I tried to draw a socialist moral for the actors, although I suppose not a dozen of them ever saw my magazine. All the "terrible unrest" that is going over the world, I explained, "is composed only of strong men and women saying the very words Marie Dressler said, with the identical emotions, and the same unescapable reasons for saying them. . . . That unrest is the one great, beautiful and hopeful thing in these sad and terrible times. It shows that the spirit of life still inhabits this bloody globe, and that out of all the devastation and death which our insane commercial civilization has brought upon itself, a new, and free, and democratic society may yet be born."

With that preacherly duty done, I gathered my notes and manuscript, and my bundle of learned works on the comic instinct, and took flight across the country to Hollywood.

It was a different journey from my "Hands off Russia!" tour of the preceding winter. Love, not revolution, was my objective now, and the American people as well as the plains, the mountains, the great rivers, and the infinitude of the desert, welcomed me. I was happier; I have to admit I was more myself. I have traveled across the country and back eight times, I think—three times driving a car—and I have always found it a tranquilizing experience. Even the daylong monotony of the central states, the plains and prairies that have nothing to sing about but space and the horizon, have a lyrical quality for me. They are like the ocean. And I never felt more like lying down in their quietude to sleep and dream that on this fast-train trip away from the turmoil of revolutionary politics into a life of meditative writing and love.

I was reminded, though, that the American people were not so grandly tranquil as their landscape in that year of the returning armies, the restoration of peace. We lynched seventy-eight people during 1919, six white men and seventy-two Negroes—one every four days. In Omaha a crowd of seemingly representative citizens twice attempted to lynch their own mayor, stringing him up to a lamppost and standing around until he was cut down and dragged away unconscious by some audacious individual. He was strung up for insisting upon due process of law. The citizens had assembled to lynch a Negro; the Negro was in the courthouse; the mayor stood on the courthouse steps and said he would defend the Negro's right to a jury trial with his life. Somebody yelled "nigger lover," and that loosed the flood. After stringing up the mayor half a block down the street, the citizens came back, many thousands of them, and burned their own courthouse, setting fire to it on all sides in order to smoke out a sturdy company of citizens inside who were still insisting on due process of law.

I am describing this incident because I saw the smoked and gutted courthouse on passing through Omaha. It was no insignificant small-town brick building such as you would imagine, but an immense pillared structure occupying, with the wide plaza in front of it, an entire block. I judged it to be twice as large as the New York Public Library, and it had evidently possessed all the austerity and majesty traditionally associated with the administration of justice.

I spoke of this, as the train pulled into Omaha, to a fellow-passenger who was getting off—a typical Midwestern business man, I thought, heavy in the jowl, meticulously clean and silky, but noisy in the throat and nose. I had heard him in the buffet car protesting his devotion to law and order, and proving it by stating that all those opposed to the

Constitution ought to be stood up against a wall and shot. I expressed a little mild surprise that citizens of his own town should burn down their own public buildings and attempt to lynch the mayor they had elected.

"Yes, it was a damn shame," he said. "Not the mayor, I guess he got pretty fresh—but it was a damn shame to destroy that building."

It was in the morning hours of September 29, 1919, that I got off the train in Los Angeles. My heart was beating high, and Florence in all her unimagined beauty was there to welcome me. She wore a summery lavender dress—unless my memory is making this up—its lines simple, a band of lace forming a horizontal neckline, no hat, just her gleaming brown hair in clouds and wavy clusters close around her head. The female costumes of the day—praise be to God—were in their tubular, not their bell-shaped or bustled phase; girls could stand straight in the shape of a human being. Hairdos also were simple, belonging to the head, not dolling it up. Thus even in Hollywood, where Florence had to obey more than she wished the dictates of fashion, my taste for what I call "natural" was never offended.

She had driven to the station in a sleek little dark-blue "roadster," and led me across the plaza to it with the urgency and gay laughter of a child displaying a birthday present. It was more than a birthday for her, it was a birth—this emergence into a salaried life in Hollywood with a contract to play leads for the Goldwyn studio. Two years had passed since *Photoplay Magazine*, naming the best actresses of the year, had listed—together with Norma Talmadge, Alla Nazimova and only three others—"Florence Deshon, the one-part wonder you may remember in *Jaffery*." The wait for a second part had been long and not easy to understand, but now it was over. The skies had opened; the sun was shining—the California sun—on her ambition, which was so nearly the inner drive and essence of her life.

Chapter 25

PLAY AND WORK IN HOLLYWOOD

I was aboundingly happy with Florence in her new paradise. I was, if you can believe it, almost normal. That inner demon of selfhood which had clutched and strangled my love the previous August was quiescent here—I suppose because I was not committing him to anything he need regard as eternal or absolute. We were in Florence's domain now, not mine. I could go back to myself whenever I chose. I was on a visit into love.

We found a long-shaped cool clean white-walled apartment two flights up on De Longpre Avenue—"Long Meadow Avenue"—and though it was only one block from the main traffic of the town, there was in fact a meadow running beside it back to the next street. Our front windows looked into palm leaves and our side windows, in the bedroom and dining room and kitchen, opened on a stretch of green grass sprinkled with some yellow blossoms—could they have been California poppies at that season? Remember again that Hollywood was then a small town, quiet though excited. Just across our meadow, and across one more open lot, was a movie studio where they were using a troop of lions in a picture. The dreamlike romance of the place came vividly to mind in the mornings when we would be wakened by lions and meadow larks roaring and singing. The two months we spent there were altogether sweet and gay; they were a second blossom-time of our love. No cloud ever passed over us, no thin veil of mist between us.

Goldwyn, alas, had not yet thought of anything for Florence to do in a picture. But that would soon be coming, and meanwhile it seemed not unreasonable for her to do a little housekeeping. It did not even injure her pride if I allowed her, at her own suggestion, to get my dinner, and perhaps invite a few friends in. She had made, as always, a circle of admiring friends, and I was able, reviving the contacts of the previous winter, to widen the circle. Among her friends, the dearest was Margarethe Mather, a slim, quietly magnetic girl, snub-nosed, grey-eyed, with this-way and that-way floating ash-blond hair. She was a devotee of photography, a close friend and co-worker of Edward Weston, who was then already becoming famous in this field. Only a something too gentle in her nature, something suggested by that softened ending of her name, prevented Margarethe, I used to think, from getting her share of that fame. She flattered me into this opinion, perhaps, by finding some kinship between me and the vast far-reaching dunelands out south of the city. (They're not dunelands any more, but a sea of hot-dog stands leading to a forest of oil wells.) Margarethe drove me out there and took some Westonlike pictures in which I was supposed to blend with the infinity—or was it more properly the vacancy?—of that mysterious landscape. The pictures were Westonlike enough so that Weston himself signed his name beside hers, and I might lay claim to the glamour now possessed by those whom he chose to immortalize in those old-fashionedly significant poses.

I took Florence one day to Charlie Chaplin's studio to pay a call, remembering his cordial welcome of the previous winter and surmising that her beauty and the lovely tones of her voice would not make another welcome less cordial. He was in one of his troubled phases, having recently buried the little malformed child that blue-eyed, empty-headed Mildred Harris bore him. Having been married to her long enough to feel lonesome, he greeted us as though we were intimate friends he had been longing to see. We soon *were* intimate friends—as intimate as one can be with Charlie, who carries a remoteness with him however close he comes. We formed almost a nightly habit of coming together, Charlie and Margarethe and some friends from the movie colony, to play charades and other dramatic games. I remember those nights' entertainments as the gayest and most enjoyable social experiences of my life.

I must explain that those charades of ours were not little impromptu guessing games; they were elaborately worked-out dramas and scenic spectacles, in the preparation of which all human experience and the entire contents of Charlie's house would be commandeered. It was Mildred's house really, for Charlie was beginning to live more and more at the Athletic Club, but Mildred never appeared at these parties longer than to say How-do-you-do. You didn't ask why, but you got the impression that she thought his friends had too many ideas and would expect her to say something. (She was only seventeen years old.) The house at any rate, though commonplace—a yellow frame house three stories high, as I remember it—was admirably constructed for amateur dramatics. The dining room opened through a wide archway into the drawing room, and had two exits at the opposite corners, one into the kitchen and one that went upstairs. There were drapes in the archway which could be drawn, and thus the whole front part of the house would be converted into a theater. Without disturbing the guests, you could sneak up those back stairs and ransack their wardrobes, if any of them had had the hardihood to come for the night. Charlie and I would always choose the sides, and we would choose them the day before, inviting to dinner those whom we each wanted on our team. We got so expert at this game that we thought a charade was not good if it didn't have continuity—the first syllable being the first act of a play, the next the second act, and so on.

It is not easy to get people into a mood at once energetic enough and relaxed enough to enter into such exploits, and that is where the speech-making game came in. It was a creation of mine, a revenge I took for my long years of suffering before audiences who wouldn't give me any help.

We played it this way: one end of the room would be cleared of people, and regarded as a platform. Everyone would write the subject of a speech on a slip of paper, fold it tight, and drop it into a hat. We always had to warn them to write a serious subject, not a funny one—the fun would come afterward. And we had to make everyone in the room solemnly agree to play: if anyone hung back, they all would. Then the host or ringmaster—whoever was engineering the game— would take out his watch, and pass the hat to the first person on the left of the platform. He—or she—had to draw a folded paper from the hat, mount the platform, face the audience, unfold and read it aloud, and make a speech one minute long on the subject read. If he could not think of a word to say, he had to stand there facing the audience just the same, until the minute was up.

It is one way of finding out how long a minute is. And it is an unfailing means of limbering people up to the point of playing charades. After they have suffered through one of those lonely minutes, they are ready for anything that is done in company.

Charlie improved on my speech-making game by passing two hats, in one of which a subject was dropped, in the other the description of a character. Then we had to make a speech *on* the subject and *in* the character. This soon involved costumes and became almost as formidable as charades. I vividly remember Charlie as a "Toothless Old Veteran" discoursing on "The Benefits of Birth Control." He rises before my mind's eye, too, completely costumed and made up as Carrie Nation, delivering, hatchet in hand, a lecture on "Some Doubts as to the Origin of Species." It was in one of our games that he first preached the sermon on David and Goliath that formed a hilarious climax in his picture, *The Pilgrim*. When I saw it my mind traveled back to the evening I first introduced him to the speech-making game, and he stood up there valiantly for one minute—fussed and embarrassed as a schoolgirl, giggling and saying absolutely nothing. He was trying to be himself. As soon as he caught on to the trick of acting a part, he loved to do it.

Charlie devised what we called the drama game to take the place of those charades after they got so elaborate that neither his picture, *The Kid*, nor my book was getting any attention at all. For this game we would drop into the hat titles suitable for one-act plays. We would divide the company into couples, and each couple would draw a subject. After consultation, and a raid on the wardrobes upstairs, they would put on a one-act play corresponding to that title, making up the dialogue as they went along.

In describing those playtimes, I have borrowed from my book *Great Companions*, which contains also a plain-spoken portrait of Charlie's wayward, subtle, mixed-up, many-sided and much-maligned character. That portrait properly belongs to this story, but it has acquired a separate identity. I must content myself with saying that, although few then realized it, Charlie was capable of loyal, everyday, untumultuous, faithful and friendly affection. His tastes on the whole were rather quiet. And I must add that he was as much entranced by Florence's quick mind and radiant beauty as I was. He was not, I think, in love with her; he merely loved to be with us both. At least, our three-cornered friendship was free from any hint of rivalry. Indeed I experienced sometimes almost a parental feeling toward the two of them, their interest in Hollywood's affairs being so much more vivacious than mine, and they liked so much better than I did to sit and talk.

In the midst of these gay times in Hollywood, I fulfilled a sober task that had been waiting at my editorial door for some months—that of answering an exalted appeal issued to the world of letters by Romain Rolland. During the war, this famous novelist had given extravagant praise to the old *Masses*, and to me in particular, in his book, *The Forerunners*, and now at the war's end he turned to me and to the *Liberator* for signatures to his "Declaration of Intellectual Independence." This was a tense and sentimental cry for the renewal of a brotherly union supposed to have existed before the war among "workers of the mind" in all countries. Composed with a little more mental work and a little less unction, it would have been a timely appeal to literary men and artists to dismiss the wartime passions, and hasten the process of reconciliation. It was signed by some big names: Jane Addams, Benedetto Croce, Bertrand Russell, Israel Zangwill, Ellen Key, Selma Lagerlöf, Stefan Zweig. . . . But it was naïve and irrational to an astonishing degree, so loosely pondered as to identify "Thought," abstract and capitalized, with an adherence to certain specific ideals such as love, democracy, brotherhood.

Let us arise! Let us set free the mind. . . . The mind knows no master. It is we who are servants of the Mind. . . . We honor truth alone; free, without frontiers, without limit, without bias of race or caste. . . . We do not know people. We know the people —one, universal . . . the people of all men, all equally our brothers. And it is that they shall become conscious with us of this brotherhood, that we raise above their blind battles the Ark of the Covenant—the unshackled Mind, one and manifold, eternal.

Notwithstanding the high names appended to this effusion, I answered it with a rather school-teacherish lecture:

"The mind," I expounded, "in abstraction from all service to the purposes of our wills, if indeed it exists at all, is of little or no moral or social consequence. . . . Moreover, when the mind does come into the service of human purposes, there is nothing essentially democratic, or revolutionary, or even social or benevolent about it."

That in the first place, and in the second: "Morally it is distasteful to me to see you and those associated with you treat of yourselves as thus forming a superior cult. . . . You speak of the calamity of 'a divorce between the higher thought and the workers.' I cannot take that expression 'higher thought' into my lips.

"In the third place, after we have acknowledged that the great question before us is a question of values to be chosen, and . . . for our part, have chosen liberty and democracy—then, indeed, mind does make a demand upon us. For there exists a science, consisting of a series of hypotheses as to the method by which this choice of ours may be carried out in the actual world. . . ." And I proceeded to expound the doctrine of democratic progress through class struggle.

"You will know," I added, "that I write this with the utmost respect for your idealism, and admiration for your moral courage which has been one of the few undimmed lights in the black period that is past. I simply have no faith for the future in the declaration of any in-

Drawn by Art Young

"JIMMIE, TAKE THE HEAD OF THE CLASS. YOU CERTAINLY
DO BETTER THAN THIS DODDERING IMBECILE."
The Liberator   October 1920

tellectuals who continue to see themselves as a class apart and aloof from the wage-laborers of the earth, or think there is any function or any place for a man of social ideals above the present battle."

It is not my intention to boast of the harm I did with my "science of revolution," but I cannot refrain from speculating as to whether my sermon, which was long and earnest, did not prepare the ground for Rolland's subsequent downslide from the realms of the "higher thought" into an automatic acquiescence in every twist of the Stalinist party line. At least it was not many years after this that the Communists succeeded—through the influence of a woman agent of the GPU, the Soviet secret police, my French friends inform me—in converting this age-ing apostle of "the mind that knows no master" into an obedient front-man for every foul trick and hypocrisy that the exigencies of Stalin's foreign policy made expedient. Our correspondence in the *Liberator* would make a good starting point when this sad story comes to be truthfully told. Especially the following, which he wrote in a somewhat irrelevant reply to my sermon:

> I love mankind. I want them to become free and happy. But if it should be at the price of a lie or a compromise, I would not tell the lie, I would reject the compromise. . . . A social community which could be saved only by the renunciation of free intelligence would not be saved in reality, but lost." *

I am, I must say, in a weak position to preach a sermon on Romain Rolland's failings. Whether influenced by my writings or not, he merely committed at a later date, and persisted in, a mistake of the kind that I at the time of our correspondence was making. By that later date, however, the mistake had become both more inept and more disastrous. People who defended Stalin's perfected tyranny, having been cool to the crude but selfless efforts made under Lenin and Trotsky to build a socialist state, belong in a different category, I think, from those who defended Lenin and Trotsky. At any rate, I will not refrain from saying what seems true to me now, that Rolland's excessively abstract rapture about "truth," "freedom," "brotherhood," "the Mind," "the People," which degenerated concretely into the loyal upholding of a patently prodigious regime of lies, hate, slavery and mindless massacre of the people, is symbolic. It might be a warning to those who elevate themselves with the term "intellectual" to make sure they are not merely sitting behind the sky. On earth they are pretty likely, I still think, to be untrustworthy.

* The *Liberator* for March 1920.

Chapter 26

AN EDITOR AGAIN

Both ambition and duty tore me from our carefree joys in Hollywood. I planned to present in Part Two of my book on humor a conspectus of all the great theories of the comic from Plato to Bergson and Freud, granting them the honor of leading up in a dignified procession to my own. For this purpose I had to have access to a more various library than was to be found in Los Angeles. My presence was also needed on the *Liberator*, where my indispensable function—according, at least, to both Floyd Dell and Louis Untermeyer, who have written memoirs of those days—was diplomatic. That is, I had a talent for persuading the contributing editors to contribute—a very ticklish and difficult trick, as all editors-in-chief will acknowledge.

So we parted in bliss and tenderness, Florence and I. We parted with dreams of her coming east again, "laden with gold" which we would spend fixing up the little house in Croton, and then taking trips around the planet in the free way people with plenty of money do.

In San Francisco on my way home, I went to see a girl poet to whom I had been acting as literary godfather, criticizing, developing and publishing her poems. Although later corrupted (in my opinion) by Stalinism and the "modernist" tendencies, she was writing richly colorful lyrics at that time. I had been romantically loving her poetry and her letters, as she had mine, and we fell naturally into each other's arms. We spent the better part of three days, as I remember it, in another sweet brief love—though I should not dismiss it as brief, for it was destined to extend, with strange and tragic interludes, a long way into my life. All that is relevant here, however, either to my story or my character, is that in that December of 1919, two days after leaving Hollywood, I spent three days in San Francisco with a young, gifted and thrilling girl, bathing with her in an emotion that can only be described as lyrical and idealistic love. She described my poems as "the best that are being written," and made me happy—as I wrote to Florence—"by showing me a copy almost worn out, with the passages marked that I myself knew were the best."

Twenty years later I saw the volume which she had praised so highly, and which I had inscribed to her "with my love," advertised as a collector's item by a second-hand bookstore. Although offered at a price I could hardly afford, I bought it and tore out the inscription—not angrily, only to protect my pride. That was the last act of a romance I look back upon with tenderness, compunction, and amazed regret.

After saying farewell to this new friend, I spent one reminiscent day-and-night with my stormy-haired love of the year before. I seem to have felt that it would be disloyal to Vera, after our vows of friendship, to pass through San Francisco without greeting her again—although, since I said nothing to her about my poet-friend and nothing to my poet-friend about her, "loyalty" seems rather a peculiar concept to employ. I also went up to Grass Valley for another day with my college friend, Sid Wood, who had helped to liberate me from my unhappy marriage, but who knew nothing, and asked nothing, about the wanderings of my heart since then. In this variety of experiences, I felt no diminution of my love for Florence—rather its confirmation with the assurance that it left me free to live my own life. I wrote her from the train east: "I wanted to come back to you from San Francisco with my whole heart. I have had enough of ego-adventure already. I have no home but where you are."

The former statement was true in its way, but the latter did not turn out quite so true. For when I got back to New York, instead of living alone as Florence did, mixing romance with its sweet friend, solitude, I moved into an apartment on St. Luke's Place with my ego-adventurous friend, Eugen Boissevain. It works a change in my nature to live with a man, to "bum around" with a man, to regard girls as slightly extraneous, a treasure to be enjoyed and indeed revered, but not domesticated. I attribute our success as living companions to the fact that we agreed, on moving in, that we would both be consciously and frankly selfish—no gestures of altruism on either side. Each would be trying to get the best of the situation and therefore all disputes and divisions would have to be settled on a basis of justice, which is another name for expediency. Eugen violated the agreement by giving me a thousand dollars to finish my book on humor when my advance ran out, but I stuck to the bargain throughout.

I do not mean to imply that I was at rest as an absentee lover—or at rest just then in any other respect. I was vigorously scheming to get back to Hollywood as soon as I could. Indeed I entertained the utopian idea of lifting the *Liberator* off of me altogether, the whole thing, and laying it on my sister's more executive shoulders. "I feel as if I were always postponing, postponing both my emotional and intellectual life," I wrote to Florence. "Crystal has gone on her speaking tour. There is money to be raised and I am working on that. I fear January 20 is the nearest date I can come back to you. I think the last number is very bad, and that gives me a terrible feeling that it really is my choice and judgment that has made the *Liberator* what it is. . . . I feel so sad when I see the manuscript of my book lying untouched all this time. Really it is unendurable." When Crystal came back she was terribly sick—"measles, acute bronchitis, a slight pneumonia, influenza—in that order." I had to postpone again my going, and give up forever the hope of laying my burden on her. "Crystal is barely walking around the room, and even when she is well she seems to have lost all her zeal for action. I am afraid I can never leave the *Liberator* in her hands. I don't think she wants to do it. It isn't sufficiently *hers*, and never can be." *

Besides these troubles, the government was on a new rampage of repression, this time ultimately directed, it truly seemed, to the total destruction of the socialist press. "Every day the newspapers seem full of threats at you," Florence wrote; and I reassured her: "The one good thing is that I don't seem to be in for an indictment. Either they haven't got a plausible case against me, or they have decided to leave Americans alone." My exposure of the Polk-Lansing correspondence had, of course, made me suspect in government circles, and I was carefully and constantly shadowed by the police. Privately I worried and felt lamentably miscast in the role of conspirator, but I had the sense to take it gaily in the magazine.

"Scientists have discovered that space is limited," I wrote in the February number, ". . . the first real setback to the spread of Bolshevism.

---

* I was beginning to realize that it had been, from Crystal's viewpoint, a mistake for her to join me in running the *Liberator*. Though our names stood equal on the masthead, and though her work and judgment were as important as mine, her position in the public mind was inevitably secondary. Crystal had her own eminence, and her own pride in it, but she was not primarily a writer—not at all a poetic or humorous writer—and on such a magazine all the wages of praise and appreciation went to the artists and writers.

" 'Political intelligence . . . $50,000,' is one of the items in the President's European expense account. A justifiable purchase, but what did he do with it?

"A force of two detectives, sometimes reinforced by a third, is deployed to watch the house where I live. One of their duties is to dig all my wastepaper out of the ash barrel and read it. This morning I sent them down a few pages from Kant's *Critique of Pure Reason* and *The Sermons of Jonathan Edwards*. Anybody who has any literature suitable for the edification of two loyal and impecunious patriots will confer a favor by sending it to the *Liberator*."

There was an exuberant solidarity among revolutionaries of all kinds and origins in those days of the shining faith in Lenin and Trotsky. One of my visitors was a two-fisted agitator from Montana, a big-muscled fighting IWW—Red Doran by name. He came around merely to thank me for the fight we had been putting up for the IWW in the *Masses* and the *Liberator*. But those detectives downstairs thought his visit mysteriously significant, and one of them followed him when he left. Perceiving that he was being shadowed, Doran took a subway train miles up to the top of Manhattan. He entered a restaurant there and sat down at a table. As it was dinner time, the spy came in before long and sat at another table. Doran called him over, and said:

"How about dining together? And I'll tell you where I'm going after dinner. I'm going to take a little walk about half a mile up north of here where there's a big vacant lot. I'm going to walk right out into the middle of that lot and enjoy the scenery for a while. If you want anything of me, that will be the easiest place to find me."

The detective, as Doran told me the story afterward, replied with a grin:

"I would enjoy dining with you, but I think, if you don't mind, I'll eat at home."

Subsequently a squad of detectives forcibly entered my apartment when, by chance, Jan Boissevain, Eugen's younger brother, was lying there deathly sick with a fever. As they started going through my desk, Jan sat faintly up in bed, and tried to protest. They paid him no mind, he tells me, until he said weakly: "If you don't get out of here, I'll call the police."

"We are the police," they said.

But they found nothing more incriminating than a few poems and some elaborate notes on the physiology of laughter.

We were being careful of our correspondence in those days. And of course in a political sense, we were far from disheartened by this hysterical reaction to our evangel. It was just another proof of what we had been saying about the savagely devouring greed of the "capitalist class"—about how the facts of economic tyranny override the forms of political freedom when proprietary rights are threatened. Only a revolution can unsettle those rights, for they have their roots in justice itself as it is conceived in a capitalist society. "There can be no judge when justice is on trial." Such was my editorial response to those "practices of tyranny" which followed so swiftly on the heels of victory in the War for Democracy.

Chapter 27

ABSENTEE LOVE

During the next several months my love and Florence's passed through profound and diverging changes that are hard to describe. It is clear from her letters that Florence was loving me more, or more unwithholdingly, after those three happy months in Hollywood. "I have given you all the room there is in my mind and heart . . ." she wrote in December. I was responding to her emotion, but I could not speak the same words, because other girls, or images of girls, had a dwelling in my mind and heart. I was conducting a more than friendly correspondence with my poet protégée in San Francisco, helping her lovingly—I remember using, although with hesitation, the word love in one of my letters—to find a way of earning her living in New York. During those same months Eugen and I were forming a habit of spending our week-ends together in the country with the Duncan girls—Isadora's adopted young dancers, with whom, while I was married to Ida, you may remember, I had been too shy or inhibited to form an acquaintance. We were gaily engrossed in a multiple romance with them now, Eugen especially attached to Irma, I to Lisa, and Anna more distantly alluring to us both. Lisa knew that I loved Florence—I could never be uncandid in so close a relation—and the fact protected her somewhat, I think. It protected me too. But her childlike grace and beauty filled my eyes; she was like a gazelle, her hair light gold and her brown eyes large and gentle.

As to whether Florence had other lovers at this time, I do not know, and in view of our agreement upon mutual independence, I did not feel privileged to ask. Men are prone to assume that the women they love are more faithful than they actually are, and I do not want to fall into that error. But a note of almost pleading entered her letters now—not pleading for fidelity, but only for unforgetting love.

"Do not desert me, dearest . . ." she wrote in January, "I need you. I long for you. We will be happy. . . ."

She was not lonesome; she had many admiring friends in Hollywood. The playwright, Edwin Justus Mayer, told me years later that her friendship lifted him out of an almost suicidal gloom when he found himself banished to Hollywood. The sonnet of love in his autobiography, *Preface To Life*, was addressed to her. Another friend was Theodore Dreiser, who created around her image the portrait of Ernestine De Jongh in his *Gallery of Women*. Dreiser's letters, which she preserved, make it clear that he, at least, was not on intimate terms with her, and his portrait corresponds only in two small remarks to my knowledge of her life and character: She was "sensuously and disturbingly beautiful and magnetic," and she was "almost abnormally ambitious."

The only man Florence mentioned often in her letters was our mutual friend, Charlie Chaplin.

Charlie is always very sweet to me.

I dined with Charlie on Christmas Eve, and he gave me a Christmas present.

Beloved, Charlie came to dinner last night and I gave him your book. He was so happy to get it. I saw his picture *The Kid* in the projection room. It is wonderful, wonderful. I cried and laughed and smiled and worried. It was the most exciting thing I ever saw. . . .

Charlie is all excited about buying a yacht. He said, "Let's you and Max and Elmer and I go off together." I said we would make movies in all the countries we touched, and he is enthusiastic about your acting in them. Well, we had a wonderful time. Anyhow as soon as he finishes this picture he asked me if I wouldn't take a trip in his car. We all had the wanderlust very strongly and were flying all over the world. . . .

To this significant communication, she added—as though to make it more significant: "I fear in each letter you write that you will describe somebody you have fallen in love with."

Although I was jealous to the point of "shaking from head to foot" about a certain stranger whose attentions she spoke of, a creature (I still so think of him) called Reginald Pole, I had no such extreme reaction to the news that Charlie had asked her to take a trip with him in his car. For some reason—perhaps because we had all three been good friends together—my thoughts of him were not disturbing. I read with a tranquil mind the interesting things she told me about him.

> Charlie speaks ever of going away, but it all depends on this picture and at the rate he is working, he will never finish it. I know I am naughty, but I become tired of Charlie's matrimonial troubles. He stays in that frightful situation at his home, and his powerlessness to move wears me out.* I did not go with him to meet Heifetz as there were too many people there. I would rather meet Heifetz with Dagmar Godowsky. You are the God of his accompanist, he talks of you all the time. Heifetz laughingly says that he himself is rich enough to be a socialist.

> Did I tell you that I met the famous French comedian, Max Linder? I spent the day at Charlie's studio, and he had a lot of callers that day. Linder is smaller than Charlie and very good looking and well dressed. He is a very sweet little fellow and Charlie was quite jealous of him for a few minutes. Then we went into his dressing room, and Charlie pulled off his cap and roughed his hair and you know he always looks charming that way. He caught a fleeting vision of himself in the glass and all was right with the world again. He is very bad about his work, he takes scenes over and over again, not because he is striving for perfection, but because something in him refuses to go forward.

Another reason, perhaps, for the calm with which I learned that Florence had "spent the day" in Charlie's studio was that my own daily emotions were becoming more deeply concerned with Lisa. I went for a second time to a performance given by Isadora and her pupils in Carnegie Hall, and this time my rapture reached its height in Lisa's solo dance to a "Musette" by Glück. I was carried away out of all reality by the blending of the movements of her lovely body with that exquisite music. There was no change in the way I wrote to Florence, but for ten days I did not find the time to write to her at all. She was so saddened by this, or some intuition of the cause of it, that she wrote, "I feel as if

---

* It was nine more months before Mildred Harris relieved this situation by securing an uncontested divorce for "mental cruelty."

the sweet house in Croton were closed against me. . . ." At the same time she received a blow that all the love letters in the world, I fear, would not have made up for. Samuel Goldwyn, after holding her six months in high-paid but soul-destroying idleness, informed her that he wished to break her contract. A letter to me, which she did not mail, but which I read long after, expressed her heartbreak and despair. A few weeks later however, her glory-dreams revived and she sent me a triumphant telegram: she had received three offers at twice the Goldwyn salary. Being still under contract she would ask my advice before making a move, but meanwhile she was thinking of me "all the time" and sent me "all her love."

Soon after that, however, came another telegram which caused a reaction in me that was disastrous to us both:

HAVE LET GOLDWYN BREAK MY CONTRACT FOR ONE THOUSAND DOLLARS AND TICKET HOME FORGIVE ME NOT ASKING YOUR ADVICE BUT HAD TURNED AWAY FROM YOU BECAUSE OF GOSSIP ABOUT YOU WHICH HURT MY HEART AM STARTING MONDAY WITH MAURICE TOURNEUR AT THREE HUNDRED FIFTY IN BIG PART I AM FREE AS WINDY MORNING LOVE

Instead of answering this with congratulations, and exulting that I too was free as the wind, and was indeed blowing two ways at once, I went into a panic of infantile compunction. Only a knowledge of my intensely moralistic childhood, my all-but-insane babyish concentration, at the age of seven or eight, upon the divinely inculcated, all day and every day business of "being good" can explain what happened to me. With the very first glance at Florence's telegram, I became a rebuked and guilty-minded child. I was certainly not the first man of honor who had loved one girl in absence and another nearby, but my feelings of guilt would not have been more obsessive if I had been the one and only perpetrator of the Unpardonable Sin. In a frenzy of moralism, I decided that the only way out of my guilt was to tell her the whole unmitigated truth. Not content to tell her I was in love with Lisa, I described how, when I saw Lisa dance in Carnegie Hall, "I was entranced away beyond any thought by the perfection of her being." A cruel and unusual remark, to say the least.

It took twelve days for her answer to come:

Shall I tell you my true emotions when I read your letter. I was sad for you. Then I was angry. Then again it all seemed so simple. If you are in love with Lisa there is no reason in the world that I should come between you. If it were not so lovely a girl as Lisa it would be someone else. . . . It is almost two years since you stopped loving me, and my first instinct was to get away, but it seemed wanton and we liked each other still. There was really no change in the basis of our relationship. Now there is. . . .

I have given up the house in the country, it is yours. Please make it your own again.

I am not turning away. Truly with my hand on my heart my feelings and emotions for you have never been kinder.

By the time I received this letter I had lost my poise altogether. My feelings of guilt had been light compared to the emotions which now possessed me. We all overvalue what we cannot have. We cry like infants when something is taken from us that we were indifferently holding onto. This is especially true, I think, of men in love. Women are somewhat civilized; they are mothers. Men are hunting animals. It is a kind of dead end for a hunter when his prey comes to meet him. But when she is slipping away into the brush—that is something else again. I say this self-excusingly, for my behavior in this storm of emotion, as I relive it in reading our letters, seems infantile. I was suffering from a desperate sense of loss—a seizure of feeling whose strength in me goes back, I think, to the shock of separation from my mother in babyhood. At least I find relief in thus explaining my inability to face up to the consequence of my recklessly meticulous truth-telling. I must have been standing strongly on two feet, thinking I had life fairly in hand when I wrote that fatal letter to Florence. Now all my supports had crumpled under me. I was dismayed and frightened. I wrote a whole series of wailing letters in the next twenty days—they were year-long days— pleading for a word from her that did not come.

I can't find what I want in the world. I can't find anything that endures. I can't make absolute choices. I have made but one, and that was you, and if I can't come back to that then nothing in the world will ever stand for me. I shall flow to my grave in a hazy and meaningless stream of emotions. . . .

After five or six weeks of such self-pitying lamentations, I received this letter:

April 26, 1920

Dearest, I am not like you. I cannot write long letters about my feelings. I must just depend upon your wonderful understanding if I don't explain but just tell you I am in love. . . .

Your letter about Lisa set me free. Until then—you were first in my thoughts. You and happy times in Croton. Then I realized I had had those things, but would never have them again. I too love love. I am not one to be content with just a friendship in my life.

I cannot write any more about it, forgive me.

You would think those words might have put an end to my wailing, and set me on my feet. I think of her eyes when I try to understand why they did not. I have said too much perhaps of the passionate wild gypsy in Florence that fascinated me by being so different from my native world, so never-to-be-found in a Congregational parsonage. It was an adventure like running away from home to love her. I have not spoken of the mother-tender warmth of her eyes, which made it a little also like coming home. That feeling of "very ownness," which I spoke of when we first lay down together, lived its life in me independent of romantic love, independent almost of sex. I am again trying to explain why I continued to behave like a baby. I wrote to her all afternoon the day I received that notice of dismissal, pouring out the whole of what I did and felt, asking only that she dwell with me once more for a moment while reading it. That letter carried me through the day, but I did not mail it. In my headstrong sorrow, I became convinced toward evening that what she had told me was not true—or not true in the absolute way in which she told it. Instead of mailing my long letter, I telegraphed that her letter was unendurably brief and I was coming out there to hear it all before I could believe it. She answered in time to stop me:

IF THIS TELEGRAM REACHES YOU I WISH YOU COULD PLEASE DELAY YOUR TRIP UNTIL LETTER I AM WRITING REACHES YOU PLEASE DO THIS FOR MY SAKE MY WHOLE FUTURE DEPENDS ON IT LOVE

The letter never came but this surprising answer might, had I been capable of logical reasoning on the question, have confirmed me in my opinion that her announcement of a new love was not too devastatingly true. She was in love, yes, but maybe no more deeply than I was with Lisa. At least it was only my present intrusion that she dreaded, only a delay that she asked. These facts were very slow to penetrate my despair, but gradually they did. I wrote her a few letters that were calmly friendly. She answered with news of her career, and thus, in a lower key and tempo, our correspondence was renewed. We were still friends.

Chapter 28

VERY CLOSE TO FAME

During that winter and spring of 1920, while so heart-stricken and drooping to the ground in my private life, I was moving publicly as near as I ever came to a position of leadership. I was not, as the *New York World* described me, "the most influential radical in the United States," but I was probably the most prominent of those who had stayed out of jail. At least I have never come so close to fame either before or since. It was a period of rebel hope and revolutionary upsurge throughout the world; the *Liberator* was waving its banner of art and poetry in the forefront of the battle; and my editorials, exclusively political now, were denouncing in harsh bold terms the "milk water and wet wool" of which the arguments of the anti-Bolshevik Socialists were composed. Nobody would dream, examining the *Liberator* in those turbulent days, that its chief editor was spending his best hours wailing at the loss of a love he had himself thrown away.

In our March number I made an expertly Bolshevik reply to the memorandum on bolshevism submitted to the Senate Committee on Foreign Affairs by Wilson's Secretary of State, Robert Lansing. I read his memorandum with respect, I said, because it was composed with a kind of "provincial honesty," but that was the extent of my praise for it.

The dictatorship of the proletariat, Lansing asserted, was acknowledged by the Bolsheviks to be "the rule of a minority," but he made the mistake of including in his appendix a statement to the contrary by Lenin himself. The dictatorship of the proletariat, Lenin asserted, is distinguished from that of the landlords and capitalists by the fact that it forcibly suppresses an "insignificant minority" instead of the "overwhelming majority" of the population. I made Lansing's really very able report look careless, at least, by playing up this contradiction.

But I dealt him a neater blow to which his honesty laid him open. His sole proof that the Bolsheviks held a close monopoly of power was that "they themselves realize what has developed in actual practice and try vainly to check the current they started."

"It is the first time in history," I remarked, "that a gang of people who had established a close monopoly of power ever tried to get rid of it. . . . Mr. Lansing's testimony that *even in the midst of war* the Bolshevik leaders are trying to dissipate that monopoly of power, and that they have adopted a constitution which opposes it, is the highest and most significant tribute that any writer has paid to these leaders. Our war is long past and the victory won, but we do not observe any similar haste to get rid of their extraordinary powers on the part of our leaders."

In the midst of the Palmer Raids—which I suspect Lansing had no love for—that was a pointed blow. And I drove it home by adducing another of his candid quotations from Lenin. Speaking of the task of building up the life of the middle peasantry, Lenin said:

"First help him, and then you will secure his confidence. . . . We must give him assistance. We must give him advice, and this must not be the orders of a commanding officer, but the advice of a comrade."

If these be "tyrannical methods," I exclaimed, "let us have tyranny in the United States. In particular let us have a tyrant in the place of A. Mitchell Palmer."

Speaking of Palmer brought me to another of Lansing's accusations against the Bolsheviks: their employment of "mass terror." My answer to this is important, I think, for those interested in my story.

Since we have now the official report of the Bullitt Commission, supported by other authorities, that the number of people put to death for plotting against the Soviet government is, at a large estimate, five thousand, we don't need Lansing's very convincing proofs that there was a terror. There certainly was; and there always will be, whenever a class government, whether bourgeois or proletarian, finds itself threatened with plots and uprisings and yet is not actually overthrown. The red terror is nothing but a revolutionary name for martial law. And "mass terror," although it is chosen by Secretary Lansing for its more terrible sound in the ears of his class, is a name which really indicates the moral superiority of this form of institutional self-defense to that "martial law"

which we derive from the Roman Empire. It depicts the masses of
the people defending their government by capital punishment from
the treasonable attempts of a small minority. . . .

In the April number I published a second song of praise to Lenin for
demanding, against the leftwing dogmatists, a signing of the Brest-
Litovsk treaty with Germany.

> Nothing is better calculated to strengthen one's faith in the
> internationalism and revolutionary integrity of the Bolshevik lead-
> ers, than to read the "Theses of Lenin" read to the party workers at
> the time of Brest-Litovsk. . . . To me this document is one of the
> greatest pieces of political reasoning ever put on paper. . . . To
> envisage an ideal aim with such inflexible passion, and yet retain
> a complete flexibility in adjudging the means of arriving there, is
> to occupy the heights of human intelligence. . . . Lenin has been
> attacked at times by the moderates, and at times by the extremists,
> in the course of his career. And this, because he has never regarded
> the emotional concept of being moderate or being extreme as of any
> importance whatever. He has known that the important thing is to
> keep a clear definition of the goal, and then be practically right as
> to the method of getting there.

In that same April number I ran up—far in advance, and somewhat
incongruously in view of my subsequent association with Trotsky—
Stalin's banner of *Socialism in One Country:*

> The breakdown of capitalism has gone so far in other countries
> that it *is* possible, little as anyone hoped it would be, for Russia to
> develop a system of socialist economy by herself. And if it is pos-
> sible there can be no shadow of doubt that from the standpoint of
> world revolution it is the proper course. Let the military and
> patriotic-authoritarian regime come to an end in one country; and
> let that country demonstrate to the masses of the people in all lands
> that happiness, and freedom, and real civilization, and the "decay
> of the state" do begin from the overthrow of capitalism; at the same
> time let that country occupy, as Russia will, a dominant position in
> the markets of the world. That is the strategy of real revolution,
> and what we have hoped for continually as we watched the
> power of the Red Army grow.

In the May number, I ridiculed the decision of the American
Socialist Party to apply for affiliation with the Third International while

at the same time repudiating what it called "the Moscow program and methods."

"Submit to your members," I lectured them, "a referendum on the principles involved, so that we can find out whether you are really a party of communism or of compromise."

This caused me some embarrassment, for the party congress whose

Drawn by Art Young

"IT'S THE STRUGGLE, MY BOY—POVERTY MAKES YOUNG MEN SUCCESSFUL AND DEVELOPS CHARACTER."
"OF COURSE YOU ARE GOING TO INSIST THAT YOUR CHILDREN GROW UP IN POVERTY?"
The Masses   March 1917

decision I ridiculed had nominated Eugene Debs for president and Debs was on our staff of contributing editors. In a recent number, his portrait in a prison cell drawn by Boardman Robinson had been titled: "Our Candidate." I escaped from the difficulty with a cheerful paragraph concluding: "Debs is a great deal more to us than our candidate for president."

Not only was I waging a joyous battle in my editorials those days, but the magazine as a whole was at the height of its trajectory. Had history traveled the road of our hopes—in other words, had we not so grossly overestimated the possibilities of human nature—the cartoons in the *Liberator* during those years, and in the *Masses* before it, would be among the choicest art treasures of the nation. As it is they would make, for art lovers and lovers of excitement (if those two things can be distinguished), a bookful of aesthetic and intellectual delights. And the text was on a level with the pictures. Floyd Dell was writing—to quote a colleague, Paul Jordan Smith—"the best book reviews in the world." He was adding a humanistic-essay flavor to the revolutionary gospel that was forever after sadly missing. He even emerged from his literary sanctum and wrote a trumpet call: "The Invincible I.W.W."; and went to Pittsburgh to do a piece of fiery reporting on the great steel strike: "Pittsburgh or Petrograd." John Reed was "covering" the supposed-to-be-coming revolution in America as vividly as he had the "Ten Days That Shook the World" in Russia. Robert Minor, an expert both of literary and graphic journalism, was giving eye-witness accounts of such tumultuous events as "The Spartacide Insurrection in Germany," "The Wars in West Virginia"—real shooting wars they were, between the miners and gangsters hired by the mine owners. Another amazing performance that Bob Minor described and brilliantly ridiculed was the expulsion of five duly elected representatives from the New York legislature because they believed in socialism—a bizarre contribution to the hysterical history of those times. I must also mention Charles Erskine Scott Wood, the grand old poet-humorist of the West Coast, on the Democratic Convention; Hiram K. Moderwell on the *putsch* in Munich and the workers' seizure of the factories through northern Italy; Jim Larkin again on the Irish revolution; Bill Haywood on life in Fort Leavenworth prison; John Dos Passos on the syndicalists in Portugal and the farmers' strikes in Spain; Crystal Eastman on Bela Kun and the seizure of power in Hungary; Frederick Kuh on the merciless repressions that followed Kun's overthrow. Fred gave us the "proletarian low-down" on many other events in Europe that he was more cautiously reporting for the United Press.

No historian of the period can afford to neglect our inside—or rather, *underside*—accounts of the popular upheavals of those post-World War years. Nor can any historian of American literature ignore the brilliant beginnings to be found in the *Masses* and the *Liberator* of almost a majority of the famous careers of the next two decades in both poetry and prose. A very distinguished critic, not given to bursts of praise for his political enemies, paid a tribute to the *Liberator* that makes anything I might dare to say look tame:

Bolshevism, which you defend, seems to me chimerical and more than a little dishonest. But I hope I know able and effective journalism when I see it. You produce the best magazine in America—not now and then, but steadily every month. It is informing, it is good tempered, it is often brilliant. Here at least is one customer among the opposition that you will have as long as you go on.

Sincerely yours,
H. L. Mencken

Chapter 29

FOREIGN GUESTS

Even beyond this country the *Liberator* was becoming a prime source of information and emotional contagion about what was going on. *La Vie Ouvrière*, the paper of the famous French humanist-syndicalist, Pierre Monatte, recommending the *Liberator* to its English-speaking readers, described it as "the best magazine now in existence." Similar comments came from working-class leaders in other countries. In August we printed a second long cable, a full page, from Robert Williams of the British Transport Workers, now a member of the Labour Party's investigating commission just returned from Russia—a momentous endorsement of the Bolshevik regime. Bernard Shaw sent us a word of editorial advice from time to time. Arthur Ransome's "Conversations with Lenin" was another important arrival from England in those exciting days—the first straight, simple, human portrait of that dread rebel whom the world was wondering about.

> He struck me as a happy man. Walking home from the Kremlin, I tried to think of any other man of his caliber who had a similar joyous temperament. I could think of none. This little bald-headed, wrinkled man, who tilts his chair this way and that, laughing over one thing or another, ready any minute to give serious advice to anyone who interrupts him to ask for it, advice so well reasoned that it is to his followers far more compelling than a command—every one of his wrinkles is a wrinkle of laughter, not of worry. I think it must be because he is the first great leader who utterly discounts the value of his own personality. He is quite without personal ambition.

A couple of months later we printed a second article by Maxim Gorky urging the literary world to follow the revolutionary torch

carried by Lenin. My report of a talk in Sol Hurok's office with the
great Russian singing actor, Fëdor Chaliapin, further clinched our faith
in Lenin and the Bolsheviks. This yellow-headed, king-sized opera-
athlete and *bon vivant*, once a cobbler's apprentice on the Volga, filling
up the room yet roaming in it, squinting his eyes from time to time in
a spasm caused, it seemed, by mere excess of energy, and praising
Lenin in a voice that made the walls shake, was enormously impressive.

"The Bolshevik government," he said (and I wrote this down),
"gives infinitely more money to art than any other Russian government
ever did. It gives us money and it leaves us free. We are free to do
anything we want to—anything we want to."

As he had been since 1918 director of the Maryinsky Theatre in
Petrograd, this testimony is worth remembering when the regime of
Lenin comes thoughtfully to be compared with that of Stalin. Our
conversation occurred in 1921. In 1927 Chaliapin was denounced by
the Soviet Government, his title of "People's Artist" taken from him,
and his summer home confiscated on the ground that he had given aid to
White Russians opposing the Soviet. His reply:

> That isn't true. The story is simple—money I give to poor
> children in Vienna who belong to those out of work. They starve—
> I have money. I give them some. I don't care whether they are
> white, red, yellow or green. They were poor and hungry.

In 1932 there was a big change of policy, and he was invited to
come back and sing in his native land—his money and property
would be returned to him. He declined the offer with a comment that
contrasts sadly with what he had said to me in 1921:

"I am a man who must be free. I refuse to be prevented from acting
as I wish."

Another distinguished foreigner I remember well was F. W. Pethick-
Lawrence, the celebrated feminist editor and British Labour Party
politician who dropped into my office unannounced one morning when I
was opening my mail. I recalled him as one who had been jailed, gone
on a hunger strike, and been forcibly fed in the cause of woman
suffrage. He had married Emmeline Pethick and attached her name to
his, as well as his to hers, in token of their equality in the marriage
relation—a precedent followed by the American correspondent, Ray-
mond Gram Swing, when he married a lovely suffragette named Betty
Gram. (We were starting a new world in those days!) My distinguished
visitor—he became Lord Pethick-Lawrence, Baron of Peaslake after

serving as Secretary of State for India in Clement Attlee's government
—was slim, polite, self-poised, already in manner an aristocrat, with a
sweet yet undeluded smile, a benevolently foxy smile. He spoke very
precisely through thin lips, but there was a Whitmanlike scope and
warmth of feeling in what he said. Among other open-minded things,
he expressed a desire to see his old friend, Frank Harris. Did I happen
to know where Frank could be found? Frank and I were then still in a
state of half-open war, and moreover Frank was never in his office in the
mornings. I knew where he lived; it was down on Washington Square
North near University Place in a red brick house with a yard and a
fence, a relic of times past as easy to find as a hairy rhinoceros. It was
also easy to direct a stranger from Union Square to that location. But in
a mood of good nature not unmixed with mischief, I offered to walk
down there myself with our distinguished visitor. Frank, as usual
in midmorning, was working in bed, and the maid came rather
hesitantly to the door when we rang the bell. I asked her to tell Mr.
Harris that his old friend Mr. Pethick-Lawrence of London had called
to see him. She vanished down a long corridor and the next thing we
heard was Frank's enormous bass voice—the voice of a Minotaur
resounding through a labyrinth:

"Pethick-Lawrence! My old friend! Why, that fails to express it!
My playmate, my workmate, my close companion. Pethick-Lawrence!
Why he's my brother! My own brother! I haven't seen him for
years!"

By that time he had got into a purple bathrobe, and as he pulled the
cords together he arrived at the door, extending his arms and beaming
with cordiality. Pethick-Lawrence by some chance had stepped to one
side, and he found only *me* standing in the doorway. Frank never so
much as drew a surprised breath or altered by a demi-quaver the
organ-tones of his great voice.

"And Max too!" he roared. "Another great man! Well, this really is
a reunion!"

Another European who came into touch with the *Liberator* in those
days was Henri Barbusse, author of *Le Feu* (called *Under Fire* in
English), one of the most popular war books ever written. Barbusse
appealed to me, both by letter and through a persuasive feminine
emissary, to make the *Liberator* the American center for a group he was
forming called *Clarté*—otherwise to be described as "The International
of Thought." Barbusse was strongly influenced by Romain Rolland,

and no more aware than he of the difference between thought and its nobler uses.

"It belongs to the intellectuals above all," his manifesto exclaimed, "to intervene in preparing the rule of the mind. . . . We call amicably to our side all who believe in the power of thought."

I made substantially the same answer to the *Clarté* manifesto that I had six months before to Rolland's letter, but permitted myself to say a provocative thing that I had refrained from saying to Rolland about the Americanness of my response. Remarking that the word "intellectual" had always seemed to me "more useful as a weapon with which to knock over a prig, than as a tribute of praise to a sincere man in humble contact with reality," I admitted that this attitude might perhaps have some connection with a bad habit Americans have of sneering at real knowledge. Quoting Edith Wharton to the effect that "the note of ridicule and slight contempt which attaches to the word *culture* in America would be quite unintelligible to the French of any class," I conceded that in this the French have decidedly the better of us. But if our attitude enabled us to see what was the trouble with his, and Rolland's, appeal to the *cognoscenti*, we need not, I thought, be too apologetic about it. On his statement that "It belongs to the intellectuals to intervene in preparing the rule of the mind," I made this irreverent comment: "If its author will imagine a group of those soulless and hard-headed schoolboys, who by some obscure process of gravitation always arrive at the back seats, deciding that it is now time to assert their superior sophistication by throwing chalk at the teacher, he will have an idea how such an announcement will be received by the average intelligent American. . . ."

"It is not intellectuality," I concluded, "that will fight and win the battle for liberty and international peace. It is the self-protective will of the exploited classes that will do it. And if there really is such a thing as an intellectual—a person whose will attaches with single devotion to abstract and impersonal truth—he will be distinguished by his *knowledge of this very fact*." *

Four months later Barbusse sent me the program of an "International Congress of War Veterans" over which he had presided in Geneva. In this "the Intellectuals" and "the International of Thought" were pretty well forgotten. The veterans were urged to "associate themselves with the great proletarian organizations of the world in order to provoke the general strike, the forerunner of the revolution and of the conquest of

* The *Liberator*, April 1920.

political power by the proletariat." And in the spring of 1920 he
changed the subtitle of his *Clarté* group from "International of
Thought" to "Center of International Revolutionary Education." This
Center adopted a Declaration aligning itself with the Communist Party
as an auxiliary in a task which "can be accomplished only by the
dictatorial preponderance of the class heretofore exploited and de-
spoiled." *

From being an auxiliary, Barbusse's organization ultimately became
an instrument firmly held in the hands of the party, and himself an
obedient servant of the dictator in the Kremlin. Like Rolland, but more
actively, he gave his aid and sanction to a tyranny over the proletariat
which mounted during his life to heights of insolence and cruelty
having no precedent in history.

In recording this sad fact, I must again acknowledge, as I did in the
case of Rolland, that he was only making at a later date a mistake like
the one I was making at the time of our correspondence. I still think, if
it comes to imputing folly or apportioning blame, that the date makes
a difference. I also feel now, after objective reflection upon it, that
another thing divided me, with my "science of revolution," from these
too long-suffering champions of Soviet Communism. There is, I must
first say, a fatal flaw in my notion of such a science: namely, that it
assumes, without making it explicit, an authoritarian power in the
hands of the scientist or engineer. It has the advantage, however, over
both philosophical and what I call literary revolutionism that it
conceives in a dynamic manner the relation between fact and idea. To
an engineer the function of an idea is to guide him in changing the
existing facts. Literary men, having organized their emotions around
an idea, and around the act of "believing in it," find it easy to ignore the
facts altogether. For their purpose of artistic creation, indeed, the facts
do not very much matter. I have felt this, not only in such extreme cases
as that of Rolland and Barbusse, but in some of my old colleagues on
the *Masses* and the *Liberator* who continued to be fellow travelers of
Soviet Communism long after it had destroyed every vestige of the
things we fought for. From the first, it seems to me, they must have had
more interest in "being a socialist"—or being a "radical," a "rebel," or
whatever they chose to call it—than in helping to create, outside of their
own minds, a freer and better society. That too, I think, is the explanation of Charlie Chaplin's incongruous flirtation, in late years,
with the Communist tyrants.

* The *Liberator*, July 1920.

Chapter 30

BERTRAND RUSSELL'S TWO SURPRISES

Perhaps the high point in our ascent to international glory was the arrival from England, in time for our May and June issues, of Bertrand Russell's long essay announcing his conversion to communism—an event like the explosion of a time bomb in the academic world.

"For my part," he wrote, "I feel convinced that any vital progress in the world depends upon the victory of International Socialism, and that it is worth while, if it is necessary, to pay a great price for that victory. . . . When I speak of Socialism I do not mean a milk-and-water system, but a thorough-going, root-and-branch transformation, such as Lenin has attempted."

Thus, England's great philosopher-mathematician cast his vote for the Bolshevik revolution. It was a great day for the *Liberator*. And like us—like so many who blamed on "capitalism" the measureless horrors of the world war just finished—Russell was ready to condone "the bloodshed and terror" that such a transformation might entail.

In the same number, let me remark, we published Lenin's speech at the Eighth Congress of the Russian Communist Party:

> We must tell other nations that we are internationalists to a finish, and are aiming for a purely *voluntary* union of the workers and peasants of all lands. . . . We must not try to decree the course of revolutionary history from Moscow.

To measure my tranquillity during this early summer of 1920, you must know that besides these reassurances about the revolution, a skyline quietness had descended into the place occupied so long in me by love's gusts and crosswinds. Florence had managed, in an amiable letter, to resolve the question—if there really was any question—as to who my rival was. Our three-way friendship had quite naturally, after I departed, grown into a two-way love between Florence and Charlie. And again I was not disturbed by this news; it seemed all right. Perhaps what I wanted more than any love just then was freedom from loving. I wanted to be selfish. Perhaps I wanted to be alone. Lisa went away on a ship to join Isadora in Europe and I had to adore her sweet, firm, fragile and unfaltering grace in imagination. My sonnet, "To Lisa in Summer," seemed somehow to consecrate and conclude our romance,

> All things that move are memories of you.

It happened that during those same days, to whose tranquillity Bertrand Russell's confession of faith in communism had made so large a contribution, Russell himself took a trip to Russia and came back with a totally changed opinion. He revoked the whole thing now, and swept it out of the record with a fervent repudiation of creeds in general and of Bolshevik communism in particular.

"Kindness and tolerance are worth all the creeds in the world," he wrote. "If the Bolsheviks remain in power, it may be assumed that their communism will fade, and that they will increasingly resemble any other Asiatic government—for example, our own government in India."

Russell was tactful enough to send his altered opinion to the *Nation*, not the *Liberator*, but it was up to me to answer him, and I did so in one of the most profound and eloquent—and mistaken—articles I ever wrote. I happened to be in the midst of an essay on Nietzsche when the bad news came—one of my periodic sermons on the hardheaded idealism that was going to save the world. H. L. Mencken had just published his translation of the *Anti-Christ*, a translation which abates none of the reckless and magnificent contempts of the original. In praising it, I had written: "If I were presiding over a course of study in communism, I would begin by asking every member of my class to read it. For until we have got purged of the contagion of this holy feeling that the world can be saved by softness, we are not even ready to begin the search for a true theory of progress. . . ."

Bertrand Russell's squeamish reaction to the "proletarian power" fell in as a pat example of the ineffectual softness that Nietzsche rose against, and I brushed it away with a like indignation: "Mr. Russell's discovery that the Bolsheviks are not meek enough to inherit the earth is simply a last will and testament bequeathing it to them."

That is a mere glimpse of my essay, which I called "Nietzsche, Plato and Bertrand Russell," and which filled five pages of the *Liberator*. It was a time of ideological stock-taking on my part, that summer and autumn of 1920. It was then that I wrote the editorial on "the Children of Light" and "the Children of Darkness," which I quoted on page 160, and in which I anticipated Reinhold Niebuhr by quite a span of time. I made Plato as well as Nietzsche do service against Bertrand Russell, and I must add that I did not call for any aid from Karl Marx. Indeed I took pains to repudiate the Marxian dismissal of Russell's recantation as a mere "class reaction."

"It is possible," I went on, "for persons of drastic and pure intellect, or militantly sympathetic emotion, to abstract from their own economic or social situation, conceive the process of revolutionary struggle scientifically, and put their personal force in on the side where lie the ultimate hopes of human life." I paid a special tribute to Russell's capacity for such disinterested logic, his championship of "scientific method in philosophy," and asked: "What is it that prevents him from bringing over that austere and celebrated method into his contemplation of the problems of society? It is the contagious Christian disease of idealizing the soft, and worshipping the ineffectual."

So I disposed of this most devastating intrusion on my state of exalted belief. I am compelled to say now that Bertrand Russell's recovery from communism was not only the quickest on record, but also one of the best informed. In that *Nation* article of 1920, he blazed the trail that the rest of us followed, some sooner and some later, but all stepping rather precisely in his tracks. He could not, of course, in his brief look-around in Russia, have made an independent investigation either of the Bolsheviks or of what they had so far achieved. Neither could his traveling companion, Robert Williams of the British Transport Workers Union, whose timely cable had contained the opposite statement: "All my previous hopes and expectations were more than borne out by my actual contact with Soviet affairs." What made their two reports so sharply differ, I imagine, was the different contacts they made with Russians who could speak English. Owing to his international reputation as a scholar, Russell must have fallen in with the sturdiest savants of the old regime, men like Ivan Pavlov, who "gave him the low-down" on the Bolsheviks from the standpoint of a high, un-Marxian, and essentially Western intellectual culture. It took but a few hours, I suspect, for this "wind of doctrine" to blow him back where he had started from.

Chapter 31

CHANCE TAKES OVER

Although so tranquil about Florence's love for Charlie, so content with my creative solitude, I cannot pretend that her image was gone from my thoughts. It had only ceased to torture me. After a month of silence between us, I wrote her asking if she was "ever thinking about me any more," recalling the scenery of our joys in Hollywood, wondering whether it was foolish to hope that "these new orbits we are traveling might some day bring us to each other as the old ones did in such noble and strong happiness?"

Before that letter reached her, Florence had written me one in which, along with light-hearted gossip about Charlie and about her picture plans, she remarked in an offhand way that she had been "sick in bed for a month." I don't know how much it tells about my love, but this announcement, without the hint of a diagnosis, the suggestion of a cure, made rest in my corner of our triangle impossible. I did not have a very high opinion of Hollywood doctors; those I knew were a little on the occult side; and I wanted to get Florence into the hands of a physician I could trust. Ignoring altogether the fact that she was living in bonds of true love with another man, I telegraphed, on receiving her letter:

WON'T YOU PLEASE COME STRAIGHT TO CROTON WHERE YOU CAN GET WELL IN THE LITTLE HOUSE I WANT WITH ALL MY HEART TO BE YOUR NURSE

While I was awaiting the answer, a second letter came saying she was feeling worse and was coming to New York. As though answering my telegram, she added: "I could get off the train at Harmon, and you could meet me in your orange sweater."

I telegraphed again:

PLEASE HAVE YOUR TRUNK PUT OFF TOO I WILL MEET YOU
WITH ALL THAT IS LEFT OF MY ORANGE SWEATER

Florence and Charlie traveled east together as far as Chicago, loitering along the way in an effort to make the trip a kind of adventure, for neither of them fully realized how sick she was. In Chicago he had professional appointments—or pretended he had, I don't know which— and she was quite obviously too sick to linger. So she arrived at Harmon alone on the morning of August 20. I met her in my bright but ragged sweater. She was not pale, but rather feverish, and her vivid colors all the more amazing to my unaccustomed eyes.

We drove back together to the little house on Mount Airy. I won't try to imagine what Florence was thinking as we approached that too familiar scene, the dwelling place of our once so perfect love. She had renounced it forever in a sadly disillusioned moment; now, just the same, she was coming back. I know all too well what I was thinking. To convey it I must give you a little plan of the house. It contained three rooms—a low roofed kitchen into which one entered from the road, then a slightly larger room, about ten by fifteen, that went clear through the house, and had a door and a double window on the porch and a high small window toward the road. One tiny room beyond contained a desk and chair and some bookshelves; the rest of the house was a bathroom with a clothes closet and a dresser. That was all. And of course the larger room in the center was the one in which we lived and ate and slept. What filled my mind was that Lisa and I, in a decorative fervor, had painted the baseboards and the slim woodwork around the doors and windows of that central room a lively Dutch red—the color they smear on structural ironwork when they first put it up. There was not too much of this brilliant color; the effect was charming. But it was not the same room. I felt the shock that this would be to Florence; I think it quite possible that I felt it more keenly that she did, for things imagined are often more disturbing to the nerves and circulation than things experienced. At any rate, there it was! And I could not pretend that I had done it alone. There was a "Duncan-dancer" quality about it.

Florence accepted the change with a word of gracious approval; she was too proud not to admire it. But I never ceased to wish that Lisa and I had done our painting somewhere else. Just then, however, I soon had something more weighty to worry about, for Florence had lost her flush by the time we reached the house, and sank into the big chair like a waning moon. I called up Herman Lorber—"Doctor Harry," my gynecological friend and the general practitioner for most of Greenwich Village—told him the story, and made an appointment to bring Florence to his office the next morning.

Harry was one of those tender-hearted doctors who only manage to be doctors by putting on a shell and manner of brisk heartless realism. He made me wait in the outer office while he discussed her symptoms with Florence. In a very few moments he came out alone and said, slicing the words off like peelings of a more compact truth:

"You came just in time. Only an immediate operation can save her from a blood-poisoning which might be fatal. I wonder what kind of a doctor she had out there."

As I was a little slow at grasping the truth, he put it in plain terms.

"Florence has been pregnant for three months and the fetus is dead. I don't know how long ago it died, but any delay might be fatal."

The operation was performed that afternoon, and Florence recovered her abounding health so quickly that my nursing came almost to nothing. But she had to rest in my house a few days, and Charlie managed to prolong his stay in Chicago during this time. I cannot write with full knowledge of the manner in which this was arranged, for I did not feel free to ask. But when Charlie arrived in New York, Florence was well enough to go down and see him—at the Hotel Astor, it seems to me—and there ensued a period in which Florence, to put it crudely, commuted between two lovers. Neither of us was jealous, or at least not troublesomely so. In Hollywood Charlie had ever since midwinter been coming to her apartment each day after work, and for the most part dining and spending the evenings with her—and how soon also the nights, I don't know. They were as close, almost, as she and I had been. But there had been no arrogance in his courtship or his love. He used to tell her—astutely as well as modestly—that he was satisfied to have sneaked in where a better man belonged. I for my part was too filled with the shame of my inconstancy to feel that I had any exclusive rights. We both had a sense of humor and of the varieties of human experience, and we both admired her extravagantly. There was something royal in her nature that gave her the right to have things as she pleased.

I do not know how seriously Charlie was waiting, during those days in New York, to see which way she was going to turn. He came up to

Croton once and took a room for a day or two at a fashionable roadhouse on the Albany Post Road. Florence spent long hours with him over there and walked with him on the hills, but she could not persuade him to come to my house. There was a three-way reticence about the details of this triangular attachment which makes it difficult for me to tell the story now. Charlie was still reticent when I reminded him of it thirty-five years later, inquiring whether he would mind my telling about it in this book.

"You ought to see what I'm telling here!" he answered, holding up the manuscript of his own autobiography. But he did not offer to help me with the task. He only contributed one heartfelt exclamation: "Florence was a noble girl!"

I venture to add, on my own, that up to that point Florence was the only girl he had ever loved with total respect and admiration. He was seeking even then, although the prurient public so outrageously misjudged him, for the happiness he finally found. For Florence it was a tragic accident that their child was not born. Up to the day Oona O'Neill led him into paradise, I used to think it was also tragic for him.

Of course our three-way romance had to end, good-natured though it was. Florence had once more to decide who was first in her thoughts. Neither I nor, so far as I know, Charlie put up any argument about it. We left her to her own sweet will, which was recklessly impulsive. Charlie was going back to Hollywood pretty soon, and Florence a few weeks later. Had she been a little bit practical—had there been, as in so many Hollywood affairs, an element of scheming in her love for him—she would have gone back with him. All Hollywood expected them to marry, and marriage to Charlie Chaplin was then the making of a movie star. Even the prospect of it had started many an earthborn beauty soaring toward the zenith. But Florence's ambition, however "abnormal," was too proudly high to be satisfied with a triumph bought at the price of her inmost self. I was still first in her thoughts, and she couldn't act on any other motive.

As she told me the story, she took a late train to Croton one night after spending the day with Charlie in New York. There was no need of her taking that train, and he had demurred. He came to the train with her, and said good-bye with tears in his eyes.

"Don't mind these tears," he said. "I'll be all right."

And in that mood he went back to Hollywood.

For me there is a sad reflection in this story: not that Florence was impractical—that was as it had to be—but that I was not practical *for her*. I knew that she was not an actress by instinct—not agile, not greatly gifted with imitation or mimicry. Once among the stars, she was dazzling enough to retain her place, but she needed some external power to lift her there. It had not dawned on me that her sudden success of the previous winter, the triumphs that followed her broken contract with Goldwyn, had been mainly due to her companionship with Charlie. This simple and subsequently quite obvious truth should have controlled my conduct. I should have advised her to go back to Hollywood with him, and she would have acted upon my advice.

Chapter 32

TRIBUTARY

Revolution was rather crowded out of my heart's attention by love in that summer and early autumn of 1920. The two Communist Parties whose birth-throes I had prayed over, or rather preached over, in Chicago the year before, had managed to grow into a quarrelsome One. Jack Reed had made his conspiratorial return to Moscow, getting across the ocean as "Jim Gormley," a stoker on a Scandinavian liner. He had attended the second Congress of the Communist International in July-August, and been elected to its executive committee as representing a "United Communist Party" of the United States. This was good news from the standpoint of revolutionary politics, but I made no mention of it in the magazine. Apparently it only enlarged my freedom from worry about the revolution. I could worry all I wanted to about love.

Florence stayed two months with me after Charlie had gone. We renewed at first the old tender companionship—the reading together, the drives and walks amid the blazing fires kindled by autumn along the roadsides, the evenings with our friends, the return under the stars to our own separate home, the fierce joy of our embraces. There was a kind of famousness about our companionship, it was so unhampered by convention and seemed so perfect.

But this perfect thing was no longer whole. It was broken into fragments by recurring scenes of rage. No ingenious schemes, no pious hopes, no deep-laid resolutions, nothing we so dearly tried to do, could put it together. I was again irrecoverably in love with Florence, and yet in some intimate way afflicted by a sense of loss in the very possession of her. It was as though I had given over my creative and controlling self, my own adventure of life, to her more powerful being. Do not mistake this to mean that she was what is called in the unpleasant sense

a "strong-minded woman"—she was essentially feminine in our relations—only that the momentum of her life force was greater than mine.
She kept me thinking about her more of the time than she spent
thinking about me!

I had enjoyed my freedom from this; I had immensely enjoyed living
with Eugen on St. Lukes's Place, and I was going back to it when
winter came. She was going back to Hollywood and her ambitions. We
were equal in this, but to me, that going back had the quality of a
return to myself. It was as if our union, though we shared it equally,
belonged to her. I was like the Missouri River, coming from farther and
quite as momentous, but after the confluence, lost altogether in the
Mississippi. I was a tributary.

> The truth is always not what we have spoken;
> We speak but when the fluent truth is broken.

So I tried to explain away our misunderstandings in a poem. It sounds
highly conceptual, but our warfare was animal enough to resemble
sometimes a barroom brawl. Of course we "made up" these ugly quarrels in each other's arms, but not with heightened passion, not without
bitter regrets.

One night during those months of intermittent rage and rapture—it
was October 2, 1920—we dined together at nearby Nikko Inn, a rustic
wooden structure hanging over the edge of a deep ravine through which
the Croton River ambled down to the Hudson. It was named after a
tourist resort in Japan famous for the sacred shrines to be seen there.
There were no shrines here, but only a bar, a kitchen, a wine cellar, a
couple of "rest rooms"—though they had not yet acquired that
simpering name—and a Japanese personnel whose dress suits and
exquisite manners made it seem all right to drive forty miles and pay
twice as much for the same food you could have had at Luchow's on
Fourteenth Street. We went down there in a mood of idle curiosity and
took a few drinks with our dinner—enough so that Florence became a
little (charmingly) intoxicated. She said things so important to my self-
esteem that before I went to sleep I wrote them down.

"My rage against you," she said, "is absolutely insane. It has no
reason. It isn't jealousy of Lisa. It isn't because I think she is not
beautiful, or because of her success as an artist. It has nothing to do
with Lisa. It has nothing to do with anything. It is absolutely insane."
She also said that she could never marry any man but Charlie Chaplin,

and if she did marry Charlie, "I would have a child by you before I married him."

We were both a little insane—at war with ourselves as well as with each other. My ambivalent behavior had divided Florence into two conflicting selves, the one proud and vengeful, the other tender and all-comprehending. We were fully conscious of this. We had a name—The Black Panther—for her vengeful self. And I, though we had no name for it, was similarly divided by my adoring love for her and my resistance to the self-surrender that love impels me to. My witty neighbor, Doris Stevens, summed me up by saying that I had a "trunk complex," meaning that I liked to have girls visit me in my little house if they came with a suitcase, but if they brought a trunk, it was all off. Well, Florence had brought her trunk—at my express invitation—and she had reawakened this conflict within me which I had never been able to escape.

We saw at last that only by parting could we conclude the destroying warfare that our love entailed. And so on the sixth of October she packed that trunk in a rather final, though far from brisk or impetuous manner, and took the train back to Hollywood.

During this time of sorrow, I was taking an optimistic part in winning American socialists to bolshevism. Although I did not see any large cracks appear in it, I think I delivered my most telling blows against the fortress of American capitalism in an argument with Morris Hillquit that I wrote in that autumn of 1920. Hillquit had been for years the unrivaled leader of the socialist movement in America. After a honeymoon period following the October revolution in which he had declared (in the *Liberator* and elsewhere) his sympathy, if not solidarity, with the Bolsheviks, he had now turned against them, denouncing the socialism of the Third International as new-fangled, narrowly dogmatic, nationalistic, "dictated from Moscow," etc. It was necessary for someone acquainted with the facts to answer him, and I undertook the job.

My arguments were based on the erroneous assumption that the Bolshevik revolution was being conducted in the spirit of experimental science—a wild thing to expect, I fear, of any revolution. Perhaps the sole point worth recalling is the one on which I agreed with Hillquit—namely, his objection to the insulting language employed by the Bolsheviks against him and against all the socialists who did not agree with them. This habit of undeliberated vituperation I objected to as he did, but I explained it as an instinctive reaction to a civil war in which their former comrades were shooting at them. "At present," I said, "I am satisfied to demonstrate very quietly—as I am going to—that Hillquit's arguments are fallacious and his statements of fact unreliable. But if he were coming after me with a machine gun I should probably agree with Zinoviev that he is a 'traitor' and 'agent of the bourgeoisie.' "

I was wrong in judging this slanderous abuse of dissident "comrades" to be a result of the civil war. It was an item in the technique formally agreed upon by Marx and Engels for conducting the propaganda of socialism, and emphatically reiterated by Lenin.* It offends me, I must say, not only as bad manners, but unscientific manners—the manners of men "putting over" a doctrine, and excommunicating, instead of convincing, those who disagree. I am very much afraid it is good campaign tactics—the public does so love a fight—but as an ingredient in a scheme for bringing in a millennium in which society is to be rationally organized, and men are to be free, equal, and so mutually tolerant that government itself will "wither away," it is assuredly perverse, warped, infantile and egregiously incompetent.

A partial glimpse of this truth in my argument with Hillquit was the first small step in my emancipation from the spell of Lenin's Marxism. How completely I was still under that spell is revealed in my reply to Hillquit's imputation of bigotry and nationalism to the Bolsheviks.

"The leaders of the Third International," I affirmed, "are absolutely devoid of the bigotry and narrow nationalism which Hillquit imputes to them. . . . The Communist International is centralized, it is disciplined, it is an 'International of Action,' but it is farther from dogmatic thinking and sectarian emotion than any other socialist body that ever existed."

To support this erroneous opinion, I could, of course, quote Lenin, and had quoted him: "We must not try to decree the course of revolutionary history from Moscow." "The situation does not exist from which there is only one way out"—a final proof, I thought, that he had no mystical faith in Marxian determinism. The conviction that Lenin fulfilled my own ideal of an experimental scientist engineering a revolution according to Marxian blueprints—supported as it was by the few documents from Moscow that got translated, and heated white-hot by the emotions of the civil war—had stamped itself deep as a watermark in the fabric of my mind.

"Now I would like to testify," I wrote in an editorial "About

* See *The Red Prussian* by Leopold Schwarzschild, Chapter X, p. 30.

Dogmatism" in that same November *Liberator*, "that I have never seen a sign in any speech or writing of Lenin that he regarded the Marxian theory as anything other than a scientific hypothesis in process of verification. . . . An active and perfect belief in a thoroughly understood hypothesis is not dogmatism. It becomes dogmatism only if it continues after the hypothesis has been disproven. And while there may be debate as to whether the Marxian hypothesis in its general outlines has yet been proven or not—anyone who says it has been disproven in the events of the last five years is either totally ignorant of the hypothesis, or totally ignorant of the last five years."

Thus I clung to my faith in Lenin. It seemed as firm and wholehearted and rooted in sound understanding as my love for Florence was changeful and divided against itself and bewildered.

My argument with Hillquit took a personal turn that I afterward regretted. It had been directed specifically against a manifesto he issued calling for a new International to occupy a middle ground between the Second and Third—a 2½ International, we called it. I began by remarking the untimeliness of his proposal—"just fourteen days after the French official paper, *L'Humanité*, stronghold of yellow socialism for years, had loosed upon its astonished readers column after column of red communist propaganda."

"However," I continued, "since Morris Hillquit will undoubtedly be one of the chief founders of that International—and perhaps the only one left by the time he gets around to it—we are compelled to read his manifesto with critical attention. Are its statements of fact reliable? Are its arguments valid? Does it succeed in making a case against the Third International from the standpoint of sincere socialism?"

I did not mean to call Hillquit insincere; nothing was remoter from my mind (I have a houndlike blindness to persons when baying on the trail of an idea). But his political lieutenant, Algernon Lee, denounced and scourged me for this insult in a long article in the party paper, making me feel that an uncrossable personal rift had opened between me and my friend and one-time legal defender. To a true-blue Bolshevik this was as it should be, but I never was as good a Bolshevik as that. I liked and admired Morris Hillquit. He had the faults, I suppose, as well as the virtues, of a skilled politician, but there was a character both firm and tender behind those strong jaws and bright dark-gleaming eyes. Our association in the first *Masses* trial had been far from purely legal; we had been comrades-in-arms.

We met by chance on a street corner many long years after. Our greeting was cordial, and we talked for a little while as friends. I told him of something I had just written that I thought would interest him.

"I would be interested in anything you wrote, Max," he said.

The memory was a comfort to me a short time later when I learned that he had died.

Chapter 33

THE CONFLICT AGAIN

I spoke of my own dividedness as insane, and when Florence was gone my conduct came near to proving it. Though a mere chance had brought us together again, love now lived in me with the old intensity— also the implacable rebellion against it. I was torn in two. And instead of taking refuge in the daily life I had been living before she came, I stayed like a hermit in the small house in Croton, living in the little rooms where we had lived together, inviting and entertaining my grief. I filled twenty pages of a notebook with renewed wailings, of which only my shame compels me to display an example: "I am in love and yet I can not love. I am out of love and yet I can not cease from loving. . . . All day my heart aches with longing and yet when I imagine your coming here again, it is with positive terror. And when I come up the stairs into the sweet house in Hollywood, the Black Panther is there too. And I know that it is going to be my death to be in her power. . . . Ah, my love, I have put these words down, but now I read them with tears of remorse. When the door of the future closes upon you, it is beyond my power to endure it. . . ."

On the day that I wrote those lines, I read in the paper the news of John Reed's death from typhus in Moscow. It seemed at first a faraway event, light-years away and yet kindred, as though some once visible star had fallen in celestial corroboration of the death in me of what we had shared—our gay reckless joy in the mere chance to live. Perhaps that is just a flamboyant way of saying that Jack's death, for the moment, didn't matter to me. I could not realize how much it mattered. I was sunk below realization in a self-centered sorrow. I sent the clipping about our friend's death to Florence without a comment.

Two more closer and more demanding events dragged me up for a time out of my abyss of self-pity. Charles E. Ruthenberg and Isaac

Ferguson, leaders in the communist movement, were tried, convicted and sent to prison for issuing a Left Wing Manifesto expressing revolutionary opinions; as editor of the *Liberator* I had to say some strong words about that. A mass meeting in memory of John Reed was announced for October 25, and there I had to make a speech. If so much of me as my sense of duty survived, there was no getting out of these two tasks. I have described that "inflammation of the conscience" from which I suffered in childhood as a weakness; here it was a strength. In a vigorous article about Ruthenberg and Ferguson, I recalled that our two great Presidents, Jefferson and Lincoln, besides asserting the right of revolutionary agitation, had themselves uttered "heresies as direct and extreme as anything contained in this *Left Wing Manifesto.*"

" 'A little rebellion now and then is a good thing,' Jefferson said. And speaking of an armed uprising of New England farmers: 'I pray God we may never be twenty years without such a rebellion!' And Lincoln in his first inaugural address made that beautiful and now, I fear, 'subversive' statement: 'This country, with its institutions, belongs to the people who inhabit it. Whenever they shall grow weary of the existing government, they can exercise their constitutional right of amending it, or their revolutionary right to dismember or overthrow it.'

"Lincoln did not mean," I explained, "that he would sit idle while revolutionary agitators recruited an army to march on the seat of his government. He would not do that unless he were in agreement with the agitators, for that is an overt act and compels the State to be equally overt in defending the side which it is destined to defend. But nobody who reads Lincoln's words could possibly imagine that he would have denied the right of those who consider a revolution necessary to present that consideration to their fellow citizens. That right is a commonplace of our jurisprudence."

Besides composing two good pages of that, I wrote and delivered a memorial oration for John Reed which began:

> We have been reading in the great newspapers of this city the last few days very appreciative accounts of the life and character of John Reed. They have permitted themselves to admire his courage and honesty and the great spirit of humorous adventure that was in him. They permit themselves to admire him in spite of the fact that he died an outlaw and a man wanted by the police as a crimi-

nal. They admire him because he is dead. But we speak to a different purpose. We pay our tribute to John Reed because he was an outlaw. We do not have to examine the indictment, or find out what special poison the hounds of the Attorney General had on their teeth against John Reed. We know what his crime was—it is the oldest in all the codes of history, the crime of fighting loyalty to the slaves. And we pay our tribute to him now that he lies dead, only exactly as we used to pay it when he stood here making us laugh and feel brave because he was so full of brave laughter. Our tribute to John Reed is a pledge that the cause he died for shall live. . . .

During the very days when I was composing that robust speech about John Reed, I issued into my notebook my most ignominious wail —the last which I will compel myself to exhibit:

> My love, I am suffering more terribly than I can possibly tell you. At all hours the tears swell in my eyes. I lie down in my little abandoned room, alone, moaning in my black anguish of longing.

Another month passed, and many such cries of self-pity went into my notebook, before I went down one day to the *Liberator* office, and amid the friendships and responsibilities to be found there, found also a realization of the maudlin depth to which I had sunk. It was a sudden and sharp realization—a recovery from disease, a complete coming-to. As though risen from the dead, I wrote a gay and self-commanding letter to Florence. "I am never going to be a baby again, and no person or thing shall ever be my mother." I have seen a renunciation of self-pity work such changes in a number of people since that day, but I was not fully aware then what it was I was renouncing.

In Florence too, the conflict of that autumn must have been filled with pain, and she could not get the relief I got from weeping into a notebook. She found only bitter disappointment in trying to revive her career where the disastrous pregnancy had broken it off. She had gradually to face the humiliating fact that not her talents or beauty, but her association with Charlie had given her the sudden rise toward stardom of the previous winter. Charlie was friendly now but impersonal. He had provided himself with a young, rosy, humorous companion, a girl with charming good sense, and no ulterior schemes or ambitions. He employed her as a secretary-companion, but also perhaps as a shield against Florence's beauty. For he was not one who, having been hurt once, would permit himself to be hurt again. This did not bother Florence, who became very fond of Charlie's new and delightfully sensible girl. But she must have been deeply, if gradually, dismayed by the absence of any offers of important roles in the movies. Her ambition was foiled, her pride hurt, and that, I am sure, made the tragedy of our unsuccessful love almost as hard for her as for me to bear. She experienced, at any rate, a mood of contrition for her part in it which was sincerely, if amateurly, expressed in a sonnet she sent me on Christmas Day, 1920.

> Forget forever those wild Autumn days
> When I returned and stared with mad surprise
> At my dreams all ended, my heart amazed.
> No hope of a new Spring met my sad eyes.
> Love hurt, only passion raised his dark head
> Darting a thin sharp tongue of hate and pain
> Kissing and scorching like a flame burned dead,
> The world turned black. Life itself seemed insane.
>
> All night closely entwined in love they lay
> In sleep, graceful and sweet, a golden pair.
> Even the moon reluctant to steal away
> Tears her light gently from the lovers there.
> Forget forever those wild Autumn ways,
> Turn back softly to lovely Summer days.

As she had never before wedded two lines with a rhyme, this achievement added a new admiration—and, alas, a new hope—to my insuppressible longing for her. I answered with a contrite sonnet of my own, agreeing to forget, "or smilingly remember," those dreadful autumn days, and joining her in the wish to turn back to the "summer days" of our first perfect union.

> Our spirits clear
> Gave light of love to our dark passion then.
> Can we not both be beautiful again?

In this exchange of poetry we met and were happy together above the battlefield where our love lay dying.

I telegraphed her in January of the new year:

IN MY HEART I AM ON MY WAY TO HOLLYWOOD ALL THE TIME I WISH I KNEW WHETHER YOU WOULD LIKE TO HAVE ME COME TO SEE YOU

She answered:

WITH ALL MY HEART I WOULD LOVE YOU TO COME

Our communications were telegraphic after that. "I wish you could find me a warm light quiet beautiful room to live in all day with my books." "If you could let me know definitely when you are leaving it would make it easier to find a room." "I am starting in a week." "I wish you could bring the lamp with the blue shade." "You made no comment on the lock of hair I sent you. Am I to pay the price Samson did?" "If I don't like your bobbed hair I am going right on to Japan." "I was so happy last night I couldn't sleep."

I did like her shorter hair. It made her beauty more appealing to a parental instinct in me that is rarely aroused by children, though always by the girls I love. But it was more than a week—it was a month and a half—before I reached Hollywood and settled the question. Many editorial duties and diligences stood in the way.

Chapter 34

THREE NEW EDITORS

I had concluded my argument against rightwing socialism with an article in the *Liberator* for January 1921: "Hillquit Repeats His Error." My final words were:

> Now I ask Morris Hillquit to lay aside his pride of authority and acknowledge that he was flatly and absolutely wrong in asserting that it was only when the Bolsheviks found themselves in a minority in the Constituent Assembly that they conceived the notion that the Soviets must supplant the Assembly and be set up as a permanent governmental organization.

It happens that Hillquit *was* flatly and absolutely wrong. Lenin astonished his followers in his very first speech on the night of his arrival in Petrograd in April 1917 by saying:

"We don't need a parliamentary republic, we don't need bourgeois democracy, we don't need any government except the Soviets of Workers', Soldiers' and Farm-laborers' Deputies." *

Whether Hillquit acknowledged his error or not, I never took the pains to find out. Our vital disagreement was deeper than that. It was not *when* the transfer of power to the soviets was proposed, but *whether* on revolutionary socialist principles the proposal was valid. On that I had taken my stand in the first issue of the *Liberator*, defending as a legitimate part of the class-struggle program the armed dispersal of the popularly elected Constituent Assembly in January 1918. That had been a defiance of political democracy, yes, but we were riding ahead with our "science of revolution," our "method of progress," to something more democratic than political democracy. That was the real thesis underlying the small chronological home thrust which concluded

---

* *The Russian Revolution, A Personal Record*, by N. N. Sukhanov, p. 282.

my duel with Hillquit. In a sense it concluded my career as an evangelist, a hard-working specialist in swinging socialist opinion to the support of the Bolsheviks. I had put all I had into that debate, and felt free, when it was done, to give my mind to more creative tasks.

Another thing that made me feel free was the success of the Red soldiers in sweeping the last remnants of Baron Wrangel's army out of the Crimea. I described in my earlier memoir how I had conceived myself as driving a kind of three-horse chariot through life: (1) earning my living; (2) doing something for mankind; (3) creative writing and thinking. The *Liberator* was "doing something for mankind," and during the civil war in Russia, while our beleaguered comrades were fighting for life on seven fronts and the armies of capitalism were invading our promised land, the duty to wage a guerilla war of ideas in the rear of those armies was paramount and absorbing. The good bay horse—"doing something for mankind"—almost ran away with the rig. Now, however, the white stallion was getting the bit between his teeth.

"The victory of Soviet Russia," I wrote to Florence, "has taken all the anguished compulsion out of the temptation to sacrifice my creative life to the revolution. It is well with the practical world, and I can live in the world of my thoughts."

Thus even before our hope of a new bliss in Hollywood was born, I had been trying to loose the chains that bound me to the *Liberator*. In the same issue with my final answer to Hillquit, I announced my resignation as co-editor—"in order to devote my time exclusively to writing."

"Our Readers will understand," I added, "that the relief from editorial and business responsibilities will result in my writing more, not less, for the *Liberator*. They may also be permitted to hope that I will know more about the subjects I write of."

It is not easy to get out of an institution that has grown up around you, rather of its own will than yours. That first attempt left Crystal as sole editor, and Crystal was not the adept smoother of ruffled feelings that I was. She was "too sincere" is the way some people put it. Besides, she was not a poet or an artist, not one of the gang, as I, in spite of the flaw of practicality in my make-up, had managed to be. With all her beauty and magnetism, she could not shepherd that cantankerous flock, and after a month's trial she became amusedly aware of it. In February she was the sole editor, but in March she withdrew from the magazine, and we announced a new set-up: Editors, Max Eastman, Floyd Dell, Robert Minor, Claude McKay. "I have enjoyed my resignation and am glad to be back on the job," I wrote, but in my private thoughts I was still groping toward a scheme that would enable the thing to flourish without me.

I am no expert judge of persons, but the three associates I had chosen seemed to possess every gift but that of running a business. Claude McKay was a rural poet from Jamaica, an untutored lyrical genius

Drawn by Gropper

"WAITER, I HAVEN'T THE HEART TO SEE THAT POOR MAN
STARVING. WILL YOU PLEASE TAKE HIM AWAY?"
The Liberator   December 1920

who is frequently compared in his native land, not fantastically, with Bobbie Burns. I think his poetry is the finest that his race has produced. In these days, when poetry is more occupied with inward attitudinizing than outward song, his exquisite note is not often remembered. But these days will pass. He was an aristocrat in the *Liberator* crowd, slightly aloof, as people of superior sensitivity have to be, but not priggish. Indeed his genial understanding and quick-witted hilarious laughter vastly promoted the spirit of equalitarian fellowship without which such a magazine could not have existed. Underneath these urbane qualities, Claude was a complex knot of tangled impulses out of which fits of unaccountably spiteful behavior would at times burst. But most of the time he was merely mischievous and altogether lovable. He was my best friend on the *Liberator*, and a good friend also of Crystal's, whom he described in his autobiography, *A Long Way From Home*, as "embodying in her personality that daring freedom of thought and action—all that was fundamentally fine, noble and genuine in American democracy."

Bob Minor possessed brilliant and original gifts both as a writer and artist, but he was in one profound sense a misfit on the *Masses* and *Liberator*. He was a natural-born fanatic. I used to feel that he would string me to a lamppost with the pained gleefulness of a Torquemada if I diverged by a hair from the fixed path of the revolution. My war against dogmatism unfitted me, he felt, for the barricades—and I guess he was right. He was the well-bred son of a Texas judge, and had fine warm intelligent humor, and a childlike delight in aesthetic values. But withal there was something like a great ape about him, the way his shaved head backed away from his eyebrows being the visible focus of it. Claude wrote that "his personality seemed to exude a kind of blind elemental brute force. He appeared to me like a reincarnation of Richard Coeur de Lion—a warrior who had found the revolutionary road to heaven and who would annihilate even the glorious and ineffectual angels if he found them drifted and stranded on his warpath."

Floyd Dell subsequently won himself a place in American literature as a novelist, but at that time he was known throughout the country as a literary critic. He had a gift in this direction that has rarely been equaled, a gift for falling in with, and exquisitely judging, the writings of others. A book of his, *Essays In Appreciation*, extending from 1909 when he entered the literary editorship of the *Chicago Evening Post* to 1922 when he stopped writing for the *Liberator*, would shed a rich light on the works and ideas of the twentieth century's adolescence. I have no doubt such a volume, or several of them, would have been published had it not been for Floyd's loyal belief in the alien and upsetting doctrine of socialism. That held us all back, and brought it about that the *Masses* and the *Liberator*, with all that they gave to American art and literature, are rather slurred over in the histories of our culture.

I must add that Floyd was free of any limiting fixation on this doctrine, freer than I was, or at least more pliant in his welcome to other ideas and attitudes. I thought it a fault in him that he could give himself so generously to any entrancing idea he happened to find in a book. I should have said then, and probably did, that he lacked stability of opinion, and I remember an example of it that troubled me. It occurred in April 1918, when I was filling the *Liberator* with pro-Bolshevik editorials, six pages of them, and "Red Russia" by John Reed was put in as the double-page feature story—it was just then that Floyd published an appreciation of G. K. Chesterton, whom he described as "one of the exponents of a mode of revolutionary thought which is older than American socialism." He spoke of its close kinship with Bakunin's war against Marx in the First International, with the American IWW, with anarchism, and syndicalism, with the teachings of Tolstoy, with Hilaire Belloc's trenchant attacks on socialism—in short, with everything *antistatist*. And he warmly recommended it to the attention of "the working class movement in America." "These older revolutionists," he explained, "regard state capitalism, as we do, as the logical outcome of present-day affairs; but precisely because it is logical, they propose to prevent it. They call it, in H. Belloc's phrase, the Servile State, and their chief anger against us Socialists is on the ground that we have been these many years engaged—oh, with the best intentions!—in helping our masters forge the fetters of an industrial slavery."

Today, I have to confess, this appreciation of the antistatists, shockingly untimely as it was, seems to me one of the wisest things the *Liberator* published. Moreover, as I look over the old copies of the magazine now, and see how much convinced and convincing argument Floyd gave to the political part of the magazine—his comment on Bertrand Russell's recantation, for instance, was much more incisive than mine—I find myself wondering why I did not offer to leave the magazine in his accomplished hands.

I had acquired three new editors; if each editor took a month and my turn came last, I would have three months to spend with Florence and my book in Hollywood. Had Jack Reed survived, I would have had four. Jack's muscular, big, boisterous, recklessly humorous yet truth-seeking revolutionary athleticism was an earth-span apart from Floyd's skilled, delicate, whimsical, rapierlike wit and reflective understanding. Their gifts were different, but they were just about equal. We were missing Jack acutely, and made the February number a kind of monument to his memory. It contained a beautiful full-page portrait of him, an account of his last days in Moscow from a letter his wife, Louise Bryant, had written me when he died, and this sonnet which says, at last, something of what he meant to me:

> Jack, you are quiet now among the dead.
> The pulse of the young lion and the fire

In that bright engine of extreme desire
That never would be tired or quieted,
That could fight, laugh, give, love and sing,
And understand, so carelessly—so strong
That you amazed us with your tender song—
It is all dead now, dead and mouldering.
They say you died for Communism—they
Who to some absent god must always give
The choicest even of the fruits of youth.
Your god was life. Because you chose to live,
Death found you in the torrent of the fray,
Exulting in the future and the truth.

No shifts of editorship, of course, could relieve me of the burden of the magazine as a business. Crystal's departure had left me, no matter how far I flew, the executive head of the company. This burden was lightened by the fact that she had organized it so well. She had installed Margaret Lane, a skilled executive, once directing secretary of the Women's Peace Party, as business manager. She had employed an efficient bookkeeper, a very perfect editor's secretary (her name was Lena Borowitz), and quite a corps of young girl stenographers and clerks—among them Bernardine Kielty, who subsequently married Harry Scherman and became the editor of the *Book-of-the-Month Club News*. With that force in charge, the subscriptions rather merrily pouring in, and my three colleagues agreeing to bring out the May, June and July numbers, I felt turned out to pasture for the spring at least. On March 20, 1921, I joined Florence once more in Hollywood. I would finish my book there, and we would make a mature attempt to find the happiness that belonged to our love.

Chapter 35

THE KRONSTADT REBELLION

Perhaps the fact that I arrived in the arms of my love, filled with a fresh ardor of hope, during the very days when it happened, will help to explain my failure as a pro-Bolshevik editor to say a word about the Kronstadt rebellion. I was on vacation from the magazine—or perhaps I should say "from the revolution," for my fragmentation goes as deep as that. I cannot even remember receiving the news of that heroic uprising of the garrison and sailors of the famous Russian naval base. It was a moment when my sense of fact might have triumphed over my fond belief—a demonstration, indeed, of the crucial fact that the "Soviet Government" was not a government of soviets, but a government of the Communist Party.

The sailors were not protesting either against the constitution or the structure of the Soviet Government. There had been, in late February, numerous strikes and meetings of the workers in Petrograd, demanding bread, freedom, reform of the soviets and a restoration of trade. The city government, then headed by Zinoviev, had replied with arrests, shut-outs and police repressions of assemblages and manifestations. The agitation had spread to the Kronstadt fortress where a giant meeting of protest was called—soldiers, sailors and workmen assembling in the open air to the number, it is said, of sixteen thousand. The meeting was addressed by the president of the republic, Kalinin, who was escorted from the station with flags, band music and cheers. Against his advice, however, and with but two dissenting votes, the meeting passed a resolution demanding free elections to the soviets; freedom of speech and press for workers, trade-unionists, anarchists, peasants and socialist-revolutionaries; liberation of all workers and peasants confined as political prisoners; abolition of the privileges of the Communist Party.

A committee was elected to go to Petrograd and establish relations with the striking workers. Zinoviev, in a panic, arrested and jailed the committee. At this the soldiers and sailors, a majority of the local Communists among them, elected a "provisional revolutionary committee," and issued a paper voicing their demands. They had no thought of military action against the government. If they had, they would have awaited the thaw which would isolate the fortress and put Petrograd under fire from the fleet. They were naïve enough to believe that the revolutionary logic and sincerity of their demands, winning the support of the proletariat of all Russia, would compel the Bolsheviks to live up to their program of a Workers' and Peasants' Republic. But Lenin and Trotsky and the Congress of their party—which happened to be in session in Moscow at that time—were as ready to shoot down a proletarian protest as a capitalist invasion. They denounced the Kronstadt sailors, soldiers and civilian workmen as Menshevik and anarchist counterrevolutionaries, led by White guards, Black Hundreds, international spies, Tsarist generals, etc. They sent a picked body of troops,* largely cadets from the military schools, against them across the ice, and shot down or subsequently executed them, to the number, it is estimated, of eighteen thousand.

Kronstadt sailors had been the glory of the October revolution, and this reversal of roles was, to all honest revolutionists all over the world, an almost unbearable, heart-sickening disappointment.

The situation was complex, of course; there were all shades of political opinion in Kronstadt as throughout the country. But the essential political demand of the rebels was for free elections to the workers' and peasants' soviets—free, that is, from the domination of the Communist Party. It was a simple demand of simple minds, a demand that the Soviet Government should be a soviet government, and that freedom should be, to a reasonable extent, free.

The assertion of the Communists, and their party histories, that the Kronstadt sailors were led by counterrevolutionary enemies of the soviet state was too patently false to discuss. It was not only false, however; it was not the justification of their act which the party leaders actually had in their minds. The whole country was in a state of frenzied depression and discontent. "Devastation, disorganization, chaos and starvation" are the words Vernadsky uses in his *History of Russia* to describe it. And Bernard Pares, in a similar history, adds that

---

* Boris Souvarine, in his *Stalin, Aperçu Historique Du Bolchevisme*, says that the Red Army as constituted refused to march.

"the markets were so empty that even dogs and pigeons stopped coming to them." There had already been a series of peasant uprisings. The Communists were finding the victory almost as hard to manage as the war had been. In these circumstances the protest of the Kronstadt sailors was, to say the very least, untimely. It was impractical. From the standpoint of Lenin's professional revolutionism, it was amateurish. Its success would have divided and destroyed the political power which, having just defended the country against a counterrevolution backed by foreign invaders, was holding it together for a new try at "building socialism."

I am afraid it must be admitted that any party, any strong body of practical men, believing in what they were doing, would have ignored the theory on which they were doing it, and taken the same or some equally drastic action. The future of the proletarian revolution as Lenin had taught his followers to conceive it was at stake, and if the proletarians of Kronstadt were too untrained and impetuous to understand this, they must suffer for their lack of understanding. Though buried in ideological top hamper, that, I think, was the real ground on which the decision to attack Kronstadt was made.*

For me, however, free from the necessity of any practical decision, free now from the passions of the civil war, it might have been the occasion for a moment of critical reflection on Lenin's whole way of conceiving the revolution. After such a showdown, could I go on believing that the dictatorship of a party was a dictatorship of the proletariat—much less a dictatorship of "the immense majority of the population"? And if I must cling to the hope that this "scientific" party was fighting for a future in which the population would rule, should I not at least have raised the question how, as that future approached, the power was to be transferred from the party to the population? Neither Lenin nor Trotsky, nor any Communist leader to this day, so far as I know, has raised that question. Their Marxian scripture tells them where history is going and they leave this too difficult problem for history to solve. But I had never believed in the Marxian philosophy of history. My blindness to this question therefore—my failure to reject in the name of truth and freedom the churchly zealotry, the ecclesiastical

* Lenin himself admitted, in a speech at the Congress, that the formula under which the Kronstadt men were attacked was false. "They did not really want the counterrevolutionists, but neither did they want us," is the version of his remark given by Emanuel Pollack in *The Kronstadt Rebellion* (1959). In Lenin's *Selected Works* (English translation, Vol. IX, p. 121) his remark reads: "They do not want the White guards nor do they want our rule."

wolf-pack fervor with which Lenin and all his followers clung to the
consecrated idea of "the party"—must be put down, I fear, to a sort
of half-fanatical glassy-mindedness on my own part.

By glassy-minded I mean offering a hard slippery surface to any
datum or idea which, if it penetrated to one's inmost thought, would
unsettle a firmly held belief. While on the subject I must confess to
another such exclusion from my mind of a vital item in the belief I was
so enthusiastically espousing. That was Lenin's demand for an "armed
uprising against capitalism" in all countries, his unqualified denunciation of all pacifist and antimilitarist notions—of which our magazine
had been full—as an insidious betrayal of the revolution. This was
contained in an article called "The Disarmament Cry," published in
1918 by a small hard-shelled Marxian magazine called *The Class
Struggle*, and brought to my attention by John Reed about a year later.
Lenin wrote:

> Our watchword must be: arm the proletariat so that it may de-
> feat, expropriate and disarm the bourgeoisie. . . . This is the
> only policy for the revolutionary class. Only after having disarmed
> the bourgeoisie, can the proletariat, without betraying its historic
> mission, cast all weapons to the scrap-heap. There is no doubt that
> the proletariat will do this, but only then, and not by any possibility
> before then. . . .

That "no doubt" rests solely on the dogmas of the Marxian
mystique. No factual mind could help doubting such an assertion. I see
this clearly now, but I was in no condition to think about it then. I found
it impossible to see, feel or imagine an assault by an armed "proletariat"
upon the controls and complicated operations of our American democratic society—bourgeois or not. Besides being impossible to my imagination, it was unhappy as a thought. Pacifism had been blindly
mixed up with revolutionism in our circles. I did not reject the idea or
accept it, but in the manner I am trying to describe with the word
"glassy" I kept it from entering my skull. It haunted me; John Reed's
solemnity about it haunted me. But I never admitted it into my mind
and said yes or no.

Now I was excluding with a similar hard surface a pointedly relevant
fact. Had I kept my mind open and alive in both directions, I might
have brought these two excluded subjects—Kronstadt and *The Disarmament Cry*—into juxtaposition, and arrived quite early at the basic
objection to Lenin's scheme of revolution: *The workers must be armed*

by the party for the seizure of power, but they must be shot down, if necessary, once the power is seized. The party, not the proletariat, will be the sovereign.

This, alas, was the doctrine-in-action of Lenin and Trotsky as well as Stalin. Absorbed in a tragic love and a treatise on comic laughter, I was in no condition to perceive it. The Kronstadt rebellion simply passed me by.

Chapter 36

ANOTHER TRY AT HAPPINESS

The train crawled into Los Angeles in the crisp early air of a California March morning. We met on the platform with so much love in our eyes that any onlooker would have been embarrassed. We were headstrongly happy and filled with naïve hope, a hope based on the poetry, not the scientific understanding, of our relation—if indeed there was, or could be, such an understanding.

We had agreed long before, when entertaining the thought of my returning to Hollywood, that for the sake of her reputation we must have—or at least seem to have—separate dwelling places. This irksome necessity now seemed a blessing, for the semi-separation, we thought, would make the conflicting currents in our hearts more manageable.

For a time it was so. We renewed all the old exciting ways of life, the privacies and the associations. We played charades and our great oratorical and impromptu drama games with Charlie and his friends and ours. Charlie knew nothing—or was deft enough to pretend he knew nothing—of the fluctuations in my relation with Florence. The fact that we had both loved her made us better friends, but not more confidential. And his new companion-secretary, May Collins, was both genial and congenial—remote indeed from what the public imagined Charlie's girl friends to be. She was plump, round, rosy, bright-eyed, unscheming, full of happy laughter. She was fun. I have the strong feeling, though whether it is metaphor or recollection I don't know, that she came from the vicinity of my home town in western New York. She was the kind of girl to make you think she came from home. She had plenty of sophistication, but wore it as a part of her nature, not an acquired adornment.

Florence was still in the apartment on De Longpre Avenue, and my room to work and somewhat live in was not far away—not out of earshot, it seems to me, of the lions and meadow larks. Charlie's motherly valet and factotum, Tom Harrington, a genius of his kind, had helped Florence secure a new Buick car at the price of a second-hand one, and we took long drives in the country together. The drive from Hollywood down to Santa Monica through orange and avocado groves and black-earth vegetable gardens, and spaces of land with weeds and wild flowers growing on them, would seem a dream of heaven to anyone visiting Los Angeles today. Well, it *was* a dream of heaven on the day that I remember. On another remembered day we visited the zoo, where an alligator was just waking up from his winter sleep, the carnivores were filling the house with short breaths of uproar, and the hawks—I jotted this down in my notebook—walked instead of hopping as a seemly bird should, taking long strides like professional athletes when going about their predatory business.

Another memory is of breakfast times when Florence would rival the dawn in some sleek silken costume, and we would enjoy after the night together a tranquillity that was rapturous. We were both happy-in-the-morning people, and scornfully pitied those unfortunates who wake up with a grouch. I have retained no image of my separate room; it seems to have lapsed out of time completely; but I remember gathering up the finished pages of some chapter of my book and going over to De Longpre to show it to Florence and profit by her sensitive and subtle comments.

With these desultory memories, I am trying to convey the many ways in which external fortune smiled upon our new attempt to reach back to happiness. There was enough power in our two contrite sonnets to keep their mood inviolate for a while—but it could not endure. I have spoken of our love as tragic, and in the deepest sense it was so. A magnetism strong as fate drew us together, and our being together as fatefully destroyed us. It might not have done so just then, I sometimes think, if Florence had been working on a picture. But she was un-occupied, and in her unspoken thoughts beginning to be dismayed by that fact.

I on the other hand was spending long hours of delicious labor on my play theory—my *"théorie ludique"*—of comic laughter, sometimes in a very ecstasy at the manner in which new facts and old ideas would fall into their places in the brand new structure I was building. I borrow the term *ludique* from a book by a French psychologist, which is almost the last word on this subject.* Perhaps if I permit myself to boast that

* *Le Rire et Le Risible* by David Victoroff (Paris: 1953).

he expounds my theory alongside those of Freud and Bergson as the three leading contenders in the field, the reader will have some idea how absorbed and excited I was in working it out. My separate room, and this separate love affair with an idea, instead of subduing, seemed only to reinforce, or bring into sharper relief, that something in me—the mood of abstraction, the withholdingness, the neurotic dread of being possessed, or should I more simply say the self-centeredness—that I am often surprised to find infuriates those who love me. It mixes oddly with my considerateness, which is largely what they love me for.

Again I am unable to conduct the reader through the subject-matter of any particular quarrels, but we were soon at war-and-peace again, behaving more like love-hungry carnivores than human lovers, snarling and caressing by turns. I can remember one incident in which the blame falls more completely on me than it sometimes did. I had been telling her with lyric abandon how happy our life in Hollywood made me, and her response raised the question how a similar division of labor, and of togetherness, might be achieved in Croton and New York. I did not say anything in answer. That was the extent of my sin: I did not say anything! My inward demon, sensing a commitment, stopped in my throat the words that should have flowed out as a mere inference from the song I had been singing. I wanted to sing it in time, not eternity—in freedom, not tied to a foregone conclusion. That was legitimate, perhaps, as an underlying principle, seeing she made a boast of not wanting to be married. But how stingy to hold back the little winged words the moment called for! We were not drawing up a contract. Another battle I remember was more easy to blame, if blame is necessary, upon her, for it rose out of my excessive eagerness, on an inappropriate occasion, to get back to my study with a new idea I had for my book.

But the specific causes do not matter much. They were trivial; all the more monstrous, however, the sudden angers and altercations to which they led. In the peace-making we would laugh about them. But that did not stop them from recurring, and recurring more often, and more suddenly. And I had a fear of the Black Panther—in the end an actual physical fear that this wild beast would arrive in the midst of an embrace and she would injure me with her teeth.

That only increased my self-protectiveness, and thus the more she raged, the more enraging I became. I must not, however, attribute all the rage to her. I have a violent temper too, which drains the blood from my face and makes me sway and strike like a snake. I could not strike

Florence, but I spat in her face once in fury at my impotence to extract a word in answer to some wildly important thing I was shouting at her while she lay in a mulish silence, to torment me, on her bed. Yes, I too could fulminate. I could deliver Greek and Roman tirades and philippics. And then I could also get down on my knees and plead like a praying Christian, an accomplishment she had never learned. In short, I had a whole repertory of responses to her anger, and no lack of skill in wielding them. But one thing I did not have. That was the strength of character and the courage to *walk out*. Whatever my faults in all this, and whatever hers, it was perfectly obvious that Florence needed discipline. But I was not man enough to supply it. I could not *endure* a rift between us, I could not simply go away, or let her go away, and stick it out until she came back or called me back. I am not sure even today that she ever would have come back or called me back, but that is a calculated risk that a brave man ought to be able to take. She knew I couldn't take it.

Ultimately and in the long run, of course, she could not bend me to her will; and she knew that too. Life had provided me with a neurosis—or did we decide to call it a religion?—which made it impossible for any woman to possess me. But in the concrete midst of these storms of our clashing natures, I was a weakling. I could not think up a strong course of action and carry it out.

Chapter 37

NEW THOUGHTS ABOUT THE REVOLUTION

Again I find that during these displays of my heart's weakness I was taking a strong line with my mind. Some of the most difficult tangles in my humor theory were untangled there in my lonely room, or chopped through like a Gordian knot. And I was not forgetting my duty to the *Liberator* either. A long telegram to Bob Minor warning him against the old enemy of "Greenwich Villageism" was my response to a copy of the April issue that he sent for my inspection. I haven't my telegram, but his answer will reveal the vigor with which I was fulfilling my role as editor.

My Dear Max,

What the devil—"surrendering to Greenwich Village studio art!!" The only thing in the paper that could even with the slightest reason be questioned on that score is the small picture by M. Kantor. And I think mature deliberation will convince you that that picture, as well, is worthy of publication and is not of morbid, mad or dilettante origin. . . .

Now that number was definitely a labor movement number of the most realistic sort. Nothing could be more timely or important or more serious than the Haywood article on the one hand and the comparison of Foster's and Haywood's labor philosophy on the other. . . .

Now, Max, damn it, I maintain that a monthly magazine cannot carry cartoons that are of the same value only as daily newspaper cartoons. I declare that to be available for use in *The Liberator*, a cartoon must contain either extraordinary "literary ingenuity" or else a distinctive artistic value. . . .

I am going to make the double-page cartoon this month, so I suppose the coming issue will be vulgar-realistic enough to suit you.

Yours as ever,
Bob

Bob would live to denounce me from the other side of this question, having become a big boss of the Communist Party in its Stalinist phase. Bohemian dilettantism was the very crime he accused me of in 1925, when I published a warning against Stalin's seizure of personal power. For those who know the story it lends an amusing flavor to this somewhat apologetic letter. He did appease me, though, with his drawing in the May number—a double page stuffed full of immense-muscled, manacled, revoltingly anguished galley-slaves in the black hold of a ship, with the caption: "Back to the Galley-Slaves—the Goal of the Open Shop." There was also appeasement in his tribute to those articles on Foster and Haywood, for they were interviews written by me and left in New York for use when the editor-in-charge might choose to use them.

In the one about Foster I drew very near, without knowing it, to a position that was crucial in the minds of the Bolsheviks. William Z. Foster, subsequently the head of the American Communist Party, was a lithe, young, wiry and brainy Irishman whom I had known as a revolutionary syndicalist, but who had then recently led the great steel strike of the conservative American Federation of Labor. Reporting my conversation with Foster, I said something surprisingly similar to what I would subsequently find Lenin saying to the so-called "Economists" in his epoch-making book *What To Do* *—published, to be sure, in 1902, but not at that time accessible in the West. To justify his shift to the A.F. of L. Foster asserted, in our conversation, that the trade unions are inherently and of themselves revolutionary.

"The A.F. of L. comprises the immense body of American trade unions," he said, "and the activities of the trade unions are the revolution."

To which I answered as though I had learned it from Lenin: "To be revolutionary is to have a clear conception of the overthrow of capitalism and a courageous will to it. . . . To invite the revolutionists

* For some reason this title is usually translated—incorrectly and pedantically—*What Is To Be Done?*

to come and be 'good trade unionists' in order to help them *become* revolutionary is a practical suggestion. But to assert that they *are* revolutionary is to weaken the suggestion."

To balance off my discussion with Foster, I described in that same issue of the *Liberator* a conversation with Bill Haywood, the founder and kingpin of the revolutionary "One Big Union," the IWW. There could be no sharper contrast than between these two men. Haywood was as big and Anglo-Saxon as Foster was thin and Irish. Foster had a keen, studious, analytic mind; Haywood's thinking was blunt and rather childishly poetic. But Haywood had what Foster lacked altogether, immense personal magnetism—a really majestic presence. His hands were small as the hands of a mountain would be, and they added to the massive appearance of his body. His motions were slow and consciously directed, never nervous. His voice in conversation was like luminous velvet, hushed and resonant. He had only one eye and he peered around with it like a tame eagle. He announced in that interview in the *Liberator*—for the first time, I think, publicly—his conversion to communism. In view of his reputation as a ruthless proletarian buccaneer, some of the reasons he gave for this change of view may still surprise the reader.

"Besides the expropriation of industry," he said, "they've accomplished three other things in Russia that would justify a revolution there, or here, or anywhere else. First is the education of the children. In Russia every child gets food and clothing and books and amusement and a real education. And, by God, for that one thing alone I'd favor a revolution in this country! Second is the relief that has been given to women in motherhood. In this country we do it for thoroughbred horses and pedigreed cattle. In Russia every woman is supported for eight weeks before and eight weeks after confinement. Third, of course, is the transfer of land to the peasants. The peasants control the land. Those are the things that make me want the I.W.W. to affiliate with the Red Trade Union International they've founded in Moscow. The I.W.W. reached out and grabbed an armful. It tried to grab the whole world, but a part of the world has jumped ahead of it."

A second subject on which I came by instinct close to the position of Lenin and Trotsky was *Literature and Revolution*. I employ the title of Trotsky's famous book because my views were an approach to his, but my subject, more exactly, was Literature and what I called the Science of Revolution. I expounded them in a long debate with Van Wyck

Brooks of the *Freeman* magazine—a debate on Science and "Literary Truth" which flared again in the next decade, and in other minds may go on, I fear, forever.

The question was raised by a new communication from Henri Barbusse in Paris stating that his *Clarté* group had revised its program in such a way as to exclude the reformers and sentimental humanitarians and adhere to the principle of class struggle. I welcomed the change in these words: "Those 'intellectuals' have comprehended—somewhat tardily as literary intellectuals always do—the practical science which can alone really give light to our steps. From being an 'International of Intellect,' they have become a 'Center of International Revolutionary Education'—a more humble title, but one which suggests that their intellects have been in actual use."

The group now acknowledged the leadership of the international Communist Party, but still thought their function was to "bring to the task of the Party a contribution of a kind more especially intellectual." With all respect for their motives, I declined to support them on the ground that this was a false dichotomy. It is not "intellect" that writers and artists bring to a revolutionary movement. It is "neither theoretical education nor a more circumspect and authentic practical information." What they do bring, I maintained, so far as it can be summed up in a word, is inspiration. And it seemed to me unwise for people carrying such a gift—"the poets, artists, humorists, musicians, reporters, discursive philosophers, etc."—to form an autonomous organization.

I still think it is a mistake for creative artists to form organizations, but to form a rival organization while acknowledging the leadership of a revolutionary party seemed to me especially inept. Creative work has to be playful, I said. "It has to be very free and irresponsible. It cannot submit to the control of a party." But if it is not to oppose the party actively—if it is not to be counterrevolutionary propaganda in disguise —it will have to be pretty carefully watched over by those whose preoccupations are practical and theoretical. They should be the only "corporate source of intellectual guidance."

This quick dash into a forest of considerations provoked quite a blast of indignation from Van Wyck Brooks. He agreed with me about the futility of an organization like *Clarté*, but he took haughty exception to my assertion that literary and artistic people are not as such "intellectual leaders," and that on the contrary they need guidance and careful watching by practical and theoretical minds. That hurt his pride of craft, and he called my view of literature a number of bad names, including *unrealistic*, *feminine* and—the worst, I am sure, he could think of—"American, all-too American." I had remarked that besides the ultimate and absolute value it has in itself, literary art "keeps up a certain warm faith and laughing resolution in those laboring in the practical terms of the task." Which enabled him to say, with some show of justice, that I conceived of art as a gay little handmaiden that "delights in trimming the beard and warming the slippers of a certain grim giant whose name is science and whose business is revolution."

I conceded to him that, besides providing inspiration for the struggle, literature plays its part in imparting great wishes to men, in raising their eyes to the revolutionary goal. If this service is at all to be described as leadership, then to that degree we must ascribe leadership to the poets and prophets of art. But that this is leadership of the will, not the intellect, is obvious in the very words that describe it. Barbusse's proposal that artists and writers should form an organization designed to "bring to the party a contribution of a kind more especially intellectual" remains inept.

These remarks, which seem to me, I must say, rather tiresomely close to the trodden path of plain common sense, looked self-contradictory when the idea of "discipline" grew to its monstrous malignancy in the thinking of Communists. Reading this idea back into what I was saying then about Literature and Revolution, Daniel Aaron in his usually so penetrating study of *Writers on the Left*, attributes to me the notion that writers and artists more than any other group need "party discipline," and that therefore, according to my conception, the revolutionary artist is "at once free and not free." It was a natural mistake to make, but nothing was more remote from my mind, or from any mind in that spring of 1921, than the idea of "disciplining" arts and letters. Nothing was more remote from Trotsky's mind when he wrote his *Literature and Revolution*. That idea was one of Stalin's unique contributions to our struggle towards a larger freedom. As Aaron himself says: "What distinguished men like Lenin, Trotsky, and Lunacharsky from Stalin and his intellectual praetorians, was their belief that the revolutionary government ought to condone all artistic groups not actively counterrevolutionary."

All this relates to a phase of my life—and the life of the Western world—that is gone and pretty well forgotten. But I said one or two other things in that debate with Van Wyck Brooks that have, perhaps, some enduring validity. I accused him of indulging in one of those protestations of cultural piety that we used to spout forth in high-school debates on the question: "Whether Poets or Statesmen Have Had the Greater Effect upon History." We lacked the courage, I asserted, to say that poets are greater than statesmen whether they had any effect on history or not. And I concluded with an exclamation which indicated how fierce would be my opposition when it came to Stalin's Literary Inquisition with its enthronement of the theory that "art is a class weapon."

"Oh, how foolish it is to try to justify poetry and art on the ground of their service to the revolution! They are but life realizing itself utterly, and only by appeal to the value of life's realization can the revolution be justified. Be a little more pagan, Comrade Brooks, and a little more recklessly proud of your trade. It has value that no movement can justify, no theory dim, no regime and no practical mandate ever create or destroy. It belongs with and replenishes the source of all values—the living of life."

More important than my instinctive agreements with Bolshevik policy during that spring of 1921 was my first unqualified objection to it. I expressed this objection in the *Liberator* for May in answering a personal letter from Robert Dell, the noted correspondent of the *Manchester Guardian.* Dell had been, like me, a leftwing Socialist, and had voted for affiliation with the Third International. But he was wiser than I, for he sensed the dogmatism and nationalistic arrogance of the Twenty-One Conditions of Affiliation—which, by the way, I had swallowed in a lump—and renounced the Bolshevik leadership at that early moment. His letter to me setting forth his position was difficult to answer because it was based on the very conception of scientific socialism which I had expounded.

"Shall we ever get a revolutionary movement," he cried, "led by men free from the religious temper, guided by reason and not by faith, content with hypotheses and eschewing dogmas!"

It was the first and only time I ever saw, outside of my own writings, the word *hypothesis* used in connection with socialist theory. He said further:

The issue really is whether the path to socialism is to be a path to freedom or not. . . . For my part I am not pining to be a slave even to a Communist bureaucracy, and it seems to me that, if the proletariat is merely going to exchange one form of economic slavery for another, it is hardly worthwhile to have the trouble and inconvenience of a revolution. . . .

I did not close my eyes tight to what Dell perceived; I closed them only part way. I said that so far as he proposed to stand guard against the establishment of a Bolshevik, or any other new religion, emotional or intellectual, I was in full accord with him. "There is no doubt that the fanatical, dogmatizing, religion-making tendency is at work among the revolutionists, as it is everywhere else—the attempt to shift off upon some God or rigid set of ideas the burden and responsibility of the daily exercise of intelligent judgment. Against this tendency all lovers of the fluent truth, and all real lovers of liberty, will struggle to the end of time."

With that as a start, I proceeded to an unrestrained attack on the Moscow leaders for drawing up the statutes of the International in such a way as to give to "the party in which the Executive Committee resides"—a crudely sly way of saying "the Russian party"—a voting control. I called this "disingenuous," "surprisingly casual," and "extremely unwise . . . unwise in exactly the same way that the invasion of Poland was unwise, because it ignored the unsurmountable fact that nationalities and nationalistic feelings exist."

This act, I reflected, was a repudiation of what Lenin had said in his "Letter to American Workingmen": "We know that circumstances alone have pushed us, the proletariat of Russia, forward; we have reached this new stage in the social life of the world, not because of our superiority, but because of the peculiarly reactionary character of Russia"; a repudiation of what he had said to the party Congress in 1919: "We must not try to decree the course of revolutionary history from Moscow."

Although going so far with Dell in his path of apostasy, I held out against his opinion that the general attitude of the Bolsheviks was dogmatic or fanatical. I still asserted that the new spirit they had brought into the movement was "the spirit of Applied Science, and nothing else." And I was still stubbornly convinced that their course was leading toward a freer world. "The Russian revolution remains the supreme social achievement of mankind."

In a box in the middle of the page containing these reflections, I published Arturo Giovannitti's triumphant quatrain:

MAY DAY IN MOSCOW

A rift of wings and clouds around each sentried steeple,
Red flags licking like flames the gold of the great dome,
Silence and sunlight and the bared heads of the people . . .
The Red Army is coming home.

Notwithstanding this sustained faith and exultation, that spring of
1921 saw the beginning of a dividing of the ways between me and my
revolutionary hero with his party of power. The divergence was
fractional, half-hearted, half taken back, destined only after many years
to be complete. But this was the date of its beginning, and this the point
on which it began: the crude instinctive nationalistic bossism of the
Russian leaders, so sharply in conflict with their creed and profession of
internationalism.

Chapter 38

A DECISION AT LAST

My parting with Florence came two months later, and was more conclusive. We had learned how fatal our conflicts were. As I recall them now, the thought comes that maybe Florence was deceiving herself in her bold certainty that she did not want to marry. Perhaps she was just too bold. But the thought never occurred to me then, nor overtly, I think, to her. Our arguments, like our exaltations, were all predicated on the assumption that our union was free as that of eagles in the air. But nothing could hide from us now the fact that we had fallen low again. The contrite sonnets, the change of scene, the headstrong resolution, the new mode of living, our whole terrible, loyal effort to reach back to paradise, had accomplished nothing. And I was able, in some intellectual, solitary, midday mood, to set this fact forth with poise and a modicum of pride. At least I found among the papers surviving from those days in Hollywood, a meditative soliloquy that would have made a fine and dignified end to our long sad effort.

It was not in a meditative mood, however, or with proud understanding, that I finally packed my belongings and prepared to abandon the love-dream of my life. It was in a mood of morbidly humble remorse. On a Monday morning late in May, after one of our tigerlike scenes, I wrote her a letter of farewell:

> My darling, I know there is nothing left I can do for you but take
> my terrible self out of the way of your beautiful brave life. . . .
> If I could live through one day of our love again I would go to the
> end of the world.

We set a date for my going, a date in June when my book would be finished and it would be my turn to get out the magazine. This quieted the demons inside us, and we spent two serene weeks together—so serene that we had to resist a temptation to postpone the date. Florence came for my books and packages in her new car and drove me in a tender mood to my train. Again the train to San Francisco, but I did not pause there now for a dip into lighter love. My heart was content to be heavy.

It took five days to cross the country then on a "fast" train, and those were sadly meditative days for me. So far as I thought of myself, at least, they were sad. I still loved the exalting great changes of mood and meaningful form that a journey between New York and California spreads before you. It is a journey between lush, rich, verdurous, emotionally indulgent beauty like that of a Persian cat, and the spare, bleak, angular, relentlessly obtruding actuality of the ribs of the earth—that an indulgence too, if one has a taste for geometry. Each time, going either direction, I looked forward to the change as an improvement, just as I rejoice in passing from classical to romantic in poetry, and from romantic to classical, happy each way, and unable to decide which chimes with my own nature best. I was going toward the lush, the abandoned, the growth-intoxicated now, so far as the view from the car window was concerned, but in thoughts of myself I was going the other way. The life of emotion, I had decided, was not for me; I had tried it a fourth time and failed. The proof was convincing. I loved Florence adoringly as I loved no other woman, but I could not subdue the conflict which love as such engendered in my breast.

I had been at home but a few days and was becoming adjusted to this humble feeling, when there came a letter from Florence expressing some humility on her part too. She enclosed a picture that Margarethe Mather had taken of us together, apologizing that she looked "sweet as a little lamb," and fearing I might not think it a true portrait of her.

> The weather is lovely once again, and the hills are green because of all the mist we have had lately. I only wish you were here. I would be so sweet to you in the morning. I would wear my beautiful green kimono and bring you your breakfast, then we would have a lovely talk and you would go away to your study to write your book which you love. . . . Do you miss me, dear? Do you think tenderly of me? There is no Black Panther. I'm all Florence. . . .
> P.S. You must send me a little love in your letter for I am lonely and very sad.

I sent her a great deal of love, and our letters became so warmly friendly that it actually seemed as though we were drifting together again—two rudderless pieces of flotsam on a mere stream of feeling. We were saved from that by the following communication, which my eyes could not see after I had read it:

> Hollywood, July 20, 1921
>
> I am not going to write to any more. You know for a long time that has been the deepest desire of my being. I am sorry but I will not read any letters from you in case you should write to me.
>
> Your neurotic selfishness has wiped any memory of you from my mind. It is though I had never known you.

The words contained no signature, no superscription, nothing but the familiar handwriting to identify them. That they were written in a blind rage was clear from the omission of two words, a form of negligence entirely foreign to Florence's nature. That gave me some hope that a gentler message would follow, but what followed was the return, unopened, of a letter I had written her the day before.

I never learned what provoked this act of enraged decision. But a poem of hers that came to light long after explains, perhaps better than any specific provocation could, the strength of her passion, and of her character:

> I once said I would not stand by and watch love dying
> I did not think
> that with burning tongue
> and brain seething with hate
> I could kill him
> I did not think
> that I would press my heel
> upon his throat
> I did not think I would bend down and pick
> up a beach stone
> and carry it for a heart
> all the days of my life
> I did not know.
> I only knew I would not stand by and watch love dying.

Chapter 39

IN FORCED FREEDOM

I cannot pretend that the shock of Florence's rejection—even with the valid insult to my pride contained in it—left me in a forlorn or loveless condition very long. I found my poise first in a mood of practical reflection: Although she made her decision in a fit of rage, there was a thinking wisdom behind it. Florence could only do such a thing in anger; I could not do it at all; but it had to be done. We could not go on destroying each other. I, most certainly, could not go through life torn by two opposite currents of emotion.

Relief, perhaps, would not be too medical a term for the feeling that stole gradually down from my mind into my heart to replace the pain I experienced on reading her violent words. I had been edging away from the *Liberator* and playing with the thought of going to Russia. Now I decided to resign my editorship at the first opportunity and go. I was free to go.

I might have gone sooner than I did, but for a munificent gift that fortune dropped in my lap during those very days of shame and sorrow. It was a six-months' subsidy for the *Liberator*. And it was paid—believe it or not—by the United States Government. A new and more liberal Postmaster General named Will Hays decided to grant us our second-class mailing privilege, and enclosed with the news a check for $11,289.69—the amount we had overpaid in first-class postage since our application had been filed. It was no time for an editor—much less a distracted money-raiser—to throw up his job.

We bought United States bonds with this money, and sat back to enjoy peace on earth good will to men for the first time in our nine long years of struggle to exist. I expressed in most unrevolutionary language my affection for Will Hays, for the United States Government, for the universe, even for old Albert Sidney Burleson, the former Postmaster, who so surprisingly "loved Max Eastman"—loved him so much, it now seemed, that he turned the U. S. Post Office into a savings bank for his special benefit. I did not, however, join the general chorus of praise for this act of Will Hays as a vindication of the principles of free speech and the freedom of the press. On the contrary, I said: "Lovely as Will Hays may be, and eleveny as those thousands of dollars, it is not the principle of free speech that has been reaffirmed, but the principle of the separation of the Executive from the Legislative and Judicial functions of the government. Hays has not renounced the powers vested in him by Congress to exclude unlawful publications from the mail. He has renounced a power vested in himself by his predecessor—according to a law enacted by his own inner consciousness—to compel a magazine which he did not like, but which he could not exclude on the ground that it was unlawful, to pay four times as much postage as any other."

In search of a more inward comfort, I went up to Glenora, my boyhood home on Seneca Lake, thinking to find there a renewal of my early delight in the mere fact of being alive. I did find it, too. The church bells from across the lake still moved me to reverence for Christianity and gratitude for my pagan freedom from it. The brook, named Cherith by my mother, was still whispering and singing past our cottage. The veery (to whom I wrote my first published poem) was spilling his cascades of song in the trees above it. The linnet (or purple finch), whose "crimson feather" had made a rhyme for my boyish song of the mere wonder of life, was still in the sky. He began singing high up like a lark, and came dropping down in little steps, one with each loop of his happy song. Yes, life was still to be loved, still something to make great and beautiful if you could find a way to do it.

But life would not hold still very long for the purpose of my contemplation. The small quiet rural space and moment I had sought for abstract reflection turned out to contain an alluring image of concrete beauty. She was an urban image; she did not belong there at all. She belonged in New York, on the East Side—metropolitan in every thought and gesture. But she was also starry-eyed and slim as a deer, and muscular, and had a head of wild, coarse, bushy hair like weeds in a swamp. She happened to be driving down to New York with her girl friend in a car with an empty seat, and I went along.

It was then, I believe, in the recoil from my too aspiring love, that I began to acquire the legendary reputation as a sort of Byronical professional love-maker—a Don Juan or Casanova—which has long pursued me, and stood somewhat in my way as a real lover. I differ from my reputation in several ways. I lack, in the first place, the consecration of those heroes to the cause; I have too much else to do. I differ also in an occasional most inopportune revival of the shyness that so long deprived me of the joys of adolescence. I differ also, I think, in the quality of my feeling. I was brought up in a prison of reverence for what is called chastity, from which, with the help of Walt Whitman, I escaped, not by abjuring reverence and letting myself down to animal passion as something profane, but by extending my reverence to animal passion. To me lust is sacred, sexual embraces nearer to a Holy Communion than a profane indulgence—a partaking, so to speak, of the blood and body of Nature. I am also, in this lyrical experience, no matter how transitory, unegotistical. I never can think of a sexual embrace as a "conquest." I esteem and admire the women who attract me, and I am still the shy child who feels surprised and elevated if they yield to him. In short, my too quick ardor for the alluring individual does not clash—as it did in Byron's case, at least—with a general attitude of male-ego contempt for the sex. That silliest and most unthinking of vanities must have troubled the very troubles of Byron's life.

I had what are called "love affairs" with three girls during the autumn and early winter after Florence rejected me. They were affairs of friendship as well as love, and there was no self-commitment, no putting out of a feeler toward the mood of everlastingness on either side. I had forsworn the attempt at sublime love, as I believed, forever, and I did not delay to say so. Those friendships were each brilliant enough to make a story, but it would not be the story I am telling. I mention them in this merely numerical way in order to make known the truth about this phase of my experience without an elaboration which, in order not to be tedious, would have to be minutely imagined and described. In the matter of being tedious, at least, I shall try not to rival Casanova.

Intellectually as well as emotionally I felt adventurous during that autumn when the conflict in my heart had subsided and I was freed from the money-raising job. My theory of laughter was also off my mind. *The Sense of Humor* was finished in August and published in November.

That book was greeted by the critics with about the amount of praise that I thought, as a work of literature, it deserved. As a contribution to psychology it was more highly praised. Indeed I received warm letters

of appreciation from such authorities in the field I was invading as G.
Stanley Hall, William McDougall, James Drever, James H. Leuba,
John Dewey. A unique surprise was a letter from Martin H. Glynn,
whom I had heard of only when he was Governor of New York,
enclosing his praise of my book. "It is done," he wrote in the Albany
Times-Union, "with a master hand. Everyone knows there are good
jokes and bad jokes, but if you want to know the laws which make a
good joke you will find them in this book." Aside from his lofty if rather
irrelevant eminence, the ex-governor's praise pleased me because I was
in fact the first student of this subject ever to discuss the differences
between a good and a bad joke—of that I was quite sure and I was
proud. Another bouquet almost as unexpected was handed me by Dr.
Frank Crane, the topnotch syndicated columnist of the day, an emotional fellow, half Christian minister, half prophet of common sense: "I
think I know a master mind when I meet it, and in this book a master
mind speaks."

This was a pleasant change from the brickbats I had been receiving
from similar sources for my political writings; a change that gave me
confidence and made me wish I had written the book better and with
fewer distractions. I had meant to have a lot of humor as well as of
truth about humor in it, and in this ambition I had less than half
succeeded. I decided to do it over again some day and have more of
both, but I obviously could not do that until a number of years had
passed. So here again I was relieved of a preoccupation, and my mind
set free to wander.

Its wanderings produced some editorials not strictly confined to
communism. A small one in December on "The Importance of Being
Unknown" is worth recalling for the larger result it had.

"Sentimentalism," it remarked, "might be defined as imputing to
things in abstract contemplation an emotional value which in concrete
reality they do not possess. And there never was a better example of it
than the spectacle of all these mighty war-generals and ministers-
plenipotentiary rushing round the world pinning medals on the coffin of
an 'unknown soldier.' They have no such impulse and no such emotion
towards any actual soldier, nor towards all the soldiers put together, as
the bread-lines and employment agencies eloquently attest. And if this
soldier should by some mysterious accident suddenly become known—
become, that is, a real individual—they would have no such impulse or
emotion towards him. Suppose he should poke a wooly head up over the
side of the coffin and murmur, 'Why for you-all reckon you's makin' dis

heah big fuss ovah me?' The bubble would be pricked, and the mighty generals and ministers-plenipotentiary would retire in cold confusion."

The result was a delightful satirical ballad, "Saint Peter Relates an Incident," written by the Negro poet, James Weldon Johnson, and published in a *de luxe* volume, which he sent me with his thanks for the idea.

Another editorial, of that autumn which seems worth remembering was about Thorstein Veblen's *Engineers and the Price System*, the foundation for a blown-up gospel of salvation which flourished for a time under the name of Technocracy.* Veblen took a very Marxian view of the evils of capitalism, and the need of "overturning" it. But instead of looking to the proletariat to provide the force for this undertaking, he looked to the engineers.

> No effectual move in the direction of such an overturn can be made except on the initiative and under the direction of the country's technicians. The chances of anything like a Soviet in America, therefore, are the chances of a Soviet of technicians. . . . It is a question whether the discretion and responsibility in the management of the country's industry shall pass from Vested Interests, to the technicians, *who speak for the industrial system as a going concern.*

The latter phrase, I pointed out, was the only allusion Veblen made to any motive, any dynamic force, by which the overturn he contemplated could be accomplished or even initiated. "And what is that dynamic force?" I asked. "It is the force possessed by a philosopher's abstract idealization of the function of the technician within the system of industry. If you catch an actual technician in substantial flesh and blood, and not just at the moment of exercising his 'instinct of workmanship' within the walls of a given factory, you will find that he does not 'speak for the system of industry as a going concern,' but like all other general classes of human beings so far as they enter into large or lasting calculations, he speaks for his own pocketbook. And Veblen himself falls short of the full stature of a human engineer, in that he can talk about a 'Soviet of Technicians' as the source of power for an

---

* This quite explicitly revolutionary book in which Veblen—so to speak— *implemented* his irony, is apt to be ignored by those who study him. John Kenneth Galbraith, for instance, in *The Affluent Society* (p. 52) says of Veblen: "The fate of man was something with which, at least for purposes of posture, he chose not to identify himself. But he also made clear his view that those who talked of progress were mostly idiots or frauds."

enormous historic change, without even raising the question what the immediate effect of that change will be upon their own economic status."

It was a fair comment, I think, and a valid forewarning of the inevitable failure of technocracy. But it carried me back, of course, to my celebration of "the developing science of revolution," and of Lenin as an engineer whose calculations were based not on industrial functions but on social forces. "We turn from Veblen's practical ingenuities," I said, "to the discourse of a truly supreme human engineer with somewhat the same mixture of minor regret and major satisfaction that we have in poetry when we turn from some exotic 'individual' to the universal classics. There is something deeper than excitement in the pure and utmost poetry, and in pure practicality something compelling rather than stimulating."

The discourse I spoke of was Lenin's defense and explanation of the "New Economic Policy" (the NEP) which had been adopted in the previous spring. This retreat from the extremes of "socialization"—a frank and open restoration, within limits and temporarily, of free trade and "capitalist" competition—was looked upon by the emotional zealots of socialism as an abandonment of principle. To me it was another evidence, like the signing of the Brest-Litovsk treaty, of Lenin's freedom from dogma, his practical flexibility. Instead of an evangelical agitator, he seemed indeed to be a social engineer.

Chapter 40

ENCOUNTER WITH H. G. WELLS

While exploring a variety of books and ideas in that autumn of 1921, I also reached out a little from Greenwich Village and made friends in what I called the Uptown Bohemia. I mean by that the *Smart Set* and *Vanity Fair* people, the writers and artists who, while leading an unconventional life, were financially successful, and in whose aspirations present-day success played a major though unacknowledged part. In Greenwich Village our aspiration was to revolutionize the world, or perhaps only to outdo Aeschylus or Shakespeare in the world as it is, but from either standpoint, being-a-big-thing in contemporary America was rather looked down on than emulated.

I am trying to describe an unseizable feeling—a feeling of shy discomfort, of bashfulness, of not-belonging, which to this day possesses me when I attend a luncheon of the Dutch Treat Club, for instance, or enter any other club, or studio, or editorial office inhabited by authors, journalists, artists, musicians—folk of my own tribe—who are a contemporary success. The Communists simplify this problem of verbal expression by calling these people "bourgeois," but that only obscures the issue, since "bourgeois" in its present development has no meaning at all.

The focus of this Uptown Bohemia was the studio of Neysa McMein, in an old rambling building at the corner of Sixth Avenue and Fifty-seventh Street. Neysa was a highly gifted painter and employed her gift in making ineffably glamorous pictures of girls for the covers of popular magazines. Her studio was a rendezvous for people like Franklin P. Adams, the light-verse poet and columnist, Irene Castle, Jascha Heifetz. H. G. Wells, when he came over to attend the Washington Armament Conference (November 1921 to February 1922) as a kind of reporter-judge for the great newspapers, was also often to be found in Neysa's studio. H. G.'s conception of the writer as a priestlike teacher rather than an artist carried him to his highest point at that momentous, or meant-to-be-momentous, conference. He was more in the news than any of the official delegates. A banquet was tendered to him at the Ritz-Carlton Hotel by Ralph Pulitzer, the proprietor of the *New York World*, and the outstanding dignitaries of the city—legal, political, financial, journalistic, literary—were invited to it. In a spirit of mischief, Wells asked that I be invited, and when the toasts began, a waiter came round with a note informing me that I would be asked to speak. I took an extra swig of champagne and spoke my mind with a mixture of candor and gaiety that was, apparently, very effective. At least I was so informed by Herbert Bayard Swope, the editor of the *World*, who called me up from his office the next morning. Of that speech I remember this much: that my tribute to Wells contained praise of his novel, *Mr. Polly*, as destined to endure long after his political opinionatings were forgotten; and I addressed an unexpected word to my political archenemy, Elbert H. Gary, the labor-baiting chairman of the board of United States Steel, who sat across the table from me. It was folly to pretend that he and I held different opinions, I said. Not our minds but our wills were in conflict. Mr. Gary wanted one kind of a United States and I wanted another. *De gustibus non disputandum est*. Therefore, much as it might disappoint some of those present, there was no possibility of an argument between us. The issue would be decided elsewhere.

That banquet was the high point of my venture among those who embarrassed me by being successful in a worldly sense. Or rather it reached its high point soon after, when Swope called me up and invited me to come to his apartment for a drink. He introduced me, among others, to a lovely and delicate widow with the brown hair and brown eyes that I like best. I suspect that there had been some conversation about our making an ideal couple. At any rate, that was my impression. But the shyness I am speaking of—the not-belonging among the arrived—had so firm a grip on me that I could not, in the presence of them all, bring the words out: "Might I come to see you some day?" I never spoke about this to Swope, and I cannot remember the woman's name.

Wells stayed a long time in New York, and I received one day this letter from him:

Dear Max Eastman,

I'd like to have a look at Floyd Dell and any others of the *Liberator* crowd that are as interesting as he is. How can I get at some of you?

Yours ever,

H. G. Wells

My answer suggested that he come down to tea or a drink at my apartment, but he replied:

I want to come to dinner and sort of go on talking. Teas are hectic and confused.

So Eugen and I, with Annie Crocket of blessed memory doing the cooking and serving, gave a dinner party for H. G. Wells, placing Floyd beside him because of their mutual esteem—for Floyd grew up almost a disciple of H. G. Wells. Indeed he will tell you today: "Wells and Shaw are *my* great writers, and I can not take seriously the literary pygmies that have followed them." Others who sat at the table were Boardman Robinson, Art Young, Mike Gold, Arturo Giovannitti—as many of the "crowd" as there was room for. I drove Wells down in my Model T Ford from Gramercy Park, and he took some of the joy out of the ride by remarking, as we rolled noisily along, that he had read my book on humor (which had just come out), adding: "I thought it a second-rate book."

While I was catching my breath, he proceeded to lay into it as a mere literary disquisition, whereas from a scientific viewpoint there could be no single explanation of laughter, it has a variety of causes, etc., etc.

I was able to answer: "I'm sorry you feel that way. I just got a letter from William McDougall complimenting me on having made a genuine contribution to the science."

As McDougall was then professor of psychology at Cambridge University, and probably the most impressive authority in the field, this had a tremendous effect on H. G. He said, "Is that so!" with cordial surprise, and began to remember a number of good points about my book that had slipped his mind.

The British cultivate, and expect of each other, a spiritual robustness that can take a critical jab like that and make a good-natured reply. In America it is physical robustness that matters. We must be able to take a sock on the jaw and give one back, but we incline to be considerately hypocritical in friendly conversation. I had observed this difference before and now tried to live up to the British code. But as a prelude to a pleasant evening H. G.'s remark was not what I should have chosen.

Wells was about as remote from our political attitude as anyone who called himself a socialist could be. "A bourgeois, boys, a bourgeois, by the sacred whiskers of Karl Marx!" Mike Gold remarked after he had gone. Nevertheless a certain rebel zest and candor twinkled in his gray eyes. They were mischievous eyes, and it was as fellow mischief-makers that Wells had sought us out. He knew as well as we did the gulf that divided the revolutionary from the Fabian socialist. But there is—or was up to Lenin's time—a fraternity among all those who like to disturb the established inanities. To this fraternity of disturbance, at least, we all belonged.

Wells conceded that we were "most of us normal," and we conceded that he had more courage than most socialists who believe that the revolution must come from the top. He was honest enough to say so. He was not trying, like many who called themselves socialists, to get on top by saying the opposite thing.

A gradual development of "the spirit of service" in those who possessed power was, according to Wells, what would give us New Worlds for Old. And as for class struggle, there were no classes—at least not in America.

"It is more proper to speak of phases. A man may be described as in the capitalist phase, or in the proletarian phase, but a class is a group of people who possess certain privileges no matter what economic phase they pass into. We have classes in England, but you have none in America. Here anyone may become a gentleman."

"You don't know Mike Gold," somebody muttered, but the joke was lost on H. G.—as I fear it will be on the present reader until I tell him something, a little later, about Mike Gold.

Chapter 41

ATTACKING THE PARTY PRIESTHOOD

Although nothing had yet shaken my trust in Lenin's scientific mind, or my belief that the Bolshevik revolution had opened a new age of freedom for mankind, my recoil against the churchlike features of the American Communist Party, and its *opéra-bouffe* imitation of Russian precedents, was becoming more vigorous the more thinking I did. I remember a talk in my office with Charles E. Ruthenberg, a leader of the Party and one of its real heroes, whose ashes when he died were carried to Moscow for burial within the Kremlin wall. He had come in to suggest some help I might give in reviving the Party, which was at its lowest ebb in that year. It was 1920, the year of Harding's campaign against Davis for the presidency, and I asked him which side the Party was on. Ruthenberg was slim, Nordic, gray-eyed, bald halfway back, but with strong sweet features and a way of smiling that made him look like a fox. He looked like a fox when he answered my question.

"We have decided," he whispered, "to boycott the elections."

The Party had at that time approximately eight thousand members, of whom only one or two hundred spoke English. Yet I was in doubt when Ruthenberg left my office whether his smile had been designed to express political cunning, or amusement at the foolishness of the pretense to it.

My effort to condone such foolishness was, anyway, growing more and more difficult. For the October number, in an editorial called "An Opinion on Tactics," I made an outspoken attack upon the conspiratorial mode of organization of the American party, its Jesuitical discipline, its likeness to a circumscribed religious order.

I began by quoting the first sentence of the original manifesto of the Third International—"The present is the period of the breakdown of capitalism"—and asserting that this was not true of the United States in the same immediate sense that it might be of Europe. An obvious fact, but a momentous heresy!

"We are not in the period of the breakdown of capitalism," I continued, "and yet we are employing tactics that could never be appropriate in any other period, tactics which have no relation to the period we are in—that of preliminary propaganda. . . .

"The Communist parties have been stressing the idea of party discipline to a degree that would seem sensible to a matter-of-fact person only on the eve of a battle. . . . They have formed an elaborate conspiratorial organization excellently adapted to promote treasonable and seditious enterprises, although they have no such enterprises on foot. . . .

"A certain plausible excuse for this state of affairs is found in the history of the Bolshevik party in Russia. . . . But the success of the Bolsheviks in leading the revolution of 1917 does not prove the correctness, and much less the adequacy, of all their previous policies in preparing the ground for that revolution." It does not prove this even for Tsarist Russia, where there had been no bourgeois revolution, and where the idea of revolution was therefore familiar, and seemed sensible to all democrats and libertarians. "To make that idea an essential part of the general propaganda of communism in a country as complacent of its democracy, and as far from a conscious struggle of classes as the United States, is to ignore the essential difference between the two situations."

In order to bring Lenin to my side, I quoted his statement that the Russian experience could not be taken without reservation as a model for revolutionary policy in other countries. "There were always two sides to Lenin's policy," I recalled. "One was to adhere loyally to the pure revolutionary truth, the other was to adhere loyally to the mass of the workers. The latter policy cannot be vigorously fulfilled in the United States by an underground organization, or by an organization operated from underground."

In conclusion, I called for the formation of a legal Communist Party and press independent of any conspiratorial control, and I denounced those opposed to it as though I were myself at the head of the Party, or near it.

"Those pure and perfect theologians of Bolshevism, whose only purpose is to establish in this country a secret brotherhood of revolutionary saints, have to be dropped aside with the same resolute practicality with which the sentimental socialists have been dropped. That is the present task. And it is to be hoped that those in the party who now evidently perceive it will have the courage to carry it through."

While dealing this straight talk to the American Communists, I excused the Russians for the enormous role played by a disciplined party *in Russia*. Although "shocking" from the standpoint of scientific socialism, I found justification for this in the fact that the Bolsheviks had seized power before "the conditions of production" made a Communist economy possible.

"It is a temporary effort," I explained (persuading myself as much as others), "depending for its success, not upon the instincts of the masses, but upon the will of the Marxian intelligentsia. Hence the extreme emphasis upon morale, the disciplinary cult, the dictatorship of an ethical organization. It is the inevitable and right thing in that particular situation . . . but it cannot be generalized. We cannot rest the hope of the international proletarian revolution upon the acquired characteristics of the devotees of a cult."

By such reasonings I clung to my belief in Lenin, while battling both the deeds and the attitudes of his American disciples. I had forgotten that Lenin, in his "Twenty-one Conditions of Affiliation" adopted at the Second Congress of the Third International in 1920, had demanded the formation of both a legal and an underground party in every country no matter how "democratic" its political system. I had endorsed those twenty-one conditions—or rather slid past them in the same glassy-minded manner in which I had slid past his essay on "The Disarmament Cry." One of Lenin's "conditions" was that the underground parties make an effort to disorganize the armed forces of the capitalist nations—a demand for a kind of treason that I certainly did not weigh and consider as a man would who was going to put it into operation. Indeed I doubt if I believed that such a measure would be put into operation in the United States within the foreseeable future. (I am not defending myself against a charge of treason, but confessing the more damnable sin of glassy-mindedness!) My forgetfulness of these "conditions" when writing "An Opinion on Tactics" only a year later, shows in what a state of defensive abstraction I had swallowed them down.

And I was wrong, of course, in distinguishing the policies of the American party from those adopted by "the Russians." As far back as 1904, Rosa Luxemburg, who belonged like Lenin to the revolutionary wing of the Socialist movement, had attacked the same features of his general policy that I was attacking in these American Leninists. She had denounced his "pitiless ultra-centralism," and rightly prophesied that under his system the entire party and the masses would be nothing but the "executing limbs" of a central committee that did all the thinking.

I would have received some illumination on this point if John Reed had lived and come home from his sojourn in Moscow, for he died in a mood of revolt against the very traits in Lenin's Russian colleagues that I was denouncing in his American disciples. At least that is what the many differing versions of the story of Reed's last days add up to. There are so many of these versions, and they differ so widely, that it is impossible to decide exactly what did happen. Theodore Draper, in his authoritative book, *The Roots of American Communism*, after faithfully reporting each version, summarizes the points on which they all agree as follows:

> At the Second Congress [of the Communist International] Reed put up a last-ditch fight against the Comintern's line and leadership that was unique even in 1920. He never gave the slightest indication of repenting his own position and, indeed, went to the opposite extreme of publicizing his opposition. His personal relations with the Comintern leadership had degenerated into an ugly feud. He made no secret of his contempt and hatred for Zinoviev and Radek, whose authority in the Comintern was then pre-eminent. On at least one occasion—when and why may be debatable but the fact is not—his anger or embarrassment or both brought him to the edge of *lèse-majesté*, as that crime of extreme insubordination was understood in the Comintern—he proffered his resignation from its Executive Committee. As far as we know, however, he was induced to withdraw the resignation, and he died before he was driven into another, irrevocable decision to revolt.

After listing these agreed-upon facts, Draper asks the question, "Was Reed a 'disillusioned' Communist?" He answers it as follows: "If disillusionment means a final accounting with the Communist movement and its ideology, there is room for differences of opinion, with the burden of proof on those who claim a definitive break. But if disillusionment is understood intellectually and emotionally rather than organizationally, Reed was probably as disillusioned as it was possible to be and still remain within the movement. . . . Death took him prematurely, not only as a human being but as a political symbol. The mystery of John Reed is what he would have done in the last act of his own life's drama. No one really knows, and everyone has written it differently in his or her own image."

My way of writing it would be to say that he would have come home to poetry and creative writing where he belonged. Perhaps this is in my own image—or what I wish had been my image—but I think Jack's image also plays a part in it. He was my friend, long loved and admired, and his enduring loyalty as I felt it was that of an individualist to his vision of the truth, and of a poet to the free and full experience of life. He was very American, and would have had a hard time learning the alien trick of identifying liberty, or the receding hope of it, with obedience to the heads of a tightly centralized and disciplined organization. His "contempt and hatred" for Zinoviev and Radek hardly foretold a life of fanatical subordination to the organization they so arrogantly controlled.

I really think more light is cast on the mystery of the unlived chapters of John Reed's life by Louise Bryant's account of his death, written to me from Moscow just after he died, than by any or all of those tales about his political feuds and arguments. He was "consumed by a desire to go home," she told me; and continued:

> He was never delirious the way most typhus patients are. He always knew me and his mind was full of stories and poems and beautiful thoughts. He would say: "You know how it is when you go to Venice. You ask people—Is this Venice?—just for the pleasure of hearing the reply." He would tell me that the water he drank was full of little songs. . . .

Whether its significance is personal or political, the coincidence of Reed's attitude to the party bureaucracy in Moscow in 1920 with mine to the same phenomenon in New York a year later, is exact. He could hardly have made any criticism of my "Opinion on Tactics," except to say that I was mistaken in confining my attack to the American party.

I must add that this "Opinion" of mine was not tossed out capriciously. It was a political maneuver as well as an opinion. The party leaders were debating the question of a legal mass party as against an underground conspiracy. It was to be decided at a convention in December, and my party friend, Jim Cannon, knowing my opinion and favoring it, suggested that an editorial in the *Liberator* might influence the delegates. It may be that, once turned loose on the question, I carried the assault somewhat farther than Jim had bargained for. His faction did win out at the convention, but I received some smashing attacks for my interference. I answered them in the December issue by sharpening the point I made, or at least the blade with which I made it:

"A critic of my 'Opinion on Tactics,' " I wrote, "tells me it would be more useful to the revolution if I would 'confine myself to trying to write poetry and leave proletarian politics alone.' He makes it plain in the sequel that he ought to have confined himself to religion from infancy. His excommunication is a testimonial. Anyone who really understands that science and not theology is the hope of the working class, must be glad to find himself in flat opposition to the rabbinical bigots of esoteric communism who are wrecking the American movement. . . .

"It is natural," I added, "that my attacks upon the extreme exploitation of the idea of discipline should call forth a bitter rejoinder from the Bolshevik priesthood, because that idea is the backbone of their church. Nevertheless, my attack is in the spirit of Marxian science, and their rejoinder is not."

And I concluded with a remark which, if there *were* such a thing as a Science of Revolution, would certainly be among its main tenets:

The revolution will not come, or coming, it will not survive, if it depends fundamentally upon discipline. It will not survive if it depends fundamentally upon anything but the conditions of production and the hereditary instincts of men.

Chapter 42

A BIT OF SOCIALIZATION

From these burgeoning wisdoms, I was caught back into my old-time business of worrying about our bank account. We had in the office a super-revolutionary bookkeeper named Edward F. Mylius—a short, round-limbed, maiden-auntlike person, very carefully cleaned and neatly stuffed into his clothes. He had a high bald dome, a soprano voice, and pale blue, politely inexpressive eyes. Although he looked rather like a doll-eunuch, he had acquired fame among the rebels by getting prosecuted in the English courts for libelling the king. I think he had fled from England under these auspicious circumstances, and had been welcomed by the rebels of Greenwich Village in consequence with open arms. How he became our bookkeeper I have no idea, for on the *Liberator* I left all these details to my sister. But like all who worked in our business office, he did a little meditative writing on the side. His pamphlet on "The Socialization of Money" was advertised in the magazine from time to time. But in October 1921—not through any dissatisfaction, but merely as a measure of economy—we decided to dispense with the luxury of a bookkeeper. Margaret Lane, our very dependable business manager, was perfectly able to keep the books. She had, however, entrusted Mylius with the keys to our safety deposit box at the bank. After a tender farewell and mutual assurances of esteem, Mylius went down to the bank and "socialized" four thousand, five hundred dollars in United States Treasury Certificates—all that remained of that precious and prodigious eleven thousand with which time and the Post Office had endowed us. The news came in a letter to me from Newark, New Jersey:

Dear Max:

I have been hoping against hope that I would not have to

write you this letter, but now I realize that I cannot keep the truth from you any longer.

When you asked me to resign I had very little money of my own, but I had the treasury certificates belonging to the *Liberator*, and in a moment of weakness, thinking I could make some money by using them as security, I had a fling in Wall Street. Unfortunately I lost, and trying to make up my loss, I plunged heavily. . . . Now everything is gone. The wreck is complete.

This is a dreadful thing. I can hardly believe it has come about. I feel unfitted for anything useful. Nothing that you may think of me can be half so bad as what I think of myself.

My only hope is that I can make eventual restitution. All I ask is a little time. Give me time and I will scrape up the money by hook or crook to send you for the *Liberator*. . . .

I know how generous you were in your trust of others and it hurts me terribly to have to tell you this . . . I am almost in despair. . . .

Not up to that point a very original letter, but it ended rather surprisingly with a piece of advice:

If you cut down on the number of copies printed per month, and dispense with a business manager, and get a cheaper printer, such economies will help out. . . .

Yours remorsefully,
E. F. Mylius

Please address me care of E. Boskin, 505 Washington Street, Newark, N. J.

Instead of addressing him I sent a detective, who found that "Mr. Boskin" had just gone away on a journey, but "Mrs. Boskin" was there and was prevailed upon to admit that Boskin was Mylius himself. She was also prevailed on—by a threat of criminal prosecution—to arrange a meeting between me and Mylius. At that meeting our neat clean little round bookkeeper looked so sick and abject, his eyes winking in a watery manner, his pose uneasy, his cuffs dirty, and his limbs somehow not fitting into his clothes any longer, that I could not be angry though I tried my best. He told me he still had something over a thousand dollars due him from two brokers. He gave me letters to these two brokers directing them to pay over to me the balance due. I promised to try to find him a job. I even went back after walking a block, and up the elevator to inquire what kind of job he would take, and how much he could live on!

That folly occurred on a Saturday afternoon—too late for me to reach his brokers. On Monday morning when we called on them we found that one had a balance of $350.00 due to E. F. Mylius, and this sum we secured. The other had never heard of Mylius, but he had heard of a Mr. Edward Boskin. In fact, Mr. Boskin had come in that very morning as soon as the office was open and drawn out a balance approximating one thousand dollars.

So much for my hard-headed idealism!

Chapter 43

THE END OF THE LIBERATOR

Although I looked pretty foolish in this episode, and felt so, it only set me forward on the course that I was pursuing in my private thoughts. I was by this time—the late fall of 1921—no longer an editor, and much less the executive head of a business. I had perceived at last that I could not run a magazine one half the day and pursue a literary career the other. Crystal's participation had made this folly plausible, but she had resigned in February and the fourfold editorship which replaced her had only given me a vacation. The responsibility was still mine, the anxiety, the being "on call" whenever a crisis arose. I have to thank blue-eyed Mylius for driving this point home. In about another month —say around Christmas time—I would have to go on a hunt, or a lecture tour, or into the meshes of a mailing campaign, to raise the subsidy for next year's magazine. It would be better, from the stand-point of my real ambition, to throw the tormenting and too wonderful creation into the ashcan.

I was looking round for something better than that to do with the *Liberator* when a helpful rebellion broke out, or rather, seeped out, among the contributing editors. The prime instigator of this rebellion was that young and highly "proletarian" revolutionist, Irwin Granich, who, after sitting out the First World War in Mexico, had come back bearing the name of Michael Gold. Mike was a dark-eyed, handsome social mutineer with wide lush lips, uncombed hair, and a habit of chewing tobacco and keeping himself a little dirty to emphasize his identity with the proletariat. As I have said, he joined our staff of contributing editors as late as January 1921, but he had been a close friend and loving contributor to the old *Masses* long before that. Born in East Side poverty, and born with a rare gift of writing, he had always brought us the very best fruits of his genius—heart-rending stories of the downtrodden, from which I had only to delete an excess of sentimentalism in order to make them firm and fine. Mike found both his artistic and his political home in the *Masses*—or perhaps I should say his school instead of his home, for he described me subsequently as his "teacher." A panegyric to the *Masses* written by him in 1918 when the *Liberator* replaced it, will convey his mood and manner as a youth:

"The *Masses!* One thrills at the name. It is hard to forget the blazing splendor of that meteor of art and revolution . . . a star of hope to thousands plunged in despair, a noble portent of beauty and fraternity across the sky . . . an irresistible pleader, a being of fire and pain . . . a temple of freedom." And as to its editor: "A true libertarian. His vision is the complete fulfillment of every man's ego, through art and fine living, and co-operation. He has a dream for a happy earth, with simple, beautiful melancholy to staunch the wounds. . . . A fascinating figure in the ranks of democracy here in America, this long symmetrical Greek, with his slow voice and graceful leisurely limbs, and face radiating calm.

"The new *Liberator*," he added, "will be more realistic and more concerned with the actual technique of revolution than was the *Masses*. It will be more 'practical,' because Socialists are being asked now to take over the management of the world's muddled affairs, and they must train themselves for the task." *

That was a fair prediction, and in its own way the *Liberator* lived up to it. But at about the time when he was elected to the staff—four years later—something strange and dangerous began to develop in Mike Gold. I cannot pretend to know exactly what—some conflict of passions so violent that they shook him into convulsions and made him behave, at unpredictable intervals, somewhat like a newly captured gorilla in a cage. He had one of these fits in a bedroom in Floyd Dell's house, sticking his head through the window glass and throwing the furniture around with a muscular power and fury that made Floyd's gentle intercession seem very brave. We all were anguished about him, and as he was dead broke, I published this notice in the *Liberator* for February 1921:

TO OUR FRIENDS

Michael Gold, formerly a contributor and recently made a contributing Editor of the *Liberator*, has suffered a serious nervous

* Published in the *New York Call Magazine*, January 1918.

breakdown. Those interested in contributing to his recovery can send money to the *Liberator*.

It must have resulted in someone's coming forward with help, for Mike got well and ten years later, when his vivid book *Jews Without Money* appeared, he sent me a copy with the inscription:

> Thanks for saving my life once.
> Best wishes always and hope you like the
> book which you helped start years ago.

With whatever help he got, Mike found a complete cure, and by the end of the year was steady enough to foment a revolt against the "long symmetrical Greek" whom he had once too extravagantly admired. Anyone who reads his book, with its brilliantly horrifying account of his pauper boyhood on an East Side block inhabited by crooks and perverts, pimps and prostitutes, will understand his fitful emotionalism; his rage of enthusiasm for the paradisal hope held out by the *Masses;* his angry recoil when the *Liberator* seemed to loiter along the straight road to paradise. It seems natural enough.

The fact is, anyway, that after a period of sickly wrestling with himself, or an angel—and on that one occasion at least with Floyd Dell's bedroom furniture—Mike found his health in a more rabid revolutionism, a more self-blinding Russia-worship than most of us on the *Liberator* could attain. He became a zealot, a being alien to the basic temper of the magazine. He wanted us to go out into the farms and factories, not omitting also the slums and gutters, and find talented working men and women who would produce a really "proletarian" art and literature. It was the first birth in America of this notion which when handed up to Lenin at an early meeting of the Bolshevik Central Committee received the answer, written on the margin of the memorandum: "Bunk!" *

In this state of mind, Mike set out to unseat the editor whose "libertarianism" had meant so much to him. Libertarianism was forgotten now; it was going down the drain for good. Proletarianism was to be the watchword, and from that viewpoint the editor was no good. Instead of envisioning a "complete fulfillment of every man's ego," he was hanging a drag on the ego of the workingman. And he was, moreover—that old point of controversy again—lazy. He was not putting enough energy into his job.

It was the opposite kind of revolt from that which I had weathered on

* The Russian word is *Vzdor!*

the *Masses* in 1916. There the objection had been that I had too much policy; here I had not enough. And it was the beginning of a profound and total split among the group which had gathered around the two magazines—a split between the emotional true believers and the thinking minds, the adherents of a faith and the participants in an effort. The division is as important as any in the world—more important, if you want freedom in the world, than that between economic classes. The war waged by our magazines against "rigidity and dogma wherever they are found," against bigotry, cant, scholasticism, sectarian loyalties and doctrinaire deductions, against regimentation whether by a church, a party, a state, an idea or a set of fixed ideas, was as essential to their character as the war against capitalism. The latter belongs after all, even in Marxian theory, to a brief period in history; the war for moral, intellectual and aesthetic freedom, the integrity of science and art and individual living, is eternal. In that eternal war, Mike Gold, a man of scars solving his personal conflicts with a rage against capitalism, was inevitably on the reactionary side. He represented the very thing that I was fulminating against in those editorials on the party priesthood. Indeed, I am not sure but it was those fulminations rather than my laziness or failure to get into the ditch with the proletariat, that roused him against me. He was on the way to becoming an intellectual robot in the cause of communism; I was on the way to exercising an independent judgment about it.

Be that as it may, his revolt reached a point where we had to call a special meeting of the editor-stockholders to debate it. A majority of the stock still belonged to me and my sister, but that was incidental. In essence, the *Liberator*—like the *Masses*—was a joint venture. Hardly a one of us was paid the market value of his work. In a crisis, therefore, it was not legal rights, but possibilities of co-operation, that mattered. I don't think anybody at that meeting ever gave a thought to the ownership question. On the question whether I was fit to be editor, Mike Gold rounded up quite a few negative votes. No record was kept and all I remember is that Giovannitti, although he hadn't been around for a long time, was among them. I remember it as a surprise. William Gropper, who had joined the staff with Mike a year before, may have been in his faction, and probably Hugo Gellert—although I am judging mainly by his subsequent career. "The Rabids," as I will call them, were naturally, in view of my ten-year editorial war against dogma, in a minority. Instead of a debate, therefore, the meeting turned out to be an eloquent discourse by Mike Gold on my lackadaisical spirit and remoteness from the suffering proletariat.

At the end of his discourse I proposed to him, in my most lamblike manner, that he take my place as editor. If I had put a squalling baby in his lap he would not have been more dismayed. He did not know whether to laugh or cry. Which of us cared more about the suffering proletariat might be a question, I said, but there was no doubt about my relaxed attention to the magazine. I was ready to forswear magazines for the rest of my life, and had only waited for this meeting in order to present my resignation. Furthermore, to make good my getaway and give myself a little education, I was going to Russia as soon as some final arrangement about the magazine could be arrived at.

An anxiously friendly and prolonged discussion followed, and in the small hours of the night it was decided that Michael Gold and Claude McKay, representing the two opposite poles of the controversy, should be the "executive editors." They together would run the magazine, and for masthead purposes the "editors," listed alphabetically, would be: Floyd Dell, Max Eastman, Hugo Gellert, Arturo Giovannitti, William Gropper, Robert Minor, Boardman Robinson.* As majority stockholder, I did make one stipulation before we parted: that if they could not keep the *Liberator* going, they should not sell it to a commercial publisher but turn it over to the Worker's Party. This they all solemnly agreed to do.

Privately I did not believe the magazine would last a year under any or all of the rather impractical bunch of creative geniuses that had gathered around it. Although I trusted Claude's political intelligence as well as his literary taste, I had no more faith in his ability to manage people than I had in Mike Gold's. They were both richly endowed with complexes, and moreover Claude looked upon Mike's tobacco-stained teeth, and his idea of "printing doggerels from lumberjacks and stevedores and true revelations from chambermaids" as the opposite of a poised loyalty to art and the proletariat. It was indeed as a foil to Mike's emotional extremism that I had suggested Claude as co-editor. Their colleagueship did not last long. After helping them with the first two numbers, I left for Europe in February, and in June they

---

* In addition there were at that time twelve "contributing editors" (and *ipso facto* stockholders): Cornelia Barns, Maurice Becker, Howard Brubaker, Eugene V. Debs, Crystal Eastman, Lydia Gibson, Helen Keller, Maurice Sterne, Louis Untermeyer, Clive Weed, Charles W. Wood, Art Young.

exploded in what came near to being a fist fight. Claude has described it:

Michael Gold and I on the *Liberator* endeavoured to team along. But that was impossible. Gold's social revolutionary passion was electrified with personal feeling that was sometimes as acid as lime juice. When he attacked, it was with rabbinical zeal, and often his attacks were spiteful and petty. One day I was informed that he had entered the Civic Club (a rendezvous of liberals and radicals) in his shirt sleeves and with an insulting attitude. I remarked that I didn't see any point in doing that to the pacifist Civic Club; that he might have gone instead to the Union League Club.

Someone repeated my comment, and one evening when I was dining with Marguerite Tucker at John's Italian restaurant on Twelfth Street, Gold came in and challenged me to box. He had been a champion of some note on the East Side. I shrugged and said the difference between us was intellectual and not physical, but that I was willing to box, if he thought that would settle it. So we laughed the matter off and drank a bottle of dago red together. However, I saw clearly that our association could not continue. Shortly after that we called a meeting of *Liberator* editors and I resigned.*

In the July number Claude's name was moved upward into the list of "editors," and the magazine was actually brought out by "Michael Gold, Executive Editor," and "Joseph Freeman, Associate Editor." Freeman's was a new name on the masthead, but in the columns of the magazine it had been signed to some very fine poetry, and the dark, sombre-staring, yet easily amused, eyes of the poet were familiar in the office and at consultations among the editors.

Joe's parents were (by this time at least) Jews *With* Money, and his approach to the proletarian revolution was different from Mike Gold's. He climbed down, you might say, whereas Mike climbed up to the platform on which they joined hands and efforts. Joe had made his first contact with the magazine in a youthfully enthusiastic letter to me—what would now be called a fan letter—mailed from Italy, saying that I had solved for him the tormenting problem of how to combine a love of poetry with a passion for the revolution. As I did this by refusing to subordinate the poetic realization of being to the practical task of

* *A Long Way from Home*, pp. 140–41.

improving the terms of it, his letter would make an interesting page in his life story, for he subsequently became a sort of unofficial commissar of Stalinist culture in the United States—tied in, willy-nilly, to the doctrine of "Art as a Class Weapon." In this summer of 1922, however, his views were not fully crystallized, and he entered his career as a revolutionary editor without, I am sure, the ghost of an idea where it would carry him.

The Gold-Freeman colleagueship lasted apparently from June until August, for the September issue announced without explanation that the Executive Editor, Michael Gold, had "left for California." In the October issue, Mike's name too was moved upward among the "editors," and the magazine was brought out by "Floyd Dell, Executive Editor, Joseph Freeman, Associate Editor." There was no November issue, and in December Floyd Dell was again a mere "editor" and the magazine was brought out by "Executive Editors, Robert Minor and Joseph Freeman."

Under all these changes, I must say, the *Liberator* flourished—it was just as good as it had been before. But in December 1922 a new and sad note sounded. The editorial page began: "The non-appearance of the November issue of this magazine meant that we were in desperate financial difficulties. . . . The appearance of a November-December issue now means that we have weathered the storm. We expect to direct our attention more than we have for some months past to political issues, and to direct attention more deliberately than heretofore to the Workers' Party, the organized political movement which, as we declared at its inception, best represents the revolutionary interests of the American workers."

That was the beginning of the end of the *Liberator*. Strangely enough, a "statement of ownership" in that increasingly party-political number describes the magazine as actually belonging to four of the wealthy patrons who had given me money for it in the old days as a free magazine of arts and letters: Ellen Scripps, Mrs. Agnes Leach, Aline Barnsdall and William Bross Lloyd. My successors had not yet kept their promise to turn it over to the Workers' Party, but they were moving in that direction. After one more year, in which straight party propaganda was shot through with occasional gleams of the old creative humor and art and poetry, the *Liberator* was combined with William Z. Foster's *Labor Herald* and with *Soviet Russia Pictorial* to form a regular propaganda organ called the *Communist Monthly*, owned by the Party and edited by its future leader, Earl Browder.

When the news got around that I was going to Moscow, my friend Jim Cannon came to me with some advice. I would have a better entrée among the ruling circles in Moscow if I carried a card of membership in the Workers' Party. He would enroll me and supply me with the card if I would drop around to the headquarters, only a few blocks away. As the Workers' Party then professed to be a mass party and its control by a conspiratorial underground organization had—formally at least—been abandoned, this seemed a decent, although distasteful, maneuver. I never used the card in Moscow, and never introduced myself, or thought of myself, as a party member.

A surprising thing happened the day in early March when I boarded the Cunard liner S.S. *Olympic* with this subversionary testimonial in my pocket. A steward came around with an invitation from the captain to sit at his table. Thinking the purely literary part of my career must be experiencing a boom, I accepted with joy and took my place at dinner with what I hoped was a patriotic as well as a poetic expression. When the coffee was being served, the captain leaned across the table and remarked:

"Mr. Eastman, I think your invention of the Kodak was one of the major events of this century."

Chapter 44

THE FINAL CHAPTER OF OUR LOVE

Florence was in New York during the autumn of 1921. My prediction of her renewed success in the movies had not come true. Her association with Charlie had raised her high in the eyes of producers, but without him she seemed to slip out of their thoughts altogether. She was acting in the Pasadena Playhouse when her last letters reached me—a sad drop downward for one who had been rising toward stardom in Hollywood. "I have reached a point in my life where I can not love myself unless I succeed in my work," she had written a year before. Now she was failing—or not getting a chance to succeed—in her work. Her self-love was stricken more woundingly than her love for me. Success in her profession would have enabled her to feel the same mixture of sorrow and relief that I did when she cut off all communication between us.

She came to New York in the early autumn, hoping to do better on Broadway. But here again, at the moment, luck was against her—the luck that so dreadfully dominates the actor's life. I knew about her coming because she stayed for the first days with Marie Howe, who had become her close friend during the winter in Hollywood, and who was an old friend of mine and my sister's. Marie was the wife of Frederick C. Howe, a noted reformer, author of many benignly progressive books, and she herself was a person of note. She had started life as a Presbyterian minister—much admired, I remember, by my mother—but she looked more like a gypsy than a Presbyterian, being short of stature with gleaming dark eyes, arched black eyebrows and jewelly teeth. To no one's surprise, she turned out to be more interested in careers for women in general than in the particular career she had chosen. She was famed as a feminist when Florence came to see her, and was writing a life of George Sand.

273

From Marie's house on West Twelfth Street, Florence moved up near Broadway to the Algonquin Hotel. But she was already in closer touch with the circle of our mutual friends than with the people of her profession. Thus inevitably and by a gravitation that seemed to inhere in the nature of things rather than in our wills, we were drawn together again. It was, in fact, an impersonal force that first opened the lines of communication. It was my book on humor. I had dedicated it to her—she had in one of her last letters called it *her* book; and I could not very well neglect to send it to her. I sent it, however, without any inscription, or any handwriting on the wrapper that might cause her to return it unopened to me. She opened it—yes—and sent me an answer the next day by messenger. It was only one sentence, but it said:

"Nothing ever made me so happy as my name in your book."

So we were friends again—much to the relief of those who had known us well, but not well enough to guess what had happened between us. Nobody, not even my sister, ever knew that. The general impression was that I had been driven mad by Florence's going around with Charlie when she visited me in Croton, and I had gone out to Hollywood in the spring to win her back. (It is as near as rumor usually gets to what really happens in a love affair.) What rumor did after I came back without Florence, and then Florence came back without Charlie, I never knew. But it pleased and relieved a good many people to know that we could be invited together to their homes again.

I did not want to ask Florence about her letter of hate. The ground of it I understood; the specific cause did not matter; and the last thing in the world I could bear would be to hear her explain it. Gods do not come down from the clouds and explain a stroke of lightning. But I did want to have a private talk with her. I suppose I wanted to make explicit our new relation as it resulted from my gift of the book and her warm response—my old folly of needing to have everything cerebrally clear. At any rate I remarked to her once, in the shadow of a general conversation, that we had never yet discussed the concluding chapters of my book. She answered, and a little more than answered:

"Why don't you come up to the Algonquin some afternoon and we'll have a talk?"

It was a long and sadly thoughtful talk, and not much about my book. I had to sit still and watch the tears well in her eyes and glisten in her lashes. I was trying to hold myself aloof enough to say the thing I had decided must be said: that although I still adoringly admired her, I had got possession of my self, my ambition, my zeal for living a life of my own, by putting our attempt at a great love into the past.

I did not succeed in saying it. I am miserably weak in conversation; I have to go off by myself in order to be strong. And now especially, seeing her so brave and tender, and so deeply wounded—as I well knew—in her ambition, I found it hard even to remember what I had intended to say. She wrote me a letter the next day which showed how far I had strayed from my scheduled performance. At the same time I wrote her a letter in which I summoned the strength to carry it through. Our letters crossed, and they will give, if not a clearer, at least a more faithful account of our conversation than my memory can call up after forty years.

Florence's began abruptly without even a dateline:

> My pride in the image you have of me in your heart is still high, and I was hurt when you suggested that my radiant freedom and your belief in it was lost to you.
>
> If I falter and strive to live a little more tenderly, and if for the first time I stop in doubt and bewilderment, surely it is better than hitting my head blindly against the wall which hurts so much.
>
> The things that made me weep before you are the same sad things that have made you weep alone in your room, and I am grateful for any change in my feelings that will release me from being cruel and hard. That was the pain I couldn't stand. I must live with Florence and I haven't liked her for a long time.
>
> The whole tragedy of us is that we cannot laugh together. If you could laugh at the little mule in me instead of expecting it to have horse sense, I know I could laugh at you and we could be happy friends.

My letter was a little more formal; it was dated December 6, and began:

> Florence dear, it is true that my vagueness is what has angered you and aroused in you that other personality, the Black Panther, that hates me and is disloyal.
>
> I am not vague now, and yet in your presence I am possessed and inarticulate. At least I feel so, and I want to tell you—even if it seems a foolish repetition—the clear truth of my feeling.
>
> When your letter came, saying you had erased me from your

heart and memory, I turned from you completely. Nothing could ever make me turn back or involve my life intimately with yours again.

The fact that I accomplished this by making of you in memory a kind of god of my life, does not alter the absoluteness of it. . . .

I can be one of your friends if you want me, because my admiration and enjoyment of you is indestructible and independent of other emotions. I always have more fun in any company where you are, for the simple reason that the people are always lovelier— more alive and more fine and elevated. Apart entirely from your sex and our memories, I love to be with you. I love to talk with you about everything.

And so I hope that you will be able to make me a friend, as you said you could. I will try to be a generous and simple one, but I will not invite you to the house in Croton any more unless someone else is there because it is too much of a strain on the habits of feeling by which I have become happy again. . . .

There was a little more—but that, I thought, was a triumph of explicitness.

We both tried hard during the days that followed to be tranquil-hearted friends, and I held firmly to my resolve not to become her lover. It is a little hard for me to say why we failed of tranquillity, but I think the reader can guess. When in love with Florence I was almost too devoted, too absorbed in her; but as her partner in a friendship, I took all the privileges of the male. Although in theory I think it is pretty outrageous, I assume by habit the man's right to the initiative— the right to go his way and let a girl wait until he chooses to come or call her up. In principle Florence accepted this convention too; she was feminine in those matters, as I have said. But this contrast with my former assiduousness must have seemed, at times, almost like an offense. I was taking quite wholeheartedly, and wholemindedly, the new regime of "friendship" as we had defined it. I was even protecting myself from her intoxicating charms by keeping up a romance with another girl. And I was planning to go to Russia, to explore a new world—an additional reason for not binding myself with unbreakable heartstrings here at home.

There were gossips to say that I was running away from Florence. If they had said I was running away from "Florence and me," they would have been right. We had too much to talk about. We loved too much to be together. Indeed we began to meet so often, and draw so close, that I felt afraid of my indecisiveness. Before long we might be in each other's arms and the old four-sided conflict would begin again.

Her angers saved me from that. Her mulish irrational angers—which she had once admitted were "insane"—had become almost a habit now. And of course my new detachment, my going-to-Russianess, accentuated and multiplied them. We sometimes laughed about this. I remember once, in one of her rages, taking her across my knee and giving her, in jest, a good sound spanking—something I should have done earnestly long before. It ended in laughter, and we came very near to making love that night, but it did not effect a cure. Florence herself was troubled about these seizures of anger, and went for help to great old George Parker, a not-too-Freudian psychoanalyst, friend and physician to Ruth and Amos Pinchot. Although it seemed incongruous that such a radiantly dynamic being should be going to a psychoanalyst, I was glad of this. It made me feel sure that, once the torment of my unsatisfactory adoration was removed, she would be triumphant again.

In December, to save money, Florence moved down from the Algonquin to a one-room apartment in Greenwich Village. It was at 120 West Eleventh Street—in a row of old houses with "front piazzas" set back a hundred feet from the sidewalk and therefore called Rhinelander Gardens. We all lived in the same vicinity, and Florence slipped naturally into our old way of life—socially close to us except for her career in theatrical circles of which we knew nothing.

I am afraid I refrained deliberately from knowing too much about that professional career. I wondered sometimes about the state of her finances, knowing that in our new relation she would be too proud to mention them. But I was in no position to help her with a loan, as I had once or twice in the early days. I was saving every cent for my projected trip to Russia. So I dismissed in our new friendship, more expressly than I might have, the impulse to take care of her that had once been so strong. It was fair, I told myself, while renouncing our physical intimacy, to keep my distance from her financial problems.

It required some effort, however, and I found it particularly difficult one day in February, when we chanced to be walking up Broadway together. She was evidently on her way to some appointment with a director, or producer, or theatrical agent, and we met by accident as I came out of the subway on Forty-second Street. We were going the same way as far as Forty-eighth Street, where I had in mind to turn east. She was more ravishingly beautiful than ever because of the cold

air on her cheeks—or was there a certain wistfulness in her expression—
the childlike pout, the perpetual challenge a little less prominent in her
lips? Or maybe it was only the dark fur collar matching her hair and the
glimpse of an orange scarf beneath it. For one or all of these reasons she
seemed like a person not only to love, but to live with in happiness for a
lifetime. Thus it was unnatural, as well as almost unfriendly, not to ask
her where she was going and how she was getting along professionally.

I succeeded in this only because, for a special reason, I did not want
her to ask me where *I* was going. I was going over to Scribner's on Fifth
Avenue to get a copy of *The Sense of Humor* which I had had bound in
Morocco leather for her, intending to surprise her with it. I would bring
it to her apartment later in the afternoon. Then she would understand
my mysterious turning away at Forty-eighth Street.

It was a beautiful dark red volume, firm for eternity, wrapped in
white tissue and tied with a gold string. I laid it on my desk when I
reached my room, and sat down to read until about five when I thought
I would find her at home. But I couldn't read; I was tired and lay down
to rest. When I woke from a brief sleep it was past five, and I
remembered that I had promised to meet some friends at the theater
that night. It would be better anyway, I thought—it would be more
fun—to bring my gift to Florence in the morning. Everything is more
fun in the morning. . . .

I had an aisle seat at the theater, and in the middle of the first act
a hand touched my shoulder and a man's voice whispered in my
ear:

"Florence Deshon has been taken to the hospital—she turned on the
gas in her room—she's in Saint Vincent's hospital."

I did not see the man, and to this day I don't know who he was or
how he found me. The whole of the real world from that moment was
my love for Florence, and my anguish—I had waited too long with that
book. Beyond that, my memory of the events which followed is stark; it
is more like knowledge than memory. With an "Excuse me" to Neysa
McMein who sat next me, I ran from the theater and across the street to
a taxi. We were west of Broadway and it was ten minutes straight down
to Saint Vincent's. A woman was in the corridor waiting for me—again
I don't know who she was. She told me a neighboring tenant had
smelled gas from Florence's apartment and forced the locked door
open. She found Florence lying on her bed unconscious. Saint Vincent's
was just across the street and they had telephoned for an ambulance.

The doctor in charge was evidently informed that I had been

summoned, for he received me as though I were a husband or brother. The patient was dying, he said, but it was just possible that a blood transfusion might save her. Would I care to give her a pint of my blood? (There were no blood banks then.) We went up one flight to an examining room, where he took a sample of my blood, and left me waiting while it was compared with hers. I did not know where he was. I did not know where she was. I only knew I had been wrong—I had been lazy and selfish—not to bring her my book. She would never know now why I turned away so abruptly at Forty-eighth Street.

"Your blood is friendly," the doctor said when he came back, placing a little ironical accent, I thought, on the word *blood*.

Florence's dying young body was rolled in on a white table, and I on another white table lay beside her while my blood flowed into her veins. She was not pale; she was still vivid, but her breathing was raucous and rapid, a fierce noisy effort of her body to get air, reminding me—as my mother's had when she lay dying of apoplexy—what a concrete real violent enginelike thing we mean when we say so abstractly, "the will to live."

I felt sure that in spite of her body's effort Florence would die. She would have her way. Even in the anguish of that last strange silent union of our life streams, I felt the more authentic purity of her will. Was it anything nobler than a brute instinct that made us try so hard to revive her? In her presence, my little personal regret about the book seemed trivial and sentimental, as I so often had seemed trivial and sentimental beside her bold heroic uncompromisingly passionate way of living a life.

During the two days that elapsed before her burial, I was possessed by an irrational, almost insane desire to go to the funeral parlor where she lay and be near her. My sister took me in hand like a mother and restrained me. She even persuaded me not to go to the funeral. I lay still in my room as though paralyzed until it was over. Friends came to comfort me—or rather, it seemed, to save me, for they acted as though I too were on my deathbed.

George Parker was sure she had not intended to kill herself. She was only twenty-six years old, beautiful and blessed with every gift—her turning on the gas had been a mere gesture of blind childish passion. But I knew it was not so. Her dear friend, Marie Howe, who was staying at the Clifton Springs Sanitarium, wrote me a letter which was more wisely comforting.

February 6, 1922

Dear Max,

I wish I could talk to you. I want to tell you one thing—the cause of Florence's mental despair was her sense of failure in her work.

Don't reproach yourself too much—it wasn't you. If she had found a job she would have been all right again. The constant set-offs and disappointments wounded her spirit. Every time she hoped for a position she was stabbed again in the same spot, so that the wound could never heal. It was always open and bleeding. And it was necessary to her pride to conceal this suffering from her friends—from you most of all.

She was with me a great deal these last few weeks. She talked to me hours at a time and I know positively that what I say is true. She needed a job. I mean she needed it psychologically. Nothing else could have saved her.

Of course her state of mind was complicated by the sort of impasse that existed between you two. But to say that it was complicated, is a very different thing from saying that it was caused by the impasse. The cause was her sense of failure in what she had started out to do.

She went out to Hollywood in the first place so filled with the sense of power and success that she abandoned you without a pang of regret. She then showed the dominant impulse of her life, the desire for personal success. I began then to be frightened for her because she soared so high that I knew how far she had to fall. When I called her joyous excitement the arrogance of youth and beauty, she laughed at me because she was so sure, so terribly sure, of fame and wealth and success.

Then after a short time there followed a continued repeated failure. The Goldwyn contract fed her ego with flattery and false hopes. The day she signed that contract was the beginning of the end. That man—or, if you like, the movies—did her an injury from which she never recovered.

All last winter I saw her meet one blow after another. She struggled on manfully. She tried to bolster up her self-confidence by brave talk. She tried to hide her hurt by silence. She would rather have died than confide all this to you. She had such enormous pride toward you.

All these last weeks in New York her state of mind was getting worse—no work, no hope of work, nothing but discouragement. She decided to leave the movies and go on the stage—again she met disappointment. Perhaps she did not tell you how many people she interviewed, how many times she tried. Then she decided to become a writer. This she talked to you about. She wrote a few things and came to realize that she lacked training and experience. She did not really have confidence that she could ever write. Her first success had been so swift and effortless that she could not face long years of slow preparation for a different work. And she wanted something important and exciting. She did not care for a dull obscure job in the business world.

Finally she faced herself—a girl with youth and beauty and no trained ability for the important position in the world that her soul craved. She saw no future. Instead of the glittering success she had expected, there was nothing but blackness.

I am so afraid that you are living through a nightmare of remorse and self-reproach, feeling that you hurt or failed her and that somehow it must be your fault.

Please try to take some comfort from my assurance that it is not so. Perhaps she talked more freely to me than to anyone else. You must believe what I tell you. She struggled to deceive everybody and you most of all, and all the time she was falling down down down until she struck bottom.

No love affair could ever kill our proud beautiful Florence. You know and I know that she could always rise above her emotions. They never conquered her, she conquered them. But with pride lost, she could not face the world.

> Affectionately yours,
> Marie Howe

On the night table by Florence's bed, I found a little notebook, familiar to me, containing her thoughts, and words or ideas that she wanted to remember. She had written there at the top of a page, in the "dark thick writing" that we used to smile about:

"I hurt you because I wanted to possess you."

I cannot know when these words were written—perhaps just before her death, perhaps soon after she recovered from the rage in which she had broken off our correspondence. But they set a seal upon my adoration of her. Her mind was supreme above those passions that she could not control. Although violently proud, she was noble enough to know what was to her a humiliating truth about herself. In a notebook of my own, during my bewildering and grief-stricken trip across the Atlantic, I wrote:

> You do possess me—yes, you have your will.
> Your dear dark hand is on me everywhere.
>
> Even the linnet's song that comes downstairs out of the sky,
> Even the beauty of life, is the song of your death.
>
> All things are bound to each by likeness or by touch in memory:
> My mind finds back the way from everything to you.
>
> Were I as brave as you who loved and hated me,
> I would lie down beside you whom I loved and feared.

PART TWO

1922-1927

Chapter 45

THE GENOA CONFERENCE

To many it was a devout pilgrimage, but I set out for Moscow rather in a mood of inquiry. By the way of a declaration of inward independence, or of the right of free thought and feeling, I wrote from mid-ocean to my friend Claude McKay:

"I feel sometimes as though the whole modern world, capitalism and communism and all, were rushing toward some enormous nervous efficient machine-made doom of the true values of life."

Claude published my letter in the *Liberator*—to the disgust, I am sure, of his co-editor, and of one or two other potential fanatics who had gathered around my banner, *Knowledge and Revolution*, having a taste for the joys of revolution but none for the sacrificial art of knowledge.

There were personal as well as political reasons why I felt so dark about where the world was going—dark enough, perhaps, to be a prophet. But my mood changed when I reached my preliminary destination, the Genoa Conference. It was the first meeting of the Western world with the despised and triumphant Bolsheviks—the first also of those international conferences attended by premiers and foreign ministers that have since become a feature of world history. At a meeting of the Allied Supreme Council at Cannes in January 1922, Lloyd George had persuaded the French and Belgians, against their instinctive judgment, to invite the whole world, or twenty-nine nations of it, to meet on equal terms with the Germans and Russians, and discuss all the questions that were driving them crazy—especially the question of Tsarist debts and German reparations. A strictly limited agenda having been agreed upon, the conference assembled in Genoa on April 23 in a mood of catlike tensity and mutual watchfulness.

Everybody was there: Lloyd George for England, a beautiful man, startling to look at after so many gray photographs, with his vivid blue eyes and young rosy skin under the silver mane; Louis Barthou for France; Hjalmar Branting for Sweden, a bristly old bloodhound, once a Socialist, now a King's Minister; Alexander Stambuliski, big, ruddy, brown, and ferocious as a Bulgarian bear, the peasant leader with a king in his pocket; Eduard Beneš, the clever boss of the "Little Entente," little himself, and as nice-mannered as a new drug clerk, with fine eyes and a neat mustache; Skirmunt, the Pole, tall, oily-faced—his lips resting on each other like those of a crocodile, not fitting together at all; and big Ion Bratianu, whose minions had scoured four countries to catch the Socialist agitator, Christian Rakovsky, and bring him into Rumania dead or alive. It was a mighty array of great men, all Europe in fact drawn up in oratorical phalanx to overawe the Bol-sheviks, and get them to be reasonable and pay the Tsar's debts, and co-operate like good boys with things as they are and must be. And every writing wild man of the decade was there who could get there, from Frank Harris (age seventy-five) to Ernest Hemingway (age twenty-three).

The hall in the Palazzo San Giorgio where the conference met was like a Yankee village church, with the press in a gallery at the back where the choir sits. Herbert Bayard Swope had given me a credential as feature writer for the *New York World*, and I sat in that gallery next to Marcel Cachin, the French Socialist leader. I looked down on Cachin then as a rightwing opportunist; though he subsequently became a leftwing opportunist. He was, at any rate, a canny and affable Breton peasant with a face like a rusty apple, and we were close enough in our views to share an amused excitement at the way the famous conference opened.

Most of the great men strolled in casually and got into their seats before anybody quite realized they were there. But there must always be one grandstand entrance, and the person to pull it off, of course, was Lloyd George, the godfather, not to say also the mother, of this world-shaping event. He did it very well—that is, just as if he weren't doing it, shuffling his papers and sitting down briskly amid a flutter of handclaps quickly suppressed as undiplomatic.

The great entrance was over, but the tension was not relieved. The lights went on full power; the president adjusted his gavel; the delegates adjusted their blotters; the audience, their chairs. Everybody stopped talking and then started again, and then stopped again.

Two minutes—three—five—ten. The tension began to grow into restlessness, impatience, vexation. The Russians were late. Russians are always late. Well, they ought not to be late when all the great men of the earth have assembled for the express purpose of letting them appear!

They did appear finally, just about one minute before the conference was going to explode. Instead of an explosion, there was a sharp whisper, almost a hiss: "Chicherin!" Every head turned.

Chicherin was Russia's foreign minister, whose diplomatic communications had been so well-phrased and irritatingly logical that he was almost as notorious as Lenin and Trotsky. He seemed very much at ease as he walked down the aisle, rather like a schoolmaster coming late with no apology to the pupils. And the five men who followed him—Rakovsky, Joffe, Krassin, Litvinov, Vorovsky, the pick of Lenin's cohorts from the standpoint of cosmopolitan culture—seemed also eminently at ease. Who wouldn't be at ease, I thought, with no social status to worry about and the victorious Red army behind him?

One could almost hear the muscles relax when they got to their seats, and the chairman, Signor Facta, rose from his high-backed chair and began speaking Italian. He was a tiny little man with a tiny winged mustache like his king's, and was wise enough to make a tiny speech.

No sooner had he sat down than a mountain of a woman got up and announced in a tremendous voice through her nose:

"Gentlemen, I assume the temporary presidency of this assembly and welcome you in the name of the King of Italy."

With that she began to stammer a little and fuss with a paper, and I realized with relief that she was not the Queen of Italy, but a woman from Kansas, or possibly Nebraska, who understood Italian and had been hired as an interpreter.

After a few other preliminaries, including his election as permanent president, Signor Facta opened the conference all over again with the following announcement:

"The present conference has been called upon the basis of the resolutions of Cannes; the simple fact of having accepted the invitation is proof that all the powers here assembled have accepted the principles contained in those resolutions."

To appreciate that, you have to know just what the great underlying idea of this conference was. It was Lloyd George's idea, and was indeed genial and startling—in fact, as I have said, historic. The idea was to hold a conference. And perhaps it is not too great an exaggeration to say that the principal delegates were in a state of apprehension lest such an extraordinary course of action might lead to a result. Somebody might do something! At least as a revolutionist I found it easy to regard the whole thing from that satirical point of view. At the preliminary meeting at Cannes, I told myself, a gentleman's agreement had been drawn up limiting the subjects of discussion to those which could not, by any stretch of imagination, lead to a result.

The first speaker, of course, was Lloyd George, and he looked so magnificent, really lionlike, as he rose in his place, that one expected some momentous oration out of him. But he was not, in my opinion, a great orator. There was a note of virtuous wonder in his voice rather like a preaching deacon, or like a mother telling bedtime stories to her children. And what he said might be summarized thus:

Gentlemen, we must hold a conference. A conference is a social thing, and therefore we must meet as equals and be free. The greatest contribution we can make is to stop snarling.

In his enthusiasm for this idea, however—and it really was a big one!—he forgot to mention the Cannes resolution. It fell to Barthou to call that to mind. Barthou was short, pug-nosed, black-whiskered, a book-writing lawyer, but with the sublime gift of elevated utterance that French grammar demands and almost imposes. His speech was equally easy to satirize:

As soon as the resolutions adopted at Cannes assured France that no question bearing upon the reconstruction of Europe could possibly be raised, France entered with all enthusiasm into this conference on the reconstruction of Europe.

After Barthou, Count Ishii, slender, ministerial, his French a little whining:

The wish of Japan is to live in peace with all people and particularly with her neighbors.

A noticeable withholding of applause by her next-door neighbors, the Russians, a portion of whose territory she then held by force of arms.

After Count Ishii, M. Theunis of Belgium to the same effect.

And then the Germans. They spoke for the first time since the war on equal terms with their conquerors, and they spoke to the same effect:

We must confer. A conference is a free thing. We must meet as equals. We must be ready to make sacrifices. We must go home in a free spirit.

Karl Joseph Wirth, the new German chancellor, was a big and

rather young man. With his head lowered to read his speech, he looked like a robust but excessively modest schoolboy. This manner delighted the French, and his speech was so courteous and inconsequential, so entirely in accord with the gentleman's agreement adopted at Cannes, that M. Barthou nodded his head in emphatic approval as it was being translated.

Chicherin wrote his speech in Russian, read it from a French translation, and translated it *ex tempore* from the Russian copy into English—an evidence of superior culture that pleased me, I imagine, more than it pleased his auditors.

As he stood with his back to the press, however, and his voice was a frail piping, I could not catch a word of it either in English or French. I had the pleasure of gathering its drift from the emotional reflection in the intent faces of his listeners. It was the expression you see on the family's face when the bad boy tells an embarrassing truth before company. But Chicherin had done a much bolder thing. He had suggested, in defiance of the Cannes agenda, that this present conference should do something and something dangerously pleasing to the war-sick world:

"We greet with satisfaction the statements of the preceding orators that they desire peace and the reconstruction of Europe, and we shall venture to propose one single thing that they might do to promote peace and save money for the reconstruction of Europe—namely, to agree now upon a limitation of armaments."

It was certainly not the part of a gentleman to come out with a practical remark like that after everything had been quietly arranged among friends for a purely oratorical demonstration. It showed no respect for the unspoken niceties of polite diplomacy. It was the act of a boor. And what made it worse was that Chicherin was *not* a boor; he was not a proletarian; he was not even bourgeois! He was by birth a nobleman of the Tsar. Blood won't tell. What is the world coming to?

Whatever it was coming to, M. Barthou was determined it should not get there.

"It is my duty to myself," he cried, "it is my duty to France, to protest. The question of disarmament is not on the agenda adopted at Cannes. I give my warning that if that question is raised, France will answer with a categorical, definite, final, decisive no!"

Chicherin's answer was quick and quiet: "We understood the French attitude upon disarmament from the speech of Monsieur Briand at Washington. But Monsieur Briand gave us a reason for the French attitude, the existence of the Russian armies. We assumed that if the proposal came from us to remove the reason, the attitude might also be changed."

Barthou was saved the labor of an answer to this thrust by Lloyd George who proceeded with the charm of a perfect master of amenities to dismiss the address of M. Chicherin from serious consideration. His speech was gay and witty beyond anybody's expectation. To me again the serious substance of it seemed to be:

This conference has all that it can possibly do in conferring. For heaven's sake, let us not try to do anything else!

Chicherin and Barthou both rose for recognition, but Signor Facta declared the debate closed.

I went down into the hall after the adjournment and asked Chicherin what he had intended to say. He answered:

"I merely wished to repeat what I had said, although nobody seemed to notice it, that while we regard a limitation of armaments as a primary point in the economic recovery of Europe, nevertheless we will bow to the will of the conference. We want to co-operate with them sincerely and harmoniously."

That was the opening of the Genoa Conference, and it was my first meeting with a *bona fide* Bolshevik. It made me happy. From the standpoint of frank and radical intelligence the game had been won hands down, it seemed to me, by my side.

The Russians had an office in the Hotel de Gênes, but they were quartered at Santa Margherita, twenty miles down the coast from Genoa. We hired a car and drove down there in the early morning, Lincoln Steffens and Jo Davidson and I. It was twenty miles of vivid excitement for the eyes. Below Genoa the coast is a steep, long hillside, that has been carved for cultivation into a gigantic stairway going down deliberately to the sea, trailing its blossoming vines and fruit trees and long grasses—wisteria and azalea and roses and black iris and daisies and oranges and cherries and sweet-smelling lemons and figs and pomegranates, and over them all the soft blue-gray mist of olives. A Garden of Gethsemane without sorrow. It is not verdurous; there is always the dry earth in Italy. But it is luxurious, and even then in early springtime it was full of summer. The houses and barns were as lovely in their soft bright plaster-colors, as lovely and old and proper to their place as flowers in nature. The churches and the little villages with their high light bell towers, were like old paintings. Nothing so mellow, so akin to soft melodious laughter, is to be seen or can be imagined in America. And nothing so blue as the blue Mediterranean, far down below, so richly cool, so tranquil, showing a little foam at the foot of the brown bluffs.

At the end of eighteen miles the road darted inland through a tunnel, revealing the black valley that lay behind this bright southern garden, and then swung back again, round a bold promontory, and down the trailing stairway to what was then the tiny village of Santa Margherita. On the hill high over the village, in an elegant hotel named Imperial Palace, the dreaded Bolsheviks were enjoying for the first time the hospitality of their capitalist neighbors. The Italian government spoke of them as "the guests of civilization." Civilization having waged a small war on them for four years and having been defeated and driven home by the Red army, the guests naturally did not feel overwhelmed by this condescension. We found them enjoying the unclouded humor of those who win, with the additional exultation of those whose victory has convinced them that their doctrines are confirmed and correct.

I have forgotten how we got past Comrade Ehrlic, the gay and athletic revolver-padded guard at the gate. I think Jo Davidson had a date to make a bust of Litvinov; Lincoln Steffens could always get in everywhere; and a copy or two of the *Liberator* was a pass to all the Bolsheviks for me. A harder thing to get past with any emotional composure was the queer and repellent creature the Russians had brought along as press representative—a cranky, neurotic, ill-mannered, sallow-skinned intellectual named Marcel Rosenberg. Never was a man in that key position so universally scorned and hated by the press—a press which included some of the most distinguished editors and correspondents in the Western world. One day, to meet an emergency—and incidentally to make myself at home in the Imperial Palace Hotel—I offered to translate some lengthy French document for Chicherin. My French was none too good, and I had to ask a question or two of this febrile monster, Rosenberg. Instead of a helpful answer, he said:

"Eastman, why do you try to do things you don't know how to do?"

I did not answer, but only walked away—in humiliation, I am ashamed to say, instead of anger. But also in dismay, for it was a calamity that Lenin's emissaries had set up this human barrier between themselves and the news columns of the world—a mystery too, for they were themselves, those six leading Bolsheviks, abundantly endowed with grace and *savoir faire*. My contact with them was close enough to confirm my still dominant impression that Lenin was a "statesman of a new order." They seemed to contrast with their capitalist opponents exactly as my conception of the hard-headed idealist, the scientific revolutionary, required that they should. Chicherin was, perhaps, the most uniquely gifted among them, a sort of prodigy, a brilliant scholar, a trained diplomat, a gifted pianist. His mother kept him in dresses, they told me, until he was ten years old, and perhaps that is why he was so quietly content to live in his mind. He seemed to be in a state of continual concentration, always either reading, or at work, or focusing his entire self upon some polite act of kindness. When he came into the Soviet workroom in the Hotel de Gênes, he never failed to greet with solemn and respectful courtesy each person who was working there. And when he went out, he would turn and say a general good-bye, even if everybody was too busy to hear him. One would never guess from his modest and slow manner that he had any revolution in him. One would never guess it from his appearance, which was in some indefinable way babylike. He held a pen in his hand like a baby. His hands were small and not graceful; he had no "build"; there was no resonance in his voice. And his perfect unity of color—mustache, goatee, eyes, eyebrows, hair and freckles, all exactly the same sandy red-brown —conveyed somehow an impression of innocence. It was only when you began to question his position that the hard clear mind and prodigious knowledge he possessed became apparent.

Among the writing men down there at Genoa was George Slocombe, representing the London *Daily Herald*. George was a mild, peaceable, blue-eyed person really, but he concealed it under a violent red beard and the wide-brimmed black felt hat popularized by William Morris and portending revolt if not revolution. George and I were natural friends, and when he was called home by a financial crisis on the paper, he asked me to take over his work for a week or so. It was my sole go at the newsman's job, and in my zeal to excel I made the first page with a statement from Lloyd George and an answer to it by Chicherin. Defending some proposal which the Allies had submitted to the Bolsheviks, Lloyd George assured us that it had been very carefully drawn up by two experts in international law. When I repeated that to Chicherin, he said: "Yes, I could tell it was drawn up by lawyers. You can never mistake their language—not at least since the thirteenth century. Now in the old Saxon times it was entirely different. In those days legal documents were composed in a language as clear and concise as that spoken by simple people." And he proceeded to give me a discourse on the history of prose style in my own language that left me wide-eyed with admiration. Here indeed was a foreign minister from Utopia!

Even more impressive to my eager mind, or more instantly so, was Christian Rakovsky. By contrast with Chicherin he had both build and bearing, a clear ringing voice and energetic utterance. Though I knew him only briefly, I remember his strong face, and brilliant warm eyes with a perpetual half-smile in them, as those of a friend. I suppose Rakovsky was trusted and loved by more people than any other revolutionist in Europe. In poise, intelligence, and I should say force of character, Rakovsky came next after Lenin and Trotsky among the Bolsheviks. Born in the mountains of Bulgaria, but a Rumanian citizen through changes in the map, he was an internationalist predestined. He spoke all the Balkan languages including Turkish, and spoke French, English, German, and Russian besides. He had studied medicine in Paris and been for a time a practicing physician, but in 1913 gave himself up to the socialist movement, organizing a Rumanian Socialist Party, editing its daily paper, and financing it with the income of an estate on the Black Sea which he had inherited from his landlord father. A man of alert mind, humane feeling, and almost supernatural energy, he played an active role in the revolutionary movements of Rumania, Bulgaria, France and Russia. He was freed from a Rumanian prison by Russian soldiers in May 1917, and joined the Bolshevik Party in time to play a part in the October revolution. While wanted by the Rumanian Government as a state criminal, he came to Genoa as Premier of the Ukrainian republic. There he took upon himself the function so fumbled by Marcel Rosenberg, that of interpreting the Russian revolution to the press of the capitalist world. He met them every evening at six-thirty in a little white-walled lecture hall in the ancient University of Genoa—a room with blackboards and rising tiers of benches for the pupils.

Those benches were always filled to overflowing, and Rakovsky always dashed in a little late with a bulging briefcase under his arm. He would make a succinct statement of the principal problems of the day from a Soviet point of view, then sit down at his desk, pick up a pen, and say with a humorous smile:

"Now, gentlemen, there are perhaps some questions you would like to ask."

On a long strip of paper he would copy out carefully all the

questions—which kept growing weightier and weightier as the opportunity to make speeches began to be comprehended by the listeners.

Rakovsky enjoyed these speeches; he never interrupted or stopped
them. He was learning from them. When all the questions were asked,
he would take another sheet of paper and classify them. Then he would
get up and reply to them, all in one speech—patiently, if possible
frankly, usually with humor, frequently with allusions to some historical parallel. He was particularly happy when he could remind a
French reporter of something in French history that he had forgotten,
for in this as in the French language he was adept.

I think Rakovsky enjoyed conducting these international classes in
the old University of Genoa as much as anything he ever did. I
remember one day at the Soviet office in the Hotel de Gênes, the
secretaries were finishing up some diplomatic communication of lofty
importance. Rakovsky had composed it in French, and the rest of the
delegation had given it their approval and gone away, leaving Rakovsky
to sign it after it was translated into English. The hour was late, and
he seemed to be in a terrible hurry. He paced back and forth like a tiger
in a cage. His mood communicated itself to those who were typing the
letter, and they, of course, filled it full of mistakes.

Well, he wouldn't wait.

"Fix it with a pen!" he said.

It was fixed with a pen, and it looked like a communication from
a hobo agitator to the business manager of the *Liberator*. Then it was
folded wrong and wouldn't fit the envelope. Somebody tried to fold it to
fit the other way, and still it wouldn't go in. Thereupon the whole room
threw up their hands, and declared it would have to be typed over again.

"No, sir!" Rakovsky said, seizing it and folding it a third way.
"That's good enough! They can read it! I must go to the University!"
He grabbed me by the arm.

"Come on! My pupils are waiting for me!"

There was something teacherlike in the attitude of all those Bolsheviks at the conference. In their Marxian fashion, they knew so much
more than their opposite numbers about history and the science of
economics—as well as about the more exact science of why they had
come here and what they wanted—that they had to offer a little
instruction before any conferring could rightly begin.

A small question which had considerably agitated the circles from
which I came, and which slightly troubled the Bolsheviks themselves,
was whether they should wear silk hats. In Moscow, Kalinin, the

president of the republic, was attending public celebrations with his shirt unbuttoned and no necktie on. Neither Lenin nor any of his followers ever dreamed of wearing dress clothes—a symbol to them of subservience to bourgeois standards. When I put the question to Rakovsky at one of his conferences, he said, suppressing a smile:

"Wearing silk hats is one of the concessions we have estimated will cost us nothing.

"Just the same I left mine home," he added with a laugh.

Adolf Joffe, I thought, came next after Rakovsky among those leading Bolsheviks in culture and independent force. He too was a physician, but with his firm thick lips, Oriental features and long pointed black beard like a mandarin's, he would have seemed more in character sitting on a mat with a circle of devout disciples around him. His forehead was too high and too meditative for the role he was playing. His poise was like Buddha's. (I am giving you the impressions, remember, of one eager to be impressed.) He had patience enough to be a teacher of philosophy to children. And he had, as I was to learn many years later, a kindness that you will not find specified in the Communist Manifesto.

Leonid Krassin was in still sharper contrast to the then accepted idea of a Bolshevik, having a sort of sorrowful gentlemanliness about him. He was so handsome with his trim gray beard, and so immaculately dressed, that one could hardly believe he had played a role in organizing the famous underground printing press with which for years the Bolshevik propagandists infuriated the Tsar's police. But his fine features wore a determined expression, the same that you see in the statue of General Sherman at the entrance to New York's Central Park. In fact he looked somewhat like General Sherman.

Vorovsky looked like the kindly friend and confidant who taught geography and good sense in a small village school because he was not strong enough in health to go and live in the city. He was the only man in the Bolshevik delegation who did not seem physically robust. He was thin-wristed and hollow-voiced, kept his head lowered when he spoke as though it were too much of an effort to hold it up. I remember a moment of feeling, when he was assassinated by an anti-Soviet agent in Switzerland two years later, that it was heartless to assassinate so frail a person!

One unforgettable thing Vorovsky said to me. I had asked him whether he found any very able statesmen among the bourgeois delegates.

"In order to be a statesman," he said, "it is necessary to be in a condition of growth. None of these men are growing."

Those words, rising so strangely with their Emersonian serenity out of a conversation about debts and dollars, trade and productivity, contracts and guarantees, made me feel again that I was among delegates from a new and better world.

It must have been the same day—for the contrast in my feelings was so startling—that George Slocombe and Ernest Hemingway and I drove over to Rapallo together. It was only a short way from the hotel at Santa Margherita, where the Bolsheviks stayed, and as I have said elsewhere, I felt as if the little red-and-white painted automobile we rode in was a time-machine carrying us from the threshold of the revolutionary future back into the previous century. For we had only to ring a bell at a little gate and climb an ingoing stairway, and there was the inimitable person of Max Beerbohm, exquisitely clad and graciously at leisure, sipping a little Marsala wine on the uncovered terrace of his villa, looking out over the blue water, and feeling quietly happy because he had just finished a series of deft and devastating caricatures of the life of King Edward VII. He was not in the least disturbed by our unannounced arrival with no excuse but a desire to talk with him.

"Not about politics!" was his only demur, and to that we agreed so heartily that before long we were talking politics with candor and abandon.

I was impressed at first by the neatness of the British gentleman in Max Beerbohm—the exquisite fit of his gray suit, the immaculately shined boots, the trousers not too slim but perfectly tailored and creased to a razor edge. There was a less painfully genteel round knobby shape to his features, and he had a boyish tan, but these were redeemed by a very neatly folded small gray felt hat that perfectly matched his small gray mustache. What he called his study was a small square hut of one room standing in the middle, it seems to me, of the broad flat terrace on which we sat. As I faced its open doors, it seemed more like a stage set than an actual study. The inside walls were painted a pure cobalt blue—a strange thing in those days—but they seemed cool in the white Italian sunshine. The blue hut contained little but a desk with blotter and pens all neatly arranged, a new shiny kerosene stove, and a cabinet from which, after a while, the wonderful pictures emerged.

I have remarked that a peculiar displacement of the light rays occurs when the chilly atmosphere of the British first touches that of the warmer-mannered peoples, and for a while nothing very much is visible on either side. It may have been that natural phenomenon that made it difficult to see Max Beerbohm in the perfect gentleman who welcomed us. It was not until we got on the subject of policemen that the blessing of mutuality descended into our conversation. We were talking of the differences between America and Europe, and I remarked that a most striking difference is in the character and conduct of the policemen. In America, I said, a policeman is a big, armed authoritarian giant who has to be bribed. In France he is a courteous being of ordinary size and social emotion who will accept a tip. It seems that in London he is even more human and delightful—actually superior in charm, according to Max Beerbohm, to the rest of the British species.

"When I return to London I am always struck by the policemen," he said. And one of us—probably Hemingway—answered that our experiences in America might be described in the same terms. That made Beerbohm laugh, and he got up very energetically and started to walk. It seemed as though he were going away on business, but in six steps he was back again with a more genial interest in the conversation.

It drifted to the subject of our common revolt against commercial journalism, his in the *Yellow Book* in the nineties, ours in the *Masses* and the *Liberator* and the *Little Review*, twenty years later. In the course of it he disavowed any interest at all in the publication of his drawings.

"For me they have achieved their destiny when they exist," he said.

I don't know how sincerely true that was, but it impressed me as an enviable state of mind—a freedom from the irksome democratic thought of the multitudes of men, and the millions of authentic values that their wills create. "Beerbohm is an aristocrat," I said to myself, "and lives content with his own values. And if you're going to be an aristocrat, that is the kind to be—the kind that remains serene and self-contented right up to the day when the revolution appears in his own kitchen."

He showed us his caricatures of the prime minister of "a proposed Labor government" in England greeting Jules Cambon, the French ambassador—a picture which had recently got him a denunciation from the *Daily Herald*, George Slocombe's Labor Party paper. We liked the picture, and he was surprised. He was disposed to defend it a little by telling us that after all the labor leader was "really a good fellow."

"He is just exactly the kind of good fellow who will run things in a Labor government," I said, "and he will run them about as you imply."

He was puzzled by this remark, but it was growing late for explanations.

"Come over to the Imperial Palace Hotel," I suggested, "and we will show you the kind of people who run things in a revolutionary government!"

He said that he was afraid he would feel a little "vexed" if he went over there—the "mess they have made in Russia," the "diagrammatic minds," "ignoring of the obvious facts of human nature."

"But no doubt you are right, I should enjoy them. I am sure I should like them better than our own delegates. I always enjoy a charming fool better than a British gentleman who happens to have his head screwed on just right!"

Again my thoughts remained unspoken: "You *would* be vexed, and vexed especially to find that they are not charming fools, but men equal to you in mental culture, superior in the scope of science their culture comprehends. In order to understand the mess they are making in Russia, you would have to put yourself to school a little under those Bolsheviks. You might find yourself, before you knew it, 'in a condition of growth.'"

The end of the Genoa conference was even more "bolshevizing" in its effect on me than the beginning. Formally it ended, so far as concerned Russia, in the appointment of a commission to examine the claims and counterclaims: the demand on one side, that is, for payment of the Tsarist debts, on the other, damages for the armed invasion. Apart from the treaty of Rapallo signed behind the scenes by Russia and Germany, that was the net result of six solid weeks of study and discussion by all the great statesmen of the earth. The Russian proposal to grant "industrial, mining, agricultural and other concessions to foreigners" was met with chilly silence.

It happened that Litvinov had said to me the day after the conference opened: "All we can get out of this is the appointment of a commission to confer some more." Litvinov was less impressive in aspect than the other Bolsheviks—he looked like a mixture of Mischa Elman and a prosperous pawnbroker, especially when dressed up in a perfectly correct morning coat and a perfectly incorrect little round felt hat. But he had a quick tight-lipped way of saying extremely acute and sagacious things. His prediction and its exact fulfillment added much to my belief in the Bolsheviks, and in the class-struggle hypothesis on which they were acting.

"This is not a conflict of ideas, but of wills," I wrote home to the

Liberator. "What the bourgeois statesmen were saying under their silence was: 'We will not let you establish a system of society in which labor possesses the capital and holds the power.'"

Lloyd George was less happy than Litvinov in this negative result. His prestige was involved, the fame of his genius for getting people to come together and "be reasonable." He was charming to the end, but he could not resist taking one ironical crack at the Russians in the closing session.

"We have some deep and incurable prejudices in western Europe," he said in effect. "One of them is that a man ought to pay his debts. And it may be perfectly sound reasoning, but it offends these prejudices of ours when a man who has already borrowed money from us, and is asking for more, prefaces his request by explaining to us at great length that it is against his principles to pay his debts!"

Chicherin was standing up with his answer on his tongue before Lloyd George got through talking: "If I come to discuss a past obligation that is in doubt and if in the meantime my alleged creditor has attacked me, destroyed my property, burned down my house and killed my son, I naturally expect the negotiations to begin with an act of restitution on his part."

Intellectually it was a body thrust with a rapier. But emotionally, Lloyd George had full possession of the house. There was no applause for Chicherin. He seemed slim and lonely, and his voice weightless, in the silent chamber. He had no friend but logic. No genial curiosity shone in any eye, no polite hopefulness as at the opening session. The attempt at seduction had failed. These strike leaders had remained true to their men. The class struggle was on. That was my thought.

It was bitter to me, though, to see this high, consecrated and brilliant man so isolated and unappreciated in a cold assembly of his inferiors. I felt hard and sad as I walked away.

"Chicherin's audience was not there," I kept telling myself, but I could not shake off the experience of my senses. I wanted to *see* his audience, I wanted to hear them applaud.

We had agreed, some of the Russians and the pro-Russian journalists, to take a parting photograph in the sunny square in front of the Palazzo after the session was closed. So I went round there to the delegates' entrance to wait for them. A bright pretty cordon of the King's soldiers surrounded the square, leaving an open space for the automobiles of the delegates, holding back the workingmen from the harbor on one side, and the merchants and plain folk from the shops on the other. For it was just the noon hour, and everybody wanted to have a last look at the great men from abroad. They came importantly out, in two's and three's—sedate or smiling and chatting, it didn't matter. We knew them well and were tired of it. So we got hold of the Soviet photographer, selected a sunny spot, grouped ourselves with our backs to the statesmen, and told him to shoot. He was on the point of pressing the bulb, when we heard behind us a few scattering handclaps, followed by a crash and a roar and a thunder of cheers and running footsteps. The whole port of Genoa had broken over that line of pretty soldiers—or rather those soldiers had melted and become one with the sailors and stevedores and coal-heavers out of the port of Genoa. They flowed in irresistibly, transforming the clean-swept little square dedicated to decorum into a place of passion and voice and motion. I never saw a happier face than Chicherin's when that mob surrounded him, proud and laughing and cheering him to the skies. His audience was there in Genoa, after all. His audience was everywhere.

For such reasons I left the Genoa Conference more firmly pro-Bolshevik than I had come, more happy in my self-identification with the international workers' revolution. I had seen the best of Lenin's following. Now I would see Lenin himself, and the Workers' and Peasants' Republic. Perhaps my journey to Moscow would be something of a pilgrimage after all.

Chapter 46

WHAT REALLY HAPPENED AT GENOA

One day toward the end of the Genoa Conference, Jo Davidson and George Slocombe and I drove down to Santa Margherita together again. Jo was working on his bust of Litvinov and I was happy in the chance to have a talk with his illustrious sitter. The sitting took place in the open air on a little second-story verandah at the front of the Imperial Palace. On the third floor, just above, was a large room occupied by the young female secretaries of the legation, four of them, noisy with their typewriters and their laughter. Jo was thumbing his clay, and Litvinov was parrying rather than answering my questions, and I was leaning with bored resignation against the balustrade, when a girl's rumpled head emerged from the window above me. As I looked up it disappeared, but in a few seconds four heads appeared, two blond and two brunette, all merry-eyed and laughing. They disappeared again as I looked up, but in their place a red rose came out of the window and dropped at my feet. I tried to pretend it was meant for all three of us, but Jo's laughter and Litvinov's grin made it plain that I must be the one to pick it up.

That evening, standing in the lobby with George Slocombe, waiting to go up for an interview with Chicherin, I saw one of the secretaries come downstairs with a skipping step, her hand sliding lightly along the banister. She was not exactly pretty, but looked so jolly, with her short nose, twinkling gray eyes and tiny front teeth, that I watched her with a feeling of reminiscent mirth. She seemed like the girls back home—not too awfully foreign. (Maybe I was a little homesick.) Anyway, when George stopped her and introduced her to me as Miss Krylenko—name of the great orator of the Bolsheviks, first commander-in-chief of the Red army, Minister of Justice in the Soviet Government

301

—I was lifted far enough out of my shyness to ask, pointing to the rose in my buttonhole:

"Was it you who threw it to me?"

She said, "Oh no!" in an offhand way, but seeing the rather chilling effect of this, added with a laugh:

"It was my idea, though."

"I hoped it was," I said, pretending I had distinguished her face among the four that looked out of the window. Then I went on upstairs, wishing I had said more, and hoping that fate would bring us together again.

Fate obliged me the next day. George and I spent the night in a small square hotel down in the village a mile or so from the Imperial Palace. I finished the translation I was working on, and to deliver it to Rosenberg—and get a little exercise—I decided to row over to the foot of the hill and walk up a path to the big hotel. Halfway up, I climbed a fence and landed almost in the arms of that merry-eyed secretary, Eliena Krylenko. She was standing all alone under a kumquat tree, weeping and eating kumquats. Before I could find an expression for my feelings, or quite decide what they were, she exclaimed:

"These tears are not for you!"

I couldn't help smiling, but managed to answer: "I never dreamed they were."

An embarrassed silence followed, which I broke finally by saying: "Even if I can't dry your tears, I might help you eat the kumquats."

She laughed without ceasing to cry, and reached up with a graceful gesture to pick one for me. I suggested that we go on up to the hotel and have a drink together. She wiped the tears from her eyes with an impatient motion and said she would be delighted.

We had barely sat down to a table however, and begun a conversation on the all-important subject of each other, when she got up:

"*Je vous demande pardon, Monsieur*," she said—all our communications, I have forgotten to explain, were in French—"I beg your pardon, Monsieur, but I have a brief appointment that I must not miss. It will take me less than twenty minutes. Will it seem presumptuous if I ask you to wait until I come back?"

It seemed anything but presumptuous—it seemed, indeed, as though we were already friends. It would have seemed even more so had I known what the "brief appointment" was. To make it known, I will quote, with some omissions, an account of this episode that she herself wrote in after years:

Our delegation, consisting of about a hundred people, filled to capacity a fine old *Hotel Imperiale* at Santa Margherita, overlooking the blue bay and the promontory of Porto Fino. We were in a mesh of romances, all of us. The sunshine, the luxury, the new clothes and good food, breaking the long drab days of deprivation and half starvation we had lived through during the civil war, made all our heads swim. We were busy enough, but not too busy for passionate flirtations. Everybody, from the heads of the delegation down, was having a love-affair. But the most engrossing and tearful affair was a real love that sprang up between me and Vladimir Divilkovsky, a young Russian attaché of the Rome Embassy, who came to Genoa to meet his fiancée. She was a sweet blonde girl who had come to Italy with the idea of meeting her fiancé and getting happily married. He was a rather neurotic young man with very green eyes, not handsome, but to me strangely attractive. When he met his fiancée he also met me—alas! Sometimes two people are drawn towards each other instantaneously, and can not conceal it. This happened between me and Divilkovsky, and there resulted one of those particularly Russian emotionally sacrificial romances. His fiancée was ready to give him up for me, but I would not have it. He would not have it either, and yet nothing could keep her lover and me apart.

In the midst of this tense tragedy I was captivated by an American whom I saw talking to Litvinov on the balcony below the secretarial office. I called all the girls to look at him.

"Let's throw him a rose!" I whispered.

There were always roses in our room, beautiful Italian roses. I brought a red one to the window, but lost my nerve and laid it on the sill. Chicherin's secretary gave it a push and down it went. With that accomplished we went back to work. . . .

The day after that, my sacrificial romance reached its climax. Divilkovsky and I said a tearfully determined farewell. He would go back to Rome and stay there until the conference should end, when I would have to go back to Moscow. We parted at the hotel gate, and he went down the hill to the station to take the little train. Left sadly alone, I wandered down toward the shore, and stood weeping under a kumquat tree. I had just picked one of those delicious fruits and was chewing it amid my tears, when my American appeared again. In a panic of foolish fear lest he think my weeping had something to do with the rose, I blurted out: "These

tears are not for you!" I don't remember his answer, but it ended
in his asking me to come back with him to the hotel and have a
drink. I didn't see any harm in that, though as we sat at the table
together, I couldn't stop thinking about my heart-torn lover going
away on the little train alone. It would be my last chance, perhaps
in all my life, to see him. I jumped up from the table finally, and
asking the new friend to wait for me, ran all the way downhill to
the station, arriving just in time to wave my lover a frantic good-
bye.

The new friend was still waiting when I hurried back. We had
our drink together. And we had dinner together. And then we
strolled down the path past the kumquat tree to the shore. We
climbed out on a big rock that glistened in the waves and the moonlight. We sat close together on the top of that perilous rock, watching and listening to the waves. He asked me to tell him a Russian
word. I told him *serébriannie*, the lovely word for silver, and
taught him how to say that the waves were silver in the moonlight.

It must have been deep into the night when we started back, for
halfway up to the *Imperiale* we met Divilkovsky's little fiancée
rushing down to the shore in a frantic search for me, fearing I
had drowned myself for grief about her lover.

Years passed before I knew about Divilkovsky, and learned why my
companion had rushed in such a hurry from our sociable drink. But I
remembered our midnight hour on the "perilous rock" in the same
tender way she did. I had, like her, the sadness of a lost love in my
heart, and yet a springtime thirst for new experience. Though I realized
how helpful it would be to have a friend so highly placed when I
reached Moscow, I did not think of our emotional relation as a thing
that would endure. I had forsworn that kind of thing forever, or
thought I had. I admired her trustfulness to the moment, her giving me
with delicate abandon a gift of love that had no roots in the past, no
questions about the future. I tried, after we parted, to consecrate with
some rhythmic words the very brevity and self-surroundedness, the
freedom from cause and consequence, of that moment.

AT SANTA MARGHERITA

Being is brief. Was that the murmured song
Of the moon-wandering waves that walked so slow

And solemnly to cast beneath our feet
Their momentary foamy jewels down?
Live now or never live; the night air holds
The sea, and our tense hearts and touching lips
Hold being as a fragrance; breathe it deep.

Chapter 47

It took me four months to go from Genoa to Moscow, and I cannot pretend there was any reason except that Paris is beautiful and I was full of "the wild joys of life, the mere living." I had crossed the Atlantic in what seemed an eternal sorrow, but deeper down, though it hurt me so keenly, Florence's death had liberated me to myself. My escape from the editorial chair had been like the flight of a caged bird into the sky. The Genoa Conference had given me a sustaining conviction that, "Lenin's in the Kremlin, all's right with the world!" My friend, Dudley Field Malone, knowing intimately of my sorrow, had expressed his sympathy on my arrival in Paris by making me a present of one of the thousand dollars he was forever borrowing from rich friends. Norman Hapgood, having taken over the editorship of *Hearst's International*, a magazine which he soon killed with similar acts of bad judgment, had advanced me another thousand on the theory that I could write for such a magazine. I had no cares, I had no connections. Nobody and nothing was depending on me. There is a bliss in living alone and a bliss in living with a girl you love; either way you miss something. And just now I was swimming in the bliss of living alone.

With Edna Millay and three other friends, I took a trip through the ravishing French landscape on the roof of a canal boat. We picked up our meals at little picture villages along the way, and peeled off our clothes and slid into the water when we wanted a bath. With three other friends—Neysa McMein, Ferdie Tuohy (who was writing for the *New York World*) and Christine Norman, a red-gold Venus who some years later threw herself from a hotel window—I made a tour of the famous landmarks of the First World War. It stirred in me a poem, "The Battlefields," in which I sang of the triumph, not of the Allies over the Germans, but of nature's life over the stricken wasteland they had left

306

behind them. It was the nearest I had come, until that time, to putting my thoughts as well as my feelings into a poem.

We drove down to Tours where I had an appointment, made for me by Norman Hapgood, with Anatole France. I left my companions at the gate of his gracious villa and strolled up the gravel drive, proud of my privilege and yet timorous, for though I could speak some French, I understood little of it when it was fluently spoken. I found him absorbed in conversation with two friends, but he came forward with an eager greeting when I entered, lifting his hand high to bring it down to mine as though he had been waiting for me as long and expectantly as I had been coming. He looked Persian to me; he looked like a grandee in the court of Cyrus the Great. He wore a soft brown-yellow cape that might have been a robe, and on his head a little round red velvet cap that was altogether Oriental. His beard was long and of a Biblical shade of gray. And there was a queer longness about his face, a face full of dark solemn shadows that contrasted strangely with the somewhat goatlike alertness and quizzicality of his expression. He was wholly Oriental until he laughed. But his laugh was such a wreathing and wrinkling-up of the whole countenance in pure mirth as no Persian grandee could permit himself. It was a genial, irresponsible, playful, impractical laugh. It was a complete laugh. Sometimes when you read the works of the masters of irony, you have the impression that they are a little held back and bitter—that they are more interested in the sting than the humor of their wit. I remember that I had this impression of Bernard Shaw, until I saw him and heard him make those keen, intellectual and stinging remarks of his with the jolly and uproarious hilarity of an infant. I perceived the same truth in my conversation with Anatole France—that great humorists are fundamentally, even when most serious, at play.

This fact made all the more moving the tragic things Anatole France said to me when we spoke seriously about the condition of France. We were joking at first about nationalities.

"The Americans came over here in sufficient quantities to demonstrate their inability to fight," he said, watching my eyes mischievously to see what would happen. But that opinion was then so general in France that I was thoroughly familiar with it.

"Considering where your ability to fight has landed you," I said, "I can only be happy at the compliment."

But he was not sure I was not offended. "You have courage, of course," he added, "but there is a military genius, an art of fighting."

"I know," I said, "but it begins to look as if we all have too much of that. Wouldn't it be better if we were like the Eskimos, who are so busy fighting the ice that they never think of fighting each other?"

He seemed a little reluctant to speak about the results of that art of fighting, and when he spoke I understood why. For there was a note of deep and troubled sadness in his voice.

"France," he said to me then, "is broken and destroyed by the war. There is no intellectual life. There is no impulse in art. There is no revolutionary intelligence in the working classes. There is no culture left. But after all, the war was not the worst thing. The war was not a deliberate crime. It was something that flowed out of the conditions of European life. The destruction of Lille was in a deep sense involuntary. The Treaty of Versailles was a *voluntary* destruction of civilization. That was the crime!

"French civilization depends upon European civilization," he added, "and there will be no civilization in Europe until the Treaty of Versailles is revised."

Such were his solemn and wise thoughts . . . but after I had said good-bye he called me back from the door.

"You mustn't go away with those gloomy things in your mind," he said. "Come back, and let's indulge in a little hope!"

And so I came back, and we talked more, and more cheerfully, about what France might become if there were any intelligence in her working classes, if there were any leisure for art and literature and for larger thoughts about social problems.

I had brought with me a copy of his book, *Le Lys Rouge*, in the hope that he might autograph it for me. By chance, he and his two friends had been discussing a volume of his in identical binding that had not yet appeared. When I whisked out my book, he mistakenly thought, in the linguistic haze in which we were operating, that I had picked up the volume they were discussing. His "Oh no, Monsieur!" while still tinted with an effort to be polite, was naturally astonished, and inwardly, I suppose, horrified.

I managed to summon enough nouns and verbs, and a preposition or two, to explain his mistake, and I added:

"*Je suis Américain, oui, mais je ne suis pas tout à fait barbare!*"

It was his turn to be embarrassed, and to make it up, he wrote in my *Lys Rouge* more cordially than he had any reason to: "A mon cher confrère, Max Eastman."

I managed to put together an article about him and about my

impressions of his countrymen, and sent it to Norman Hapgood as I had promised. I knew well it could not be published in *Hearst's International*, but I hoped it might persuade Norman to bid a friendly good-bye to my thousand dollars. The magazine had expired when we met again, and he never mentioned the subject.

My reputation as editor of a magazine containing the works of great American artists got me a ticket, which American millionaires could not buy, to the Quat'z Arts ball, and I was able to satisfy my childish curiosity as to what an "orgy" is like. This survival of the once-religious heathen jamborees, rutty, drunken and licentious, driven by the Bible out of respectable Christendom, was—and for all I know still is—permitted annually to the art students of Paris. For one night in a year, the streets were given recklessly over to their libidinous pranks and shenanigans. The various "art clubs," some invented for the occasion, paraded the town in costumes, or lack of costumes, that no other police force in the world would tolerate. I was bronzed all over to represent an American Indian and had the pleasure of marching down the Boulevard St. Germain, across the Place de la Concorde, and through the principal thoroughfares of Paris like the last of the Mohicans through the forest with nothing on but a jockstrap. I cannot describe the all-night orgy which followed in a dance hall except to say that everything took place which I cannot here describe. These spring-time carousals were, indeed, the old pagan "fertility rites" in their full glory of abandon, but even more ingeniously licentious because infertility rather than fertility was the sole practical concern.

In contrast with this perpetration of frivolity, I remember a gloomy dinner and a dismal evening of conversation with my correspondent on the *Clarté* question, Henri Barbusse. He was the most somber, the most heart-darkening creation, next to a hearse with black horses, that I ever encountered. Tall beyond all probability for a Frenchman, thin and angular, black-browed with a black mustache, he looked like Paganini—a cadaver of Paganini. He wished to greet me cordially, but had no smile with which to do it. He told me that in the army the *poilus* had given him as a *soubriquet* the name of the leading funeral parlor in Paris, but even in telling that joke on himself he could not dredge up a smile.

There was nothing left, it seemed, of our disagreements. Indeed I judge he was already overconverted into a fanatical "Marxist," and was well launched on his career of mixing to order a dry pabulum of circulars and manifestoes, trying to lure "literature" into the Communist

Party corral, obliterating in the effort every trace of the rare gift of metaphoric utterance he had possessed. Never, I think, was a world-famous fountain of imaginative language more completely stopped up and dried at the source by an idea.

A more gracious and growing figure that my revolutionary editorship introduced me to in Paris was Pierre Monatte, an intellectual leader and kindly teacher of the syndicalists. His essays in *La Vie Ouvrière*, and subsequently—even up to the date of his death, 1960—in its successor, *La Révolution Prolétarienne*, introduced a literary charm into the French labor movement that has had few parallels in other countries. He was then defending the Bolsheviks as I was, but with a mind free from political dogma—saved from it, perhaps, only by the antipolitical dogma of the syndicalists. His bright brown eyes, high wise forehead, and sly urbane humor, formed, at any rate, a relieving contrast to the somber fanaticism of Barbusse. Although we did not communicate for thirty or more years, and I have ceased to see any hope of a more free society in the prosecution of the proletarian revolution, I still subscribe to his magazine and still think of him as a departed friend.

I must add to this sketch of the people and pleasures that delayed me on my way to Moscow, that I was engaged in a romantic love affair with the French language and, smiling amid the wreckage I made of the language, with a teacher named Renée. She was slight, blonde, with largely wondering eyes like a doll, but with a most undoll-like flexibility in perceiving life's values, and a hard, brave courage in seeking them out. She was interested in psychic experiences, and asked me one day if I thought I could hypnotize her. She also asked if she could trust me not to take advantage of the power a hypnotist is said to have over his subject. I said yes to both questions, rather recklessly, but managed to make good. Afterward I described the experience in a French poem which I called "Magnétisme," and which I preserve as a memento of this twofold love for a girl and a language. The poem was its only fruit, although it lasted, in a distant, intermittent, unfulfilled and unperfected fashion, for another forty years. I mean that Renée and I remained friends, and I remained in touch—at times quite closely, and again at a disheartening distance—with the French language.

Chapter 48

THE PILGRIMAGE TO MOSCOW

Among the friends I made in Paris, two charming and important ones were Albert Rhys Williams and Josephine Herbst. Important, because Albert like me was on his way to Moscow, Josephine was going with him as far as Berlin, and they invited me to go along. Albert was an ex-Christian minister, who had found a temporary refuge from the exigencies of his faith in the old *Masses* and the *Liberator*. Becoming a free-lance reporter and world-wanderer, he had by chance arrived in Moscow just in time for the October revolution. That monumental event had overpowered and enraptured him, lifting him so out of himself, that, like St. Paul after the trip to Damascus, he became an apostle, dedicating his life, or as much of it as he could spare from a certain princely leisure that he liked better, to preaching the gospel of Lenin and Stalin to the unillumined. Albert was a jovial and delightful companion, if you did not rely on him for acts of judgment which might disturb his faith in the eternal and unchanging values that descended into the world in October 1917. And Josephine Herbst was possessed of gaiety, kindness and a fanciful humor that was inexhaustible. She became subsequently a successful novelist—rather switched out of her own character, I think, by the influence of Hemingway—but she was then in the stage of being urged to write books by friends who delighted in her humorous and poetic letters.

We went to Germany together, and finding ourselves, thanks to the inflation that was ruining the country, fabulously rich, we paused a few weeks in Bad Homburg to enjoy the life lived by millionaires. We stayed at the sumptuous hotel patronized by King Edward VII as Prince of Wales, dining on the best viands and sipping the most expensive wines, at an average cost of twenty cents a day. While we were in the hotel it was a lark, and I made tremendous progress in my new adventure of learning German. But when we walked the streets and saw the acute and sickly misery of the people, our holiday joy became mixed with shame. We hired a car finally—it cost us a few dollars—and fled from our guilty feelings toward Berlin. I stopped off in the Hartz mountains to pour the rest of me into my poem, "The Battlefields," joining them in Berlin after it was finished. Albert and I then made our preparations for the trip to Moscow.

I had arranged with Chicherin in Genoa to have a visa ready for me at the Soviet Embassy in Berlin; his secretary had shown me a reply from the Embassy confirming this. But time had passed, and the functionary now in charge turned out to be a snarling desk-dog who deemed it his duty, as representing a proletarian government in a capitalist country, to be as surly as possible. He looked me over and decided that either the cut of my clothes or my manners were essentially bourgeois—as indeed they both were—and denied that he had any authorization to admit me into the Promised Land. I do not know how long he might have found it necessary to demonstrate the class struggle in the privacy of his office, had I not happened to meet Chicherin himself in the hallway just before entering, and been pleased to find that he remembered me.

"I will wait here while you telephone Comrade Chicherin," I said to the functionary.

The result was not only a passport, but a passport bearing the magic word *byezplatno*, the literal translation of which is "without payment" but which meant in effect: "In spite of his good manners and the cut of his clothes this guy is all right."

Perhaps nobody remembers now the almost tremulous circumspection with which one prepared in those days for a plunge into Soviet Russia. Political hostility had painted the country as brimming with typhus, cholera, malaria, dysentery, jungle fever, bubonic plague, sleeping sickness, dying sickness, every human woe and affliction known to the textbooks of medicine. Albert and I were both inclined to get sick on a slight provocation, and imagine we were sick on a slighter one. We had the motives, but not the constitution, of the adventurer. Moreover, my friends had been telling me for three years that it would "do me good" to go to Soviet Russia, and I always know when my friends tell me something will do me good that I'm in for a bad time. So we went to the Koch Institute in Berlin and had all the up-to-date antitoxins injected into our veins. We made a tour of the drug stores and bought all the remedies and preventives that two morbid imaginations could dream up. Coming home with these bundles we met a little biology professor from the University of Texas who was taking to the Socialist fatherland a series of prophylactic cultures, the gift of some medico-philanthropic society to which he belonged. He had an even more nightmarish idea of the miasmic jungle into which he was venturing than we had. He told us that all our drugs and concoctions were no good. In order to protect ourselves against the numerous diseases then raging in the land of our dreams, we would have to have a series of carefully compounded powders—eight of them, if I remember rightly —which we must mix together and hang in little linen bags from certain nicely calculated points of our anatomy. There were different powders for each of these several points of attack, and the mixtures had to be renewed every morning as it was only the fresh contact of the powders which produced the peculiar odors and emanations calculated to repel the onslaughts of all these various tribes of invisible malignities.

Josephine actually made the little white bags, and I found mine in my suitcase the next morning. But when we looked up the professor for specifications on the powders, we learned that, having finished his own prophylaxis, he had chartered a plane and taken flight for Moscow. The thought of him winging through the heavens with all those tiny chimes of odoriferousness tinkling about him, was too much for our sense of humor. We threw away most of our medical supplies, and took the train for Moscow with little but a toothbrush and a change of clothes. I did have with me, however, two little red dictionaries, Russian-English and English-Russian, a condensed Russian grammar, and a volume of Lermontov's poems, in communion with which I proceeded to forget the German language as fast as I could.

Traveling always contains disillusionments for a poet, and it was the poet rather than the politico in me that set out on that journey. Things excite a poet in idea, and he wants them still to be ideas after they have become facts. I felt this disillusionment very often on my pilgrimage to Moscow. Only two things on the way to the Russian border seemed very different from a ride on the Erie Railroad. One was the sharpness of the borderline between East Prussia and Lithuania. On the German side green fields, gardens rich with glossy vegetables, roadways trim and white, roofs a fresh yellow-red, and every human being hard at work. On the other, everything gone to rack, fields gray with aged weeds, gardens half cultivated, roads meandering and made of mud, roofs all sagging in or missing altogether, having been blown up at the beginning of the war ten years before. Albert and I took a little walk in Lithuania while our baggage was being examined, a twenty-minute walk at three o'clock in the afternoon, and I saw four people asleep. One was falling unhappily out of a broken hammock; another had thrown himself away in a vacant lot among tin cans and burdocks; a third lay in his wagon at the side of the road behind a horse that had stopped going; a fourth was leaning against a tree opposite his front gate, having given himself the task of keeping a pig from going through the gate. I've never had much doubt about the existence of national characteristics since I crossed that border between Germany and Lithuania where they were as plain to be seen as the colors on a map.

Having to wait two days in Riga for our train to Moscow, Albert and I took a steamboat down a marshy river to "The Strand"—a wide gray wind-rippled beach with languid half-briney waves running up on it, and a great many—too many—sun-tanned girls and women bathing there. They all seemed to speak Russian, and we surmised they were the wives and daughters of Tsarist aristocrats killed or ruined in the civil war. Their soft tones sent me back to my Russian books with renewed enthusiasm—and here I must tell a brief tale with a moral.

It takes only a few hours to learn a foreign alphabet, and I was already able when we reached Riga to look up words in my little Russian dictionary. Instead of wasting my patience on paradigms and memory exercises, I picked out a short poem by Lermontov and began at once to translate it. Having found the words in the dictionary, I would of course have to guess their cases, tenses, and so on. This I managed with a little help from Russian passengers, and by the time I reached Moscow I had made an English poem of Lermontov's "Utyos," which I called "The Mountain." It was published years later with other translations of Lermontov that I made after I had learned the language, and even to Russian-Americans it did not seem inferior. The moral of this slightly immodest tale is—and it is often overlooked—that the language on the receiving end is the one a translator must have in command. He must be primarily a writer, not a reader. Perhaps a profounder moral is that no poem is ever really translated.

After a night in a comfortable hotel by the sea, we went back to Riga to secure our tickets to Moscow from the Russian Embassy. The passport functionary here was as gentle as a lamb, and I judge it was due to that magic word *byezplatno* on our passports. We had to wait three hours while our railroad tickets were "drawn up," but when we got them we saw that they called for a seat in the "diplomatic coach," a comforting piece of news, for we had been overfed with tales of the "filth and congestion" of these trains to Moscow, and how the passengers were "herded in like animals." There was no filth or congestion on our train. The third-class cars, to be sure, had no upholstery, the berths were made of wood, and as there were two upper ones, the effect was like shelves in a pantry. It is a little funny to see people going to bed on shelves like dishes, but, come to remember, in American coaches, unless they are Pullmans, you can't go to bed at all. So here again things were not so different as they were supposed to be. "The idea that they are herded in like animals," I wrote in my notebook, "is probably due more than anything else to the fact that they are animals. Speech is the main thing that distinguishes man from the less cerebral species, and when you can't understand his speech it is easy to ignore the distinction."

Our own compartment was so luxurious that it troubled my proletarian faith a little—a big square space like a two-story room, with a table between the beds, and a space like a haymow upstairs. Clean white bed linen was to be had at a small price, and a friendly young host in a workman's shirt came in every once in a while to know if we wouldn't like some tea. We belonged quite obviously to an upper class—a political, not a pecuniary one, to be sure, and I tried to settle for that. In this I was aided by the absence of a uniform on the young man, and his easygoing manners. Thus I was able, when we crossed the Soviet border, to feel the emotions that my faith expected of me.

It was night when, reaching the border, we drew up beside a little shanty occupied by Red Guards. An earnest and kindly-faced boy of high-school age came through the dark car examining our passports by the light of a stable lantern. The Red Guards, in long dust-colored coats, stood sentry at intervals along each side of the train. I could see them dimly out there, a colonnade of tall silent figures disappearing into the dark. I was deeply moved—so deeply that it disturbed me when some comrades in a neighboring compartment began to sing the "International." To me the ceremonial expression of an emotion, its socialization, so to speak, is unpleasant. I wanted to be alone with my feelings. I wanted to savor in my own way the thought that those soldiers were defending a new and more just and beautiful world, a world in which the workingmen instead of the rich men ruled. The sounding bugles, the parades, the public banquets, the pomp and ceremonials of sovereignty would all be in honor of the poor.

A sharp little whistle tooted outside the window, the engine gave a big round hollow puff, and we moved on into the mystery I had come to explore. We went about three miles, and then came to a stop by a little way station alongside a pond. I went to bed while we were still standing there, expecting to wake up the next morning in Moscow. After a sound sleep I woke up the next morning and went swimming in that pond. What woke me was the familiar strains of "The International," being rendered by a soprano chorus outside my window. I pushed aside the curtain and saw a procession of six female section hands, young, rotund, ruddy, and with powerful bare legs and feet, carrying a railroad tie over their shoulders and singing that song as they walked. It might have been the dream of a feminist and revolutionist—or perhaps a piece of propaganda. But it was neither; it was a simple and natural fact. The "International" had become a folksong in Russia; in Russia people sing when they work or march together; and in Russia women do all those heavy kinds of work which American women are taught in infancy that they cannot do.

It was late afternoon when our train finally got under way, and my great experience began. Again it was, to the adventuring poet in me, a disillusioning experience. Rolling along through green farms and forests, I could not feel that I was in any strange or distant place. I was happy to be moving and happy to be at home on the earth. But what a familiar earth! The same black baby cedars dotting the open meadow, and gathering in elderly groups at the fence corners as they do in New Jersey and along the shores of the Hudson; the white birches among them like ghosts of graceful ladies, taller than in America, but of the same delicacy; the rich purple-brown earth plowed up and combed for the fall planting; the lines of the harrow standing soft and sharp in the slanting light; the shocks of wheat turned upside down and tied at the top, like rows of demure nuns in wide skirts; the slim aspen saplings along the brooks shaking their leaves to make them glitter; the horses and cows, and the white-faced calf who shook his head mischievously and mocked the fixed motion of the train with a series of cavorting leaps. It was all well known and dear to me. Some children were gathering berries along a fence as we passed by—eager-bodied, peering among the bushes. They looked around without straightening up, their plump cheeks thoroughly smeared with purple.

A big surprise came, however, when we pulled into the stations—so many stations, and such enormous, lively, eager, excited crowds of vigorous people pacing back and forth on their platforms. I do not know what I had been expecting—whether the same, dull, worried, wearied-out world I had seen in France and Germany, or whether something worse, a starved and half-expiring people—or perhaps only a few people scattered here and there in a vast tract of woods and wilderness. What I found was a land brimful of people and a people brimful of energy. Many of them, to be sure, were dressed in rags. Indeed, a very large number looked as though they had just stepped out of a meal bag—or what is nearer the truth, had just stepped into one. But even the poorest looked healthy and had plump cheeks and a surprising vigor of movement.

At a press conference in Genoa, when I had asked Lloyd George why the Allies did not send a commission into Russia and *find out* how much she was able to pay, he said: "You can go into that unhealthy country if you want to." It got him a big laugh, but now it seemed a joke on him. No one traveling from Western Europe into Russia in that year 1922 could have failed to receive the impression I did of an abrupt step-up in vitality and health. It was like passing from age to youth. Although many have agreed privately with me about this, I have never read it in a book or article. And yet it may have some relevance to the political history of our times. Biologically, the Russians seemed to be on the upswing, the West by comparison in decline.

As we approached Moscow I learned from Albert that the amiable young proletarian who had been making us so comfortable would be expecting a correspondingly generous tip. In the mood of exaltation I had been enjoying since we passed those Red Guards on the border, this hurt my feelings deeply. It was one of the big steps down. There was no tipping in my utopia; no such indecent exposure of class relations was tolerable. Obsequious hope on the one side, a free choice between benevolence and meanness on the other—what place has that in the "classless society?" Albert laughed at my naïve idealism. A cynical humor about the entire human race, combining oddly with his devout adoration of the Bolsheviks, was one of Albert's most engaging charms. It is a charm one sometimes finds in priests and parsons who officiate in an ideal world but live in a real one. I learned later to enjoy this trait in Albert, but at that point my recoil was painful. I must truly have believed, in some part of my nature, that this diplomatic coach was taking me to paradise.

My first feeling in Moscow, where we arrived on August 23, 1922, was a kind of disappointment to find it so much like any other big city—Cleveland or Baltimore or Minneapolis—so immense and noisy, so jammed full of streetcars and trucks and cars and horses and people, rumbling and roaring and chattering and earnestly proceeding this way and that, with no more reason than the earth has for going so fast around the sun.

But that was, I judge, still the poet in me, forever disillusioned that the real continues to be real. Had I been in a more political phase, I might have found weighty significance in the fact that Bolshevik Moscow's mode of life in 1922 seemed familiar to me. The first attempt at large-scale socialism—military communism, as they afterward chose to call it—had been abandoned in March 1921, and a large measure of competitive trade restored under what was called the New Economic Policy. The discarded force of "personal interest" had thus been in operation eighteen months when I arrived, and the whole country, even those parts of it recently devastated by the great famine, was in a state of excited revival. What I saw in Russia was not socialism in embryo, but free enterprise reborn. But I was in no mood to realize this fact. I took all the good things I saw, and the familiar things, as proof that the collectivist experiment was in the main succeeding. Socialism *did* work; life went right on just the same! This first impression quieted the sober critic within me, and colored with a too utopian joy the experiences that I am now going to relate. How ignorantly wrong it was, may be inferred from the following remarks by Victor Serge, who was in Russia both before and after the NEP was adopted:.

> The NEP, though it had been in existence only a few months, was giving marvelous results. You could tell the difference from week to week; food was easier to get; there was less speculation; the restaurants were opening their doors. More incredible still they were selling pastries, edible pastries, mind you, at a ruble apiece. . . . You had the feeling that money, dethroned, had been restored to its kingdom.*

If these lines had fallen under my eyes when I arrived in Moscow, you would have found much more wisdom than you will find in the pages which follow.

* From "Vignettes of NEP," to be found in Julien Steinberg's *Verdict of Three Decades*, p. 136.

Chapter 49

HOW I LEARNED RUSSIAN

We were driven from the station straight to the Lux Hotel where a room had been reserved for us. The Lux was an old second-class hotel, vulgarly ornate, fronting on the busy Tverskaia thoroughfare, reserved, after its confiscation by the government, for delegates to the Communist International and close friends of communism. Bill Haywood, the old iron-fisted head of the IWW, soft now and sorry-hearted, was living there. He had jumped his bail two years before, and made his way underground to this land of what he tried to hope were his dreams. But his dreams were of a free society of workingmen, in which politicians, even of the democratic socialist stripe, would not exist, and not much hard thinking would be done. Lenin's powerful mind and party-dominated state was as alien to him as the Russian language. The party tried to use him, and he tried faithfully to find a place of service, but what could he do? He was homesick for America and for the prestige enjoyed there by his childlike faith in what the One Big Union was going to do. He withered away as the state he despised was supposed to, and died in miserable idleness.

The Lux was a free and easy place in those days, not hedged around by passes and police officers, not infested by spies and informers, and stinking of suspicion, as it later grew to be. But it was infested by bedbugs. Albert and I waged a bloody war on them during the few days we spent in that hotel. We called them "the Red army," and left some fifty on the battlefield when we moved out.

Through some sort of wire-pulling, Albert had secured rooms in the "Sugar Palace," the governmental house across the river from the Kremlin. It had been the sumptuous home of a family who made millions trading in sugar, and what remained of its sumptuousness—the beds, at least, and the chairs that were too heavy to carry off—was being carefully preserved for the comfort of visiting diplomats and high-up guests from the "bourgeois" world. Albert and I enjoyed all the privileges accorded to these despised emissaries of capitalism without losing those accorded to us as esteemed friends of the proletariat. These privileges included luxurious sleeping-rooms and three meals a day—not too nourishing, but the best that Moscow could produce. It was an anomalous and unfair position, and no doubt played an unnoticed part in promoting my eagerly formed conviction that— barring a few painful details which I succeeded in pushing to the fringe of perception—all was well with the proletarian revolution.

Resting in this conviction, I turned my thoughts from politics altogether, and gave myself to the joy of making friends with a new people and a new language. After two or three days spent pecking away at Pushkin and Lermontov the way we used to at Homer and Virgil in college, I decided to plunge in and really learn the Russian language. This gave me an extra reason for going up to the Commissariat of Foreign Affairs in search of the friend I had made in Genoa, Eliena Krylenko. Although wearing in my thoughts an aura woven of tearful laughter and silvery moonlight, I found her clad in a prosaic brown shirtwaist and hard at work in front of a filing case with a bunch of long-shaped papers in her hand. She was excited to see me—I could tell by the tremor in her voice—but she could mix laughter with tremors as well as with tears. Her welcome, though warm, was light-hearted and unassuming. "She is everything that one could love," I thought. But I did not want to love. I wanted to learn Russian.

I did, in fact, take a few lessons with Eliena, and found her the most quick-witted, kind, and blithesome teacher imaginable, but she led a busy life and the lessons were not frequent. Besides her secretarial work, she was studying at the Moscow Art Theatre—wanting to be an actress—and doing most of the dinner-getting for an equally busy mother and aunt and cousin and sister. I never saw anyone who could do so much, so swiftly, so *gladly*, and without nervous tension or the remotest thought of getting tired. My mother could *do* as much, but she compensated for it with sick-headaches and moods of melancholy. Eliena flashed along through life like a comet on its course. Lessons are solemn things usually, but ours were gales of laughter. And besides this mental stimulation, she began, as we drew closer in friendship, to supplement the rather short rations of the Sugar Palace by bringing me across town every evening a bowl of rice with raisins, keeping it warm under a fur coat. When I got home to America, I would amuse my audiences by saying that I gained thirty pounds during my first six months in starving Russia, and that was literally true, though not exactly an index to the living standards of the country.

It was not easy to abandon such a friendship and so much hilarious education. But I needed more than once-in-a-while lessons. I needed to talk Russian all day long. Albert could speak the language after a fashion, but his vocabulary was meager and his pronunciation execrable. He needed practice as badly as I did, and we consulted together how best to get it. The first step was, of course, to get away from our English-speaking friends into "the Russian Land." Since it was still summer, we judged that the Russian land would probably yield the most pleasure where it borders the sea, and for that reason we took the train south to Yalta—a place of cloudy and too political repute today, but still brightly famous then as a Slavic Riviera. We chose Yalta because the Tsar used to have a summer palace there, and because Rakovsky had said when we were standing on a balcony over the blue Mediterranean at Santa Margherita: "If you think this is beautiful, you ought to see Yalta!" We felt that where the Tsar and a leader of the revolution agreed we had something that was in all probability true.

Rakovsky was now head of the Bolshevik government of the Ukraine—president, that is, of its Council of Commissars. He had certainly not been elected to that office by the liberated workers and peasants of the region, none of whom had ever seen him before, but such reflections were not bothering me then. I was only too happy to be invited to dine with him and his rosy-cheeked, robust, and lovely-mannered wife in their house in Kharkov on the way south. The house was small, the furniture ill-matched and inadequate, the dinner austerely frugal, for Rakovsky was one of those Bolsheviks who remembered the dictum of Lenin that the income of a state official should not exceed that of a well-paid workingman. He was one of the "idealists," as William Reswick called them, and much as all Marxists despise that term, I do not know how else to distinguish the Rakovskys, Rykovs, Bukharins, from the hard-boiled type who regarded high living as the legitimate loot of those who had led a victorious revolution. I remember, on the other hand, the genteel solicitude with which he asked an aide to find Albert and me a lodging where we could have comfort and privacy, in case we found occasion for a little *ukazhivanie*. It means flirting or love-making. I also remember how, after dinner, when in the course of an argument Rakovsky got around within range of a window, his wife jumped up in anxious haste and pulled down the shade. Heading a Bolshevik government in the Ukraine was a hazardous trade just then. I also remember that no "comfort and privacy" was to be provided in Kharkov, no matter how high up the order came from. We slept on a bare bedspring and a broken-backed couch in a room about as suitable for *ukazhivanie* as a looted cow barn.

In Yalta we found a small white hotel fronting the sea, neatly kept, and in American money immoderately cheap. We selected rooms remote from each other, and in deliberate isolation, entered upon our solemn enterprise of having a good time learning Russian. I have my own rather celebrated system for learning foreign languages which I put into successful operation in Yalta—so successful that within a month and a half I was expressing my inmost passions in Russian poetry. I hope the reader will be patient if, before describing the details of this particular application, I recall the general principles of my system.

The first thing to do is to go to the capital of the country where the language you choose to learn is spoken and buy a grammar, two little red dictionaries, and a railroad ticket. The railroad ticket should take you as far away from the capital as possible, clear out of the sound of your own language, and preferably to a summer resort. The reason for this is that you are going to have a good time and you need company.

On the train, on the way to your summer resort, you have some hard work to do. It is the only work called for by my system, and it has to be done thoroughly. You have to learn the name in the language under consideration for noun, adjective, adverb, verb, participle, conjunction, pronoun, and preposition. And if you do not know in your own language just what these wonders are, you have to find out. And then you have to learn to say "What does that mean?" and "What is the word for this?" and a few handy remarks like: "Do you speak English?" "Do you speak Italian?" "It's too bad." "Let's take a walk."

With that equipment you go into the dining room of the principal hotel in your summer resort and pick out your teacher. You may do this quite boldly for, if you have equipped yourself as I direct, you have a power to ensnare that teacher which reaches beyond the charms of your personality. Moreover it is advisable to have an eye to her physical beauties, for you are going to spend a good deal of time gazing on them in comparative silence.

After dinner you may go and lean against a pillar, or the railing of a little footbridge in the garden, or somewhere—I need not be too specific about this—and when she comes by, you will say in your poor broken tongue with a forlorn expression, "Mademoiselle, do you speak English?" When she says "No," you will heave a sigh and say, "Do you speak French?" At a second "No" your expression will become disconsolate, and you will say, "Do you speak German?" At a third "No" you show real consternation, and offer to speak Italian, or Bohemian, or Chinese, or what you will. If God is with you, she will decline all these offers, and you will find that she is at once seriously distressed over your plight, and in a somewhat humbled condition as to her own talents. You will find, if I am not mistaken, that you are already taking a walk with her, and you may assume that her next statement is, "Too bad you haven't a Russian dictionary," or something to that effect. At the sound of these words—no matter how bad they sound— you will produce your two little red books, and hand her the one marked "Russian-English."

Here the work, properly so called, comes to an end. She will be very curious to see what the words in your language look like, and she will examine the little red book and pretty soon point to a word, probably the word "hot," or something equally uninteresting under ordinary circumstances. Under these circumstances it acquires the charm of an incantation. It begins to open just by something less than the shadow of a hair's breadth the gate of a possible romance.

And so, in a gentle fever of delight, you look up the word "too" in your dictionary, and you say, "Too hot?"

It is one of the signs of our human kinship, and a blessing we rarely pause to appreciate, that in widely separated regions, however the words may change, the vocal inflections retain the same meaning. You do not have to learn how to melodize a question in Russian, or a doubt, or a suspicion, or a declaration, or a caress. If you did, this industrious romance would probably run on the rocks in the first three minutes.

To your question, "Too hot?" she will no doubt answer rapidly and at some length, forgetting your limitations. Perhaps she will say: "Not if we could find a shady tree to sit under."

She will be a little shocked at your inability to grasp this simple proposition. A flicker of impatient contempt will cross her face. She has forgotten about your magnanimous offer to speak English, French, German, Italian or Bohemian. She has forgotten that there are any such languages. She just primitively and quite properly feels that a person who can't talk is a fool. And here you must bring forward the second part of your equipment. But use it gently, use it sparingly, for it is possible the experience may be too bitter, and her pride not strong enough to hold her to the task.

You may, I trust, have been able to isolate one word in that insane rush of syllables that came out of her mouth. Look for it in your dictionary, and while you are looking, murmur somewhat abstractedly in her language: "Is that a preposition or a participle?"

You will see that look of contempt upon her features give place to a flush and a catching of breath, and your companion will wrinkle her brows and lean over your shoulder to watch you find the word in your dictionary, and her hair will brush your cheek helpfully, and her voice be all gentle sympathy as she says, "Why, now, let's see, that must be—there it is! You understand?"

By this time no doubt you will have arrived at the shady tree, and at something far better than understanding, a consciousness of your power. You are in the peculiar position of knowing more than your teacher about the very subject she is going to teach. And if you employ your power with delicacy, as I have advised, so that she does not either run away in fright as from an intellectual monster, or in a fit of mad pride buy a grammar and learn her own language, you can retain this position of lofty helplessness throughout the duration of the romance. For at every stage of the proceeding your mind will know more about the language than hers, her knowledge being in her tongue.*

Although in the form of an abstract dissertation, those words describe pretty accurately what happened to me in Yalta. My teacher's name was Nina; she was beautifully formed, brown-haired, her features keenly chiseled, her eyes almost too alertly bright. She was twenty-seven years old, the wife of an engineer in Kharkov, and was taking a holiday at the seaside during his absence on a long construction job. . . .

That sounds as though our romance were furtive, but nothing could be less true to the quality of it—or of the times in which it flourished. Although there were disputes among the party leaders about the principle involved—should the revolution follow the example of Marx or Engels?—among the intelligentsia in general, the restrictions upon freedom of choice in sex relations were much relaxed in those begin-

* My system was set forth more completely in Mencken's *American Mercury* and republished in my book, *Art and the Life of Action.*

nings of the "new world" of socialism. No ghost of the Seventh Commandment, no wraith of a marriage vow, not even, I think, the memory of a talk about fidelity between Nina and her husband, haunted the sky-covered scenes of our embraces. The October revolution, whatever it was going to do for the proletariat, had already done some liberating for the cultured classes. It had cut down a number of artificial barriers between the beautiful and the good—one of them the habit of putting on clothes to go swimming. It was true at the time, and startling enough so that Will Rogers made it the title of a travelogue: *There Is Not a Bathing Suit in Russia*. There would be a space of a hundred-odd feet between the parts of a shoreline allotted by mutual consent to men and to women. But if a couple, or a small group of differing sexes, strolled up the beach to bathe together it caused no commotion. At home I had been a little squeamish about this kind of liberation when indulged in by radical friends on sequestered beaches. I wanted all to myself the nakedness of my own girl at least, and in general I thought this custom deprived life of some delightful excitements. But here—in the new land of freedom—it became symbolic of a kind of candid realism, a living in the truth, that I thought the abolition of class status might bring into the whole world.

At any rate, this Garden-of-Eden-like freedom, the absence of both prudishness and prurience, fitted well into the natural beauty of that coast of the Crimea. It was a dry and savage coast in comparison with Italy at Santa Margherita, but no less beautiful. There was rock and sand at the peaks of the high mountains, giving a gray austere color and a sense of still space in the daytime, and in the evening those sculptured shadows that seem softer the sharper they are. It was like California at the top, like the wild hard West, but at the bottom it was tropically rich. The sea rolled lazy pebbles musically on a warm shore, and innumerable acres of imperial vineyards sloped gorgeously down to the edge of the bluff above it. Their rows were clean, and their leaves rusty or scarlet or light-green or yellow or black-purple, according to the kind and the degree of ripeness of the clusters of cloudy-transparent luminous round cool grapes that were hanging under them. These vineyards were high-fenced and patrolled by Red Guards as carefully as they had been by the Tsar's soldiers, and it was still an adventure to steal any of the grapes. One day we asked a Red Guard whether he would shoot us if we took a few bunches. He glared at us ferociously, and then shouldered his rifle and marched away long enough to let us fill our hands full and go down over the bluff to the sea.

We used to walk far southward along the shore, beyond Livadia, I think, beyond the Tsar's estate, out of sight of all human life, and make love on the beach in the sunshine. Although married for nine years, Nina had not had the baby she longed for, and the answer seemed to flow from the mere logic of the beauty of our love when she asked me if I would give her one.

Those days in Yalta are among the happiest in my memory—an experience as far off from the adventure in desolation I had promised myself on taking the plunge into Russia as paradise from the life of man. Only once did the stark fact of political terror come to my attention. Two Red soldiers strode down the beach one day and picked up an innocuous-looking baldish, pot-bellied little merchant who had been sunning himself in benign relaxation in my vicinity. He walked back naked between the two burly soldiers, trailing a tiny white towel. I tried to turn away from that heart-piercing incident, and from all it implied—"After all, people get arrested everywhere"—and I must confess that I largely succeeded.

It was our purpose, Albert's and mine, to return to Moscow for the fifth anniversary of the October revolution, and the Fourth Congress of the Third International which was timed to coincide with it. Thus on a sadly resolute day in late October, we hired a team and driver and went straight up the face of the mountain peaks we had been admiring—not really straight, but on a zigzag road that rises steadily above Yalta for six hours without departing from it. The tropics dropped gradually away, the rich fragrant leaves and the luxurious surf became something small that I could see far off as though I imagined them. Around us a grim forest of gigantic pines roared softly in a cold northern wind. And then even those pines dropped away, and a scramble of crooked and laboring scrub oaks and gray weeds appeared—and then nothing but rocks. There was mist in the wind, and we could see far away and below us little ridiculous clouds floating out over the corrugated sea and pouring their shadows down on it. I laughed at the summery brightness of the sun on the backs of those clouds while a bleak autumn hurricane was roaring round our wagon, and I piled on my sweater and big winter coat to keep warm. A cold, wet gray fog poured across the summit like a flood of water, and the horses leaned forward against it with their heads down.

We were glad to descend again into the low-level plateau which forms the interior of the Crimea. Our driver took us to the home of a Tartar merchant, who gave us dinner and allowed us to sleep on the floor of his parlor for the night. In a burst of extra-genial hospitality, he offered us each a plate of well-aged rancid butter. Here I achieved a triumph over my too fastidious nervous system—not that I ate the butter, but I succeeded in eating something else while it was within smelling distance. Speaking again of national differences, what could exceed that between a man who laps up this dish with avid satisfaction and one to whom it is, even in imagination, an emetic?

My love for Nina and for her language blended into a poem which I kept making up in Russian all the way back to Moscow. I called it "Words," and in each stanza reminded her of the mood and circumstances in which she had taught me the name of some significant thing or emotion. Obviously it cannot be translated. I will just have to assure you it was a terrific poem, full of "star-tossing waves" and "rebel pulse-beats" and "passions" and "dangers" and dactyls and anapests and spondees and diaereses and amphibrachs and internal rhymes and alliterations—a plethora of alliterations. No poem was ever more sincere in its love for an experience and a language, the twin loves out of which all poetry is born.

Chapter 50

MEETING THE BIG CHIEFS

For favored visitors, it was a momentous event, that fifth anniversary of the October revolution followed by a Fourth Congress of the Communist International. It was an opportunity to hear Lenin and meet the great Bolsheviks, to see also the variegated assemblage of hard rebels from all countries who had been drawn to Moscow like fragments of steel to a magnet by the triumphant revolutionary power.

My interest in these events was enormous, but my joy in them was cooled by a small circumstance which to the fact-loving vein in my nature seemed ominous. The celebration was of the triumphant liberation of the "proletariat"—the toiling masses, that is, or in the language of those who despise them, "the populace." And yet from early morning on the day of the celebration, which was to consist of flag-flying and oratory on Red Square, not only the Square itself, but the whole surrounding section of the city, including a public park, was blocked off and denied to that same "populace" by guards mounted on horses and armed to the teeth with weapons of war. To my eye they were not distinguishable from the Cossacks of infamous memory. But that last was a poetic objection. What troubled me practically was their distance both in space and time from the actual celebration. I said to Albert:

"Since dawn this whole damned city has been locked up against the people to whom it belongs in order to celebrate their coming into possession of it."

Again he smiled at my naïveté. "This is Russia, remember, not America. It's the way things have always been done here."

So I cooled off, and remembered that this was Russia. But that was another considerable step down from my utopian exaltation. It was not the way things would be done if by "proletariat" the Bolsheviks meant the people comprised in that concept, and not just the concept. The whole Bolshevik revolution, I was to learn, was conducted by men living among ideas which, because they took the form of a metaphysical belief, did not have to be checked against facts. They were not celebrating the triumph of the proletariat, but the triumph of the idea of the proletariat.

That, however, is a subsequent reflection. I only felt indignant for a while, then folded the feeling away where it would not spoil my happy thoughts about the coming great society. The main part of the celebration was to be held in Petrograd, and the delegates to the Congress of the International were brought there from Moscow in trains decorated with revolutionary streamers, red flags and portraits of Lenin and Trotsky. Lines between party and nonparty were not sharply drawn in those days, and Albert and I went along with the delegates by a natural gravitation which no one resisted. We went along as friends and companions of the revolution. The train made whistle-stops along the line, and was welcomed by crowds of excited people, eager to see and hear from the foreign delegates. Karl Radek, who acted as a kind of head usher of the expedition, led them out on the platform, and introduced them with some witty and laudatory remarks. Each made a brief speech, and then Radek or one of his confreres would translate it. I noticed that while the speeches averaged about three minutes in length, the translations would often run to nine or ten. Evidently the Russians had their own ideas of what the foreigners ought to be saying. To outwit them, I retired into a corner with my two little red dictionaries and wrote out a short speech in Russian. By the time my turn came, I had learned it by heart. The surprise when I began to speak was complete, and the applause that greeted my first word, and every word thereafter, would have satisfied Demosthenes. Radek threw his arms around me in a great bear hug and the story of my prowess was printed in *Izvestia* the following day. It was better than a party card in gaining me entrée among the Bolshevik leaders, for they were themselves, with few exceptions, men of ardent intellectual culture. It both pleased and surprised them to see any one of these political tourists from other countries, delegate or not, doing a bit of hard work with his brains.

As I am depressed rather than exalted by parading crowds and public demonstrations, I missed the impassioned joy which others found in the Petrograd celebration. But I was, in my less gregarious way, happy to watch it. I found it uplifting to see what I still conceived to be the triumphant Russian people filling the vast square surrounding the Winter Palace, scene of the Bloody Sunday massacre and of so much else that symbolized the Tsar's cruel despotism—filling the square with triumphant oratory, and shouts for the heroes of the Workers' and Peasants' Republic. As always, I felt a bitter pathos in these bright eyes and fervid shouts—no reality can ever equal man's ever-springing hopes. But my confidence in Lenin's mind sustained me, and I believed that, however illusory might be the ultimate dream of communism, "progress toward liberty" was assured as never before.

Returning to Moscow I attended the opening session of the Fourth Congress of the International,* and made further acquaintance with the brilliant galaxy of revolutionaries who had gathered around Lenin. At one time or another, you could meet them all, seated among the delegates or strolling in the aisles and corridors between sessions. For they were still thinking in terms of world revolution then, and these meetings of the International were of primary strategic importance. "The Fourth World Congress reminds the workers of all countries that the proletarian revolution can never be victorious within a single country, but only in an international frame as a world proletarian revolution." So they spoke publicly in the resolutions of this congress, and so in their private conversations.

Felix Dzerzhinski, the revolution's Lord High Executioner, I did not meet, but only gazed at him with mingled horror and respect. This "Saint of Terror," as he appeared to those within the circle of the faith, was pale and slow-moving and held himself very level as he walked. He suggested a Chinese statue in porcelain. His image merges also with that of Lincoln Steffens, perhaps only because of the gray goatee, but Steffens' famous preachment that bad men are better than good, that we must abandon "old exploded ideas like right and wrong," would lead very nicely into the practice of murdering a few to keep the many in terror. The notion that Dzerzhinski was "bloodthirsty" is, however, entirely erroneous. He was chosen to head the Cheka† for the opposite reason. He had been a poet in his youth, and his tenderness toward subordinates was notorious. Nor was he, according to my information, exceptionally well-informed or astute. But he was, to quote Trotsky, "a man of tremendous will, passion, and high moral tension." You felt sure, as you observed him, that those traits might, with a different life story, have led him to martyrdom instead of murder. In general, it was the ideas they believed in, not their instincts, that distinguished Lenin's lieutenants from other consecrated men.

* It lasted from November 9 to December 15.
† Abbreviated name for the secret police—soon changed to GPU.

This was most obviously true in the case of Kamenev, a mild-eyed, soft-bearded gentlemanly humanitarian in aspect. In America he would probably have become the head of a settlement house. How he turned up among the Bolsheviks, instead of the Mensheviks, would make an interesting psychological study. Were his motives perhaps similar to those which brought me to my gospel of "hard-headed idealism"? I called on him once in his office in the city hall—he was president of the Moscow Soviet—but what we talked about I cannot remember. I only remember thinking that he was as little designed by nature to lead a revolution as I was.

His name is often linked with that of Zinoviev, the president of the International, mainly because they both opposed the seizure of power in October, and did so in a nonparty paper. Lenin in his "testament" felt obliged to warn the party that this act of apostasy "should not be held against them," but of course it was. Zinoviev had been for years so loyal and close a friend and intellectual companion of Lenin, that his standing against him on this question must have been a painful surprise. He was regarded by the other Bolsheviks as something of a coward, and perhaps the idea of becoming responsible for an insurrection against established government frightened him as it would you and me. At any rate, he was no hero in my eyes, and when he took his place on the rostrum as president of the International, I was merely curious. He was rather bean-shaped and was not vigorous in his bearing. No American school or college boy would have liked him. His manner was languid and his features sad and suggestive of a woman. Had he actually been a woman, he would have possessed a certain beauty. But that sorrowful languor was not attractive in a man, and his handshake was like receiving the gift of a flattened-out banana.

Stalin, whom I had never heard of, may have been among the visitors to this congress, but not often I think. He knew no foreign language, and suffered from a sense of inferiority among his highly educated colleagues. They, on the other hand, in part for the same reason, had no notion of his extraordinary acuity and force of character. He hovered in the background, thinking very steadily, I suppose, as all supreme political bosses and tyrants must, of the problems of personal power.

My friend Rakovsky turned up one morning with his lovely wife, and when he asked me where I had been I showed him a poem called "Yalta" which I had composed for Nina as a part of my homework in Russian. He gazed at me in amazement. "I've talked Russian all my life," he said, "but I couldn't do that!" And he passed it around for inspection by other members of the presidium. With all respect for the principle of organization, I believe that poem did more for my status among those pre-Stalin Bolsheviks than would my card of membership in the Workers' Party—which, so far as I can remember, I lost promptly and never showed to anybody.

Another more political episode lifted me out of the class of mere "sympathizers." I had an earnest criticism to make of the way the communist movement was being conducted in America—the place of honor being monopolized by Russian immigrants instead of native Americans. I wanted to impart this rather obvious piece of wisdom to someone in high command. The chance came one morning when I saw Trotsky sitting far over in the middle of a row of delegates. I recognized him, of course, from the cartoons with which the journals of the day were filled, though he was surprisingly unlike those cartoons. They gave him a fierce, nervous, high-strung, Mephistophelian character. But he sat there listening to what was going on with composed and quiet attention, his head high, his cheeks rosy, more like a carefully washed good boy in a Sunday School class than like Mephistopheles. During a pause in the proceedings, I summoned my small store of social and linguistic audacity, and slid along the row until I could introduce myself in French. Trotsky and Rakovsky were the closest of friends, and I think he already knew something about me. At any rate, he was very cordial, and when I said I would like to tell him a few things about the situation in America, he gave me an appointment the very next day at the War Office—the "Military Revolutionary Soviet."

Trotsky was certainly the neatest man who ever lead an insurrection. He was immaculate, and so was his office. We had tea together and some sort of breadstuff to go with it, and I remember the swift concern with which he brushed the crumbs from his desk as soon as we had finished. I remember my surprise at the largeness and pale-blueness of his eyes, and again his quietude. In press descriptions his eyes were always "flashing" fiercely, and he was lean, nervous, and excitable. Bob Minor's double-page cartoon in the *Liberator*, "The East Side Jew Who Conquered Europe," seemed almost a libel against this gracious person who listened with such courtesy to the bad French in which I wrestled forth my ideas. I told him, or tried to, that the self-importance and organizational dominance of Russian-Americans in the party councils, made it impossible to get an American revolutionary movement started.

"Though most of them were Mensheviks until October 1917," I

said, "they think they created the October revolution. You know the way a young rooster will crow in a loud falsetto voice because some hen who is old enough to be his grandmother has laid an egg."

The idea amused and interested Trotsky, and I remember one of his remarks verbatim:

"Mais nous sommes prêts à brûler quelques milliers de Russes afin de créer un vrai mouvement révolutionnaire Américain." (But we are ready to burn up a few thousand Russians in order to create a real American revolutionary movement.)

I was really out of touch with the American movement, and my picture of the situation, although still true as a social fact, was politically somewhat belated. The split between Americans and Russian-Americans had by that time been pushed aside by a split between the advocates of a legal party and those who wanted the party to remain underground. Besides painting my own picture, however, I made an appointment with Trotsky for two American delegates to the International, James Cannon and Max Bedacht, who brought him up to date on the factional dispute as then existing. In conversation with them—so they reported—Trotsky decided, and promised, to support the program of a legal party for America. (The limited result of this decision I have described on page 168.) If my report to Trotsky had any effect, it was to be found in a supplementary instruction which read:

> The immigrants who have migrated to America from Europe play an important part in the American labor movement. But it must not be for a moment forgotten that the most important task is to arouse the American workers out of their lethargy. The party must systematically and willingly assist American-born workers to play a leading part. . . .

As we parted, Trotsky asked me to put my ideas in a memorandum which he could show to Lenin. "Lenin will want to talk to you himself," he said, "but he isn't fully recovered from his illness yet, and I'm afraid that will have to be postponed."

Lenin's illness was the first of those cerebral hemorrhages which brought him to his death, and he never did recover. Thus I missed the prize of a personal contact with the man in whose head and heart I trusted (far more than in any proletariat) for the success of this experiment in socialized production. I did, however, attend on November 13 the session of the International at which Lenin spoke (it was, with one brief exception, his last speech) and I sat close enough to the platform so that my impression of his personality was vivid. In a note surviving from those days I described him as "the most powerful man I ever saw on the platform."

"I do not know how to define the nature of his power," I added, "except to say that he is a granite mountain of sincerity. His gestures are extraordinary in their variety and grace, but otherwise he is not distinguished-looking. He is a little bit funny-looking, perhaps, with his wide small eyes and broad nose and black-painted brows under a great bald head. I could almost think he was 'made-up' to look funny. But if a man ever walked across my vision that I would trust to the edge of doom, that is Lenin." It was not oratory exactly, I wrote, but something above and beyond that. "He is simple in his heart like a peasant who knows proverbs, but in his mind subtle and mighty. And this you feel while he is talking. You feel that he is all there for you—you are receiving the whole of the man."

I can see still how he walked briskly up to the tribune amid roars of applause like a conflagration, pulled a big bluish-white handkerchief out of his pocket and cleaned his nose vigorously and thoroughly in the face of that applause, bending an ear meanwhile to discuss some matter of notes and papers with his secretary, turning occasionally to the audience to see if they weren't getting through with the noise, taking up a more elaborate question with his secretary, and so on, until the lull came, and with no salutation he began speaking in brisk, earnest terms about the objective situation we had come there to discuss. I remember only one thing he said, and that because it fell in so well with my high conception of his wisdom. He criticized a resolution that had been adopted by the congress on the ground that it was "too Russian." Seeing that this startling remark needed elucidation, he added with a laugh:

"For one thing it is so long that nobody but a Russian would read it!"

He continued to laugh a little at the memory of that remark after he had begun to say something else. Both the remark and the manner of it delighted me.

I was undoubtedly in a state of Pindaric rapture, due both to my still unqualified admiration for his mind, and my innate disposition toward hero worship, for he was speaking German and I did not continuously understand what he was saying. Moreover the blood was not flowing freely through his brain. He lived only fourteen months longer, and physicians who performed an autopsy expressed surprise that he had been able to think at all during the last two years of his life. Russians who had heard him speak in his robust days were conscious of a "weakness" or "hesitance" in his diction on this occasion. But I attributed this to the fact that he was speaking a foreign language, and I thought it was customary, and quite charming, when Karl Radek stepped up beside him and like a cupbearer passed him from time to time the word he was groping for. It added to my feeling that here was something more important than oratory. It was as though a selfless intellectual had at last been found, the only one perhaps in history, and with expert help he was taking us inside his mind and showing us how the truth looks.

Notwithstanding my rapture, I believe there was a validity in the impression made upon me by the presence of this extraordinary man. Although he was the fountain source of the direst calamities that have afflicted mankind in these thirty years since he died—I mean the totalitarian one-party states—he was as selfless as any of the saints. Every act and every judgment of his was directed toward the goal that, as a Marxist, he believed would free the world from its age-old miseries.

The Russians have a long word, *tseleustryemlyennie*, which describes Lenin's dominant characteristic. It might be translated, with a view to the music of it, as "streamlined to the goal." Literally it means "to-the-goal-tending" (or swooping—they use it of a hawk). And that is the quality you feel in every essay or printed speech of Lenin's. The very commas and semicolons seem to be chosen with a sole view to the race for the revolution and the socialist state. I spent a great many hours while in Russia reading Lenin, deriving a kind of rapture that I can only call poetic from the pure and almost ecstatical *practicality*—the total absence, that is, of poetic divarications—in every word and sentence he put down. He had imagination, he had figures of speech, but he used them for one sole ever-present purpose, to clarify the road to socialism—never for fun.

In that, I think, lay much of his power, sometimes described as hypnotic, to subdue both minds and hearts and compel strong men to accept his leadership.

Chapter 51

A CHOSEN TASK AND A WONDERFUL FRIEND

That winter of 1922–23 was one of the happiest in my life, although there were no outstanding events in it—only a gay-hearted friendship and long hours of work on a task that I myself had chosen. I learned Russian better than I have learned any other language, and I read in their own tongue the classic works that had guided the various sects and parties in the Russian revolution. Shameful though it is, I first really came to grips with the complexities of Marxism in Moscow and in the Russian language. I inherited from my father the aptitudes of a scholar, but I exercise them only spasmodically and under pressure from some creative purpose. My purpose now was to write the life of Leon Trotsky, and with that as a vehicle, explain and justify to Western democratic minds the Bolshevik revolution.

I was not troubled here as in Germany by the inordinate value the collapse of the national currency had given to my few handfuls of dollars. I was "serving the cause" with my life of Trotsky, and had a right to be free of financial worry. If I also hoped that the book when published would earn me many more dollars—for Trotsky's name was a torch throughout the world just then—that too was legitimate. Perhaps I could imbue it also with a long-time literary value, and thus keep all three of the horses of my troika on the run.

For the main thread of the story, since there were no documents, I would have to depend upon Trotsky himself, and for sidelights, upon his friends. I asked for an appointment, which he granted promptly, and put this ambitious idea before him rather shyly. He was obviously pleased. He was also, I think, a little relieved, for Anna Louise Strong, who was in Moscow at the time, had made him a similar proposal, and he had left the answer in doubt.

"I agree in principle," was Trotsky's answer to me, "but I have hardly a moment of spare time. If you'll remain in the vicinity, and allow me to send for you suddenly and brusquely whenever I do have a moment, I'll try to co-operate."

He gave me a letter of introduction to a list of his friends, asking them to talk frankly with me. The list included his first love, his first schoolteacher, his wife, and his closest associates in the Soviet Government. The opportunity to know a great man, and through him a great current in history was exceptional. I have sometimes thought, during her career as an apologist for tyranny in Russia, that my intervention may have prevented Anna Louise from acquiring the kind of knowledge she needed in order to serve the truth and the labor movement, as she so fervently wanted to.

Although it never brought me the money I hoped for, this arrangement with Trotsky enriched my life in Moscow with connections that were invaluable. I was a frequent visitor at the War Office, which vied with the Kremlin in prestige, if not in beauty. I had many gay and informing conversations with Trotsky himself, at first in French but gradually in Russian. And in conversations about him with his friends, I entered into the emotions of the Russian revolution more intimately, I think, than in any of the books I read about it. A visit in Petrograd with his early sweetheart and motherly first wife, Alexandra Ivanovna Sokolovskaia, was especially rewarding. In conversation with her I touched the warmer side of that somewhat ambivalent creature called Bolshevik who swept away so much rubbish and left so much havoc in its place. This creature has faith, hope and charity in him at his best, but he has also the gift of hate, and he has the disease of doctrine in its most virulent form.

Unafflicted with doctrine and more congenial to my mind was my friend, Eliena Krylenko. She found me a "furnished room" over in a used-to-be-elegant section of the city—furnished mainly with a narrow iron bedstead and a chair. But she had now, for herself, a better-furnished room in an apartment house taken over as a dormitory by the Foreign Office. By better-furnished I mean that it contained a bed large enough to recline on against pillows if one were careful not to slide into a mysterious hole in the center of it. She also had a *paiok*, or ration, which enabled her to invite me to a breakfast which she would cook on a primus—a portable small stove that burned oil with a loud woosh. We had coffee and fried eggs sunny-side-up, and that delicious "black bread" which is really brown and keeps the Russian peasants plump and round-cheeked even in a famine. For the Moscow of 1923, those breakfasts were sumptuous, and the mixture of Russian, French and English big words with which they were organized flavored the whole experiment with humor and the joy of mental growth. "Oh, I overthrew an egg!" Eliena exclaimed one morning, and that phrase lived as a symbol of the continual fun we had manipulating our three languages. We soon managed between us to hire a woman to come in and cook our dinner, and the lengthening hours we spent together in that dilapidated room with its funny wiggly chairs and ill-matched drapes and dishes, came as near as anything in the Soviet Bohemia of those days to being a marriage.

Eliena plays so central a role in the rest of this story that I think I must tell the reader who and what she was: a girl, in the first place, so muscular and agile that you could plunge her headfirst into a ten-foot snowdrift and she would dive up in the space of seconds, laughing the snow out of her eyes and tipping you into the drift before you knew she was back. I composed a Russian verse about our playtimes in the snowy woods surrounding Moscow. I had been reading a prose poem of Turgenev in which he describes a resurrection of the wild god Pan, and the nymphs that used to troop laughing through the landscape with him. My poem only says they were still alive—they could not be dead.

A poet's joy is the deadly enemy of death.

And I compared her "funny triumphant gait" and mischievous glance with those of Pan himself. While not of the "ravishing" type, Eliena was *captivating* in that recklessly life-loving, ready-for-anything, wild-god way. Dick Simon took a picture of her years later which would illustrate my poem.

She was born of Russian parents in Lublin, Poland, where her father was controller of taxes for the Tsarist government. He had taught natural science in a Russian university until revolutionary indiscretions lost him that post, and then tried editing a liberal paper in Smolensk. But a family of six growing children compelled him to find a better-paid job. Thanks to a friend in the bureaucracy, he was assigned to this lucrative task of extracting money from a conquered people. To the good fortune of his children, he so conducted it that everybody loved him, from the haughty Polish landlord to the humble Jewish tobacconist. To their further good fortune, he lined the walls of his house from floor to ceiling with books both of science and poetic literature in three or four languages. "There was always a pile of books beside his bed," Eliena remembered, and "he carried a little worn copy of Goethe's *Faust* in his breast pocket wherever he went."

The memory of his intellectuality and gentle-hearted love was an abiding force in all her deeds and judgments. "Kindness and tolerance, sympathy with one's fellow men, a love of beauty, a love of life, a thirst for knowledge—those were the things he tried to plant in our little selfish and arrogant souls."

So Eliena wrote of him. Undoubtedly she had a flourishing "father complex," and that was my good luck, for I was eleven years older than she and was already turning gray.

Her mother was harder-grained and more impetuous than her father—a character differing from his, Eliena said, "as a roaring rapid differs from a mountain lake." But she was equally idealistic and, like all liberal idealists in Tsarist Russia, absorbed in the one divine all-comprising ultimate event—"the revolution." She was still living, a grandly handsome and dynamic old woman, when I was in Russia, still toiling in self-sacrifice to help that revolution make good its promises. I remember a visit with her in Yalta where she had taken twenty-eight orphan children down from Moscow, a three-day train trip, for a vacation by the sea—a task beyond the strength, you would think, of a woman seventy years old. While cooking a little fish for my supper, she asked me why I had come to Russia.

To simplify the answer in a half-learned language, I said: "Just for the adventure."

"You'd better not let any of our people hear you say that," she said sternly, correctively.

She did not laugh as much as the rest of the Krylenkos, and was intolerant of a disposition to take things easy now the civil war was won and the starvation past. "Nobody in this house is really doing anything!" I can hear her exclaim as a person choking with dead air might cry, "For God's sake open the windows!" Action to her, it seemed, was the breath of life.

This trait had been inherited by her two oldest children, Nikolai and Sophia, both of whom went in for conspiratorial agitation in its most dangerous forms. But Volodia, the second son, became an engineer; and Vera, the second daughter, a pianist, was aggressively uninterested in politics. Eliena and her pretty sister Olga were eleven and nine at the time of the defeated uprising of 1905; too young even to have dwelt with the idea of revolution as a pure rosy hope. To them it was a catastrophe. The elder brother, Nikolai, who had joined the party of

Lenin, was arrested and imprisoned in St. Petersburg. The elder sister
Sophia arrived home from "the underground," demanding help for an
escape over the border. The nonpolitical Vera was jailed in Lublin and
joined the other prisoners, for solidarity's sake, in a hunger strike. The
home, with its precious books, was raided and ripped to pieces from top
to bottom by the Tsar's police.

That turbulent year of 1905 was for Eliena the end of a serene
childhood passed within the circumference of her father's love. And it
was followed by a more shocking catastrophe. Her father's job had
survived the aborted revolution, but he was transferred from Lublin to
a small rural town eighty miles from a railroad. The loneliness, the
political disillusionment, financial hardships, a sad love affair perhaps,
and the jealous disposition of his wife, then going through a neurotic
menopause, were more than he could bear. On one of his forlorn solitary
trips through the country on a job he despised, he committed suicide. I
do not know just when or how this happened, for Eliena would never
talk of it. But there was always a sadness in her voice when she told me
how he taught her to be happy.

Some light is cast on the tragedy by a childish vow she made that
when she grew up she would marry a man like her father and let him
love all the other women he wanted to. She was generous enough by
instinct to make good on that. In love at least, she was generous almost
beyond belief. Love in her heart meant giving. She had lived in a
common-law marriage with some soldier before I met her, and when I
asked her why they parted she said: "He wasn't selfish enough—he
wouldn't let me do things for him." There was a cat named Seashell
whom she loved, and who would come and sit by her at breakfast. I
remarked once, when she herself came to the table hungry, that she
seemed more interested in feeding Seashell than in satisfying her own
hunger. She was ready with an answer that tells how extrovert her love
was:

"It's because I can see her enjoy it—I can't see myself enjoy
it."

Besides being so generous—and maybe there is a connection between
these traits—Eliena was the gayest person I have ever known. She had
that instinctive joy in the mere fact of living, which makes all wailings
over a lost "meaning" of life—all such cry-baby philosophies as ex-
istentialism—look as futile as they are. And she had a power of
controlling her emotions that I have never seen equaled. It was a power,
I suppose, of deciding to what feature of an experience she would give

her attention. She thought, for instance, that drawn-out feelings of remorse were futile, and although humbly and for a moment bitterly regretful when she had committed an error, above all an unkind one, she wasted no time on it. She turned her attention, as simply as from one page to the next, from the past to the future. Even from so quick-biting and poisoning an emotion as jealousy she could, as though from a snake on a bypath, turn completely away.

She gave evidence of this when I told her about my romance with nude-swimming Nina in Yalta. She made a little "moue-mouth" at first, as though she did not want to hear about it. But seeing my disappointment, and hearing perhaps a brief lecture on the glories of a friendship that stands above jealousy (I had indeed vowed never again to come within the fringes of a possessive love) she changed her expression without visible effort to a laugh.

"Tell me all about Nina," she said. "And you can tell me about all the other girls you have loved, and those you may love in the future—or not tell me, just as you wish. I won't be jealous in either case. I don't want to possess you. All my love asks is to see you happy."

I don't know how many women there are in the world, or men either, who could live up to that, or who could honestly say it. Was it a result of that childish vow she had made, that passion of sympathy for her adored father? To me it seemed too instinctive for that, and was too easily achieved.

If I seem to be describing someone almost perfect, that in itself is relevant to my story, for it was the perception of her as a perfect companion which, as you will see in the sequel, came near to accomplishing my ruin. She was not always gentle—except to those she loved—not always good. Her genially mischievous blue-gray eyes could turn into cold steel with anger, and anger could congeal into hate. She was phenomenally generous only toward those she loved, and she had an underlying vein of egotism, never untastefully expressed—an egotism that in a gifted person is hard to distinguish from self-knowledge. And she was indeed gifted in almost every direction. She could dance and paint and write poetry in two languages (I mean dance and paint professionally and write poetry that was published in distinguished magazines). She could cook, keep house, keep garden, keep bees. As an orator, had she chosen to be one, she might, I think, have run a close second to her famous brother. And with a few drinks to overcome her hesitance, she could sing Russian songs. She had no mechanical sense or sense of dynamics, and was not a skillful driver—not one whose instinctive reactions could be trusted in an emergency. And she lacked a quick sense of what an act or a word spoken might mean to others—even I could sometimes tell her about that. But this failing was inherent, perhaps, in her gift of unhesitating concentration and speed—speed without nervous tension—in whatever she undertook. In this she was the most un-Russian person I met in Russia.

Some part of her father's warm place in her heart had been filled by that brilliant brother Nikolai, who was likewise gentle-hearted and poetic in his youth, but who hardened up under Lenin's influence, or put on a hard shell, and became a ruthless Bolshevik, the greatest orator of the party until Trotsky joined it. Released from prison in 1906, thanks to the tireless intercessions of his mother, he taught history and literature for a while in Polish schools, and then went back to St. Petersburg to study law. For no better reason than hero worship of that gifted brother, Eliena followed in his steps. She lived through the revolution of 1917 as a law student, graduating and receiving her diploma on the very day when the established system of law and court procedure—all that she had learned—was triumphantly abolished by her brother's party.

Although she adored that brother and was, like him, a revolutionist, she never joined his party. She was repelled by the vicarious class hate and not-so-vicarious thirst for power which Lenin's Marxism had imported into the rather naïvely moralistic mood of the Russian revolution. The Marxian trick of uniting man's most heavenly aspirations with a satisfaction for his most brutish instincts awakened in her a childlike distrust. And she was too strong a child to be swayed even by her strong-minded brother. She was proud when Lenin appointed him commander in chief of the All-Russian army. She was proud when, on Trotsky's accession to that post, he became Commissar of Justice—or in our terms Attorney General. She hoped he was right with his abstruse philosophy which asserted that a day of universal freedom and brotherhood would be the final outcome of this cruel and unscrupulous fight for power, but she was not convinced of it. And she had no impulse to profit by his high advancement.

These feelings, and a wish to be of some help in the hard days following the October revolution, led her to join her elder sister in an expedition sent by the Bolsheviks to the Ukraine in search of wheat. After many months of wandering through the war-torn country, they arrived in the city of Kiev. It was in 1919, a critical year of the civil war, when White and Red armies swept back and forth over Kiev like waves of a raging sea, each setting up a government and holding a massacre of its enemies.

The Reds were in control when Sophia and Eliena arrived there, but the Whites soon bombarded the town and took over. Sophia "went underground," and Eliena, not realizing her danger, got picked up by White Guards while roaming the streets. Her name was enough to condemn her, and she was marched through the town as an enemy, while crowds loyal to the new regime were hooting and spitting at the leaders of the old, and the guns of the firing squads executing them were still ringing in her ears. She marched bravely and proudly—"taut as a string," according to a friend who watched in terror from the sidewalk—and escaped death by something very like a miracle. A social revolutionary, who while politically anti-Bolshevik had been a friend of her mother's, happened to be in charge at headquarters when she arrived there. He put on a sort of mock court-martial, permitting a number of pretended "witnesses" to fulminate against her. Having dismissed the witnesses and closed the doors, he turned to her, shaking his head:

"Well, you certainly got yourself into a mess!" he said.

He managed, in the general confusion, to contrive her escape. And she managed, after some further adventures which hardly belong to this portrait of her character, to find her way back to Moscow. She applied for a job in the Commissariat of Foreign Affairs in the hope that it might someday entail a journey to other countries—perhaps even to America. And thanks to the stories of Huck Finn and Tom Sawyer read to her as a child by her father, she had always thought it would be fun to live in America.

Chapter 52

ACQUAINTANCE WITH THE BOLSHEVIKS

Thanks to my friendship with a Krylenko, my collaboration with Trotsky, and my learning the language, I came much closer than most foreign visitors, even most delegates of the International, to the inner circles of the early Bolshevik regime. Up to then the language barrier had not been leaped by any sympathizer, no matter how deep his sympathy. Everybody was sick and tired of conversations, and above all speeches, that had to be translated in both directions before the "Workers of the World" could unite even for an evening's entertainment. By January, I had progressed far enough, with Eliena's help, to make a speech at a mass meeting dedicated to international art and literature. I was the last on a four-hour list of speakers, all of them foreign, and all translated at intolerable length, and I began my speech with these words:

"*Yesli Vy budete ochen tyerpilivi, Ya budu ochen khrabri.*" (If you will be very patient, I will be very brave.) Again as on the train to Petrograd, a cheer went up as though I had made a great oration. *Izvestia* gave me another flattering notice, and I moved some degrees further into the good graces of those exceedingly highbrow big Bolsheviks. A group of them, keenly interested in literature and aware of it as a thing independent of politics, were starting a new monthly magazine called *Zhizn* (Life). Sosnovsky, the charming *feuilleton* writer and editor of *Izvestia*, and Demian Byedny, the party's beloved poet-columnist, were among them, and both Trotsky and Rakovsky stood behind this effort to liberate creative art from the too strict dictature of the party. The group invited me to join them, published one of my articles in translation, let me make a speech on creative freedom at their inaugural banquet, and made me a member of the editorial staff. It was a brief honor, for the magazine died with its second number, the funds having been withdrawn by the party, which alone, of course, could supply them. It was a lesson to me, or should have been, for the magazines I edited in America, although supported with funds raised mainly from the hated "capitalists," enjoyed a creative freedom that the heads of that "proletarian" party, even the most broad-minded, could not imagine. I do not mean merely that they would censor counterrevolutionary writings, which goes without saying, but writings that seemed—I remember the words on Rakovsky's lips—to be "slipping back from Marxism into Populism." *

All those *isms!*

I did not feel at home among them intellectually. There was something alien here, an atmosphere of theology rather than science. Rakovsky spoke as though recalling our wandering minds to an infallible scripture. Could it be that I had been wrong even about Lenin? Could it be that his agile mind too, so imperiously at ease among facts, was confined within a system of dogmatic ideas? Well, I would have to find out. I would have to dig into the intellectual background of the whole romantic tale of revolution in Russia, from the Decembrists of 1825 to the Bolsheviks of—almost 1925. Almost a century of revolutionary deeds and ideas to master in a foreign language!

My book about Trotsky became rather incidental to that very much larger, and yet relevant, purpose. And then also I had a revolutionary novel germinating in my mind. I would have to go off in a corner before long and concentrate on that. No wonder I was happy with these big things that I really wanted to do, and an insuppressibly gay and devoted friend to help me do them. The truth is I was too elated and too busy to be keenly critical of the progress of what in sober moments I still called the "great experiment." A glow from my own happiness will color, I fear, the next few chapters of this book.

It probably colored a visit I made to the Butirki prison where certain enemies of the regime belonging to the Socialist Revolutionary Party were confined. Eliena telephoned her brother, the Minister of Justice, asking him to give me a pass. He received me with a ferocious scowl, and a harsh question: "What do you want to visit a prison for?"

He looked so almost exactly like Eliena, though, that I was not intimidated.

"To see what it's like," I said. "I'm not asking for a room!"

---

* *Narodnichestvo*, a name for the pre-Marxian, and anti-Marxian, forms of revolutionism in Russia, which based its hope upon the people (*narod*) rather than the proletariat.

Of a sudden the harshness fell off his face and he laughed—genially and with the same brimming-over of joy-in-life that made Eliena's laughter magnetic. He had to put on that hard shell in order to be a prosecuting attorney—in order to be a Bolshevik at all, as I have said. Eliena had told me what a charmed and charming lover and reciter of poetry he had been in his youth, and what a tender-hearted brother. Later I watched him in court, demanding the death sentence for a counterrevolutionary conspirator. I saw him work himself up to the degree of histrionic fury that earned him the nickname in the Western press of "bloodthirsty Krylenko." But that was not his true nature. Like the other ardent Bolsheviks of those early days, he was actuated in his "tough-mindedness" by a "tender" idea. He was hard because he was convinced by Karl Marx and Lenin that it was necessary to be hard.

Moreover I found the Socialist Revolutionaries in the Butirki living more comfortably than anybody would be allowed to in an American prison. One of them with a long brown beard, I remember, was sitting comfortably in a folding chair, with his cell door open, reading a book. I cannot pretend that I made an investigation of "prison conditions in Moscow in 1923." My visit was brief and casual in the highest degree, and may conceivably have been prepared for. But the very fact that I made such a visit on the spur of the moment, and with a pass from the Attorney General, would be worth remembering when the balance is drawn between the regime of the earlier and later Bolsheviks.

I was investigating ideas, not conditions, and as the ideas were printed in a foreign language, they kept my attention pretty steadily occupied. George Grosz,* the German artist, who visited Moscow during that same year, included in his memoirs an impression of me that bears this out. A group of visiting artists and writers had been called together by Zinoviev to discuss plans for a grand alliance between Soviet culture and the revolutionary culture in foreign lands.

"There were about eight of us writers and artists from different capitalistic countries," George wrote. "Arthur Holitscher was elected

---

* George Grosz won fame in Germany with caricatures of her feudal-military and capitalistic society so obscenely horrible that they can only be described as a masterly apotheosis of the art of the back-house wall. Even Trotsky, I remember, pushed away with a squeamish gesture a book of them that George had given him. "To me they seem cynical rather than revolutionary," he said. Subsequently George Grosz emigrated to America, where his mood changed, and he painted some tenderly beautiful landscapes. He died in 1959, a few weeks after returning to his native land.

secretary for Germany, first because he was old and esteemed, second because he believed almost everything anybody told him. (This led later on, when he discovered the truth, to a harsh embitterment.) Martin Andersen Nexö was the natural delegate from Denmark; he didn't believe everything quite so fast or quite so fervently, but he had been designed by nature for an office manager. Max Eastman was there too; he appealed to me with his specially beautiful American sneakers with red rubber soles. I can't say much about him since he took little part in the discussion, but kept reading away in an English-Russian dictionary while the rest of us argued hot-headedly. Did he know more than we did? He was good-looking, had white hair and always a friendly laugh, which pleasantly distinguished him from many of the fanatically-believing Apostle-faces among us."

I did know, it is true, what George himself learned later, that "this whole supercolossal project was . . . a word-circus and talkfest, probably only a scheme for diverting us and keeping us busy." But this was not because of my closer relation to some of the big shots in the Kremlin—no outsider got within suspecting distance of their secrets—but only as I know in general that real art and literature cannot be evoked or promoted by a planning commission. On these questions my dissent from the Marxian philosophy left my intelligence free.

My contact with the leading Bolsheviks had not altered my opinion that their attitude to revolutionary movements in other countries was rank with nationalistic egotism. They were indeed men of unusual character and high culture, but they were not the only ones in the world. An American I then admired, and liked as a political friend, was William Z. Foster, who had led the great steel strike of 1919, and whose adherence to the Communist Party had been a signal event. We met in Moscow on the Tverskaia Boulevard one day, and he showed me a letter that had just been handed to him by Zinoviev, the president of the International. It was addressed to the membership of the American Party, and his job was to take it home and sign it and send it out. I was indignant. "How in hell," I said, "do these people think a revolutionary movement can be led in the United States, or anywhere else, by people whom they treat like kindergarten pupils. Don't they know it takes a full-grown man to lead a revolution?"

Folding the letter and putting it back in his pocket, Foster said:

"Max, a lot of things happen here that I don't like. But we can't do anything about it. They've got the prestige. No revolutionary movement anywhere, as things stand now, can prosper without their backing."

I couldn't answer him. I suppose it was true. You had only a choice between the spry and lively and unprincipled course he was taking, and the lethargy and heavy-hearted dying-out of the hope of revolution so painful to perceive in Bill Haywood. I have spoken of the contrast between these two men; in Moscow it acquired a tragic significance. Haywood had a vision of the future and a poetic way of talking. Some of his figures of speech—"The IWW is socialism with its working clothes on," for instance—were once collected and printed, if I remember rightly, in the *International Socialist Review*. But he was no student and had no quickness of mind—not even enough to be "taken in" by the fast-talking highbrows of Bolshevism when he got to Moscow. They merely dazed and overwhelmed him, and left him inarticulate and sad. Foster was keen-witted, versed in the revolutionary lingo. Although he had started off with what Lenin called anarcho-syndicalist opinions, and indeed worked as an agitator for the IWW, he was flexible and practical-minded enough to catch on to the importance of the party—of the unscrupulous struggle for party power which Lenin pitted against the unimplemented aspiration of the syndicalists and "compromising" socialists. Lenin's sense of the indispensability of a disciplined party and its struggle for power, if the revolution was not to be shot down or expire in lofty talk, was unanswerable. It was also, in its implications, a demonstration that the goal of the revolution is unattainable. But that never occurred to Lenin, and if it occurred to Foster, he was too far gone in service to the party to admit it. While Haywood languished and died in Moscow, heartbroken at the frustration of his faith, Foster shifted his gears and became a zealous bureaucrat, helping along the frustration.

I had an opportunity, not long after that exchange of opinions with Foster, to make the same point with Trotsky. He had agreed, as a part of our collaboration, to visit with me the old Tsarist prison in which he had been confined on his way to Siberia as a young man of twenty. It seemed a good time to raise my objection, and I said:

"I don't see how you and your colleagues, who know by experience what it takes to lead a revolution, can imagine that in other countries mere puppets whom you move around on a string can play a similarly heroic part." And to illustrate, I told him about the letter which had been handed to William Z. Foster, precomposed by a Russian committee, and only awaiting his obedient signature.

"That isn't the way to treat potential leaders of a world revolution," I said.

Trotsky's answer was revealing.

"In general we treat each of them according to what he deserves."

"You miss my point," I said. "My point is who set you up to decide what each one deserves?"

But he hardly heard me, or if he did the point was beyond his apprehension. It was beyond any of those triumphant Bolsheviks to realize that their successful seizure of power in a crisis mainly due to the backwardness of their country, did not constitute them kings and captains of every similar attempt in every other country. They constituted themselves, without the shadow of rational support, or support in the Marxian Scripture, autocratic bosses of the world revolution.

Chapter 53

I ATTEND A PARTY CONGRESS

It was a rather overwhelming experience for a Mark Twain democrat, hating all false eminences whether of caste or class, to attend a congress of the Russian Communist Party in the resplendent reception hall of the Tsar's palace. That is a really-truly palace, the kind they have in fairy tales, a climbing hive of gleaming and "sumptuous" chambers full of "porphyry and gold," with thrones and coats-of-arms, and crystal chandeliers containing millions of tiny lights that fill its grandiose spaces with a delicately aristocratic glow. In that glow those chambers now became homelike in spite of themselves, and the great gold-freighted doors that you had to buck your back against to move, seemed to stand open as hospitably as though the delegates, plain folks who might have come from a farm in Idaho, or a factory in Pittsburgh, or from Greenwich Village or the Henry Street Settlement, were the original proprietors. The palace had got used to them, I suppose, by the time I arrived there.

The Twelfth Congress, sitting from April 17 to 25, 1923, was the first one from which Lenin was absent. It was an orphan congress, and everybody was on his good behavior. I do not remember how many sessions I attended—perhaps only the first and second and the last—but in any case I could have seen nothing of the sullen currents of schismatic passion that would swell to a riptide in the coming months. They were undercurrents still—rigidly held under by common agreement. Lenin, had he been there, would have "exploded a bombshell against Stalin," to use his own expression. He would have opposed Stalin's re-election as general secretary and prevented in every way he could his rise to further power. He had confided to his wife a letter written on his sickbed, warning the party against Stalin and advising the election of a secretary "who in all respects differs from him only in

superiority." He had asked Trotsky to substitute for him in this attack
on Stalin and his clique, begging Trotsky to make no "rotten compromise" for the sake of peace in the party. But there was no substitute for
Lenin. His wife, still hoping for his recovery, withheld the letter. She
never mentioned it. And Trotsky made all the compromises necessary
to bring off a peaceful congress, not even opposing Stalin's re-election
as general secretary.

All this was as far as the moon from my knowledge. And to further
mislead me, the congress debated and decided, on the days I attended,
an issue which I thought went to the heart of the question whether
the Bolsheviks were really going to produce a "socialized" economy or
not. Leonid Krassin, coming back from a trade mission in London,
made a ringing speech protesting against the nagging and hampering
of legitimate enterprise by party politicians occupying posts where
experts in commerce and industry were wanted. Krassin was the only
businessman in the whole assembly. He had been a manager for years
of the Russian department of Siemens & Schuckert, a famous Berlin
firm like our General Electric. He knew what he was talking about and
he talked well. But more was at issue here than just flexible good sense
against the mounting bigotry of the party. The very viability and survival of the state-operated economy was the issue. Krassin's pro-
posals would undoubtedly promote recovery, but they would also lead
farther along the road back to capitalism that had been opened by
Lenin's New Economic Policy. Lenin was out of the fight now—
paralyzed, perhaps for good—and his disciples had no more consuming
fear than that this policy, so carefully explained by him as a maneuver,
should turn into a retreat. They undertook the chastisement of Comrade
Krassin in good order and with unanimous enthusiasm.

Zinoviev came first. He delivered in Lenin's absence the "Political
Report" of the Central Committee to the party. He looked sadder than
ever—sad, cold and sincere. The smile of his eyes never quite connected
with that of his mouth, and they both quickly vanished as though
smiling were something you do in order to get it done. His voice was
almost soprano and his oratory a series of short high vibrant complaints,
each a phrase long and very rapidly uttered. The rapidity and monotony
and equal spacing of these little wails of speech had a gradually
inebriating effect, like the beating of a tom-tom, and turned your
wonder at the unfaltering speed and lucidity of his thought into a kind
of crazy passion. He was a rabble-rouser if there ever was one.

"Comrade Krassin finds himself on the verge of making a very, very serious mistake," he said, picking up a copy of *Pravda* in which Krassin had set forth his views. "Listen for yourselves! Dwelling on the role of politics in the state Krassin says: 'Render unto Caesar the things that are Caesar's. A strongly maintained political line of the party in the state must not hinder the revival of industry. Politics—that is a necessary evil, but at least let it not hinder the revival of industry.'

"It did not occur to Krassin that politics not only does not hinder, but it helps. His attitude to the role of the Communists you can gather from this further quotation: 'You find that a power independent of you has thrown one of your workers into another department, perhaps into another establishment. Without even asking you whether you need them or not, they sprinkle you with a dozen or so more of human material belonging to the party, sometimes absolutely unsuitable either for work or for control in the given department.'"

Here Zinoviev drew a deep and reproachful sigh.

"You can imagine Comrade Krassin's psychology. They sprinkle him with Communists, with whom he does not know what to do! . . . You find yourself, Comrade Krassin, on the verge of a very grave mistake."

After this rather painful and motherly-serious spanking, the paddle was passed to Karl Radek, who thoroughly enjoyed manipulating it. Radek did not approach the erring child with the well-known "this hurts me more than it does you." On the contrary, his expression said: "I am very glad to see that you have made an ass of yourself, for I have known all along that you were going to, and ever since you were born I've been aching to roll up my sleeves and hand you a good crisp wallop!"

Radek had the attractiveness of a thing that you didn't like at first. You thought he was weak-eyed and coarse-lipped, and that you could never endure that old brown stocking of whiskers under his ears and chin. You found that behind the big spectacles his blue eyes were not watery, but queerly penetrating. You found that the coarse lips had a delicate line between them. What you learned to like about them was an expression of serenity. Radek dressed his hollow frame in a strange square costume with unusual flaps and buttons, slick and aristocratic in material, but in design suggesting a New England deacon rather than a Bolshevik agitator. He carried a cane, which was usually in his way when he was not using it to poke somebody halfway across the room. He would flit about through a meeting on fine threads of intellectual interest like a spider-grandmother, seeing that everything was revolutionary and all right. You couldn't help liking him. You gradually became reconciled to that brown fringe of whiskers under his chin. I even reached a point where the news that it had been removed for the sake of a conspiratorial sortie into Germany, struck me not as a maneuver but a compromise.

Radek's more expert chastisement of Krassin concluded with these unambiguous hints:

"I do not suppose Comrade Krassin's remarks were a candidate's speech, but if they had been a candidate's speech, they would have been rejected by the congress, and the candidate would not have arrived in the Central Committee. I must say that if there is any one enormous obstacle to the general appraisement of the situation, that obstacle is Comrade Krassin."

Dzerzhinski's opinion was influential because he was supposed to be a great executive, but it was really sentimental.

"How often as industrialists," he said, "we turn to the party with reproaches—with reproaches not because it controls, but because it does not control enough, does not interfere enough, does not give that help which is the one thing real and essential."

In the process of driving home a point there is usually a moment when it sticks a little on account of some purely intellectual friction, and it was a part of the recognized technique in Moscow, when this point arrived, to telephone for Nikolai Ivanovitch Bukharin, a very small, young and inconspicuous-looking man who carried with him an enormous Marxian pile driver. He was inconspicuous from a little distance. Indeed he was just a healthy, clean, rosy-skinned boy who looked happy—seemingly because he had been elected president of his class, and was going to play quarterback on the college team. He was quick and wiry and popular like that, and he toed in a little, and stood very firm on his legs. You would see, if he came nearer, that the outline of his head and ears and features was delicate as a seashell, and you would guess that he must be very talented in a polite and lovable way. But you would never prepare yourself for the sparkling torrent of witty argument that flowed out of him when he got on the platform. He just strolled about, holding some paper in his hand, his blouse unflapped at the neck to make it easier to talk, and his whole being would become talk. Although rosy in color, he reminded me of a canary bird. A canary will start to sing, you remember, and the performance is so brilliant that you think he must soon stop—but no, there is nothing left of him but song. Bukharin had a way, too, of repeating a phrase but varying the melody:

"What may *this* mean?"

"What *may* this mean?"

"What may this *mean?*" he would sing.

I think from reading his books that Bukharin's gifts as the "theoretician" of the Bolshevik party were vastly exaggerated. Lenin himself, in his last letter to the party, called him "scholastic," and said he did not "understand the dialectic,"—a deathblow from a Marxist. A simpler way of stating the facts would be to say that his exquisite head was so full of all kinds and varieties of ideas, learned by heart and never critically assimilated, that he could tie up any practical question in a web of theoretical big talk which the other Bolsheviks were unable to penetrate. He was not the theoretician, but the saint, the one they all loved, the "favorite of the party," as Lenin called him. He lived not in the Kremlin but in the heart of Moscow, among the people, a simple and devoted life—one man whom power could not corrupt.

Trotsky did not say anything about Krassin in his report on the problems of industry, and Krassin in discussing the report did not say anything about himself either. He did not deny that he had been "on the verge of a very serious mistake." He made a charmingly disarming speech on the need of foreign credits for the revival of Russian big industry, and the peculiar difficulty of securing them. He told the delegates that in London years ago, when the revolution was burning low and Lenin needed funds for the publication of his journal, somebody suggested they might get a contribution from a rich British capitalist who sympathized with the revolutionary movement in Russia. Lenin decided to tackle the capitalist, but as he could not then talk English, Plekhanov went along as interpreter. They shook hands and sat down, and Lenin began:

"Of course we recognize in you a political enemy, a representative of the exploiting class, but we understand that you are liberal-minded, and in spite of your unfortunate position we thought perhaps. . . ."

Plekhanov had to translate this speech.

"Our esteemed friend," he began, "knowing that you sympathize with our struggle for freedom in Russia, and with all the libertarian efforts of mankind. . . ."

They got the money, Krassin said, and moreover the esteemed friend came around recently to the Russian Trade Commission in London, presented a bill, and got it back. Krassin drew the moral from this tale, that if you are going to get money out of bourgeois governments you've got to approach them in a somewhat conciliatory spirit. That was as near as he came to answering his critics. They all laughed, happy in the reminiscence of Lenin, and one felt that the chastisement of Krassin was about finished.

Every man in the party who could get there attended the congress on the evening when Trotsky made his summing up. The ovation to him had been the big moment of the congress. And now the entire constellation of "big Bolsheviks" sat around him, either at the long table or on the steps leading to the platform: Bukharin, Radek, Litvinov, Krylenko, Chicherin, Piatakov, Rakovsky, Zinoviev, Kamenev, Krassin, Dzerzhinski, Antonov-Avseenko, Rykov, Stalin, Preobrazhensky—everyone who was not away on a diplomatic mission. There was still a hope that Lenin would be back, and Stalin had not yet shown his hand. Whatever their thoughts, they all looked friendly and congenial. They looked, to my admiring eyes, like a good-natured family. And Trotsky, in summarizing the decision against Krassin, came as near as he knew how to being diplomatic.

"Comrade Krassin tells us," he said, "that if we are going to get credits out of foreign governments it is necessary to know how to do it, and he tells us how Plekhanov translated Lenin into English and got money for the revolution. We knew this, and that is exactly why we sent Comrade Krassin to England. We did not intend to change our policies, we just wanted him to translate us into English!"

Amid the laughter this evoked, he turned toward Krassin, who was sitting on the edge of the platform. "The only flaw in your illustration," he added with a smile, "is that Plekhanov got the money and you didn't." *

I have dwelt at length on this congress of Lenin's party because it confirmed and strengthened my pro-Bolshevik convictions. One does not defend the blood and violence of a revolution unless he believes it is going to change things profoundly, almost absolutely, for the better. It seemed to me that no meeting like this of a political party had ever been held before in the world. There was nothing extraordinary in the aspect of these people. Except for the fact that none of them was very well dressed, you could hardly distinguish them from any gathering of earnestly thoughtful men of affairs in the United States. But the things they said and thought about seemed to me extraordinary. Throughout

* My quotations at this point are not verbatim.

the sessions that I attended there was not a sentence or a phrase of what could be called political oratory, either of the spread-eagle or the tub-thumping variety. There were two moments devoted to emotion: one when at the opening they rose and sang their sadly undulating hymn in memory of those who died for the revolution; the other when Trotsky first entered the hall and they rose to applaud. For the rest it was more like a meeting of directors to discuss the balance sheet of a corporation than the convention of a political party. Even in the dispute with Krassin the question was predominantly of increasing sales and promoting production. The average American, I thought, would find it difficult to believe that so many able brains, and such a wealth of practical thought and information, could be brought to bear upon a problem of production and distribution by any consideration less mundane than million-dollar profits. But the problem these men were discussing was how to develop a system of business such that all men and women should have a chance to live rich lives and be free and happy.

Such were my thoughts. And I must confess they took place in a rather opaque cloud of optimistic emotion. I was unaware of the beastlike struggle for power that was in progress behind the scenes of this high-minded discussion. I was unaware of the existence of Stalin. And I was uncritical of the momentous implications of the discussion itself. Something in me, some vein of practical good sense, felt a sympathy for Krassin, but my hopes in the other direction were too strong. I was content to rejoice in the mere topic of the discussion, the cool-minded and resolute concentration on a goal so remote from that of Big Business in the United States. This erased my doubts. It put me back into a mood of unqualified belief. I had come to Russia "to find out whether what I had been saying was true." I thought I had found out now that it *was* true.

Chapter 54

DOWN THE VOLGA

Thus confirmed in my easy hopes by a look at the ruling group, I wanted to have a talk with the ruled. I also wanted material for stories and articles I could sell in America. Beyond that, I wanted to get away somewhere and write my novel—I wanted to have fun. Albert told me about Sochi, another resort on the Black Sea, beautiful as Yalta, and we agreed to meet down there where he would be finishing his book on *The Russian Land*. A steamboat trip down the Volga was not the short way to get there, but it was one that would teach me much and be most thrillingly enjoyable. Indeed all I needed to make it paradisal was Eliena's company.

She managed, somehow, to persuade Litvinov that my trip was politically important, that I needed a courier from the Foreign Office, and that she needed a vacation. I did, in fact, need help in talking with the Russian people, for they did not all speak quite the stately language I had been learning. Moreover I am much slower at understanding a foreign tongue than speaking it, and understanding was, alongside of pleasure, the business in hand.

Sochi is on the high shore of the Caucasian peninsula where Jason came seeking the Golden Fleece, and Prometheus was chained to the rock. A romantic end to our journey, but the whole journey was romantic. We went by train to Nizhni Novgorod, by steamboat miles down the Volga to Tsaritsyn (subsequently Stalingrad and now Volgograd), by train again across the Steppes to Armavir, then down the Kuban river to Novorossisk, and by steamer along the Black Sea coast to Sochi. The journey gave me, I think, a fairly representative view of the country, the public mind, the way of life, in the second year of the New Economic Policy. If my notes and recollections of it have any value now, it will lie chiefly, perhaps, in their refutation of the notion that things were "just as bad" under Lenin and Trotsky as they became after Stalin seized his despotic power. The notion is disproven by the mere fact that I wandered so far and so freely, talking with all kinds of people, and, whether I merely introduced myself as a visiting American or presented a document attesting my friendship with the Bolshevik government, no man or woman ever hesitated to enter into friendly relations with me, or withheld, so far as I could judge, his frank opinion both of the Communist idea in general and of the government.

The name *Nizhni Novgorod* had always carried a flavor of Far-Eastern dreams in moonlit gardens to me. The words mean nothing more romantic than *Lower Newtown*, and that, when we got there, was about all we saw, for our boat was leaving in two hours and it took me most of that time to buy a ticket. The Volga was dishwater brown like the Hudson at Albany. It smelled of steamboat smoke, and resounded with whistles and the yells of draymen and stevedores. Nothing here to feed my thirst for the unusual—except, indeed, some mighty-limbed Percheron stallions that crowded the quays and the streets along the waterfront, dragging immense loads of bags and barrels. Why did we never use stallions as draft animals in America? Was that puritanism or pusillanimity? It gave, at least, a slight flavor of novelty to Lower Newtown. So did the fuss and palaver at the ferry station, where it was necessary to buy tickets not only for yourself, but for your baggage, which a porter carried in a queue fifty or sixty paces behind you, and for which you had to wait until he fought his way forward to where you stood. This would give rise to a great deal of humorous laughter, some amiable swearing, and endless excited arguments as to the proper way in which a ferryboat ticket office ought to be conducted. I don't know how it is now, but in those days Russians conducted all these social operations as though they had just opened the place, and were in process of establishing a system. They never could seem to establish the system, and this kept them mentally active, and made them all very intellectual as well as impractical.

The steamboat was another disillusionment, it was so cleanly white and shining, with polished deck and cool gray-painted wicker chairs and tables, immense plate-glass windows, a dining room with palms and flowers, white tablecloths and clean silver on the tables, a smoking room enclosed in glass and furnished with deeply receding leather armchairs and divans. My cabin was twice as large as it used to be on the Fall River boats to Providence, the bed was good, the electric lights were working, and the water running in a washbowl in the corner. Of course it was a survival from Tsarist days, but there it was, and it made me feel quite hopeless about the Volga.

In Kazan, where we stopped for three hours, I did get a little taste of desolation. There seemed to be nobody there. The streetcar was down at the pier exactly where my prehistoric Baedeker said it would be, but it was empty of people. Eliena and I hopped on and rode as far as the base of a high rose-yellow tower like a pyramid, a graciously beautiful colored form, that we had seen from the river shining above the city. It brought us in contact with the government, and I spent my three hours in the company of the Vice-president of the Council of Commissars of the new Tartar Republic of Kazan. He introduced us first to the District Committee of the Communist Party which happened to be meeting that morning—the people, that is, who were running the town. They impressed me as "exceptionally young, gentle and intelligent," to quote my notebook, and they asked me clamorously for news not of Warren G. Harding, but of Upton Sinclair.

I have already mentioned the distinction between idealistic Communists and the hard-boiled place-hunters, and without that distinction—whatever Marx may say to the contrary—it is impossible to understand, much less to feel, the history of the Bolshevik experiment. Those young, gentle and intelligent Communists showed me proudly all over the newly autonomous Tartar Republic, confirming in my willing heart the trust inspired by the top-level congress of the party I had just attended in Moscow.

"Your republic looks fine," I said, as we started off, "but there don't seem to be any people in it."

He lowered his eyes and looked a little humbly ashamed, and I wished I hadn't said it.

"You've come too early," he said.

"What do you mean," I asked, "you haven't got started under the NEP?"

"Too early in the morning. We haven't got up yet."

I looked at my watch and of course realized my mistake. It was only eleven o'clock. Even in Moscow they had only been in the office an hour. You would hardly expect Kazan to keep the lightning pace set by Moscow.

We visited the new state theatre, where for the first time the Tartar people, 53 percent of the population, could hear plays from their own literature rendered in their own language; the three new hospitals, where for the first time a sick Tartar could get well, or a Tartar mother have a baby under hygienic conditions. They showed me their famous old university and told me of the new wonders of modern science that were being taught there. It was a propaganda tour, and they frankly confessed it, but the joyous hope in their eyes was not propaganda. They fervently believed, as I did, that a new and better world was coming to being along the lines indicated by Marx and by Lenin and Trotsky.

As the boat drifted out into the current, I saw an elderly man in high boots and a gentleman's coat leaning against the rail. The quietness of his eyes was sad, and his strong figure sagged.

"I guess it's a different Volga," I said, "from what it used to be."

"Oh, but it is!" he said. "Why, this place used to be *full* of boats. You can't imagine what a beautiful thing this river was. It was *alive* with traffic. Salt, grain, petroleum, fish, timber. Motion everywhere. You wouldn't go three versts without passing a string of barges. Now what do you see? Just a little petroleum going up the river and tanks coming back. It's gone. It's all gone. Look at that town!"

His gesture expressed both scorn and despair, but the town looked so beautiful to me, with that salmon-colored tower shining in the sun and no smoking hanging over it, that I could not feel his emotion.

"I suppose it will be built up again in five or six years," I said.

"You don't know!" he exclaimed. "It would take fifteen years to revive the Volga, if we had the chance."

"If you will permit me to ask," I said, "who do you mean by *we?*"

"I am a fish merchant," he said amiably. "I was a big merchant before—one of the biggest. The Volga is my home. I've lived here and in Tsaritsyn thirty-five years. I am doing a little trade again."

"What do you think is the cause of this condition," I asked, "the revolution or the civil war?"

He was surprised at the question. "The war," he said. "There was nothing destroyed here by the revolution. The war and the famine. They were so hungry in some of these towns that you didn't dare go on the street after dark. They would drop a lasso on you and pull you in for food."

He turned away from the memory. "What do *you* think of the Volga?" he asked.

I said that, as a poet, I thought it was very fine without so much traffic.

He laughed. "But you would have loved the luxury," he said. "The life on these boats was wonderful. People took the trip just for a rest. A different class of people. Such costumes! Music! Songs! This would be just the time for it—high water and a full moon. You would have loved it then. The food was magnificent, the beds were comfortable, and there was running water in your room."

I told him there was running water in my room now.

"Yes, but that's nothing," he said. "In those days it was *luxurious*."

"Do you think things are improving at all?" I asked.

"Very little."

"Do you think they will improve under the present regime?"

"There can't be much improvement," he said, "so long as labor dictates the conditions. You've got to set a limit to what labor can do. Now, for instance, I make a contract to sell caviar. I've got to pay for the caviar, and then I've got to send it by rail. I never know when the railroad workers are going to decide to take a bigger wage and raise the rates. You can't do business that way."

Another man joined in the conversation here, a Volga merchant also, slim-faced with multiple wrinkles and big teeth. He was absolutely convinced of something, and eager to define it exactly.

"What you've got to do"—he paused impressively—"is to *restore private property*."

His tone made it clear that he had thought things through to the bottom, and knew that on that account he might be regarded as a little utopian.

"At least," he added, "the government has got to encourage private enterprise. They've got to quit stifling us with arbitrary taxation. The taxes change every three months. You just get something started, and they walk in and take away your profit in the form of taxation. And meanwhile you are competing with the state enterprises which have all the advantages. The government doesn't care anything about us. It only passes laws to protect the workers."

To me, of course, this last remark gave further glory to the Bolsheviks. They had really turned society upside down, and were holding it firmly in that position. These rich merchants would have to *become* workers—that was all—and then we would have real democracy. But I did not say that, and I cannot pretend that I pondered deeply about it. I was occupied now with the poetry of life, the full thrill of living it, no matter under what "system." I was riding down the Volga—that was enough—the classless society could take my attention later on!

Sometimes in those days I experienced a feeling akin to shame because of this trait of my character. In a country where so many of my friends were consecrating themselves, in a superhuman if not almost divine tension, to the effort to build a new world, I was so largely engaged in merely experiencing the world as it is, or learning with a wayward interest whatever could be learned about it. But these moods of compunction for my sin of enjoying life were not frequent enough to redeem me.

We slipped past Simbirsk, the birthplace of Lenin, in a drizzling dark and I saw nothing of it. But the next day in sunlight we entered the "gates of Samara," where the river narrows and grows swifter; and the sky narrows too, for hills rise on both shores, and the too peaceful long meadowy Russian landscape gives way to a small patch of mountain scenery. Leaves grew on those mountains rather than trees; they must have been recently shaved for timber; but they were jungles just the same. The river swirled past them almost as fast as the steamboat, a yellower brown since the Kama flowed into it. And most unrevolutionary of surprises, a strong moist wind blew steadily into our faces the fragrance of millions and millions of lilies of the valley that were blossoming under those leaves.

There is nothing in nature more thrilling than a river at the flood. Below Samara in the valleys, whole forests were swimming in the Volga, high stately oaks, and lindens and waving poplars trailing their longest branches in the swift water. As we slid rapidly past in the twilight, following the channel from one bank to the other, we could hear nightingales singing in those forests. And once we heard a cuckoo—so much like a cuckoo clock that we laughed aloud at his cleverness. The old wild rich brown silent river cares little for the politics of the republics along its banks, cares little for revolutions, parties, nations, for races, for man. Unimaginable ages it has poured magnificently down through those drinking valleys, only to dry up in the desert and disappear into the air.

Russia as I saw it from the Volga was a nation of poor people. It always had been a nation of poor people, with an incredibly small class of owners and rulers putting a shiny frosting on it. Now the owners and rulers were gone; the new Communist aristocracy had not yet caught hold; *everybody* was poor. And poorness in Russia was unredeemed by any color. There was never a fleck of paint in all these farmer and fisher villages along the Volga. Never two stones were laid up together for a house. All the human dwellings were little one-story squares, dull gray or wet-straw brown, drabber than the earth they clustered on, and the dwellers were clad in that dusty yellow flour-bag type of cloth that made Russian poorness look poorer than any other. Sometimes a girl would have a white towel around her head, but never a gay ribbon. Never any single thing was vivid or picturesque. Only the church! That indeed was newly painted, was made of stone, and was big and almost always beautiful. White in its body and with high silver-green domes or golden-domed towers, you could see it shining in the sunlight long before you distinguished any sign of the poor sad cluster of huts surrounding it. You would think it incredible that life so destitute and so barren of color could build such a bright-hued temple to an un-answering God.

In calling the Russia I saw a nation of poor people I do not mean to suggest a "classless society," or the faintest beginnings of it. I never saw class division more distinct and disheartening than on that Volga steamboat. The first-class and second-class passengers, to be sure, were merged together, and some of them, I was happy to note, had patches on their pants. Even among them the question how much dinner one's money could buy and whether one could afford an extra cucumber today, or perhaps tomorrow, was a general one. But down below all this on the under deck, was an impenetrable mass of packed-in peasants, sleeping on crates like dried apples with only a lath between them, squatting all day in a dark gangway, nursing their babies or munching their bread and sausage in serflike forbearance, and smelling to heaven as they had for centuries. I was surprised and shocked by this fact; it did not fit in very well with some of the oratory of the Bolsheviks. But I comforted myself by asking and answering a question: "Can Russia raise herself up very gradually as a whole people, decreasing instead of increasing these class differences with the increase of wealth?" And my answer: "I do not see how any person of historic imagination or human sympathy could fail to be glad that, in the person of her government, she is determined to try to do it."

In Tsaritsyn I presented my letter from Trotsky at the office of the President of the Soviet, and was shown immediately into the presence of that important character. I found him a slim-faced, scholarlike young man with a high clear brow, a jocular mind, and a talent and taste for conversation. He told me that I had made a great mistake in coming down the Volga on the *Memory of Comrade Markin.* I should have taken the *Comrade Trotsky* or the *International*—those were real boats—this was an ill-appointed old tub. Moreover when he found that we were leaving the boat at Tsaritsyn and going overland to Armavir and the Kuban valley and the Caucasus, he took delight in painting the glories of the lower Volga, of Astrakhan and the trip on the Caspian Sea to Baku. His charm and his feeling for the adventure of our trip were persuasive. He almost made me believe that the smell of fish in Astrakhan and the smell of petroleum on the Caspian were the two chief attractions this side of Samarkand. He had taken the trip himself in a rowboat, escaping from Denikin with two companions stricken with typhus, rowing the boat and nursing those patients for twenty-seven days on a breathless ocean, and pulled them both through. Every long-time Bolshevik in Russia had some such tale to tell. I stopped him by saying that I had only a day in Tsaritsyn, and wanted to see all the fine points of the town.

"We haven't any fine points," he said. "We can show you graves, and we can show you factories wrecked and destroyed by the civil war—that is about all. This town is a ruin."

How much more dreadful a ruin it would be twenty-two years later when its name had been changed to Stalingrad, was beyond the reach of our thoughts. And indeed it was not a ruin, but like all Russia in those days of the NEP, half ruin and half reviving life. He sent us out in a troika to explore and examine the town, and I spent that day confirming, as best I could, by the aspect of an industrial city far from Moscow, the statistical reports published by Lenin's government of the rate of industrial revival throughout Russia. My conclusion was that those reports were, to the degree humanly possible, reliable. When that too heated question of the relative merits of Lenin's and Stalin's government comes up at last for thoughtful settlement, I trust this detail will be remembered. Lenin faced his ledger and made others face it; he had no use for falsified statistics.

Chapter 55

SOCIAL OPINION UNDER LENIN AND TROTSKY

It was a talkative trip on the all-day train from Tsaritsyn to Armavir, but the talk as I remember it was not about politics mainly, but about "the meaning of life." It is a subject that Russians are readier to discuss with perfect strangers than Americans are. And I need not add that the only conclusion arrived at was the end of the journey.

Armavir, a trading center with a population of about seventy thousand, nestles in a bend of the Kuban River, and the river, approaching it, cuts a wide clean curve through acres of vacant dark-green meadow. So it was, at least, in 1923. And on a sunny afternoon a good half of the population, it seemed to me, the youngest and the healthiest half, the alive half—if I may pretend that a half of any city's population is alive—would ramble out there, strip off their clothes, men, women, boys, and girls together, or very near together, and go swimming in the cool water. From the bridge in the city you could see them strung along the banks for a mile in each direction, their flesh rosy in the setting sun, their little mounds of clothing white in the dark grass.

A mile up the river beyond that meadow I saw a tall smoking chimney, and decided to go up there and find out what the workers in a factory might think about the revolution. On the way we passed a cavalry barrack with four vast brick stables and hundreds of highly polished, powerful Arab horses, saddled and bridled and ready for battle, standing in a restless line outside. "Cossacks!" I said to myself almost with a shudder. But they were on my side now, and I had a letter from their commander in my pocket. The Cossacks paid no attention to us, and we contented ourselves with admiring their horses. Approaching the factory we ran into a barbed-wire fence that was evidently intended to keep us out, but wasn't very serious about it. It was not a factory exactly, but the city's waterworks in a state of partial restoration. A group of some twenty men, day laborers and mechanics, were grouped around an outdoor table over the river bank, studying some blueprints in the hands of an engineer. They were surprised at me and my strange grammar, and it took me some minutes to overcome, with Eliena's help, their suspicion that I had an ulterior motive in asking them questions. We became very friendly, however, and our conversation lasted for over an hour. I made elaborate notes of it because of my surprise at its sophistication. We discussed the war, the revolution, the Bolshevik government, the hopes of peace and democracy, much as they might have been discussed by a mixed assemblage of rebels and revolutionists, pacifists and humanitarian socialists, at a highbrow gathering in the Rand School for Social Science. Perhaps a glimpse of it is worth preserving even at this distance.

The engineer was the first to speak up frankly, a big man with level eyes under burly eyebrows. When I told him I had come all the way from New York to study conditions and states of mind under the Soviet Government, he said:

"We're sick—that's our condition. We *were* sick, but we're beginning to get well. You can hear those wheels going round." And he pointed proudly to the open door of the shop.

"You'll be sick too," he added with a grin.

"No, they won't!" a lively little mechanic in a blue blouse interrupted. "Only countries on a low level of culture will go through this experience. Countries like China may. America never."

That was forty years ago. How little the basic question has changed!

"What do *you* think about it?" the engineer asked me.

"I don't call it a disease exactly. I call it an experiment, a very interesting experiment."

"Interesting to *you* to see *us* make it!" he said, and a good laugh drew us together.

"I'll tell you what we think," a pale young man began—younger than the rest, but also, I thought, better educated. "It may be possible to develop a society under the Communist dictatorship, but it will take a long time. It will be the younger people who will grow up to it. For us it is hard. We Russian people are accustomed to a life where everybody has his own private ambition. Everybody wants to get a little piece of property."

"At present you don't feel that the Bolsheviks represent you, then?" I asked.

"Self-appointed representatives!" said a ragged worker leaning against a tree at a distance. Dressed in greasy clothes of a patched yellow color, with wisps of yellow hair in his eyes, his face lean and seamy, this man pounced on our conversation.

"Self-appointed representatives!"

"You see," the pale young man continued—and this was the first time I had heard it explicitly stated—"all the important offices in our trade union are occupied by Communists, and they are decided upon from above. For instance, I think I can say that I represent the workers in this shop, but they can't elect me to an important post because I'm not a Communist. I have no power. I can't decide anything."

No one opposed this, and in the pause that followed, a deep warm voice from behind and over the young man said: "God give us peace! That's what we want—peace!"

At this the rebel against the tree spoke up again.

"I want peace too," he said, as though making a concession. "I enjoyed the war. I fought on both sides, and they both treated me fine. But I've had enough."

To my inquiry how he came to fight on both sides, he said:

"I fought with the Reds first. The workers in general sympathized with the Reds. The Whites came and drove us out. We swam right across this river here under fire. Lots of us were drowned. I retreated with them and came back with them. And then the Whites came back and I was tired of retreating, so I stayed where I was. The Whites mobilized me, and we drove the Reds all the way to Tsaritsyn. There they licked us and we started to retreat. We ran like hell day and night. I ran all the way home here and then I stopped. I never left home again. I had enough."

"And you liked one about as well as the other?" I repeated.

"Yes. Only I'll say this: The Reds didn't hang. They killed people, shot them, but they didn't hang. The first thing the Whites did when they took a town was to put up a scaffold."

They all began to tell me at once how they had seen the bodies of their friends hanging for days, and had not been allowed to remove and bury them.

I knew enough and too much about that. To bring them back to the present, I asked what they thought of Lenin and Trotsky.

"I'll tell you what we think of Lenin," said the engineer. "If there were ten of him there wouldn't be any problem."

"Trotsky also is a big man—he has the respect of all the workers," said the young mechanic.

"I might have an altogether different opinion," said the rebel against the tree.

"You always might," I said, and he gave me a smile.

"Lenin we can acknowledge," he said. "He's a Russian citizen and speaks for the Russians. Trotsky's a Jew, and Jews are always for the Jews."

"You know the Jews say just the opposite thing about Trotsky," I said. "They complain that he has no racial loyalty."

He started to answer, but the large warm voice chimed in again:

"Comrade American, I want to say something there. You will find among the Russian workers that every man has his own view. Now for instance. . . . " Those in front moved a little to make room for his expansive gestures. "For instance, in my opinion it makes no difference at all what race or what nation a man belongs to. Whether you're an American and I'm a Russian, or you're a Jew and I'm a Tartar, what difference does that make? The question is what kind of a man you are. All men ought to meet each other as men. And I say if a man is defending the working class, he's a good ruler."

The word he used was not *ruler* exactly, but *administrator*.

The rebel's feelings were not strong on this point, and he yielded with a magnanimous gesture.

"All right. That's all right, if he works for the working class."

"If he works for the population!" said a milder voice.

"The working class!" he snapped back. As though they were bored with that argument, the others began to pick up their tools and stroll back to the factory.

Sochi, which has since become a grandiose playground for Stakhanovists and the Soviet aristocracy, was a humble little vacation town by the sea when we came there. It was divided into two "sides" by half a mile of woodland and a deep ravine. One side was the "town" with market, stores, church, the soviet, or town hall, and a once-fashionable hotel standing on a cliff over the water. The other was just summer cottages, eighty-four of them, to be exact. After a few days at the hotel, Eliena and I moved across the ravine and into the front room

The MASSES

"Gee, Mag, Think of Us Bein' on a Magazine Cover!"

A

B

C

D

(A) A Stuart Davis cover drawing (B) Max Eastman and Claude McKay (C) Floyd Dell (D) John Reed

(A) John Sloan (B) Art Young; (C) Crystal Eastman (D) Boardman Robinson (from a drawing by Robert Minor)

Four views of Florence Deshon (the actor
in the second picture is C. Aubrey Smith)

A

B

C

D

(A) Lisa Duncan (B) the little hous
Croton (C) the "orange sweater" (D
the trial of Eugene Debs (right, Rose
tor Stokes) (E) with Charlie Chapli
his studio, 1919 (right, Isaac McBr

IV

B

A

C

D

(A) Christian Rakovsky (B) Maxim Litvinov, Vorovsky and Adolph Joffe at Genoa (Underwood and Underwood) (C) Albert Rhys Williams (with Soviet writers) (D) Bill Haywood, Jim Cannon and Max Eastman in Moscow (E) Eliena Krylenko

E

V

A

B

C

(A) Trotsky at Prinkipo, painted by Eliena Krylenko (B) Trotsky and his first wife (C) Serebriakov and his daughter (D) the Humor lecture

D

VI

(A) On the dunes at Martha's Vineyard (B) on the beach with Marion and E. E. Cummings (C) Ernest Hemingway in the twenties

A portrait of Eliena by Richard L. Simon

of one of those cottages. The gentle young lady who had owned it before the revolution was still allowed to live there, but only in the two back rooms and on the back porch. Theoretically she rented these rooms and the porch from the government, but actually she paid her rent by taking care of the house—as much as any Russian house in those days was taken care of. Russian houses always looked to me as though the family were just moving in or moving out, but here it looked as though they were just moving out of a barn. There were no rugs or carpets, the furniture was falling apart, some essential hinge, knob or handle was missing from every object in the house. Seventy thousand Cossack soldiers, they told me, had been quartered in this little town of eleven thousand souls.

Our landlady—for notwithstanding her precarious perch in those back rooms, we called her that—would have made in America a nice and respected Sunday-School teacher. She had an unsensuous prettiness, a thin nose, thin legs, and a belief that God required her to be nice and not do anything wrong—a requirement which she fulfilled by being nice and not doing anything at all. For company she had two girl friends, a peachlike blonde called Ruzha and a little slit-eyed brunette whom we nicknamed Gipsy. They were dispossessed like her, daughters of the bourgeoisie, but impressed by the name, Krylenko, and disposed to be extra cordial, rather than resentful of the disaster Eliena's brother had helped to bring upon them. For further company there were two goats who lived in the cellar, and a stream of fleas who came up from that direction every day at dawn when the goats left for the communal pasture. It was primitive living, but Eliena's tireless energy and ingenuity made a happy home of it. My bed was a rusty woven-wire spring which she covered with a mattress of hay and leaves, freshening them up in some magical way every morning. For cooking she had another of those antique blow-torches called by the lordly name of "primus"—I never could find out why—and she used the outdoors for a kitchen. We found Albert in a rooming house called Teremok not far off, but high on a hill that rose between us and the sea. His rooms had a view and were less shaken to pieces by the earthquake of the war than ours. At least he had good chairs and a big desk, and we would meet there every evening and, with Eliena as umpire, gamble our depreciated rubles on who could define the largest number of words in a column of the Russian dictionary. It is the same way I learned Greek at Mercersburg with

my classmate Reuben Reed, and as a method of education it has
no rival.

I was rather impolitely curious about the thoughts and feelings of the
different classes of Russian society represented in this summer resort or
its environs. The main fruit of my curiosity was a large surprise at the
number of well-off people dispossessed of their property and leisure
who recognized a certain justice in the principle involved. "It's all
right, I'm not afraid of work," they would say. It was a first intimation
of the folly of our socialist assumption that the "capitalist class" would
fight with ferocity any attempt to dispossess them. In England, as
Norman Angell has remarked, "the capitalist class, once a parliamentary majority for a socialist government was obtained, was to reveal
itself as completely impotent to prevent widespread socialization and
even its own pretty complete dispossession. We were to see not only the
millionaire, but virtually the whole of the 'country house' opulence
. . . abolished, and the standard of living of the whole bourgeois
order most seriously reduced, by a socialist government that had not
even a clear electoral majority. . . . This social revolution was accepted without any attempt at revolt."

As an experiment one morning, I decided I would stop the first two
interesting people I met on the way to market and inquire what they
thought about bolshevism. It was early and I met nobody at all until I
reached the top of the stone stairway going up the other side of the
ravine. Here in a little shanty by the sidewalk with a table in front of
it, a soda bottle on the table, and a tray inside containing bright-
colored fruits and melons, sat a tall hulk of a man with steel-
rimmed spectacles and a drab mustache. I had passed him often, and
noticed that the roof of his shanty was so low that he had to bend over
when inside, and that he never took the trouble to straighten up when
he came out. Undoubtedly he had been intending to raise that roof for
years. Russians are always intending to do something; they never rest
from their intentions. Here are his exact words in answer to my
question.

"It's all damn nonsense, if you want my opinion. Liberty! The
Russian people haven't got enough spunk to be free. Communism—
Phh! What they need is just what they had before, an oak club over the
back. All this nonsense is ruining the country. The only thing that
would put it to rights is a Tsar!"

"Do you really mean that?" I asked.

"Why, of course," he said, and he swept in the whole country with his long arm. "Can't you see that these people won't work unless you stand over 'em with a club?"

My next victim was standing proprietorlike in front of a quick-lunch restaurant on the market square. He had the black eyes, black beard, and audacious big nose of those Caucasian mountain races. Although standing under a palm tree and sweating, he wore a tight-fitting cap of shaggy fur, and a stiff black fur cloak the size of a barn door. Thrown open to let in the air, it revealed the inlaid handle of a dagger hanging against his stomach, and a string of cartridges inserted in a braid that was looped across his chest. If he really was the proprietor of that restaurant, and not a Circassian bandit, I felt sure it was owing to circumstances over which he had no control.

Bandit or not, he turned out upon inquiry to be a devoutly religious man, painfully disturbed by the unorthodox faiths that were creeping into the Caucasus from other lands. After expressing himself eloquently on that subject, he suddenly asked me:

"What did you come to Russia for? I'd get out of here in an hour and a half if I had the chance. It's a damned hopeless place. I know what it is. You needn't say anything. I've lived abroad too. You've got some reasonable kind of freedom there."

He looked me over in a comradely way.

"If I live in America and I hate a man, I can go and kill him, can't I, and then explain myself to the police?"

He brushed his thumb over his fingers to show what he meant by "explain."

"What can I do here if I hate a man?"

I was, for the moment, at a loss for an answer, and he continued:

"Here in Russia if you kill somebody, this Bolshevik government comes right along and kills you!"

"I suppose they've had a good deal of trouble establishing order," I timidly suggested. "They had to be a little strict at first."

"Order!" he shouted. "What kind of order is that? They never give you a chance to explain yourself. They just clap you in jail, and then when they get ready try you for murder and shoot you. That's no kind of order!"

I looked for a smile in his scowling features, but could not find a trace of one.

"A government," he said, "ought to take a man's feelings into consideration."

I must add one more sample from my collection of social opinions, though I culled it in a different time and place. It was one of those clear sunny days when the Black Sea turned almost a Mediterranean blue, and the nude bodies of the Elysian bathers along our curving shore were so rich in color that man seemed, for the afternoon, to be at home on the earth, and belong to its beauty as do so many of the more kindly animals. One young woman especially seemed warmly lovely to me. She was formed like the Venus, not of Milo but of Cyrene, which is for me to say that she was the most perfectly formed woman I ever saw. Her hair too, ash blond, was knotted in a Greek fashion, and her face had a carved and quiet dignity. She bathed near me, and I cannot pretend that it was in the mood of a social investigator that I swam over to where she lay in the sun. I cannot pretend, either, that I am bold enough when dressed as a savage to make such an advance without encouragement. The encouragement came, however, little as you may incline to believe it, from my vicariously adventurous friend Eliena. I did, in the course of our acquaintance, remember to ask The Venus what she thought about the Bolsheviks. She had evidently done some thinking about the question, for she answered instantly and with an earnestly regretful shake of her beautiful head:

"They haven't done enough killing."

I want to mention, by contrast, a trait I found among the Russian people which had nothing to do with the revolution, or the regime of Lenin and Trotsky. The Greeks had a word for it, but I have never encountered it except in Russia. The word is *philoxenia*, and it means "love of the foreigner."

Two examples of this trait stand clear in my memory after thirty years. The checkroom for personal baggage in the Kharkov station was a long corridor running along a whole side of the waiting room. Your bags went in at one end, and to get them out you presented your check at the other end. I was in a hurry to catch a train and there was a big crowd at the outgoing end, so I went up to the ingoing end, and asked the clerk if he couldn't get my bags out in a hurry. He gave me a disapproving look and said rather brusquely: "You have to stand in line over there. Don't you know the end from the beginning?"

To parry the rebuke, and still hoping to get my bag, I started to explain that, as a foreigner, I hadn't caught on to the Russian way of doing things. I had no more than got the words "I'm a foreigner" out of my mouth, when he exclaimed: "Oh, you're a foreigner!" and rushed way down that long corridor and back with my bag as though I had said I was the president of the republic or the commander in chief of the Red army.

I did have in my pocket a large paper bearing the seal of the Red army and the signature of its commander in chief, asking every citizen to give me whatever help I might require in getting acquainted with the country. But this seemed, at least on one occasion, to command small deference compared to what was due me as a mere foreigner. I was on a train in the vicinity of Rostov-on-the-Don at the time when Trotsky had set going a campaign to teach the Russians to be clean. One of its stern, and apparently unheard-of, decrees was that anybody using the toilet while a train was standing in a station would be subject to a fine of, say, half a ruble. I probably have the amount wrong, but it was enough so that when a little boy of seven or eight years transgressed it and was collared by the conductor and dragged back to his parents to collect the fine, he bawled like a branded calf. His parents too, poor peasants whose lunch had been a small hunk of black bread, protested with outcries and tears of dismay. I got out my impressive document and, showing it to the conductor in what I thought was a magisterial manner, complimented him on his enforcement of the rules, but explained that they could not be applied to a child who was unable to read them.

The conductor examined my paper curiously and handed it back to me.

"I have every respect for the Red army, Comrade," he said, "but that doesn't alter the rules. This boy has broken a rule, and I have no choice but to impose the fine."

"But you're not fining *him*," I argued. "You're fining his parents— they didn't break the rule."

There ensued one of those hourlong and highly abstract arguments which are also characteristically Russian. The principles of law and equity were invoked, the age of maturity, the differences between a child and an adult, between hygiene and morality. At every descent into the concrete, he would say: "But the rules are explicit, and my duty is to enforce them." When driven into a corner, he would add: "I have to make a report, Comrade, and if I don't impose this fine I'll be fined myself."

A dozen of the passengers in the car had gathered around us, and most of them were on my side—or the little boy's. So the conductor felt obliged finally to back down. The impact of my powerful document, however. with its great seal and signature, was negligible.

"All right, Comrade," he said, taking out a pad and a pencil. "I'll put it down in my report that you, a foreigner, advised me not to impose the fine."

That satisfied them all, and they returned to their seats feeling that a principle had been invoked more honored than law or equity, or even the mandates of the Red army.

Chapter 56

A NOBLE FAMILY

If you come from a country town you will remember that there was in that town, or somewhere on the outskirts of it, or over the hill in Factory Hollow, a family of professional "poor folks." Other people were poor, too, but in a feeble, meager, half-hearted sort of way. This family was the real thing. Their poverty was an art. It was something to go to see. The bare, dirty, hen-trodden dooryard, the windowless, paintless, leaking and sagging house with a rusty stovepipe sticking out of the front window, the mangy rabbits and sick cats and dirty-faced, pretty children around the door.

Well, there was one of these families in Sochi, and in proportion as Russia was poorer than the United States they were poorer than the most absolutely destitute household that ever dug in on this side of the graveyard in our country.

There were six of them—a feeble, gentle, bewhiskered old man, who could do nothing because his hands shook violently all the time; his wife, beautiful, but practically blind; her mother, an aged lady in a wheelchair; her sister, still ineffectually walking on her feet; her daughter, whose arm was paralyzed but who earned a crust or two "giving lessons"; and the little granddaughter, five years old, blue-eyed, delicate, beautiful and wholly absorbed in the care of the above-mentioned cats and rabbits.

This was a noble family, the former owners of two estates in Russia and a villa in Nice, friends of the Tsar, hobnobbers with W. K. Vanderbilt and James Gordon Bennett, members of the *Petit Cercle* in Paris, international aristocratic joy-livers. And their name, Rimski-Korsakov, is known all over the world because one of the family was a great composer, and because the mother of that feeble old man I have referred to was an internationally famous beauty whose portrait hangs in the Louvre.

The husband of the daughter who gave lessons had been an officer in the Tsar's army, was mobilized by Baron Wrangel, and shot by the Bolsheviks when they occupied the town. She tramped sixty miles through the snow at night with a friendly Communist trying to intercede for him, but arrived too late. He shared the fate of all the officers captured on either side in that deliberately savage war.

I was told about this family by one of the members of the local administration and I asked him to take me round and introduce me to them. It sounded like a good story, and I approached that blind, broken-down, and half-burned-up old house with the practical eye of an enterprising journalist.

There was a sort of lopsided porch to it, but the roof of the porch had been broken off, and the splintered beam-ends of that roof stuck out into the air like mangled limbs. The window-holes were empty or stopped up halfway with old pieces of board and paper, and so the house looked blind as well as crippled.

And inside there was nothing, or almost nothing, but dirty and pit-marked walls, an aged thin-legged table, some tottering chairs and the strange sway-backed relics of a few beds. An old square reddish stove had its existence there but gave no warmth since there was no fuel to put in it.

On the chimney-piece was a photograph of that famous beauty whose portrait hangs in the Louvre, and of the present Madame Rimski-Korsakov in court attire, beautiful, too, and famous for her elegance in the most elegant circles of Paris and St. Petersburg.

To an "enterprising journalist" all these facts were admirable and exactly as they should be, but unfortunately I had stopped being a journalist and turned suddenly and somewhat shamefacedly into a human being before I had set a foot on the first step leading up to that lopsided porch.

"Oh, how good of you to come to see us!" said the old man, running feebly but with a most graceful geniality to meet me. "We heard that there was an American in town and we have so many friends in America. At least we had once—I don't know what may have become of them now."

He enclosed my hand in both of his trembling hands, looked in my eyes with that frank and real interest that is the only courtesy, and led me into his poor, dirty barrack with a sweetness of manner which made me feel that I and all enterprising journalists were criminals and fools.

"Now I wonder if you will happen to know any of my friends in America," he said, sitting forward in his chair with gentle animation. He was clad in some sort of loose baggy pants like flour bags, and an old faded blue coat with patches and the pockets hanging wide open like hungry stomachs, and there was no button on his shirt, but just some admirable attempt at a loose necktie, made, I should imagine, out of the tail of his shirt.

His shoes had white strings and they had little of anything else. They lay down sideways on the floor when he walked.

"There was Vanderbilt—W. K. Vanderbilt—we used to be together in the *Petit Cercle* in Paris. He had a private car there. I remember riding down to Trouville with him. You know him perhaps? But then you are younger. This was long ago. I lived almost all my life, you know, in Paris. I really speak French more naturally than Russian—"

He was speaking English as naturally as I could.

"And James Gordon Bennett—what can you tell me about him? Oh, that is too bad. We always thought he was a very unusual fellow. Well, you see I myself am an old man, but I forget about it!" And he laughed merrily, and with a humorous gesture toward his surroundings added, "You see how the times change—I won't live very long either at this rate!"

There was not a flicker of self-pity—not a false note in his merriment.

"But you," he went on, "you are young yet. You will see something come out of this. For us old people there seems to be nothing left to do but die, and that isn't very interesting. I try to tell them sometimes what they ought to do here in Sochi. I tell them how life is conducted in France, where they have a republic. But they tell me that is 'bourgeois,' and they don't want any of that. They don't want a bourgeois republic. They want something new. Well, perhaps they will get it. I wouldn't mind seeing Russia do something new—such a lazy, impractical, backward country. It would be quite a surprise if she showed you Westerners something you never heard of! But now, let me see, there was a very charming and dark-eyed Mrs. Mackay, Mrs. Clarence Mackay. Perhaps you would know something of her. But here is my wife, who very much wanted to meet you and she can remember all about those people far better than I."

His wife came in from out-of-doors carrying a long staff, standing slender and straight and gracious in the doorway, holding out her hand very far and a little indefinitely, because she could not see clearly where I was. She was dressed in a slim rag that used to be crêpe-de-chine, torn and dirty and delicate.

"I am so glad to meet you," she said, and her English too was perfect. "I don't know how an American ever strayed way off down here into the Caucasus. I can easily imagine all the people in Russia going to America, but what ever brought an American here I don't know."

"I think this is the most interesting place in the world," I said.

"Ah, you think it is interesting," she said, and the tone of her voice was just the least bit ironical as she dwelt on that word "interesting." She was smiling, and her face was very beautiful, exceedingly dark and thin, but with finely formed eye sockets and firm, sweet, intelligent, humorous lips. She had been a great beauty in her youth—that was evident—and in a way perhaps she was more beautiful now, for the bony structure of her features was so clear.

Her husband caught the irony in her tone and, although it was not bitter, he was moved to apologize for it.

"My wife is a little intolerant of this change," he said. "She cannot accustom herself to the personal hardship as well as I can."

"We are simply becoming savages," she said, looking about at that barren room with glowing eyes like a lynx in a cage. "We have moved seven times in three years, and each time to a more horrible place and with fewer things to take with us. I don't know where we shall end. But then, as you say—or perhaps you didn't say it, but you thought it—what becomes of us doesn't matter. We are old, and we have lived, and the question is, what is going to become of the world? Yes, indeed, you are right to say it is interesting. And what do *you* think about it? Do you think the whole world is going to be socialist?"

I did not commit myself on that question, because I wanted to know what she thought. So I brought the conversation back to Mrs. Clarence Mackay, whom I could discuss from personal acquaintance. From her we passed on to Mrs. O. H. P. Belmont and her daughter, the Duchess of Marlborough, whom also as a feminist I had known. She remembered all these people vividly and many other Americans of whom I knew only the names, and we had a long, gossipy, jolly, personal conversation that carried us both back ten or twelve years, and thousands of miles from where we were.

"Oh, I like Americans," she said. "We were always with them in Paris. My husband spent more than half of his life in the American bar."

She laughed lightly as he spread out his hands in futile protest.

"Now, that is not true!" he said. "How can you say such a thing?" But she was enjoying herself.

"Oh, yes. He was a fine fellow and he had such beautiful manners. There is very little left of him now, as you see! He used to change his shirt three times a day in Paris, and then when he came home to Russia he thought it was only necessary to change it twice a day. Now he only has one shirt, and he takes it off once in a great while, when we can afford to heat up a little water, and washes it in his bare skin!"

She laughed, and then she became more serious again.

"You know," she said, "that is the one thing of all that I find it most difficult to endure—the fact that I can't have hot water when I want it. It seems to me now as if I have learned to stand everything but that. I can't be clean. That is unbearable. But let us talk about pleasanter things. You didn't tell me whether you think something good is coming out of all this. Do you?"

"I think so, yes," I said. "The Soviet Government is at least trying to solve a problem that all other governments refuse to face."

"Yes," she said, turning her head toward the window as though she were looking far off there where I could see white clouds moving in the wide Russian sky but she couldn't. "I suppose that the condition of a majority of the people in Russia is better now than it was before. We are a little group, and we don't count. But it is hard on old people. There is no place for us."

The slight sadness of her expression troubled her husband again, and he explained it. "They tell us," he said, "that those who don't work shall not eat. And that is perfectly just, but it is a little hard on those who *can't* work." He made this explanation with an expression of happy triumph, as though a knotty point in the problem had been overcome.

"It is impossible, you see, for me to work." And he held up his shaking hands, beaming at the irrefutable proof of his proposition.

His wife was not listening any longer; she was still seeming to look out of the window. She turned suddenly in the pause that followed his demonstration.

"And American cocktails!" she said. "How I love American cocktails! Do you know I don't believe you could name a drink that I couldn't make with my own hands—Martini cocktails, and whiskey sours, and highballs and Jack Rose and Tom Collins—oh, I know all those American names!—and gin fizz and gin rickeys. Your compatriots used to keep me busy all the time. How I would love a gin rickey right now in this hot weather, wouldn't you? But I can't even afford a bottle of that awful white soda they sell at your boarding house!"

She chuckled as though at something too ridiculous for hearty laughter. "When my daughter comes she will give you some of our 'tea,' and you mustn't be afraid of it. It is not made out of dirt. It is made out of chestnuts, last year's chestnuts.

"And no doubt you like pastry. Our pastry is made out of the very best leather, as you will see. My husband, you know, was a terribly fastidious gentleman, when he used to be a gentleman, and two things he never would eat were pastry and vegetables. Now he lives on pastry and vegetables, nothing else—and very little of those."

You could make no answer to these remarks, which flowed so musically and humorously out of her throat. You could only laugh as she was laughing. It was the whole-hearted and yet moderate laughter of an imaginative person, who has seen every side of a situation and decided that the humorous side is the best.

Her daughter was larger and stronger than she, a school-teacherly woman of thirty-five or forty. She seemed to have a similar intention not to be bitter—or rather, perhaps, not to be stupid about what had happened. But she had not the same humor to help her, and she did not succeed so well. She spoke, however, with a surprising degree of sensible judgment about her husband's death.

"The tragedy of it was that he was captured in another town, where they did not know him. He would not have been shot here, because everybody knew him and knew that he worked hard and worked for the people. He did not share the views of the Communists, and he made no pretense of it, but he was not in favor of the war against them. He was mobilized, and as an officer in the army merely felt that he had to go. I had the help of one of the Communists here in Sochi, and I could have saved him, if I had got there in time.

"I resent that accident, that unnecessary misfortune, but I have no personal resentment against the Communists because he was shot. That was the way war was conducted. That is what a revolution is, I suppose, and the revolution was bound to come. I can see that. I don't know whether any good will come of it or not. I am afraid there are too many beasts in this world. But it was inevitable; it was bound up in the war and the conditions of Russian life."

"I think it is wonderful," I said, "how little bitterness, or personal resentment, you feel about it all. You never even mention the loss of your property."

"Oh, the property," the old man explained, "the land and all the care of those estates—I am really glad to be rid of them! They belong to the peasants, and anybody who thinks they will ever be given back to us by the government of Russia, is a fool. That is all done and settled, and a good thing it is.

"I do wish I had kept my villa at Nice," he added. "I sold it just before the war. I had only then decided to come back and live in Russia. In consequence I have absolutely nothing, and that is too bad, when I cannot go to work. But as for owning land and having servants wait on you—if you want my opinion, they are quite right, it is all humbug."

He spread his hand out, and smiled again that conclusive and delightful smile. "Servants especially," he added.

His wife looked at him with a kind of incredulous tolerance while he made these extreme statements. Perhaps she was saying in her heart: "Well, after all, we take care of you." But I do not know about that: it was merely a guess. She had grief in her heart, and he for some reason had not. Perhaps he was too old, or perhaps he was a Christian—a real Christian. There have been such beings. He had recently endowed the family with two poods of flour which he earned by giving a young boy lessons in English, and that had made him happy. It was the first cent of money he ever earned in the whole seventy-one years of his life.

I do not want to exaggerate the political liberality of this family. I could not exaggerate that of the old man, and his wife had a mood of grief and humor that was above politics. But the daughter was able to speak bitterly about the local government. She enjoyed describing the hypocrisies and follies of the soviet, for which she worked for a time in the capacity of tax assessor.

"I had to go around and pry into people's personal lives," she said, "to find out how much taxation they were able to stand. At one time they were taxed on the basis of whether they used tooth powder or not. And I had to find that out. If they wanted to put a tax on tooth powder, why not collect it at the drug store?

"And oh, the falsehoods!" she went on. "At one time I had to ascertain the number of cows owned by each peasant in the district. And I would come in and report that a certain peasant had one cow and another had fifteen, and they should be taxed accordingly.

" 'That figure one is all right,' my chief would say to me, 'but this fifteen—that is too many, make it seven.'

"Now why should I make it seven when it was fifteen? Can you explain such wanton falsehood and injustice?"

I could explain it quite easily, I thought, as but one evidence of the central difficulty of the Bolshevik government—that of accommodating a proletarian revolution to an agrarian people. But I did not explain it, for I wanted to hear the worst.

"What do you think about it all?" I said to her mother. "Do you think the Bolsheviks are false and hypocritical?"

"Oh, no," she said. "There are many sincere and able people— especially among the leaders at Moscow. And they may be right. Something may come of it after fifty years—but for us nothing. We see nothing but the world turned upside down. We are too old." She paused, and it seemed as though she were holding herself back from the abyss of that thought.

"It is not for us," she continued quickly, "but Lenin, it seems to me, is a man of great sincerity and idealism."

"That is one man of whom everybody in Russia speaks well," I said.

"Yes, and Trotsky, too," she added. "They must be geniuses to have taken hold of this country in the condition it was and made it go. You don't know what a task it was, you don't know Russia. Russians literally never do anything. They have to have a German or an Englishman come and show them how to get up in the morning."

"What is your mother's state of mind about it?" I asked. "Is she as reasonable as you are?"

"Oh, don't ask mother," she said quickly. "She can't realize that it might be better for other people, even if it is so hard for us."

But her mother had heard my question, and leaned forward in her wheelchair, sharp-eyed and crackly voiced. She reminded me of a predacious bird, suddenly waking up at the scent of prey.

"If you ask me," she said in Russian, "I say horrors, horrors! That's all. Horrors!"

Madame Rimski-Korsakov smiled. "Now you mustn't get her roused up about it. She sees only one side. She remembers how we used to live on our estate. Oh, it is too bad you couldn't have visited us then. Did you ever ride in a troika? Oh, yes, that is fun, and we had such lovely horses. We could have gone riding every day, and I would have made you all kinds of wonderful food and drinks. I will tell you now how to make a delicious salad and when you get back to America and start living again you can try it.

"You take some new potatoes, and you boil them in a very perfect lamb broth. And then you take a few truffles and boil them in champagne. And then you take the best Italian olive oil, and make an exquisite mayonnaise dressing. You mix the dressing with the potatoes at the last moment, and then sprinkle the truffles delicately over the top. That is delicious."

I could not help laughing, she described this salad with such a wistful smile, and looked so trim and elegantly and raggedly destitute down to her feet, which were clad in large, shapeless, flat peasant's clodhoppers made out of rope. She noticed my glance.

"You would never think," she said, "that I was known in Parisian society as the 'queen of elegance,' and that my father was Master of the Court at St. Petersburg. Look at me!" And she spread out her hands, laughing musically and delightfully.

"I might think so, you know," I said, remembering the fairy stories.

"Well," she said, "now let us talk a little about beefsteaks. This is one of my great pleasures, talking about beefsteaks. I will tell you how we used to do, to make them especially good. We used to take two beefsteaks and while one of them was cooking we would squeeze the juice out of the other in a press and pour it on the first one. My, didn't that make it rich and juicy!"

"If you used up two beefsteaks every time you ate one," I said, "you certainly have no right to complain of the revolution."

She laughed and looked friendly.

"I knew that was what you were thinking," she said. "You think we got just what was coming to us." And when her daughter came back into the room, she repeated our conversation.

"He says if that is the way we lived we ought to be thankful there was a revolution."

"No, I didn't," I corrected her. "I said you ought not to complain."

"I guess you are right," she said. "And you know I don't complain. I just laugh. I think it is all so indescribably funny. You know there are six of these workers' sanatoriums right around the vicinity of this house and every time any of them serves a meal they ring a little bell. And they each of them have five meals a day, counting tea. I sit here with practically nothing to eat and I hear these little bells ringing merrily all around me all day long. It reminds me of a passage in one of Tolstoy's novels. I've forgotten which one it is, but a servant comes back to the servants' quarters, after being in the dining room, where the master was giving a dinner to his friends. And—do you know what the Russian word *zhrat* means? Then I must find just the right word in English. I think it is gobble. 'How can they gobble so!' That is what the servant said.

"And that is what I say to myself when I hear these little bells ringing all day long and I know that those who used to be our servants are having their turn.

" 'How can they gobble so!' I say, and I find it hard to feel very resentful about it."

Mme. Rimski-Korsakov's tea and pastry lived up to all that she had said about it, and I was as glad to get home to my own place for dinner as I was to go back there the next day for a glimpse of her beauty and a taste of her inimitable conversation. To me she was heroic, and I was glad I had no fixed system of ideas in my head to block the path of my admiration.

Chapter 57

A JOURNEY TO NO GOAL

I lived almost two months in these primitive yet joyful conditions, cared for and guided by an expert in love and the Russian ways of life—convinced that the whole world was being made over on super-democratic specifications and that I was helping it along with my hard study and writing.

An interruption came in early August, a message from the War Office that Trotsky was taking a rest and could see me in Kislovodsk, an inland *kurort* under the shadow of Mt. Elbruz. Eliena received at about the same time an intimation from Litvinov that he could use her services in Moscow. We went the long way round, taking a boat from Sochi down the shore to Sukhum where we paused a day or two for exploration, then on to Batum—from Batum across Georgia by train to Tiflis. There we got in touch with the Red army command, and they gave us a ride in a military truck across the famous Georgian Military Road to Vladikavkaz. From there we went by train north to Pyatigorsk, where I took a branch line down to Kislovodsk and Eliena went on to Moscow. I was still trying to be a social investigator on that trip, but my chief memories are of the keen air and singing landscape high up on the watershed near Mount Kasbek, and of the Terek River, roaring like a wild yellow dog or catamount furiously down among tumbled boulders through its cavelike canyon in the northern slope of the Caucasus Mountains.

One of the first things to strike my eyes after finding a room at Kislovodsk was a bright gold and rosy scarf fluttering down breeze from the throat of no less astonishing an apparition than Isadora Duncan. Standing beside her was her most dynamic daughter-in-the-dance, Irma, Eugen's best girl when we all played together two years before. I liked Irma and would have loved to renew our friendship in that strangely far-off place, but my feeling toward Isadora was not so simple. It was a mixture of adoring hero-worship with annoyance and recoil. There was something in her in private life that embarrassed me and made me ill-at-ease. She looked, in the first place, like one of El Greco's Irish Mick-like angels with a turned-up nose—a very difficult kind of nose, in my opinion, for an angel to wear, and still more for a Grecian dancer. She was not of heroic size as you expected after seeing her on the stage, and even her body was not excitingly beautiful. She had in supreme degree only the powers of expression and motion. Thus when not dancing, her physical presence did not make up for a certain overriding force in her—a sort of didactic, almost blue-stocking assertiveness. She was always lecturing me on things that I knew a great deal more about than she did. And this began right there at the railroad station in Kislovodsk, where I had gone down to buy a bottle of milk from the peasants who sold produce to the incoming trains. We had hardly finished an astonished embrace when she began explaining bolshevism to me in terms of a romantic leap toward the unattainable, and assuring me that Yessenin, from whose blows and drunken clutches she was just then escaping, was a great lyric poet. That too was a subject on which, since I could read his poems, I felt it would be more fitting to ask my opinion than overwhelm me with hers. I am recalling all this in order to explain my rather peculiar behavior on meeting these old friends from America in a far-off Russian forest. I find it described in these terms by Irma in her book, *Isadora Duncan's Russian Days:*

> After two and a half days' not too comfortable journeying, the travelers reached the little town at six o'clock one August morning. As they stepped off the train, amid the bustling and shouting, the first person their astonished eyes lighted on was an old friend from New York—Max Eastman, the poet and writer. He was down at the station at that early hour, he replied in answer to their first question, to buy some milk.
>
> Eastman very helpfully piloted the two newcomers about the place, helped them find rooms at the hotel, and then entertained them at lunch. After lunch he went off and was seen no more, either closely or at a distance during the remainder of their stay in the resort.

My recoil against Isadora's didactic romanticism must have been pretty strong, for I was badly in need of company at Kislovodsk. I was drearily lonesome. I used to boast that, though often melancholy, I was never bored. But here in this vacation resort, once filled with the gay life of a ruling class, and now invaded by a mixture of proletarians and zealots, neither of them acquainted with the art of enjoying life, I did come very near to boredom. I was also exasperated because Trotsky, who had got me there with a promise of leisure, found himself too busy to see me at all. His wife was sick, and I couldn't see her either—only a smug, female-hipped male secretary, who kept putting me off in a mysterious manner as though he were the guardian of an explosive secret of state. I was making no headway on my biography, and was rapidly losing my zeal to create it. Besides that, there was no coffee in the region and I had a hard time keeping awake.

"I am very lonely," I wrote to Eliena, "also sleepy and good-for-nothing. I haven't seen the twin peaks of Elbruz yet, though I went wandering way up in the high mountains yesterday, alone and disconsolate and fervently longing to see something the shape of a woman's breast."

In despair one day, I approached a little comely girl who looked at me in a funny slanting way.

"Mademoiselle, why do you never take a walk?" I asked.

Her answer sounded like water plumping out of a bottle.

"What did you say?" And again that queer noise.

"You must please speak very slowly, for I don't understand Russian very well."

Again only an unintelligible spasm in her throat. But I had disciplined myself to be stubborn in these linguistic matters. I repeated my question more loudly—this happened in a street opposite the Grand Hotel—and while a large public assembled to watch and listen to our agony, she made that painful noise once more. I saw that her face had turned red, and felt that I had turned both red and wet, when suddenly it dawned on me: That isn't Russian—it's just nothing—she's a deaf mute!

I gave the onlookers a fierce glance, said, "Pardon please!" as gently as I could, and fled.

After about two weeks of this frustrated existence, I went up one day to Trotsky's headquarters to get my mail. His vague and self-important secretary had learned from the courier who brought the mail that Eliena had had an attack of malaria. He had also learned that she was very much better, but he advised me to go to Moscow nevertheless, and suggested, in what I learned was meant to be a significant manner, that

I could have a place on a certain train. I did not take that train because of a previous hint from him that I was to have extended conversations with Trotsky where I was. My feelings when I learned that Trotsky had gone on that train, and that his conspiratorial secretary had been attempting in his best secret-of-state manner to convey this information to me, were not conducive to creative effort.

A sole gleam of light during those gloomy days at Kislovodsk had been a letter from Charles Scribner's Sons saying they had five hundred dollars of royalties on my *Enjoyment of Poetry*, and where should they send it? In Soviet currency that was a year's living as I lived, and I decided to go back to Sochi and write my novel.

Chapter 58

AGAIN THE INWARD ENEMY

Albert was still in Sochi when I came, living in his high room on a hill where he could see a good stretch of "The Russian Land," and our two rooms in the house down in the hollow behind him were still vacant. Our "landlady," Niura, and her two friends whom we had named Ruzha and Gipsy, agreed eagerly to my moving in and occupying alone the two front rooms that Eliena and I had lived in. They had been wondering, I suppose, what bureaucratic stick or brutal Red soldier the government would quarter in those rooms, and were happy to see a friendly face. For me too, it was a happy situation, for though all three were comely and possessed of charm, they were not exciting in a way that might have got in the path of my work. Gipsy was small, brown, slanty-eyed, sensually attractive but frigid; Ruzha, a big pretty doll-like blonde, sensual enough but "slow to catch fire," as she would amiably explain. Niura, the landlady, was in every way a nice girl, but shaped by destiny, one felt, to be an old maid. I hired a tall, dark proletarian woman, a native Georgian of middle age, to come in daily and cook my lunch and dinner. Her name was Liza, and she was handsome in an angular way. We all became, it seemed to me, notwithstanding differences of class and opinion, genial if superficial friends.

Albert and I were rising early and working hard, but keeping healthy by swimming when the work was done, or wandering along the beach and over the hills throwing stones at trees, or into abandoned wells, betting millions of rubles on each throw. "Gambling takes the place of love with us both," I wrote to a friend. The ten-million-ruble banknote, as I remember it, was then worth about a half a cent, but as a stimulus to the gambling instinct it had a higher value. My royalties at Scribner's were slow to arrive, and Albert had funds in the

Co-operative Bank. Also I was a better shot than he, but only slightly so, not steadily enough to discourage him. It thus resulted that I earned a good share of the twenty-five dollars a month on which I lived by betting on these contests of skill. We devised another way of gambling that I would like to advertise to those who share with me, and with the ancient Greeks, a belief in the importance of play. There was a small stream that meandered down through a valley not far from Sochi, and we would take a couple of "boats"—any little chip or twig properly shaped to avoid the snags would do—and start them traveling down that stream, each backing his own boat with a few million rubles to arrive at a distant harbor first. It is an active, outdoor, meadow-and-woodland game of chance that far surpasses pinball or roulette.

The situation was ideal for that combination of creative work and fervent study that was keeping me happy so far from home. Indeed it was ideal for the creation of a great novel if I had one in me. For a short time I thought I had, for my imagination put on such a tropic storm of passion-drenched and tumbling thoughts, events and scenes and actions as it had never dreamed of doing before. Up to then my creative life had been continually diluted or crashed into by practical, political, social, romantic, or financial concerns and diversions. I had never quite got down to business as a writer. Here at last I could do that.

Eliena in the distance was, of course, a vital factor in this perfect situation, for her love sustained me and yet asked nothing but that I accept it. I did adore her, and said so in a letter every time a little steamboat went up to Tuopse, where the mail train came down to the coast. I needed that much of the joy and security of love, but not any more. A little self-knowledge, a little remembering, a little disciplined and pure devotion to what I was doing, would have held me there without emotional change until the novel was written. But my capital vice of self-dispersal, of wanting to live all lives at once, diluted me.

"I have no desire and no purpose now but to finish this novel," I wrote to Eliena, "I want to do something with all my heart once before I die. . . . " and then in folly and contradiction I added: "I am always thinking that you will be with me, and whether you will come, and when you will come." And I proposed that she resign her position in the Foreign Office and become my secretary instead of Litvinov's. The salary in American money would not be too much to pay—especially after my life of Trotsky was published throughout the world—and aside from the financial contract there would be no responsibility on either side. Our emotions would be free.

"It is a big step for you to take," I cautioned her, "and I am not sure a wise one. I might go away in the spring—perhaps to publish my book—and you might not be able to leave the country. We don't know what wars are coming, what changes." And for full measure of caution (or self-protection) I added: "I don't know what I will do, or what I will be, after I finish this novel. I only know that I will defy every expectation, and betray every duty that people think I have, in order to finish it." More persuasively, I concluded:

"It is so beautiful, so unbelievably warm and beautiful here—the sea velvety and wild, the sun full of love for all animals and birds and the race of men—it seems a folly for us not to pluck the flower of happiness while it blooms for us. Maybe you will be sad afterward, and maybe I, but we will have been happy. I will meet you at the station in the sun with joyful and careless love in my heart if you come."

She did come, and seemed to come with reckless abandon, although I learned years afterward that her "resignation" as Litvinov's secretary had been offered with a certain prudence. She was wise enough, and he magnanimous enough, to leave the way open for her return if I should turn out to be unreliable either as employer or lover. It might have been better if I had known that.

I was waiting a car-length away when she stepped from the little train in Tuopse where I had gone to meet her. Her feet had not touched the ground when my old inward demon clutched me with an unanswerable emotion:

"I do not want her here. She is alien to me. My sublime joy in her companionship is gone. Being gone, it can never return, never believe in itself again."

These thoughts, these certainties, flooded my mind in the few seconds that carried me to her side. They kept up their willful tumult within me while I threw my arms around her and greeted her as though in the happiest moment of my life.

I was too shockingly astonished to recognize in this the old evil work of my demon—too horrified to remember that the same thing had happened within me twice before: once with Ida Rauh, when I woke to find us on a boat to Europe together, again with Florence Deshon. No, I believed that on this particular occasion I had made an error in judgment: Eliena was not after all, now that I saw her, the ideal companion I had been loving in my dreams; I had committed myself by mistake to a line of action I could not carry through.

I did carry it through all that afternoon and the night long, falling back on my well-learned art of kept-up lovingness. But in the morning when I sat down to my desk to continue the novel that had been so turbulently pouring out of me, not a word would come, not an image, not a thought. I was dried up completely. I was dead. I sat there for a long time trying to put down words, but instead of the words, and blocking their flow, a tangle came into the muscles of my brow, a knotted tension that became increasingly painful. I gave up finally and proposed that we take the first day off and go swim in the sea.

But I could not keep up such a deception very long. We were too closely thrown together, and Eliena was too sensitively intelligent. She had secured and brought down with her one of the rare copies of Pushkin's forbidden poem, "Gavriliada," which had cost him his liberty and almost his life. It is a long poem, a sort of epic song, both boldly erotic and blasphemous in the highest degree, but saved by sheer lyrical beauty from being crude or coarse. When she saw me translating that poem all morning instead of continuing with my vaunted novel, Eliena knew that something had gone wrong. It was, indeed, a crafty stratagem of mine, since I could not write words of my own, to busy my mind with words already written. It kept me at my desk. It untangled the knots in my brow.

I think my translation carried over into English a real breath of Pushkin's fluid grace and gaiety. At least no one reading it would guess that I was clinging to the task to hold me up from a pit of absolute despair.* It was not long, however, before Eliena knew it, and she had no wish but to help me out of it by whatever sacrifice she could. There was something almost beyond nature in the gay courage, the spiritedness, with which Eliena would take such a misery of disappointment. She would take it, like a race horse, "in her stride." I can think of no better expression. She took everything—took death itself, when it came—in her stride.

I could not long deceive myself that my judgment of her had been a mistake; her rare qualities were too obvious. But that only made more devastating my creative paralysis. Groping for an explanation of it, I arrived at the conclusion that what I needed was to be alone with my

---

* With the title "*Gabriel*" my translation was published in *Transition* (Paris, July 1927), and in a limited edition with Rockwell Kent's illustrations by Covici-Friede (New York, 1929).

book. Although I would not accept her offer to go back to Moscow, I also could not live with anybody, it seemed, and be creative. To this rather baffled and baffling ideological concoction, Eliena responded by going down the road toward the sea and hiring a room of her own to live and sleep in. She would have to come back to cook my meals over the primus—only a Russian could do that—and also to freshen up my bed of leaves and dried grass. That had to be done every morning, and the whole contraption renewed every third or fourth day. In the afternoons, of course, we continued to swim and play together, and we still spent our evenings with Albert in the old study-game of betting on the definition of Russian words. But she accepted, as though it were the most natural thing in the world, the dogma laid down by my neurosis that I must "live" (and that meant occupy a dwelling place) alone. She must have seen the folly of this, but she loved me and she had no fears for herself. She would go home sometimes on a black night in a tumult of thunder and lightning past a brace of fierce dogs that ran out snarling at her heels. She did not want me to "see her home"; she wanted to put me to bed and go home by herself. She told me long after, with laughter, about the dogs, but I am not sure she was in a mood to laugh about the situation then. My needs were so in conflict with themselves that she must have known I was sick—too sick to be left completely alone. I had to have her with me, though the cause of my sickness was that she was there.

I hope the reader, with whom I agree in condemning my selfishness throughout this episode, will realize what a devastating thing it is for an ambitious author in the full flush of creation to be stopped dead in his tracks. The problem, although an inward one, was far from imaginary. And it was not solved, alas, by this scheme of nightly separation. It became evident that Eliena was braving the dogs in vain. So one morning she said, as though prompted by a sudden happy thought: "Maybe you should try living completely alone for a time and see if your inspiration would come back. It need not be a final separation, but it would be a genuine one, if I went over to Yalta to visit my aunt. She is living in the cottage we used to spend our summers in when I was a child. I would be happy there, and you could send for me if you should want me back. If not I could go home by way of Kharkov to Moscow."

Divine Powers, it seemed to me, could hardly have thought of a scheme more perfectly adjusted to still the conflict in my breast, giving me a free chance at solitude yet with the future open, with neither dismay nor apprehension—no cause even for troubled thinking. I accepted her offer with feelings of hope, fright, shame, reluctance, eagerness, gratitude—amazement. So much goodness of heart, such gallant goodness of heart, I had never imagined.

The old steamboat that ran from Sochi to Tuopse and Novorossisk went on around the north coast of the Black Sea and down along the shore of the Crimea to Yalta—a trip of three or four days. Eliena booked a passage on one of those steamboats—it was named the *Kerch*. There was no landing place at Sochi; the steamers would anchor off shore beyond the high bluff where the hotel stood, and passengers would be rowed out in dories to clamber on board. Between trips and at night those big dories lay upside down on the beach. We knew that the *Kerch* was to leave sometime in the night, but we had no way of knowing when, so we had to wait over there a couple of miles from our house. As the boat did not arrive until dawn, we spent the whole chilly night in each other's arms under one of those upturned boats. We were dreadfully in love. I don't know how she managed to be so, but she was. And her love seemed as clear-hearted and happy as mine was confused and baffled but aching with remorse. The tears of our parting were mutual, and hers turned magically into smiles as she took her place in the dory. She waved her hand to me as she climbed from the tossing dory onto the big ship with as joyous a grace as though she were off on the adventure of a lifetime. She was doing something for me—that is why she was happy. That was her nature.

It will add a valid shadow to the picture, however, if I recall a dream she related during the previous days, and which I wrote down in a mood of compunction. "I was bringing a ship to the shore," she said, "full of silk or something—thread, I think it was, or kitchen utensils— and there was nobody on the shore, no way to land. I was the captain and was all alone on the ship, and didn't know what to do."

I did not preserve Eliena's letters from Yalta, or if I did, I thought best to destroy them for political reasons that will appear later. But I remember what a stream of joy in the adventure of her journey they poured out—the sights and sounds, the sailorly and social adventures, and then the homecoming to the scenes of her childhood, a stream of delight in mere action and perception, like that in Gorky's poem "The Stormy Petrel," which we had been reading. How strong-hearted and avid of life those two Russians were!

I wrote three letters to Eliena in Yalta, mailing one every time the steamboat came by. One of them, written in Russian, describes a disagreement between Gipsy and Liza as to who should prepare my dinners. It was a contest between amateur hospitality and professional paid service. Liza won out by giving me "a very, very tasty meal of cabbage and boiled potatoes and cocoa"—a banquet which Gipsy was not up to producing. The other two letters are in English, and are not about cabbage and boiled potatoes, but about my abandonment of the novel, my "wounded" self, my adoration of her. "Never did a poet, or any other kind of a lunatic, have such a friend. Never was there such a friend."

She came back in December, and we tried again, with a more analytical understanding of my psychology—my pathology, rather, for I had now remembered the previous performances of my demon. I told her the whole story, and we discussed our problem in a more therapeutic manner, trying to think up ways to outwit my neurosis and get me back to my desk in a free-flowing condition. We had no success. The springs had gone dry. I could still study and learn; I could still translate. But I could not write. I could not express my own self.

We decided in mid-January that Eliena should go more conclusively away—that is, she should go back to Moscow to find a job, and I would take up my work in a final solitude. It was the third time I had sent her away, and it seems as I look back on it now, more laughable than tragic, for I was irremediably in love with her. If I had been a cotton broker or a hardware merchant, I could perhaps have adjusted myself. I could at least have settled down to sell stocks or tend store. But I was a writer and I could not write, a poet and I could not sing—a problem which could not be met by just making the motions. . . .

It was not quite accurate, by the way, to say that I sent Eliena away. It was her proposal, just as it was hers to take a room beyond the snarling dogs, hers to visit her aunt in Yalta. We were treating me jointly like two doctors, she the family physician, I the specialist called in for consultation on the symptoms of a crazy patient.

I did not realize how crazy the patient was until the night came when we walked once more over to the beach under the high cliff, and she climbed again with a smile into the dory that rowed her out over a windy sea to the steamer. I did not stand there and wait for the steamer to pull away; the torture was sufficient without that. I took the long walk home, empty in my solar plexus, wiping the tears from my eyes, all the time listening, only listening, for the low moaning whistle that would tell me the steamer was gone.

A strange and truly terrifying thing happened that night. I did not hear the whistle and I went to bed, sure at any rate that the boat had gone. Four times in the night I woke in a panic, cold and wet, convinced that I had made a terrible, irrevocable, life-destroying mistake, and each time I heard that fateful, groaning whistle. The boat seemed to be leaving all night long. And the fourth time it whistled, I jumped up and dressed and ran through the woods, up a hill and down to the brook in the ravine, almost half a mile on the way to where we had parted, believing—yes, actually believing—I would get into a dory and row out to the steamer and drag her off before it started. The whistles I heard—if I really heard them—were those of another steamer traveling south. Indeed it was the appearance at the brookside of two men carrying a suitcase on a stick that brought me to my senses.

"Did you come on the southbound boat?" I asked them.

"Yes."

"Has the other boat gone?"

"There wasn't any other boat."

I realized as they spoke that the sky was already pale with the first rays of a new dawn. I turned round and dragged myself up the hill again and went back to bed, whimpering, and amazed to be whimpering, like a child.

In the morning I wrote down what I had done, for it was a story hard to believe about myself. I had always thought of myself, no matter how romantically impulsive I tried to be, as irretrievably sane. My brain, even when drunk or frightened, would aways remain logical and clear. I used to be chosen to drive the rig back to Williamstown when, as college boys, we went over to North Adams and got lit. But here I was, after all, cast loose from both fact and reason, behaving like a lunatic.

Chapter 59

END OF A GREAT HOPE

While I was in this condition a thing happened in the world outside myself so momentous, and so largely tragic, that my personal woes dwindled for a time to their true size. Early in the morning of January 23, I heard a burst of laughter from my housemates, ending in cries of "Hurrah! Hurrah!" The hall door banged open, and they shouted: "M'sieu Max! M'sieu Max!"

I went into the hall, and Gipsy and Ruzha, with loud laughter and a look that I can only describe as frisky, shouted:

"Niurochka was over at Teremok and learned that the market has been closed because Lenin is dead."

I stood transfixed; I could not for a moment say a word.

"That's not true—you're not serious!" I cried finally.

Gipsy saw my expression and, becoming frightened, said:

"You know there are lots of stupid rumors in this town—maybe this is only a rumor."

I must have turned pale with rage, for fear filled her eyes and Ruzha sneaked away like a scared cat. I grabbed Gipsy by the throat and threw her back through the doorway.

"That's the way you greeted the rumor!" I said. "I despise you! You're rubbish, nothing but rubbish!"

I was trembling and felt a tumult of emotion, but rubbish was the only Russian word that came to my aid.

Gipsy came back after a while and said: "M'sieu Max, don't be angry!"

"I'm not angry," I said. "This isn't rage, it's contempt."

And she went out.

The local Soviet held a memorial service in the market square on that same day, for Lenin had died two days before. There were drums and soldiers and speeches and some pathetic music, and above five thousand people from the surrounding country crowded the tiny village. Lenin, they felt, had delivered them from the Tsar and from all tyranny, and offered them an almost supernatural hope. It is a common human weakness to attribute divinity to the holder of supreme power. I was hardly free of this feeling toward Lenin myself, although I thought I had deeper grounds for it. I spent the afternoon on the beach where the sea lay quiet as a pond and the air was warm and moist as in spring. Grief, grief was in my heart, and a feeling of unworthiness. It seemed to me that I had sat out my whole life just as I was sitting there by the placid sea, doing nothing while the earth quaked to its center, and the greatest man in history lived, acted, and died. So I wrote to Eliena, and to prove it I concluded: "I am tired out with grief and I'll go to sleep."

The next day Gipsy came into my room and told me they had not been laughing about Lenin's death, but about some other joke which she proceeded to relate. There was still fear in her eyes—she had remembered my friendship with the Bolsheviks—but also, I thought, a tear of regret that she had hurt me. I pretended to believe her story.

A few days later, I received a letter from Eliena, which I will quote, with but a minor correction or two, just as she wrote it in English.

Jan. 25, 1924

Darling, Lenin is dead. You do not need many words to understand what it is. The newspapers will come to you and tell you many words about his death. But you know better than they what it means. The brains of the Revolution went away last year when Lenin became sick, the soul of the Revolution is gone now. We have yet his body.

All the streets and squares from Lubianka to the Moscow University are full of people standing in curved lines and flowing to the sacred place where he is lying—the Dom Soyuzov. The doors are open all day and all night and all day and all night two lines of people, three in every row, are going through those doors. Nobody stays home. Small children from the kindergarten, school girls and boys, workingmen and women, students, soldiers, the last ragged tramps, and the fat Nepmen, all are there in those lines. They pass by him in deep silence with bared heads and broken hearts. And he lies so quiet—thin and pale. His mouth is silent and his eyes are closed. I saw him last night. It was five o'clock in the morning. I was in one of those lines. Nobody can stop for a minute but they go through the hall with their heads turned toward his body. In the full light of all the lamps he looks pale, very pale. You can see his forehead so well known, and the little mustaches, the same face that you used to see every day and everywhere. And you can not understand what has happened. You know that this is Lenin, but you can not understand it.

Four members of the Party Committee are standing at the four corners of his tomb, replaced by another four every ten minutes. And his wife is standing there, looking at his face. She is standing there all the time. Nobody can replace her. Sometimes his sister comes and they stand there together, old, bowed, white-haired. And the chain of people continually, endlessly passes by. It has been passing now, moving at 4 miles an hour. And yet there is no end. The funeral procession is postponed two days because of it, and delegates from all the Russia are coming to Moscow in a hurry to get there in time. The red flags with black hems, the black-red sash on the right arm of many people, the black-red frames of Lenin's pictures in every window, many people selling little picture-brooches of Lenin, and his small white bust and small white statue, and over all, the white bright snow, the thick cold air, the frosted hair and furs, white smoke from the mouths and the red fires in the street at night. That is Moscow of these days. . . .

Darling, after I had written that much I got a pass from my brother to enter the Dom Soyuzov and I stayed there almost two hours. You can imagine what a great and heavy impression you receive there. Mothers lift up their children for one look at him, hysterical women fall on the floor crying "tovarisch Lenin," three strong men in white suits are there to lift them and carry them out, and they cry so terribly that your blood becomes cold. One of them died there from a ruptured heart. I went away quite sick. But I had to run all the way to my brother's house because I had promised to give back the pass at six o'clock, and it helped me very much, that run. I was sweating and felt bold when I got back home. And you have to be bold, darling. I will not write anything more in this letter, but I will write you another tomorrow not so sad as this is.

Chapter 60

MY DEMON BECOMES SOMATIC

Besides enlarging my sorrow, Lenin's death helped forward in another way my struggle to begin writing again. Though my imagination was jammed, I could still think, and one of the subjects of my thinking in Russia had been the problem of Lenin's relation to the Western understanding of Marxism. I was not yet equipped to deal, as I did later, with this problem, but the moment was opportune, and I launched prematurely an essay to be published in the *Liberator* called "The Wisdom of Lenin." It was, in the essence, a defense, or at least an explanation, of what would prove the most disastrous feature of his teaching, the identification of the dictatorship of a party with the dictatorship of the proletariat. I pointed out that back in the 1870's and '80's before Marxism arrived in Russia, a great dispute had arisen among the Narodniki—the champions of "the people's will"—as to whether they ought to act in the *interest* of "the people" when the *opinion* of "the people" was against them—even when that opinion was that they should be hanged for their acts. The question had been decided by the stalwarts in favor of action in any case, the opinion of the people being, in the view of these consecrated democrats, of "secondary importance." Tracing the development of this attitude down to Lenin's time, when the concept of "the people" had been replaced by that of the proletariat, I explained, or thought I did, why Bolsheviks never felt obliged to apologize for their emphasis on the independent role of what they called the "conscious vanguard" of the proletariat.

"The fact that the dictatorship of the proletariat can be realized only through the political party of the revolutionary vanguard leading the proletariat, is to them an entirely obvious thing which every intelligent person took for granted from the beginning of the discussion. . . . There is so little hypocrisy about it, and it has lain so long and so solidly at the bottom of the whole development of Russian Marxism, that

Bolsheviks are entirely unaware of the necessity of commenting on it."

So I wrote—with some historic truth, I think, though without critical judgment. At any rate these thoughts helped me toward finding myself—or my self-importance—in solitude. The success was spasmodic, however; I was sinking and swimming by fits and starts. In one letter I told Eliena: "I am getting back to my writing." In another: "I sit at my desk every day but nothing comes out." In another: "I have got over the panic of sadness, but I want to go home, and I have no home but in your heart." In still another: "I am writing an essay on the wisdom of Lenin." But a week later: "I can not write. My neurosis has got me for the time being."

One thing at least I could write, and that was love letters to Eliena. Like other love letters, however, they contained little that is of interest except to the lovers—indeed only two pieces of news: that Eliena was a perfect object of love, and that the conflict begotten in me by this fact was absolute. In early February she wrote that she was working again as Litvinov's secretary, and that the Foreign Office had allotted her a new apartment in Gnezdekovskaia Pereulok, a little alley branching off from the famous Tverskaia Boulevard. I telegraphed, "Is there room for me?" and she answered: "Yes, but why should you come to Moscow? Be stronger. . . ." That exhortation, or reproof, so foreign to her ways, shocked me into writing a veritable treatise on my malady, demonstrating with remorseless logic the reasons why I should go to her in Moscow. I never sent it, but it sets forth so well and wisely the decision I had to make—and after a further period of purgatory did make—that I think a bit of it is essential to this story. It is dated February 5, 1924.

I will tell you now why I think I should come to Moscow, and you can judge whether it is just weakness. I am filled almost all the time, or more than half of it, anyway, with an almost unbearable grief. It is the same feeling I would have if you had died, or we had parted forever. This is the result of the fact that something *inside of me*, my "complex," whatever it is, has decided that I shall not love you. I both loved you and did not love you when you were here, as you know. And in my past life the end of this divided condition has been my going gradually away, and finally getting in love with somebody else, and *doing it again*.

But in those past cases I could see a reason for going away, because those loves were not helpful to my work, to my egotism, which is the real force in me. With you it is just the opposite. You gave my self to me as I never possessed it before. I never was so creative before in any happiness as I was this last year in my happiness with you. Even now I can only get back to my work by *deciding* that I am coming to Moscow, and that I am going to conquer the feeling that I can't write unless I am alone, calling it hysteria, and going entirely back to you in my heart. Then I get a little peace, and a little time with my head clear.

In short, this experiment—this attempt to find out whether it is a fact that I wanted to be alone with my writing—has given a doubly negative result. I not only don't want to, but I *can't*. I have exactly the same continual struggle about my relation to you in my heart and my head that I had when you were here.

Thus I have two alternatives: One is to struggle towards clearness and creative joy alone. The other is to struggle for it with you. Here it is the yearning infant, there it is the rebelling adult, who gains the upper hand emotionally. But in either case it is the *conflict* and nothing else which prevents me from flowing out into my work: and it is the conflict which gives me those terrible feelings in my head.

Once the terms of the problem are clear, it can have only one intelligent solution. Your infinitely patient and understanding love gives me the sole hope I have of really solving it—the one hope short of going to Vienna and asking Freud to recommend me a psychoanalyst. And Moscow is on the way to Vienna, so there is simply no reason left for staying here!

I did not go straight to Moscow after setting forth so carefully the reasons for doing so. I thought I would take a try, since poetry was failing me, at being purely practical. The practical thing, quite obviously, was to finish my life of Trotsky and gather in a fortune while his fame was at its height. He happened to be recovering from one of his mysterious fevers a little way down the coast from Sochi, and I asked him in a letter whether it would be convenient for us to continue our work there. He answered by telegram: "In view of my illness, better later on in Moscow." At which, I must say, I drew a breath of relief, for I was tired of that endlessly intermittent task. I decided to quit where I was and call my book *The Portrait of a Youth*.

Even then I did not go back to Moscow, but only to my essay on

"The Wisdom of Lenin." "I am writing it joyfully," I told Eliena, "and am getting back my equilibrium." But that proved to be a very perfect mistake. I was not getting back my equilibrium, but driving down out of my consciousness the conflict of impulses that was destroying it.

One afternoon during our play-and-exercise hour, Albert and I set up an old driftwood box on the Black Sea shore, and, standing off twenty-five feet, made bets on our ability to drop pebbles into it. This was a game at which Albert almost always beat me, for my arm has no skill in actions below my shoulder. But on this day I rolled up a score that astonished us both. As though supernaturally guided, I dropped nearly every stone I picked up square into the box. I felt flushed and exhilarated while doing this, as though some more than earthly power had entered my body. As I walked home I became aware that this celestial power was my own heart, beating fast and with abnormal power against my ribs. That night I awoke with an emotion of fear such as had accompanied the nightmares of my childhood. There was no nightmare, no object of fear, simply the emotion, acute and painful, but again the heightened heartbeats strong and rapid. No doubt the two were in a deep view identical, but it is clear in my memory that the heartbeats and their stepping-up of my physical skill preceded by several hours this first seizure of fear.

I don't know whether the reader can imagine what it is to feel a sheer piercing terror with no thought or object upon which to fix it, no action possible, or even imaginable, by which to evade it. I remember it as the most unmitigated pain I have experienced.

It would arrive suddenly day or night, like a malign visitation, and endure from one to four hours. And there would remain, in the intervals, the all too rational dread that I was losing my mind—that I would end my life, if help were not found, weeping and shuddering as I had seen patients afflicted with melancholia weep and shudder in some corner of a bench in the incurable ward of an insane asylum. It did not turn out so, but it turned out badly enough. I never recovered my rather arrogant self-confidence, one of the chief blessings with which nature and birth, and Emerson and Walt Whitman, had endowed me.

Thus it was not in the mood of my severely self-knowing letter of February 5, that I did finally, in early March, return to Eliena in Moscow. Nor was it, alas, in the mood of a rapturous and romantic lover. I loved Eliena: I enjoyed her company better than that of any other person I had ever known. She had every gift, every quality that I admired; and I had placed in her keeping my most shameful and carefully guarded secrets. She was my own—she was *rodna*. (It is a Russian word that has no parallel in English.) But I came to her at that moment rather as an emergency patient to a nurse, an injured child to his mother. Madame Rimski-Korsakov, in tender sympathy, had advised me to "go home"—and there was, I suppose, a strain of home-sickness in my trouble—but my inward answer had been: "Eliena is the only home I have."

It was a two-and-a-half day trip up the coast to Novorossisk, where one took the direct train to Moscow. I had what I thought was a rational dread of taking that boat trip alone; it seemed plausible that to escape the pain of one of my paroxysms I might jump into the sea. At any rate, I was baby-scared, and I asked Madame Rimski-Korsakov's sturdy middle-aged daughter, the ex-schoolteacher, to accompany me as far as Novorossisk, paying her a nurse's wage for the service. She was wise and kindly-understanding, and I think the necessity of relating myself to a stranger brought back my normal self in some degree. At any rate, by the time she put me on the Moscow train, I was feeling completely cured. All I had needed, I was telling myself, was to make a firm decision and act upon it. So I paid her a double wage, and bidding her an everlastingly grateful farewell, climbed almost gaily into the train. No fears, no palpitations any more! I was sane. I was carrying out my own well-thought-out decision as to what I ought to do.

It was a sleeping-car I climbed into, a rather odd, outlandish one, unless my memory has distorted it, for the upper berth in which I was to pass the night seems to have been a sort of box with a sliding door and openings only for the air to come in. It did not matter, I thought, I was well now and would have a sound sleep. But my head had barely touched the pillow when my heart jumped into action like a steam drill, and my consciousness became a single globe of fear.

I was alone with it now; I was trapped. It would be easy to slide back that door and get out, but what help would I find? What drowsy passenger would give comfort to a man who jumped out of his berth at midnight and announced that he was in terror of nothing at all? No, there was no remedy. For some reason none of us, not even Madame Rimski-Korsakov who had been so concerned about me, had thought of such a thing as a sedative, so I could only lie there and cling hard to my mind's knowledge, no matter what feeling told me, that there was nothing to be afraid of. I did cling hard, and in a matter of hours my heartbeats slackened and I went to sleep.

To avoid another anguish in such a coop—and to fulfill a solemn promise—I stopped in Kharkov to spend the night in the home of my friend Nina, of the happy days in Yalta. We had exchanged a few letters—indeed we continued to exchange them occasionally even after I left Russia, remaining in touch until Stalin's meticulous fury, creeping along the least tiny thread of a remote association with Trotsky, made it unsafe for her. She was tender and not painfully disturbed when I told her of my condition—regretful, I think, that she could be only a way-station mother to me. These Russians, reared on Dostoyevsky, have a surprisingly calm way of taking it when you tell them you have gone crazy. Nina at least was not for a moment shaken by the story of my malady in her wish to have me for the father of her child. To her bitter disappointment, she had lost through a fall and a miscarriage the one that had been conceived in Yalta, and now . . . It was the presence of her parents in the tiny undivided apartment where we slept that troubled her—not the problem of my sanity. I promised to come back. But there was no trust, only tears, in her brilliant eyes when she put me on the morning train to Moscow.

Eliena accepted what seemed to me my desperate condition with a calmness that again surprised me. And on my side too there was little turmoil. My demon, it seemed, was too frightened to put up his semaphore against her. She had a bed ready for me, and a desk, in the large room the Foreign Office had allotted to her. The room was on a top floor with light windows overlooking roofs, and it had an alcove with a stove where meals could be prepared. In the Moscow of those days, it was a luxurious dwelling for two people, and for me it was a haven in a storm. I had a sweet long quiet sleep the first night, and the next morning she took me to Dr. Kutirin, the family physician, a slender middle-aged man with a blond mustache, highly trained and educated, though dressed like most of Moscow in patched and worn-out clothing. He too took my seizures rather as a matter of course, calling them hysteria—and I suppose they deserved no more calamitous name—and giving me a sedative to take when they recurred. He also taught me to quiet my pulse by putting a bag of ice over my heart. And though he was innocent of psychoanalysis, which had been very slow even to make its existence known in Russia, he urged me to come and talk a while with him whenever these seizures occurred. A wise and sweet man to whom I owe an eternal debt of gratitude!

But of course it was Eliena, ever-giving Eliena, and the home in her heart, that gradually made the life in me flow out again. I untangled the knot in my brow—that first night and many times after—by lying close to her and pushing my forehead like a baby's into her cheek. She would prepare the ice bag to place over my heart, and she would get my meals and care for me with a speed and lack of effort that made life seem a thousand times more simple than it is.

My recovery was swift, and was interrupted by only one alarming interlude that I remember. Eliena had invited her two sisters and engineer brother and his wife to dine with us in our big room. They were strangers to me, and I experienced as we sat down at the table a clutching impulse, almost like an intention, to run and hide in a corner of the alcove where the cooking was done. I did not do it, to be sure, but the strength and specificity of the impulse, replacing the abstract feeling of shyness that would be natural to me in such circumstances, alarmed me in my rational self as much as anything that happened throughout this whole shameful story I have told. Suppose I had done it! Where would they have put me?

I was soon forgetfully absorbed—not, alas, in my novel, that would have to wait—but in something perhaps better fitted to my gifts, a criticism of Marxism from the standpoint of scientific method. Within two months I was proposing to Eliena, if she could find a way to get out, that we leave Russia and go live together by the seaside in France. We made no mention of marriage or of marriage vows. Rather the opposite: we made a compact of mutual independence. Eliena still had the impression, frequent among newcomers to English, that the word "any" all by itself was a negative, and I can still hear her exclaim: "You will have *any* responsibility—*any!*" It became a byword between us. I can also hear her say:

"I'll be anything you want me to be—sister, sweetheart, secretary, slave—I'll be your mother if that is what you want."

"And what will you get out of it?" I asked, laughing.

She answered: "What a mother always gets—ingratitude."

In Sochi, during our first sojourn there, Eliena had worked for a little time in a half-built hospital where two pretty nurses were training. They were bemoaning the dearth of marriageable men in the wake of the civil war, and she advised them at least to have children. A Russian-American heritage, she thought, would be a good one, and she assured them that it was not difficult to have a love affair with me. Neither of the pretty nurses accepted her invitation, but it did happen one night, after she had gone, that a young woman who saw me in the hotel came across town at midnight to knock at my door and ask if I would kindly become the father of her child.

"Light the lamp before you say no," she said.

She proved on acquaintance to be rather lacking in intellectual charm, but the lamp had nothing against her.

Such were the mores of the time and region in which we made our pact of independence. I must add that the pact was not one-sided. Released from my demon, I became a steadfast companion of Eliena, and my love for her, though adequately physical, was not sensual enough to make me jealous of her physical relations with other men. It was more a realistic than a romantic love.

Chapter 61

BEGINNINGS OF THE TROTSKY-STALIN CONFLICT

While I was lingering five months in the Caucasus, preoccupied with
my own inner conflict, the Russian Communist Party was entering
upon an inner conflict that marked the beginning of the end of its health
and of the high hopes that millions had placed in it. I have described my
own morbid condition during those months in a degree of detail that I
hoped might make it interesting to a psychologist. If the reader has a
political mind, and a little patience, I would like to describe in a similar
way what was happening during those same months to the Russian
Communist Party.

The first intimation I had of its morbid condition was the news that
Trotsky did not hasten to Moscow on learning of Lenin's death. He was
in Tiflis on his way to take the cure in Sukhum, he tells us, when the
word came—sitting in the working end of his car "with the high
temperature that was usual at that time." In ten minutes he could have
had a locomotive on the other end of the train and been on his way north
to attend the funeral and make a funeral oration that might have been
crucial, and would certainly have been historic.

Instead, this is what he did: "I got the Kremlin on the direct wire. In
answer to my inquiry I was told: 'The funeral will be on Saturday, you
can't get back in time, and so we advise that you continue your
treatment.' Accordingly I had no choice. As a matter of fact, the funeral
did not take place until Sunday, and I could easily have reached
Moscow by then. Incredible as it may appear, I was even deceived about
the date of the funeral. The conspirators surmised correctly that I
would never think of verifying it. . . ."

So he sat there for half an hour, knowing "only one urgent desire—to
be alone," and then went on to Sukhum.

These facts should be sufficient to refute the newspaper myth that

Lenin's death was followed by a struggle for power and party leadership between Trotsky and Stalin. "Accordingly I had no choice." "Incredible as it may appear, I was even deceived about the date of the funeral." The idea that he might *make* a choice, that he might have his own say about the date of the funeral, never entered his mind.

The truth is that Trotsky had side-stepped the power long before that. When Lenin first fell sick he suggested that Trotsky take his place as vice-chairman of the Council of People's Commissars, a move which would have published to the world his choice of a successor. When Trotsky told me this, I asked him why he had rejected the suggestion. "I couldn't wield Lenin's authority in the Politburo," he said. "Zinoviev and the others had already combined against me." That was, of course, true. And he could not have wielded the authority in the Politburo whether they had combined against him or not. He could command men; he could inspire them to action with great oratory; he could expound the grounds and principles of their action; but he could not manage them. He could not *lead* them. Leadership requires tact and adroit personal understanding as well as magnetism. It requires a certain craftiness which Trotsky lacked altogether. In the Bolshevik Party, which he had joined only a few months before the revolution, he could not even pretend to the position of leader. And owing to his superior intelligence and his greater prominence throughout the country and the world, this put him in a very difficult position. I think it had more than a little to do with those fevers—and even occasional fainting spells—to which he was subject. I remember his telling me of the unsuccessful efforts of a group of German physicians who were attending Lenin to find an organic cause for his affliction as well as Lenin's. One of them, more by way of flattery than diagnosis, reminded him that Julius Caesar had been afflicted with epilepsy.

"Yes," Trotsky said, "but the trouble is I don't happen to be Julius Caesar."

Those doctors might perhaps, on investigating his life story, have concluded that his high temperatures—which, he says, "paralyzed me at the most critical moments, acting as my opponents' most steadfast ally"—were more psychic than somatic. He never fell sick when required to command an army or organize an insurrection. It was this intra-party sniping and conniving, this crafty, scheming, dizzying, and dreadfully important business of backstage politics that sickened him. He loathed and recoiled from it. He knew besides—he could not have failed to know—how miserably unfit for it he was. He would remark later, ironically, that he "made the mistake" of falling sick at the height of the party discussions in 1923, but I think there was more truth than irony in the word "mistake." His mind as well as his bloodstream took part in the decision. At any rate, sick or well, if Trotsky had aspired to party leadership, he would have been on his way to Moscow ten minutes after hearing of Lenin's death. Of that there is no doubt.

I must add that I was aware of this at the time. I was not greatly surprised at his holing up in Sukhum while others took charge of the nation he had defended. I hadn't a notion then, however, of the fact that Stalin as general secretary of the party had already gathered the principal reins of power in his hands. I did not know who Stalin was. With all my reading and study I had never seen his name in print; I had barely heard it spoken. And I note that Alfred Rosmer, who was in Moscow both earlier and later than I, and who as a member of the executive committee of the Communist International was close to the sources of information, had the same experience. In his book *Moscou Sous Lenine*, Rosmer says: "If the name of Stalin does not appear in my account, it is because he was never mentioned in the debates, although they touched upon all the varied aspects of the workers' movement during those four years. No more does he figure in the book of John Reed, *Ten Days That Shook the World*, the author, an eye-witness, never having seen Stalin among the heroes of those memorable days." I do not mention this in order to belittle Stalin, but merely to place him correctly in history—a history which, in the exercise of his incomparable genius for manipulating men and institutions, he found it expedient to rewrite and distort beyond recognition.

In the inner circles of the party, the conflict between Stalin and Lenin had been in progress since before my arrival in Russia. It was on Christmas Day, 1922, that Lenin wrote his "Testament," or last letter to the party, warning them that Stalin as general secretary had concentrated too much power in his hands. His postscript advising that Stalin be replaced by someone more loyal, less rude, capricious, etc., was written on January 4, 1923. Two months later Lenin in a brusque communication broke off "all comradely relations" with Stalin. (What a gruesome thing if some voice had told him then that their embalmed corpses would lie side by side for years in a mausoleum on Red Square!)

Lenin's wife did not present his "testament" to that Twelfth Party Congress which I watched with so much satisfaction in April 1923. She thought there was still hope of his recovery. There was no hope; the delay only gave Stalin another year in which to perfect his control of the party machinery, appointing men of his gang to key positions throughout the country. I use the word gang advisedly for it is here that the distinction between idealistic Bolsheviks and the place-hunting roughnecks, often criminal and not rarely psychotic, who so eagerly stepped into their places, becomes important. Stalin's cultivation of these gangsters was positively frightening to his higher-minded colleagues, though their philosophy prevented them from ultimately judging any political change in moral or psychological terms. Historians will need a freer wisdom in describing what happened during the year in which Lenin's warning against Stalin as rude and disloyal and possessed of too much power was held in abeyance. Their histories will be blindly inadequate if they ignore that change in the moral quality of the official personnel throughout the party which accompanied and made possible Stalin's rise to autocratic power.

At a party conference in Kharkov, answering an enthusiastic greeting from a suddenly intruding throng of nonparty workers, Trotsky said:

"This greeting lays a great responsibility on our party. The principal task is not yet accomplished. We haven't even started on it. We still have relics of capitalism; unemployment, homeless children, poverty, prostitution, old people without anyone to support them, a mass of wrongs and injustices. Who dares to say that we have accomplished the principal task? We have only cleared the road. The principal task is the creation of a society founded on brotherly labor, where all men and women are brothers and sisters, where science and art are not the privileges of a handful, but the property of all. If you keep in sight this great aim, the creation of such a society, it is clear that the principal labors lie ahead." *

I find it impossible to imagine Stalin, or any of his henchmen, making such an impromptu answer to a crowd of nonparty workers—or to anyone else. And yet I think it is a thought that might come to the lips of any of those whom I call, in defiance to their own terminology, the idealistic Bolsheviks. They were ruthless enough, God knows, but they were ruthless on principle—in behalf of a superhumanistic dream. The very taste of the air changed when the natural-born gangsters stepped in.

Unfortunately, the only *constitutional* charge that could be brought against these manipulations of Stalin's was that those key men he was

* *Pravda*, April 4, 1923.

appointing, the local secretaries mostly, were not supposed to be *appointed* at all, but elected by the members. In September 1923, an effort was made by a group of the old Bolsheviks, including Trotsky, to recall this constitutional provision. Forty-six of them addressed a letter to the Central Committee protesting against the unlawful system of appointment-from-above, and asserting that the time had come to put in full operation the resolution on "inner-party democracy" which had been adopted at the Tenth Congress in March 1921. Drawn up and introduced by Bukharin, the resolution had been at that time little but a pious wish, an obeisance to abstract principle. Concretely, thanks to the Kronstadt rebellion and Lenin's dread of disintegration, the congress had actually moved in the opposite direction. Resolutions were adopted limiting the freedom of discussion, forbidding "fractions" or organized groups within the party, and smashing the unforgettable "Workers' Opposition." The secretarial trio, Serebriakov, Krestinsky and Preobrazhensky, who had really believed in workers' democracy, were replaced by more uninhibited bureaucrats.

Such had been the drift of Lenin's counsel at that time. At this later time, however, Lenin's dread was no longer of disintegration but of bureaucratic regimentation. His final acts and writings leave no doubt of that. In spirit his name was signed to the letter of the forty-six old Bolsheviks. In response to it, the Central Committee appointed a subcommittee consisting of Stalin, Kamenev and Trotsky to draw up a new resolution in favor of "inner-party democracy." In the wording of this resolution, both sides made concessions. But it said plainly enough that the bureaucratization of the party was threatening to cut it off from the masses, to break its once close bonds with the nonparty workers, and convert it into a body of self-appointed officials instead of the "vanguard" it was supposed to be "of the working class." The resolution, dated December 5, was passed unanimously by the Central Committee, and a conference of all the leading officials of the party was called for December 8, to discuss and prepare to implement it.

In the interval Trotsky fell sick with one of his fevers, and instead of attending the conference, addressed a letter to it, outlining the things he would say if he were there. In content it was a very wise letter. Expanded later into a pamphlet called *The New Course*, it gave unanswerable advice as to the path to be pursued if the party dictatorship, with centralized power in the party, was not to degenerate into the bureaucratic police state, into which, as we know now, it did degenerate. As a political directive, Trotsky's letter was unimpeachable, but as a political maneuver at that moment it was inept in the extreme. Trotsky stood so high above his colleagues both as an independent thinker and a writer, that a communication of the kind would be irritating to the normally small-minded among them in any case. But in this case a compromise resolution had been agreed upon, and Trotsky's letter did not stick to the terms of it. He gave free rein to his racing thoughts, as a gifted writer will. In superb prose and perfect concatenation, he set forth the evils of the present tendency toward bureaucratic regimentation, and the fine points of excellence to be aimed at in the new program of workers' democracy. To characterize the present evils, he invented the offensive phrase "degeneration of the cadres," cadres being a Communist euphemism for the party officialdom. And he broached for the first time the indubitably relevant problem of the interrelation of the younger and the older generations. He remarked that the youth are "the barometer of the party," a metaphor which added the sin of being literary to that of being Trotsky and not Lenin. Of this there had been no mention in the resolution agreed upon. Indeed Trotsky himself had not brought it up—or so Stalin asserted—when he and Trotsky and Kamenev drafted the resolution.

This wise yet fatal letter (which was published in *Pravda*) gave Stalin, as though on a golden platter, the opportunity he had been awaiting with such eager patience. How easy for him now to assert that Trotsky had double-crossed the committee. How easy to say that after a compromise program had been agreed upon, Trotsky had come out with a totally new program. He had started a new wave of discussion. He had broken the inner-party peace so painfully arrived at. He was forming a faction. He was slandering the trusted leaders. He was stirring up the young against the old. He was "playing a trick on the party."

In this tone and manner, Stalin and Zinoviev—and after hesitation, Kamenev—managed to make of Trotsky's wise and moderate, but atrociously ill-timed, letter an open threat to the hegemony of the party, to the dictatorship of the proletariat, to everything that Lenin stood for and the Bolsheviks held dear. Under their influence, the conference, instead of implementing the new program of workers' democracy, adopted a resolution condemning, not Trotsky only, but all the forty-six signers of the original protest against control from above. The whole lot of them were guilty, it declared, of violating the party law against factions, of abandoning "Leninism," of a "petty bourgeois deviation from the line of the proletariat."

The proletariat, to be sure, never had a look-in on either side of this fight. But that Trotsky and the forty-six were defending what hope there was (if any) that the proletariat might ever *get* a look-in, must be obvious, I should think, to anybody primarily interested in knowing and understanding. To me, when I found out about it, the question seemed clearly and conclusively posed: Is the Bolshevik experiment going to result in the hoped-for Workers' and Peasants' Republic, or is it going to tie the country up in a dictatorship of the officialdom of the Communist Party, the evident first step toward a new ruling class?

To return to my personal story: I have to confess that in my brain-sick isolation in Sochi I knew nothing about these critical events and arguments. I was so innocent of it all that I could not guess what it meant when after Lenin's death I stopped receiving my mail in Sochi, and Eliena in Moscow failed to receive my letters. I went over to the local office of the Cheka to inquire about it, and was frankly told by a slightly shamefaced official that my letters were being held for examination.

"Don't you know that I have credentials signed by Comrade Trotsky?" I exclaimed.

"We know about that, Comrade Eastman," he said, with deference and yet firmly, "but we have orders to examine the mail, and we have had trouble finding a translator for some of the letters that come for you. You will have your letters in a few days."

My letters did come in a few days, and I assumed that some local misunderstanding had been cleared up. That my precious credentials from the commander in chief of the Red army had become a liability instead of an asset was slow to penetrate my mind. But the incident did not make me feel any more at home in Sochi. It gave me something besides my self to think about on my retreat to Moscow.

In Moscow, as my nemophobia began to clear up, I came back gradually to my political self, and began to find out, by reading old copies of *Pravda* and *Izvestia*, what a desperate war had been going on between the idealists and the machine politicians in the party. The idealists, with their inept, unskilled and intermittently sick leader, were already beaten—that was obvious. The party press was filled to nausea with unscrupulous misrepresentations of Trotsky's views and those of the Opposition, lies and slanders and base distortions of fact and idea, a "smear campaign" against the leading member of the Politburo that, had he answered them, would have split the party right down the middle. The dishonesty of the attack was so flagrant, its motive so obvious, that Trotsky was urged by some of the best of the old Bolsheviks to send a detachment of soldiers into the Kremlin, arrest his opponents, and restore elective life to the party by armed force. I was told that Muralov, the commander of the Moscow garrison, begged for the privilege of heading the detachment. But Trotsky declined to use either his power or his eloquence. He made no answer to the vilifications of him in the press. He made no public appearances, no speeches, no motion whatever against the fire-hose stream of slander that was poured against him. By the simple device of not reading it, he retained his composure and continued his work. But that was no help to the cause he had fought for. As I believed the true aim of the revolution was at stake, this course of events made me sick at heart. There might have been no snow in Moscow that second winter, my memory of it is so dark by comparison with the bright hope-filled days of 1923.

Chapter 62

A NEW AND LARGER PROJECT

March and April are still winter in Moscow, and I spent most of those
months, and May too, in the library of the Marx-Engels Institute, or at
home in Eliena's big room with heavy volumes in my lap and
dictionaries perched on the furniture around me. For I had found both
cure for my sickness and distraction from my sadness about the
revolution in a new and more exacting intellectual project. I have
described how, with a view to my biography of Trotsky, I had been
reading and studying the ideological history of the Russian revolutionary movement. These studies were to me a prime source of
enjoyment all the time I was in Russia, but during this winter they
acquired a new critical edge and a new purpose. My investigations into
what I called "The Wisdom of Lenin" had led me at last to the
reluctant apprehension that, with all his keen and seemingly freethink-
ing practical sagacity, Lenin was after all a Marxian fundamentalist.
He believed in the whole highly elaborated, cloudy, and to my mind
obviously unscientific mystique of "dialectic materialism." This state
religion, it seemed to me, would wreck the hopes of a free society even if
the "bureaucratization of the party" did not, and I became possessed of
the grandiose idea of exposing its antique and unscientific character.
I've told how, long ago, without knowing much about it, I had
dismissed Marx's philosophic system as "a rationalization of his wish."
But I had not realized the naïve credulity with which that rationalization
had been carried through.

I cannot remember the exact date, but I can remember my astonishment when one winter evening it fully dawned on me that these supposedly advanced thinkers, these champions of revolutionary progress,
were actually stuck fast in a pre-Darwinian system of wishful thinking
—an imputation of their own human plans and purposes to an external

world which, to fool themselves, they called "material." To me Marx's trick of turning Hegel's philosophy "other side up"—imputing to matter, that is, the essential attributes of mind—is one of the most transparent pieces of hokum in the history of human thought. It took me months of hard labor, working in a foreign language, to convince myself that these revolutionary heroes of mine did sincerely and fanatically believe in it.

Lenin's philosophical work, *Materialism and Empiro-Criticism* was the crowning disillusionment. Jack Reed had told me, when he came back from Russia, that Lenin, besides his great political speeches and pamphlets, was the author of "a work on philosophy and scientific method." In my state of exaltation the mere phrase had confirmed me in my belief that my hero possessed a maturely scientific as well as universal mind. But now that I was able to read the Russian text, I found his book to be a mere political harangue from beginning to end. Not once in the whole treatise does Lenin invite, or permit himself to enjoy, a moment of speculation or inquiry about the universe, the nature of being, the significance of mind, or about any philosophic question whatever. His only question is: Which side are you on in the class struggle? And the beliefs you will hold if you are on the working-class side have been settled by Marx and Engels finally and for all time. Contemplation is impossible. Philosophy is and must be partisan—and worse than that, for the Russian word *partini* means "belonging to a party." In order to be true, it must belong to the party of the working class; it must reflect the socialist "method of production." I could hardly believe my eyes. And yet I was to learn, as I pursued my studies further, that this was not a madness of Lenin only. It was orthodox Marxism. The idea that there is a "proletarian" philosophy, a "proletarian" mathematics, a "proletarian" logic even—this total retreat from reason which many have blamed on Russia's barbarism—was not Russian, it was German. It was set going by Karl Marx, and Karl Kautsky, Marx's chief expositor, laid it on the line as insanely as Lenin did. "Every method of production," he declared, "is connected not only with particular tools and particular social relations, but also with . . . a particular view of cause and effect, a particular logic, in short a particular form of thought." *

In 1955, a squadron leader of the Canadian Air Force captured in Korea, a man named A. R. MacKenzie, described in the *New York Times* his "interrogation" by the Chinese Communists.

---

* *Ethics and the Materialistic Interpretation of History.*

"One day one of the interpreters gave me a little lesson in Communist dialectics. He explained that truth is partisan, and that what helps the people is the truth. In other words, even if I had not been shot down over China and said I had been, this would be the truth because it would help the people propaganda-wise. 'If you tell the imperialistic truth, you hurt the people,' (he said). 'But if you tell our truth . . . you serve the people, and nothing is a greater honor than to serve mankind. . . .'

"I knew it was a crazy word game. I knew I was lying, and I knew he knew I was lying. Yet in some fantastic way he was convinced that these lies were the truth."

It *is* fantastic, but the nub of it—"truth is partisan"—is practically a quotation from Lenin's exposition of the dialectic philosophy. That this infantile scheme for elevating political passion above both reason and factual judgment, could be adhered to by educated, astute and high-powered intellects like Marx, Engels, Kautsky, Rosa Luxemburg, Plekhanov, Martov, Lenin, Trotsky, was to me, I must repeat, a devastating discovery. I think I should have waked up sooner to the practical failure of the Bolshevik experiment, had I not been so absorbed in confuting this folly in their theoretic assumptions. It was a full-time job, and one which I felt had practical implications more vital to the success of the socialist experiment than any other service I could render.

For I was beginning to realize that the atmosphere of cant and bigotry and theological cocksureness which dismayed me more than any other feature of life in Soviet Russia—cerebral automatism taking the place of reasoned inquiry on so many human problems—flowed inevitably from this system of disguised supernatural belief. Dialectic Materialism had become a state religion, and in that I saw the germs of priest rule and police rule, an end to the advancement of learning, a locking behind rusty bars, where I had looked for a total liberation, of the mind of man. I had been wrong ten years before to abandon my pretentiously titled magnum opus, *Towards Liberty, the Method of Progress*. I had shirked my real task. That was the way I felt now.

"Forget the grandiose title, get down to business and really do the work," I said to myself.

And that is what I did—for the rest of my stay in Moscow, and for months and years thereafter. Indeed the final result—my book, *Marxism Is It Science?*—was not published until 1940.

Chapter 63

TROTSKY FADES OUT

What I have done with my life has been to a humiliating degree determined by external forces. I drift along and become entangled in some sequence of events that engages not only my mind and talent, but my will. I had a novel to finish, poems to compose, a treatise on Marxism to write; I had to think up ways to earn my living. Nevertheless, by a chain of highly improbable little accidents, I was pulled into the task of explaining to the world what happened among the Bolshevik leaders upon Lenin's death. The accomplishment of this task, and its consequences, occupied my mind and energies, and roiled up the precious reservoir of my feelings, for twenty times the length of time I had thought to give it. Although my opinions about Trotsky were far as the poles from discipleship, I became more widely known as a Trotskyist than I have ever been known as anything else.

Here is the accidental way it came about.

The Thirteenth Congress of the Russian Communist Party was announced to assemble in Moscow on May 23, 1924, while I was buried to the ears in my study of Marxism. At that congress the question of "workers' democracy" against command-from-above would come up for settlement by the party itself. Trotsky, as a member of the Politburo, would speak in defense of his program, and would answer, it was assumed, the campaign of slander against him. His speech might resound through history. I knew this, but did not feel impelled to make it my business. My business was in the library of the Marx-Engels Institute.

The library was not open Sundays, however, and on Sunday, May 25, as I strolled over to the Foreign Office to have lunch with Eliena, I felt a stab of self-reproach.

"Here you are in a far country where you came seeking experience.

A great historic scene is being enacted within a few hundred yards of
you, and you are missing it! You wouldn't miss the Battle of Waterloo,
would you? Did you ever even miss the circus when it came to
town?"

The stab was sharp because it was too late, I assumed, to get a card
of admission to the Kremlin. Trotsky was to address the congress on
Monday—it would be open at ten—and now, on Sunday, everybody's
office would be closed. How could I secure a pass?

Eliena said: "Trotsky *might* be in his office—let's try it."

"Well . . ." I said. "All right . . . if you want to."

By accident he *was* in the office, but his secretary said very
brusquely:

"Comrade Trotsky is busy preparing his speech for tomorrow's
session and cannot be disturbed."

By another accident, Eliena did not hang up instantly, and the
secretary added: "Who is calling?"

She answered, "Eliena Krylenko." And by a third accident—most
unpredictable of all—the secretary did not hear "Eliena," but only the
word "Krylenko." If Nikolai Krylenko, who had not yet committed
himself on the issue at stake, was calling Trotsky on the eve of his
speech, it was important. For *that* he could be disturbed! So Eliena's
call was put through, and Trotsky's voice answered:

"Nikolai Vassilyevich!"

"It isn't Nikolai Vassilyevich," she said. "It's Eliena Vassilyevna,
Comrade Litvinov's secretary, and I'm calling for Max Eastman."

"Oh," he said. "Oh—"; and then, relaxing a little, "What can I do
for him?"

"He wants to hear your speech at the congress tomorrow."

"Tell him he will find a pass in the hands of the guard at the gate
of the Kremlin at nine-thirty," was the crisp answer.

Thus it fell out that I was a spectator of the great historic scene
after all—sharing a chair-seat with Nikolai Krylenko right under the
rostrum.

Trotsky has observed that "the last real congress of the Bolshevik Party took place in 1923, the Twelfth Congress"—the
Thirteenth and all that followed it were "bureaucratic parades." So far
as concerns the two which I attended I can pretty well confirm his
statement. This Thirteenth was plainly a packed congress—as different
from the one I had attended the previous April as cold is from warm.
Everybody in the room was tense; every object in the room seemed to sit

square and expectant; the delegates themselves sat more like objects than people. They were awaiting a battle, but not with minds active or prepared to act—not with doubt or speculation—rather as the Greeks watched a tragedy or the Spanish a bull fight, to see the inevitable happen and be purged of pity and terror. Zinoviev and Stalin had each made a "report of the Central Committee" on Saturday; Sunday had been by-passed for the funeral of Comrade Nogin; and this, ostensibly, was to be a discussion of the two reports.

There was a special reason for the tension. The delegates were all thinking about something they were not permitted to mention. I did not know the whole story then, but I knew that Lenin had written a sort of "testament," a deathbed letter to the party, which was being suppressed. The whole story is this: Lenin's wife, Krupskaia, who had held back his letter at the previous congress, brought it before the leaders now and proposed that it be read to this congress and discussed. The triumvirate, Stalin, Zinoviev and Kamenev, who dominated the Politburo, proposed to suppress it altogether, but could not, or dared not, overcome her resistance. After heated discussion a compromise was reached. The chairmen of the various delegations were assembled before the congress opened, and Kamenev read the letter aloud to them. Then, by a further concession, it was read aloud separately to the members of each delegation. But all this under a pledge of absolute secrecy. The delegates were not permitted to make notes, and they were forbidden to make any reference to the letter on the floor of the congress. It had been, they were told, a confidential letter to the party.

It was, indeed, a descent into the realm of personalities unusual in Lenin's political writings. The Marxian dogma that personalities do not matter to the course of history—a dogma sufficiently disproven by the example of Marx himself and Lenin—had this rather depersonalizing effect on the writings of all the devout Bolsheviks. They outdid the British upper classes in personal reserve. But in this deathbed letter, Lenin came right down to cases, and what he said was about as harmonious with what was going on in this congress as a blockbuster at a picnic. Among other things, he said that Trotsky was the "outstanding" member of the Central Committee; he reminded the party of the "strike-breaking" of Zinoviev and Kamenev on the eve of the October insurrection; and he accused Stalin of disloyalty, rudeness, and caprice, recommending that he be replaced as general secretary by someone superior to him "in all respects." Needless to say this document cast a shadow as from the grave over the present assembly, packed as it was with men who owed their jobs and prestige to Stalin, and whose heads were fattened with Zinoviev's and Kamenev's slanders against Trotsky. Its phrases hung in their memories, ghostly-vague no doubt, but painful to think of.

The party's old-time trouble-shooter, Kamenev, was in the chair— soft-bearded, soft-spoken, gentle but not innocent. He gave the floor first to Leonid Krassin. "The word belongs to Comrade Krassin," is the way the Russians say it. And Comrade Krassin mounted the tribune— very little like the world's conception of a "Bolshevik," with his natty English tailored suit and carefully sharpened beard. But his speech was Bolshevik enough: there had been a police raid on the Soviet embassy in Berlin, and he urged that the Soviet Government raise hell about it. (No pretense that this party congress wasn't the Soviet Government!) Applause for his bold vigor, and then:

"The word belongs to Comrade Trotsky."

In a silence like death or absolute zero, Trotsky stepped forward to the tribune, meticulously neat as always in his military uniform—neat, clean and erect. He was their great orator—not only the leader and organizer of the insurrection that gave them power, not only the organizer and commander of the armies that preserved their power, not only the one man among them who could command the loyalty of the troops surrounding them right now, but their great orator, an orator whose eloquence history would remember. And his position was right. It was profoundly and irrefutably right. What a moment for a great speech!

Trotsky has often been accused of admiring his own image in the mirror of history. A pity he did not glance in the mirror then. Instead, he guided his conduct, as always, by a conscientiously thought-out plan of duty to the revolution. And as always, in matters calling for finesse in the management of men, his plan was wrong. He had not wanted to attend this congress at all, but urged by his friends to put his position in the record, he had decided he must do it "diplomatically." Above all, he must not "take the offensive." To speak the plain truth would be to take the offensive. He was being accused of "forming a faction" in the party, when every man possessing a twelve-year-old IQ knew that a faction had been formed against him, with an explicit program to isolate him, destroy his prestige, suppress his books, silence his oratory, revile his name, and forestall his possible inheritance of the authority of Lenin. To state that fact would have left an image in history. It would have raised a standard to which the wise and honest might repair. But in the state of mind imposed upon its members by this party-church, with a monster fortress of pseudo-realistic theological belief looming behind it, such a bold free simple human action would look sinful, uncanonical, anti-Bolshevik, "against party discipline," against "Marxism-Leninism." Trotsky, moreover, never having been a Leninist until the eve of the revolution, was overimpressed by this inviolable Frankenstein that Lenin created. Many of its members still thought of him as an outsider, and in a sense he was. He was too much an outsider to dare say what Lenin once said when a majority of the Central Committee were cool to his plans for an insurrection:

"If you want a split, go ahead—take the power in the Soviets and carry on. We'll go to the sailors!" *

So Trotsky leashed his genius for emitting lightning strokes and thunder, put a lock on his real thoughts, and acquiesced by his unproud behavior in the plan of his enemies to put him in the wrong.

"Comrades, I will discuss a very limited number of the questions which were developed or touched upon in the reports of the Central Committee. I will focus your attention (or try to) upon the question whose illumination the congess (or the greater part of it—more truly the whole congress) expects from me. In doing this I will set aside in advance—and I think the congress will understand my motives in doing so—everything that might in any degree exacerbate the question, introduce personal factors, and make more troublesome the liquidation of the difficulties which have arisen before the party, and out of which we all want to bring the party with advantage to its further work. . . . If I do not touch upon a series of acute personal factors with which my name has lately been associated, it is not because I would decline to answer any question that might be asked. . . ."

Nobody was going to ask him a question—that was the last thing that could possibly happen.

Against the charge of stirring trouble in the ranks of the party between congresses, Trotsky defended himself by saying that "the Central Committee itself had found it necessary in the interval between congresses to announce a change of the party course."

The fact was, as I explained, that ever since Lenin failed to appear at the Twelfth Congress, Stalin had been building his machine control by appointing new secretaries throughout the party, and Trotsky and his forty-six colleagues, in an effort to check the process, had *compelled* the

* *The Bolshevik Revolution,* Hoover Library publication No. 3, p. 195.

Central Committee to announce a change of course. The course had not been changed, and the anti-Trotsky solidarity of this Thirteenth Congress was proof of it. But Trotsky said no word of that. He was trying to be conciliatory—a thing for which he had no gift whatever.

"The statement that I was for permitting factional groupings is not true. Comrades, that is not true. I made the great mistake, to be sure, of falling sick at the critical moment of the party discussion, and was unable to appear promptly to refute that statement, and many others. But I never and nowhere thought, and nowhere stated, that I think, besides forbidding factions, we may permit groupings. . . . A grouping is in the given historic situation only a faction by another name. . . ."

As for the accusation of petty bourgeois deviation: "Exaggerated party democracy and exaggerated bureaucratization are both channels for petty bourgeois influence."

As to the charge of inciting the young against the old: "We must guarantee the leadership of the old underground generation, but also the free, active, independent participation of the youth in the political life of the country.

"Comrades, none of us wants to, or can, be in the right against his party. The party is, in the last analysis, always right, because the party is the only historic instrument given to the proletariat for the fulfillment of its fundamental tasks. . . . Nothing is easier than to say in the face of the party: All those criticisms, all those declarations, warnings, protests were a bunch of mistakes. I however, Comrades, can not say that because I do not think so. . . . The English have a saying 'Right or wrong, my country.' With greater historic truth we can say: Right or wrong in certain separate, particular, concrete problems, it is my party. But if I, in the opinion of certain comrades, have mistakenly offered certain reminders, if I, in the opinion of certain comrades, have mistakenly pointed out certain dangers, then I, for my part, think that I am only fulfilling my duty as a member of the party, who warns his party of what he considers the dangers. . . .

"Great difficulties still confront us, Comrades, and I hope that in overcoming these difficulties we will proceed like good, like compact, soldier-Bolsheviks. It may be a little funny for me to make here a personal declaration, but I hope, if it comes to that, I will not be the last soldier on the last Bolshevik barricade!"

There was no applause for Trotsky's speech. How could there be?

The word was passed to a Comrade Uglanov, a Moscow party secretary, not important, but of working-class origin. He has left no image in my mind. I will quote only the conclusion of his raw, and yet in a manner justifiable, remarks.

"As to the general character of Comrade Trotsky's speech, I think that anyone who wants to fight along with the party and through the party ought not to make parliamentary speeches! . . . [Applause. Voices: "That's right!"] Comrade Trotsky says, 'We do not think of ourselves as in a struggle outside the party, we do not think of ourselves as outside the ranks of Bolshevism, and if it comes to that we will do our bit on the Bolshevik barricades.' For us, Comrade Trotsky, that is not enough. We do not regard you as a rank-and-file rifleman, we regard you as a commander. We expect from you not just mere rank-and-file participation in the barricades, we expect from you words of command—but words of *intelligent* command and *clear* directives."

It was the *coup de grâce*—and delivered by a second-string *apparatchik*, whom one flash of the ironical lightnings that poured out of Trotsky in the tempests of the revolution would have laid dead in his tracks. In an intermission which followed, I could not refrain from going up to Trotsky where he stood apart from the others—isolated, self-possessed—and offering him a little 100 percent American advice. I had spoken to him before the session began, and he had told me, drawing me into a hidden corner of the palace, the principal phrases of Lenin's "testament." As we parted, I had said: "I guess this is good-bye, for I'm leaving very soon."

"What are you going to do when you get home?" he asked.

"Nothing," I said. "I'm going to write books."

He smiled a deprecating smile, and to make it worse I added: "I believe in the class struggle, but I love peace."

"You love peace—you ought to be arrested!" had been his parting shot to which I modestly agreed.

Now I came to him again and was not so modest.

"In God's name," I said, or words to that effect, "why don't you peel off your coat and roll up your sleeves and sail in and clean them up? Read the testament. Don't *let* them lock it up. Expose the whole conspiracy. Expose it and attack it head-on. It isn't your fight, it's the fight for the revolution. If you don't make it now, you'll never make it. It's your last chance."

He looked at me in some surprise. I had been on the whole a

respectful biographer. I thought he even weighed my advice a moment —at least he paused for reflection. Then he assumed a quizzical expression.

"I thought you said you loved peace!" he said.

It was indeed his last chance, for only at an annual congress could he address the party as a whole and in freedom from restraining rules. His half-sick and fitful leadership—which at least *resembled* malaria in being on one day and off the next—was disheartening to the Opposition. All the best minds knew his policies were right, but they also knew he could not cope with the party machinery. He could not run the country. His speech made this abundantly clear. And that speech was only the first of a series of personal maneuvers every one of which was as gauche, inept, tactless, and calamitous as his political judgments and outlines of policy were correct and far-seeing.

Following Uglanov, a procession of approximately a dozen routine party speechmakers mounted the tribune and poured their grapeshot into Trotsky's political dead body while Trotsky listened without apparent emotion. However many may have wished they dared to do so, one sole intellectual, Preobrazhensky, co-author with Bukharin of the official textbook, *ABC of Communism*, came bravely, though without eloquence, to the defense of the Opposition. Thereafter his body, too, was raked with grapeshot. Krupskaia, Lenin's wife, tried earnestly to make peace—poor ageing Krupskaia, with her bulging eyes and unrelieved ugliness. If the party is always right, why do we debate its decisions? she asked quite sensibly. And then:

"Comrade Trotsky's statement that he is against factions and groupings is enough—we can't afford the luxury of doubling and redoubling these discussions."

But it *wasn't* enough. The dead body had to be danced and pranced on, laid out and buried in another flood of vituperation when Stalin and Zinoviev made their summations. Trotsky's favorite epithet for Stalin was "mediocre," and Stalin was indeed undistinguished by any grace or brightness of thought, speech, presence or address. But if Trotsky had deigned to listen to the skillfully marshaled, deadly aimed, and from the standpoint of lethal administrations, superlatively concocted extemporaneous discourse with which Stalin finished him off, he might not have been so glib about mediocrity. It was a masterly display not only of ruthless force and Olympian dishonesty, but of skill in the *ex parte* manipulation of facts and ideas. Stalin was a genius—a genius of "patience, continuity, cruelty and fraud," as my Greek friend Papandreou described him. But he had also a quick, shrewd, and retentive mind. Among the tyrants of history, he may well stand supreme. It was a serious mistake to dismiss him as "mediocre."

Zinoviev, to be sure, with his high-tenor delivery, got three times the applause that Stalin did. He filled the very air in the corridors with Trotsky's sins of factionalism, anti-Bolshevism, antiproletarianism, betrayal of Lenin, petty-bourgeois deviation. A majority of the delegates probably thought, as he undoubtedly did, that Lenin's mantle had fallen, or was about to fall, upon Zinoviev. He pronounced the benediction at the end of the congress:

"The Thirteenth Congress will go into the history of our party as a congress absolutely unique in unity and solidarity."

A truer benediction was never pronounced. That the author of that "unity and solidarity," sitting behind him with no glitter in his hard cold eyes, would employ it to do him in and destroy him the moment Trotsky was out of the way, was far indeed from Zinoviev's elated thoughts.

Chapter 64

THE PASSPORT PROBLEM

What stood sharpest in my mind on leaving the Thirteenth Congress was that I had heard three grown-up and apparently sane men seriously discuss the question whether or not the Russian Communist Party could make a mistake. For Stalin had found it necessary to adduce arguments from the Leninist Scripture to prove that it could: Lenin taught us that the party should learn from its mistakes—if it didn't make mistakes, how could we learn anything? And Zinoviev had chimed solemnly in: "Comrade Stalin has said that the party can make mistakes, and I am in full accord with him."

The connection between this display of ecclesiastical casuistics and the Marxian philosophy of history may not seem obvious to the reader. To me, engaged as I was in the demonstration that this philosophy has all the attributes, save only personality in the godhead, of a supernatural religion, these echoes of medieval theology seemed to follow as a matter of course. I was more than ever convinced of my duty to disabuse the revolution of this incubus. Fate, however—which I have previously and more accurately called a series of accidents—had pushed me into the midst of this momentous conflict, which owing to my independent position I seemed uniquely called on to explain in the West. Trotsky had entrusted to me the carefully guarded secret of Lenin's Testament —probably the biggest news story in the world at that moment. His close comrade, Rosmer, and my admired political friend, Boris Souvarine, both members of the Executive Committee of the International, supplied me with further information accessible only to insiders. They all three assumed that I would take upon myself the task of defending the Opposition, or in other words, stating the facts to the workers of the world, and I had no power to resist them. For light on a few remaining problems, Rosmer and I visited Trotsky at the War Office on the last day before I left. Trotsky was still president of the Military Revolutionary Soviet and commander in chief of the Armies of the Republic—then and for a few weeks longer the most powerful man in Russia—and he added a flourish to my brief and only friendship with a government by driving me home through the streets of Moscow in his famous military car.

I have called the political conflict between Stalin and the Opposition, led by Trotsky, momentous, and before proceeding with my story, I want to say a word about that. The whole world imagined that the dispute between Stalin and Trotsky was about the international revolution, Trotsky wanting to promote it, Stalin to withdraw and devote himself to "socialism in one country." Stalin contrived that the world should believe this; he was delighted with Trotsky's attempt to defend a negative thesis: We can *not* build socialism in one country. It was a typical example of Stalin's craft and Trotsky's ineptitude. In practical terms, as very soon appeared, there was not the slightest differerence between them on this question. *Build all the socialism you can in Russia while promoting to the extent you can the world revolution*, was their common policy. It would have been so stated if Stalin had been candid, or Trotsky less inclined to Marxian schematism. The real issue, as we have seen, was the antibureaucratic program called Workers' Democracy as against Stalin's regimentation of the party. *No other question was raised until after the battle was over and Trotsky defeated*.

In retrospect there is a certain pathos in that program of Workers' Democracy. It was an attempt to correct the basic defect in Lenin's entire scheme for creating a Workers' and Peasants' Republic. Lenin was keen enough in his knowledge of men to ridicule the idea that one could "realize the dictatorship of the proletariat without a party rigorously centralized and possessed of iron discipline." He scorned as "infantile leftists" those who thought this possible. "Just let them try it!" he said. But he never planned or proposed any means by which the power might be transferred from such a party to the Soviets—to say nothing of transferring it to the proletariat as a whole. He watched without protest the transformation of the Soviet congress into a mere false front or passive instrument of his party. He acquiesced in the gradual replacement of the once-celebrated Council of People's Commissars by the Politburo of this doctrinal organization. Alarmed by the Kronstadt revolt, he even suppressed the opposition and tightened the hold of a small knot of orthodox officeholders within the organization.

This is the basic tragedy of Lenin's life and work, the seed and source of our modern monster, the totalitarian state.

Again I attribute this to his belief in the Marxian theory of what economic evolution was going to do. The separation of that *a priori* belief from his keenly sagacious perception of facts, prevented his confronting this problem—prevented his *knowing* that once the power and the wealth of a nation was in its hands, the centralization of his party would make a plaything of its democratism. The attempt to forestall this with a program of Workers' Democracy enacted by the party itself—"inner-party workers' democracy," to use their own phrase—was worse than futile. It was pathetic.

At the time I am discussing, however, those who had joined in Lenin's audacious effort, and yet retained a minimum of political sagacity, saw clearly enough that Trotsky's demand for a thorough-going implementation of this program was a demand that Lenin's effort be continued toward its original goal. That is why the conflict seemed momentous to me—momentous enough so that I postponed the more fundamental task I had undertaken, and spent my last few days in Moscow gathering all the newspapers, documents and items of information that were essential to a complete account of the conflict. A fervent help in gathering these documents was rendered by my friend, the Bulgar-American, George Andreychine, who knew Russian like his native tongue. George was a kind of human torch; he was lit up and burning from head to foot with zeal for poetry and the proletarian revolution. Handsome, eloquent, voluble, and reckless, he had got arrested and convicted with Bill Haywood and the IWW's in Chicago, but had jumped his bail of ten thousand dollars and fled to Moscow— abetted in this maneuver by our generous friend, Betty Hare, who had put up the bail.

I was able on leaving Russia to take along a bulging package of these papers, notwithstanding the attention I was now receiving from the GPU, because I left in the "diplomatic car" chartered by the Foreign Office to carry Maxim Litvinov and his delegation to the London Conference of June–July 1924.

To explain that, I must go back a little and remind the reader that I had been tried twice for sedition in the United States courts; I had made myself notorious by defending the Bolsheviks at their most unpopular moment. In the files of the foreign offices I was on a black list. I had been unable to get a visa to visit my sister in England on my way east, and had got a passport out of my own government only after sitting three days, so to speak, on the steps of the State Department. My passport was valid for only two years, and was stamped in big letters: "Not To Be Renewed Without the Express Authorization of the Department of State." I had forgotten all about that, and the prescribed two years had passed when I began to think of going home. There were five countries requiring transit visas between me and the Department of State in Washington, and there was no American consul or minister in Russia. The British had a trade representative in Moscow, however, and Eliena persuaded him, as a favor to the Foreign Office, to give me a sheet of brown paper stamped with official permission to "land at Folkestone on June 7th 1924 on condition that the holder does not remain in the United Kingdom longer than one month." To get to Folkestone, I would be compelled, it seemed, to travel underground. But here again Eliena came to my help with a brilliant idea: I should go along with Litvinov as first assistant to his secretary. Litvinov's feelings toward his secretary were not such as to make the company of a first assistant seem absolutely necessary, but he was kindly in his brusque and tight-lipped way. He took me along with my brown paper passport, and moreover enriched my understanding by telling me the whole story of his political life on the way. He was at that time, in my opinion and Eliena's, disillusioned to the point of cynicism about the outcome of the revolution. He took no part in the intra-party disputes; he advised Eliena not to join the party, when she feared it would be necessary in order to hold her job. "Why waste your time in those futile squabbles?" he said. He subsequently survived—somewhat mysteriously—the wholesale purge of the old Bolsheviks, although, as they used to say, "he had three secretaries shot from under him." It was bad luck for history that the so-called *Diary of Litvinov* turned out to be a forgery, for his comments on the bloody events he survived would have been unique. He had lived long enough in England, out of the jurisdiction of German metaphysics—which dominated the whole Russian intelligentsia—to acquire an unclouded sense of fact, realistic and potentially cynical. He told me his life story with very simple common sense, and none of the pious lingo of the Hegelian-Marxian religion.

Chapter 65

A ONE-WAY MARRIAGE

While our plan of departure was still in suspense, a difficulty arose which held an element of horror for Eliena, and which might have changed the whole course of her life and mine. Her elder sister, Sophia, the intemperate rebel, was so irate against the Bolsheviks for the Kronstadt massacre that she joined a tiny anarchistic organization, the first to be called Fourth International, which imagined it was preparing another and better revolution. It had an underground network, or the beginnings of one, in Western Europe, and Sophia was in secret correspondence with its "center" in Berlin. Eliena knew nothing of this, and quite innocently, when returning with Litvinov from the Genoa conference, brought along in the diplomatic pouch a letter for her sister supposedly from "an old friend" in Germany. The letter was opened and read by the GPU and found to contain material relating to this new "Leftist" movement. When Eliena entered her request for a diplomatic passport to the London Conference, she was informed that a visa had been refused, without explanation, by the heads of the GPU. She reported this to her Commissar brother, and he called the GPU and insisted that, whatever the difficulty might be, they explain it to her. So Eliena went over to the Lubianka, up that flight of stairs where many before her had abandoned hope. . . .

But here I am going to quote her own account of what happened:

I spent four hours in the GPU that day. I was questioned by a sly creature with flabby lips and soft hands, one for whom I can think of no other epithet but smutty worm. He would question me for an hour, then let go of me for a half-hour, only to start again another hour of foul, stupid, insinuating questions. As he wrote down what I said, and as I did not have much to say, I had to compose quite a discourse—about my sister's being critical of the present party leaders, about her calling me and my other sister, who were "honest Soviet workers," *bourgeois*, and *philistine*, about her having been always in rebellion against anything established. I oiled thick all this sort of thing, because if I did not, it would seem that I had things to hide, and because I knew that my sister's psychosis made her safe. She was at the moment in an insane asylum, and had formed a protective habit of going actually crazy and getting committed whenever her rather fantastic conspiratorial activities came near to detection.

At the end of four hours, my inquisitor began to relent, but he asked me one final question:

"What would you do if, now, when we give you a passport to go abroad, someone should come and ask you to carry a letter to your sister, or to some other friend in Moscow?"

"Good God! . . . I will tell them to go to hell!" I said.

"Ah," he murmured with a practiced smile, "we don't want you to do anything so rude. We want you to accept the letters, tell them you will be glad to transmit others, and send them to us instead of to the persons addressed."

"I *can't* do that," I cried. "I'll tell them to go to hell and that's all I can do!"

"Aren't you interested in defending the government you work for?"

"Of course, but there are certain moral standards one has to live up to, otherwise life isn't worth living."

"But those are bourgeois standards, and you are in the service of a proletarian state," he began, and in the course of a brief lecture on ethics and the Marxian philosophy of history, managed to make it clear that my receiving a passport to London depended upon my coming over to the morals of the proletariat.

"I can't!" I cried again. "I cannot do that!"

"Well, you think it over," he said finally. "Don't give me your answer today. If you should change your mind, come over tomorrow and I will have a paper for you to sign."

"I assure you that I won't think about anything else," I answered, "but I can tell you now that my answer is *No!*"

I used the word horror to describe Eliena's state when she came home from that interview. She was pale and tear-stained, feverish, and was shaking her hands as though she had reached into some loathsome substance and could not get it off her skin. Deeper than disgust was the torturing thought that our whole plan of life and love must be sacrificed if she did not surrender her moral principles to this loathsome power.

"What on earth has happened to you!" Litvinov exclaimed when he saw her the next morning.

She told him the story with a flood of tears and he answered with an ironical small puff of his tight lips.

"Why do you get so excited about a little thing like that? Bourgeois or proletarian, what does it matter? It amounts to nothing. Go over immediately and sign the paper."

Pausing—but not long enough for her answer—he added in a lowered voice:

"You don't have to *do* it, you know."

So Eliena left Russia enrolled as a spy and an *agent provocateur* for the GPU.

"It meant that I was leaving Soviet Russia for good," she wrote, "and I was glad."

Aside from my passport, and Eliena's, there was one other small matter that had to be fixed up before we got on the train. Unlike so many Russians, Eliena had longed all her life to get away from her native land, and live in a larger world. Her recoil from the deeds of oppression and violence that followed when her big brother's party seized the power, had not diminished this sentiment. Although she never tried to influence me—she tried, on the contrary, to share my political views—she did not in her heart *like* bolshevism well enough to believe enthusiastically in it. She wanted to live in the West, and it so happened that we wanted to live together. So we decided that, after the London Conference, we would find a little cottage on the French Riviera by the sea where a warm sun would shine on us while I finished my novel and my book on Marxism—and now, incidentally, this third book or pamphlet that I had undertaken. The difficulty was that a Soviet citizen's passport was no good in Western Europe at that time, and Eliena's diplomatic passport would presumably be withdrawn when she left the service. The only way we could carry out our plan was to get her name on my passport, once I had one. And the only way we could do that was to get married.

Marriage, as I have remarked, was not much in vogue in revolutionary Russia in those days. Together with bathing suits and epaulettes, lawyers, and other impediments to social freedom, it had been largely swept away by the revolution of October, and had not yet come back. The Moscow I lived in was, in its sexual code, a sort of generalized Greenwich Village. Getting married, when it did happen, was commonly called by the rather disrespectful name of "registering." It consisted of appearing together in a small dingy office about the size of a hall bedroom, and signing your two names in a paper-bound ledger—also the names you intended to be called by after the feat was accomplished. The process was made still more casual by the fact that divorce could be obtained by as simple a process and without mutual consent.

Eliena did not belong to a registering family. Although her pretty young sister Olga had an Esthonian lover whose life ambition was to persuade her to register, neither she nor Eliena had any taste for it. They were devotees of freedom. As for me, I have always felt that this intrusion of the state, or society, or public law, into the sanctities of a private romance is disagreeable. Besides that, Eliena and I had been living happily together in unregistered bliss so long that this necessity of a common passport in Western Europe did not occur to us until the very day the diplomatic train was to leave. We rushed across town to the marriage bureau at about noon—the train was leaving at two-fifteen—signed our names in the book, paid down a ruble to the glum and perfunctory young woman in charge, and were about to rush out again, when she came to life and shouted:

"Wait! You can't be married without establishing your identity. You have to have two witnesses."

"We haven't got time," I said. "Can't we omit that formality?"

But no, we weren't married until two witnesses had signed their names here—and she showed me the exact space on the certificate allotted to this indispensable addendum. After a rather hilarious consultation, we ran to a telephone and called up Olga's unregistered husband, Drauden, who ran a party publishing house halfway across town.

"Bring a friend and rush over here as fast as you can," we said breathlessly. "We're trying to register before the train leaves, and we need two witnesses."

"Don't move!" he said fervently. "I'll be there in ten seconds!"

His fervor was due to a hope that, once Eliena was registered, Olga, who adored her, would fall in line. But as always in Russia, ten seconds meant half an hour.

"The bags aren't packed," Eliena said finally. "I can't wait any longer—I've got to be on that train."

"So have I," I said. "Married or single, I've got to get out of this country."

As we hurried toward home, we met Drauden and his friend coming our way, one on each sidewalk, combing the street for fear we might elude them. We held a conference on the curb, consulting our watches and striking an average of the different times they told. It was too late. The thing was impossible now. We couldn't count on the train being late—not absolutely.

Drauden was almost in tears, and I, but for Eliena's infectious laughter, would have felt pretty bad too. But just as we were saying good-bye, an ingenious idea came into my head—one of those supremely simple ideas, like Newton's about the apple, that occur perhaps only once in a century.

"Eliena will pack the bags and I'll go back and tend to the getting married!"

So that was how it fell out, and I suppose I am the only man in history that ever got married without a bride.

Chapter 66

HUNTING FOR SUNSHINE

All went smoothly until we arrived from the Hook of Holland at Folkestone. There when the ship docked I was called downstairs to confront a handsome young official of Ramsay MacDonald's government. He sat at a table gazing at my improvised passport.

"There's something the matter with you," he said. "What is it?"

"The only thing against me I know of," I answered, "is that, like your Prime Minister, I was opposed to the war."

He laughed generously at the gibe, and asked why I wanted to come to England. I told him I was merely paying a visit to my sister who lived in London.

"All right," he said. "I'll telephone the Home Office and see if they'll agree to your entering the Kingdom. Just wait here on the boat."

I waited, and Eliena, much to the distaste of her boss, insisted on waiting with me, though what she would have done if I had been turned back—or what I would have done—I can't imagine. The Home Office relented toward evening and I was allowed my two weeks in the Kingdom.

During those two weeks I managed, by cabling young Senator Bob La Follette, to get a fresh passport delivered to me at our London consulate, and with that in hand I persuaded the Home Office to let me stay another four weeks. Those weeks were mainly filled with an attack of lumbago and a lonely visit to the Isle of Wight to try to find some sunshine. I did, however, have one or two tastes of English social life that were as characteristic as the climate.

On a visit to Cambridge I met Lytton Strachey hurrying across the campus like a lean scrawny bird out in a storm and eager to find shelter. We were introduced where two sidewalks met, and his eyes seemed to be darting up one and then the other to see which would get him away the quickest. I met John Strachey, too, at a dinner of distinguished people, and admired the sturdy spirit in which he affirmed views that antagonized everybody else at the table. That surely is an English trait, that robust give-and-take in the realm of spirit.

We dined at the home of a young man named Ivor Montagu, who, though his father was a lord and the head of the Bank of England, had just come out in print for the Dictatorship of the Proletariat. His apartment was small, there were only six of us, and the dinner was served informally at a small square table. Highballs were served to the men, and the ladies each received a thin-stemmed glass of sweet wine. Eliena, who did not care for sweet wine, asked politely if she might not also have a drink of whiskey. Our host, who was out to aid the proletariat in overthrowing the foundation and framework of the British Empire, giggled in an embarrassed way, squirmed painfully in his chair, and managed to survive this dreadful breach of upper-class conventions only by ignoring it. That too, I thought, could happen only in England.

I was an "expert on Soviet Russia" now, and compared to the average expert, who had stayed two weeks in Moscow and learned to say "*Sukinsin*" and "*Ya vass liubliu*," I was a fairly good one. I had lived in Russia a year and nine months, mostly with Russians, and not only spoken the language but done much of my explicit thinking in its terms. At a luncheon given by my friends Francis and Vera Meynell to celebrate the publication of *The Week-End Book* by their Nonesuch Press, I shook hands for a second time with vain and delightful H. G. Wells. He begged me to come down with "Miss Krylenko" and spend a week-end at his country home in Kent.

"I want to ask you a lot of questions," he said, and added with generous warmth: "You are the one person whose judgment about conditions in Russia I regard as worth listening to."

I accepted his invitation delightedly, of course, and Eliena and I put the needed clothes in a suitcase and took a Saturday train south as directed. Wells had been given to understand that we were not married, and being himself a famed believer in free love, was pleased at the idea. I for my part, since our marriage had been a reluctant concession to expediency, felt no urge to enlighten him. As we drove into the spacious front yard of his home, he ran out cordially to welcome us, but when the chauffeur took our suitcase from the back of the car, his face fell. He put his hand to his lips a moment, then said with embarrassment:

"I was going to put you in separate rooms but since you've brought only one bag I'm afraid I'll have to put you together and call you Mr. and Mrs. Eastman. I hope you won't mind."

"Oh, no indeed," I said, "it doesn't matter to us at all."

The bag went into the house, and he led us out to a sort of pavilion where other guests were playing a tennislike game with inflated balls and a net. He left us there and went back to the house, but after we had played a while he appeared again, and coming up close to me said in a semiwhisper:

"After all I think I can put you in separate rooms and call you Mr. Eastman and Miss Krylenko. I've managed to arrange things."

I said: "Oh, it's all right either way. It doesn't matter to us at all." And he disappeared again.

After another while he came back and, approaching closely, communicated to me that on further consideration he had decided in view of our one bag, that it would be better to put us in the same room and call us Mr. and Mrs. Eastman.

I said: "It's all right either way—it doesn't matter to us at all."

When the game was over and we all approached the house again, Wells ran out and, drawing me aside a fourth time—I am afraid I will be accused of exaggerating, but this is the exact truth—he confided quite earnestly:

"You are to sleep in separate rooms after all, we have to put the bag in Miss Krylenko's room."

"It's quite all right," I said. "It doesn't matter to us either way."

That too could only have happened in England, where so often social appearances count more than the substance of things. Once H. G. had got this dreadful anxiety off his mind, he became a charming host. Mrs. Wells, handsome and whole-minded, put everyone at ease. Their grown son, handsome as his mother and adept in general conversation, was at the dinner table, and I remember his quoting in some neat connection the murmur attributed to Galileo after his condemnation: "*Eppur si muove.*" Another of those stray floating bits that get caught in the stream of consciousness and hold fast for no discoverable reason—unless perhaps in this case the gratifying fact that I too remembered that phrase in Italian.

The conversation was sprightly and intellectual; but H. G. never throughout the week-end asked me one of those promised questions about Soviet Russia. For this I was not sorry, for my opinions were revolutionary, and a painful clash would have occurred had we both said vigorously what we thought. Still it revealed a self-absorption that surprised me in a man who knew so much about so many things outside himself. I should not say "surprised me," for I am continually wondering how people who never listen manage to know so much as they do.

At the close of the London Conference Eliena said a fond and last farewell to Litvinov, who kindly, and somewhat irregularly, permitted her to keep her diplomatic passport. We set out then, early in August, on a serious search for sunshine. After a look at St. Jean-de-Luz, and Hyères and St. Tropez (where we rented a house but went back in two hours and unrented it), we found our haven in Juan-les-Pins, a small seaside village nestling beside a pine grove at the base of the Cap d'Antibes between Cannes and Nice. That village has since become a recreational boom town, a built-up and crowded resort of fashion with a casino almost rivaling that in Cannes five miles away. But when we were there an old barnlike attempt at a casino had been boarded up and abandoned. There were no sports shops, no apartment houses, no crowds on the beach, nothing in this little corner of the coast to disturb a poet, a novelist, a political philosopher—whatever I might turn out to be—and yet much to attract a person who loved to dive and swim.

We had hardly any money at all, my friendship with Trotsky having cut me off from the shower of gold rubles that was beginning already to baptize those foreign writers who stood for Stalin's tyranny. I had written my sister from Moscow as late as April 28 of that year a glowing account of my prospective wealth.

The amazing news is that I have sold all my articles to a magazine here for about $45 a piece, untranslated. I have also had an offer of $200 down and big royalties for my Trotsky book, and a promise to translate *Enjoyment of Poetry* and advertise it on the back page of the Trotsky. The magazine that bought my articles also promises to bring them out as a book. And another guy with a literary magazine is translating the preface to *Colors of Life* and some of the poems. Another poet is translating "The Battlefield." In short I am just about to burst into bloom as a great American writer—in Russia! But Russian money, you know, is now made out of gold and silver, and it really is going to be the solution of my problem. I only want to find a *nook* now in Europe where I can keep warm and study and write. I am simply wild with the creative impulses that come to me every day and the little time and strength life gives me to realize them. I don't dare go home; I should have to make speeches and be political. . . .

We found an upstairs room in a Villa Martha, with two windows looking down upon a multitude of leaves, and the sea sending an occasional glimmer through them. But the rest of my bright financial hopes had died a quick death between April and the party congress in May. Only a royalty check from Scribner's for *Enjoyment of Poetry*, a small but unfailing trickle, a smaller one for the *Sense of Humor*, and an advance of five hundred dollars from a publisher named Greenberg who bought the American rights to my portrait of Trotsky, stood between us and destruction—meaning by destruction the disaster of a regular job.

Eliena kept house, typed my manuscripts, and washed my shirts in a cold well with a fig tree beside it that stood in Villa Martha's front yard. In my memory of those days she is usually up in that fig tree eating figs, but somehow the clothes got washed, and the manuscripts, although she still did not know what many of the English words meant, were typed and retyped and typed again with inexhaustible energy and patience. The Russians have a single word that I miss in our language, *rabotosposobnost;* it means "ability and readiness to work"; and the exemplars of it that come first to my mind are Lenin and Eliena and Floyd Dell.

Under the leaves down in front of Villa Martha, lived Gelett Burgess, grouchy-faced author of one of the most famous poems ever composed in America:

> I never saw a Purple Cow,
> I never hope to see one;
> But I can tell you anyhow,
> I'd rather see than be one.

I made the mistake of mentioning this to him, and aroused his indignation, for he had written funny books by the dozen and hated to be remembered for this one immortal work of art. We exchanged a brief greeting, and I never saw him again until the mid-fifties when he spent an evening in my house, arguing with fanatical vigor, and a fervor surprising in such a master of frivolity, that the Earl of Oxford wrote the plays attributed to Shakespeare.

Chapter 67

WORLD-WIDE DISGRACE

At first when we settled in Villa Martha I went to work on *Marx and Lenin*, for after reflection I had no wish to write the projected defense of Trotsky's opposition. Knowing that he was not and could not be a political leader, it seemed futile to argue at length that he was right. More important, I thought, to show that the dogmas underlying the whole dispute, so strangely reminiscent of theology, were unscientific.

Accident, however, had other plans. My London lumbago had turned into a fierce pain in my sciatic nerve, and after four months of it I went to Paris late in November to consult a specialist. In Paris, Rosmer and Souvarine took hold of my mind and dragged it back into current politics. Stalin and Zinoviev were falling out, they reported, the Opposition, on the other hand, was firm and growing stronger. All it needed was a clear and strong demonstration of the issues at stake. The time was ripe for a body blow against the bureaucrats. It would be effective in Moscow no matter what language it appeared in.

So I yielded again to the old temptation. Returning to the Midi—sciatica and all—I laid aside my larger task, got out my collection of notes and newspapers, and went in once more for political journalism. I would dash off a pamphlet in a month or two, I thought, hand it over to Souvarine, or whoever was heading the Opposition in the West, and return to the major task of my mind. In both these tasks my inflamed nerve conspired with me, for it would not let me lie down or stand up. The one thing I could do with comfort was to sit in a straight chair, and I could do that as well with a typewriter in front of me as without.

A thing I could not do at that critical moment was pay my bills. Eliena and I had moved into a single room in a dirt-cheap, dilapidated old house with its back to the seashore—Aigue Marine was the name of it—but even so we were down to rock bottom. Eliena offered to go to

Paris and look for a job, and I thought that was a grand idea. I had never been driven by the urge, amounting to a neurosis in many males, to be the money-earner of the family. Indeed I had often thought how sensible it would have been to find a wife who could support me and enable me to write with no motive but the writing. More organic motives had always stood in the way, but now at last it was going to happen—provided Eliena found a job! We had just twenty-five dollars left after buying her ticket to Paris. She took the train on December 18, and telegraphed me on Christmas Eve that she was employed as secretary in the Russian embassy. She sent me a New Year's present of enough francs to equal about twenty-five dollars at the prevailing rate of exchange.

By that time, and quite as miraculously, my sciatica had let go its hold, and all my happy welfare asked for was her company. On January 8, 1925 I joined her in Paris and we moved into an apartment on the rue de Vaugirard where I had warmth and a good window for my work. It was there, with much critical help from Souvarine and Alfred Rosmer, that I finished my "pamphlet," which turned out to be a small book called *Since Lenin Died*. It contained a complete exposure, backed by unanswerable facts and quotations, of the conspiracy of falsification and slander by which the "triumvirate" had demoted Trotsky and destroyed his authority. It also contained the first world news of the existence of the document called Lenin's Testament, with the quotations from it which Trotsky had whispered to me. I could not, of course, cite my authority, but my information was too detailed not to be authentic, and moreover because I was a friend of Trotsky—my "Portrait of His Youth" having already appeared—there were strong presumptions in my favor. *Since Lenin Died* was bound to make a sensation.

I was keenly aware of this, and although Trotsky himself had endorsed the project, I did not feel free to publish the result without assurance that it would be, in the existing conjuncture, useful to the Opposition. Souvarine thought it would not, and was against its immediate publication, but Rosmer took the contrary view. Obviously I could not consult Trotsky, but his closest friend and political colleague, Christian Rakovsky, was in Paris as Soviet ambassador. I sent him the manuscript with a promise to publish it or not according to his decision. It was read by him and by his wife, and returned with their enthusiastic approval.

While these things were happening, news came of my father's death in Florida on February 7, 1925. He died in a little house he had built for himself next door to his aged sisters, Miriam and Luna, in Daytona Beach. He died as he had lived—serenely, just lay down with what they thought was a "cold in his chest," and passed into a coma from which he never returned. My surgeon brother, Ford, raced down from Erie, Pennsylvania, but not soon enough to say good-bye. It would not have made much difference. My father was strangely remote from his children, or they from him. He was remote from everybody, it seemed to me, although "admired and loved" to quote the common expression, by the whole city of Elmira. It was a respectful kind of love, almost reverential, not intimately warm and on-two-sides confiding. I can picture him sitting at the table of an adoring parishioner; it would be an event for the man's whole family, but they would not be really together—not any more than if he were, what some of them probably thought he was, a messenger from God. He never had a pal or a crony. You couldn't imagine anybody coming up and slapping him on the back with: "Hello, Sam, you old son-of-a-gun, how are you?"

Even his love for God, I suspect, was not very intimate. It was not religion that made him so serene. I asked him once whether he really believed in immortality, and he said: "Max, I hope for it." He was more at ease with Nature than with God—that is my impression—at ease, as an animal is, with life and death. That was his serenity. And his love for Nature *was* intimate. He knew how to, and he adored to, make plants and animals flourish and grow. As a farmer he had genius. He had also a true gift of scholarship, and a zealous enjoyment of it. His "Lenten Lectures" on Biblical history and the lives of the saints—composed in the mood of the "Higher Criticism"—meant much more to him than his sermons. Indeed he was happy to leave most of the preaching to my mother, whose gift of eloquence was as instinctive as his for making things grow. Above all he was good. He had courage and character. He had never to wrestle with remorse.

I give these glimpses of him, or my thoughts of him, in order to explain, before saying it, how little disturbed I was—in my preoccupation with the tragic things happening to the world revolution in Moscow—by the news of my father's death. It seemed—as a quiet death always would if we could be wise—a simple and harmonious part of his life.

My little book, *Since Lenin Died*, was published in London by the Labour Publishing Company on May 10, 1925. In America it was published subsequently by Horace Liveright, and reviewed on the front page of the *New York Times* book section—the only time that honor has fallen to me. Gallimard brought out a French edition in the summer, and a translation into Czechoslovak appeared in Prague a few months later. The book was indeed a sensation, and one for which I had to pay in anguish.

What with Eliena's earnings, some small royalties, and a thousand dollars inherited from my father, we felt free once more in the spring, and wanted to go back to the Midi. Eliena begged for a vacation from the embassy, and even offered to resign, but they liked her too well. "You are indispensable," was the only answer she could get. So we lingered in Paris unwillingly until June, when our problem was solved by a telegram to the embassy from Chicherin, Commissar of Foreign Affairs: "Chinovnik Krylenko will return to Moscow." It was the first official reaction to my book, and the first, I suppose, of thousands of telegrams recalling suspected heretics into the jurisdiction of the Kremlin. Eliena, at any rate, was the first of these heretics to refuse to go—the pioneer of the Nyevosvrashchentsi (the "Non-Returners"). There was no hesitation in her choice.

"You may never be able to go back to Russia, if you don't go now," Davtian, the acting ambassador, told her.

That intuitive prescience which kept Eliena from joining the Bolshevik party, did not desert her now. She told Davtian, in effect, that she was surer of certain other things than of ever desiring to go back to Russia, and she composed a telegram to Chicherin announcing rather mysteriously, that "family considerations" made it impossible to obey his order. She was relieved immediately of her duties, and we were free, as we wanted to be, to return to the Midi.

There is a spacious residence near the end of the Cap d'Antibes called Château des Enfants. It was built by an elderly gentleman named George Davison who made a fortune as British manager, and a considerable stockholder, of the Eastman Kodak Company. In midlife he got converted to anarchism and maneuvered an amicable separation from his employers—so the story went—by marching past the offices in a May Day parade. His health failing, he moved down to the Midi with a woman he loved, who had been his nurse, and who shared his beliefs and humanitarian intentions. They built this vast dwelling and adopted eight children, besides producing one of their own. There was room in the "château"—which was shaped more like an orphan asylum than a castle—for any number of guests, and Mr. Davison loved to have it full. It was George Slocombe, I think, then representing the *London Daily Herald* in Paris, who told me all this and gave us an introduction to the

Davisons. It resulted in our being invited to move into the château and stay as long as we liked. We stayed three weeks or a month, time enough for Eliena to buy paints and brushes and begin her career as an artist. And we carried away when we left the most precious of privileges on the Cap d'Antibes—that of diving "whenever we pleased" from the Davison's cliffs into a deep blue beautiful and secluded arm of the sea. We moved back to our first happy dwelling in the Villa Martha at Juan-les-Pins, but hardly an afternoon passed that did not find us out at the end of the Cap diving and swimming.

In these lucky circumstances, and with my duty of "political journalism" done, I plunged into my more deeply gratifying work about Marxism. I was lost in meditation on it one morning, standing between my desk and my bed, when Eliena came in with the mail. She gave me some warning, some "prepare for bad news" as one does when announcing a death in the family, then handed me a copy of the *Sunday Worker*, the Communist paper published in London. It was open at a page with bold headlines:

TROTSKY TROUNCES EASTMAN
Lenin's 'Will' a Myth—
Eastman No Warrant for His Assertions
By Leon Trotsky
(Special to the *Sunday Worker*)

I read in a glance or two the main sentences of Trotsky's disavowal of my book, and of me, my friendship with him, my "Portrait of His Youth"—he made a clean sweep of everything. I groped toward a chair and sank into it, so pale that Eliena thought I was going to faint. I did not faint, but I was sick to my heart. Throughout the world I would be known only for this disgrace. Trotsky wrote:

> There is in this little booklet a not inconsiderable number of obviously fallacious and mendacious assertions. . . . Eastman alleges that the Central Committee has "hidden away" from the Party a number of important documents written by Lenin in the last period of his life. . . . This can not be called by any other name than a slander against the Central Committee of our Party. . . .
>
> As for the famous "Testament," Lenin never left one. . . . All talk about a secreted or infringed "testament" is so much mischievous invention. . . .
>
> When making use of Eastman's "information," and quoting his

statements, the capitalist, and more particularly the Menshevist press, have invariably underlined his near relations to me as the author of my biography, his alleged "friendship" with me. . . . The question is about a perfectly harmless booklet relating to my youth up to 1902. . . . My relations with Eastman differed in nothing from my relations with a number of other Communists or foreign "sympathizers" who have asked my assistance in studying the October revolution, our Party, and the Soviet state—not more than that. . . .

With a vulgar self-assurance, Eastman writes sarcastically about my "quixotic" attitude toward my nearest Comrades on the Central Committee. . . .

We have seen above on what a rotten foundation Eastman is trying to erect his building. He exploits single incidents of the Party discussion in order to blacken our party and undermine all confidence by perverting the meaning of facts and distorting all and every proportion.

No honest worker will ever believe the sort of picture drawn by Eastman. It contains its own refutation. . . .*

Soon after, there arrived a series of similar lashings written for world publication by Lenin's wife, Krupskaia. My book, she said, was "a collection of petty gossip." I knew nothing of the task which "history has imposed upon our Party." I understood nothing of the Bolshevik attitude to the workers. To me, with my "petty bourgeois anarchist leanings," the workers were "merely pawns, waiting to be led by any leader." I had invented "various fictions" about Lenin's letters to the party congresses—calling them "testaments." I had no interest in "the real testament of Lenin," his last articles relating to "fundamental questions of Party and Soviet work." I was too busy calumniating the Central Committee "by alleging that the 'testament' [meaning the letters above mentioned] has been 'concealed.' " I had woven "a network of lies . . . around the question of our Party differences with Trotsky," and so on.

---

* Trotsky also denied my statement that Lenin, when he first fell sick, proposed to make him "President of the Council of People's Commissars." There was a mistake in my statement; I should have said "Acting President" or "Deputy Chairman," and I had already corrected this in the French edition. But Trotsky did not correct me, he merely contradicted me. It is of some historic interest that Lenin did make that proposal, and that Trotsky told me he did. I have since learned that he repeated it several times.

These official maledictions were, of course, repeated and enlarged upon with variations by the lesser lieutenants of the Kremlin throughout the world. "Since Eastman Lied" was the title of the six-column article in the American *Workers Monthly*, which had absorbed what was left of the old *Liberator*. In a special supplement to the *Daily Worker*, my once-envious assistant editor, Robert Minor, reveled in a two-page spread under the title, "Max Eastman Blows Up." It was a field day for the trained Stalinist sharpshooters in all countries. There is hardly a civilized language on the globe in which the party militants did not learn to pronounce, and execrate, my name.

A puzzling detail of the disaster was that in the French Communist paper, *L'Humanité*, Trotsky denounced me *twice!* His first effort printed July 12, although it seemed sufficiently devastating to me, was itself denounced by the Central Committee of the French Communist Party as "equivocal, unclear, uncategorical, almost *à double sens.*" My book, the Committee averred, was "a vulgar counterrevolutionary job, a collection of *ragots*, lies, calumnies, and unseemly insinuations, written with the obvious purpose of discrediting the chiefs of the Russian Communist Party and the Soviet Government," but Trotsky's response was "even more dangerous in its ambiguity than the book itself." Trotsky had dismissed the book as trivial, but the Central Committee maintained it was of tip-top importance. The tone Trotsky employed toward the author of this "indecent book," the Committee declared "was that generally employed in a discussion among friends." And it concluded: "The Central Committee of the French Communist Party is of the opinion that Comrade Trotsky can no longer occupy so equivocal a position among the worst enemies of Communism and the Communist International, and that a clean, clear answer without ambiguity on any point, is imperiously necessary, and this without delay."

The "clean, clear answer" was forthcoming, but only after a considerable delay. It was not until August 18 that *L'Humanité* published the full denunciation as it had appeared in the *Sunday Worker*, giving its approval as though to a naughty boy:

"Comrade Trotsky having modified the text of his letter, we now publish the definitive text. This text, which categorically condemns Eastman's book as counterrevolutionary, gives full satisfaction to the Party."

Although I could not agree that the first text was either friendly or equivocal, it did lack some of the punches to be found in the second. My "vulgar self-assurance" was a new idea, my "rotten foundation" also, and my "exploiting single incidents of the Party discussions in order to blacken our Party." But a more significant difference lay in the maneuvering of the denial that the document called Lenin's Testament existed or had been concealed. In his first text, Trotsky alluded quite frankly to Lenin's "famous 'testament'," and gave away the fact that it had been read privately to each delegation at the Thirteenth Congress, instead of being openly considered at the congress. This misstep was corrected in the second version. It now appeared that "Lenin left no testament," that "all the talk about a 'testament' concealed or transgressed is nothing but ignoble lies directed against the real will of Lenin and against the interests of the Party created by him." As to any letters that Lenin did leave, it now appeared that they were—quite simply—"all brought to the attention of the members of the 12th and 13th congresses and had their influence upon the decisions of the Party."

These and other substantial changes made it plausible that there had been a struggle over this disavowal—that Trotsky, after putting up a resistance, had been forced to the wall. And this, we learned later, was what happened. It happened in Moscow, of course; the French Party was merely adding a little pressure on orders from the Kremlin. News came to Boris, "from one of Trotsky's closest friends," that on arriving in Moscow my book was hastily translated into Russian, and a committee appointed consisting of Stalin, Zinoviev, Kamenev, Bukharin, Trotsky and Tomsky to draw up Trotsky's answer to it. Trotsky, his friend reported, "fought them step by step all the way."

That crumb of comfort arrived in my hands six months later, in January 1926, when I went up to Paris to work on *Marx and Lenin* in the Bibliothèque Nationale. In reporting it to Eliena I wrote: "I know one thing—it did those guys a lot of good to read my book and try to answer it."

My wound had healed over by that time. But in Moscow, in the breasts of the Opposition—or of those in whom the Marxian religion had left a trace of moral sensitivity—there was a discomfort not easy to cure. William Reswick, then Associated Press correspondent in Russia, has described in *I Dreamt Revolution* the sensation the book caused in Moscow. Copies were "smuggled in somehow and traveled from hand to hand." Wherever he went he heard people discussing my revelation of Lenin's "testament" demanding Stalin's removal as secretary, and

"Trotsky's denial of this truth, which for over two years had been known not only in high party circles but in many a Moscow home." Trotsky's denial, according to Reswick, "robbed him of many a friend and earned him many a new enemy." He quotes Yenukidze, the most humane of Stalin's henchmen, as remarking in mitigation of Trotsky's act that he was not alone in subordinating truth to pary discipline— Krupskaia did the same thing. "But Krupskaia is not an idol," he added, "while Trotsky is, or was. An idol must never leave his pedestal." It is true, at least, that a political leader cannot do what Trotsky did. Even if I had not consulted Rakovsky, and were as politically irresponsible as Trotsky thought, he would have done better to stand his ground on the facts, and let Stalin expel him, if he could, from the party.

If my book had been crude or clumsy, the plight of these party-disciplined heroes might not have been so distressing. But apparently it was a pretty good book! * As Rakovsky's imprudent enthusiasm indicated, it said just what they all wanted in their inmost thoughts to hear. Many of them, I learned long after, yearned to send me some word of trust or reassurance. But for the time being that was impossible. I was untouchable. I was dynamite. A pathetic effort was made by Trotsky's sister, Olga, Kamenev's wife, to convey some hint of the general feeling by sending me in a tiny envelope her calling card—all that she dared to do.

A pathetic relic of those sad days is the mass of letters I wrote to various publications in France, England and America, answering these unanswerable denunciations from the Kremlin and from Communist officials everywhere. Piled all together, these letters size up almost to the manuscript of another book. What a waste of brain and energy! But I must say gratefully that a number of publications, notably, *La Révolution Prolétarienne* in Paris, *Plebs* and Landsbury's *Labour*

---

* I will be excused, I hope, for jumping over a quarter century and quoting Leonard Schapiro's statement, in his authoritative treatise on *The Russian Communist Party of the Soviet Union*, published in 1959, that in *Since Lenin Died* I "not only correctly reproduced long extracts from the 'Testament,' but also gave an accurate (as we now know) account of the political conflicts since Lenin's death."

The only error in *Since Lenin Died* that I wish to correct was the unqualified manner in which I attributed to Lenin the program of "Workers' Democracy" which Trotsky and his friends were defending. I had not then read the report of the Tenth Party Congress in 1921 where, upon Bukharin's insistence, that program was adopted. As I have remarked in Chapter 61, Lenin's mind, under the conditions prevailing *at that time*, had been moving in the opposite direction.

Monthly in London, gave ample space to my futile reassertions of the truth. In England even the Communist press had not then absolutely abandoned the habits of honorable journalism. A long polite letter from R. Palme Dutt, the editor of the Communist magazine, discussed with courtesy the possibility that "the Politburo might decide" to publish my reply to his bitter attack upon me. Indeed he pleaded with me to discontinue the dispute; he "found it difficult to believe" that I wanted to place myself "in opposition to the whole international," and so on.

Nothing like that could have happened five years later, when Moscow had the whole international movement under taut control. In January 1926, returning to Paris to do some library work for my book on Marxism, I went unhesitatingly over to the Soviet embassy to consult the works of Lenin. While those particular books seemed always to be locked up and the key missing, I found the attitude of the personnel, as I wrote to Eliena, "*extremely* cordial." "Some special feeling seems to pervade the atmosphere." When, however, I approached the acting ambassador, Davtian, with a complaint against the sequestration of Lenin's works, he said:

"We don't feel sure, Comrade Eastman, that you are going to use those books for the benefit of the revolution."

My utopian illusions still survived sufficiently so that I went into a rage at this remark.

"What sort of a revolution is it," I said, "that locks up its scriptures, and picks and chooses who shall read them? Is that what you seized the power for? Is that what is to become of the heritage of Lenin?"

I don't like to quote myself *verbatim* when I get mad—which is not often—but I think I told Davtian in unvarnished Russian to go straight to hell and take the library and the whole embassy with him. I told him loud enough so that a visitor in the corridor when I emerged—it was the well-known French Communist, Amédée Dunois—was in a state of extreme agitation. We stood there for some moments discussing in tremulous voices the Rights of Man, the doctrine of Economic Determinism, and the Historic Mission of the Proletariat. The incident will suggest to the present-day reader how far from *sewed up* the regime of dictatorship was at that time. My presence in the Soviet embassy six months after an official denunciation from the Kremlin seems hard to believe in as things go now.

The sewing up was under way, however. Within a few months it became evident that Stalin was courting and then degrading his rivals one after the other in order to gain personal power. To trick people and fool them and betray them was one of the delights of Stalin's life. He was a *schemer* of unflagging zeal and genius—patient, inscrutable, ruthless, absolutely solitary. The story of his colossal achievements will not be rightly told, I think, by anyone who ignores this personal trait.

The Opposition won many recruits as these maneuvers of Stalin became clear. It began to assume almost the aspects of an organization. With couriers bringing the news back and forth between Moscow and Western Europe, such a debacle as the publication and subsequent repudiation of my book seemed no longer possible. In September news came through that on a date in October the Opposition was going to stage a *Vystuplenia* in Moscow. All its chief leaders—Trotsky, Radek, Piatakov, Sokolnikov, Yefdokimov, Zinoviev, Kamenev (for these latter two had come over to the Opposition now, as had Lenin's wife, Krupskaia)—were going in a body on that day into the big factories to address the genuinely proletarian party locals. They were going to rouse the workers themselves against Stalin's bureaucratic incubus that was strangling the party. A role in the operation would be played by Lenin's Testament—now called without apologies by that name—which warned the party against Stalin's excessive power, and recommended that he be replaced as general secretary. This deathbed letter of Lenin, the Opposition now decided, should be published throughout the world. In turning a copy over to the Executive Committee, Lenin's wife had kept the original in her own possession, and from this a new copy was made, and it was carried by a trusted messenger to Souvarine in Paris. Both for moral and political reasons, I was the one chosen to give it to the press. The act would indemnify me in some degree for the blow dealt me when its existence was denied. And my name, already so widely advertised as friend and biographer of Trotsky, would, so far as this was possible, guarantee its authenticity.

I went up to Paris the first day of October to translate the Testament and arrange for its publication. It had to be accompanied, of course, with an article explaining its significance, and this must be done in such a way as to chime with the news of the coming appeal to the worker Communists against Stalin's machine. My news would be released on the sixteenth, and I understood that the news of the revolt would be in subsequent issues of the papers. It turned out that I had quite a treatise to write, and I spent the best of two weeks—always in co-conspiracy with Souvarine—composing and verifying it. The *New York Times* bought it for a thousand dollars, and gave it a front-page headline and the entire second page of the paper. A Paris news agency had meanwhile cabled it to the ends of the earth, and I suppose it had a similar display in every great city. The world stage was perfectly set, in short, for the great news from Moscow.

For two days I went out early each morning to get the great news and when it finally came on the eighteenth, it was accompanied by the news that after their effort failed the Opposition led by Leon Trotsky had capitulated, confessed they had done wrong to agitate against the Stalin regime, and promised never to do it again.

Their capitulation, although not then textually published, was accurately reported. "We consider it our duty," they wrote, "openly to confess before the Party that in the struggle for our opinions . . . we have taken steps that were a violation of party discipline and have transgressed in the direction of factionalism the boundaries set by the party for intra-party ideological struggle. . . . We hope the cessation of struggle on the part of the Opposition will make it possible for expelled comrades, having acknowledged their mistake, to return to the ranks of the party. . . ." A passage was inserted declaring it "absolutely unpermissible" for comrades in other countries to support such oppositional groups as that of Bordiga in Italy, Maslow-Fischer in Germany, and Souvarine in France. The concluding sentence read: "We promise the party all possible co-operation in its . . . struggle against a recurrence of such violations of discipline in the future."

The promise was not kept, of course, nor ever intended to be. The whole thing was a lie to the public, worked out in private by the majority of the Central Committee and forced on the minority in the name of party discipline. What really happened was that the Opposition's final bold appeal to the proletariat, so logical from the standpoint of Marxian theory, was blocked by the untheoretical device of sending strong-arm squads into the proletarian meetings to hoot and yell, and lining up cars and trucks outside the buildings to blow their horns and sirens, until not a word of the appeal could be heard. As an inference from this—not quite so logically Marxian perhaps, but in accord with the mores of the Russian Communist Party—the Opposition made a peace offer to Stalin. Stalin's terms were the signing of the above capitulation, the substance of which he himself undoubtedly dictated. Signed by Trotsky and his co-leaders, it was the first of a long series of capitulations which continued for over a decade, until finally the last trace of any objection to Stalin's dictatorship, or any private fireside murmur against it, was wiped out in the Great Purge of 1936 to 1939.

As for me, I was out on a limb once more, and it now seemed I was out there permanently, for the lips of everyone in Moscow who might have authenticated my text of the Testament were sealed by this pledge of subservience to the party.

My feelings in this second debacle can best be conveyed by quoting a letter I wrote to my sister in London.

> Trotsky's capitulation is complete and to me appalling. Such things can happen only in Russia, and only in a religious church. It makes my book about the *Science* of revolution seem more important. But I am sad—I feel I'm *out of it* now for a long time. Nobody will read my book.
>
> In a fight to the bitter end it seemed legitimate to publish Lenin's Testament in the bourgeois press, or anywhere. But such a pathetic little attempt! And then when they failed, to sign in humiliation a declaration that they *had no right to try*—and a repudiation of all their friends!
>
> The science of communism is replaced by the mystic religion of the communist party.
>
> There is no place for me, and in publishing that article just at that moment I only advertised the fact. I can't be an anarchist and believe in magic, and I can't be a Marxist and believe in the materialistic God.

It remained for Stalin himself, a year later when his power was secure, to confirm the existence of the Testament and quote from it phrases enough to confirm my text. By that time it was Trotsky—and on his side now Zinoviev, Kamenev, Krupskaia—who protested that Lenin's Testament had been "concealed." Stalin jeered at them with good effect.

"There exists a certain Eastman," he said, "a former American Communist who was kicked out of the Party. This gentleman, having hung around among the Trotskyists in Moscow and collected some rumors and gossip about the 'testament' of Lenin, went home and published a book entitled *Since Lenin Died*, where he spared no colors in blackening our party . . . and where the whole argument rests on the assertion that the Central Committee concealed the so-called 'testament' of Lenin. . . . Let me read you a passage from an article by

Trotsky on the question whether the Party and its Central Committee did or did not conceal the 'testament' of Lenin."

Stalin then read an extended passage from the disavowal of my book that Trotsky had signed—under Stalin's pressure—concluding in the statement that "all the talk about a concealed or transgressed 'testament' is so much malicious invention."

"That seems clear enough," Stalin exclaimed. "It's Trotsky writing that, not somebody else. What basis, then, have Trotsky, Zinoviev and Kamenev for flapping their tongues now about how the Party and its Central Committee 'concealed' the 'testament' of Lenin? Tongue-flapping is 'permissible,' but there ought to be a limit to it.

"They say that in this 'testament' Lenin proposed that the congress, in view of the 'rudeness' of Stalin, take up the question of replacing Stalin with some other comrade as general secretary. That is perfectly true. Yes, I am rude, comrades, in relations with those who are rudely and treacherously splitting and destroying the Party. . . ." *

Thus he turned all to his advantage, both the lies and the truth.

Stalin had no further need to conceal Lenin's advice that he be removed as general secretary, for by now he had offered his resignation to a hand-picked plenum of the Central Committee and got it rejected. That Lenin advised his removal because he was *disloyal* as well as *rude*, he omitted to mention, but since the Testament actually had been concealed, nobody was in a position to check up on this slight omission.

* Speech to the combined plenum of the Central Committees of the Soviets and the Party, October 23, 1927. Stalin's *Works*, Vol. 10, pp. 172–77 of the Russian edition. An English translation was published in *Inprecor* No. 64, Nov. 17, 1927, p. 1429.

Chapter 68

A QUICK RECOVERY

Fortunately I had other interests as strong as my interest in revolutionizing human life. One was in living it; another was in finding out the truth about it. The revolution having tossed me and my political contribution to the scrap heap, I did not devote myself, as a consecrated soul would, to suffering over it. A little suffering, yes, but I soon had my life stream flowing in other channels.

In February 1926, Eliena and I took a ride through Corsica with Bill Taussig, a son of the great Harvard economist. Bill had a fine brain, but felt that his father had done all the hard work that was required of the family. His sardonic humor seasoned a joyously beautiful trip. After he and his wife had gone back to France with their car, Eliena and I stayed on for a few days, and while she painted, I forgot my woes in composing poetry and admiring the wild alien aspects of that still primitive island.

Incidentally I admired the clear and chiseled beauty of an American girl we saw there, an artist named Marion who was staying in a hotel where we dined. I went into one of my adolescent raptures about that girl. We had smiled to each other across the dining room and I became obsessed with the notion of the romance our smile had promised. I couldn't get it out of my head, and I am afraid, from a mature point of view, that speaks very badly for my head. However, as I have explained, there was so large an admixture of the all-giving mother in Eliena's love for me—she stood so firmly and without visible effort by our compact of independence—that I felt free to be as adolescently romantic about other girls as I liked. Indeed, she gave me two kinds of freedom in the enjoyment of brief or uninvolving loves. I was free, in the first place, from any doubt or hesitation on my own side. I knew that I would never part from Eliena; she was my savior and sustainer in the joys, as well as the ambitions, of my essential life. She was more fun to be *with* than anybody else I ever saw. And in the second place, the girl I was enamored of would know this too. She would have no choice but either to turn me down or accept this limitation upon the degree and measure of the infinitude with which she gave herself. The skill with which some, and I had better frankly say many, lovely and delicate girls accomplished this inward maneuver might surprise the philosophers of love.

If Eliena did not like a girl I was enamored of she would offer no obstruction, but I might find it uphill work to maintain my dissenting opinion. If she did like her, or even join me in a feeling of love for her, she might invite her to come and stay with us a while—an experiment in the *ménage-à-trois* which had the advantage of temporal limitations. It was a risk for me because most people who knew us both ended by liking Eliena best.

I seem to have spoken as though these love affairs came in droves, but that is not true. It was not an addiction, but only a privilege that none but a fool having my temperament would fail to enjoy. And I must again recall that the privilege was two-sided. I remember a jocular discussion in which it was agreed between us that my amours would best be left unnumbered, but that Eliena had had, by actual reckoning, seven. I am sure there will be—and there always were—critics who doubted whether Eliena was, in her heart, as celestially giving a lover as I have described. I think they confuse a custom of our culture with an instinctive trait of human nature. There are hundreds of sex customs in man's history that place no such dominant accent as we do on physical jealousy—the Eskimo's, to name but one. At any rate, I can only describe, as accurately as I know how, Eliena's behavior as the wife of a poet much given to falling in love.

In this matter of the clearly chiseled girl in Corsica, understanding no doubt better than I did the infantile sense of a lost poem that was afflicting me, she said:

"Why don't you go over there again alone and see if you can find her? Even if you don't, the landscape is still beautiful, and a little going off by yourself will do you good. . . ." Words to that effect. And so, with no sacrifice of the possessed, I fared forth in search of the un-possessed, the ever-beckoning.

There was a little old-fashioned seaplane—old-fashioned even then—that flew over to Corsica in an hour and a half every morning. To avoid eight hours of seasickness on the boat, I decided to take that plane.

Quite a flock of Americans were staying in Antibes that summer, among them Ferdie Tuohy, who was in Paris writing for the *New York Times*. He came down to the dock with Eliena to see me off. I invited him to join me, but he took a skeptical look at the engine of the plane, which was attached in a precarious fashion to the underside of a wing.

"Drop me a line and tell me how it goes," he said. "If you have a good time I'll join you later."

A violent gale had been blowing and there was some hesitation about taking passengers that morning. The authorities finally decided to accept two—myself and a teetering old man who seemed to be hurrying home to his own funeral.

It was my first trip in a plane, and I was surprised to find what a dull mode of travel it is. As I looked down from five thousand feet, the billowy sea was no more interesting in aspect than a sheet of corrugated iron roofing. There were no clouds in the sky, no motion anywhere—not even that of the plane, so far as my senses could report. We were about halfway to Corsica, out of sight of land in both directions, and I was indulging in these derogatory reflections on the romance of human flight, when the small engine that clung so precariously to our wing began to stutter, and the plane to descend. In a few seconds the last stutter died off, the engine burst into flame, and we were swooping down toward my despised iron roof, trailing clouds of very smoky glory. The pilot was unmoved, as Frenchmen always are in a crisis, and his assistant calmly crawled out on the wing, clinging to a stay, and sprayed the engine, or the wing above it, with fire extinguisher. My sheet of corrugated iron was fast growing into a tumbling and foam-tossing ocean. I was not too frightened to admire the skill with which the pilot set his plane down in a trough between two raging billows. They were dying billows, but they were as big as houses, and a tiny error in his calculations might have turned our landing into a dive.

His assistant crawled back into the plane, rushed into the forward compartment where we two passengers sat, and getting down on his knees, lifted out of a perforated box: a carrier pigeon!

He scribbled a note on a slip of paper, tied it to the bird's leg and threw the fluttering thing into the sky. It circled twice and then winged away as though having found a path through the air straight on the course we were traveling.

Within an hour or two a plane from that direction circled above us as the pigeon had, verifying its story, I suppose. And in a few hours more a French destroyer came in sight. The destroyer had to stand by until the waves subsided sufficiently so that the old man and I, both green and staggering, could clamber up a gangplank from the wallowing plane, and the plane be slowly towed to the port of Ajaccio. I had left Antibes at nine in the morning—to avoid seasickness, you remember— and I arrived in Ajaccio still green, at 8 P.M.

Next morning, I wrote the promised letter to Ferdie, and I have to quote a few phrases of it in order to reach the climax of this story. I advised him if he decided to follow me to come in an ark.

"We sent out a dove over the waters and he came back with a branch of the French navy and lifted us right out of the flood. Which shows, as I've always told you, that the old ways are the best after all. The fat pilot was very skillful and heroic. I tried being heroic but found it made me seasick. . . .

"Air is all right in its place, Ferdie, even water has its uses, but for purposes of navigation, earth is best."

Ferdie put my letter on the cable, together with his story of the crash, and my wisecracks appeared, if you can believe it, in a box on the front page of the *New York Times*—just as though I were Will Rogers.

That was the crown and whole real harvest of my adventure, for the girl with clear and chiseled beauty proved cloudy and complex in her emotion—neurotic, it seemed to me, though perhaps only preoccupied with a half-forgotten romance. No pride was injured on either side, but our attempted union turned into an altercation about the manner in which, and under whose guidance, operations should be conducted in the bedroom. It was almost a stand-up fight as I remember it. I know at least that vexation and anger took the place of passion, and we were at one only in the decision to meet for breakfast and try to enjoy the scenery instead of each other. We did this amicably, however, and have remained friends to this day.

Chapter 69

MY "SCIENCE OF REVOLUTION"

I have indicated the kind of adventures in mere living which lifted me out of the gloom of my political disgrace. I must say though, that, underlying them, the intellectual task I had undertaken gave me a more solid ground to stand on. My investigation of the relations between Marxism and scientific method was, just then, as exciting an exploration as one with my limited knowledge of either could possibly undertake. It absorbed my whole working time during the year after I finished *Since Lenin Died*—much of my playtime too, for I amused and flattered myself, in almost a Joycean manner, by making my own translation of every passage I quoted from a foreign tongue. By January 1926 I was in Paris putting the finishing touches on the notes. Eliena had typed the book all out clean—for the third time!—and we were looking for a publisher.

The title, *Marx, Lenin and the Science of Revolution*, was clumsy, and it telegraphed the fact that the book was revolutionary—not the best of salesmanship. Moreover, American intellectuals, revolutionary or not, had then no interest in theoretic Marxism. Neither, indeed, had the British. But Stanley Unwin expressed a venturesome wish to publish my book provided I would contribute fifty pounds toward the cost of publication. That was two hundred and fifty dollars in those days, and no small sum, but I had that much in the bank. He published the book in May 1926—just a year after *Since Lenin Died*. I got my money back in due course, and more too, for he managed to sell a fair-sized edition in England; Albert and Charles Boni subsequently sold one in America; and translations appeared in both French and Spanish.* For the present, however, my labors were rewarded only by

---

* *La Science de la Révolution* (Paris) and *La Ciencia de la Revolución* (Madrid).

the privilege of sending the book where I thought it might be appreciated or do some good.

Bernard Shaw sent me a surprisingly prompt postcard with his cocky picture on it: "I read your book right through, and think it a much needed and most competently executed contribution to the literature of Socialism." Sigmund Freud, to whose relations with Marxism I had devoted a chapter, welcomed my book as "really important, probably also right." My old teacher, Preserved Smith, author of a three-volume *History of Modern Culture*, sent me from Cornell a letter of high praise: "Some of your phrases put a whole book in one sentence; for example, that one about Marx substituting a World Robot for Hegel's World Spirit."

A copy I sent to the Marx-Engels Institute in Moscow was returned by the Post Office marked, "Denied admission by the Department of Publications," but through Adolf Joffe I got one to Ivan Pavlov, who startled me with a letter in his own hand sent fearlessly through the mail: "I endorse in full your criticism of the philosophical foundation of Marxism." Pavlov added this contribution to my painfully slow escape from the prison of socialist belief:

"There isn't any science of revolution, and there won't be for a long time. There is only a groping of the life force, partly guided empirically, of those who have a much-embracing and strong common sense. Our Bolshevik Revolution, with its details so disastrous to our intellectual and moral development, I consider an anachronism which (of this I am convinced) will be repeated in this form never and nowhere in the civilized world. Such is my deepest understanding of these matters."

H. G. Wells, who was living now in a villa called Lou Pidou on the slope of the mountain between Antibes and Cannes, took a copy of *Marx and Lenin* with him on a trip to London. He sent me, before starting, a disparaging postcard beginning, "Dear Max," but on reaching Aix-les-Bains took it all back: "My dear Eastman, I scribbled you a postcard from Lou Pidou, telling you I liked the book but accusing you of an imperfect knowledge of the Realist-Nominalist controversy. On reflection I think that was all nonsense. . . . So please scrap my postcard except in so far as it expresses my accordance with (and approval and admiration for) your very important book." When he published somewhat later his sanguine prophecy, *The Shape of Things To Come*, Wells listed *Marx and Lenin* among the handful of books that people were still reading in the far-off golden epoch he imagined.

It would be more false than modest to omit from my story these words of praise from men eminent just then in the world of ideas. I am humble enough to be elated by such things at any time, but in my state of disgrace in the year 1926 they were uplifting events.

Still it was only halfway to a good book. It had to be rewritten ten years later. My criticism of Marx's Hegelian philosophy was, I think, cogent and scholarly. But my proposal that, following the line of Lenin's instinctive heresies, we convert the whole thing into an applied science of social transformation, had the serious defect I have mentioned: it ignored the question who is to be the scientist and whence comes his authority. It also accepted from Marx the defective blueprints that were justified only by his philosophical belief. To him with his philosophy of universal progress "from the lower to the higher," this defect was a virtue. "The workers have no ideal to realize," he said, "they have only to set free the elements of the new society which the old bourgeois society carries in its womb." That being so, it was sufficient to remark that "in the higher phase of the Communist society . . . the limited horizon of capitalistic justice will be left behind entirely and society will inscribe on its banners: From each according to his abilities, to each according to his needs." If instead of fooling ourselves about the goal of the historic process we are going to make a scientific effort to *construct* a higher phase of society, we must have careful blueprints. But if any earnest student of human nature and history had set out, with the mental energy of Marx and Lenin, to draw the blueprints of a society combining freedom with common ownership of the instruments of production, I think he would soon have seen that the goal is unattainable. That, perhaps, is why my mind dodged this problem when attempting to make an applied "science of revolution" out of the Marxian mystique.

It was at least a strenuous effort, and it led me to one experience so delightful that I must describe it. In selling the book to Gallimard for publication in France I rashly promised to find a translator, and the translator I found was a gifted French writer and *penseur* named Lucien Monod, who did not know a word of English. Lucien lived only a few miles from us on a leaf-hidden road up a hill above Cannes, and for several months I took the train over there every afternoon, climbed up to his aerie in the Chemin de Bénéfiat, read my text to him sentence by sentence in atrocious French, and watched him convert it into that most stately creation of the intellect of man: perfect French prose. Lucien was a cripple, helpless in both legs from birth, and traveled only from his bed to his tiny living room or his garden; but he led a happy life. He had more fun with his heart and brains than most people have with the full use of their bodies. I dropped in to see him in 1955 and he welcomed me with the same gay wise tender smile that had greeted me every morning thirty years before. He was in bed when I came, surrounded with books and papers, finishing the fourth volume of a *History of Religions*. He is gone now, and I don't know what will ever become of that *History of Religions*, but it served him well.

For the rest of that year my energies were occupied, apart from an occasional poem, with completing the novel I had begun at Sochi. I was calling it *Breaking Through*, and I had surmounted the inner roadblock which stopped me in my tracks when Eliena came to Sochi. Eliena was my companion in the effort now, typing and endlessly retyping my messy pages, and I was again joyfully speeding along the track of the story. Of a sudden, however—or so it seemed—I discovered that the money we were living on had given out. There were no on-the-side sources of income for me in France, no lecturings, teachings, translations, no embassy job for Eliena. The roadblock was external now, but it was serious. I had barely begun to inspect it, however, when my old friend Albert Boni—now a newborn publisher—dropped off a train to Paris, and offered me an advance of two hundred and fifty dollars on the novel. He was returning from Constantinople where he had met Leon Trotsky on his arrival in exile with an offer to publish his *History of the Russian Revolution*, and take only half of the income from subsidiary rights. In my state of frustration I was as easy a mark as Trotsky. I only stipulated that he should also buy five hundred sheets from the English publisher and issue an American edition of *Marx and Lenin*.

Chapter 70

A FLIGHT OF WRITERS

I was at least surrounded by novelists while trying so hard to become one. American literary men were flocking to Europe like crows to a cornfield during those years of the debased currencies, and most of them would alight for a few months in the vicinity of the Cap d'Antibes. Ernest Hemingway kept his typewriter in a loft up in a spare corner of "the rampart," where I also found a hideaway. He was staying, as I remember, with Gerald Murphy, son of the wealthy wit and politician, Charles Francis Murphy, in a villa out toward the end of the Cap. Ernest was unknown and broke then, and rode in to the rampart and back on a bicycle. John Dos Passos and Archibald MacLeish also alighted for a time in the charming home of Gerald Murphy, who seemed to have a liking for literary young men. The Murphys invited Eliena and me to dinner there once and we thought we had a rare good time, but whether they agreed or not I don't know, for we had nowhere to entertain them, and were not invited again. Their swimming place was the more populous one in front of the Hôtel du Cap, and we of the Davison tribe used to go over there occasionally because of the springboard. The Davison tribe included the English dancer and dancing teacher, Margaret Morris, her husband, the Scotch painter, John Ferguson, and six or eight young English girls who were studying with her. Those girls were all excellent swimmers and each was in some delicately individual way molded to fit ravishingly into a bathing suit. I still fancied myself somewhat of an amateur diver, and was showing off on the springboard at the hotel one day a few badly executed jackknives and one-and-a-half dives, when Archie MacLeish—then best known as an ex-captain of the Yale swimming team—came strolling modestly down the path in professional swimming tights. He did ten or a dozen

464

of the most varied and beautiful dives I had up to that time ever seen. It was quite an event in my life, as a firm and convincing setback to one's excessive pretensions always is.

On another day I was basking out on the float when a swimmer approached with a slow deliberate stroke from a westerly direction. Mooring himself beside me in the water, he said:

"Aren't you Max Eastman?"

"Yes, I am," I answered.

"I'm Benchley," he said.

Being constitutionally behind the times, and especially so then because of my long absence in Russia, I had never heard of Robert Benchley. In my confusion I said the first thing that came into my head:

"From New York?"

Laughing about it afterward, we agreed that he should have had the port of origin painted on his stern.

Scott Fitzgerald was another American who alighted at the Cap d'Antibes while we were there. He and Zelda and Eliena and I had several good times together, and would have had many, if the quantity and continuity of their drinking had not made it impossible. They drank not out of conviviality or even eagerness to drink, but automatically. It was a reflex action like breathing and as little within the control of their wills.

My great joy in having these people from home turn up in Antibes was the manner in which they all fell for Eliena. Here was a treasure I had found in a far country, and what a treasure it was! Could pride in oneself be as joyous as that?

Sitting on the floor one night at a party in the Château des Enfants, I heard Scott say to Eliena: "You are one of those persons who when they smile everybody smiles, when they come into a room the room is lighted." To Eliena's demur he added: "It isn't only I who say so—Zelda thinks so too." And John Dos Passos—since I am citing the authorities—remarked that there was "a sort of greatness about Eliena, a Roman sort of greatness." My concurring opinion I expressed to some small degree, in these lines:

ELIENA

Nimble with laughter, loving to be,
Courage quick and as quick a skill,
Pride that contains humility,

Love that adoring is thinking still—
Most men love in a girl some star,
I love you for the things you are.

About Zelda, a strange thing is that, although I learned years later
in Turnbull's *Scott Fitzgerald* how muscular and boldly athletic she
was, I perceived her then—almost prophetically—as exceedingly frail. I
admired her beauty as one admires an exquisite vase on a shaky table
and would not touch it for the world. Indeed I sensed a similar fragility
and hazard in Scott himself, whose beauty was almost as delicate as
hers. He surprised me with his robust and reckless thirst for experience.
His daring pranks and exploits reminded me of the hero of my college
days, Sid Wood. Instead of thinking up stories, Scott kept thinking up
ways to make real life read like a story.

One night we four were drinking very late and alone at a newly
opened restaurant and dance hall. I had been teaching him to play the
cockfight game. It consists of two people hopping on one foot with arms
folded and seeing who can knock the other off his balance—compel him,
that is, to put the other foot down. Scott, being a beginner and very
much lighter than I, was easy to defeat, and he wanted a little more
drama. He called the head waiter, who had been watching, and told him
to go into the kitchen and choose the best man they had out there, and
he would give him a hundred dollars if he could knock me off my
balance. After an interval there entered the room a two-hundred-
and-fifty-pound meaty bruiser—either the chef or the bartender—with
all the employees following to see the show. I was rather wrought up,
and perhaps a little lit, as everybody in Scott's company always was
around midnight, and I decided I would have to knock this giant off his
foot instantly or I never could. I went after him like a whirlwind, and
knocked him not only off his foot, but through a big glass window that
opened onto the verandah. It was a rather bloody scene and actually
satisfied, I think, for one evening, Scott's thirst for experience.

Scott loaned me a copy of *The Great Gatsby*, and I loaned him the
manuscript of my novel. He came over to our tiny Villa Parthénite one
afternoon and we each praised the other's book. Of his praise the only
thing I remember is his allusion to "that wonderful era of liberal
enthusiasm" through which I had lived, and of which for him my novel
was a "beautiful record." This jolted me, for I thought my novel concerned the proletarian revolution, and that the proletarian revolution
was still engaged in building a new world in Soviet Russia. I was soon

to receive other jolts of this kind, for I had been away from America almost five years, and was unaware how far and fatally those years had removed me into the past. *The Great Gatsby* might have taught me this, if I had realized how famous it was, for although I found it a good story and easy to praise, I failed to see anything significant enough about it to "symbolize an era." For me a sense of conscious artifice, not quite so perfect as the conscious artifice of Robert Louis Stevenson, makes Scott's prose seem immature. I thought this quality was at its worst in the description of a certain scene on the estate of the Great Gatsby. Scott, when I praised the book, opened it and said: "Let me read you just this one passage that I'm particularly proud of." It was that same description, the worst example of what I considered his principal fault.

On another afternoon Scott brought over T. S. Eliot's "The Waste Land" to read to me, I in my geographical and political isolation having never heard of it. He spoke of it as a great poem, a new and wonderful event in the world of letters. Again I felt that I was behind the times, and made an honest effort to curb my envy and keep my mind open, but I could not find any sense at all in what he read. When he had finished, I asked him what Eliot meant by a certain passage which he had rendered with special eloquence.

"I don't know what it means," he said, brushing from the page the idea of meaning, "but just the sound and feeling—isn't it wonderful!"

I couldn't agree, and I cannot agree yet. I can enjoy the sound and feeling conveyed by music because it does not challenge my verbal understanding. But when my understanding is appealed to with meaningful words and is baffled, I find it hard to give myself to any feeling but one of bafflement.

Perhaps I am too intellectual, I thought, and the old boyhood sense of American shame about having brains came over me. But I couldn't very well express that to a comparative stranger. Another feeling I could not, or did not, express was one of dismay, the gropingly cosmic dismay that afflicts you when, keenly and for the first moment, you realize that your time is past, the generation you belong to has been laid away, your life and opinions are history. I cannot pretend that this moment lasted very long. I was soon time-scorningly convinced that my reaction to those musical, yet unintelligible, lines had been on the side of surviving civilization, Scott's on that of the decline into a new Dark Age.

Closest to my heart of the literary men that alighted on the Cap in 1925 and 1926 was my old friend and co-editor, Claude McKay. I met

him quite accidentally on one of my trips to Paris, when our two trains
going in opposite directions stopped side-by-side in the railroad station
at Marseilles. The brainstorm that obliterated our friendship in Moscow
had swept over, and we embraced laughingly as though nothing had
happened. Claude was writing his first long story, "Home to Harlem,"
and I persuaded him to come to Antibes to finish it. He took a room in
the aerie where Ernest and I had perched, and came over to Parthénite
to eat with us and help Eliena get lunch and dinner. They two were
washing and wiping the dishes one evening when Scott Fitzgerald came
to the door. Eliena ran out of the kitchen to greet him, but Claude, who
did not know him, continued to wash the dishes. Scott naturally took
him for a Negro servant and sat down with his back to the door of the
tiny kitchen. There was a mischievous glint in Claude's eyes as he came
out to join us, but when I introduced them, instead of trying to cover his
surprise with some verbo-gymnastic pretense, Scott said quite simply:

"Oh, I thought you were the cook!"

It made us all like Scott, and we spent a delightful evening
together—three novelists, and a Russian girl who could tell them things
they did not know about Gogol and Tolstoy and Turgenev.

With one exception, Claude was the only American identified with
the revolution who had a good word to say for *Since Lenin Died*. "It
seems to me," he wrote right after its publication, "that you have given
us one of the finest and most balanced political treatises of these times, a
crystal-clear analytic study of the co-operative work of Lenin and
Trotsky, their faults, their weakness, their greatness. And whatever
happens to Trotsky this little book of yours will live and interest the
world as long as it remembers Lenin and Trotsky. An electric thrill
runs through it from beginning to end."

Those were extreme words, and sounded fantastic in the atmosphere
of obloquy in which I read them, but I had always esteemed Claude's
political intelligence only a little less than his lyrical genius, and they
were a comfort to me. A further sentence from the same letter reveals
the advancing boldness of his judgment: "Incidentally, you're doing
more than anyone can imagine just now for the proletarian movement—
you are lifting the clumsy hand of Moscow off of it."

Another novelist nesting on the Riviera in those days was Glenway
Westcott, in whose room at Villefranche Claude and Eliena and I
passed some unforgettable hours. Paul Robeson was there, and his
strong-minded wife Essie, who seemed to me to have the faults without

the virtues of my conception of a "revolutionary engineer." At least I've always thought she was at the wheel when Paul, a man with a gentle heart and magnanimous understanding of America's slow progress toward race equality, veered from his path, and became a blustering yet manipulated advocate of totalitarian tyranny over all the races. Paul sang for us in Glenway's little room—it was the first time I heard that solemnly celestial voice—and it so surrounded and drowned my faculties that I have no other memory of what must have been a brilliantly interesting evening.

Still another literary friend and swimming neighbor of those days was slim, delicate, and very British Lloyd Osbourne, Robert Louis Stevenson's stepson, who lived with his strong-limbed and very American wife in a red stucco villa at the top of the rocky steep next door to the Davisons' diving place. In his driveway one morning I ran into Waldo Peirce and Rockwell Kent, who were tearing around the Alpes-Maritimes looking for adventures in an immense truck with beer barrels for a back seat. I have a photograph of myself sitting on one of those beer barrels, but I cannot remember what it was all about—except that the general idea was to get out and raise hell in a juvenile manner, an idea with which, as author of "The Folly of Growing Up," I heartily sympathized. In Rockwell this business of raising hell—or to speak more respectfully, having adventures—was then so steady a preoccupation that I've never been able to regard his subsequent espousal of communism as anything but a prank. Waldo, I remember, was privately disgusted with the unbalanced extremes to which Rockwell wanted to carry it, and this I think caused the truck to be returned to its owners without memorable eventualities, or at least without running over a cliff into the sea.

Waldo was just beginning to try to paint in those days, and I spent some agonizing hours in his studio, while he produced a portrait of me that looked like the wrapper of a cake of facial soap. Other such faces were leaning against the wall of his studio, and the idea of his ever becoming an artist of distinction was incapable of entering my mind. To me he was a writer, though so known only to his friends. His poems, for the most part too Rabelaisian for publication, were composed with equal fluency in Spanish, French and English. For a taste of his charm as a correspondent, I will quote a poem that he once sent me from Key West where he was sailing and fishing with Ernest Hemingway. It was called "La Mort de Myrtle, le Turtle."

La grande Tortue est morte en plein amour
Harponnée dans la mer envers le neuvième jour,
Où le Gulf Stream commence son énorme parcours.
Parce que ses mille cinq cent oeufs se vendent pour
Soixante sous la livre pour mettre dans le four—
La grande tortue est morte, est morte en plein amour
Harponnée dans les reins. Eh bien qu'il soit mon tour,
Je serai mort d'amour avant le troisième jour.

At the time of which I am writing, Waldo was living at Cagnes-sur-Mer, a few miles east of Antibes. Rex Ingram in nearby Nice was making his spectacular film of Blasco Ibañez's novel *Mare Nostrum*, and he recruited Waldo with his great beard and magnificent figure to play the part of Neptune rising from the sea. Subsequently Waldo left for home, and Rex recruited Claude and Eliena, and some dancing companions of hers, to do a rustic dance in another film. I wrote Waldo urging him to come back and join the fun, but he replied that he was preparing for a one-man exhibition at some art gallery in New York. I am telling all this because, having quoted the poem Waldo sent me, I want to quote one I sent him. There was a slim, mysterious girl in Cagnes named Harriet, who also claimed to be a dancer, but danced only to a phonograph record of Chopin's Funeral March, and that only after locking her door and consuming large quantities of rum which she bought at a tiny bistro run by a pear-shaped woman named Rosa. All these further details are necessary, I fear, if the reader is to participate in my poem.

TO WALDO PEIRCE

We need you, Waldo, as the fifes the drum,
Your beard of Neptune and your breast of Mars.
We're all of us becoming movie stars—
Claude dancing ragtime and the Mumbo-Jum,
And Harriet the dirge of Rosa's rum,
Eliena skipping to the scribbly bars
Of Scriabin like a sprightly train of cars—
Why not pack up your poetry and come?

"An exhibition in New York!" you call?
Sweet Virgin, Waldo, with the beard and all?
The fringed belly and the beveled bum?
You super-Tarzan of the Apes-to-come,
If you exhibit there the city's lost.
Remember Sodom, Waldo—count the cost!

Next door on the other side of our diving rocks, and with access to the same private bight of clear deep blue water, lived Jan Boissevain, a younger brother of my dear friend Eugen. Jan had married Charlotte Ives, an actress whose warm-hearted charm, and delicious meals, and private swimming place, seemed also to exercise a special magnetism upon novelists. I first met Somerset Maugham reclining in nothing but a blue bathrobe on the curved bench of wave-washed gray rock that belonged to Charlotte and Jan. I also first saw in their house—to interrupt for a vivid memory's sake this list of distinguished novelists— the justly famous and still lustrous eyes of Maxine Elliott. But Charlotte's crowning feat as a social being was to be a close friend for many years of both H. G. Wells and Rebecca West. Rebecca really loved her, and H. G. was often to be found lunching and entertaining the guests at her house.

On one of these occasions he invited Eliena and me for a weekend at Lou Pidou, and we spent gay hours with him and his sharp-angled girl friend, Odette, in that tree-shaded villa. This week-end was less densely populated than the one in England, and Wells did get around, finally, to asking my opinion about events and prospects in Russia. It pleased and stimulated him to hear that I regarded the Byzantine Marxian scholasticism prevailing there as the most ominous thing about it. We agreed that Marx's philosophy of dialectic evolution was remote from science.

"I always suspected," he remarked, "that Marx got it all out of Darwin."

"I'm afraid your dates are wrong," I said. "Marx and Engels formulated their philosophy in 1845 and *The Origin of Species* was published in 1859."

It was a bad break for the author of a *History of the World*, but Wells accepted my correction as though accustomed to such checkups. Indeed he accepted it so jauntily that I thought he was not vain. But he was vain, in a trivial way, as I learned when we played badminton one day down at Charlotte and Jan's. With a rare stroke of beginner's luck I beat him the first set six-two, and he suffered visibly. He was positively stricken down with disappointed pride. He played the game, as a matter of fact, better than I, and that became clear in the next two sets. But clearer than anything else was the total change in the color of his universe when he began to win.

My brother was quicker than I at his studies, and stronger physically. In general I thought him a superior being, and largely for that reason never got the habit of regarding myself as a show-piece—or indeed of habitually regarding myself at all. For that accidental blessing I am profoundly thankful. I don't know any social trait more disagreeable than the constant itch to shine and be admired. Gifted men and beautiful women are apt to acquire this affliction in their youth, and it rides them through life, sucking their charm like an insect. People who get famous even in late life sometimes acquire it, and become a bore to the friends who used to enjoy them. They sit aloof now, wrapped up in themselves like vultures, peering into the conversation to see where they can pick up a scrap of meat for their insatiable egotism. Frank Harris had this itch to a pitiful degree. He could not attend a meeting where somebody was making a successful speech without shouting out "Hear, Hear!" every little while in his booming bass-viol of a voice, drawing attention away from the speaker to the little great man who happened to be sitting in his audience.

Frank was spending his last years in Nice, a short run on a bus along the coast from Cap d'Antibes. I did not know it until one day, sipping a cup of coffee in a garden crowded with resting swimmers, I saw Isadora Duncan coming toward me in an ambience of flowing scarfs which almost hid a small companion making his way among the tables behind her. I had not seen her since our meeting at the railroad station in Kislovodsk, where I promised to call and failed to keep my promise. Her reproach and the need to think up an explanation, combined with one of her secretly erotic embraces, preoccupied me, and I was slow to realize that the little man behind her was Frank Harris. When I turned to greet him he was looking intently at a battleship out in the bay.

"Why, Frank Harris won't even speak to me!" I said in genuine surprise.

"Well, you passed me by, my boy!" he said, drawing himself up like a fighting bantam.

Frank was consumed almost to an ash by the desire to be, and be known as, a "great writer." He was indeed a brilliantly gifted critic, but since the only creative things he wrote were short stories, the way to his heart was to compare him to de Maupassant slightly to the latter's disadvantage. Once when we had offices in the same loft on Union Square, I brought him a copy of my newly published poems, *Colors of Life*. As I had just been reading with enthusiasm his fascinating book, *The Man Shakespeare*, I wrote on the flyleaf: "To my friend, Frank Harris, the discoverer of Shakespeare's heart."

He opened my little volume, turned quickly to the inscription, and looked up, crestfallen.

"Oh, you thought only of the Shakespeare!" he said.

Another flame that consumed Frank Harris was the desire to be a sporting English gentleman, spending an income of twelve to twenty thousand dollars a year. This mixed badly with the desire to be a great writer, and made something of a mountebank out of him. Hesketh Pearson puts this rather extremely when he says: "Nothing could turn him from his strenuous, blatant, truculent, independent and undependable course, except hard cash, spot cash, and plenty of it." But Frank's own biographer, Hugh Kingsmill, is almost as extreme: "No one but a salamander would risk the stake for the accuracy of a single statement in Harris's autobiography." His intimate conversations with the great men of his time, pretty near all of them—and they all called him Frank—had, I suspect, a little more to do with reality than that dull and colorlessly erotic book, *My Life and Loves*. They were at least good reading. When delivered in the form of conversation, borrowing color from his magnetic voice and great jovial guffaws, they were, for the first few hours, unexcelled entertainment. I do not think Frank himself knew when he was romancing and when telling the truth. But he was astute enough to know that his anecdotes of great men were universally taken with a grain of salt. He had, however, a scholarly and quite prodigious memory, and it was not easy to catch him in an anecdote that *might not* be true.

One day dining at his apartment in Nice, I tried to discourse a little about the fallacies of Marxism, but Frank cut me off.

"I told Karl myself," he said, "that he was overdoing that class-struggle business. History would be a bore if it all consisted of class struggles.

" 'Frank,' he said, 'you're talking about history as literary entertainment. It's the inner dynamics of the thing that I'm trying to work out.' "

I happened to remember, for no better reason than that I was born the same year, that Marx died in 1883. It seemed doubtful that Frank Harris was old enough to have been hobnobbing with Marx about the class struggle before I was born. So I asked him, in as casual a manner as I could assume, just when this conversation with Marx had taken place.

He looked at me with a mischievous grin which said as plain as daylight, "I know what you're up to!" Then, speaking very slowly so as to keep me as long as possible in suspense, he said:

"Max, that was a long time ago—that was in the . . . late . . . autumn of . . . eighteen . . . eighty . . . *two!*" He put a great emphasis on the word *two*, and we both laughed heartily without a word as to what we were laughing at.

A favorable thing to remember about Frank Harris was his devout love of literature. In appraising the great writers, if not in gossiping about them, he had a fine unswerving integrity. He was a bold, generous and resourceful editor. If he did not find the lyric soul in Shakespeare's dramas, he dreamed one up that is plausible and worthy to inhabit them. And he was kind. I never saw any meanness in him.

A little farther down the coast and over the Italian border at San Remo, Lincoln Steffens was nesting in a rose-embowered villa with his brand-new wife, Ella Winter, and their small baby. He had been stirred by my reports of happenings in Moscow since his disappointed departure. Indeed he had written me one of the few enthusiastic letters I received from political friends about *Since Lenin Died*, and had planned to come to Antibes for one of those long talks about the revolution that meant so much to him. Instead, Eliena and I went down to San Remo for a week-end. The term "brand-new" slipped out inadvertently when I mentioned Ella Winter. She was so crisp, so neatly put into her clothes, unmellowed by experience, excessively positive, and handsome in a perfectly unwrinkled way that both attracted and repelled me. Her brain action was swift and continuous, unimpeded, it seemed to me, by any inclination to exercise judgment. Intellectually she was born to be a zealot. I cannot presume to measure her influence upon Steff, but what with her capture of him and Stalin's capture of his beloved revolution, he was transformed, during the decade left to him, from a sentimental rebel preaching Jesus on both sides of the class struggle to a hard-cut propagandist of the party line. His autobiography, published in 1931, a fabulous best seller, was almost a textbook of revolution, and he did as much as any American to swing the idealist youth of the thirties into the pro-Soviet parade. His deathbed in Carmel, California, was a place of pilgrimage for devotees and dupes and fellow-travelers of Stalin's tyranny from all over the country.

More frankly than his followers, Steffens confessed that his motivation in becoming a Communist was purely emotional. His conversion, he wrote to Marie Howe, was a "process, not of thought, but of psychological revolution." And to Sidney Hook, who challenged him at the end of his life to explain rationally his defense of the Soviet dictatorship, he replied that he had given up the effort to think things out; he "felt" that the Communists were right.

This process of feeling was not completed at the time of our visit. In fact, less than a year before, he had been trying hard to think things out, as is evidenced by a letter he wrote me on June 16, 1925. (It is not to be found in *The Letters of Lincoln Steffens*, edited by Ella Winter.)

Dear Max,

Your book, *Since Lenin Died*, came in last evening's mail. Thanks. And I read it last night. Thanks. It clears up the whole situation for me, as it will for others. It is a fine example of clean reporting, clear thinking and extraordinarily simple writing. I am absolutely convinced and I should think you will have convinced not only the revolutionists outside but the Communists also, everywhere. You and your book can not go to Russia. And maybe the book should not.

I too have had some letters from Moscow. They have taken your view of the facts, not so clearly, but I got it just the same. And I got also and I still rather hold to the view that Trotsky's attitude, not yours, is right, in the sense of what is revolutionary. The fight must be fought out within the party, not in public, and meanwhile the party—the machine, as we used to call it—has to be supported, even as against Trotsky. It is liberalism to resent the injustice done to Trotsky, it is liberalism to feel as strongly as you do, I think, the crookedness of the methods of the bosses of the machine. These things are not worse, morally, than the red terror, which we have learned to understand. I am not criticizing you, Max; I am really inciting you to answer a question in my mind ever since this situation began to dawn upon me.

Would it not be better to assassinate Zinoviev and Stalin than to write this book of yours? How are men to deal with a situation like this, which rises in every such movement (and therefore is "natural" and typical), and yet hang on to the party as a weapon and tool of the revolution? . . . Trotsky is clearer than you are in his evident view that nothing must jar our perfect loyalty to the party and its leaders. Even as it stands, a menace, not only to him and to the best of the followers of Lenin, but to the revolution, it is the main spring of the revolution and has to be identified with it—always. Or doesn't it? That is my question. How are we to beat Paul and keep from beating Jesus?

My impression was, and is, that this letter came nearer to a vital process of thought about the revolution than anything else Steff wrote. Although based on the erroneous assumption that I had published my book without consulting the Opposition, his question was deeply pertinent. We did not find an answer to it on the beach at San Remo. I doubt if an answer could be found without unsettling our basic premise—that "the revolution" was an indubitable good. We were neither of us ready then to assail that premise. But the developments of the next twelve years, which so abundantly vindicated my book, also led me to the conclusion that the revolution—meaning the October seizure of power by the Central Committee of Lenin's minority party—was a misfortune. Steff did not live the whole of those twelve years; he died in 1936, just at the beginning of the Great Purge. That unmitigated horror might have shaken his "feeling" that the Communists were right, but I hardly think so. Ella Winter took it in her dashing stride. In the letter I quoted, Steff was already (in 1925) choosing the party as against the true aims of the revolution—even against the revolution itself, he seems almost to say—and he continued on that course. It was the only way to hang on to his premise, but it was the very opposite of what Steff throughout his life had stood for. In the days of the old *Masses* and the *Liberator*, he had called himself an anarchist and jeered at the idea of organization, while I lectured him on the scientific concept of a method of procedure.

Chapter 71

SOME MORE NAME-DROPPING

There are two kinds of name-droppers: those who tell about their famous friends in order to enhance their own prestige, and those who do so in order to be interesting. With this latter purpose I am going to drop a few more names in this chapter, and I will begin with Stefan Zweig, from whom I borrowed twenty marks in Salzburg.

It happened this way. My prep-school task of learning German, an unfinished task that has nagged me all my life, took me by the collar in earnest one spring morning in 1926.

"Look here!" it said. "While wasting your worktime writing books, why not at least in your playtime be finishing me up?"

It struck me as a frugal idea, and Eliena chimed in with timely longings for a taste of mountain air. One would naturally go to Germany to play at learning German, but we had both been in Germany. Austria was something new; Vienna and Salzburg were sights that every poet should see; and the valleys of the Salzkammergut were said to excel in beauty all known containers of mountain air. So we packed our belongings and took a romantic train up through the Tyrol to St. Gilgen on the Wolfgangsee, pausing in Salzburg and detouring to Vienna for history's and our heart's sake. In Salzburg our cash ran out, and not a bank or a hotel in the defeated town, bled white by the war and bleeding from the peace, would honor our check on the Guaranty Trust Company, though it had an office in Paris. We must pay our lodging in Austrian coin or sleep in the streets. We must sleep in the streets for several nights, since it took time to get a draft from the bank in Paris. After plodding from bank to hotel and hotel to bank for twelve hours, I fell back on the notion, always rather distasteful to me, that I am a citizen, after all, of "the republic of letters." Stefan Zweig lived in a fine and enviable house halfway up the steep hill that springs

477

like a skyscraper right out of the middle of Salzburg. It took a lot of courage to climb up there and knock on the noted author's door. I didn't ask him for a loan. I told him our plight and asked him what we should do. He looked more like a businessman than an author, with his piercing eyes and close-clipped mustache, and he met my question in a coolly businesslike manner, securing us a room in a hotel by telephone, and providing me with a handful of marks for incidental expenses. His wife surrounded this transaction with the warmth and hospitable grace and abounding good will that he did not seem to have, on such short notice, at command.

I knew little of his writings then, and I am sure he had never read a word of mine—except perhaps my correspondence in the *Liberator* with Romain Rolland. Years later, I read some of his writings, among them the wonderful story, "Amok," and learned what a greatly gifted man he was. By that time he had parted from the wife I remembered so warmly and had been driven from Austria by Hitler's lunatic assault upon the Jews. He died by his own hand in Rio de Janeiro in 1942, leaving a note of farewell to the world whose dignity of thought and phrasing filled me with regret that our meeting had been so brief.

"After one's sixtieth year unusual powers are needed in order to make another wholly new beginning. Those that I possess have been exhausted by long years of homeless wandering. So I think better to conclude in good time and in erect bearing a life in which intellectual labor meant the purest joy and personal freedom the highest good on earth."

Another famous man we made friends with in Salzburg was Andreas Latzko. He was far more famous just then than Stefan Zweig, his rebellious book, *Men In War*, having had a vogue second only to that of *Under Fire* by Henri Barbusse. He was a constitutionally unhappy man, dark in color and dour in manner, who, I felt would have raged against man as eloquently in peace as in war. His grouch seemed unjustified, for his wife, a Georgian by birth, was as beautiful and charming a woman as I have seen. I had been told before going to Russia that the most beautiful women in the world are to be found in Georgia, but I had traveled in vain from Batum to Tiflis, and over the high range of the Caucasus, in search of a single example of it. Here at last I found one, and she and Eliena and I, leaving Andreas alone with his gloom, talked Russian together with gay disregard of the behavior of men, dreadful though it truly is, in peace as well as in war.

We spent a month in St. Gilgen, Eliena and I, but found no

mountain air, only water pouring out of the heaven—and no German either, but a bastard dialect which bade fair to ruin what little of the *echte Sprache* I had left in my head. The landscape was beautiful beyond our dreams, but we were lonesome in the rain. We were homesick for the sun and the swimming and the pleasure-loving friends from all countries that turned up at Antibes or Juan-les-Pins. They included my sister Crystal, her husband and two winsome children; Charlie Chaplin and a comely girl friend; Dudley Field Malone and Doris Stevens, my neighbors in Croton; Frederick O'Brien, whose book about his life in the South Seas was a furious best seller; the painter Jerome Blum and his wife "Frankie"; Hutchins Hapgood, whose auto-biographical *A Victorian in the Modern World* is unequaled in plod-ding honesty; William McLeod Raine of "Western story" fame and of humane, intelligent charm—indeed many a friend about whom a live-lier book could be written than this one about myself.

In early June my generous friend Betty Hare—generous friend also of the old *Masses* and the *Liberator*—arriving in Paris, asked me to join her in a visit to the institute for the cultivation of physical health and intellectual nonsense run by the handsome Armenian or Georgian, Gurdjiev, at Fontainebleau. Gurdjiev had been made famous along Park Avenue by his apostle, A. R. Orage, once a British economist and prophet of Guild Socialism, who came over and earned a fine living teaching our wealthy intelligentsia how to "expand their consciousness" and escape from the rigors of verified knowledge. Gurdjiev had been made still more famous by the dwindling away to death in his institute of the sensitive British girl-of-letters, Katherine Mansfield. Betty had always a wistful feeler out toward the super-mundane, and I, ever since my experiments with hypnotism in Dr. Sahler's New Thought Sani-tarium at Kingston, have enjoyed toying with its pretenses. Besides Betty's invitation, I had word from my British publisher of some problem that required, or could be made to seem to require, my presence in London. With these two excellent excuses I got out of St. Gilgen by train to Paris the first of June, leaving Eliena to paint the rain-drenched landscape alone.

Gurdjiev had a lovely place in Fontainebleau—all places there, indeed, are lovely—a woodsy farmlike tract of land, with cottages for his disciple-patients, riding horses, Russian baths, an oriental-style pavilion for purposes of mass hypnosis. He kept up an atmosphere of mystery with curtained divans, exotic costumes and dancing motions, and with spiritual sessions in which he read words from a scripture dictated to him, as he explained with a disarming smile, by his tutelary divinity, Beelzebub. Betty and I attended one of these sessions, and I watched his fervent disciples listen, with rapt and exalted attention, to some of the most banal and corny drivel that ever entered my ears. To break the spell, I put in an irreverent question, and received in response that disarming smile:

"Beelzebub only speaks, he never answers questions."

It seemed to me as though Gurdjiev knew that I knew he was a faker, and did not care. He was making money; and he was doing good at the same time, disrupting the corrosive habits of the idle rich by putting them to work digging ditches or shoveling manure from six to eight hours a day. He also taught them esoteric dancing motions, which must have done them good, although probably not so intimately related to values in the world of spirit as he pretended. He did not try to put me in touch with that world of spirit, but on the contrary urged me with surprising cordiality to join him in a Russian bath. I was scornful of his charlatanism on the train back to Paris, and thinking about Katherine Mansfield's gullibility, said things about the absence of intellect in fiction writers which Betty pointed out were unbecoming in one who had been trying so hard for a year to write a novel.

I spent a day and a night in London. Then Eliena, who had found it difficult to paint landscapes in a continuous rainstorm, joined me in Paris and we fled home to Antibes. A holiday resort, for those who carry the tools of their trade with them, can be a paradise of hard work mixed with play. With that profound reflection I drowned the voice of my conscience, still pleading with me to *learn German*—as I now fear it will plead to the end of my days.

Chapter 72

VIENNA AND THEN HOME

Nothing I ever received through the mail surprised me more than a registered letter from Adolf Joffe written in his own hand and dated "Moskva, 30-1-1927." I thought my friendly connections with Moscow, and above all with the big chiefs of the Bolshevik party, were cut off forever. Joffe, you will remember, was the darkly oriental-looking emissary of Lenin whom I had admired at Genoa. I had met him again at a dinner with the Rakovskys in Paris before *Since Lenin Died* was published. He was one of the really big Bolsheviks, chairman of the first Soviet delegation to Brest Litovsk, negotiator of the treaty with Poland in 1921 and of the pact of friendship with Sun Yat Sen, Lenin's ambassador to Berlin and again to Japan, at critical moments. There was no tinge of the demagogue in Joffe, but a prestige which rivaled that of many who were more talked about. We had exchanged some words about science and Marxism at Rakovsky's dinner table, and when *Marx and Lenin* was published in London I sent him a copy to Moscow, in care of the Soviet of People's Economy. Since the other copies I sent into Russia—to Pavlov, to Bechterev, a noted psychologist whom I had met, and to the Marx-Lenin Institute—had been returned or reported undelivered, I assumed that no Russian would ever look into my book. It made my proposal to educate the Bolsheviks about their own theory look as fantastic as indeed it was. But now, at the depth of my political disgrace there came a letter from a leading Bolshevik, telling me I had sent the book to the wrong address, and would I please send him another copy? He was working, he said, with the Commission on Foreign Concessions. Reflecting that the foreign mail of such a commission could not very well be effectively censored, I sent him two copies, asking him to forward one to Pavlov.

In March I received another letter from Joffe, saying that he had sent my book to Pavlov, but had been too busy and sick to read it himself. He was taking it with him to Vienna where he was about to undergo a month's cure. His illness, "polyneuritis," was such that he needed a whole year in the care of Western physicians, but the party had denied him the necessary funds, and he wondered whether he could get an advance from a foreign publisher on a story of his life. He asked me to advise him what were the chances of this and how to go about it.

The faith of the Russian intelligentsia in Western doctors and sanitariums was as fixed as the admiration of the muzhik for foreigners as such. A sojourn in "European" *Kurorts* when one was tired out, or sick, or nervous, was an abolute good. Nobody ever questioned this, and the refusal of the party—that is, of Stalin—to grant the privilege to Joffe was like withholding quinine from a malaria patient. It was political persecution. Joffe had been a long-time friend of Trotsky and was with him heart-and-soul in the antibureaucratic opposition. Knowing this, I wanted very much to help him. I also wanted to see him and learn from a top source the plans of the Opposition, their prospects, their attitude to my book. He would be in Vienna in late March, he said, and he asked me to address him at the Russian embassy. I wrote him very tentatively that I might be in Vienna in late March myself, and if so, we might possibly have a personal talk. To my further surprise, he answered promptly:

"I will be very glad to see you in Vienna, but am not sure I will be in a condition to talk! I am taking a strange cure (bromnarcosis) which entails my being practically unconscious for several days. If you come too soon or stay too brief a time, you will hit upon the very days when nobody will be allowed to see me. And I should be very sorry to miss you and Eliena Vassilyevna. In any case call up and find out about me. . . ." And he gave me the address, Parksanatorium, Hessgasse 29, Wien XIII.

Eliena and I had by this time decided to go home to Croton where my little house was now waiting with vacant rooms for me. A cogent reason for this move was that we were broke, and a lecture tour in the United States, where I thought I still had an oratorical reputation, seemed the natural solution of our troubles. Having dreamed of a life in America since childhood, Eliena was eager to go, and I was joyful in the thought of bringing her home. Thus instead of going to Vienna together, we went to Paris to book our passage and begin what promised to be a long argument about her visa. We stopped at the Hôtel d'Alsace in the rue des Beaux Arts. It was an old haunt of mine, and I slept once, by chance, in the room where Oscar Wilde died. It had now become a headquarters for the underground agents of Stalin's Comintern, but I was ignorant of this mixture of shadows. I cheerfully left Eliena among those agents while I set out for my conference in Vienna with a leader of the Opposition.

I did arrive in Vienna too soon, for Joffe was "out of this world" when I telephoned, but he had told the nurse that my visit was important and she must urge me to wait until he came back. While waiting I explored Vienna in the company of "Sonka," a Communist poet of oppositional leanings, who had come to see us with his sweet young wife Roszi in Antibes. Sonka's real name was Hugo Sonnenschein, and Roszi was a round-faced, full-lipped, almost roly-poly Jewish girl, merry and kindly and good. She spoke Russian as well as German, and that was a help, for neither she nor Sonka knew English or French. Roszi went along to show me the way to the hospital when it came time to call upon Joffe, and I assumed she would leave me in the hallway, or at least at his door. But she came right on in, and I was too shy—the confession is ignominious, but is a characteristic truth—to tell her I wished to talk with him alone. I had not yet learned the maxim of the socialist fatherland that everyone is to be considered an informer until proven an accomplice. I was still a greenhorn as a conspirator; indeed I am yet, as we shall see. But I might, if in adult control of my faculties, have realized that her presence made impossible an entirely intimate talk with Joffe about the plans and prospects of the Opposition. The nurse had warned us that the talk must be brief, and it mainly concerned Joffe's proposed memoirs, of which I promised to translate a chapter or two for advance sale to an American publisher.

Joffe spoke apologetically about "the beating we gave you," and assumed in the name of the Opposition a collective responsibilty for it He conveyed, as well as he could in Roszi's presence, the fact that the disavowal of *Since Lenin Died* had been signed under pressure, and not without sympathy and regret for the awkward position in which it placed me. His warm and kindly manner enriched the meaning of his words. In after years, my most vivid memory of our meeting was a Rembrandt-like picture. It was a picture of Joffe's dark sick face sunk in the pillow, his big eyes and rounded features somewhat babylike in that position; of Roszi sitting bright-eyed, upright and healthy beside the white bed; and of his pleased languid glance at her. The scene stands out vividly as though it were a painting hung forever, and never to be forgotten, in the galleries of time—a memorial to them both. For within a few months Joffe shot himself in despair at the uselessness of his life under Stalin; and within a few years Roszi was put to death in a gas chamber by monsters in the employ of Hitler.

A letter to Trotsky which Joffe left by his deathbed contained a rather unusual treasure, an avowal of motive, a glimpse into the heart of one of those resolutely impersonal idealists who captained the October revolution. It also contained a comment on Trotsky's political character that has relevance to the story I have been telling.

It is thirty years now since I adopted the philosophy that human life has meaning only in so far as it is lived in the service of an infinite—and for us the infinite is humanity. Even if humanity must have an end, this will happen at an epoch so remote that we can regard it as absolutely infinite. And if one has the faith I have in progress, one can very well conceive that, even in case our planet is destroyed, humanity will find means to go and inhabit other younger planets; and then all that has been accomplished for its good in our time will find its reflection in remote ages.

It is in this, and this only, that I have always seen the meaning of life. And now glancing back over my past, twenty-seven years of which were passed in the ranks of our party, I have the right, I think, to say that during *all* my conscious days I have remained true to this philosophy, I have lived according to the meaning of life: work and struggle for the good of humanity. . . .

We are bound together, dear Lyev Davidovich, by ten years of common work, and I dare to hope of personal friendship, and this gives me the right to tell you, at the moment of parting, what in you seems to me a weakness.

I have never doubted the correctness of the course you have pointed out, and you know that for over twenty years, ever since the "permanent revolution," I have marched with you. But I have thought you lacked the inflexibility and intransigence of Lenin, his resolution to remain, if need be, alone in the course which he has recognized as sure in view of a future majority, of a future recognition by all of the justice of that course. *Politically* you have always been right, commencing with 1905, and I have often told you that with my own ears I heard Lenin acknowledge that in 1905 *it was not he but you who were right*. One does not lie in the face of death, and I repeat this once more now. But you have often renounced your truth for the sake of an agreement, a compromise, whose value you overestimate. That is a fault. I repeat: politically you have always been right, and *at present you are more right than ever*. Some day the Party will understand this, and History will be forced to recognize it. . . . But the guarantee of the victory of your truth lies in a strict intransigence, the most severe rigidity, the repudiation of every compromise, just as that has always been the secret of the victories of Ilych.

I have often wanted to tell you this, and have summoned the courage only now, at the moment of farewell. . . .

I wish you energy and valor equal to those you have heretofore revealed, and a swift victory. I embrace you fervently. Adieu.

Yours,

A. Joffe

While in Vienna, I summoned the courage to send a note to Sigmund Freud asking if I could have a talk with him. I had two claims on his attention: way back in 1915 I had written for *Everybody's Magazine* the first popular American account of psychoanalysis, and more recently he had sent me the gratifying words I quoted about my book on Marx and Lenin. His praise had been qualified, I neglected to state, by the remark: "I liked it much better than previous books of yours." And moreover when I asked his permission to quote his words, he had answered: "I will thank you for *not* mentioning in public any of the remarks in my letter. I seem thus far to have failed to accustom myself to the American life forms." To which I had answered that I did not mention his remark in public, but only asked permission to, and I intimated that the American life forms were such as usually to make the difference between these two things quite easily perceptible. So although he answered my note immediately and with an appointment, I was not sure of a warm welcome when I went around to Berggasse 19. I was feeling a little frightenedly bold.

I waited, only a few minutes, in a richly carpeted and rather sumptuous drawing room—nothing to suggest a doctor's office, except for Rembrandt's "Anatomy Lesson" which hung like a diploma on the wall, and Fuselli's well-known picture, "The Nightmare," which advertised the more medieval side of Freud's genius. An attentive monster sits, you remember, with a half-evil leer on a sleeping maiden's naked breast. She is not screaming: "Oh, oh, oh, what shall I do!" nor the monster answering: "That's up to you, dearie, it's your dream!"

Without Freud we should never have had that joke. But there is a sort of two-way look on the monster's face that is consistent with it.

"What did you want?" in perfect English, was Freud's greeting when he hurried in.

"Nothing," I said. "I just wanted to look at you."

"You want to quote my commendation of your book. But why should I support you? Can't you stand on your own feet?"

"I'm trying to," I said, "but I don't see why you should make a secret of your opinions."

It was a rather acrid beginning, and bore out my fear that Freud was going to punish me for my sins against his theory of wit, for no doubt *The Sense of Humor* was what he meant by "previous books of yours." However he mellowed gradually, and before I left was laughing merrily with me over his jokes at the expense of America.

(I quoted these jokes in an essay that is to be found in my *Great Companions*. Indeed I described pretty much verbatim our whole conversation, and illumined it with facts derived from a careful study of his life story and his writings about the concept of the unconscious.)

"I don't see why you talk about unconsciousness as though it were a thing," I said. "The only thing present when we are unconscious, is our brain and body. Wouldn't it be better if instead of saying 'the unconscious,' you said 'unconscious brain states?'"

"Well, haven't you read our literature?" he said tartly. "The unconscious is not a thing, but a concept. It is a concept that we find indispensable in the clinic."

That silenced me for awhile, but before long he forgot about it and began lecturing me to the opposite effect:

"You mustn't confuse the *psychic* with the conscious. Psychic entities are not necessarily conscious."

"So after all the unconscious *is* a thing—an entity—and not only a concept." I did not say this, of course; you don't say things like that to a great man. But I'm not sure he didn't know I was thinking it. At any rate he grew more affable after that, and we had a jovial, although still rather anti-American, conversation. His farewell was double-barreled, a combination of the malicious jab with the effusive handshake so ingenious that I must quote it verbatim.

"What are you going to do when you get home?" he asked with warm concern. "Have you any definite plans?"

"None except that I am going to write."

"I'll tell you what I want you to do. I want you to write a book on

America, and I'll tell you what to call it. *Missgeburt*—what is that word in English?"

"Abortion?"

"No, not abortion."

"Monster?"

"Well, that will do. You write a book about the monstrous . . ." He paused. "The word is 'miscarriage.' *The Miscarriage of American Civilization!* That shall be the title of your book. You will find out the causes and tell the truth about the whole awful catastrophe."

He was standing up now.

"That book will make you immortal. You may not be able to live in America any more, but you could live very happily somewhere else."

I had risen too, and he extended his hand.

"Now I want to see that next book of yours without fail. So please remember to send me a copy, and I'll read it with happy memories of this conversation. . . ."

My regret, when I recall this disagreement with Freud, is that the IBM machines, which come so near to thinking without consciousness, had not yet been invented. They would so effectively have backed up my opinion that no mysteriously psychic creature called "*the* unconscious" need be imagined to explain that thoughts and impulses are followed out by us after we have ceased to be conscious of them. Those machines will be an increasing help in exorcising the demonology from Freud's contributions to science.

From my visits with Joffe and Freud in Vienna I went back to the rue des Beaux Arts, and to the problem of Eliena's permission to enter the United States. Marriage did not, according to our law, give her American citizenship, but on the other hand, it did, according to Soviet law, deprive her of Russian citizenship. All she had now by way of passport was a paper given her by the American consul at Nice requesting that, in view of her marriage to me, she be treated *as though* she were an American citizen. Fortunately the American authorities in Paris were bold enough to recognize the validity of a "Soviet marriage," a precedent then generally regarded as dangerous to America's morality. They appended a visa to the strange paper that Eliena held, and we boarded the single-class ship, the *De Grasse*, for New York.

We felt uneasy while crossing the sea about Eliena's highly informal ticket of admission to the United States, and we approached the immigration officials in New York Harbor with some trepidation. As I have confessed, I always encounter any uniformed authority with my heart in my boots, and in Eliena, with her bitter experiences both under the Tsar and the Bolsheviks, this feeling was a hundred times as strong. She was actually pale when we were separated into two lines in the dining saloon—American citizens on one side, aliens on the other. She was at the tail end of her line too, and much to her dismay the big sheet on which names and data for each alien were being inscribed, got filled up just before they reached her. She was left waiting alone, neither in nor out of the country, for an hour-long twenty minutes while somebody left the saloon to go and hunt up another big sheet. Finally the chief customs officer, seeing her standing there looking like a small child on the verge of tears, walked up to her—he was a great big man—put a protective arm around her shoulders and said:

"You can come in, little lady. Just step along. We'll fill out the papers when they come."

I was proud of my country, I must say, and Eliena fell in love with the United States for good and all.

PART THREE

1927–1941

Chapter 73

OSTRACISM AND MY NOVEL

My three years in France are bright in my memory; the return to America in the spring of 1927 and the three years following it are dark. Five years is too long to stay away from home—especially a home in New York, where the fabric not only of social life, but of stone and mortar, changes so fast. In that racing city even the scenes I would seek out for romantic remembrance no longer existed. In Croton my "little house by the side of the road" awaited me, but the life I had lived there as "a friend of man" was not to be found. In revolutionary circles where I had moved so confidently, shining with no reflected light, I was extinct. The Communists had taken the trouble to expel me from their Workers Party, though I had by that time forgotten the futile episode of my membership. But worse than that, they had ostracized me by party decree: No fraternizing with Trotskyists! My old friend and co-editor, Bob Minor, now a neighbor in Croton just across the road, would pass me in the morning with his eyes on the treetops. Once when we met face-to-face in Floyd Dell's living room, he bowed ironically low, and neither spoke nor extended a hand. There was, moreover, no sharp line where the party's influence ended. To all the rebels by instinct, the Greenwich Villagers, the liberal sympathizers with Bolshevism, if I was not unclean, I was at least unclear. There was a doubt about me. "Is that man a skunk or a weasel," Claude once said when we turned away from an insulting doorkeeper. And I thought I could feel similar words being spoken behind my back. Not a single friend of mine in the revolutionary intelligentsia, or among Socialists, or IWW's, or the political left anywhere, took firm sides with Trotsky in his conflict with the new ruling class. Trotsky was "impulsive," "impatient," "capricious" (the very word Lenin had applied to Stalin in his testament); he was a "stormy petrel"; he was "rocking the boat."

491

That was the most lenient view on the left. And on the right, among the vested interests, there was no lenience either. In the general mind the pseudo-conflict about world revolution as against socialism in one country had entirely replaced the original and real point at issue between Trotsky and Stalin. The program of workers democracy for which Trotsky had fought, far from being understood, was never, so far as I can remember, once mentioned in the public press. "Socialism in one country" sounded fine, to the vested interests, whereas "world revolution" made them quite unhappy. As a defender of Trotsky's Opposition I was therefore as lonely on the right as on the left.

A year before I came home, a new magazine had been started by a group of insurgents ranging in political color from Marxian Communists like Mike Gold and Joe Freeman to intellectual rebels like Rex Stout, and aesthetic free spirits of the type of Egmont Arens, once editor of the super-Bohemian *Playboy*. The new magazine was to be "free" and "revolutionary," and though "primarily a magazine of arts and letters" it was to "express radical economic views." The group had thought of calling it *Dynamo*, but after strenuous debate, and mainly for reasons of quicker promotion, had decided to name it after the old *Masses*. In its second number, however, this *New Masses* printed an editorial rhapsody by Mike Gold entitled: "Let it be Really New!" A few sentences by Mike at this juncture (June 1926) are essential to my story:

"What I deny is that I, or any one else, demands of young Americans that they take their 'spiritual' commands from Moscow. . . . Moscow could not have created John Reed, Upton Sinclair, Jack London, Max Eastman, or Horace Traubel. American life created them. It will create others like them and better. Let us forget Moscow in this discussion. Let us think of America, where you and I have spent the better part of our lives."

The active editors in those first issues were: Egmont Arens, Joseph Freeman, Hugo Gellert, Michael Gold, James Rorty, and John Sloan. These names suggested the same mixture of "free expression" with adherence to a program of socialist revolution over which I had presided in the *Liberator*, though here nobody seemed to be presiding. I had received a letter in France asking me to become a contributing editor, and had agreed. Indeed, I had contributed while still in Antibes translations from the Russian of two stories by Isaak Babel, a couple of book reviews, and my rendering in English verse of Pushkin's *Message to Siberia*. And now, on arriving in New York, I attended an editorial meeting at Egmont Arens' penthouse apartment—a rough-hewn penthouse at 120 East Sixteenth Street—and was promoted from "Contributing Editor" to "member of the Executive Board." Most of those present were old friends of mine, and I attended two or three meetings and contributed during the summer three articles made out of chapters of *Marx and Lenin*, which was still unpublished in America.

My theoretical heresies in these articles gave the party heads the pretext they wanted to attack me with intemperate vituperation, and the editors, now dominated by Gold, Gellert and Freeman, made it clear that no more "free expression" on my part was wanted in the *New Masses*. My letter of resignation dated January 27, 1928, tells the story:

The New Masses
Dear Comrades:

I herewith resign from the Executive Board and withdraw from my association with the *New Masses*, and I want to explain my action briefly.

When I was invited to join the Executive Board, its members were aware of my association with the opposition in the Russian Communist Party. They were also aware of my theoretical position as set forth in my book, *Marx and Lenin, the Science of Revolution*. Their invitation implied that the *New Masses* was independent of the dictation of the Workers (Communist) Party and the International, from which they understood I had been expelled. They had, moreover, from the beginning advertised the *New Masses* as independent of all dictation—a "free revolutionary magazine." It was with this understanding that I joined it.

At the invitation of the acting editor, I published in the magazine, among other things, an article on Sacco-Vanzetti and the relations between anarchism and the science of revolution, and an article called "Lenin was an Engineer." Although neither of these articles touched even indirectly the questions at issue between the opposition and the ruling group in the Communist parties, they were objected to by the heads of the American Party. I was denounced for my "lies" in large type every day for over a week in the *Daily Worker*. Instead of offering me space to reply, or even to continue explaining my ideas, the *New Masses* gave me to understand that no further contributions entailing any expression of my theoretical position would be accepted.

My offer to explain the conflict between the opposition and the ruling group in the Russian Communist Party, giving some supporter of the ruling group an opportunity to reply to me in the same issue, was also declined. A previous invitation to review the philosophical books of Lenin and Bukharin was revoked. It was suggested that I write an innocuous "literary" book-review.

It goes without saying that I am not going to contribute articles without remuneration to a magazine that denies me the expression of my views.

I withdraw from the Executive Board, because I think a magazine with this confused and pussy-footing policy is harmful to the advancement of a genuine revolutionary culture in America. No practical person will deny the value of a party magazine, and no person understanding the present situation in America will deny the value of a magazine of independent expression and criticism. But a magazine which announces itself independent, and then obeys the dictation of the party heads through fear of the loss of patronage or circulation, or through mere fear of stating the facts of life, is worse than useless. A professedly "free" and "revolutionary" magazine which will pass in silence such an historic event as the arrest and banishment under police surveillance of the entire leadership of the opposition in the Russian Communist Party— not through fear of taking sides, but through fear of telling the American workers and radicals about both sides—is merely a new weakness and a new deception.

Yours sincerely,

My letter of course was not published, the magazine being now completely in the clutches of the totalitarian party, morally and I suppose financially. Its pretense to be free from the "spiritual commands" of Moscow was soon forgotten, and three of its editors, Michael Gold, Joseph Freeman, and Hugo Gellert, became obedient priests of the new cultural bigotry developing in the Kremlin. In June the magazine was reorganized with Gold alone as editor, and to salve his sick conscience, he adopted the subhead: "A Magazine for Rebels." For further relief, he declared in the September number, speaking of three schools of writing in the United States: "I choose communism because its discipline is not of the barracks or church hierarchy, but is a creative self-discipline." Poor Mike!

Well—on the old *Masses* and *Liberator* we had pursued together

four arrogant aims or ideals: freedom of mind and spirit, unqualified
truth-telling, proletarian revolution, and state ownership of the means
of production. This compound had created, in the innocence of those
days, a vivid revolutionary magazine, but when put to the test of
experiment it proved unstable. Truth-telling and freedom would not
combine with loyalty to the regime of revolutionary state-ownership.
Thus as a consequence of the Bolshevik revolution the old *Masses*
crowd exploded. I adhered to the truth-freedom nucleus; Mike Gold
stuck by the ideal of revolutionary state-ownership. We each tried to
hold the old four aims together: I deceiving myself that by truth-
telling in freedom we might hold back the collectivist state from its
destined union with tyranny and hypocrisy, Mike struggling fitfully to
make tyranny and hypocrisy look like freedom and truth.

Mike's fate was sadder than mine because it destroyed him morally,
but mine for the time being was lonely. I had no political companion in
the United States; I had no magazine or printed sheet in which I could
express my anxious thoughts about the revolution. In Europe there
were small voices of protest against Stalin's usurpation—in America
absolute silence. I wrote during that year of 1928 a sonnet entitled
"Eleventh Anniversary," which began:

> Trotsky is banished; Lenin lies in state.
> The sword, flung off, still flickers in the sod;
> The god-destroyer, dead, becomes a god.

It concluded:

> Speak, if you have no deed; the truth is great.
> They rot to earth who only stand and wait.

But nobody spoke. There were a few close friends who, like Claude
McKay, believed in my facts and my understanding of them. There
were plenty of pleasantly intellectual people who sat on the fence,
awaiting without partisanship the fate of the Russian revolution. But
they were new people, new friends to be made. The kin and comrades of
my popular days as editor, orator, and almost-leader of the radical
intelligentsia, were gone forever. One *New Masses* editor, Egmont
Arens, who unlike most of them was interested in science, had got hold
of an English copy of *Marx and Lenin* and was enthusiastic about it. He
conceived in a glow the idea of giving me a belated dinner of welcome.
Thinking I was still a big thing, he reserved an immense long table at
a popular restaurant. There were places for twenty or thirty people, and

three came. We sat like the few remaining hairs on an old dog's tail at one end of the table. And I, while inwardly suffering, exchanged super-hilarious wisecracks with Louis Untermeyer, who, though on his way to become a fellow-traveler of Stalin, had retained a quixotic loyalty to the old *Masses* and the *Liberator*. Louis is quicker with wisecracks than I, and that increased the inferiority pains I was concealing under my laughter.

The worry about cash, which exacerbates every human woe, was another cause of my gloom. Arriving in April, I had barely time to set in motion a lecture tour for the coming fall and winter. Moreover, to make money lecturing you have to be on the crest of a wave of some kind or other. Politically I was in a backwash; even my literary books belonged to a past decade. W. B. Feakins, my old impresario, turned me down cold, and Leigh-Emmerich, who consented to speculate on my future, took a big percentage and held out little hope. Meanwhile, Eliena and I lived largely by grace of a total stranger, a jovial big blond moon-faced Croton grocer named Bill Harmon, who for some reason stopped in to say: "Don't pay my bills till you get good and ready." By contrast, a long-time friend who had rented my house two years before moved out owing me fifty dollars—a momentous sum, and he refused to pay it. What kept us going that first spring and summer was a most improbable accident. Walking along Forty-second Street, I ran into an Elmira boy named George Ingraham, one of the suave and sporty contingent with whom, as a humble minister's son, I had gone down to Mercersburg Academy in 1898. Although in my memory a crack shortstop before whom an honor student could only bend the knee, he seemed now rather pathetically pleased to see me. He was doing publicity, he said, for a new magazine just starting, to be called the *Smoker's Companion*. I mustn't be misled by the title; it wasn't to be about tobacco; it was to be about everything. And it was to be read by everybody because—you see—when you get right down to it, everybody, or practically everybody, *smokes*.

"You've been in Russia," he said. "My editors are interested in what's happening over there. How about giving us a series of articles explaining the whole thing."

"But I'm *for* the Bolsheviks," I protested. "You wouldn't want to launch a magazine with a series of articles favoring the Bolsheviks."

"It doesn't matter at all," he said. "It's a magazine about everything and for everybody."

He was right! We went up together to a little office-room near Grand Central Station, and when I came down I was signed for three articles on the subject "What Is Bolshevism?" at three hundred dollars an article. They were to be illustrated with a series of portrait-drawings of the big Bolsheviks, prints of which had been given to me by the artist, Georges Annenkov, in Paris. They would appear in the June, July, and August issues, and be paid for on publication. I went home and wrote what, as I read it now, seems to me as devastatingly convincing a pro-Communist pamphlet, especially for American readers, as could be devised. It defined bolshevism by means of three differentia: its ideal aim; its definition of existing facts; its plan of action for proceeding from facts to ideal. The articles were beautifully published and the *Smoker's Companion*, I need hardly add, was soon a memory.

Deeper than my financial depression was the distress I lived in about my three books. My portrait of Leon Trotsky had been sold by an agent to an obscure publisher while I was in Europe and they between them had decided that I need not see the proofs. While I, no farther away than Antibes, was eagerly awaiting the opportunity to perfect my work, jotting down endless corrections in the carbon copy, and re-solved, if necessary, to pay more for author's corrections than I would earn in royalties, the book itself arrived, all dressed out in the inevitable red binding. No mutilations could make you so furious, for mutilations you can disown, but this ungroomed and blotchy monster was forever and inexorably myself. Subsequently I sold the book to Faber and Gwyer in London and had the pleasure of seeing an edition decently born, but in America, when I came home, this miscarriage was all I had on the market. It sickened me particularly because I had taken a mischievous pleasure, while Trotsky was being portrayed throughout the world as a satanic demon, in describing somewhat tenderly his well-behaved and blue-eyed childhood. Now, with these new clouds around him, this sounded a little sentimental, a little, as one critic remarked, "like a bedtime story." It nourished the sadly mistaken notion that personal rather than political passion had fed the fires in *Since Lenin Died*.

A sadder fate befell my other books. I had, as I've said, in a moment of pecuniary frustration sold them to the newly fledged publishers, Albert and Charles Boni, who had sung me the old song that a small publisher will put more money and effort into selling your book than an established firm. Indeed Albert's promises to me in Antibes had been prodigious. He would make my novel, *Breaking Through*, "the book of the season"; he would put *Marx and Lenin* on the map; he would "get behind me with all his force"; he would "put me across."

"There are a thousand ways to promote a book and get it reviewed and talked about, Max, if the publisher gives it his personal attention."

That was the sales talk which, flooding in on my desert of penury, had induced me to accept a tiny advance from unknown publishers. But now the publishers were known. They were publishing *The Bridge of San Luis Rey*, the biggest best seller of the season, and the English translation of Marcel Proust besides. I, on the other hand, having once been a potential luminary, had faded from the sky. I do not know to what degree a political motive entered into their seemingly aggressive neglect of my books. Albert Boni is a brilliant and acute business man; so is Charles, and they are both good friends of mine. Moreover they long ago dissolved their business, so it will not damage them, if I tell the truth—that their dilatory manner of putting my books on the market, whether caused by a valid estimate of my lost prestige, or by the balmy condition in which they were raking in profits from *The Bridge of San Luis Rey*, was one of the most devastating disappointments of my life. I wrote them a list of specific complaints five pages long, which I refrained from mailing, and which I now refrain from quoting, but I must, for biographical purposes, mention the state of woe which led me to write it. Although ostensibly published in 1927, there was not a mention of my books in the press until the winter and spring of 1928. I had to call up the *Nation*, and send them a copy of *Marx and Lenin* myself.

Meanwhile the Communists had got hold of the English edition of my book on Marxism, and assigned to Bertram D. Wolfe the job of sneering at me as a piffling ignoramus. I was, more exactly, "a profound intellectual snob gazing upon the seductive image of himself in the role of a great social engineer, standing a little above Lenin, mountains above Marx, and of course 'above society.' " Ten pages of these sneers in the party's theoretical organ, accompanied by briefer demonstrations in its daily press that my "intellectual gymnastics" consisted "simply of arrogant snobbery and deliberate falsification of Marxism-Leninism," were in circulation four months before my book found its way out of the maze of its publisher's office.

Bertram Wolfe recovered from the Communist obsession a while after this, and is now among the most reliable authorities, not only on its history, but on its strategy and tactics. He knows them; he knows how to combat them; and I must add that he too is my friend. But I can hardly tell the sad story of my return home after sinning against Stalin without citing his toplofty contribution to the general gloom.

A more painful contribution, and totally unexpected, was an assault upon my book—no milder term will do—delivered in three different journals by a young graduate in philosophy, a brilliant pupil of John Dewey, named Sidney Hook. Since Sidney has grown up to be one of the wisest defenders of the real values of democratic culture, and we also are friends, I am not going to characterize those early animadversions against my study of Marxism. Suffice it to say that no such bitter pain of humiliation was ever caused to me, before or since, by a critic of one of my books. Sidney had the academic status which I had renounced—we were both in our day the "bright boys" of John Dewey—and he used this status to make me look like a flip and irresponsible amateur. It struck me like a bolt—not from the blue, for there was no blue, but from the dead gray weight of fog that hung over my intellectual life in those lonely days.

It had one good result: it led me to an acquaintance, which later ripened into an important friendship, with V. F. Calverton, who had founded an independent magazine of radical opinion called the *Modern Quarterly*. Calverton gave me space for an affirmative statement of the thesis of my book, an essay entitled "The Doctrinal Crisis in Socialism," and also for a counterattack on what I described as Sidney Hook's misrepresentations of it. There were twenty-four of these, I averred, but I let the reader off after boring him to death with a violently logical and carefully numbered promenade of fourteen. Sidney replied with equal vigor and violence of logic. We were both well equipped with adjectives and laid about us in a manner that became quite notorious— rather as a contribution to the literary prize ring than to the critique of Marxism. We were still at it in 1933, when Calverton, in what had now become the *Modern Monthly*, stepped into the ring with a "Letter to Sidney Hook and Max Eastman"—an admonition that we both calm down and obey at least the Marquis of Queensberry rules.

There was a real and deep theoretical difference between Sidney Hook and me. I set it forth to the length of fifty pages, a year later, in a pamphlet called *The Last Stand of Dialectic Materialism.** But I am inclined to think that the unrestrained passion with which Sidney attacked me in those earlier days was due as much to my darkening of

* Reproduced in Part VII of *Marxism Is It Science* with revisions and a new title, "The Americanization of Marx."

the hopes of socialism in Russia as to our disagreement about Marxian theory. Long after, when we were in agreement on the disaster contained in Stalin's seizure of power, he wrote me so magnanimous a letter that I came within an inch of regretting the violence of my reply to his attack on *Marx and Lenin.* He wrote:

> Whatever may have been our differences on Marx-interpretation —differences on which another generation of Marxist scholarship will have to decide—I have always admired the steadfastness and courage with which you fought, for years single-handedly, against the spoliators of the revolutionary tradition. It is better to fail fighting as you have fought than to win in any other way.

But that was in 1937, and I am writing about the darkness of the sky in the first years after my homecoming ten years earlier. As a result of that darkness, and an inward diffidence that seized me in those years, I took some bad advice about the title of my novel: I called it *Venture*, instead of using its true name *Breaking Through.* That and the fact that it was, perhaps, a little too "clever" to be absorbing, made it difficult even for a sympathetic critic to grasp the seriousness of the effort I was making. My novel had both a geometric shape and an underlying idea. The shape was that of a letter *T* with arabesques and variations. The main stem of the *T* was the impulse of my hero, a youth made out of traits borrowed from my college friend, Sid Wood, and Jack Reed, and that part of me which admired them both—his impulse to experience to the full and recklessly the very *reality* of the world into which he was born. To reach it, he had to "break through" a Bohemian or Greenwich Village phase, and also the retiring room of occult and mystical belief. He came out finally, driven by his passion for downright reality, in close association with two hard-headed enterprises. One was the effort of an imaginative but ruthlessly realistic capitalist to establish an overt financial aristocracy in the United States; the other was the effort of Bill Haywood and the IWW to overthrow the capitalists in violent revolution and establish an industrial democracy. My hero got mixed up personally and with passionate emotions in both of these grandiose exploits. In each he found that bold strong sense of reality, the downright, uncompromising confrontation of fact, which he was seeking. That was where the cross of the *T* came in. He had reached the heart of the contemporary reality, but found that it had two opposing sides or essences; it went off in two directions. It was, in short, the class struggle—a plausible thesis in the America of the teens. His effort to live on both sides got him into some dramatic troubles—at least I think they were dramatic—and got him treated on both sides as a traitor. There was love, of course, in each direction, love for George Forbes, the great industrialist, the dominant character in the book, drawing him one way, love for a Russian girl in the Paterson silk strike drawing him the other. I left the story there—although it was fairly clear that the girl at least, whatever might come of the IWW, was going to win out.

I called my novel "clever" in a tone of deprecation. It is full of aphorisms and aphoristic sayings, too full to carry a reader spellbound into the story. I was myself rarely spellbound when I wrote it. It is hard for me, except when composing poetry, to give myself body and soul to the imaginative experience of events that did not happen. Sometimes when at work on my novel, I would get into a mood of hilarity in which I had to stop myself from burlesquing the story instead of telling it. *Venture* had, nevertheless, a considerable success. The *Nation* described it as "a he-man's book that should appeal to every red-blooded American, tired to death of the soul-tripping subtleties of contemporary fiction. A book full of stirring narrative, plots, counter-plots, society ladies and silk strikers, love and life." To the *New York Evening Post* it was "thoughtful, sensitive, intelligent and entertaining." To the *New York Times*, "vigorous and powerful, extremely well written, extremely well characterized." To the *Saturday Review of Literature*, "arresting and capable . . . Max Eastman's notable quality is his vigor. His novel in character as well as incident is rich and meaty. He has imagination, restraint, energy, and a gift for full-blooded narrative." Stefan Zweig described it as "really a living book." Upton Sinclair called it "extremely brilliant." "A new novelist has appeared," he said, "one with both wit and wisdom." Scott Fitzgerald read it all over again, and wrote from Wilmington: "I think it's fine. It's so beautifully written and tells me so much about what are the dim days, 1910–1917. You make it all very real and vivid—nothing so sane on that terribly difficult subject has ever been written." Sinclair Lewis was "disappointed." "I'm tired of your main character," he said. "He's after all the hero of Poole's *The Harbor*, Sinclair's *Coal* and *Oil*, of *The New Machiavelli*, of *Comrade Yetta*, and a dozen dozen novels. . . . To me it was so much better when you dealt with the real out-and-out, non-literary, non-Bohemian IWW's in Paterson, and with the Irish anarchist. I thrill to think what you could have done with a Bill Haywood. I hate these free young intellectuals—like you and me!" The

Hartford Courant agreed: "The book is but a repetition of a thousand and one pieces of fiction." To the *Baltimore Sun* it was simply unreadable—"packed full of a fearful jumble of ideas and theories with a few rather questionable facts thrown in." A meditative critic on Toronto's *Saturday Night* remarked: "One has no quarrel with hash as a whole—at its best it is a satisfying and easily absorbed preparation. It is the meaner, mess-room type one has in mind in referring to this book *Venture* as hash, composed as it is of half-baked Red propaganda, warmed-over platitudes, coarse cynicisms, and fermenting finance, all hopefully spiced with great plops of sex." To the *Chicago News* it was "altogether an uninteresting waste of printer's ink."

It had the honor, at least, of being translated by writers of note into both French and German, acquiring in the process two very much better titles: *L'Apprenti Révolutionnaire* and *Der Sprung Ins Leben*. It might, I think, if unhowled against by the Stalinists, have had a wide reading among revolutionaries. But it made small head against the current of passion aroused by *Since Lenin Died*, the official Communist tabu on me and all my words and works.

Nobody in any country, so far as I know, ever mentioned the theme and meaning of the novel as I have described it above. Even Edmund Wilson, who liked my aphorisms—finding them "acute and beautifully put"—and praised the book quite highly as an "idea novel," did not exactly apprehend my idea, though he substituted a very good one of his own. For this I suppose I must thank my meaningless title, the result of a morbid loss of self-reliance which afflicted me in those days.

Chapter 74

A DEEPER SORROW

My homecoming was further darkened by the sickness and early death of my beautiful and inspiring sister, Crystal. I want to place here some words more convincing than those of an admiring brother to convey the magnetic phenomenon that Crystal was. I take them from an article by Freda Kirchwey published in the *Nation* of August 8, 1928.

> Crystal Eastman is dead. And all over the world there are women and men who will feel touched with loss, who will look on a world that seems more sober. In her short life Crystal Eastman brushed against many other lives, and wherever she moved she carried with her the breath of courage and a contagious belief in the coming triumph of freedom and decent human relations. These were her religion. Her strength, her beauty, her vitality and enthusiasm, her rich and compelling personality—these she threw with reckless vigor into every cause that promised a finer life to the world. She was a great leader. Those who knew her, know these words are not too strong. When she spoke to people— whether it was to a small committee or a swarming crowd— hearts beat faster and nerves tightened as she talked. She was simple, direct, dramatic. Force poured from her strong body and her rich voice, and people followed where she led. . . .

I knew and had seen the truth of these words about Crystal's public character; I described in Chapter 2 the service to America, the probable impact on history, of her act as head of the American Union Against Militarism. But my own admiration of her had little to do with those qualities of leadership, or even with her eminent beauty. As a boy of ten I used to announce that I would never marry any girl but my sister, and I suppose a passionate attachment underlay this firm resolution. Of all Freud's plain and fancy inventions, the concept of an "incest barrier" is the one most easily verifiable in my experience. My mother and sister were both beautiful women, but I grew to manhood without knowing this. Even when I learned about it, the knowledge was academic and objective. There was no rejoicing in their beauty, no sinking into the joy of it.

The qualities in Crystal that I most rejoiced in were her ruthless sincerity and logic; the inexhaustible fountain of understanding love that made these qualities bearable; a supervening humor which kept that "belief in the coming triumph of freedom and decent human relations" from becoming fanatical; a gift of entering into the problems of other people as though she had no problems of her own—a veritable genius for friendship and wise counsel; and withal a passionate joy in the adventure of living her own life.

"To live greatly—that's the thing, and it means joy and sorrow both," she wrote in an early letter to me. In that key her life-symphony began and ended.

She owned a house near me in Croton, and she came back from England in August 1927 to live there with her two children, leaving her husband to follow as soon as it became financially possible. Instead of his coming, there came in less than a month a cablegram saying that he had died of a brain hemorrhage.

Crystal herself, although she did not know it, was mortally sick when she received this heartbreaking news. Her kidneys had been impaired in childhood by a savage attack of scarlet fever, and now, after a life of strenuous and abounding passion and achievement, they were giving out. She had come home joyful in our renewed companionship and that of her many American friends, filled with the ambition to find in America the work that had eluded her in England. It was not only an ambition, but a necessity now, and she met the challenge with her head high. She found a job organizing for the *Nation* a grandiose celebration of the tenth anniversary of the editorship of Oswald Garrison Villard. But she had barely the strength to carry it through.

"She was obviously fighting a tremendous battle," the associate editor, Lewis Gannett, wrote me after she died. "I'm glad I had that last picture of Crystal fighting with head up and a smile in her eyes, and never telling how hard she had to fight. You had a glorious sister, Max."

There was a failure of diagnosis, or of candor on the part of the regular physicians, and Crystal hung desperately to the hope of returning health, going from treatment to treatment, from cure to cure, adhering to any healer, even though pretty near to a charlatan, who would hold out the promise of some ultimate recovery. I had never then seen death courageously and calmly faced; I had myself an infantile horror of it; I played up to her successive illusions, hiding my heart from my true judgment of them. This habit of concealment remained with me to the end, and I regret that. For Crystal, when finally she did confront her close-approaching death, was as calm and humorously brave as any battle-tempered soldier would be. I think her last ten months would have been happier and better worth living if she had lived them in the mood in which she died.

Her search for salvation brought her to Dr. Kellogg's sanitarium in Battle Creek, Michigan, in June 1928. My brother, a surgeon in Erie, Pennsylvania, drove up to see her there, and sent us a telegram which made us feel that she had not long to live. We set out for Battle Creek as soon as we could pack our bags. She was six weeks dying, and all that time I would have been dying too but for Eliena, whose buoyancy combined with a heavenly tenderness was to me a miracle like the coming of Christ. Crystal, who had never wholly accepted Eliena—or indeed any girl with whom I became deeply involved—fell in love with her during those six weeks. Eliena gradually, yet actually, took our mother's place in her heart, bringing an almost mystical peace into those final days. Even to me it seemed sometimes as though we were back home in the Eastman family, the three of us, reproducing quite perfectly the state of affairs that had prevailed in our youth—Crystal and Eliena closer and more constantly together, I a member of the trio, but a little aloof, always sneaking away to my thoughts and writings.

"Well, here we all are," Crystal said one morning as Eliena and I sat down beside her bed, pouring that sweet radiant smile on each of us. "It's as if we were going away somewhere together.

"Isn't it funny, death is here. Death is right here. And the funniest of all is to think of me dying in Battle Creek Sanitarium—of all the bourgeois institutions. Think of me dying in Battle Creek Sanitarium!"

Her old humorous laughter! I told her how dear it was, and she said: "Well, that's all there is left to do now—that's all there is, isn't it?—laughter."

"Children," she said on another morning, "I'm ashamed—so ashamed of the trouble I'm causing. This dying business I mean. But I've never done it before, you know—you must remember that. I'm just making Max's life a burden. I think that is what I was put in the world for, to make Max's life something of an effort. He was born with a silver spoon in his mouth and nothing to do, and here I've provided him with children, cares, responsibilities. Every woman, you know, was put in the world for some particular purpose having to do with some man. And that was why I was put in."

Her two much-loved children—Annis, five, and Jeffrey, ten years old—were in a summer camp in the Adirondacks, and my first task as their guardian was to drive up there and tell them of their mother's death. It was a dreadful task. But the sweet strong poise of those children in their lonely sadness was a lesson and an inspiration to me. Children know and understand so much more than we imagine they do!

"I thought she would live," Annis said in a voice with only a tiny tremor in it. She had been meditating and waiting, with hope and yet with fortitude.

I would like some day to tell the whole of Crystal's story, but now I am only describing the darkened world I lived in when I came home an outcast after my visit to Russia. There was also a source of despair about myself, an inward thing, a thing that seemed for a time pathological. It was the complete and mysterious loss of my gift of eloquence, or that ability to speak effectively in public, on which I had counted as a source of income. My first engagement under the Leigh-Emmerich management was at Yale—it was the old humor lecture that had been so hilarious. Now it was an hour of dogged hard labor on my part, and politely curious attention on the part of the audience. I could not understand what had happened to me. Something I had possessed in glorious abundance had been pulled back from the inside. Was another demon in there, a neurosis, a purpose alien to mine, frustrating my ambition and earning power? Was the change in me? Or was it America that had so changed in my absence? Had I myself become an alien? I thought at first that this had happened, and tried so to explain it to Eliena, for she, having enjoyed my success at the international meeting in Moscow, was as surprised and bewildered as I to find me a flop in my own language.

We went together to a symposium at the New School for Social Research on "Liberty in the Modern World." My speech was an essay—good enough to be published subsequently in an anthology—but I delivered it as though I were mixing concrete. I stood there rolling it around and out in complete aloofness from the audience. I could not bring one of them to life. I was not alive myself; I was a reciting machine. . . .

This mystery dulled and appalled me. It also alarmed me, for I had no job, and I was still unwilling to hire myself out as a writer. Eliena came once more to my rescue, teaching Russian and taking a job with an exhibition of Arts and Crafts that Amtorg (the Soviet Trade Bureau) was putting on in Steinway Hall. She earned most of our living during the months that I was plodding my way through a lifeless tour of lectures.

That lecture tour was so pathetic and awful a phase of my experience that I must try—as deeply as I can—to explain why this was so. I was a noticeably rambunctious and commanding baby, but I was torn away from my mother's arms at the age of three and put out to live among strange people on a farm while she went to work as a boarding-school teacher in a distant village. The village, as a fact, was only three miles distant and the strangers were dear friends of the family. But never mind that—I was scared. I was scared and bewildered and didn't know what to do with my feelings. Strangers have abashed and paralyzed me ever since, and night-fears have been my companions. In the book I called *Enjoyment of Living*, I attributed this "shadow in my soul" to my mother's sorrow over the death of her eldest boy and the end of her physical relation with my father. But that I see was romantic. The separation from my mother herself was more probably the cause of these fears, and of a morbidly extreme reaction to any experience of loss—even the saying good-bye for a brief absence to someone I love and live with.

My art of oratory—derived also, by the way, from watching my mother—had thus a strong obstacle to overcome. I had to devise ways of surmounting my shyness before I could even begin to make a good speech. For one thing I had to write out the speech and learn it by heart so that I would feel sure of having something to say. The greatest orators, in my opinion, do write out and learn their speeches when they have time, but I am compelled to do this because I cannot depend on the presence of an audience to stimulate instead of abashing me. When the moment comes, a fit of diffidence is as likely to seize me as an impulse to talk. And a fit of diffidence, as all shy people will agree, is in every way similar to a stroke of paralysis. After I have delivered a successful speech and got on the top side of my inferiority complex, if a question is asked, or I am heckled, I can speak *ex tempore* almost as well as I wrote. Cicero, in advising orators to write out and learn their speeches, tells them that this will happen, and I have confirmed it many times. Indeed it has been one of my egotistical joys to hear myself make a good extemporaneous speech once I had got possession of myself and the audience. But before that, I have to lift myself out of the rather languid, unassertive, gestureless, slow-spoken creature I normally inhabit; I have to plant myself in a more aggressive soul and body. It can be expressed by saying that I am not an orator, but an actor who knows how to act the part of an orator.

I had forgotten this during my long absence from the platform. I was in the depths of me too, for personal as well as political reasons, on the underside of my inferiority complex. I was trying to make speeches from that position and in my own character. That was the trouble. And the truth of it dawned on me one midnight—November 24, 1928, to be exact—in Madison, Wisconsin. I was booked to speak the next day in the auditorium of the University of Wisconsin on "Poetry in the Age of Science." It was in large part a militant speech, the beginning of my long war on the "Cult of Unintelligibility." I could not go to sleep because I so dreaded my incompetent delivery of it—I so pitifully longed for the old gift of eloquence now mysteriously withdrawn from me. Of a sudden as I lay there in the darkness a memory was lighted.

"You are not, and never were an orator," I said to myself. "Oratory was something you put on as an actor puts on an act."

I put on my act the next day. I had some papers to read from in the course of my lecture, and I strode up to the lectern, and slapped them down there with the gesture of a man challenging the sun to stand still. The attitude and gesture worked an inner revolution. The mother-hungry baby was cast out; my self was cast out; I knew my lines and could be anyone I chose to be. It was a strange kind of triumph, but a life-saving one. For twelve years thereafter I made a good living acting the part of an orator—or shall I say, more analytically and with more comfort to my pride, overcoming my acquired timidity and getting back to my hereditary rambunctiousness.

It was, at any rate, an immense event, the beginning of a brighter phase in my life. Eliena preserved the telegram in which I told her the good news: "I made a grand speech in Madison. Just like old times. I've found out what was the matter."

For no better reason than that I am on the subject of lecturing, I want to relate a strange thing thing that happened long after. I had a lecture called "The Art of Enjoying Poetry" in the course of which, ostensibly by way of illustration, I read some of my own poems. I gave this lecture one night at the New School for Social Research—in a new top-floor auditorium which had been equipped with unusual intersecting planes and crossing lights. At the end of the lecture I was asked to read the idyll which I call "Swamp Maple," a poem ten pages long and much more of a strain on my shyness than I had undertaken before. In the midst of it I discovered that only exactly half of me was there—the right half. No other words will describe my state of consciousness. I feared that I was going to fall in a faint or a fit of epilepsy, but nothing else happened. That right half of me went right on reading intelligibly, and, it seemed, eloquently. The seizure lasted a little more than a minute, at the end of which my left half came back and joined in the performance. Eliena and I, discussing it afterward, tried to believe that it had been an effect of the peculiar lighting in that modernistic auditorium, but I remained unconvinced of this. I blamed it rather on the hypnotic rhythm of the poem, though I could not see why it should have divided me in half. Twenty or twenty-five years later I learned that the artist Karl Knaths has (or believes he has) the gift of seeing people's auras. He first learned of this gift, I was told, when hearing me read a poem at the New School for Social Research, where as I read my aura rose up and stood for a brief time above me!

Strange things happen when one is spellbound by an audience, but that is the only incident of this seemingly occult kind that I have to relate.

Chapter 75

A TASTE OF REHABILITATION

Other and more objective lights began to dawn during the winter of 1928. A well-known New York radical, Ludwig Lore, called me up one day and asked me to come to his apartment to meet a Russian friend. Lore, as editor of the *New York Volkszeitung*, had been for years a leader of the German-American socialists, a leftward leader who took sides with the Bolsheviks when the party split. He had dark eyes and a dark mustache, and might, but for his affable manner and a twinkle in those eyes, have played the part of a dangerous conspirator. He actually was a conspirator now, for the Russian friend he had asked me to meet was a man named Eleazar Solntsev, ostensibly an economist working with Stalin's Amtorg, but secretly a devout agent of the Trotsky Opposition. Lore too, although I had not known it, was sympathetic to the Opposition, and Solntsev had appealed to him to call together a *Kruzhok*, which might become the nucleus of a Trotskyist party in the United States. Lore had called together the *Kruzhok* (it means a small circle) and it had five members: Solntsev, Lore, Antoinette Konikow, a noble old-time socialist who had come down from Boston, and Eliena and me. We talked about the miserable plight of the revolution in America, my unwillingness to become an organizer being one of its most regrettable features, and then broke up and went home. But Solntsev had another mission to fulfill: that was to get the platform and related documents of the Trotsky Opposition, which Stalin had suppressed in Russia, translated into English and published in the United States. He broached—somewhat hesitantly in view of my reward for similar services in the past—the idea of my taking on this job. We had several tête-à-têtes on the subject in out-of-the-way nooks and corners, and I finally succumbed—more because of my shame at not being an organizer, than through any persuasiveness of his. He was a tall,

510

slender man of about forty, with earnest gray eyes and a sweet but infrequent smile, brilliantly intelligent according to Victor Serge, who wrote of him in his *Russia Twenty Years After*, but with nothing about him to suggest that he was risking his life for a cause. I learned afterward that on returning to Moscow he was arrested and jailed for three years without a formal accusation, kept for an additional three years "by administrative order," and then deported to Siberia. Before he could join his wife and child who had been deported elsewhere, he was arrested again and again sentenced without trial to five years in prison. Preferring death to this cat-and-mouse torment, he replied with a hunger strike, and after eighteen days of it was liberated by the gangsters of the GPU, who seemed to take more pleasure in killing people than watching them starve. Although emaciated to the last degree, he insisted on leaving immediately to join his wife in a distant village. On the way an infection of his inner ear became violently inflamed. He was removed from the train and operated on, but died in a hospital while his wife was still waiting. In my thoughts he stands for hundreds of thousands of sincere and lucid-minded people who died in that holocaust for the crime of knowing what was going on and being courageous about it.

Solntsev had turned over to me the precious suppressed documents he had smuggled out of Russia. I sorted them, made the outline of a book, and took it up to Alfred Harcourt of Harcourt, Brace & Company. Harcourt was curious, as every thoughtful person was, as to what had really happened in this four years' upheaval among the Bolsheviks. He called in his partner, Donald Brace, and I explained as succinctly as I could the nature of the documents and their importance to an understanding of the real situation in Russia.

"That's a good title," he said. "Would you embody what you've been saying in a sufficiently extended introduction so that we could call it a book and not just a bundle of political papers?"

I agreed to that, and he turned to Brace: "It's a long time since we've had an adventure in this business. What do you say we take it on?"

Brace agreed with a smile, and in that light-hearted way an historically important book, *The Real Situation in Russia* by Leon Trotsky, came into being. I signed the contract on March 14, and went immediately to work on my task of translation, and my effort to dissipate with a preface and editorial notes the smoke screen of lying propaganda poured over the earth from the Kremlin about the issues at stake between Trotsky and Stalin. That smoke screen mingled so perfectly with the fog of wishful thinking rising, it seemed, from the earth itself, that facts were hardly visible in any direction. When stated, they looked like fictions grossly magnified. I remarked, for instance, in my part of the book that Stalin was "moving toward the physical destruction of the Opposition," a truth which then seemed insanely fanciful to the American intelligentsia, but which soon enough proved true.

Solntsev was much impressed by the diligence and speed with which I did the work—also, I believe, by the fact that in agreeing to do it I never reminded him of the poor thanks I got for a previous effort in the same direction. This must have seemed to him magnanimous, or something of that nature, though the truth is that I had ceased to think about that previous incident. Trotsky's capitulation of October 1926, his renewed attempt to arouse the masses in 1927, his exasperating silence followed by a more exasperating burst of sudden straight talk in *Lessons of October*—in short, all his maneuvers—had been so badly timed and ill-advised that I felt he had abdicated any lingering ghost of a claim he may have had to political, as opposed to intellectual, leadership. Less than ever was it Trotsky I was working for, more than ever his irrefutable demonstration of the true course, if there was one, toward a workers' and peasants' republic. Thus when Solntsev asked me one day, after receiving an underground communication from Trotsky, whether there wasn't some favor I would like to ask of "the old man," I replied rather caustically and without realizing what he meant:

"Yes. Tell him I want him to be the leader of the international proletarian revolution!"

Solntsev withheld his answer, but what he had meant became apparent some weeks later when he handed me a document signed by Trotsky, formally retracting his disavowal of *Since Lenin Died* and more than compensating for the injurious adjectives it had contained. His retraction took the form of a letter to his good friend and hunting companion, N. I. Muralov, commander under him of the Moscow military district, and one of the truly great old Bolsheviks. Muralov was a giant of a man, a brawny hero of the insurrection and the civil war, one whose good opinion would be especially precious to a mortified litterateur. I have to quote this letter as end and climax to the story of my political disgrace, although some of its sentences, as I read them today, give me once more, I must say, a feeling akin to mortification. It is dated Alma Ata, September 2, 1928, nine months after Trotsky's forcible deportation from Moscow.

Dear Nikolai Ivanovich,

You ask me about Comrade Max Eastman whom our press holds up from time to time as a horrible example, picturing him as almost a hireling of the bourgeoisie who sold the state secrets of the USSR. That is a shameless lie! Comrade Max Eastman is a revolutionary American of the type of John Reed, one of the most loyal friends of the October Revolution. A poet, author, journalist, he came to the Soviet Republic in the first hard days of its existence, learned the Russian Language and entered closely into our life, in order with the more assurance to defend the Soviet Republic before the popular masses of America.

Max Eastman took the side of the Opposition in 1923, and openly defended us against political accusations and especially against insinuation and slander. I will not speak here of the theoretic disagreements which divide Comrade Eastman from the Marxists. But Eastman is an absolutely irreproachable revolutionist, who has demonstrated his ideality and his political disinterestedness in everything he has done. He stands in that respect several heads higher than most of these functionaries who are slandering him. Eastman thought that the Opposition was not waging a sufficiently energetic struggle and started a campaign abroad at his own conscious risk.

Not having access to the official communist press, and desiring at any cost to publish for general public information the Testament of Lenin, Eastman gave it to an American bourgeois newspaper. Every one of us has been compelled at times, both earlier and during the epoch of the Soviet Power, to use the foreign bourgeois papers in order to issue information to wide circles inaccessible otherwise. Lenin more than once gave out such information in the form of interviews to foreign journalists. And to that you must add that the American workers, with insignificant exceptions, read only the bourgeois press. . . .

At a time when the Opposition was still hoping to correct the party line by purely inside methods, not carrying our differences outside, we were all, and I in the number, against the steps taken by Max Eastman in defense of the Opposition. In the Autumn of 1925 a majority of the Politburo forced on me a declaration, prepared by themselves, containing a sharp condemnation of Max Eastman. Inasmuch as the entire ruling group in the Opposition thought at that time that it was inexpedient to carry the political struggle into the open, and had resolved upon a series of concessions, it naturally could not start a struggle and develop it over the personal question about Eastman, who had taken a step, as was said, at his own conscious risk. That is why, upon the decision of the entire guiding group of the Opposition, I signed the declaration about Max Eastman, forced on me by the majority of the Politburo with an ultimatum: Either sign the declaration as it stands or join an open struggle on that issue.

There is no use entering here on the question whether the general policy of the Opposition in 1925 was right or wrong. I now think that at that time there was no other course. At any rate my declaration about Eastman at that time can be understood only as a constituent part of our then policy of compromise and conciliation. It was so understood by all informed and thinking members of the party. That declaration casts not the slightest shadow, either personal or political, upon Comrade Eastman.

As far as rumors reach me about Eastman during the last year, he remains what he was: a friend of the October revolution and a defender of the views of the Opposition.

With Bolshevik greeting,
L. Trotsky

Three years later, when I was corresponding with Trotsky I told him that I had shown the manuscript of *Since Lenin Died* to Rakovsky before deciding upon its publication, not wanting him to think that I am as negligent of the problems of practical politics as his letter implied. He answered me—and this was the last time the subject was mentioned between us:

"Your communication about the circumstances in which you published your book containing Lenin's testament is very interesting. A vague rumor of the facts you relate had reached me. But when Rakovsky arrived in Russia, events had so piled up one after another that we had no chance or occasion to talk of the past, and I went into exile with the impression that you had acted completely on your own. I will find a way to correct that erroneous part of my letter, for the matter has both personal and political interest. It will be impossible to name Rakovsky in the press, since the Stalinists will use that against him instantly and in the foulest manner. But it will be possible, without mentioning names, to make the essential correction. I will do this in the next number of the Bulletin of the Opposition." *

One day in that spring or summer of 1928 the telephone rang, and a familiar voice said:

"Max, this will surprise you, but it's your old friend Jim Cannon speaking."

It did indeed surprise me, for, as I have said, Cannon was an outstanding leader of the American Communist Party.

"I thought there was a law against fraternizing with Trotskyists," I said.

"There is, but I am breaking the law at present, although for the time being secretly. Things are happening and I want to come up to Croton and have a private talk with you."

We talked far into the night, and I learned that he and Max Schachtman and one or two less prominent members were on the point of leaving the party, and forming a new organization backing the principles of the Opposition. As I was in the midst of my task of translating the documents involved, I had those principles on my tongue's end, and was better able than ever before or since to godfather an organization. I think "godfather" is a fair description of the role I played, for Jim knew too much to expect me to join it, and I was still passionately concerned—it surprises me now to see by surviving documents how passionately—to get some practical action taken in behalf of what I so clearly conceived to be the true program of the revolution. I fulfilled a godfather's role, at any rate, to the extent of turning over to the new party my royalties on *The Real Situation in Russia.*

The book itself was a more precious gift than the royalties. It was and still is the arsenal of the Trotskyists, a source book, indeed, for all who want to set free the truth—imprisoned in solid walls of silence and lies by Stalin and Khrushchev—about Trotsky's struggle to keep alive the fading hope of a free collectivist state in Russia. I had not realized then that this hope is impossible of realization, in Russia or anywhere else. There was evangelical fervor still, as well as a fair statement of the existing facts in my introduction. "Trotsky and the opposition," I explained to the reader, "are defending the Bolshevik forms of organization as conceived by Lenin against Stalin's perversion of them

---

* Whether Trotsky remembered to mention this subject in the Bulletin or not, I do not know. One could hardly expect it.

in the direction of bureaucracy, clique-rule, and personal dictatorship. And they are defending scientific thinking against dishonest political big talk, demagogism, juggling of statistics, jesuitism, and a deliberately adopted campaign of all-Russian and international lying."

A fair-sized edition of the book was sold, and excerpts from it have been purchased by writers of history ever since. But I fear a pleasure in the adventure was about all the profit that Harcourt and Brace got out of its publication. The only critic well enough informed and judicial enough to write an adequate review of it was Herbert Solow in the *New York Evening Post:*

"In this book Trotsky again proves himself a polemical writer of amazing force and clarity. Every sentence carries conviction; he piles fact on fact, epithet on epithet, quotation on quotation, to build a monumental structure on which to expose the shame of Stalin."

Solow pointed out, however, that "the bureaucratic sclerosis on which Trotsky blames much of the evil in Stalinism is a common enough phenomenon. After the prophet come the disciples, after the disciples comes the church, and with the church comes the hierarchy. If this has been the fate of Marxism, the Communist revolution has ahead of it its hardest struggles, and they will be internal, not foreign, struggles."

The internal struggles, alas, were soon over, for the head of the hierarchy was one of the most adroit and ruthless tyrants in history. In foreign lands, however, the struggle still continues. The Trotskyist parties are small, but you are apt to find them almost anywhere. A dispatch from Ceylon not long ago described such a party as playing a vital part in a national election. In this country Jim Cannon is still the leader, no longer very active, I judge, but undismayed and on hand when his unusual gift of eloquence is needed. Max Schachtman split off from the party in the thirties, and is now a member of the national executive committee of the American Socialist Party.

I fear the Trotskyists, like the Socialist Labor Party, will be with us till the end of time. They have a truly great man and a powerful thinker and writer as their hero. And Trotskyism, after all, is nothing but the Marxism of the Bolshevik revolution expounded with agile intelligence and without accommodations and corruptions—even those introduced of necessity by anyone who tries to hold power in its name.

Chapter 76

THE LITERARY MIND

There was unconscious irony in Trotsky's endorsement of my political integrity and revolutionism, for it arrived at the crux of one of my sharp turns from politics to poetry. Ever since Scott Fitzgerald had brought "The Waste Land" across the Cap and read it to me with so much enthusiasm and so little reck of understanding, a storm had been gathering in my breast. At home I found all the literary vanguard to which I had once belonged thronging along the same road into a fog. I met Hart Crane one day in the home of Charmion von Wiegand. He was showing her a sheaf of poems, and she handed me one to read. It had by way of subtitle a Latin quotation about *Ultima Thule* which I could not translate. I was simple-minded enough to want to know, before reading the poem, what the quotation meant. Crane gave it a hasty glance over my shoulder and said:

"I don't know what it means—I don't understand the language at all."

In the world I was familiar with that would have caused a hitch in the conversation, and somebody might even have laughed, but he and Charmion went right on seriously talking as though nothing had happened. I settled back to wrestle with the English parts of his poem, which I found as impossible to make sense of as the Latin.

Hart Crane was not famous then; I had never heard of him; he was merely a handsome, lanky young man with a blond mustache. The incident was but one of many which convinced me that some dreadful plague or pest was settling over the realm of poetic literature. I am not opposed to obscurity in poetry, and I am not so dry-hearted as to imagine that all the values of a poem, or of any work of art, must be capable of reasonable exposition. Moreover I am the last to insist that poetry must have a practical significance. In my lectures on poetics at

Columbia and my first book, *Enjoyment of Poetry*, I had defended the opposite thesis. If poetry preaches a moral, or conveys a message of some kind, or makes a "criticism of life," as Matthew Arnold thought it must (and I. A. Richards belongs to the same school) that is so much velvet. But it doesn't have to in order to be good or great poetry. It has only to communicate life. To live is—or it can be—a great thing. To live vividly is greater. To live together is still greater. Pure poetry is living vividly and living together. That was my view. And if a poem is *obscure* or "difficult," if one has to make a penetrative effort to reach the quality of the life communicated, all well and good. But when the poem is unintelligible, when no matter what effort you make, the thing communicated remains a blur, then it is no longer a question of good or bad poetry. Intelligence itself, civilized intelligence, is being abandoned.

With these thoughts I turned back from my preoccupation with revolutionary politics to my earlier intense interest—the psychology of poetry. I had found an intellectual friend in Lee Hartman, the editor of *Harper's Monthly*, a man whose subsequent decline and death dealt a blow to my hopes, for he gave me for the first time in my life an urgent welcome into the pages of an American magazine. He published in April (1929) an essay, "The Cult of Unintelligibility," in which I waged impudent war on the principal heroes then towering on the literary horizon; T. S. Eliot, Hart Crane, E. E. Cummings, James Joyce, Gertrude Stein, Edith Sitwell. It was a lovely war from my point of view, all weapons permitted and no holds barred. Of course I lost the war. A gap in my memory indicates that I was carried unconscious from the field of battle. But I recovered in the course of a year or two and came back with another essay called "Poets Talking to Themselves." That was the end of the war. I disappeared under a cloud of awfully overwhelming language called the New Criticism, and as a critic of poetry I have not been heard of since. But I enjoyed my side of the war immensely. I have been told that if I had not been so polemic my essays would have had more effect. But how can you wage war without being polemic?

I don't mean to imply that I was frivolous. I was indeed, and still am, irritatingly cocksure on this subject, but my thesis was carefully weighed and considered. I distinguished two traits in the movement then called modernist: a tendency toward pure poetry, and a tendency toward privacy combined with a naïve sincerity in employing as material the instruments of social communion. I defined and defended the former tendency in a separate essay which *Harper's* also published, and in the essay on unintelligibility my main drive was not against the poets who are spontaneously so naïve, but against the critics who coddle them by pretending there is communion where there is none. I pointed out that Hart Crane, in explaining the metaphors in his lyric, "At Melville's Tomb," had given incontrovertible proof that *without the explanation* no human brain could conceivably guess what he had in mind. And yet a pretentious critic had described the poem as "far from being one of Crane's more difficult compositions." Of James Joyce, while appreciating, among other qualities, his humor, I remarked that his most original contribution to English literature had been to lock up one of its most brilliant geniuses inside his own vest.

It happened that I was in Paris a month or so after this piece was published, and strolling down the rue de l'Odéon I dropped in to see my friend Sylvia Beach, who ran the charming and historic bookstore called Shakespeare & Company. Sylvia is the heroic woman who first published Joyce's *Ulysses*, and I entered her delicately audacious sanctum with more trepidation than the phrase "dropped in" suggests. Instead of the scowl I expected, she came forward with a jovial greeting and her first words were:

"Joyce likes your essay in *Harper's* so much—I wonder if you could find time to have tea with him while you're in Paris?"

And she handed me an autographed copy of *Anna Livia Plurabelle* that he had left for me. I could find time for the tea of course, and it was arranged over the telephone that I should come out to his apartment the following afternoon.

Joyce's greeting was as affirmative as Sylvia's had been. He welcomed me as though I had gone to war in his behalf and won a great battle. He said that my essay was not only "delightfully witty," but in his opinion, *"sound criticism."*

Words which I saved carefully and have used with rather bewildering effect when attacked by his disciples for my "philistine" opinions. Irish words, I should say, for I don't know who but an Irishman would so commit himself in speech when the dominant stream in his nature was running the other way.

Joyce seemed a gentle, earnest and very quiet person—poised and mildly indignant about his blindness—an intellectual and yet not a thinking type. He began our conversation by saying how glad he was that, even though I found so much of him unintelligible, I had enjoyed his humor.

"It would be terrible," he said, "to think that I had done all that work and not given you any pleasure at all. I spent six hundred hours making that little book I sent you. Six hundred hours, and what a waste if it had brought you no pleasure at all. For certainly the motive of an artist—of all artists, whether they are conscious of it or not—is to give pleasure to others."

"It surprises me to hear you say that," I said.

"But it is true, isn't it?" he answered earnestly.

And then he told me that into the prose of *Anna Livia Plurabelle* he had woven the names of five hundred rivers. The book seems to have at least one of these rivers flowing through it, for he explained, before reciting a passage from it, that either two people, or a rock and a tree, or the principles of organic and inorganic nature—all three, or any one of the three, I assumed—are talking to each other across a river. One of his learned commentators has since issued a paper to the effect that it is the two sexes, male and female, who are talking across this river; another maintains that it is two washerwomen; but I choose to believe what Joyce told me. As he spoke the lines, I watched him, and saw how much every syllable weighed and carried to his mind and feeling, and since I could not myself understand the syllables and therefore could not think and feel what he was thinking and feeling, my mind wandered a little from the music and I thought what a wonderfully different thing an intense artist is—or a man in the mood of artistic rapture—from an ordinary practical-minded adult. An artist might be described as a man consecrated to the child's attitude toward values, and yet translated by his consecration into a world in which childhood is the sovereign thing and growing-up a mere incidental necessity.

Joyce had handed me the open book, asking me to follow the text and prompt him if he went wrong, for he had learned these pages in order to make a recording and was not sure he could trust his memory. But I had no prompting to do, and gave my attention half to the music and half to my thoughts as I so often do at a concert. Here was a famous author reciting his lines for me—lines on which he had worked six hundred hours and woven into them the names of five hundred rivers. And yet I did not detect one river. I have examined them since and have not yet found but three-and-a-half rivers. Moreover, having had something to do with inductive and deductive logic, I know that if it took six hundred hours to weave those rivers into his prose, it will take somewhere near six hundred thousand to weave them out. When Joyce told me in his most melting and most Irish voice, that he liked to think how in some future day, far off in Tibet or Somaliland, some lad or lass reading the little book would be pleased to come upon the name of his "home river," my smile was a trifle ironical. If his motive as an artist had been to give pleasure to that sweet lad or lass, he might, I thought, have provided some little key or pirate's chart of some kind which would enable them to dig up their river without doing all that unnecessary hard labor. I do not know whether I said this or not, but to something I said Joyce answered:

"The demand that I make of my reader is that he should devote his whole life to reading my works."

My answer was: "You absolutely insist on giving them all that pleasure!"

I did not make the answer, of course, I rarely make the right answer until I have gone home to bed. I only thought what I have often thought before, both in reading Joyce and in reading the encomiums written by his disciples, that the first and very principal thing to say about them all is that their minds are untrained and incoherent. They do not know how to think.

Joyce thought he was writing the extremely unintelligible prose of *Finnegans Wake* because, whereas *Ulysses* gave us a day in the life of a man, the new work would give us the night.

"In writing of the night," he said to me, "I really could not, I felt I could not, use words in their ordinary connections. Used that way they do not express how things are in the night, in the different stages—conscious, then fore-conscious, then unconscious. I found that it could not be done with words in their ordinary relations and connections. When morning comes of course everything will be clear again. I'll give them back their English language. I'm not destroying it for good!"

It was impossible not to be charmed by the mild high delicate voice and the gentle smile with which Joyce uttered this grandiose reassurance. But one would have to be simple-minded indeed to believe that the idea of writing about the night was anything more than an interior pretext for amusing himself with words in the rather old-maid-knitting fashion he chose to. The tendency appears often enough—and with no such imposing reason—in *Ulysses*. Would an author who sincerely desired to convey to his reader the experience of falling asleep— "through the various stages, conscious, fore-conscious, unconscious"— begin by taking the names of five hundred rivers and burying them so deep and secretly that the reader would have to stay up a fortnight with a couple of dozen foreign language dictionaries, a brace of encyclopedias, an atlas, a world almanac, and several pounds of coffee in order to dig up a hundred of them?

Pondering on the mystery of this descent of a prodigy-begotten fog over the bright pages of great literature, I came back from revolutionary politics to my more proper subject, the relation between science and poetic art. It seemed to me that among the obvious causes of such a retreat of poets into unintelligibility was the advance of science into fields once proudly occupied by them. Poets could no longer think of themselves as discoverers and announcers of vital and reliable truths —that was the trouble. During those same years a literary epidemic called "the New Humanism" was sweeping through our cities, and that too, I thought, was caused by the advance of scientific method into fields once sacred to the "humanities." The "New Humanists" were resisting the march of science; the poets were fleeing before it. That was my thesis, and what would the outcome be? What would be the position of the literary mind in a world so dominated as ours was going to be by science? Out of these questions, and my answers to them, I made in the years 1929 to 1931 a book which I called *The Literary Mind: Its Place in an Age of Science.*

I had always wanted to expound in a more thorough fashion the theory of metaphor which I arrived at while teaching poetics at Columbia University. I had hushed it down somewhat in my first book, *Enjoyment of Poetry*, not wishing to make that book too technical. But now I dug it up from its hiding place in the *Journal of Philosophy, Psychology and Scientific Methods*, refashioned it in two chapters, "Art and Biology" and "What Poetry Is," and published them in *The Literary Mind*. I also made a long and painstaking criticism of I. A. Richards' books on poetry, which I think are based on an erroneous psychology. His conception of "thought," and of science, as merely a "pointing to things," without regard to attitude or active response, leaving to poetry the task of organizing attitudes and practical actions, is false to the whole history and nature of the mind. Science is an outgrowth of practical effort, and its connection with and dependence upon action is and always has been direct and continual. Poetry was begotten upon magic ritual by daydreams and play. Whatever one's ultimate philosophy, whether pragmatist or intellectualistic, these facts are hardly subject to question. Thought might more truthfully be credited with creating "things" out of an undefined flux of experience, than with merely pointing to them. . . .

Out of such elements, with a concluding speculation on the future of the poet, the novelist, the critic, the teacher of literature, I made up my book *The Literary Mind*, which was published by Scribner's in the autumn of 1931. Its fate was a kind of corroboration of its thesis. It was devastatingly denounced, or as devastatingly ignored, by the advanced men of letters, but by progressive scientists, philosophers, students of history and sociology it was highly praised.

Allen Tate, being appointed by the Library of Congress to prepare a list of American books for presentation to the Soviet Union, described it as not worth sending along because it was based on a superficial conception of science. But Edwin Hubble, our foremost astronomer, wrote: "You are one of the few people who understand the meaning and the limitations of that much abused word, science."

Robert M. Coates concluded a comment in the *New Yorker:* "Mr. Eastman, let me say that you, a poet—you ought to be ashamed of yourself." But Bernard Berenson, who shared my interest in bringing psychology to bear on the enjoyment of the arts, greeted me in a thrilling letter: "I can not tell you how exciting I found your *Literary Mind!*" George Santayana wrote: "I heartily agree with the gist of your definition of poetry. . . . I also agree with you in thinking that aesthetic feeling involves the inhibition of action and transitive intelligence."

I. A. Richards assured the readers of the *Criterion* that the "Science of Psychology"—in capital letters—"annuls and abolishes" me. But six professional psychologists gave me their warm approval. Robert M. Yerkes, Yale's famous psycho-biologist, wrote: "I am confident that the view of the relation of scientific ideas and progress to literature, perhaps even to all the fine arts, which you have set forth, is correct and will prevail." Another eminent scientist, C. Judson Herrick, of the University of Chicago, placed a quotation from my chapter "Art and Biology" at the base of his *Neurological Foundations of Animal Behavior!*

I must not exaggerate the preciseness of this contrast. A few distinguished literary men spoke favorably of my book. Henry Seidel Canby, H. G. Wells, Sinclair Lewis, Joseph Wood Krutch, even Walter de la Mare had a good word for it. Edmund Wilson gave the book a literary thumbs-down when it appeared, but afterward took this handsomely back. "A glance into *The Literary Mind* today," he wrote in 1941, "reveals, rather surprisingly to one who was prejudiced against the book when it first appeared, that it was distinguished by a deeper comprehension of the real issues raised by contemporary literature than almost anything that had been written in the twenties.

. . . Max Eastman was almost alone in his attempt to work out as an enlightened modern man the larger relations of art and science to one another, and of both to the society behind them."

Notwithstanding such exceptions, the general lineup of progressive scientists in my favor and vanguard litterateurs against me, was definite enough to be instructive. You might think that a book about literature so highly praised by men trained in the definition of fact would have played *some* part in criticism and the philosophy of criticism during the decades that followed. One of my scientific eulogists, I remember, went so far as to suggest that my book would probably mark the beginning of an epoch in literary criticism. If it did, the epoch was distinguished by an aggressive neglect and total disappearance both from criticism and from learned discussions about it, of every thesis advanced and every thought expressed in my book. To the vanguard literati, the travelers in "New Directions," the exponents of the New Criticism—identified with the *Criterion, Horizon*, the *Kenyon* and the *Partisan Review*—my discussion of the relations between literature and science does not exist. Once and for all, in T. S. Eliot's *Criterion* for October 1932, I had been "annulled and abolished."

To me these facts bear out my thesis about the literary mind and its relation to scientific knowledge—or even to an amateur attempt to achieve such knowledge. They do make me wish, however, that I had written my book better. They keep me thinking of bright ways to do it over again as I did my books on humor and Marxism. It should contain a chapter on John Donne and the trend in seventeenth-century poetry called "metaphysical," exploring its merits yet noting its reduction to absurdity in the inanities of Gongorism; and one on the trend in French poetry called by the equally ill-chosen name of "symbolism"—its reduction to absurdity in the more perfect inanities of Gertrude Stein.

I will say, at least, that if I did thus rise from the dead, I should prove unregenerate. I still think the most famously "modern" poets, while commendably interested in poetry as a thing by itself, an evocation of the sheer qualities of their experience, have mixed this up with an obdurate neglect of the strategy of communication. Their poetry is not only pure, but private. It is something whose enjoyment they share only with themselves, and perhaps a small coterie of studiously adoring friends. I have the same opinion about what I have called, in a more recent essay, "Non-Communicative Art." To put it as decently as I can, a habit which might be described as auto-erotic seems to have become fashionable among all the creative arts. It requires little skill or discipline, little social magnetism—anybody can do it—and so it has naturally accompanied "the revolt of the masses," the surging upward of untrained and uncultivated multitudes into regions once occupied by a class possessing the leisure for trained aesthetic perception and creation. This thought gives hope, at least, that when the masses have had time for a like training, the Cult of Unintelligibility and the reign of Non-Communicative Art will gradually come to an end.

I belong, of course, to a past generation, and the hypothesis that my views are merely antiquated has to be entertained. But the more I entertain it, the less convincing it becomes. I find, for instance, a sustaining place in the "modern tendency" occupied by William Empson's praise of what he calls "The Seven Types of Ambiguity." Empson finds ambiguities "beautiful." To me ambiguities are not beautiful, and that may indeed place me among the antique. But I also think that ambiguities are not *good*, and the point I occupy in time has little to do with that judgment. To my mind a habit of enjoying fuzzy images and conceptions, though it has furnished a handy avenue to a new and exclusive literary fashion, is a step down from our high inheritance from the ancient Greeks.

Another sustaining prop of the modern tendency is a frequent allusion to Freud's psychology. Freud's theory of unconscious motives and the psychoanalytic technique by which these can, over a period of weeks or months—and if the patient can afford it, years—be brought into consciousness, gives the modern poet an excuse for abandoning creative purpose, and making an esoteric art out of undirected speech. The notion that he gets some precious values up from the depths of him by this process is not sustained either by Freud's theory of what lurks in these depths, or by Freud's method of getting it up. In this maneuver the poet seems merely to be borrowing a little prestige from science. It is part of a general attempt these days "to make . . . the arts respectable by showing that they are semi-scientific." (I quote—to show there is no hard feeling—from Allen Tate.) And I add that Freud himself might fairly be described as semi-scientific, so thus the poets who borrow their respectability from him are doubly unconvincing.

But I forget . . . I was not writing *The Literary Mind* over again, but only saying I would like to. The book unfortunately is not a systematic treatise, but a series of essays composed in the by-paths of a life occupied with too many other things: wrestlings with dialectic materialism; defences of the "Soviet System"; lectures to the general public about its surpassing merits; warnings to insiders about Stalin's corruptions of it; and one other fantastic interruption of my proper life which I will describe in the next chapter.

Chapter 77

MY CAREER IN THE MOVIES

I have mentioned the shamefully great role played by chance in determining what I do with my life. If chance sets me down headed in a certain direction, I travel in that direction like a mechanical toy, with inward commotion and much apparent determination—but I could as well be going somewhere else. I do not refer to my opinions here, but only to what I do about them. I had hardly got started on my study of the relations between science and the arts—my real task in life, according to wise friends—when chance picked me up and set me off on a career in the moving pictures. It was an evil chance too, for besides absorbing a full year of my creative life, it involved me in a series of courtroom litigations which ate up my time in small mouthfuls intermittently for no less than twenty-four years.

In the late autumn of 1928, a young man named Herman Axelbank came to see me—a persuasive young man. He was broad and short, hairy enough so that his chin was always blue, and his skull, which he kept close-cropped, was so shaped as to give him—but for his eyes—a rather formidable appearance. His eyes were deep blue and warm, and could be very convincing of his nobility of spirit. And he had in his possession a thing of great value to mankind: a collection of all the important films, or most of them, that had been taken of momentous events and personalities in the Russian revolution. He had come down from the Bronx merely to ask me whether I thought a consecutive narrative could be made of them, but before we parted he had offered to give me complete editorial control, and split the profits fifty-fifty, if I could convert them into a "visible history" of the revolution.

Axelbank had himself arranged the film in a rough chronological sequence—the years at least were not mixed together—and the idea of making history visible was his own. He had a ray of imagination and a stubbornness of purpose which, if combined with an adult regard for the purposes of others, would comport with the idea of genius. Ever since 1920 he had been collecting these pictures with unflagging energy, ingenuity, a shrewd sense of historic values, and a matchless skill in getting what he wanted without losing anything he already had.

His proposal was that, besides supplying the technical knowledge, I should sort and cut and edit the films, and write the captions. In short, I should produce an authentic pictorial history of the Russian revolution—and incidentally, raise the money with which to do it. It was a large order, but I was foolhardy enough to show the films to Otto Kahn —our Lorenzo the Magnificent, as Horace Liveright called him—and he was generous enough to bind me to the job with a check for twelve thousand dollars. With some help from other excited sources, and a reckless promise from the eminent attorney, Arthur Garfield Hays, to "take care of the legal end of it," I was launched on my career in the movies—and the law courts.

Axelbank's offer to me dwindled considerably by the time we met in Art Hays's office to draw up a contract. My share of the profits had shrunk from 50 to 30 percent. Also, a brother-in-law was found to be in possession of the negatives and would need twenty-two hundred dollars before they could be released. Besides which he, Axelbank, must have an advance of one thousand dollars for the help he would give us in making the picture. We acceded meekly to all this—"we" meaning Eliena and I, Art Hays and Art Hays's cousin, Alan Hays, a keen-minded, generous-hearted youth who was as much caught up by the grandeur of the enterprise as we were.

The tale of our adventures in law and diplomacy, and what I may call psychological tightrope-walking, is too long and complicated for this book. "One goes to court with one lawsuit and comes back with two," the proverb says. And I add: "One goes with two and comes back with four," for that is the number we actually became involved in before the tale was ended.

It must suffice here to say that the contract was signed on the twenty-eighth day of February 1929, and after four months spent in rapturously tinkering with his films, Axelbank brought the collection to my house in Croton. I purchased a "moviola," and with Eliena as splicer and adviser on things Russian, and Axelbank as contact man with the film laboratories in New York, I actually made the film—in riotous contempt, I fear, of the fire laws—on our dining-room table.

By the end of August, I had it sufficiently shaped so that I knew what scenes I would need to complete it. I also knew that most of them could be found in the film laboratories of Pathé and Gaumont in Paris, or similar institutions in Berlin. By a lucky chance I was compelled just then, as guardian of my sister's two children, to make a trip to London. That brought it within my means to visit France and Germany, and I spent an exciting month hunting for those missing scenes. In Paris I found, among other things, the brilliantly strong picture of Lenin addressing the workers, which forms a high climax in the earlier half of our picture. I also called on Kerensky and induced him to let the noted photographer, Man Ray, make some motion pictures of him, and I sent Man Ray to Prinkipo where he made portraits of Trotsky in exile.

In Berlin I found a beautiful picture of the Tsarina walking up the aisle of a cathedral, and of the Tsarevitch feeding sugar to his pony. Of the Tsar himself, I found a sumptuous shot in which he strides down a carpeted stairway clothed in all the majesty of his sublime office, and one of him swimming in the royal pool, not clothed at all, naked of majesty, stark naked, shiny as an otter, which is certainly a unique contribution to pictorial history. That picture cost me a thousand dollars, which I raised by cable from a personal friend who had already contributed to our subsidy.

While in Berlin I found that Romain Rolland, my famous correspondent on the subject of revolution and the "intellectuals," was spending a night in the hotel where I stayed. I sent my name up and we had a fervent handshake and an hour together. He was still un-Stalinized, and our conversation was warm and friendly, but for some reason—my old shell of shyness, I suppose—we never touched upon the difference of opinion which had made our correspondence interesting. We did little more than take the measure of each other's presence—a thing that animals more poised than man can do without wiggly motions of their lips and tongue. The impression he made upon me was not unlike that of his unctuous "Declaration." His pear-shaped head with high unwrinkled dome, thin ash-blond mustache, and strangely colorless eyes set close under the brows, suggested the weakly drawn portrait of a saint. And to increase the impression of saintliness he wore the high black vest and round collar buttoned-at-the-back which gave notice to the world of some priestlike superiority. Although I liked him and was charmed by his cordiality, I came away feeling again crudely and assertively American—again thinking of Mark Twain, a greater novelist and as arrant a warrior against hypocrisy. Imagine Mark Twain dressing himself up in those self-righteous garments!

What I searched for in Berlin, more anxiously than for Lenin or the Tsar in swimming, was a newsreel shot of Stalin. For Axelbank had only five feet of him, standing in a crowd, rear view, shifting from one foot to another. Gaumont's Berlin representative told me I could probably find others at the film department of the Soviet Trade Delegation where they had a whole vault full of Russian newsreels. He gave me a card of introduction under an assumed name, and I spent an entire morning ransacking their film library in search of a picture with Stalin in it. Failing to find one, I asked the manager to telegraph Moscow, which he did, or said he did, and assured me that up to the funeral of Lenin no newsreel containing Stalin existed. So we redoubled our five-foot strip, and made Stalin shift from one foot to the other *twice*. That's all he does in our picture, but history is to blame, not I. Another important character in the revolution, Victor Chernov, head of the Social Revolutionary Party, was also missing among the newsreels, but he was living in New York, and when I got home I invited him up to Croton and Axelbank took his picture making a speech on our tennis court.

Owing to these cumulative needs and seekings, the film was not complete and ready for the market until January 1931. That was late, but not too late for a big success. Interest in the revolution was intense and still largely free-minded—not yet channeled and controlled by the remakers of history in the Kremlin. I mean that intelligent Americans were still permitted to remember that Trotsky organized the October insurrection and led the Red army to victory, and that Lenin was able to cross the street without help from Stalin.

Just here, however, the psycho-legalistic obstacles to our adventure began to pile up. The completed film belonged, you must understand, to Axelbank, who kept it in the vault at Lloyd's Film Storage on Seventh Avenue at Forty-ninth Street. You must also know that when I was paying him a salary of fifty dollars a week, as I had been during the making of the picture, Axelbank and I were very good friends. (He never offered a word in criticism of any editorial decision I made.) And now that the picture was done, he wanted my help—or agreed to accept my help—in putting it on the market. As he lived way uptown in the Bronx, we agreed that a mutual friend named "Ruby," who sold movie equipment in the same building with Lloyd's, should have the right to withdraw it from the vaults at my request. Ruby, whose real name was

Benjamin Rubenstein, was regarded with trust and affection by everybody who knew him—not only by Axelbank.

It happened that Charlie Chaplin spent some weeks in New York that winter, and as a step toward selling the film, I brought him over to Lloyd's projection room to see it. Charlie was still an unrivaled king in the movies then, and he was immensely impressed by our film. Discussing it next day with A. C. Blumenthal, he spoke so enthusiastically that Blumenthal, without seeing it himself, promised to distribute it for me. As A. C. was not only a man of enormous wealth, but also a large shareholder in Columbia Pictures, it looked as though our best hopes, if not even Axelbank's dreamed-of fortune, were coming within reach.

When Blumenthal saw the picture, he was even more enthusiastic than Charlie had been. He called me on the telephone, and renewed his promise to distribute it. As to how that should be done, however, he wanted to get the advice of Florenz Ziegfeld, and for that purpose requested my permission to take it over the week-end to his country home. We were dealing with the big shots now, and Ruby and I were more than delighted to grant his request. He asked us to take the films over to Columbia Pictures, nearby, and leave them for him.

By a diabolical mischance, Axelbank chose that moment to put on one of his disappearing acts. His wife had no idea where he was, and neither had anyone else. Recognizing the importance of the opportunity, Ruby and I together decided to withdraw the reels from Lloyd's and take them over to Columbia Pictures. But when they came out of the vaults, we found that Axelbank had placed them in three padlocked metal boxes and gone off with the keys. I was ready to give up, but Ruby, on his own responsibility, broke the locks, and took the films over to Columbia Pictures.

By another mischance, Axelbank chose that moment to reappear. He flew into a violent rage at Ruby, and stormed over to Columbia Pictures to demand from a frightened attendant the immediate return of his stolen films. On getting them back, he bought new locks for the boxes and refused with the stubbornness of a bronze mule to let Blumenthal, or Ziegfeld, or anybody else, have a look at them without a down payment in cash.

"If Blumenthal is serious, he ought to be glad to advance a couple of thousand" was his ultimatum.

It was the end of the good Ruby as mediator, and it was the end of Blumenthal's offer to distribute our film. He had never heard of

Axelbank's connection with it, and I never tried to explain the situation to him—it would take too long. Axelbank supplemented his ultimatum with the information that he himself was a distributor as well as a collector of films, and that he would put *Tzar to Lenin* on the market without help from anybody.

That was where things stood in the spring of 1931. I was finishing a book and was glad enough when Art and Alan Hays advised me to give Axelbank two years in which to try out his own grandiose ambition. After that we would move in court for the appointment of a receiver to hold the film and handle the marketing of it.

Toward the end of those two years, while dreaming of himself as the distributor of a film that would earn sums to be estimated in millions, Axelbank began to leak the actual film out in small private showings, for which he received sums like fifty dollars and eighty-three dollars—enough to pay some pressing personal obligation. For a like purpose he began to sell frames taken from the film as newly discovered portraits of the leading characters portrayed in it. That is where the lawsuits began, and lawsuits being what they are, it took us three more years to get *Tzar to Lenin* out of Axelbank's dream world into the world of reality where it could be put on the market and exhibited. In the end, Arthur Garfield Hays himself—whether as a generous friend or a public-spirited citizen, or both—spent an entire week in court presenting the situation in its psychological as well as legal terms to a judge with the patience to study it through. It was Judge Aldrich in the New York State Supreme Court in White Plains who had the acuity to discover that in giving into Axelbank's possession the films I had bought in Europe, I had not made them his property. Those parts of *Tzar to Lenin* belonged to me. Therefore, although I was not a partner under the terms of our contract, the making of the film had been in fact a "joint venture," and a receivership was the lawful solution of our dispute. His decision was rendered in the winter of 1936. Another year passed before *Tzar to Lenin* was presented to the public and my career in the movies reached its climax. But that story belongs in a later chapter of this book.

Chapter 78

ON THE EDGE OF THE RED DECADE

There were cracks and windows in the Communist boycott against me as the twenties came to a close. Eliena and I had good friends in Greenwich Village, and enjoyed many a swim in the ebbing tide of the irresponsible gaiety of the Jazz Age. The Communist Party itself was lonely enough in those years. Its dictates did not ray out with almost binding influence into the radical and liberal intelligentsia as they were to do in the thirties. Moreover, even in Russia the Trotsky-Stalin split was slow to reach its murderous extremes. Trotsky, in exile at Alma Ata, was still corresponding with his adherents in the Soviet Union in 1928. It was February 1929 before Stalin felt strong enough to push him out of the country. And this sharpening of the issue in Russia found its reflection among American radicals with a considerable time lag.

Joseph Freeman came often to Croton to visit his close friend Floyd Dell, and my meetings with him were not unfriendly. William Gropper and Hugo Gellert both moved up to Croton for a year or two, and they too were neighborly associates, although gravitating toward their future servitude. Things were still fluid enough so that Eisenstein, the famous Russian film director, came over with a friend to my house and sat like a vigorous schoolboy on my porch rail, talking of everything but politics. He wanted to have a look at me, I suppose, for I was a celebrity in Russia if not anywhere else. With Boris Pilnyak, the novelist, another famous visitor from Moscow, I had a friendly meeting in the home of Charmion von Wiegand and Herman Habicht on Macdougal Alley—a center of warm gay life that for a time became almost our home when Eliena and I came to the city. Only the strict active Communists, the party militants and finished bigots like Bob Minor, then regarded the barrier against me as absolute.

As late as January 1929, Eliena was working for the Russian

Amtorg, which was putting on in the Grand Central Palace a spectacular exhibition of Russian Arts and Handicrafts. The situation was fluid enough so that my name floated into the list of Americans to be honored with an invitation to its preview.

You will be keenly interested in the revelation of the amazing artistic wealth of the U.S.S.R. and, we trust, will also enjoy the musical program which will be provided for the occasion.

Looking forward to the pleasure of meeting you at the Exhibition, I am,

> Very truly yours,
> Saul G. Bron
> Chairman Board of Directors, Amtorg

Just before the date of the preview, I received another letter, which illustrates the situation I am describing: Soviet divisionism mingling in uncertain whirlpools with the general stream of social good fellowship in America:

My Dear Mr. Eastman,

A clerical error occurred in our office as a result of which an invitation was sent to you to the Special Opening of our Exposition.

We regret exceedingly that this error occurred and ask you to be kind enough to return the invitation to us.

> Very truly yours,

One bold and real revolutionist who crashed all the fences on arriving in America was Leonid Petrovich Serebriakov. Of small stature, but thick-set, calm and magnetic, a loved and trusted Bolshevik, he had been one of Stalin's predecessors as secretary of the party. He had bunked with Stalin in the civil war, being sent down to Tsaritsyn by Lenin with instructions, among other things—so he told me—to "keep that troublemaker quiet if you can." Although he did not entirely succeed in that, he smoked so many companionable cigarettes with Stalin, that, when the rest of the opposition leaders were arrested and exiled, he was merely sent off to New York as an unofficial appendage to the Soviet trade delegation. His job, as he explained it to me, was to stay away from Moscow. With a little more prudence he would have stayed away from me too, at least in public places, as every other visitor from Moscow did. But he was scornful of prudence.

"Look at my back," he said when I asked him why he came openly to our house or dined with us in popular restaurants. He stood up and turned round to show me the rigidity with which his backbone held his shoulders square.

"Does that look as if I could cringe?"

I remembered those words when in the show trial eight years later he recited a "confession" dictated to him at Stalin's bidding by Andrei Vishinsky. He made his recitation, according to Walter Duranty's news dispatch, "in a dreamy voice" that suggested he had been drugged. Drugged or not, I felt sure, after his confession, that no human organism exists which could withstand the technique of psychological breakdown invented by Stalin and his educated gangsters of the GPU.

In describing Serebriakov as my friend, I have not told quite the whole truth. He and Eliena were lovers, and though this brought us all three close together, I cannot say how warm his response would have been to my admiration alone, or how great a risk he would have taken to make friends with me. He was warm and tender, as well as sternly courageous, and I loved him almost as much as Eliena did. Moreover, I was happy in her "unfaithfulness," which gave a sort of parallel status to my own. She was getting up early to go to work at the time, and before sitting down to my desk I would wash the breakfast dishes and straighten up our little one-room apartment in back on Commerce Street. I wrote her a poem one morning which I think belongs in this book. I called it "Interlude."

You trembled when your lover came beside you;
You trembled as the April bird her wing.
Of all that may in mortal time betide you,
  That is the sweetest thing.

I cleaned our tranquil room for you this morning;
I pulled the purple deep shades very low.
The milkman's wheel will give you early warning.
  The neighbors will not know.

Some day perhaps when both our heads are whiter,
And our great friendship still is clear and true,
I will sit down in pride—I am a writer!—
  And type these words for you.

But now when love's pale fire has sanctified you,
And brought your burning lover to your breast,

Let no profane consent of mine divide you,
No blessing be expressed.

I must recall one more thing that Serebriakov said on the afternoon
when we discussed the risk he was taking in coming to our home. I
remember it almost verbatim:

"What difference does it make? Stalin will get us all in the end. He
will kill every single one of us who ever opposed him. He is the most
vindictive human being alive. You know what he said when they were
discussing the highest taste of bliss to be had in life: 'To get revenge on
an enemy and then go home and quietly to sleep.' That isn't a myth. It's
exactly what he said. Stalin will wait, if necessary a lifetime, for that
taste of bliss. And don't think you're immune because you're on the
other side of the planet. He'll never forget that you published Lenin's
blast against him. Some day, it may be thirty years from now, a very
disagreeable thing will happen to you, and you'll find, if you look
around, that Stalin is at the bottom of it."

That astonishing prediction came accurately true as we shall
see—not in thirty but in eight years. Every single one of the leading
Bolsheviks who had opposed Stalin was put to death, and as an incident
in the general massacre a very disagreeable thing did happen to me.

To those days before political lines were drawn too sharply, belongs a
friendship with Theodore Dreiser which had, by accident, a long,
wonderful and momentous consequence in my life. We met at an
evening party in Lawrence Langner's house, and being bored by the
rapid and vacuous chatter, retired together into an alcove to discuss in
more private detail a question which had arisen—that of contraception.
Our talk began solemnly enough, but ended in one of those gales of
foolish and almost hysterical laughter, which are among man's happiest
and most uniquely human delights. What the world really needs, we
decided, both for joy and procreation, is Fatherhood Insurance. Not
theft or fire, but unexpected fatherhood, is what makes life such a
hazard for the unprotected male. It was our duty, we realized, both to
our sex and to mankind—and we agreed to meet for the purpose at
ten-thirty the next morning—to found a Fatherhood Insurance Company. Shared laughter is a sure road to friendship, and TD and I were
friends forever after that evening.

A rumor exists, I am told, that he and I were hostile, but I cannot
imagine its origin. I received recently a letter from Charles Morrow

Wilson, once a close friend of Dreiser's, saying: "He held you in tremendously high regard. I never heard him speak more favorably of any man."

Well, we were both rebels—though we never quite got together as to what we were rebelling against. Our correspondence consisted mostly of efforts to bring each other into the same orbit. He urged me to write for the *American Spectator*, I urged him to sign statements in defense of the honest revolutionists whom Stalin was holding in jail. In 1931, when he went down to Harlan, Kentucky, to investigate labor conditions and arouse the public against a murderous persecution of the striking miners, he was arrested and accused of sleeping with a girl in his hotel room. His reply: "I couldn't have, I'm impotent," left the prosecutor and the magistrate—and indeed the whole country—speechless. I don't know who else in the world would have had the nerve to say it. I must have expressed my appreciation in a note, for I have his answer: "Dear Eastman, Thanks for your letter. You are the first, of all those I know, to get the real point I was trying to make."

It was sad news to me, more sad than his death, that in his last year Dreiser joined the Communist Party—a throwback perhaps to his Roman Catholic childhood, a loneliness. But it was no great surprise. I never admired him as a man of judgment. He was a man of passion, deep and commanding passion in a day when so many literary men were merely cerebral. That is how I thought of him, and even, as one loves a mountain, loved him. He was reckless of all rules and standards, reckless even of knowledge if it got in his way. I can see him standing, giantlike and uncouth, with harshly irregular features yet innocently brooding blue eyes, on the hearth in front of his fireplace guffawing at some critic of his style.

"He tells me I should use a conjunction instead of a relative clause. I don't know what a conjunction is. What the hell is a conjunction?"

That ignorance of, or superiority to, grammar really was his style, and like the similar style of Dostoyevsky, it caused the reader to believe absolutely in the truth of what he was laboring so hard to tell. He kept up a like superiority to science, although intrigued and fascinated by it. Scientific knowledge confined him; it pinned him down. He was a libertarian defender of superstition. One day in Charmion von Wiegand's house on Macdougal Alley, he got up and walked across the room with his fist doubled as though to knock me out when I made the innocent remark that, although the laws of probability confute it, we can't help feeling that there are such things as lucky days and streaks of luck. I was lounging in an armchair, and he came at me so ferociously that I got up, thinking to meet the attack on my feet. But he unclenched a finger before reaching me and only shook it angrily in my face.

"You and your scientific laws! Let me tell you something. There exists a man that I have seen just twice in my life but if I should pass that man on the street tomorrow morning, I would know as surely as anything science can tell me that some terrible misfortune is going to befall me!"

"What a world to live in!" I murmured. But again I admired and envied his passion.

Among my letters from Dreiser is one which reads:

Dear Eastman,
　　Thursday evening here at 9 a small and so intimate group which you and Eliena will like I think. My Scotch artist friend John Ferguson, now here for the first time, is coming, and Angna Enters. Also Boris Sokoloff and Mrs. Murray Crane. If you two are free, will you let me know? As they say in Chicago—howbow?
　　　　　　　　　　　　　　　　　Theodore Dreiser

If we joined that intimate group, it is gone from my memory, although John Ferguson was our good friend from the days in Antibes, and Angna Enters was climbing to her high fame as a painting dancer or dancing painter. But I shall never forget another group in which among the intimates were Margaret Monahan and her adopted daughter, Yvette Szekely. Yvette was in her late teens, half Hungarian and half French, lithe and dark-haired—dark-eyelashed, and her lashes curled upward from eyes sparkling with joyous interest in everything that was said. She was alluring to me in every smile and motion. I learned afterward that she was a dear and very special friend of TD's, but I did not know it then, and wished with unhindered longing that I were young enough to go to school with her. That thirty years later—after I had lost Eliena—she and I would be joyfully married was remote indeed from my dreams.

Chapter 79

VINEYARD SUMMERS

Martha's Vineyard, an island in the Atlantic, south of Cape Cod, is another love of mine that had its beginning on the edge of the Red Decade. It was in the summer of 1929 that Boardman and Sally Robinson, who had become our next-door neighbors in Croton, invited us for a week-end in their camping place, The Barn House, toward the rural west end of the island. The Barn House was a tiny tribe or colony of writing and painting and thinking folk who had bought a farm, and used its big barn for dining and being sociable, and for sleeping the rooms in its small house, and then the woodshed and chicken house, which they cleaned up and made over to hold a couple of beds and a washstand.

Stanley King, who on graduating from The Barn House became president of Amherst College, knocked me out in a game of cockfight on our first night there, I remember. And along with that I cherish an image of him on the beach in a pair of blue trunks, standing on his head for five consecutive minutes—an achievement never rivaled, I believe, by any other New England college president. I mean only to indicate that it was a gay as well as a thoughtful crowd at The Barn House, and a wonderful introduction to the island we were destined to love.

The focus of our love was a cottage farther along westerly toward Gay Head, a village which had been an Indian reservation, and was still dark-skinned and unassailed by tourists. The cottage we rented was a made-over sheep barn, equipped, by way of plumbing, with only a cistern and a kitchen pump. For the morning bath we would pour the soft cistern water over us from high white pitchers that stood on a bench outside the kitchen door. Humanly speaking, though open to the moors and the sunshine, those baths were private, for there was no other dwelling in sight except our landlady's modest farmhouse, which crouched behind a grove of trees-of-heaven on the other side of the cottage. For drinking water I would walk down every morning with a pail to the landlady's well a hundred yards away. For my work I had a little woodshed-study, and behind the trees-of-heaven there was a tiny one-car garage for Eliena to paint in. Besides painting, she was teaching Russian dances—which she had studied with Pavlova's partner, Mordkin—to the Indian children in the Gay Head town hall. And she was cooking our meals on an old rusty and smoke-blackened kerosene stove which grew steadily older and rustier and blacker for twelve years without ever provoking from her a word of reproach or complaint. Besides being Eliena, she was Russian, you must remember, and that senile stove was an improvement on the primus with which she had kept me well fed and flourishing in Sochi and Moscow. It could at least cook two things at once.

Please remember, then, while I tell you the rather lonely story of my struggle against the current of radical opinion in the Red Decade—the deaths and humiliations of our friends in Moscow, the ostracisms and literary frustrations here at home—remember that for three months of every summer in that decade Eliena and I were happy together on a quiet island, with a beach and a tennis court nearby, and friends who, although disapproving, were willing to overlook our sin of knowing the truth about Stalin, and play with us just the same. And remember that, wherever I dwelt, I had in the same house with me a wise counselor and a center-of-buoyancy like the earth itself—

> Her cool hard rocklike courage ever beside me,
> Her measureless wealth of tenderness never denied me. . . .

But I feel that any further praise of Eliena from me would be judged *ex parte*, and would seem like boasting. Instead I will quote a bouquet of paragraphs from his notebook that E. E. Cummings once made me a present of. In the first paragraph he is telling me, or reminding himself to tell me, what it was like to have his portrait painted by Eliena.

> describe to M my posing for Eliena (sitting
> on a chair on a dias in her tiny "studio"
> adjoining the garage) and she muttering
> things—only half to herself; half to me,
> to make me less grim and more cheerful (to

bring out of the posing effigy a myself) and
I heard E say something like "why don't you
feel like a swallow, who comes s-woo-ping up
into the sky, because she's so perfectly happy
because everything's wonderful and new,
because it's spring and she has her babies"
there (i tell M) is an artist—who feels what
IS; not merely spring but a bird, not merely a
bird but a mother & therefore all joy and all
mystery—
"she should have had children" says M tenderly
Well (i answer) i don't know: that i can't say or
gainsay. But of this I am more than sure—being
an artist, she has children without having them:
look, she is a bird; in spring: "with her babies"
—how (i continue) could you bribe a person like
that? If an ordinary person is poor, you can say
to him: do this, & I'll make you rich. But the
artist is rich while being poor!
O he's a terrible fellow, the artist
& E is he

"There's one poem of Jeffers" I tell Eliena "which
makes me feel worse than any of his others. A mob
of infrahuman dwarfs (our earliest ancestors) has
trapped a mammoth. They're yelling and capering
around the pit in which the huge great noble
creature flounders hopelessly, & they're putting
fire to him so he'll burn alive. That makes me
feel sick."
E's whole being flashes out—"yes" she exclaims
with ferocious indignation "we know that, we have
too much of that. But so what? For also we have
some people who are like you and me; they will put fire to
to themselves rather than to the beautiful creature: these
are the human beings; and they exist too! Why forget them?
Why leave them out?"
                         wonderful gal
The dancing at Gay Head's townhall (or some such structure)

delightfully informal. . . . When Eliena—as the "faun"—comes to after swooning, she does so with a rapt solar psychic vitality which lifts everybody in the house.

Extraordinary human being!

I must add that Eliena was also an extraordinary painter—not just in my prejudiced view, but in the general opinion. She painted sometimes almost in a classical manner, but usually in the free and beauty-guided style of the Impressionists. To me, in whom literary art consists so largely of deliberated purpose and impassioned effort, the ease and speed with which her love of life flowed out into a painting was a continual surprise. There was no problem of "representative" and "nonrepresentative"—just a conspiracy between her and a scene or subject to create a new thing of beauty. And besides being beautiful, her paintings were strong. If influences must be referred to, I suppose Jules Pascin would be the chief. He was our good friend, and once when he stayed for a time in George Biddle's studio in Croton, he and Eliena painted together, and each made a portrait of the other. Hers was not successful, but his picture of her is a treasure of grace and energy. To Eliena, as to me, his gift of "materializing" substantial creatures by the sole means of pearly light and shadow seemed almost a kind of magic, and I think it made a lasting impression on her. Eliena painted over seventy portraits. She had five successful one-man shows in New York, others in Paris, Boston, Guatemala City, and, of course, Martha's Vineyard. She earned the praise of the best critics and attained a celebrity that is still remembered among them. I think that if ambition had been as strong as love in her heart, she might have become quite a famous painter.

Our friendship with Cummings and his wife Marion Morehouse was gay and orchidlike. We had known Marion long before their marriage, when she was a fashion model and *Vanity Fair* published her picture as one of New York's four most beautiful women. It was through her that we met Cummings. By orchidlike I mean not only that our friendship was colorful and gay, but that it did not have roots in a deep community of conviction. On my side, much as I admired them and was exhilarated by their visits to us in the Sheepbarn cottage, there remained always something unspoken between us. I suppose I am a little fanatical in my zeal for the principle of human equality, not only before the law but before the bar of moral judgment. I recoil violently against any least hint or shadow of the suggestion of a validity in caste or class or race or color distinctions—group distinctions of any kind. I react inwardly as a puritan does against lewdness when someone takes for granted a superiority which rests on such distinctions. Marion and Cummings had no such "democratic" reluctances—Marion liked indeed to call herself a royalist. And I with my wish to avoid a clash would have to hush down my rabid feelings on such subjects.

Another topic unspoken of in our friendship was the cryptograms and punctuational pranks and acrobatic tricks of typography with which Cummings would adorn his books of poetry. Perhaps he was trying in this way to make his readers stop still, and give some attention—at last—to the qualities and interconnections of words. I don't know. At his best he is a great lyric poet, and you have to let him do what he wants to. I only know that when one has succeeded in extracting a few nuggets of poetry from one of his cryptographic clumps of words and syllables, there is little gleam left in them. The mood of hard work has expelled the mood of realization. At least that is what happens to me with all these moderns who, instead of inviting us to know and enjoy them, challenge us to understand them.

What made poignant our silence about this difference was the fact that I had been mirthfully disrespectful about it in *The Literary Mind*. I am sure that Cummings—or Estlin, for we called him by both names—had read my ironical praise of him as the contributor of new kinds of freedom to the Cult of Unintelligibility—the inventor, in fact, of "free punctuation."

"With all respect to his typographical genius," I had concluded, "he is a mere infant in the free art of punctuation. Why content oneself with meagerly redistributing a handful of tame signs, dried up, stale, and dead, and familiar to all Western European civilization for upwards of three thousand years. Can you wake a man up with an exclamation point that was known to his father and his grandfather and his great grandfather before him? Can you stop the modern breath with a colon that was a bore to Cleopatra? Let us have a little creative activity in these fields. A little cross-breeding between plus signs and semicolons would be a good beginning. By crossing the minus sign with the colon we got the sign of division; a cross between a plus sign and a semicolon might give us something even more remarkable. . . ."

That was my tone, and there was more of it. But Estlin never mentioned the subject, nor did I. Although he gave me, or gave us, an inscribed copy of every volume he published, I had not the courage in personal contact to approach his poems in the manner of an inspector general. They were not the fruits, I felt, but the essence of his individuality. Merely the way he carried himself, as though with a ramrod down his back, announced that that individuality was not to be impinged upon by so much as a question. My feeling about this was confirmed on the one occasion when I did summon the courage to ask him what he meant by one of his most impenetrable cryptograms.

"Don't you think it's pretty?" was all he said.

I do not mean to dismiss as cryptograms his disposition to play leapfrog and other acrobatic games with the parts of speech. All the little connective words and phrases that we don't pay much attention to were his intimate friends. And this trait of his verse was no affectation; it was an ever-present charm in his conversation. I remember once when I was driving to town, leaving him and Eliena and Marion sitting in lazy-legged chairs on the lawn, or what would have been the lawn if the Sheepbarn had one. The beds had not been made or the dishes washed and I said as I got in the car: "Now in my absence I want to see you children get something done!"

"How large is your absence, Max?" he said. "Are you sure there is room in there for us to do anything?"

He was the only person I ever knew in whose conversation fancy played a major role. Fancy is rare enough these days in poetry itself; in conversation it is all but nonexistent. Cummings would catch up some drab remark you made, or some phrase within the remark, and weave a sudden little fairy tale out of it—quite a long tale sometimes, like those of the brothers Grimm or Hans Andersen. In this as in all ways he was more unlike me than any other friend I held dear. A capering mind he had—sleek and rebellious like a kitten or a young kid. You couldn't argue with him; he would refute a point in logic by turning an intellectual somersault and coming up somewhere else. But underneath those quips and capers, and notwithstanding his fanatical individualism, and an irrepressible determination, after a few drinks, to shock the bourgeoisie and yet more the proletariat, with four-letter words, he was a gentle person, reverently concerned with life's deepest values.

Chapter 80

MY DOUBTS BEGIN

On March 29, 1930, addressing a luncheon of the Foreign Policy Association on "Present Trends in Russia," I voiced publicly for the first time a particle of doubt, a carefully limited particle, about the ultimate success of the Bolshevik experiment.

"I should describe the situation as highly satisfactory in the economic and cultural fields," I said, "unsatisfactory and fraught with extreme dangers in the field of politics in the narrow sense."

But I used up five sixths of my time telling how brightly everything was going along in culture and economics, and got cut off by the chairman before I was well started on my more critical conclusion. Lenin's party, I explained, combined the essential features of a professional association, a scientific society, an ethical brotherhood, an army, and a political party in the usual sense. I asserted that its composition and therefore its equilibrium in the general population was determined by drawing certain proportions from all the economic classes. Besides which, it was surrounded by a whole group of nonparty organizations that leaned upon it, and whose relations with it were adjusted "so subtly" that this party extended its roots clear down to the bottom layers of society. "By means of this altogether new political instrument, Lenin brought it to pass that when he seized the power and said he was seizing it in the name of the masses, he really *was* seizing it in the name of the masses, and although he held it in his single hand, all the powers of the world could not overthrow him."

All of that, which seems to me now an irreproachable ground plan for the enthronement of a tyrant, I described in a tone of eulogy, only adding in the tail of it a gentle word of doubt:

"This Communist Party now occupies a position in the Soviet society similar to that occupied by the Tsar under the old regime. The relation

545

of its members to the different classes of society, and more particularly their relation to each other within the party, is the essential political question. It is the question of the location of the sovereignty. It is just here that I think the political situation in the narrow sense is unsatisfactory."

That was as far as I got, but it seems clear now where I was going. The mystery is that it took me so long to get there. After describing Lenin's system of social engineering in such uncompromisingly practical terms, peeling off the last shred of metaphysical rubbish about historic dialectic and the "mission" of the proletariat, any free mind might have seen, I should suppose, that dictatorship was the inevitable outcome of it—that Stalin was to be regarded, not primarily as an enemy but a result. My mind was not free, however, from an eighteen-year commitment to the alluring concept of a world-cleansing revolution.

Perhaps if I had not done so many other things, I would have traveled more rapidly toward a thoughtful wisdom on this vital question. My thoughts were occupied elsewhere almost all the time. Those years, 1929 to 1931, were the most chaotically busy years of my life. Besides my lectures, and *The Literary Mind*, and *Tzar to Lenin*, I composed the sixty stanzas of my romantic idyll, "Swamp Maple," during those years. I collected, revised and published all of my lyrics that I thought worth preserving, calling the collection *Kinds of Love*, tempted by the idea that it would appeal to more readers than the book's proper title, *Swamp Maple and Other Poems*. It appealed to enough, at any rate, so that Scribner's sold out a first edition and made me known to the literary public as something besides a "Trotskyist." It was published in 1931, and in 1930 I lectured in twenty-eight cities from Brunswick, Maine, to San Diego, California, on subjects ranging from "The Russian Soul and the Bolsheviks," to "Why We Laugh Like Human Beings," and "The Art of Enjoying Poetry." I spoke in a four-cornered debate in Carnegie Hall with Harry Elmer Barnes, defending against Rabbi Stephen S. Wise and John Haynes Holmes the Soviet policy toward religion. America was in one of its epidemic fevers on that subject just then. The hall was jammed to the doors, and the crowds outside were paying seven dollars for tickets.

During that same period I functioned as the ringleader in getting together a little dinner and cocktail club in Greenwich Village called "The Meeting Place"—pursuing the quixotic dream of reviving in New York a haunt for the intelligentsia like the old time Civic Club or

"Polly's" of prewar fame. I functioned as Leon Trotsky's literary agent in the United States, a labor of love which involved an exchange between us of over 150 letters. I translated two of the three volumes of his *History of the Russian Revolution*, and supervised their publication in the English language. That this was not merely a quantitative achievement was best testified to by Trotsky himself who confided to me that his book is better in my translation than in the original—a remarkable statement from a man reputed to be so vain and egotistical.

"I am just now engaged in verifying the French translation with Perezhanine," he wrote, "and whenever he gets stubborn and insists that this or that 'cannot be rendered in a foreign tongue,' I answer: 'Let's see what Eastman did with that phrase.' In every case so far I have found in your text a maximal exactitude in rendering all the nuances of the original."

While propelling myself in all these directions I was steadily building up the reputation that has pursued me through life, of being, to quote a letter from my friend, James Henle, the head of the Vanguard Press, "the laziest man in the United States." He had suggested that I write a book about Wat Tyler, and when I replied that I was busy with other things, expressed his disappointment with this familiar observation.

One more considerable task that I performed during those same two busy years, was to prepare for the *Modern Library*, and edit with an introduction, a volume called *Capital and Other Writings by Karl Marx*. Bennett Cerf advanced me six hundred dollars on that book— and, by the way, has been paying me from two to five hundred a year ever since. He advanced me another six hundred on a contract we made for a similar edition of Lenin. But Eliena and I managed to spend both of these six hundreds before I so much as approached the second task. It involved an enormous amount of translation, and as it grew near we decided we had no room for it in our lives. We just couldn't tackle it. What could we do, then, about that almost equally enormous six hundred dollars which we had already spent? We were lying awake nights over this problem, when by chance Bennett and Max Schuster came to visit us on Martha's Vineyard for the week-end. While we were chatting together on the beach after a swim, Bennett began to say something hesitantly—an arresting phenomenon, for he has not a hesitating flow of thoughts. What he said was that since the split with the Trotskyists had grown so bitter, it would cost the firm "at least two thousand dollars" if I, instead of someone more orthodox, edited and introduced the works of Lenin. I tried to look pained and suggest without saying so that, in spite of political conjunctures, a contract is a contract.

"If you'll call it off, Max," he said finally, "I won't ask you to return the six hundred we advanced."

I agreed with a mournfully magnanimous expression, and I don't think Bennett ever guessed how glad I was.

Chapter 81

OUR KIND OF LOVE

Notwithstanding the doubts so hesitantly expressed to the Foreign Policy Association, I was in 1932 still keeping my faith in "scientific Marxism," and the super-democratic Soviet state which it enabled Lenin to build. Privately and in little esoteric meetings or publications I was warning against Stalin as an enemy of the faith, but in public lectures I was still defending the Soviet system and "explaining the Bolsheviks." Indeed I think I was, during those years, with the exception of Maurice Hindus, the most prominent pro-Soviet lecturer in the country. To convey the mood of my lectures, and also—more significant—that of my audiences in the early years of the Great Depression, I will quote a letter I wrote to Eliena from Texas, in January 1932.

It is incredible and could only happen in America: My speech was a complete exposition of communist theory—the word *communist* even being used in the discussion; an audience perfectly representative of the "elite," not only of the proletariat but of the capitalists, came to hear me—local officials, newspaper editors, Mike Hogg, the son of old Governor Hogg, who owns a large part of the state. They were all there, everybody, as I was advertised on the front pages as a great orator and everything else you like, including a "liberalist." I denounced America forty ways and held up Lenin and the Soviet system as the only way out, denounced religion too, in perfectly unqualified language. I was applauded and cheered. Only a single one-hundred percenter got up in the gallery and tried to attack me for "talking nothing but theories of government." I said: "Have you got anything against theories of government as such? If you have, you're a perfect example of these pro-

549

vincial American intellectuals that I am trying to educate!" And
I was applauded to the roof by the whole audience. The next day I
had lunch with Mike Hogg and a bunch of big business men in a
swell penthouse office up on top of a skyscraper. They told me they
all agreed with what I said about religion, and added that if I had
made that speech six, or even four years ago, I would have been
tarred and feathered and ridden out of town on a rail. . . .

Such was my political experience in the year of Roosevelt's inauguration. It has some bearing perhaps on the question whether he averted a
considerable upheaval in the United States. "They are all willing to
overthrow the government," I wrote, "if only for the pleasure of
watching Hoover slide off." But I was not serious those days about
American politics. My serious thoughts were about the economic
system, and I didn't think it mattered much whether Hoover or
Roosevelt was in the White House.

My playful thoughts I find expressed in another letter from Texas,
which will bring us back for a moment to the personal part of this story.
Eliena had forwarded a request from some organization for a public
statement on "The evils of prohibition from a psychological point of
view." I excused myself on the ground that I hated issuing statements
as much as I enjoyed taking a drink, and added:

> Down here in Texas they bring the whiskey down from the
> attic in tubs and pitchers and there is hardly any psychology to be
> found anywhere. They keep the whiskey in the attic because if
> anything happens they want to have the law on their side. I think
> they refer to the law of gravitation. Moreover last night my boy-
> hood dream—and everybody's—came true. Just as I laid my head
> down on the pillow, my host's slim, slanty-eyed daughter slid
> through a secret panel in the wall—she called it "the other door
> of the closet"—in shimmering topaz-golden pyjamas, and an-
> nounced that I was in her bed and she was going to get in too.
> You can't expect me to be psychological today. . .

Not many a husband could write a letter like that to his wife and be
sure she would smile. But Eliena had ways of writing to me that made it
easy on my side to trust our compact of independence.

"It's too bad you are not having any love-adventures up there."

"I went to tea with the tall girl who dreamed about you. I told her you were ready to go to bed with her if she wanted some more sweet dreams, and she said: 'Any time.'"

It is not good portraiture to quote, in isolation, these light-hearted remarks of Eliena's. They were only a froth on the surface of her letters, but they kept me assured that I could be as frank with her as I could with a man. Jack Reed wrote to Louise Bryant during a love-quarrel they had: "No one I love has ever been able to let me express myself fully, freely, and trust that expression." If Louise learned to do it, Jack was lucky, for he was a truth-teller by nature, and truth does not often mix in a perfect emulsion with love. Too many have to fall back on the assurance of Ovid:

> God in his Heaven laughs at the lies of lovers,
> Cancels, and bids the South Wind blow them away.*

In living with Eliena lies were unnecessary. So also were forced blushful truth-tellings. Our agreement was that we should confide our private experiences to each other or not, just as we chose. And for a professional lecturer to "advanced circles," this is important, for he has a good many such gifts and opportunities as the one I have just described. I can remember counting twelve in one journey of two months' duration.

I must say here that I am not offering the kind of love that flourished between Eliena and me as a model, or pretending that there can be a model, or any universal rules laid down, in such a matter. I merely assert that, with no more than the usual displays of selfishness and miseries of self-reproach, it did flourish. We were happy.

Eliena, by a lucky chance, was born happy. She woke up happy every day, and went to bed happy. It took some measurable sorrow or disaster to bring a sad look into her eyes. She had no kinship—I hope it is clear—with those meek or masochistic wives who assume that love consists intrinsically of suffering long rather than of being kind. She was proud. She reminded me more than once that she had left her former husband because "he wouldn't let her do enough for him," meaning that the too *motherous* girls who moved in and tried to take her place in our home were not welcome, no matter how enamored of them I might be. She made that very clear several times, and once expressed it quite alarmingly in one of the casual verses she was accustomed to jot down on scraps of paper in her studio.

* *Ars Amatoria*, I, 633–4. (It is my translation.)

> A sparkling laughing stream, whose rapid course
> Has been impeded by a fallen tree
> Will swell its waters at the lowest shore
> And seek another channel for its course;
> And so do I in my despondency
> Look for new gods to worship and adore.

Another possible misapprehension of Eliena, is that she was so generous toward my amours because she was sure of her own possession of me. She was not sure of that. It had not been so in the beginning when my demon was awake and I suppose he was always only sleeping. Indeed I have to confess that one day in 1930, on my return from a lecture trip in California, where I had enjoyed a rather collegiate visit with my old friend, Sid Wood, and his two teen-age daughters, that demon awoke again. I had to go into seclusion and "psychoanalyze myself"—by which I mean write down for confrontation my inmost thoughts, dreams, and wishful emotions—in order to free myself from his clutches. It took me a week, and Eliena meanwhile was again uncertain, for I had confided to her in bald terms the recoil against her which was devastating me. She knew why I had gone away.

No, it was not sureness of my love, but of her own firm stance on the earth that enabled Eliena to be so generous. She had courage, and she had confidence in her own genius for living—a confidence that was magnificently well founded. I used occasionally, aside from the lecture business, to go away on a trip for the pleasure of being alone, or being with someone else, or just being "away from home." I cannot remember an occasion on which, when I got back, I did not learn from the out-gushing chronicle of events and activities which greeted me, that she had been having "more fun" than I had while I was gone. She stood on her own feet, and her fund of interests and things to do was inexhaustible.

I too had a habit of jotting lines down on scraps of paper in my study, and here are some that I fixed up afterward and made into a sonnet:

> Although you care for me as would a mother,
> I love you as my child. I love to see
> You play all kinds of work so vividly
> And now-alive in them that not one other
> Creature except the earth, I think, ever
> Possessed so unconfined an energy
> Or was of fore-and-after fret more free—
> The earth or some full-channel mad June river.

I will not dim your kindled eyes, or smother
Your gay talk and mountain-brook-like laughter
With steads and purposes, this logic-bother
To drag my scattered parts through life so needed.
You are what I am only seeking after.
You are life's self, unargued, unimpeded.

Chapter 82

AN EXTRAVAGANT JOURNEY

If 1929 to 1931 were the busiest years of my life, 1932 was the most rich in outward experience. I fear I cannot explain why without speaking a little immodestly about my private fortunes. The truth is that while the rest of the country was in the depth of the Great Depression, I was, for the first time in my life, rich. I mean that I had upwards of four thousand dollars in the bank. To avert suspicion of larceny, I must explain this unprecedented opulence. In the first place, the publishers paid me a cent a word for my translation of Trotsky's three-volume history, and Trotsky added ten percent of his fees and royalties. His actual fee from the *Saturday Evening Post* for serial rights was forty-five thousand dollars, but half of that, as I have said, had been signed away to the Boni Brothers on his arrival in Turkey. Still, there was a big sum left. And then the Bonis—after a fracas with Trotsky, who denounced the contract as "an unheard-of robbery, made possible only by my ignorance of American conditions and customs"— sold the book rights to Simon and Schuster, and they made generous advances on the translation.* At the same time *The Literary Mind* was selling at a brisk if academic rate. I gave twenty-seven lectures during the fall and winter, 1931–32, and my lecture fees were mounting. I got five hundred dollars for my share in that theologico-political foursome in Carnegie Hall. Eliena's rare gifts as a painter and draughtsman were developing, and she was beginning to sell pictures. In short, we had so much money we didn't know what to do with it!

We decided to go to the Holy Land. It was part of a larger

---

* Trotsky, by the way, suggested an appeal to the "conscience" of the Boni Brothers to let him out of his contract, and I had to remind him that, according to his own gospel, there is no such organ in the anatomy of a capitalist corporation.

decision—indeed one of those momentous turning points in my life when I made up my mind, once and for all, to be a poet. I shall die wishing I had devoted myself to poetry and not let the political torrent wash me in. My feeling is opposite to that of Heine, who said: "Poetry, dearly as I have loved it, has always been to me but a divine plaything. I have never attached any great value to poetical fame; and I trouble myself very little whether people praise my verses or blame them. But lay on my coffin a sword; for I was a brave soldier in the Liberation War of humanity."

As a soldier in the liberation war of humanity, my bravest act was to confess that I had fought on the wrong side. As a poet I lacked self-confidence and resolution. I did, however, conceive a great poem, or series of poems: a retelling in vivid realism of the prodigious stories the Old Testament is full of. Much is said truly of the splendors of poetry to be found in that book, but its tiny epitomes of fiction, if unrolled and given room for their potential of suspense, would prove as wonderful. If told without superstition, and in terms of the lives actually lived by the Semitic tribes of the Near East at the time of their creation, they could also be made to carry a more life-enhancing morality than the pinched and negative one which they now expound.

This, then, was the mild ambition with which I set out for the Holy Land: I was going to rewrite the Bible! I had found one day in my bundle of "ideas for poems," which has pursued me through life, a slip of white paper on which was written: "Praise Lot's wife for looking back." That would be the subject of my first poem. But that would be only a beginning—"only one chapter, or one Song rather," as I wrote to a friend, "of a complete epico-philosophical rhymed Bible, in which I intend to tell the world everything that it needs to know. My poem will be made into a moving-picture serial—for by the time it is finished I will have the public educated up to this Unholy Bible—and the movie will be used in Sunday Schools instead of painted cards with velvet saints and angels on them to illustrate the obvious advantages of virtue when it is rightly understood."

The whole Western world, in my opinion, is full of suppressed indignation at having the surviving scraps of a thousand years of the superstitious literature of one small primitive tribe in Judea put over on them as the source of all moral wisdom and all access to Deity for the whole race of man. This, I suspect, is one main cause of the rancor against Jews with which this world is filled. I hoped that, by first telling the unvarnished story of this madman Lot and his wife and daughters, a story of sodomy, arson, treason, massacre, and incest, weeding out all the plush and elegance and patriarchal dignified virtue that sanctimonious sermons and stained-glass cathedral windows have infused into it, I would relieve my mind and blare forth my unreverent intentions. Then I could go ahead and unroll all the great story-plots, even the very wise and gentle ones, with honest historical and geographical realism. To do that, besides reading widely in the anthropology of Biblical times and regions, I had to see the regions. That was the prime reason why we spent our bewildering riches on a trip to the Holy Land.

But there were incidental objectives. I had been translating the third volume of Trotsky's *History of the Russian Revolution*, and I carried the proof sheets with me when we took ship for Paris in early June. In Paris we bought a Ford car, and had the windshield altered to lie flat down on the hood in sunny weather and let us enjoy the air. We were in no fevered haste to reach our ultimate objective—there were too many lures of pleasure along the way. One of these was Genevieve Taggard, writing poetry in a house by the sea in Mallorca, friendly to me now for a time, and eagerly inviting us to visit her. We examined that island thoroughly for two days and judged it a less fertile soil for poetry than Martha's Vineyard. Then we sailed back to Barcelona, and along the coast of the Mediterranean, pausing to gather emotions in our old haunts at Antibes, and through the Alpes-Maritimes to Italy. We left our car in Milan and took the train to Istanbul, arriving on July 6. The next day, after some hours in the time-hallowed cathedral at St. Sophia, and a view of the ancient city from an ancient vehicle, we got on the boat to Prinkipo island to pay our visit, long promised and supposedly of long duration, to Trotsky and his wife in exile.

Chapter 83 *

WITH TROTSKY IN PRINKIPO

Prinkipo is a small island in the Sea of Marmora, famous in the Middle Ages as a place of banishment, and later as a place of recreation, for very important people from Eastern Europe. Trotsky had rented one of the unoccupied villas on a seaward slope looking toward Istanbul, an hour or two away, as I remember it, by steamboat. As the villa was full of political adherents and secretaries, carrying on the immense work of literature and propaganda, from which Trotsky never took a rest, he had engaged a bedroom for Eliena and me in another villa a little way down the street. We came to his house only for meals, and evening and teatime arguments, and to start off fishing with him. But he welcomed us, and so did Natalia Ivanovna, as though we were the closest of friends.

Although Trotsky's eyes were a rather pale blue, reporters were always calling them black. Not only Frank Harris, with his genius for remembering what didn't quite happen, but John Reed, a keen and careful observer, made this mistake.

"To look at he is slight, of middle height, always striding somewhere. Above his high forehead is a shock of wavy black hair, his eyes behind thick glasses are dark and almost violent, and his mouth wears a perpetual sardonic expression. . . ."

So Reed described him in a dispatch from revolutionary Petrograd to the *Liberator*.

"There's something fatal about it," Trotsky commented. "Those black eyes figure in every description of me, although the eyes nature gave me are blue."

---

* Most of this chapter, although originally belonging here, was published as an essay in my *Great Companions, Critical Memoirs of Some Famous Friends*. It is here republished with the permission of Farrar, Straus & Company, and of Collier Books.

I for my part can testify that in Prinkipo in 1932, nothing less dark or violent was to be seen on the horizon than Trotsky's pale blue eyes. His mouth, in repose, might almost be described as cherubic. He could *be* sardonic; he could cause an oratorical opponent to shrivel in the air with a single shaft of sarcastic logic. This seemed a black art, and its Mephistophelian character was emphasized by that wavy black hair and a short pointed goatee. But it was a spiritual, not a physical, attribute.

Eliena and I spent twelve days with Trotsky and his wife and retinue of bodyguards and secretaries on Prinkipo island. It was there that he and I got really acquainted. It was not on my side a pleasant process—or rather it was pleasant while superficial, but harshly unpleasant as the acquaintance deepened. This was no great surprise to me, for although I took Trotsky's side in the conflict with Stalin, and do not see how any understanding mind could have failed to, I was far from enamored of him personally. I hero-worshipped him and do still, especially after reading Isaac Deutscher's glowing account of his revolutionary deeds,* but I did not, even in Moscow while writing my own little portrait, feel any affection for him. I used to say this frequently when coming home to Eliena Vassilyevna after a conversation with him at the War Office, but I could not explain why. He was not egotistical; he was forever wandering from the main subject to expatiate with thoughtful penetration about the lives and qualities of his friends. Yet to me he was not a friend. With all those intimate talks about his infancy and youth—about all infancy and youth, all growing into life and grasping it—we never came together. Therefore it was not with happy excitement, but with an under-feeling of reluctance, that I accepted in 1932 his urgent invitation to "come and spend several weeks with us in Prinkipo, and we'll work and go fishing together."

Although it happened twenty-five years ago, my impressions of Trotsky at the time of that visit are entirely fresh for I wrote them down and saved them. I wrote them at two separate times: one in the evening after the first three days, the other on the train to Jerusalem the morning I left.

I. *After Three Days*

Trotsky seems the most modest and self-forgetful of all the famous men I have known. He never boasts; he never speaks of himself or his

* I refer to the first volume of his biography, *The Prophet Armed.*

achievements; he never monopolizes the conversation. He gives his attention freely and wholly to anything that happens or comes up. With all the weight of world-wide slander and misrepresentation he struggles under today, the peculiar position he occupies, he has not so far breathed a syllable suggestive of preoccupation with himself or even the ordinary quite human touchiness that might be expected. As we work on his book, if I pay him a compliment, he says some little thing—"I am glad"—and then passes hastily to another subject. I agree with Lunacharsky after all, although I did not when I came here, that there is "not a drop of vanity in him."

Like all the great men I have met he does not seem altogether robust—not altogether masculine. There is a frailty associated with great intellect. I wonder about Lenin. But Trotsky, especially in our heated arguments concerning the "dialectic," in which he becomes excited and wrathful to the point of losing his breath, seems to me at times almost weak. He seems too small for the struggle. He cannot laugh at my attacks on his philosophy, or be curious about them—as I imagine Lenin would—because in that field he is not sure of himself. He is not strongly based. I get the impression of a man in unstable equilibrium because of the mountain of ability and understanding that he has to carry. In what is he unequal to the load? In self-confidence? Is it the Jew's inferiority complex after all? Is it that he has never played, never loafed and invited his soul, or observed that the sunshine is good whatever happens? When I remarked that fishing with a dragnet is interesting work, but not a sport, he said:

"Two pluses—it is interesting and it is work! What more can you ask?"

I wonder if that is the mood in which he will go fishing—intense, speedy, systematic, organized for success, much as he went to Kazan to defeat the White armies.

He seems to me oversure of everything he believes. I suppose that is what Lenin meant in his testament when he warned the party against Trotsky's "excessive self-confidence." But I suspect that his weaker point as a political leader would be that when that cocksureness breaks down he is nonplused. He does not know how to cherish a doubt, how to speculate. Between us, at least, to *confer* is out of the question.

His magnanimity, his freedom from anything like rancor, is amazing. I see it in his portrayal of his enemies, but also in smaller things. Yesterday we reached a point of tension in our argument about the dialectic that was extreme. Trotsky's throat was throbbing and his face was red; he was in a rage. His wife was worried, evidently, and when we left the tea table and went into his study still fighting, she came in after us and stood there above and beside me like a statue, silent and austere. I understood what she meant and said, after a long hot speech from him: "Well, let's lay aside this subject and go to work on the book."

"As much as you like!" he jerked out, and snapped up the manuscript.

I began reading the translation and he following me, as usual, in the Russian text. I had not read three sentences when he suddenly, to my complete surprise, dropped the manuscript and, looking up like an excited child proposing a new game, said: "I have an idea. What do you say you and I together write a drama of the American Civil War!"

"Fine!" I said, trying to catch my breath.

"You see we would each bring something to it that the other lacks. You have a literary gift that I lack, and I could supply a factual knowledge of what a civil war is like!"

This man has the childlike charm of an artist. Perhaps my feeling of his weakness, of his being inadequate to his load, derives from the fact that his character as a man of action is the result of self-discipline and not of instinct. He has made out of himself something more, or at least other, than he is. I do not know. I merely record these two, or rather, three impressions: an utter absence of egotism, instinctive magnanimity, and something like weakness, as of a man overburdened with his own great strength.

II. *Ten Days Later*

It is fortunate that I recorded the above impressions immediately, for now, after twelve days in Trotsky's home, my mood has changed to such an extent that I could hardly write them down. I feel "injured" by his total inward indifference to my opinions, my interests, my existence. There has been no meeting either of our minds or feelings. He has never asked me a question. He has answered all my questions as a book would answer them, without interchange, without assuming the possibility of mutual growth. My pointed criticisms of his policy—that he has not thought out the implications of the national problem on a world scale, that he never should have let Stalin make "socialism in one country" the issue, thus jockeying him into the defense of a negative slogan— were met with mere dogmatic lordly-hasty rejection. I was an amateurish creature needing to be informed of the technical truth which dwelt in his mind.

On the disputed question of Trotsky's "vanity," I still agree with Lunacharsky. His failing is subtler than that and more disastrous. He lives instinctively in a world in which other persons (except in the mass or as classes) do not count. In youth he stood so prodigiously high above his companions in brain, speech, and capacity for action, that he never formed the habit of inquiring—he was always telling. *His* knowledge and true knowledge, *his* view and the right view, were identical. There is no bragging or vanity in this, no preoccupation with himself. Trotsky is preoccupied with ideas and the world, but they are his own ideas and his own view of the world. People therefore, who do not adulate, go away from Trotsky feeling belittled. Either that, or they go away indignant, as I am.

Opinionated minds are usually far from wise; Trotsky is opinionated in the highest degree, but with wise opinions. Cranky people are usually old and barren of fruit; Trotsky is cranky, but young and fruitful.

I want to dwell on the manner in which his arrogance differs from vanity, or self-centered egotism. It is not a conscious thought, but an unconscious assumption that he *knows*, that he is the truth, that other people are to be judged and instructed. It is a postulate laid down in his childhood, as I said, and by his instincts. That, I now suspect, is why he is weak and indecisive and lacks judgment, when frustrated. That is why he became almost hysterical when I parried with ease the crude clichés he employed to defend the notion of dialectic evolution. The idea of meeting my mind, of "talking it over" as with an equal, could not occur to him. He was lost. Similarly, in the party crisis when the flood of slander overflowed him, he was lost. He never made one move after Stalin attacked him that was not from the standpoint of tactics a blunder. Trotsky is much concerned with the task life imposes of making decisions. He told me once that in youth he passed through a period when he thought he was mentally sick because he could never make up his mind about anything, but as commander of the Red army he often astonished himself by the prompt assurance with which he gave orders to generals and colonels trained for a lifetime in military science.

It was in revolt against an inferior father's stubborn will that Trotsky developed the "excessive self-confidence" that Lenin warned against. What he needed, when that self-confidence cracked, was a father—an authority to defer to. That is what Lenin supplied. If you read Trotsky's *History of the Russian Revolution* carefully—as carefully as I, the translator, did—you will find that, although he praises others, he never attributes fundamental importance, either of initiative or judgment, to any Bolshevik but Lenin and himself. (That comes near, I must say, to being the objective truth about the October revolution, yet I think a diligent search might have discovered exceptions.)

Trotsky's idea of our collaborating on a play was, he confessed later, merely a scheme for making money. He is spending one thousand dollars a month according to his wife—his secretary tells me it is nearer fifteen hundred—keeping up the establishment he has founded here and in Berlin. There is here in Prinkipo, besides the secretary and stenographers, a bodyguard of three proletarians, one continually on sentry duty at the door; there is another secretary in Berlin, an ingenious system for transporting books from the library there, and getting them back on time. Besides that Trotsky is supporting a sick daughter and her child in Prague. He does not live in luxury; there is practically no furniture in his villa; it is a barrack; and the food is simple to an extreme. He merely keeps up the habits of a war minister after he has become the leader of a tiny proletarian party. His secretary, Jan Fraenkel, confided to me his anxiety approaching despair because Trotsky, still living like a Commissar, ignored completely the problem of financing his new party and his own gigantic labors. This was not a newly developed trait in Trotsky; he was always, even in his poverty-stricken days in Paris or the Bronx, incapable of hanging on to his earnings. Even the small change in his pocket would dribble away, thanks usually to some transparent form of *chantage*, in the course of a short walk down the street. In his present situation, however, it was a calamity, for it made him overestimate the revolutionary integrity of certain dubious characters who chipped in generously to the ever-dwindling treasury of his Fourth International. Money, of course, is beneath the contempt of a revolutionary idealist—gold, according to Lenin, was to be used for public urinals in the socialist society—but while we are on the way there it deserves a little steady attention.

The lack of comfort or beauty in Trotsky's house, the absence of any least attempt to cultivate the art of life in its perceptual aspect, seems sadly regrettable to me. A man and woman must be almost dead aesthetically to live in that bare barrack, which a very few dollars would convert into a charming home. The center of both floors of the house is a vast hall—not a hall exactly, but a room twenty feet long and fifteen wide with great double doors opening on a balcony which looks outward to the richly deep-blue sea and downward to this bright red-cliffed island that lies down beside the sea like a prehistoric animal drinking. In these vast rooms and on these balconies there is not an article of furniture—not even a chair! They are mere gangways, and the doors to the rooms on each side are closed. In each of these rooms someone has an office table or a bed, or both, and a chair to go with it. One of them, downstairs, very small and square and white-walled, with barely space for table and chairs, is the dining room. The garden surrounding the villa is abandoned to weeds and these are running to seed. To save money, Natalia Ivanovna explains. Through sheer indifference to beauty, I should say. Trotsky talks a good deal about art in his books, and lays claim to a cultivated taste, but he shows no more interest in art than in that garden. I brought home one day from Istanbul photographs of the rarely beautiful sarcophagus of King Tobuit of Sidon that is in the Museum of Antiquities.

"Do you want to see one of the most beautiful works of sculpture in the world?" I said to Trotsky.

He grasped them hastily, and handed them back to me almost with the same gesture. "Where were they found?"

"They were dug up in the ruins of Sidon."

"Who dug them up—Schliemann?" I said "No . . . " but by that time he was out of the door and on his way down to dinner.

His sole reaction had been, it seemed to me, to avail himself of the chance to reveal his acquaintance with the name of Schliemann. At least he had no interest whatever in the sculpture.

Although it is not so in his books, he seems in personal life to lack altogether the gift of appreciation. I think it is because no one ever feels appreciated by him that he fails so flatly as a political leader. He could no more build a party than a hen could build a house. With all his charming courtesy, and fulfillment of every rule of good manners, including a sometimes quite surprising attentiveness to one's comfort, his social gift, his gift of friendship, is actually about on the level of a barnyard fowl. His followers, the followers of the great brain, make pilgrimages to him, and they come away, not warmed and kindled, but chilled and inhibited. Those of them, that is, who have individual will and judgment of their own. Hence he has no *influence*, properly so called. He does not sway strong people but merely directs the weak.

Trotsky is playful, and proud of being so, but I notice that his humor consists almost exclusively of banter. A perpetual poking of fun at the peculiarities of others, their nationality, their profession, their circumstances or tendencies—good-natured, smiling and charming fun, to be sure, but not varied with an occasional smile at himself, or any genial recognition of the funny plight of mankind in general. And when you take part in the game, when you poke fun at him, he does not laugh, and his smile is never so cordial as when he himself lands a blow. I feel it is a little mean and picayune to make this hypercritical observation of Trotsky at play, for he can be delightful indeed if you are firm enough on your own feet to accept his banter and give it back, but as a student of laughter—and of Trotsky—I can't refrain. To me it is all the more significant since it is a superficial trait.

As to his angularity, his cocksure terseness, that quality which led Lunacharsky to describe him as "prickly," I could not honestly be silent. It is a failure of instinctive regard for the pride of others, a lamentable trait in one whose own pride is so touchy. But he also disregards, when his own schemes are involved, the personal interests of others. And he is not forthright about it; he is devious even with his friends. As Trotsky's gift for alienating people has a certain historic importance, I am going to set down here the otherwise rather inconsequential details of an episode which alienated me.

I had functioned for some time as a sort of unofficial literary agent for Trotsky in the United States. I got my pay in royalties in the end; I am not pretending to be extravagantly generous; but I did when he first arrived in exile quite a mountain of unpaid work for Trotsky. In the fall of 1931, however, he sent me an article to translate and sell for him, offering me 20 percent of what I got for it. He said he hoped for a large sum, as much perhaps as two hundred dollars. I translated it and took it to George Bye, a popular literary agent, who sold it to *Liberty* magazine for fifteen hundred dollars. Of this George took 10 percent for the sale, and I 10 percent for the translation. This seemed not quite fair, and George, who is very generous, agreed in the case of future articles to let me have 15 percent for the translation and take only 5 percent for the sale. This arrangement was reported to Trotsky; we sold two or three more of his articles; and he was delighted.

All went well until an article about Stalin arrived while I was absent on a lecture trip and the translation was delayed a few weeks. During those weeks Trotsky, impelled by his book publishers to give an interview to the press, gave out the substance of the article. After that it could not be sold at a high price, but George persuaded the *New York Times* syndicate to pay one hundred dollars for it and give it the wide publicity that Trotsky, whatever the money payment, so much desired.

The delay, and the small fee, and his own costly mistake in giving out the interview, irritated Trotsky beyond measure. He decided to throw me over and deal directly with George Bye, trusting him to find a translator. I suspected this because a long letter from George was lying on his desk the day I arrived in Prinkipo. I said nothing about it, but noticed the next morning that the letter was gone. As he had never heard of George Bye or had anything to do with him except through me, this piqued my curiosity, and at the risk of impoliteness, I decided I would force him to be frank. To my seemingly casual question about the letter I had seen, he answered nervously; "Oh yes, when you told me you were going to Palestine and might not come to see me until afterward, I thought it might be best to get in touch with the agent directly."

I said: "It is all right for you to deal with George Bye directly if you want to, but please remember that I have a contract with him giving me 5 percent of his commission, and if you deal directly with him without mentioning this, it will deprive me of a part of my earnings."

He was not impelled either by friendship, or by a recognition of my many unpaid services, to make any response to this. He was angry about that Stalin article. I was by this time heartily pleased with the prospect of not being interrupted every week or so with a too-long article to translate, but I ventured to remind him that George Bye did not have a Russian translator at his elbow. He merely said very sharply:

"No, it is absolutely impossible when you are traveling around Europe. The fate of that Stalin article showed me how impossible it is. I prefer to deal directly with a responsible agent."

My breath was taken away by the harsh, irascible tone in which he said this. If I had been at home when the Stalin article came, and had translated and sold it immediately—say to *Liberty*—for a high price, it would have been in print and ready to publish when he gave away the substance of it to the press. The result would have been an explosion in the editorial rooms and a refusal to have anything to do with "Trotsky articles" in the future. I tried to say this, but he cut me off again sharply.

"No! Such delays are impossible. It is quite impossible to have the translator in one place and the agent in another."

In short, I was fired—and being in my heart mighty glad of it, I took it in silence, and we changed the subject.

We both loved languages, and one of our pleasantest diversions was for him to dictate to me in his horrendous English answers to his American and British correspondents, which I would take home and bring back the next day polished off and typed on my portable machine. That same afternoon he drew out an illiterate inquiry from some woman in Ohio about her relatives in Russia, asking me if I knew who she was. When I answered no, he said: "I guess there's no use answering." I agreed and crumpled the letter, or started to crumple and throw it in the wastepaper basket, but he stopped me with an outcry as though I were stepping on a baby's face.

"Is that the way you treat your correspondence? What kind of a man are you? That letter must be filed!"

I straightened the letter out, laughing at my mistake, and passed it over to him, remarking, however, that it didn't seem to me very important to file a letter that wasn't worth answering.

There followed a certain amount of playful banter on that subject, and we went on with our fun, entirely friendly and good-natured.

The next day, however, I got to worrying, as everybody in the household did, about Trotsky's money problems. (In that respect, at least, he was a faithful follower of Karl Marx.) Realizing that if he sent articles to George Bye to be translated by anybody with a Russian accent who came along, he would spoil his last chance of getting the needed fifteen hundred dollars monthly out of the American press, I ventured to raise again that question on which he had been so crisp. (Trotsky was a hero, you must remember, and moreover he had been through such nerve-shattering experiences at the hands of the implacable avenger of excellence, Stalin, that no one could hold a grudge against him.)

"I feel a little embarrassed to resist you in this matter," I said, "because my own financial interests seem to be involved, but I can't help warning you that if you leave to a commercial agent the choice of a translator, you can easily lose in a month the position you've gained as a writer available to the American press. Of course you can get statements on questions of the day published, because you are Leon Trotsky, but that is a different thing from being a highly paid contributor to American magazines."

That was, at least, what I set out to say, but he interrupted me halfway through with an exclamation impatiently snapped out: "No, no! I prefer not to send my articles to a man who grabs up his correspondence and throws it in the wastebasket!"

He imitated my gesture of the day before, but now without playfulness. He was still angry, I suppose, about the low price he got for that Stalin article. You would have to have in your memory, as I had, the painstaking drudgery of my two years' effort to protect his financial interests and teach him to get what was coming to him from the American press, to appreciate my indignation. Had he been any-body but Leon Trotsky, I would have given a red-hot expression to it and walked out.

Instead, I sat still until there came a brilliant inspiration. It was one of those few times in my life when I thought of exactly the right thing to say.

"Lyef Davidovich, I can only answer you in the words of Lenin," I said, and quoted, in perfect Russian, from the famous Testament: " 'Comrade Trotsky is apt to be too much carried away by the administrative aspect of things.' "

At this Trotsky relaxed and dropped back into his chair, laughing genially and completely, as though to say, *"Touché!"*

In a moment, however, he was forward and at it again, insisting now that I had been negligent about other articles—"the one on Hitler, for example." This was an article that, after several high-paying magazines refused it, George had finally sold to the *Forum* for three hundred dollars. There was nothing else to do with it and nobody was to blame.

At that point I gave up. Repeating once, and more insistently, my warning that a single article published prominently in the usual bad translation might ruin his chances, I added that I would let him know as soon as I was settled somewhere, and he might send me his articles or not, as he pleased. What he will do I have no idea, but that he will do anything out of consideration for my interests, or my legitimate stake in the enterprise, I regard as *ausgeschlossen.*

By "gave up" I mean that I abandoned the attempt at friendly conversation with Trotsky. I abandoned it about practical, as I had previously about theoretical, questions. I got away as quickly as I politely could, pleading the need to get back to the West in time to correct the page proofs of the third volume of his history. To the end Trotsky kept insisting that we stay for several months—so that he and I might continue to "work together and go fishing." He was, so far as

I could judge, blandly oblivious to the unwarmth and unfruitfulness of our relation.

On my way home from Prinkipo, I met in Paris Alfred Rosmer, one of Trotsky's closest friends—the closest, I think, after Christian Rakovsky—and we spoke of the subtle contradictions in Trotsky's character. To my hesitant and groping effort to say that he seemed to me to lack a feeling for others as individuals, his friend said shortly:

"*C'est tout-à-fait vrai. Il n'a pas d'humanité. Elle lui manque absolument.*"

Notwithstanding this startlingly extreme confirmation of my impression, I feel that I left out of my memorandum something which, in justice to Trotsky, ought to have been included; a confession, namely, of my own failure of regard for the interests—indeed the most vital passions—of another. It was far from tactful of me to descend upon this intellectually lonely exile with a headful of fresh hot arguments against the religious belief by which he had guided his life to triumph and to this tragic end. It must have put him on edge against me. Perhaps that underlay some of the responses which I attributed to more trivial causes and to the general traits of his character. I find in our subsequent correspondence a letter in which, as though to heal an unmentioned wound, he took pains to mention that he had sent a certain manuscript direct to George Bye only because he had been given to understand that I was away from home.

I think Trotsky earnestly wanted to be regardful of the interests of others, but except in small matters and in the case of his wife, toward whom the most exquisite consideration was unfailing, he did not know how to do it. He lacked the gift of mutuality. He could apprehend, and discuss at times with keen penetration, the currents of emotion prevailing in other people, but he could not flow with them in a warm common stream.

Chapter 84

IN A SPANISH DUNGEON

We were on the train from Istanbul headed for Beirut when I scribbled down, in conscientious haste, those final impressions of our famous host. As I folded them away and forgot them, I folded away the revolution also for a time. I was a poet of history now, and my task was to see and feel. I must get the actual colors and smells of the surroundings of the life lived by those Biblical characters whom I intended to lift down from their stained-glass-window elegance and bring to earthy and honest life. It was a disturbing and thrilling experience. I grew up going to church and Sunday School, and the very names of the places in Palestine carried a sacred flavor, not remote in my mind from the flavor of unreality. To get out on a pond called "Sea of Galilee" in a squeaky-oared old rowboat, to dip my hand in a small weedy stream called "River Jordan" less lovely than the "crick" I used to fish in when I was a kid, to hail a taxi at the gates of Gethsemane and nip over to Bethlehem in less than a quarter of an hour, was a rather soul-bleaching experience. It increased, however, my sense of the validity of the thing I had set out to do to: the Bible. And to find Christ, even in the stable in Bethlehem where he is alleged to have been born, supplied with a swanky manger of marble, increased my contempt for the motivations of the devout to such an extent that "Lot's Wife" became more violently and vulgarly realistic, if that is possible, than it had set out to be. In general, the manner in which a supposedly worshipful Christendom has tricked out the remembrance points of the tender and spirited legend of its religion makes the human race seem vulgar beyond redemption. A rather penurious "conspicuous consumption" would seem to have been, judging by the behavior of his tourist-disciples, the essence of the gospel of Jesus.

But this is not a travelogue, and I must content myself with mentioning the high points of our journey until we got back to Spain, where an event occurred startling enough to belong in an autobiography. We spent the night on Mount Lebanon with my friend Ameen Rihani, Syrian poet and patriot, whom I had known in the old, old days in New York. We traveled through Palestine lengthways and crossways in a touring car with the top down under an August sun, visiting Tel Aviv, the Plains of Esdraelon, spending the night at a co-operative farm with some friends of the old *Masses*; we examined the relics of Solomon's palace, the ruins of Jericho, swam—or rather floated like helpless corks—in the Dead Sea, located Sodom as best we could, and the "stumps of salt" where Lot's wife died for looking back. We spent ten days in Palestine, and since that country is only sixty miles wide and one hundred and forty miles long—about the size of the state of Vermont—I think I may boast that my purpose, to fill my eyes with it, was adequately accomplished. I tried hard not to be political, and but for an irresistibly instructive evening with Hans Kohn in Jerusalem, and a rhymed reflection on the problem of Zionism, which I called "The Much Promised Land," I succeeded pretty well. Although I do not believe in Zionism and think it has been a disaster to the world, I was swept along, I remember, by the pervasive happiness, the plump and healthy happiness, of those Jews who, by swarming into their "homeland," were driving the Arabs out of their homes. Jews when gathered together had always until then conveyed to me an impression of sadness. Here on their Sabbath they thronged gaily along the streets of Jerusalem as though just to be alive was a picnic.

To complete my Old Testament imagery, I had to have a glimpse of Egypt, and from Palestine we took the train for Cairo. We visited the Sphinx and the Pyramid of Cheops on camel-back at high noon with the July temperature around 140° in the shade—gaily, for we were almost Arabs by that time both in color and constitution. And we spent four days beside the Nile, most of them in the museum of Egyptian art, subdued to a tragic wonder about the mystery of being and nonbeing by those rigid figures gazing at us out of the remote past, so sternly bent on immortality. They made me wonder, also, what causes determine the unique styles of art developed by different peoples. Is it some prevailing trait in each one's character not common to the human race? That seems unlikely. Is it, then, in spite of all the learned talk, an accident or a series of accidents? Did some painting, or some piece of sculpture happen by chance to possess a trait that became popular, and the whole thing follow, not through discriminative taste, but through loyalty to an accidentally established convention?

On August 2, we returned by train to Haifa, then north by car past Acre, Mount Carmel, Tyre and Sidon, back to Beirut, and from there by boat to Italy. We stopped at Cyprus long enough to go down the shore and take a nude swim where we decided Venus had risen from the sea. We by-passed Athens because I love it too much. I wanted to keep distinct among my images of ancient history the birth-home of the Bible. Picking up our Ford car again in Milan, we made our way back to Spain where the colors of the earth and the gaiety and cordiality of the people had so captivated us. King Alfonso had departed without abdicating and been replaced by a revolutionary republic in the previous year. The republic had recognized the autonomy of Catalonia just before we came. It was a time of peaceful popular revolution; perhaps that is why the people seemed so gay and cordial. At any rate, I found Spain in that republican interval between De Rivera and Franco so delightful a place that I felt like staying there and becoming a Spaniard.

Going over the border from France into Spain in the evening is like coming out of a cave into the light. The streets of the typical French village are deserted as though stricken with the plague, and all the houses locked tight, so that no ray of light escapes through a crack, by about seven-thirty or eight—a dismal state of affairs associated with the saddest moments of childhood, and attributable rather to the fear of spending money, I suspect, than to a distracted love for the home circle. In Spain life doesn't begin until some time after eight o'clock in the evening. Life doesn't begin until the work is done—that is the general assumption upon which affairs are conducted in Spain—and it lasts until morning. And so as we waved to the hospitable vigilantes on the border and plunged into this "backward" country, we felt as though we were attending a series of village fairs or birthday celebrations. We toured the whole of Spain on the excellent roads that De Rivera had built for military purposes, meeting so few cars that he seemed to have built them for us. . . . Again resisting the temptation to write a travelogue, I will content myself with the music of the names of some of our stopping places: Tarragona, Tortosa, Castellon de la Plana, Valencia, Murcia, Cartagena, Granada, Motril, Malaga, Tarifa, Cadiz, Sevilla, Cordova, Toledo, Madrid.

In Madrid the story of my life as something besides a poet's perception of qualities begins again, for there by force of circumstance I became scientific, or at least political, and to the usual extent, revolutionary. Exploring the newsstands, I hit upon a small vermilion-covered magazine called *Communismo*. I bought it and read a few pages of thoughtful editorials couched in a prose so limpid that I could skip along without a dictionary. I went home and wrote a letter to the editor of *Communismo*, telling him that I was loitering in Madrid and would like to have a talk with him if he knew French. The next morning a handsome youth with shining brown eyes appeared at our door, and said that while the editor would find it embarrassing to come to my hotel he would be glad to meet me in a café in the evening after dinner—that is to say, in the small hours of the morning—and talk French as long as I liked.

We met that evening, and I found the editor as thoughtful and limpid as his magazine, although far more pale in color. Moreover, he too, with his well-chiseled and almost too luminous features that reminded me of Alfred de Musset, was good to behold. In fact—to return for a moment to my character as poet—I will make this one black mark against Spain, that the men are far better-looking than the women.

The editor told me that Andres Nin, an agitator known and admired from prewar days, was coming down from Barcelona, and other Trotskyists from all over Spain. They would be gathering informally on Saturday evening, and would we not come over and join the conversation? We came, of course, and had a most illuminating talk, most soothing also to my scientific conscience. At a very early hour in the evening, however—that is, about one o'clock in the morning—we took our departure, saying a final farewell, since we were planning to leave for Paris the next day. As we emerged into the street, an alert citizen stepped up from the shadow, very respectfully but with a significant hand under the lapel of his coat—an international gesture which I fortunately had not forgotten, for the badge was a mere glimmer in the dim light—and invited us to accompany him. We accepted the invitation with the usual mixture of reluctance and alacrity, and soon found ourselves in the local police station, trying to explain to a slow-witted but persistent old professor of genealogy how our mothers spelled their maiden names.

It was no time to bother with the traditions of the Lucy Stone League, but I had a determination to call Eliena by her own name, which had settled into a habit, and as I happened to be doing the stammering at the moment, the name, Krylenko, and the birthplace, Russia, were on the bill-of-lading before I had time for reflection. Krylenko was then a name to conjure with in a magistrate's court in the Soviet Union, but in a country whose infant government was tottering away from the outstretched arms of the Communists on one side and wriggling out of the embraces of the Monarchists on the other, it produced something like a convulsion.

"Russian! Oh, aha, Krylenko!"

We were loaded into the police wagon and rushed across town to the Prefecture, and upstairs to a department designated—hopefully rather than with scientific precision—*Seguridad Social*. Here a more quick-witted magistrate, and one who by the grace of God could talk French, undertook to find out what we were doing in the heart of the proletarian section of the capital, in the office of an extremely vermilion-covered and limpidly intelligible revolutionary magazine called *Communismo*.

I have explained it to the reader, and it seems simple enough. All you have to do is understand the nature of poetry and the peculiar relation it bears to a scientific generalization. But we found it exceedingly difficult to make this entirely clear in a foreign language at two o'clock in the morning to the chief of the department of public security in the turbulent capital of a somewhat trembly republic. He decided to send an officer and search our room in the hotel for incriminating evidence. Meanwhile we were put out on two kitchen chairs in a side room to wait.

When the evidence arrived—at about four o'clock in the morning—it consisted very largely of poetry. Fortunately I do not belong to the cryptographic school of poets who write in a secret code for a close conspiratorial group of intimate friends and initiated critics. If I had been E. E. Cummings I would never have got out of there alive. My poetry is both rhymed and reasonable. It always says something. What it says, moreover, has not up to the present date overthrown any republics. However, that limpid and revolutionary editor had been kind enough to present me with a complete file of his vermilion-covered magazine, which seemed to stand up some three meters high there on the chief's table, and looked very much like concentrated provender to be ladled out to the hungering proletariat as we toured the leading cities of the republic. I was unable to explain where I was going with those magazines. It seemed improbable to those who had heard me try to talk Spanish that I was intending to lug them home. Moreover, this man had got an idea that Comrade Krylenko had been there three months already, and that I had only come along with my innocuous poetry after the work was done. It shows what's in a name. We never did disabuse him of this idea. He found no incriminating evidence, however—for that magazine was quite legal, being on sale, as we pointed out to him, on the newsstands. And so he fell back on our passports. I think there is always something the matter with a passport, if reason arises for finding it out.

"Why haven't you got a visa on these passports?" he said.

"We have. They're in perfect order."

"No, you haven't. Where is your visa?"

"Right here—page twelve."

"I'm talking about your visa for the province of Madrid." He said this shamefacedly; he couldn't look me in the eyes.

"What on earth do you mean by that?"

"Don't you know that on entering any province in Spain you have to go to the local police and get your passport visaed within twenty-four hours?"

"No, I don't, and neither does anybody else traveling in Spain. There wouldn't be a tourist in the country if they did."

He made no answer.

"Would you mind letting me read that law?" I said.

He looked about feebly. "Well, I haven't it here at the moment."

"I'd like to read it before I'm convicted under it. I'm an American citizen and I suppose I have some rights."

This "American citizen" set me off on a wrong track. I did not really believe that President Hoover would send over a fleet of battleships to pull me out of a Spanish hoosegow. I merely wanted to work up some "positive self-feeling," and I did.

"Your law, if it exists, which I doubt, has nothing to do with the cause of our detention," I said.

That was true and he did not like to deny it, so he retreated gently into the Spanish language—so gently that when we found ourselves back on our chairs in the next room, it was with an impression that we were about to be released.

We were disillusioned by another official who beckoned and started us down into the bowels of the earth. Down, down—and so far down that it was quite obvious we were headed for the dungeon keep. But when we questioned him with signs of indignation, he said, "to another office." We crossed a small court, open to the sky way up like an Egyptian tomb ready for the mummy, and peering down a long thin stairway saw bars at the bottom. Here we rebelled and bolted back like sheep in the stockyards. "No!" we said. "Not in the least! We are not going to jail without telephoning our consul." We were so positive about this, and we so eloquently—and in such alarming distortions of grammar—invoked the principles of international law and the comity of nations, that our guide took fright and went back upstairs to find out what he should do. He went back twice. But meanwhile the place began to fill with heavy-bodied policemen and it was clear what the answer was to be.

I must say for those heavy-bodied policemen that they manhandled us with a dexterity and self-control that seemed almost paternal, and once the bars closed they became as courteous as though we were the royal family. It is not easy to search a man and deprive him of his weapons with courtesy—especially when the weapons consist of his necktie, belt, garters, safety pins, whatever he was most confidently relying on to hold him together until he got to bed. However, I can honestly affirm that I was never more graciously disarmed, and I was ushered into my cell like the prince of the underworld. Comrade Krylenko was taken to another vault and as graciously turned in with the prostitutes.

There were about twenty criminals in the dim cold cell in which I found myself, most of them lying flat with their feet toward me on a wide raised floor of cement, which was all the cell contained, and which *was* the cell, except for a little trough to walk in next to the bars. I felt very much like an intruder, and could find no words to explain my unexpected arrival. As I stood there in the trough holding my clothes on with some difficulty, my embarrassment became evident and one of the criminals said:

"There's plenty of room. Come on, lie down and sleep. Where were you arrested?"

I described the location.

"Are you a Trotskyist or a Stalinist?"

Wondering whether the whole Spanish underworld was up to the fine points of Marxian theory, I answered that I was Trotsky's American translator.

"Never mind, we're all friends in here! Lie down and make yourself at home. We're Stalinists."

I then learned that a general roundup of some two hundred and forty revolutionists of all colors had been effected that night in preparation for the visit of Herriot, the French premier—it was, after all, a mere gesture of hospitality—and I felt better in that large company. The morning was enlivened with some animated political discussion, and the Stalinist law against "fraternizing" with friends of Trotsky was heartily broken.

At ten o'clock I again demanded of a passing official that I be permitted to telephone my consul. The answer was short and ominous.

"Here you can't communicate with anybody."

To me that meant that if I had been arrested for any ordinary crime, like high treason, for instance, and were in a regular prison cell, I might have some rights—but not in this lowest pit. "Here you can't communicate with anybody."

What he really meant, I suppose, was that this was merely a preliminary detention, and as soon as they got round to my name I would be examined and either liberated or sent to a regular prison where such things could be bothered with. But he did not say that, and I should probably not have understood him if he had. "Abandon hope, all ye who enter here!" was what I understood.

It was four o'clock in the afternoon before that gloomy thought lifted, and I will not dwell upon it because it now seems naïve. At four, Eliena and I were removed from our cells simultaneously, and led back upstairs to be sentenced. We were fined five hundred pesetas each— about eighty dollars in all—for not having secured a visa for the province of Madrid! And we were told we could stay in jail until we paid it.

We again demanded the right to telephone our consul, which was again refused, and upon that we said that we would stay in jail until they let us communicate with our consul. Comrade Krylenko further explained that we had only about eighty dollars to get us back to Paris and that if we paid their fine we would have to stay there in Spain forever. She also inquired whether they would take a check on a New York bank—a proposal which seemed to me ludicrous, but which so impressed our interlocutor that he put us back in jail until he could consult his chief. This time, moreover, out of respect for that check on a New York bank, he put me into a cell with arrested Monarchists.

At seven in the evening we were called up and informed that the fine would stand against us—asked in fact to sign a receipt for the information—but that we were granted ten days in which to pay it and could now *marchar.*

We "marchared" with a pleasure that, brief as the restraint had been, was truly poignant and unique. And we were welcomed back to our hotel—where those detectives had made their midnight incursion—with a joyfully laughing hospitable enthusiasm in which law and government seemed one of the most amusing of all the preposterous things with which, to a civilized mind, this earth is so obviously encumbered.

The next morning we called on that American consul, who had taken on the proportions of a protecting deity in the dark hours of our adventure, and found him surprisingly anthropomorphic—indeed positively human. He advised us to continue our journey to Paris as though nothing had happened—hoping, although we could not of course be sure, that no hindrance would be interposed to our crossing the border. Meanwhile he would make efforts to explain to the Spanish Government the difference between science and poetry, and get the fine forgotten.

No hindrance was interposed at the border and the fine was forgotten—at least by me—and my love for Spain survived to make more painful the bitter and awful things she has had to live through after that day.

Chapter 85

A LONG POEM AT LAST

By the time we reached home, the stream I was swimming against was turning into a torrent. The entire radical and left-liberal intelligentsia were going over to "proletarian" art, "proletarian" literature, pro-Stalin politics, and the glories of the workers and peasants republic which I was beginning to suspect had died in embryo at the hands of a tyrant.

Edmund Wilson says, in an essay in his *Classics and Commercials*, that my political writing during this period was "damaged by a peculiarly disgruntled tone," and I guess he is right. I was opposed and rejected by two dominant currents of opinion: Stalinism and what is called the New Criticism—although the whole trend both of poetry and poetic criticism would be a more accurate designation for the latter current. If I had time, I think I could demonstrate certain consanguinities between these two currents, or tidal waves of opinion, but I must remember that I am only telling a story. The story is that I brought home enough money from our trip to Palestine—and managed sufficiently to distract my thoughts from the agony of the revolution—so that in the summer of 1933 I settled down at last to writing the long poem I had in mind.

Edgar Allan Poe thought there was no such thing as a long poem, poetry being by nature a momentary rapture. Leigh Hunt and the circle Keats grew up in maintained, on the contrary, that only a long poem could establish one's claim to *be* a poet of consequence. Up to the late twenties I had inclined to Poe's romantic opinion, but at this time for some reason—a conversation with Edna Millay played a part in it—I began to realize that I had left a great deal of myself out of my poetry. Owing perhaps to my early preoccupation with the problem what poetry is, and how it differs from practical and scientific language, I had made an artificial division in my own creative life. My feelings I was inclined to express in verse, my thoughts, no matter how deeply felt, in prose. It was a division somewhat like that the Hebrews made in the week, with poetry in the role of the Sabbath. My love of poetry had been born at family prayers when my mother took to reading Sidney Lanier instead of the Bible, and I fear it remained for me, no matter how pagan it became, a little bit like prayer. There was never any humor in my poems for one thing—until that summer of 1933.

It was not a change of views or definitions that occurred then. I still hold to my definitions, and regard my account of the psychology of metaphor as of enduring importance. But I was realizing now that for a creating artist, *any* division of himself, no matter how valid conceptually, is detrimental. In short, I was unlocking some closed doors—I was turning my *self* loose—on that morning when I sat down in the little woodshed alongside the Sheepbarn cottage, and began to write my *magnum opus* on the subject: "Praise Lot's wife for looking back."

"Don't try to be more poetic than you are" was one of the slogans under which this inner revolution was conducted—oversimplified, as all revolutionary slogans are—but ever present in my mind. "Don't bother where the rhymes come in" was another. Rhymes reinforce the waves of a rhythm as a paddle struck in from time to time will heighten the ripples in a stream of water; it doesn't matter for this basic purpose between just what ripples you strike it in. "Don't be prissy and meticulous about laws of versification—trust your ear." "Don't think about caesuras—only grammarians ever did—just pour it out." That is how I wrote "Lot's Wife," starting off with two lines indecent enough to serve notice that I was abandoning the refined Christian hush-hush in which I had been brought up.

> Lot climbed his thin pale woman every night,
> Plunging and thudding in her till she groaned;
> And hoisted her when morning was half light
> To fetch and pray and figure what he owned.
> She by his faithfulness worn down too soon,
> Sagged forward head and belly, like the moon.
> The blue veins ambling down her legs were thick;
> Her little whims and wishes were all sick.
> Desire felt in her bosom like a swoon.
> A smell would waft against her, or a tune,

And weakly like a weak rope she would give,
And vow still, still before she died to live;
But she would gasp and stagger from that sin,
And drive it back and drive it down and in.
She fed him forty years of help and hate;
He wallowed in it blandly, and all ate. . . .

What came out of me was, all through, as angry and barbaric as that. All Christendom's suppressed revolt against the merciless Old Testament God and the superstitions of his Chosen People seemed to gush forth, as it does in Mark Twain's so long withheld and recently published "Reflections on Religion." * Without some gentler companion piece, some sign of a realization that there *are* tender and noble tales in the Old Testament, I was certain that no American publisher would so much as glance at my poem. So I put it away in a folder and went back to my disgruntled and futile polemics against those who were trying to take over the world for Stalin.

Before resuming that sad story, however, I am going to tell how, after lying in darkness for six years, my poem came surprisingly to light. It must have been in 1939 or thereabouts that Cass and Jane Canfield came one night to dine with us in the Sheepbarn cottage. It's a sin against etiquette, I think, for an author to read his writings to his guests. But on that occasion, at Eliena's suggestion and with all three insisting, I dug up "Lot's Wife" and read it aloud. To my utter astonishment, Cass, when I stopped reading, asked me if Harper & Brothers might have the privilege of publishing it!

To my further astonishment, the poem, in the exquisite little book he made for it, was highly praised by every critic, except one, whose opinion I cared about. Edna Millay sent me a poem-telegram almost, telling me how much she liked it. E. E. Cummings wrote: "Livingly and wholly your poem delights me." André Maurois, Granville Hicks, William Rose Benét, Frances Winwar, Somerset Maugham, even Max Lerner—who politically was as disgruntled against me as I against him—had words of praise for it. "Delightfully wicked," "Not for the squeamish," "Stuffed shirts should shun it like rat poison," were some of the comments. Stephen Leacock wrote: "Whether it should be put in the hands of anyone under seventy is questionable, but I am seventy-two." Henry L. Mencken named it to the *Herald Tribune* as one of the

* *The Hudson Review,* Autumn, 1963.

three best books of the year. "To my barbaric mind," he wrote, "it makes T. S. Eliot's 'Waste Land' sound childish."

But Marianne Moore wrote to the publisher: "I do not like sanctimoniousness any better than Max Eastman does, and on various grounds I am bold enough to regard myself his friend, but I do not like the book."

Chapter 86

I LOSE FAITH AND LOSE FRIENDS

It was in 1933 that my resolute faith in the Soviet system began really to break down. The news from Russia, and things that crossed my eyes in the Soviet press, grew steadily more disheartening. The *cultural* backslide was following the *political* one now, and I wondered if things could be much better in the sphere of economics. I had a lecture called "The Russian Soul and the Bolsheviks," nicely calculated to bring Americans around in a happy but not humiliated frame of mind to the idea that the Russian system was really better than ours. I still hoped it was, but I could not be eloquent with a doubt in my heart. On the other hand I couldn't say that their system was *not* better than ours. You can't make a living out of suspended judgment. So just when this lecture was becoming most popular and remunerative, I had to cross it off my program. I think I delivered my last pro-Soviet lecture in Ridgewood, New Jersey, in 1933. A speech that had been set for Lexington, Kentucky, January 13, 1934, I canceled.

I must boast that I did not surrender to my doubts without a prolonged and hard-fought battle. Laying aside my lecture manuscripts, I sat down to my desk and composed a disquisition forty pages long, designed to convince myself first, and then others, that all was going well in Russia. I called it "What the Soviet Experiment Proves," and it ran in substance as follows:

> We did not expect everything to come right after a socialist revolution. Our expectation was that, once the interest of profit-takers in maintaining the capitalist system was removed, the *efforts* of idealists to make things come right would not have so pitiably tiny a result as they do among us. These efforts would, in fact, succeed beyond all the world's previous hopes.

I asserted, or my typewriter did, that whatever might be said about *political* developments, this *social* expectation was being realized in the Soviet Union. I took up *seriatim* all the major fields of endeavor in which, under capitalism, social reformers and evangelists preaching only good will and sound reason have such a hard time getting anything done: prison reform, public health, education, matrimony, sexual morality, substitution of real values for "conspicuous leisure and consumption," elevation of the press and the movies, establishing of the rights of national minorities, extermination of anti-Semitism, inauguration of mental hygiene, enthroning of the "moral equivalent for war," universal disarmament, world federation. It was a scholarly performance. I did not rely on my own outdated memories, but quoted from books written by various Depression-haunted liberals who had gone over to Russia in the mood of one who, about to die, is permitted a quick peek into heaven, and can even hear, although without comprehension, the mellifluous tones of the celestial language. (I have thirty-five of these books.) It was a heroic effort and I laid it away, as is my custom, to cool for a few weeks until, in revision, it would be an external object rather than a vital part of myself.

Those weeks stretched into months, and during the months news of the cultural counterrevolution in Russia—a subject still awaiting its historian—piled in as though expressly to refute my thesis. I gave up the fight finally, and filed away that forty-page effort of faith among the other expendable relics of my trade. I was beginning now, by painful steps, to learn how premature, how propaganda-happy, I had been, both in Russia and after my return, to believe that a one-party dictatorship could usher in a "society of the free and equal."

I learned this faster—perhaps largely because I could pass the language barrier—than most of my similarly motivated friends. Roger Baldwin, for instance, prophet of Freedom in the Absolute, abandoned the religion of a lifetime to come out for "a class position, anticapitalist and revolutionary." "When the power of the working class has been achieved," he wrote, "as it has been only in the Soviet Union, I am for maintaining it by any means whatever. . . . If American champions of civil liberty could all think in terms of economic freedom as the goal of their labors, they would accept—regretfully of course—the necessity of dictatorship while the job of reorganizing society on a socialist basis is being done." Roger published this self-stabbing confession of faith in September 1934, just when I was canceling—regretfully, of course—my last pro-Soviet lecture, and laying aside as hopeless my forty-page attempt to prove that some basic blessing to man had come out of the victory of Lenin's party in Russia.

Another mind moving in the opposite direction from mine during those years was that of Norman Thomas, the leader of the American Socialist Party. In 1933 he came out for a united front with the Communists; in 1934 he was saying: "The time has clearly come when it is the business of Socialists to get socialism and not bother about reform." He was asserting the rights of Socialists to "conceive of circumstances that would justify armed insurrection," and rejecting the "blind belief in romantic parliamentarianism." In 1935, on the same platform with the Communist leader, Earl Browder, he announced to twenty-five thousand people in Madison Square Garden: "I want to make it as clear as words can make it that I regard the achievement in Russia as . . . the one bright pillar of hope in the turbulent, confused world. . . ." In 1936, he split the Socialist Party on such issues. I was just then finishing an essay—published in *Harper's* magazine in January 1937—entitled "The End of Socialism in Russia."

In August of that same year, Lincoln Steffens died, an abject captive to the Stalin propaganda. He had become so adept in the Marxian "Religion of Immoralism," so far gone on the road back to barbarism that he wrote seriously of "old exploded ideals like right and wrong, liberty, democracy, justice." His wife, Ella Winter, whose combination of maximum brain action with a minimum of horse sense I have described, had followed along this road. A few months after his death, she did a thing which I think the old exploded ideals of right and wrong would have made it difficult to do.

"Dear Max," she wrote me, "we are going to publish a volume of Lincoln Steffens' letters. As you are one of his old friends, I wonder whether you have any letters from Steff. . . . If you would very kindly send them to me I will copy and return them promptly and carefully."

I did have a letter from Steff—not the one I have quoted, but another almost a thousand words long and obviously, on the face of it, marking a turning point in his mental life. It was dated January 7, 1927, and was an acknowledgment of my criticism of the Marxian philosophy, and of anarchism and syndicalism, in *Marx and Lenin, the Science of Revolution*. Instead of sending the letter to Ella to copy, I had a copy made for her, feeling distrustful, not of her, but of her too close pals, the Communists. (They had stolen from my shelves in Croton a presentation volume of Steff's autobiography inscribed to me as "the poet of this whole period"; I did not want to give them another chance.) A sentence or two from that letter will show that a compiler loyal to the truth about Steffens rather than to the party line on me, would have felt bound to include it.

"This book cleared me up like a sunrise. . . . You have done me good, Max. I wish you had done it earlier. . . . I am feeling now that I can be a disciple of yours."

Ella experienced no compunction about omitting this avowal from her collection. She felt no need to explain, much less apologize. She merely assumed that I would understand.

Dear Max,

    Thank you for that letter. I thought Steffy had written you quite a lot those years we were in Italy. It's a pity the ones from "the olden days" don't exist still. . . .

In old friendship,
Ella

I did understand—all too well. The surrender of principle to expedience is itself a principle among those moving in the ambience of Soviet communism.

"Old friendship" gave rise to other odd incidents after Stalin erected a new barricade for friends to reach their hands across. You remember my old playmate and traveling companion, Albert Rhys Williams, for whom the October revolution had taken the place of Christ's Second Coming. He had been a preacher, and was still a preacher—a preacher of salvation by faith. He wrote five books telling Americans how to keep faith in the Communist leaders, whatever they might do. After many years of separation, and some pretty bitter exchanges of opinion in the columns of the *Nation*, we met one day in Monterey, California, and for old times' sake had a drink together. It was in 1936, just before the beginning of the Great Purge, and to spare him as well as myself, I tried to keep off the subject of recent developments in Russia. When it came up of its own momentum, I contented myself with the mild remark that there seemed to be rather less democracy under the Soviets than under capitalism. Albert pounded his fist on the table.

"I'm going back there next year, and if you're right, if things aren't proceeding democratically, I'm going to call my friend Yenukidze on the carpet. 'Look here,' I'll say, 'How about it? What have you got to say for yourself!' "

He pounded the table once more to emphasize this, and I remained silent—only saying to myself, "You must remember to note down those words, for they are truly remarkable."

Albert did go to Russia the next year—it was 1937–38—and while he was there his friend Yenukidze was put to death along with the last loyal remnant of the disciples of Lenin. Albert came back preaching the glories of the Soviet super-democracy just the same. That is one example of the prodigious things that faith can accomplish. Faith can not only move mountains, but turn them upside down.

Another old friend I met on a lecture trip was Anna Louise Strong, an even more influential evangelist of Soviet communism in the United States. On another trip to California, I was invited to dine with my munificent friend of the old *Masses* days, Mrs. Kate Crane Gartz of Altadena, California. Mrs. Gartz was an ardent pacifist, but she loved above all things an intellectual cockfight. You would rarely accept an invitation to her house without finding someone there who disagreed with you violently about some vital question. On this occasion I found to my dismay that Anna Louise, who had been telling the Women's Club of Los Angeles how gloriously free and democratic everything was in the Socialist Fatherland, was staying as a house guest with Mrs. Gartz.

Anna Louise had been a contributor to the old *Masses* and the *Liberator*. We had met, besides, in antiwar committees, where she had esteemed me far beyond my worth. At least I remember a poem she sent me beginning, "You came into the committee like a light, like a flame"—a sincere poem, I thought, for in those days words like "committee" did not appear in faked-up dithyrambs. Later in Moscow, I had got in the way of her plan to write a biography of Trotsky. Thus our meeting now, on the opposite sides of a barricade, was a little constrained. It was, in fact, an ambush carefully prepared by pacifistic Mrs. Gartz with a view to enjoying a fight. I tried to outwit her and gallantly avoided to the best of my ability any clash of opinions. But by chance the news had just come from Moscow that my friend Christian Rakovsky had been condemned to death, having "confessed" to a life of treason and involved me in the confession. Of a sudden Mrs. Gartz asked Anna Louise whether she thought Rakovsky was really guilty.

"I can't tell from here," she answered briskly, "I'll have to wait till I get back to Moscow and examine the testimony."

That was too much.

"Anna Louise," I said, "you're not talking to the Los Angeles

Women's Club. You're talking to me, and I know as well as you do that on your return to Moscow if you dare breathe a hint of Rakovsky's possible innocence, your husband will be picked up by the GPU the same night, you will never see him again, and you yourself will be jailed or kicked out of the country without ceremony. Why don't you tell Mrs. Gartz the truth? Why don't you tell the truth?"

Anna Louise flushed to her hair-roots, jumped from her chair, throwing down her napkin, and fled from the table and upstairs to her room.

I never saw her again, but that evening she mailed me a long letter, not answering what I had said, but sorrowing like an anguished mother over my arrogance in thinking my own thoughts. You must learn, she pleaded, the art of "collective" thinking—the great new discovery they have made in Soviet Russia which is molding a new, harmonious and happy future for mankind.

By a fantastic irony, Anna Louise was *both* jailed and kicked out of Russia, and for a much less heinous crime than hinting at Rakovsky's innocence. Her crime was trying *too earnestly* to get a passport to Manchuria when Stalin was scheming to beat his Allies in replacing the Japanese armies there, and get his hands on their munitions. She had by that time written no fewer than twelve rapturous books, and numberless newspaper and magazine articles, extolling the life, the laws, the government, the economic system—in short, the happy future for mankind—contained in the Soviet civilization. To express the fervor of her conviction, she had called one of her books *I Change Worlds*. She had also founded and edited the *Moscow News*, an English-language paper which published for tourists the same happy tidings of the new world being born.

In Moscow, on the night of February 4, 1949, she was lying in her bed, happy in the consciousness of the consecrated life she had lived—twenty-nine years of unstinted labor in the service of this new world of freedom, justice, and benign relations among men—when she heard the fatal midnight knock on her door. It frightened her, for it was a sound that she knew all about—though you may be sure she never told about it in her books. Going to the door in her nightgown, she was ordered by three armed agents of the GPU to put on her clothes in a hurry, and was whisked away with nothing in her hands but a coat and her vitamin pills, to the dread Lubianka Prison. There, without a word of explanation, she was locked in a cell. She remained in that cell five days, undergoing frequent "investigations" but receiving no hint of the charges against her. She was then taken by plane, auto and jeep, still under armed guard, to Poland and almost literally kicked over the border—"chucked over" is her expression—at a lonely river on a broken-down bridge. Fortunately she had taken the precaution, when she "changed worlds," not to change her passport. That saved her life. It enabled her to get home. But her arrival was preceded by an announcement, broadcast to the world, that she had been expelled from the Soviet Union as a "notorious spy."

This shattering experience has relevance to my Altadena anecdote because, in a published account of it,* Anna Louise confirmed with naïve candor my intimation that she knew a great deal more about what was going on in the land of her dreams than she was reporting to Mrs. Gartz, or the Los Angeles Women's Club, or the world at large. She knew, the moment she heard that midnight knock on her door, the whole gruesome truth.

"How shall I ever get out of here!" was her inward cry, when the doors of Lubianka closed behind her. Though relieved that no one "laid hands" on her, she was "scared stiff and dazed." When given a routine physical examination, she "wondered in panic whether the doctor was deciding how much I could stand." And when the prison warden asked, "How is your health?" his words, she reported, "knocked me silly. . . ."

"My health? For hard labor in the woods or for what?" she asked herself.

So she had known all along, while writing those songs of praise to the Soviet heaven, that elderly people, innocent of crime, were being sent to the forests of Siberia to work themselves to death. Undoubtedly she knew there were millions of them. . . .

But perhaps it is wrong to say that she knew it. Might it be truer to say that while it recorded itself in her brain and memory, she did not, until the threat of pain approached her own person, permit herself to know it? Even then, however—even after that crushing rebuke to her soul and body—she declared her continuing faith in the Soviet heaven.

Anna Louise is a good girl—Sunday-School good, I mean—the daughter of a social-minded Congregational minister, and she had followed in his path and beyond. She has lived a dedicated life. But because of a brittleness of mind and emotion, she could not veer away when she found unqualified evil in the object of her dedication. I suppose it requires brittleness, it requires rigidity, to be dedicated to

* Her story, entitled "Jailed in Moscow," was published in six installments in the *New York Herald Tribune*, beginning March 27, 1949.

anything. But how shall that rigidity be combined with flexible good judgment? I don't know. I can only say that, as between the two, I would rather have judgment. I would rather be able to change my mind when reason and the facts demand it, on no matter how fundamental a question.

An old friendship that blew up with a considerable repercussion was mine with Ernest Hemingway. It was not overtly concerned with faith in the Soviet heaven, but with the lesser question of how much hair Ernest had on his chest. But I venture to think that if I had not been the Judas of the proletarian salvation, that great question—important though it may have been in the development of Ernest's character— would never have come up in the semiviolent way it did. The Communists themselves called it a "political gesture" when Ernest pushed into my face a book in which he professed to believe I had accused him of sexual impotence.

I have described elsewhere how our friendship began in Genoa while Ernest was still a young reporter. He had an essentially boyish charm, and for me he retained that even in his most bullfighting and blood-lusty writings. While reading him, I don't have to think of him as entirely grown up, and perhaps that is just as well, for he has immortalized the attitudes and emotions of a heroic adolescence. Perhaps his extreme and almost Byronic fame in these times is partly due to that. They are times in which there's small pleasure in grown-up meditation on what life is and where it's going.

Ernest first won my affection by telling me he was "scared to death," as I'm sure I would have been, in the war. He didn't tell me about his shrapnel wounds, and I never knew till long after that he spent weeks in a hospital in such a state of fright that he could not go to sleep in the dark. That he built himself up from that neurotic condition to a point where veterans and professional soldiers of the Second World War declared him to be "quite simply the bravest man they ever saw" strikes me as a manifestation of moral character as superb as anything to be found in the life histories of literary men. Ernest lived the life he believed in—he lived up to the code he preached. That also certainly stands among the causes of his celebrity. His fame will not endure in a degree comparable to Byron's—there is not enough intellect involved. But like Byron, he proved himself in action. He was not just a voice in the air.

Of course I think he concentrated too much on one particular phase of character-building. In order to be brave he felt he had to turn himself into something of a bruiser. He had to go around being exaggeratedly masculine and spoiling for a fight. I ventured to express this opinion in a review of "Death in the Afternoon," his book in praise of bullfighting. I thought his way of talking about bulls and matadors was, in a reverse sense, sentimental, and I called my essay "Bull in the Afternoon." I made another remark in that essay which has been many times quoted, and usually misquoted. Even in the scholarly obituary which the *New York Times* allotted to Hemingway, I find this raw and impossible remark attributed to me: "Come out from behind that false hair on your chest, Ernest, we all know you!"

What I wrote was as far as you could get from that without changing the subject. Here are my words exactly:

"This trait of Hemingway's character has been strong enough to form the nucleus of a new flavor in English literature, and it has moreover begotten a veritable school of fiction writers—a literary style, you might say, of wearing false hair on the chest."

I think the difference is very great, but the effect of this remark on Ernest was as extreme as the raw taunt would have been. It resulted in a tussle, or fracas, in Max Perkins's editorial office at Scribner's which was alluded to in almost all of the obituary notices published when Ernest died. "Both sides," said the *Herald Tribune*, "claimed victory" in what it called a "fist fight." There was no fist fight. I would have kissed the carpet within forty seconds in a fist fight with Ernest Hemingway. What happened, briefly, was this: Ernest blew in—at first with a friendly greeting, but then, suddenly changing his tone, with an accusation: "What did you say I was sexually impotent for?" The book containing my essay was lying on Perkins's desk, and I offered to show him that I neither said nor implied anything of the kind. Rejecting my offer with "You know damn well what you said!" he pushed the open book into my face—not hard enough to hurt, just enough to be insulting. I grabbed him by the throat and threw him, or backed him up, over Perkins's desk and onto his back on the floor. It was not an act of prowess on my part, but rather the opposite—a device for saving my pride without giving him a chance to hit me. Lying flat with both shoulders touching the floor, he changed tone again and, smiling genially, reached up and patted my shoulder. Perkins was urging in my ear: "Max, please don't do this!" and we both got rather hastily to our feet. After we had picked up a few books and pencils in a laughing mood, Ernest patted my shoulder once more, as though to say, "Well, you're not so soft as I thought." But then suddenly, changing again, he stalked across the room, cursing me in foul language and challenging me to meet him in the ring.

I said to Perkins: "Max, who is calling on you, Ernest or I?"

"All right, I know!" Ernest said, and adjusting his collar and necktie, strode out of the room still cursing me.

Thanks to Eric Knight, with whom Eliena and I dined that evening, the rumor got around, and the next day the evening papers called me up. I gave them a very accurate account of what happened. Indeed, I *read* it to the *World-Telegram* over the telephone, for suspecting that Ernest would invent a fantasy, I had written the whole thing down as soon as I got home. The evening papers printed my account of the facts, and the next day, Ernest's fantasy appeared in the morning papers. Here's a sample of it:

"Eastman sat there on the window seat trembling with rage. 'Ernest, you're a big bully,' he said. I was laughing at him all the time, and I said: 'Max, if you were ten years younger I'd knock the hell out of you.' He came for me then and I backed him up against the desk, still laughing. I said: 'Make this guy stop being silly. He's too old.' I just held him off. I was trying not to hurt him."

In a television interview long after, Mike Wallace asked me what really happened in Max Perkins's office and I gave him my account of it. When I finished, he pulled out a clipping containing Ernest's account.

"What would be your comment on this contrast?" he asked.

My answer was not very conclusive.

"Do you remember Irvin Cobb, the American humorist, and what an awfully ugly mug he had? Once in the old days when he was conducting a column in the *Daily Telegraph* he made some slurring remark about Lillian Russell, the reigning beauty of Broadway. A correspondent wrote in vigorously protesting, and concluded his letter by saying: 'After all, you're no great beauty yourself.' In answer, Cobb published side by side a picture of himself at his worst and Lillian at her best, and under them in big letters the caption: 'Let the Public Decide!' "

I could make a more conclusive answer now, for I have a letter from Whitney Darrow, Sr. (then vice-president of Scribner's) who saw the whole fracas from the doorway, stating that my account of what happened was "substantially correct." * I cite his testimony because,

---

* He had read it, and read the whole account of my friendship with Hemingway, in my book, *Great Companions*.

while it doesn't matter much what happened—neither of us did anything praiseworthy—it does matter vitally, at least to me, who told the truth.

Among the many amusing sequels of that much laughed-at episode, was Westbrook Pegler's allusion to Hemingway as "one of the most talented of our fur-bearing authors," and a picture Waldo Peirce sent me of Ernest on the beach at Marquesas Key when he was not by one half so fur-bearing as he subsequently became.

In "The Snows of Kilimanjaro"—which is, I think, a poem of his own struggle toward the heights, a poem of the need of an artist for moral force—Hemingway says of his hero: "He had destroyed his talent by not using it, by betrayals of himself and what he believed in, by drinking so much that he blunted the edge of his perceptions. . . ." So Ernest knew what he was doing when he was drinking "15 to 17 scotch-and-sodas over the course of a day," and "holding them remarkably well," as he was during the time of our fracas. (I quote from his brother Leicester's biography, excerpts from which were published in the December 1961 and January, February and March 1962 issues of *Playboy*.) He was certainly not drunk on that occasion, but two physicians to whom I described his rapid shifts back and forth between smiling friendliness and explosive hostility, said that I was describing a typical case of—one said "alcoholic degeneration," the other "alcoholic psychosis." I think those scotch-and-sodas explain much about Ernest's life and death that will otherwise never be explained. He thought of tossing off liquor in a he-man way as a part of his literary personality—and he was admirably determined to live the way he wrote—but he might have done it with a little moderation.

A friendship whose cooling-off cost me more than Hemingway's was that with Louis Untermeyer, our Anthologist Laureate, as I call him with a touch of malice. His numberless anthologies have, in the public mind, almost fenced the domain of American poetry. Louis never became a Communist, or even a fellow traveler. He was just a political innocent whose name was to be found among those supporting, in the name of freedom, a notorious conspiracy of the totalitarian Communists against our relatively free institutions. In my better-informed attack on the conspirators, I seemed to him to have betrayed this ideal of freedom. Or as he put it, I had "so devoted myself to negatives that I had forgotten the affirmatives which were once our aim." In short, and less politely, he shared the general impression that I was a turncoat. In 1936, at the depth of my obloquy, he threw me out of the fifth edition of his *Modern American Poets*. Up to that time, my "Coming to Port" and my well-nigh famous "At the Aquarium" had occupied a place in his anthologies. I existed, at least, as an American poet—for "modern" in his title means any poet since Whitman.

My poetry, I have to admit—though I am far from humble about it—is out of the present fashion. It would be glad to make room for some thirty "more progressive" poets, or maybe fifty, or even seventy-five. But there are a hundred and eight modern American poets in Louis' book, nine of whom I have never heard of—and there is room in there for fourteen poems by my old friend and co-editor, Louis Untermeyer. I hope I am not vain in regarding my sudden ejection in 1936 as another "political gesture."

While thus divided from my friends in the Liberal and Socialist as well as the Communist camps, I found myself once more sharply at odds with the Trotskyists. Indeed, I had hardly got home from Prinkipo when Trotsky came out with a letter in his American organ, the *Militant*, warning his followers against my crime of unbelief in dialectic materialism. (If this is becoming a hard-luck story, be patient—there are happier chapters coming.) Trotsky wrote:

Dear Comrades:

Recently I have repeatedly had opportunity to convince myself that Max Eastman is carrying on a systematic fight against materialist dialectics, the philosophical foundation of Marxism and scientific Communism. In its content and its theoretical tendency this fight does not differ in any way from the other varieties of petty bourgeois revisionism. . . . If Eastman while so doing keeps his warm sympathy for the October revolution and even for the Left Opposition this crying illogicality is subjectively honorable for him but does not raise by one iota the value of his criticism of Marxism.

I could have left the Croton variety of revisionism silently to its proper destiny, if I had not been bound for a long time to Eastman himself by personal and literary ties. Eastman recently translated three volumes of my History of the Revolution into the English language. As is generally acknowledged, he has carried out this great work in an excellent manner. I have expressed to him my sincere thankfulness for this, and am prepared to repeat it here. But as soon as Eastman attempts to translate Marxian dialectics into the language of vulgar empiricism, his work provokes in me a feeling which is the direct opposite of thankfulness. For the purpose of avoiding all doubts and misunderstandings I consider it my duty to bring this to the knowledge of everybody.

On reading this, I addressed this letter to Trotsky:

My dear friend:

This is not a reply to your recent letter to me, but to the one in the *Militant* expressing your feelings of ingratitude for my criticism of the dialectic philosophy. You are quite right that I am carrying on a systematic fight against this philosophy. What else is the life of a writer but a systematic fight for the ideas he believes in? You speak of the "crying illogicality" of my support to the October revolution and the Left Opposition. I supported every step taken by the Bolshevik party and by you and Lenin from the seizure of power and the dissolution of the Constituent Assembly (horrible to all other American editors) to the condemnation of the Social Revolutionaries. I was for six years alone in America in supporting the Left Opposition. I *was* the Left Opposition. Moreover, my support, as you know, survived a blow that emotional attachments do not survive. I cite these facts not in reproach, but in evidence that the "vulgar empiricism" of twentieth-century science can be as clear-headed and clear-purposed as your nineteenth-century metaphysics.

If you had read my book on *The Science of Revolution*, before judging my position, as I have repeatedly urged you to, you could have not been so glib with the word "vulgar." I argued that Engels in describing the materialism of natural science as "vulgar," revealed himself to be defending a rationalistic metaphysics—that is, a "religion in disguise." "Whence indeed this word vulgar on the lips of a revolutionist?" I asked. "It is the Marxian way of saying *profane*." The only weakness in my argument lay in the ambiguity of the word *materialism*, which may imply vulgarity in another sense. You hand me the phrase "vulgar empiricism" which can mean nothing to a thinking mind but thorough-going empiricism, courageous empiricism, radical empiricism—a plain man's belief that knowledge does actually come from experience and not from somewhere else. Thereby you concede a rationalistic or *a priori* element in the dialectic philosophy. That is the best help you could give me in my effort to keep dialectic materialism out of America while bringing the Marxian science in. . . .

I treasure your answer when I sent you my book: "I am terribly sorry you have taken such a theoretically incorrect position on Marxism. . . . I have as yet only leafed over your book and will read it in the near future," as a classic example of that fault of yours which Lenin described, in the very mild language of his testament, as "excessive self-confidence." And I promise you I will keep up my fight until you are compelled to answer my arguments with brains, and not only with feelings of ingratitude.

With warm regards as always.

It seemed futile to send this reply to the *Militant*, or to Trotsky, either, and I laid it by for a month or so. Finally, however, having to write Trotsky about some other matters, I enclosed it. In doing so, I remarked that since his communication to the *Militant* had seemed to contain "a note of personal feeling not absolutely necessary to a political clarification," I had an idea that perhaps he did not care to continue our correspondence. He answered:

Dear friend,

Your idea that I am not inclined to continue our correspondence is wholly unfounded. The harsh tone of my letter in the *Militant* was due to the (in my opinion) improper tone in which you write about dialectic materialism—only that. You wish to conduct a philosophical dispute by way of correspondence. I can't take that road: I have too many present-day political letters to write. If you remember, I tried by word of mouth to settle things with you about dialectic materialism, in the presence of Eliena Vassilyevna. Nothing came of the attempt, for the reason that you never let me finish a single sentence. If I succeed in completing my book about Lenin, a big chapter will be devoted to this question of dialectic materialism. Meanwhile I have to postpone our quarrel.

According to Eliena Vassilyevna, Trotsky finished as many sentences as I did in those disputes at Prinkipo, though she conceded that few were finished on either side. At any rate our friendly correspondence continued. He left Prinkipo in the summer of 1933 and I had a letter from him in France, but then another letter from his secretary saying that he was too sick to write. After he found a final refuge in Mexico, I translated two more of his books, *The Revolution Betrayed* and his unfinished *Life of Lenin*. Eliena and I spent two light-hearted hours with him in Coyoacan in February 1940, seven months before an emissary of Stalin's vengeance plunged the blade of an alpenstock into his brain. He had grown more mellow, it seemed to me, instead of more bitter, in consequence of his persecution and the defeat of his hopes. His faith in the disguised religion, or "optimistic philosophy" as he called it, of dialectic materialism was absolute. He died believing that, through whatever miseries and contradictions, what massacres and assassinations, mankind might have to pass, the goal would yet ultimately be reached—the "society founded on brotherly labor, where all men and women are brothers and sisters." To that goal all the rigorously intense studies and researches, the meticulous long humble labors of organization, the executive decisions, frightening in their boldness and often their bloodiness, the sacrificial silences and lies, the self-imposed humbleness, the excruciating efforts to be what he could not be, a political leader—to that unattainable goal they all were directed.

My translation of his *Life of Lenin* is in the archives at Harvard University and will, I surmise, some day be published. The substance of our dispute about dialectic materialism can also be found, if anyone happens to be interested in it. For although he never finished the *Life of Lenin*, Trotsky did set down independently his promised discourse on the dialectic philosophy. It is to be found in the *New International* (theoretic organ of the American Trotskyists) for March 1940, and my answer forms the concluding chapter of my book, *Marxism Is It Science*. I called it "Trotsky Defends the Faith," and was looking forward to mailing him a copy, gleefully sure that he would at last feel compelled to read what I wrote. He was murdered by an agent of Stalin while my book was in the press.

Chapter 87

POLEMICAL YEARS

One of the chief values to vanish from the world with a totalitarian polity, whether communist or fascist, is the obligation felt by every self-respecting editor, having printed a damaging attack on a man, to allow him space for an answer. These new brutish regimes assume, along with other despotic rights, that of shameless character assassination. I think this change is one of the most momentous to have been introduced into civilized societies in our time, and yet it is rarely mentioned. It crept across the world from Moscow almost unnoticed.

I felt it very sharply in those first years of my disagreement with the Stalin Communists—especially so because I had no publication on my side in which to reply to their attacks. The *Modern Quarterly*, you may remember, had offered me a pillbox from which to snipe at the academic artillery Sidney Hook moved up against my critique of Marxism. But I did not realize until 1934, when I got acquainted with its editor, V. F. Calverton, that this paper, now become the *Modern Monthly*, stood for free debate even on so touchy a subject as "Trotskyism." Although in the intellectual camp of revolution, Calverton was too much interested in anthropologic and social science, and he had too bold and original a mind to adhere to a party church. He looked, at first glance, a little like a "smooth guy," with his plump, too-shapely face, keen black eyes, and snug black mustache. He had, besides, as smooth a flow of words and ideas as any man I ever knew. There were no periods, colons, semicolons, not even a comma, not any pause at all, in a speech by Calverton. There was a wealth of incisive conceptions and they were connected in some way—they must have been—but you felt, when he stopped talking, that you had been doused with a stream of intellection rather than presented with an argument. You wondered how he *could* stop. I think he did his writing in the same rapid way, and with so prodigious a memory that he would sometimes, in referring to another scholar's thoughts, reproduce the man's words almost verbatim without knowing it. This got him a monstrous accusation of plagiarism from the Stalinists—an accusation which he met by pointing out that accompanying each alleged plagiarism was an accurate reference to the book, the page, the author, in which they had been so astute as to find it. As a scholar, he checked and rechecked his references with a care that must have been difficult for a man whose thought-stream ran so fast, and in personal relations his honesty and candor were as fully to be relied on as his energy and intelligence. A close friend, and almost co-editor of the *Modern Monthly*, was Ernest Sutherland Bates, a gentle and wise man whose book, *The American Faith*, traces all the roots and little rootlets of our democratic idealism. That book would be most timely now, and might, if republished, have the great success it failed of in those days when everything American was under assault from the Russia-worshippers.

Notwithstanding its small circulation, Calverton's magazine played a memorable role in the growth of thoughtful opinion in America during the years of its life—1923 to 1940. I am proud to say that during the last six of those years it published fourteen of my essays or advanced chapters of my books. Indeed, for a brief time I was listed on the masthead, along with Edmund Wilson, Rolfe Humphries, Ernest Sutherland Bates, Sterling Spero, Diego Rivera, Tom Benton, and George Grosz, as a member of its editorial staff. I raised money for it on my lecture trips, and Eliena and I numbered its ever gracious editor and charming managing editor, Nina Melville, among our dear friends.

I have elsewhere explained how exactly the *New Masses* was *not* an inheritor of the spirit, body, or editorial staff of the old *Masses* and the *Liberator;* I might add that the real successor of those magazines, in so far as they had one, was the *Modern Monthly*. Calverton once begged me to take over the editorship and let him serve as my associate, but I knew too well all the kinds of harpies, hags, and vampires that suck blood from the capillaries of an editor's cerebrum. I had had enough of that.

It saddens me now too, on glancing through the *Modern Monthly*, to see how much of my life force was expended in ephemeral polemics with minds controlled by the Kremlin. The editors of *New Masses* had received special orders from Moscow to expose my "treacherous role" as a "Social-Fascist ideologue." "The liquidation of these traditions of rotten liberalism," they were told, "is a task which must under no circumstances be put off." * The task fell, in the main, to Joseph Freeman, who with Michael Gold was the responsible editor of the *New Masses*, and a sort of unofficial captain of the cultural activities of the American Communist Party. The scheme adopted for my "liquidation" was to portray me as a Bohemian aesthete—a sort of beatnik, to use the modern phrase—who had lost his way among proletarian revolutionists. The old *Masses* and *Liberator* were to appear, correspondingly, as adolescent attempts to achieve the viewpoint of the working-class struggle. My policy of nourishing universal human interests, not pounding incessantly on the propaganda note, lent color to this, and also my liking for beauty and lucidity in art and poetry. But at bottom, it was a replica in miniature of the mode of attack with which Trotsky's prestige had been destroyed in Moscow. It was a New York way of saying, "petty-bourgeois deviation."

Joe's task was made easy by a book called *Garrets and Pretenders*, a history of Greenwich Village in which much space was devoted to the *Masses* and *Liberator*, and it was made plain that, like the Village at large, these magazines, "being middle class, revolted for revolt's sake, and not for the sake of reshaping the world." All Joe had to do in order to "liquidate" me was to write an appreciation of Albert Parry's book, agreeing with him that the magazines I edited represented "romanticism of mood rather than firmness of purpose and clarity of thought." "The Bohemian," he further specified, "hates order. As a confused adolescent or frustrated adult . . . he becomes a literary anarchist. . . . He can not distinguish between law and capitalist law. . . . He revolts against certain aspects of capitalist society which belong to all organized society. . . . They are the well-known virtues: such dull matters as honesty, sobriety, responsibility, and even a sense of duty."

It wounded Joe a little to do this, and to spread balm on the wound, he described me as "the brightest star in the Bohemian firmament." As though that were not enough to finish me off, several other consecrated proletarians, newly hatched but firmly anti-Bohemian, came forward with hearty denunciations of me—among them the unwashed archpriest of Bohemia, Maxwell Bodenheim, who demanded that the proletarian poets "oppose with every atom of their spirit the well-fed, well-educated and cultured Max Eastmans, the Calvertons . . . the whole rotten bunch put together." An equally unexpected help in the process of my liquidation was offered by Bob Brown—once upon a time, Robert

* The *New Masses*, September 1932.

Carlton Brown—a talented wag who had been for two and a half years a
contributing editor of the old *Masses*. His contributions had been
cleverly amusing stories, as near to the mood of revolt for revolt's sake
as the magazine ever came. Since then, he had wandered among Latin
Quarters both of Europe and South America, publishing in Paris a dada
book called *Bob Brown*, and winning himself a reputation as a sort of
amiably grinning Play-baby of the Western World, a detachable
gargoyle on all the Ivory Towers of Art. In this world crisis of the call
for my liquidation, however, he rushed to the barricades with a red flag
in his grip and delivered a fusillade of proletarian revolutionary wisecracks against my reign of bourgeois terror on the editorial board of the
old *Masses*. His contribution, which he called "Them Asses," was
published, somewhat to my surprise, in H. L. Mencken's *American
Mercury*. Its thesis was that under its first editor, Piet Vlag—who was
in fact a pious advocate of Consumers' Co-operatives, supported by a
gentle-hearted vice-president of the Metropolitan Life Insurance Company—the *Masses* had been a flaming organ of proletarian revolution. I
had debauched it with my policies of milk-blooded compromise and
reformism, and, subsequently, under Mike Gold, it had "completed the
flaming circle" and come back to march at the head of the militant
battalions of the revolutionary proletariat. To those who knew the story
of the *Masses*, and knew Bob Brown, this was a hilarious joke, and I
answered it in that vein. My answer was illustrated with ironical
drawings by my one-time co-editor, John Sloan, the one man who had
participated in the founding of both the *Masses* and the *New Masses*.
Collaborating for the last time, Sloan and I created in the staid pages of
the *Modern Monthly* a little island of artistic and literary satire
reminiscent of the old days.

On the question of my adolescent Bohemianism, I was able to
produce from my files a letter to Norman Thomas in which I said: "I
have fought off the encroachments of Greenwich Village's provincialism
on the *Masses* from the beginning"; also the letter I have already
quoted from Robert Minor, objecting to my accusation that, as
pro-tem editor, he was "surrendering to Greenwich Village art."

"Now that number was definitely a labor movement number of the
most realistic sort," he protested.

As Minor had now become a mighty hero of the Stalin party, this
offered rather authoritative proof that as a socialist editor I had at least
been grown-up.

But I had other proofs. Indeed I had far too much to say in refutation of these crudely manufactured slanders, a waste of two long essays in the *Modern Monthly* which I called "New Masses for Old" and "Bunk About Bohemia." I was moved to write so much, I suppose, by the fatal results of Trotsky's policy of silence when similarly attacked. That my opponents were as little bothered by the truth as his, was brought home to me when the *New Masses* published what it called a "Twenty-fifth Anniversary Number." As the magazine was only eight years old, this involved a pretense that it was identical with the old *Masses* and the *Liberator*, the latter being described disingenuously as "this magazine under the *Liberator* title." That was an exercise of imagination that might perhaps be excused in a fervent propagandist. But in writing what he called a biography of this triune magazine, Michael Gold omitted my name altogether from a list of those who had created its first two incarnations. As I was the editor of the old *Masses* as well as president of the Masses Publishing Company, and with my sister, founder, editor, publisher and owner of the *Liberator*, this was not imagination but deliberate assassination. It was again a replica in miniature of what happened to Trotsky at the hands of Stalin—his elimination from the history of the Russian revolution.

While wasting my time in these ephemeral polemics, I was preparing to take the offensive in a work of scholarship which, I think, had a more permanent value. It was a study of the fate of creative arts and letters under the dictatorship of the Communist Party in Soviet Russia. It must have seemed to my opponents as though I were spoiling for another fight, but in truth this major turn in my career was caused, as usual, by an external accident. A strange, plump young man named Eric Estorick, slow-spoken and a little uncouth, but possessing acumen, arrived at my house in Croton one day and showed me some pages from *Voices of October* by Joseph Freeman, Joshua Kunitz and Louis Lozowick. They contained so rapturous a boast of the joyful upspringing of poetry and art in the free soil of the Socialist fatherland, that he had come all the way up on a train to ask me if it was true. I happened to know from inside sources—by which I mean public documents printed in the Russian language—that Stalin was holding the party whip over artists and writers as well as workers and peasants. I was incensed to see these Americans—once my comrades in a fight for freedom—bend to a whiplash that could not reach them. In a conversation with Estorick I decided to write a brief article refuting, with textual references, some of their more preposterous assertions.

In order to do this, I had to go into the public library and ascertain in detail just what had happened to Russian art and literature since Stalin confirmed his personal hold on the Russian Communist Party. I learned that this master manipulator had set up an inquisition over arts and letters such as mankind had never seen before in all history. The thing was so prodigious and so exactly opposite to what his American apostles were shouting, that my brief article grew of its own volition into a book. I called the book *Artists in Uniform*. It was published by Knopf in June 1934, and was praised highly by a few reviewers who were not swimming in the stream of pro-Soviet fanaticism. The newly founded *American Spectator*, edited by Ernest Boyd, George Jean Nathan, Theodore Dreiser, James Branch Cabell and Eugene O'Neill, gave it the blue ribbon as the best critical book of the year. But their praise did not altogether rejoice my heart, for their premises were "counterrevolutionary," and I was still holding to the conception of myself as a revolutionist. I had said in my introduction: "I am on the side of the Soviets and the proletarian class struggle. But I think that truth-speaking is an element of that struggle essential to its success. . . . The efforts toward socialist construction in the Soviet Union must inevitably serve the world movement in some sense as a guide. These efforts should not be followed, however, as a seamstress follows a pattern, but as a scientist repeats an experiment, progressively correcting the errors and perfecting the successful strokes."

The controlled detachment suggested in these lines got quickly lost in the fiercely polemical pages of the book, which was—to quote the *Herald Tribune*—"charged with a vigor born of fury." I am afraid my fury had as its unconscious aim a larger target than the topics treated of. I was, perhaps, farther along toward a rejection of the whole setup out of which this inquisition arose than I realized. The result, at any rate, when my vital chapters appeared in the *Modern Monthly*, was a storm of abuse which made my previous "liquidation" look like a birthday celebration. Joseph Freeman now devoted six full double columns in the *Daily Worker* to a circumstantial demonstration that I was "a liar," a "literary jesuit," a falsifier of quotations, a libeler, a slanderer, a charlatan, a morally and intellectually irresponsible person, a writer of "scurrilous diatribes." He even called me a "forger." In two more double-column spreads, Michael Gold added the epithets: "Shameful! Disgusting! Horrible! Nauseating! Criminal!" "I have never turned away from a friend who lost his path through drink, disease, or personal weakness. But Max Eastman, former friend, you have sunk beneath all tolerance. You are a filthy and deliberate

liar! . . . Nay, you are worse, since you yourself were once the
Bolshevik leader of a generation of young intellectuals. The world has
always loathed the Judases more than the Pontius Pilates."

The specific cause of this outcry was the following sentence of mine
which Mike quoted: "To appreciate the literary situation in Russia
under Stalin, it is necessary to remember not only that the life of the
Russian author who will not sell his pen to the bureaucracy is a social
misery and a literary death, but that the life of the author who *will*
sell, is, as lives go in Russia, luxurious."

The statement seems mild enough now, for in the subsequent course
of Stalin's inquisition, thirty writers were condemned to death (or total
disappearance) for refusing to follow the party line in literature, and
the high incomes of those who survived is now undisputed. But in those
days, all this was concealed by the language-curtain, and by the cloud
of paradisal dreams with which the skilled propaganda machine of the
Kremlin befuddled the minds of liberals throughout the world.

By a miracle of faith, Mike Gold has stuck fast to his creed of
salvation from Moscow, and even to this day contributes to the Communist press. The faith he clings to he himself defined in the old *Masses*
in 1917, when reviewing *The Autobiography of a Super-Tramp* by
W. H. Davies:

"Davies never grew into much of a socialist, yet reading his strong
and simple picture of the incredible life of the poor, we become
reconfirmed in our faith that the world must be set free, and society
made friendly to the tenderest, most innocent temperaments."

Would you expect that so gentle a faith could move out of its way a
mountain of cold cruelty such as the world has not seen since Nero and
Caligula, purges and prison camps, millionfold murders of innocent
men and their wives and children, whole villages transported and
dumped to die in the desert, poets put to death by the dozen,* tyranny
in the highest and slavery at its lowest depth of pain and degradation?
Faith in a "world set free," a society "made friendly to the tenderest,
most innocent temperaments?" Isn't it truly a miracle that such
mountains can be moved out of the way by such a faith?

Joe Freeman's faith was diluted by a more critical intelligence than

---

* In an "Open Letter to Rockwell Kent," published in *Plain Talk* for April
1950, I presented a list of thirty doomed writers. Compiled with the collaboration of Vera Alexandrovna, then the outstanding authority on Soviet literature,
it was—so far as was possible at that time and distance—a work of careful
scholarship.

Mike was bothered with. Joe had suffered more, too, in reviling a former friend than Mike had. A letter from Stephan Naft, who worked with Joe in the office of TASS, the Soviet news agency, described to me his recoil against a first confrontation with this political duty:

> I see the scene as vividly as though I had the actual picture before me. It was at the time of the first attacks of your comrades against you—I believe in connection with your book, *Since Lenin Died*. Kenneth Durant, the director of our New York office, and an obedient official of the Moscow Foreign Office, showed Freeman a prepared declaration condemning you in the strongest terms. Very curtly Durant asked Joe to sign it. Joe read it, began to stammer and turned alternately white and red. Durant then became quite imperative. Sit down—he ordered—here is the pen, sign it. Joe looked at him helplessly with eyes wide open and mouth trembling like a child about to be spanked for a reason it cannot understand. Joe sat down. Behind him bending over his shoulder stood tall, skinny Durant, with that parchment skin of his tightly drawn over his skeleton of Torquemada, enjoying the torture of a heretic who still hesitates to confess that he has sold his soul to the devil. Durant's eyes expressed a mixture of vindictive hate and the expectant joy of striking. I still see Durant bending over helpless Joe, pointing with the index finger of his skinny long hand, and commanding, almost shouting, "Sign it—SIGN IT!"
>
> Joe signed it, got up without a word, and for hours did not speak to a soul.

Joe's sacrificial devotion to the Communist Party lasted until late in the thirties, when it died a slow and strangely silent death. In his autobiography, *An American Testament*, published in 1936—the best and most engaging book written by an American Communist—his fervor was still at its height. Indeed but for one mistake, or one act of defiance—who knows which?—that book might have served the party as an instrument of propaganda among intellectuals for a long time. While taking a firm stand against Trotskyism, Joe ventured to speak of Trotsky as a person instead of a reptile—even to assert that "you could not question his intellectual powers, his character, his integrity, his devotion to the cause, nor his brilliant services to it." I find it hard to understand—except through his own description of himself as "a daydreaming romantic"—how Joe Freeman could have deemed it possible to publish those words and remain in good standing with the Stalin gang, who were already eliminating Trotsky from human history. But Joe's consecration was persistent. He went so far as to "kill" his own book when ordered to do so by the party, calling off a lecture tour designed to promote it, asking the Workers' Bookshop to cancel a large order, forbidding any mention of it in the *New Masses*, and refusing to accept advertising for it. Thanks to these efforts, Daniel Aaron tells us, "a potential best seller sold about 4000 copies." *

Notwithstanding such deeds of self-sacrifice, Joe's book was, in 1939, formally denounced from Moscow as "an underhanded defense of the Trotskyites," and his career as an evangelist of communism came to an end. Cold-shouldered by his friends in the party, he drifted as though windblown into the camp of the anti-Communists. But his silence offended them; he never explained himself; he never retracted the insults he had directed against them when in the top councils of the party. He thus found a chill wind blowing against him from both sides. I remember an enraged philippic delivered against him by one of the victims of his pen, Charles Yale Harrison, and I myself worked up enough rage to denounce him in unmeasured language when once we met by chance at a party on Washington Square. I thought afterward that my rage had been a little histrionic, the inner and honest stream of my feelings being tinctured with pity. But I have followed his example and refrained from apologizing. In 1943, in a novel entitled *Never Call Retreat*, Joe seems to have tried, by brooding over various historic parallels, to make his mum retirement from a position of loud influence understandable. The title was inspiring, but I could not quite find the meaning of the book.

Another and better-placed authority who took a crack at *Artists in Uniform* was Boris Pilnyak, the famous Russian novelist, whose visit to America after the publication of *The Naked Year* was a triumphal tour. In a chapter entitled "The Humiliation of Boris Pilnyak," I had told how the Literary Inquisition compelled him to recant and repudiate his own writings. In a long and cleverly sarcastic article in *Partisan Review* (then a pro-party organ) Pilnyak denied, and challenged me to prove, that there had been any such humiliation or recantation—trusting perhaps to my limited acquaintance with Russian sources. In a reply which I called "Artists in Strait Jackets," I said, among other things:

* *Writers on the Left*, p. 370.

Since Pilnyak challenges me to show *where* he has published any unctuous recantation or repudiation of his own work, implying that he has not done so, I must, I suppose, prove that he has— though I should think he might spare himself this additional humiliation.

In *Novy Mir* for April 1933, after quoting from his book, *Roots of the Japanese Sun*, he offers the following prayer: "These pages were written by the author, Pilnyak, Boris Andreyevich, may the Soviet god give him Soviet health! . . . The author Pilnyak of the year 1932 brings to the attention of the reader that his *Roots* are worthless. The author Pilnyak requests his readers to throw out of their shelves the seventh volume of his collected works published by the State Publishing House. . . . Pilnyak is destroying his *Roots*. This must be done in the interest of literacy. This must be done out of respect to the profession of letters. . . . Pilnyak ought to be arraigned before the courts for defamation, granted indulgence on grounds of illiteracy, not this first time sent to prison, but deprived of the right to publish his works until he has attained literacy. . . ."

Pilnyak made no reply to this. The reply was made by the "Soviet god," who, instead of giving him health, arrested him and shot him as an "enemy of the people."

Besides refuting Pilnyak, I wrote a thirteen-page reply to the criticisms that Joe Freeman and Mike Gold had leveled at my *Artists in Uniform*, taking up and answering in detail every point they made against my account of the plight of literature in Moscow. It was a quixotic performance on my part, for I knew there was no room for it in the *Modern Monthly* or anywhere else but in my files. I seem to have felt an imperious need, facing such a set of slanders by old friends, to demonstrate, if only to myself, my true knowledge of the facts. Trotsky had assured me of it in a private letter: "It is needless to say that you write with a full knowledge of your subject." But owing to our disagreement about dialectic materialism, he could not heartily recommend my book to his American followers. And they, while grateful for my revelation of "the ghastly depradations of Stalinism on the body of art," made haste to dismiss my remarks on Art and the Marxian Philosophy as "childish prattle."

Said one of their pundits, writing under the pseudonym of Chester Ernest:

"The present fire-cracker boyishly placed by Max Eastman under the great chair of Papa Marx is but the latest of a whole series of similar adolescent pranks that have won some public notice. It is hard to take seriously these utterances, which together constitute the Defiance of the Lone Rebel of Croton, the Last Survivor of the Old Masses gang, to the invading hordes of Marxism. . . . No Marxist-Leninist can rest content while the best available attack on the pseudo-Marxist regimentation of the artist (squeezing art into army-cap and high-boot uniform) remains one written from the viewpoint of a Left Wing nudist."

This annihilation by the Trotskyists would have been even more complete, I imagine, if my book had been published in its original form. For as I presented it to Knopf, the chapter on Marxian aesthetics was followed by an eighty-three-page essay presenting my own view of art and its relation to the revolution, or to any practical enterprise. I called it, "Art and the Life of Action." * The defining feature of art, I declared, is its arrest of action in order to heighten consciousness. This heightened consciousness can be used for a variety of purposes, and in a review of the history of aesthetic theories, I argued that each one had been an effort to justify art on the ground of its service to some contemporary prevailing purpose. According to my conception, art needed no justification, being worthy of defense and championship, as life is, for its own sake. As an "adolescent prank," this would no doubt have amused "Chester Ernest" even more than did my comments on the Marxian attitude. But unfortunately, Alfred Knopf's publicity manager (and subsequently editor), Bernard Smith, decided that the polemical book would lose its force if this treatise on aesthetics were appended. He persuaded me, by adding a few miscellaneous essays, to make a full-sized second volume of *Art and the Life of Action*, and promised they would publish it six months later. His expressions of enthusiasm for these two books treating of the position of art in all history as well as in the Soviet society, raised me to quite a height of hope and self-esteem.

Moreover, his promise was carried out; *Art and the Life of Action* was published in the same format the following autumn. But although praised extravagantly by one or two critics, among them George Santayana, it sank from the public view without a splash. As best I can remember it sold under three hundred copies. I am reminded, however, by a letter which recently turned up, that even *Artists in Uniform*,

* It was republished with revisions in an enlarged edition of my *Enjoyment of Poetry* in 1939.

although its title at least became famous, sold less than five hundred. I
learned many years later, in Daniel Aaron's *Writers on the Left*, that
Bernard Smith, whose enthusiasm for those two anti-Marxian and
anti-Communist books was so exhilarating, had been "an orthodox
fellow traveler throughout the thirties." This was not known to Knopf,
who was innocent of such opinions, but it may have had more than a
little to do with the meager publicity and low sales of my books. Their
failure does not require that explanation, however, for whatever their
send-off, those poor little green books—excuse my parental tenderness
—had not only to breast a turbulent current of contrary opinion, but to
wrestle with an underpull from saboteurs and secret agents planted by
the Communists and their accomplices in bookstores, mail-order houses,
and distributing agencies all through the country. Next to the government itself and the munitions industries, these centers of communication
were then the main target of the party in an astute and unremitting
campaign of infiltration. Not only were *anti-Communist* books mysteriously turned down in manuscript, ill-advertised when accepted, sabotaged in sales departments, and slipped under the counters in bookstores, but nonpolitical books by authors *known to hold anti-Communist
opinions* met the same deadly impediment of underground hostility.
While the Communists were continuing the old wail about the suppression of their views, we who opposed them saw their views riding to the
surface everywhere while ours sank and were drowned. A prominent
publisher frankly told me years later that one of my books had been
sabotaged by pro-Communists in his employ. A man personally well-
known to me as a card-carrying Communist, occupied for years a key
position in one of our book clubs. The president of the club was no
Communist or fellow-traveler, but when I called his attention to this
man's affiliations, he laughed at the notion as outlandish. The man was
a faithful worker, he said, and had no "political prejudices" whatever.

I am in a poor position to report these facts, since a question
naturally arises whether my books about art had sales value in any case,
or any value at all. But that the queer sad death of my next book was
due to political forces is fairly obvious, since it was explicitly political.
Indeed, it was a body blow at the "proletarian" or pro-Soviet frenzy
that Stalin's agents and adjutants were so successfully fanning up—a
reprint in book form of my essay in *Harper's* for January 1937, *The
End of Socialism in Russia*. The magazine had not been out a month
when I received in Florida an urgent telegram from the president of
Little, Brown & Company, asking me to call him on the telephone. He

had read my essay, he said, and discussed it with Dorothy Thompson, who considered it vitally true and important, and between them they had decided to make a little low-priced book of it, and spread the news all over the country. Dorothy would write a blurb, and give it a thundering send-off in her syndicated column. Little, Brown would get behind it with all the sales and propaganda force at their command. We had to rush things through, as the book must be on the stands by early spring.

We did rush things through—at least I did. The contract was signed and the revised manuscript delivered within a week. Within another week the cover was designed, the pages started rolling off the press—at least I thought so—and Dorothy's pen was poised to announce to the public that I, a lifelong socialist, had not only declared, but proven with figures and statistics, that all hope of a classless society in Russia was dead.

At that critical moment something happened—I do not know exactly what. Within a year, a new president took charge of Little, Brown, and that staid old New England firm had a seizure of pro-Soviet enthusiasm. I call it a seizure because it was so astonishing, and the recovery has been so complete. But it seems quite possible that the germs were in its body and already at work while my little book was on the press. I know only that when it slid off the press, Dorothy Thompson, although she had not so far as I know changed her mind, had gone to Europe and become, for some unclear reason, "inaccessible." No blurb was written; no column mentioned the book; no effort was made to sell the book or even adequately announce its existence. The public at large was off in a spree of "Russia Worship," and I suppose those entrusted with the book's distribution were swept along with the rest. Had it really been published, my announcement of the end of socialism in Russia would have coincided quite exactly with Stalin's announcement that in Russia, socialism was fully and finally achieved—a contrast that might have been employed to promote its sales. As it was, my royalty sheets for the entire period when the book was supposed to be on the market showed sales, if I remember rightly, of fewer than two hundred copies.

Of course I am now telling this tale, not with tears, but somewhat boastfully. I had announced twenty years before Milovan Djilas got around to it that a new exploiting class was coming to birth in the Soviets. I had proven, with statistics which remain, I think, unassailable, that the gulf between the exploiters and the wage workers in the "Socialist Fatherland" was wider than in the United States. At that time, however, this sad announcement aroused in me feelings nearer to shame than to boasting. The warmth of emotion toward me among New York's liberals and radical-minded progressives sank to absolute zero. At Charlie Studin's cocktail parties—the nearest thing we had to a literary salon—I stalked about like the Masque of Death at the soirée in Poe's horrible story. Eliena and I found it pleasanter to stay at home. Except for occasional evenings with our friends of the *Modern Monthly*, we spent the nights and days in Croton, hugging our fireside and our too private knowledge of a bitter truth. Fortunately we were not disturbed by any *doubt* about the truth. The forty pages of my strenuous effort to convince myself to the contrary were lying in my desk drawer—the dead body of a dream. Moreover Eliena had, with all her gift of joy and tenderness, a rocklike fortitude under attack. She knew how, without supernatural rationalizations, to make me feel upheld by truth itself as "by the wings of the Eternal." I hope it will not be considered a boast of anything but her imaginative gift and the reckless force with which she supported me, if I quote, in concluding this tale of my obloquy, a sonnet which she made for me in one of its darkest moments.

> Keep high your proud head, my beloved friend.
> You spoke the truth against their God and Law;
> As panic-stricken swimmers grab a straw
> They grab at lies in order to defend
> Their peace of mind. Let cowards use what blend
> They will of slander and abuse—they glow
> With shame in private. In their hearts they know
> For what high ends and ventures you contend.
>
> In the Grand Canyon rock-hewn temples stand
> In silent magnitude amid the gutted plain.
> They stand unchanged, unchanging, while the sand
> And dust are swept away by wind and rain.
> So history in ages singles out
> A few bold lonely minds who dare to doubt.

Chapter 88

MY BIG SUCCESS

I crowded so many unpleasant experiences into the preceding chapter that I fear the reader will think I was in a gloomy storm from 1933 to 1937. It was true of my political self, and no exaggeration. But I must again explain that I had divided my active life—my conception of it—into three parts. Beginning on January 12, 1933, the part of me devoted to creative play-work was having the time of its life. On that day I signed a contract with Simon & Schuster for a book on the psychology of comic laughter. They gave me generous royalty terms and an advance of a thousand dollars, and I went to work on a second attempt to fulfill my high-flown ambition to write a scientific explanation of humor and have the humor there while I explained it. That, I thought, was the most difficult task a writer could set himself. I had not succeeded in *The Sense of Humor*, mainly because I hadn't worked out my theory completely enough to hold it lightly and be playful while I wrote. I still believed that I could accomplish this feat, and was happy in the chance to take another try.

How I combined this with writing *Artists In Uniform*, *Art and the Life of Action*, *The End of Socialism in Russia*, a folly of polemics in the *Modern Monthly*, and a life-sustaining stream of lectures—twenty-eight of them all over the country in 1935 alone—I will never know. I am not a hard worker; I rarely tire myself out. Could it be that this dividing of oneself into three parts is a good thing—that a three-horse team is easier to drive through life than a single nag?

At any rate, you must understand that while undergoing the punishments described in the last chapter, I was also enjoying my natural life. I was by profession—at such times as proved convenient—a humorist and a psychologist, uninterested in politics, and writing a book which was to be, from a sales standpoint at least, my *magnum opus*. Simon & Schuster had also at that time little interest in politics, and what they had was rather anti-Stalin, if only because they were still selling my translation of Trotsky's *History of the Russian Revolution*. They were generous friends too, and published my *Enjoyment of Laughter*—its title suggested by Max Schuster—with a blast of publicity that practically painted my name on the literary sky. Dick Simon, who is a gifted photographer, got Eliena and me out in his garden in Connecticut one day, and his merry-hearted wife, Andrea, fed me cocktails and funny stories until we were all hilarious. Dick meantime strolled around taking pictures of me in all the aspects of my own enjoyment of laughter. The most abandoned of these pictures adorned the jacket of my book and appeared in numberless announcements of its joys and glories—one of them actually a full page in the *New York Times*. A tribute to the salesmanship of my publishers was paid by the *New Yorker*, whose "Talk-of-the-Town" editor remarked that he had been wondering why he felt so mournful the last few weeks, but finally realized it was from "having to look every morning at a picture of Max Eastman laughing."

To convey my elation in that autumn of 1936, I must add that, besides being generously published, my book was as generously received not only by the critics, but by the most eminent psychologists, and by all our leading humorists and comedians. Joseph Wood Krutch said in the *Nation* what every writer since time began has wished every critic would say: "This is certainly one of the best books ever written." The psychologists, William McDougall, Margaret Floy Washburn, C. Judson Herrick, Robert M. Yerkes, John B. Watson, James H. Leuba, Karl Koffka, Floyd H. Allport, and others, hailed it as a contribution to their science. W. C. Fields sent me a "big old-fashioned hug" through the mail, and Fred Allen said that "if all the hyenas in the world were laid end to end, you would still get more laughs reading *Enjoyment of Laughter*." Bob Benchley praised it to me privately, and wrote a delightful burlesque of it for the *New Yorker*. Anita Loos said she was sure it would become a classic. Max Beerbohm signed his letter about it "Max the Lesser." Edgar Bergen told me every hard-working comedian had a copy of my book at his elbow, and I verified this in the case of Olsen and Johnson, who were putting on their great hit, *Hellzapoppin*, during that winter. Johnson threw his arms around me when I went backstage, and led me into his dressing room to show me *Enjoyment of Laughter* lying open on his make-up table. Although proudly happy at the reception my theory has received in scientific circles, I regard this tribute from professional merrymakers as the ultimate proof that my theory is on the right track. Literature and the scientific journals are full of essays on laughter and the comic, but no other one, I think, ever proved of any use to a person who wanted to crack a joke.

I once clipped from the *New Yorker* a comic drawing of three polar bears on an ice floe, a mother and father bear and a little child bear. The child was protesting:

"I don't care what you say, I'm cold!"

I stowed it away in my billfold for employment when I find myself compelled, as being a hypo-adrenal type I frequently am, to make the same protest. A year or two later, I was lecturing on humor for the Institute of Arts and Sciences at Columbia University, and a young man named Ed Nofziger traveled all the long way from Brooklyn to hear me. He came backstage after my lecture to tell me how helpful my new book had been to him.

"I am trying to be a little something of a humorist myself," he said modestly. "I haven't got very far, but I did have one comic drawing in the *New Yorker*—just a picture of a couple of polar bears on an ice floe."

I drew the billfold from my pocket, showed him his drawing, carefully folded and preserved. "This is the biggest day of my life!" he exclaimed, and wrote these words with his signature on the picture. I met him a few years ago in Hollywood, flourishing among the makers of animated cartoons.

I fear the success story in this chapter may cast doubt on what I said previously about the boycott even of nonpolitical books written by anti-Communists. The sovereign position occupied by humor in American culture has something to do with that. A laugh always has the right of way in this country; even a funeral can't stop it. And Simon & Schuster sold my book primarily as a book of laughs. I used to go into their office armed with a sheaf of tributes from eminent men of science, begging them to remind the public that I had proposed a new theory of the cause of comic laughter, a new definition of wit, a demonstration of the differences between a good joke and a bad.

"Oh Max, don't bother about those highbrows, they'll buy the book anyway. We're selling it to the public," they would say.

They did sell it to the public, I had to admit, and seemingly right over the heads of the pro-Soviet fanatics. I have to record, however, that they sold far less in the long run than the early returns led them to expect. Notwithstanding its brief ride on the best-seller lists, its success was pretty rapidly stopped down by the organized boycott of the Stalinists. With all the magnificent publicity and press notices, the sales of the first and second editions reached less than twenty-five thousand. Subsequent editions have been published, and the book is still selling at this date, but Dick Simon told me, when the big sales were over, that they had spent more on publicity than they got back in profits on the book.

At any rate, I rode high during that spring of 1937, and made enough money with my pen to free me from the lecture business for two good years. I can find in my files only one unfavorable comment on *Enjoyment of Laughter*. It was written by William Saroyan, who was just coming into popular fame at the time and was published by Ben Abramson in his little Chicago paper called *Reading and Collecting*. A month later a strange and I believe unprecedented thing happened. Saroyan, whom I happened to meet at the house of a friend in Croton, apologized for having reviewed my book without reading it! He must have been very honorably disturbed by what he had done for he also wrote me two long letters explaining it.

"The kind of people I found chattering about your book burned me up," he said, "and kept me from reading it and made me think it was no good. . . . I would have liked seeing you again and am sorry I didn't. I wasn't in New York many days after that Sunday. I was living on borrowed money. . . ."

I would have liked seeing Saroyan again too, for his letters made me admire him and wish him success—a wish of which, as it turned out, he had no need.

Chapter 89

A TRIUMPH AND A DEFEAT

I have described how, in 1936, our film history of the Russian revolution was placed in the hands of receivers. It was promptly leased for production to the Lenauer Film Company, but another year passed before it was produced—this mainly because I had made it with printed captions, and these now had to be replaced by a sound track carrying my spoken words. On March 6, 1937—nine years after this entrancing affliction began—*Tzar to Lenin* was presented in the Filmarte Theatre at 202 West Fifty-eighth Street in New York.

Its success with the critics exceeded our extremest expectations. The *World-Telegram* described it as "a magnificent and unforgettable panorama . . . the most vivid and tremendous record of its kind yet compiled."

The *Sun:* "These newsreels are history, and tremendously interesting history . . . well-edited, clear and dramatic."

The *Times:* "Max Eastman's *Tzar to Lenin* is an important work, neither hymn of hate nor paean of praise . . . a complete, impartial and intelligent film history of the Russian revolution."

The *New York Post:* "The most important moving picture I ever saw in my life. . . . The most vital and absorbing film, to my mind, in the history of the movies."

Not only the critics but the public were enthusiastic. People flocked to the Filmarte in the throngs those press notices foretold. Our anticipation of similar successes throughout the country, and perhaps the world, were intoxicating. But here the old obstacle to all my efforts rose up in the path. Trotsky had led the October insurrection and organized the Red army—the films said so—but Stalin was now in total power. *Tzar to Lenin* never got the distance of a few dollars beyond the Filmarte Theatre. Five days after the outpouring of praise I have quoted, a big-headlined article appeared in the *Daily Worker:*

"Max Eastman, chief apologist for the Trotsky band of traitors to the Soviet Socialist land, has assembled news-reels and documentary clips. This man is an expert in distortion, chicanery, trickery, innuendo, and outright lies. . . . *Tzar to Lenin* must be boycotted. . . . Protest to the management of the Filmarte Theatre. . . . Make it clear to other theatres that *Tzar to Lenin* is unadulterated Trotskyist propaganda, and as such cannot be tolerated by the friends of freedom. . . . Boycott *Tzar to Lenin!*"

That was to be expected, but it was only an advance notice of what was coming. Orders arrived from Moscow to the American distributor of Soviet films to notify all patrons that if they exhibited *Tzar to Lenin* they would not receive any more Russian pictures. Thanks largely to Eisenstein, Russian pictures were having a tremendous vogue just then in the very theatres where, but for this boycott, *Tzar to Lenin* would have had its longest run. It never had any run at all. Its triumph at the Filmarte was, for all present purposes, the end of it. A few sixteen-millimeter copies were bought by history departments in certain universities. I deposited a copy in the Library of Congress at Washington, where it is still available to those who want to see the Russian revolution happen. . . .

For those who enjoy a tale of trouble, I must add that in this sad denouement, Axelbank felt that he had been cheated by the Lenauer Company, by Alan and Arthur Hays, by his own former attorney, Harold Blackman, by Judge Aldrich—subsequently by the Modern Museum, Metro-Goldwyn-Mayer, and several other men and institutions who had used copies of some of the films that appeared in our picture. And he finally got around to me. He sued me for a hundred thousand dollars on the theory that I had shown my copy of the picture for profit, although I did not know how to show it without his help. I happened to know that he himself was earning a good part of his living by showing or selling the film, or parts of it, in little ways here and there, the percentage of these earnings due me according to our contract having escaped his memory. But I had had enough. Instead of filing a countersuit, I signed a paper relinquishing all my rights in the film in return for a "General Release" from "all and all manners of action and actions, suits, debts, dues, sums of money, accounts, reckoning, bonds, bills, specialties, covenants, contracts, etc., etc., . . . which he ever had, now has, or which his heirs and executors or administrators hereafter can, shall, or may have, for, upon, or by reason of any matter, cause, or thing whatsoever, from the beginning of the world to the day of the date of these present."

I was, in short, free from the wordy entanglements of the law! My career in the movies was at an end. In thus belatedly defending my peace of mind, I made one mistake: I neglected to specify that in exploiting the film Axelbank must make no changes in it. My peace of mind was slightly disturbed, I have to confess, when I saw this picture, which had cost me over a year of study and creative effort, announced on the billboards of the Fifth Avenue Cinema as "Herman Axelbank's TZAR TO LENIN—Commentary by Max Eastman."

Chapter 90

A JOB AND A HOUSE OF OUR OWN

I had hoped throughout the long years of toil and exasperation over *Tzar to Lenin*, that it might solve my old problem of earning a living without writing for hire. Lecturing, now that my political opinions were unpopular, was becoming less lucrative as well as more tiring, and I was beginning—for the first time in my life, it seems to me—to think of "looking for a job." In the spring of 1938, a job sprang at me out of a clear sky, a job that required no writing, and not any thinking either—just a few spontaneous bright remarks.

I think it came my way through a misunderstanding, for I am not in my own true nature a witty talker. Only once in a while, in the euphoria which follows a successful speech, my brain suggests the right answer while I am still there to make it, instead of waiting till I am home in bed wishing I had thought of it. This happened one night in 1938 after I had addressed a large audience on the Soviet religion of Marxism. I had made disparaging remarks about determinism as against free will, and in the question period some Marxian highbrow in the audience got up and said portentously: "I would like to ask the speaker whether he thinks that a river when it is flowing in its bed is acting through its own free will, or is determined by pre-existing causes?"

After a breathless pause, I answered: "Comrade, what a river wants in its bed in so different from what I want in mine that I can't very well answer your question."

It was the rumor of this stroke of mental good luck that led Earl McGill of CBS to offer me four hundred dollars a week to monitor a new program to be called "The Word Game." My job would consist of questioning four competitors first on the spelling of certain words, then on the definition of them, and then—after a pause in which the preliminary scores would be added up and I would fill in with a small speech—on the definition of slang words. It was fun, and it lasted five months, running neck-and-neck for a little while with "Information Please" on NBC. But it was a terrific strain on me, for my real job was to kid those competitors, and kid their definitions, and in general keep things gay and jocular for the infinite stretch of a half an hour.

The way we accomplished it was this: an audience of two or three hundred people would fill the studio, and before we went on the air I would get them laughing with some sure-fire jokes I had learned by heart. This convinced them that I was going to be funny, and it had a similarly inebriating effect on me. Our program went on at nine in the evening, and it would be three the next morning before my heart would stop thumping drunkenly against my ribs.

One day the big boss, who had a gruff throat and a ferocious manner that kept everybody scared to death, called me into his office and said in a roaring voice: "Eastman, you have the highest class of fan mail that ever came into this building."

I said: "That means I'm on the skids, doesn't it?"

He said: "Yes, it does."

I had that much warning, but I forgot all about it when the hurricane came. It came on the night of my program. Eliena and I had driven down from our cottage near Menemsha on Martha's Vineyard, and we approached New York and the CBS studio through torrents of water, thunder and hellfire in the heavens, and a wind that almost blew us off the road. When we got there, the studio, of course, was empty—not a soul there to laugh at my jokes and convince me that I was a bright boy. But the show had to go on just the same, so Earl placed Eliena directly in front of the microphone and told her to laugh a mouthful whether anything I said was funny or not. (She was good at that.) And he sat down beside her to help.

"Now do your best, Max," he said. "Never mind the vacant seats! Never mind this local hurricane—we're on a nation-wide hookup."

I didn't mind. I was prepared to be witty or bust. But just as the clock reached nine, the announcer said: "We will take a moment out for two important news dispatches."

The dispatches were that Hitler had marched into the Sudetenland, and that the village of Menemsha on Martha's Vineyard Island had been swept into the sea.

And he had a third piece of unexpected news which he proclaimed in the same voice of doom: "This will be the last appearance of Max Eastman in the Word Game."

Now all I had to do was be gay and witty once more. Which according to Earl and Eliena—though this is a bare-faced boast—I was. But I failed to snare a sponsor—I only got one exciting "bite" from Wrigley's Chewing Gum—so this new hope of a nonwriting job was snatched away as abruptly as it came.

In an indirect way, however, I owe something better than a fortune to that engagement on the radio. It emboldened me to borrow the money to buy a hilltop in Gay Head that Eliena and I had yearned for as "the most beautiful site on the island." I think it also emboldened a Vineyard banker to lend me the money with which to buy it, for I had no assets but my notoriety as a broadcaster. The whole of Vineyard Sound is spread before that hilltop, the Elizabeth islands with Buzzard's Bay behind them, Menemsha Bight and its little harbor village to which artists and poets flock like deer to a saltlick—Menemsha Praecox, we sometimes call it. All that on the north side, a lagoon the size of a small lake to the east, and to the south a freshwater pond the Indians named Squibnocket, some dunes and the ocean beach, and then the entire Atlantic ocean with the little wild island called Noman's Land afloat in it. That hilltop with a corridor down to the lagoon was priced at four thousand three hundred dollars. We had five hundred dollars to spare. The rest was supplied by the bank.

"All we can lose is five hundred," we would tell each other when approaching this adventure into high finance. "You can't lose any more than you've got."

The argument seemed so convincing, and the pictures Eliena kept drawing of a house on that hill became so intriguing, that by the end of the epoch—I mean before Pearl Harbor and our entrance into the Second World War—we had borrowed three thousand five hundred dollars more and built the house. We hired no architect; Eliena's pictures and a plan on squared paper were enough. And Roger Allen, a farmer-builder in the old New England tradition of self-taught perfection, brought them beautifully, and with sturdy frames and foundations, to life. Although a smallish house, it is a palace compared to the Sheepbarn cottage, and we looked back sometimes with a pang of regret to the simple and charmingly inconvenient life we had lived down there for so long. But this is a sentimental weakness which plumbing facilities, better than anything else, help one to overcome.

Chapter 91

SHADOWS OF THE GREAT PURGE

Politically, things were growing steadily blacker during the days of my success with *Enjoyment of Laughter*, and that blackness entered like a personal executioner into my very family and home.

Let me recall that in December 1935 the popular Bolshevik, Kirov, who had inclined to take Stalin's democratic pretensions seriously, was assassinated—with the connivance, it is supposed, of Stalin. At least Stalin made Kirov's death the prelude, or pretext, for the arrest and execution of thousands of the most prominent citizens of the country, both within the Communist Party and beyond its ranks. It is hard to identify in general terms the victims of Stalin's Great Purge, except to say that they included almost all the old Bolsheviks who were sincere and strong and forthright in their interest in the ultimate ideals of socialism. In numbers sacrificed, it was an operation unmatched, I think, since the worst days of the Roman Empire. And it was covered and excused before the world by a series of "show trials," in which dozens of the most trusted of Lenin's colleagues "confessed" that in collaboration with the exiled leader, Leon Trotsky, they had conspired to betray to a foreign enemy the party, the Soviet state, and the cause of socialism.

The first of these trials involved Leo Kamenev and Gregory Zinoviev, two of the best-known Bolsheviks, top officials when I was in Moscow. With both of them I had a friendly acquaintance; Eliena's sister, Olga, was Kamenev's private secretary. Their lurid mockery of a trial, inane confessions and summary execution occurred in August 1936, two months before *Enjoyment of Laughter* was published. And in the following January, at the height of my joy in its best-selling, another of these travesties of truth, justice, and rationality struck our hearts down. Our friend, Yuri Piatakov, with whom we attended a circus on one of our last days in Moscow, and Karl Radek, who signed himself "with friendship" in a book he gave me, were among the victims this time. And Leonid Serebriakov, our dear friend—who had predicted, you remember, that Stalin would kill them all—recited his "confession" and was condemned and shot. He had boasted to us that he could not cringe, but he had also shown us a picture of his little daughter who was dearer to him, he told us, than anything else in the world. A promise of immunity for their families, according to Alexander Orlov, was the principal means by which those confessions were dragged from the old Bolsheviks.

A half a year later the great Soviet general, Michael Tukhachevsky, and seven other generals of the highest rank, commanders of the principal military districts in the country, were seized and executed. And this was followed by the arrest and execution of their subordinates to the number, some said, of twenty thousand, others thirty thousand. Walter Krivitsky, who was at the time an official of the GPU, placed the number at thirty-five thousand. Who knows? Who will ever know?*
It included all who owed their positions or personal loyalty to the murdered chiefs, and was undoubtedly a feat of arms and strategy on the part of the GPU and its police army that has no parallel in military history.

After an agonizing lull of some eight months, another show trial was put on. This time, Nikolai Bukharin, "the favorite of the party," Alexei Rykov, the premier who had succeeded Lenin, Christian Rakovsky, and even Yagoda, who as head of the GPU had engineered the earlier phases of the purge, were its victims. While the show trials were being put on in Moscow, thousands of equally eminent Bolsheviks throughout the country were executed in the secret chambers of the GPU. Stalin killed his closest friends like flies. Of the ordinary citizens, hordes numbering into the tens of millions were rounded up and shipped to hard labor and death by starvation in the innumerable prison camps that dotted the whole map of the country. Walter Krivitsky summed up in the following words the harvest—so to speak—of the last twenty-six months of Stalin's great purge:

A partial list of Yezhov's victims includes almost all the eighty members of the Soviet Council of War created in 1934; the majority of the members of Stalin's own Central Committee and his

* Boris Souvarine, in an article on "L'Affaire Toukhatchevski" in *Le Contrat Social*, Vol. III, No. 4, quoting six sources, puts the number of officers of the army and navy slain in this purge at "more than 30,000."

Control Commission; most of the members of the Executive Committee of the Soviets, of the Council of People's Commissars, of the Council of Labor and Defense, of the leaders of the Communist International; all the chiefs and deputy chiefs of the OGPU; a host of ambassadors and other diplomats; the heads of all the regional and autonomous republics of the Soviet Union; 35,000 members of the officers' corps; almost the entire staff of *Pravda* and *Izvestia;* a great number of writers, musicians, and theater directors; and finally a majority of the leaders of the Young Communist League, the cream of the generation from whom the greatest loyalty to Stalin was expected.*

George F. Kennan, in *Russia and the West under Lenin and Stalin,* sums up in these words what happened after Yezhov was appointed:

From that moment on, the purges took that fantastic course which defies the powers of description and nearly defies the imagination. Heads rolled by the thousands, probably even the hundreds of thousands. A process of terror and panic, mutual denunciation and mutual extermination, was set in motion which is probably without parallel in modern history. In a vast conflagration of mock justice, torture, and brutality, at least two thirds of the governing class of Russia literally devoured and destroyed itself. The jailors and judges of one day were the prisoners and the victims of the next. And over this whole macabre procedure Stalin presided, with diabolic, cynical composure, with his customary self-deprecating manner of having nothing to do with it all—but presumably enjoying every minute of it, relishing every new exhibition of the misery and degradation and helplessness of his former aides and associates.

My little personal story hesitates, I must say, to lift its voice in such a hurricane of tragedies. My older brother died in the midst of this holocaust, the last of my family. I have described our boyhood friendship, our love and warfare, in a previous memoir, and I need not repeat it here. My sorrow for his death was a sorrow that mature life had not kept us close together, rather than that it had. The news came while I was driving through the mountains and across the desert to California, and brought a feeling of cosmic wistfulness, in which the innumerable untimely deaths in Russia, the loving hearts torn apart by

* *In Stalin's Secret Service,* p. 177.

a tyrant in order to drink their pain—millions of them, millions of men, women and their little children, freezing and starving and writhing toward death in torture at that moment, to satiate one ruffian's greed of power, overawed my personal sorrow. I could not, in such a world, adequately grieve for my brother, who died as we all hope to—suddenly, of a brain hemorrhage, in mid-career as a brilliant surgeon, a father of three strong gifted sons.

Eliena's brother was dragged from his bed at midnight by green-uniformed gunmen, whisked to Lubianka, and from there shipped to Lefortova, a prison notorious as a place of torture for high-up Bolsheviks. He must have refused to "confess"—to speak his humiliating piece at the bidding of Vishinsky. That was Eliena's sole consolation, for he was never heard from again. We only knew that because of the fame of his great service to the revolution and the state—often a cruel service too, we had to remember—his entire family, Eliena's family, three sisters, another brother, a beloved aunt, a cousin and five or six little nieces and nephews, disappeared from the earth. From the day of Kirov's assassination, Eliena never received a word from any one of them, nor could she, by any manipulation of influence or pulling of international political wires, uncover so much as a rumor of their fate. To this day, so far as can be ascertained, no member of the family of Krylenko, one of the half-dozen proudest names in the heroic days of the Bolshevik revolution, remains in existence. Even after Stalin's death, an effort of our former Attorney General, Francis Biddle, to get word of the fate of Eliena's family and relatives, bore no fruit.

Our wound from this tragedy in Russia was exasperated daily by the stupidity with which so many Americans swallowed down the phantasmagorial "confessions" with which its true meaning was concealed from the world. To me it was sickening to see supposedly intelligent people surrender their good sense to the self-refuting notion that all the known leaders of the October revolution, builders of the Soviet state, had been treacherous and contemptible fiends, except only one, and that one, by a sublimely improbable accident, the very man who had managed to concentrate all power in his hands. He alone was loyal enough to kill all the others and stand firm for the original ideal of a society of the free and equal. Up to that time, I had tried to respect those who believed in the "socialism" of Stalin's Russia. I had tried to maintain an attitude of humble thankfulness for my more intimate knowledge of the facts. But here the tension grew unbearable; tolerance became a pose. I permitted myself to feel derisive of the childish minds of those American intellectuals who were hoaxed by the burlesque show with which Stalin camouflaged his seizure of absolute totalitarian power.* Especially disillusioning to me was the fact that his new constitution, adopted simultaneously with these operations, and described by him as "the most democratic in the world," was not unmasked in America as the most dishonest in the world. It was not, indeed, a constitution at all, but the proclamation of a one-party police state. While containing every conceivable guarantee of the sovereignty of the people, it nullified them all with a single sentence providing that the Russian Communist Party "shall form the directing nucleus of all organizations in the country both social and governmental." In short, it provided for an absolute sovereign who should stand outside the constitution; it even *named the sovereign*—an abandonment of the very concept of the reign of law. I was more dismayed by the failure of the American intelligentsia to detect this demagogic trick than by the trick itself. The trick confirmed me in my knowledge that socialism had failed in Russia, but this voluntary blindness of independent American minds made me doubt whether socialism would ever succeed anywhere.

As I explained at the beginning of this book, my belief in class-struggle socialism grew out of a low rather than a high estimation of human nature. But I did assume that educated minds would be able to tell the difference between the goal finally achieved and the embodiment into fundamental law of its very opposite, the tyranny of a designated clique.

Gloomy as all these events and reflections were, they brought me a personal honor and distinction which caused envy among some of my Trotskyist friends and enemies. It was a denunciation of me by Stalin himself, broadcast throughout Russia and the world by the Communist press, as a "notorious crook" and "gangster of the pen." He was discussing before a plenum of his Central Committee (on March 3, 1937) the menace of "Contemporary Trotskyism," which he declared "is not a political tendency in the working class, but an unprincipled band of wreckers without ideas, diversionists, intelligence agents, spies, murderers, sworn enemies of the working class, acting in the hire of the intelligence service organs of foreign states."

After dismissing four other "rotten theories" on this subject, he said:

* The story of this American phenomenon is fully preserved in *The Red Decade*, by Eugene Lyons, a not-to-be-forgotten source book for the history of our culture.

"It is necessary to shatter and discard a fifth rotten theory which alleges that the Trotskyite wreckers have no more reserves. . . ."

He then cited the example of the Fourth International, of Opposition groups in Norway and Germany, "the group of Souvarine in France," and continued: "Or for example, the well-known gang of writers from America headed by the notorious crook Eastman, all these gangsters of the pen who live by slandering the working class of the Soviet Union—are they not a reserve for Trotskyism?"

Serebriakov was right about Stalin's unforgetting vindictiveness. One wonders how, with all his practical cares, the man found time to remember all these little purely artistic obligations. He even managed, in a peculiarly distressing way, to drag me into the pitchy cloud of shame surrounding the authors of the Moscow Confessions. In the last of the show trials, that of March 1938, he compelled my good friend of Genoa, Christian Rakovsky, in alleging his own ten years of treachery to the revolution, to name me as an accomplice. The two hostile nations preoccupying Stalin's mind at the moment being Great Britain and Japan, it was with their governments that Rakovsky recited the tale of his "conspiracy." In the course of it, he mentioned my name as the man who had introduced him to the British Secret Service. The *Daily Worker* came out with a streamer across the top of its front page: "MAX EASTMAN IS A BRITISH AGENT." I found it hard to believe that anyone who knew anything about me—even those who had to headline it—would take this invention as anything but a further proof of the craziness of those "confessions." I learned later however, that in censoring a booklet by Joseph Freeman, party critics V. J. Jerome and Robert Minor declared that "he had been much too kind to Eastman— he had not mentioned the $50,000 Eastman got from the British Secret Service." (I can see Bob Minor's astute expression when he decided on that sum of $50,000.)

Although not "disagreeable" in the simple way Serebriakov had predicted and Stalin must have hoped, this sideswipe from Moscow was in two other ways disturbing to my mind. As a general rule, anyone casually mentioned in one of those trials either turned up as a victim in the next or disappeared in the interim. Thus it seemed plausible and to some of my friends probable, that Stalin was planning a new trial in which, by using Eliena's brother, her interview with the GPU as described in Chapter 65, her former employer, Maxim Litvinov, and my well-known friendship with Trotsky, he would include me in a frame-up not easy to get out of. The mysterious arrest in Moscow at about this time of the American photographer and former passport forger for the Communists, Adolph Arnold Rubens, gave an additional boost to the idea that Stalin was planning some character assassinations that would extend his megalomaniac vengeance into the Western Hemisphere. And this seemingly casual mention of my name among the "spies and saboteurs" coming atop of his previous denunciation of me suggested that I might be a victim of it.

It disturbed me in another more immediate way. Carlo Tresca, the anarchistic agitator, called me up on reading the news and the headline in the *Daily Worker*. "This means it's an open season on you, Max," he said. "Stalin has killers in every country in the world and they are looking for work. If they can't get Trotsky, there's no reason now why they shouldn't take a shot at you. They've got his okay on it."

That is the substance of what he said, and he gave me two pieces of advice:

"Keep off of the vacant streets at night, and in particular never go down from Fifth Avenue to your house on Thirteenth Street without a companion. That will make it hard for them, at least.* But more important: play up your public character as an opponent of Stalin. That's your main protection. If I were you, I would sue Earl Browder and the *Daily Worker* for libel. It will be a sensation, and once it's in the papers, your life is safe. They will be afraid to shoot you then. Publicity is your main defense."

On Tresca's advice, I did sue Earl Browder and the *Daily Worker*, and also its editor, Clarence Hathaway, for libel. I hoped for a time that, besides protecting myself, I could get them into court and expose in a big way the whole criminal fabrication of the Moscow trials. By the time we were ready for trial, however, Browder was in jail for falsifying a passport, and Hathaway had resigned, signed an "acknowledgment of his mistakes," and disappeared. As there was no further point in wasting time on a lawsuit, I permitted my lawyer, Morris Forkosch, to settle with the *Daily Worker* for a payment of fifteen hundred dollars.

Thus Stalin's revenge on me for publishing Lenin's judgment of him can hardly be called, by his standards at least, a grand success. Indeed it brought me one pleasure and profit that he could not possibly have contemplated. Being so well advertised by him as a gangster, and having my name inscribed among his chosen enemies in the typescript of the Moscow trials, I became a sort of little Mecca to whom

---

* Tresca himself was shot subsequently less than two blocks from my house.

thoughtful refugees from his tyranny, on seeking asylum in the United States, naturally gravitated for friendship and advice. There were others in this position of course, but none of them had quite the claim to distinction I had, a title of nobility conferred by the tyrant himself. I collaborated with Alexander Barmine on his expert and important book, *One Who Survived;* he and his beautiful Greek wife, Mari, became for a time our very good friends and companions. I translated part of Krivitsky's startling articles in the *Saturday Evening Post*, chapters from his historic book, *In Stalin's Secret Service*. I sold to Charles Scribner's Sons Kravchenko's famous and influential *I Chose Freedom*. I helped and encouraged Leon Volkov with the articles which won him his job as Russian consultant on *Newsweek*. Alexander Orlov, whose *Secret History of Stalin's Crimes* climaxed with intimate and gruesome details the vital truths set forward in these other books, brought his text to me in strict secrecy a year before any other American knew of its existence. Kyrill Alexeiev, another brainy defector, who crossed the border from Mexico where he had been commercial attaché of the Soviet embassy, came also by a natural gravitation to our house. Eliena helped his gifted wife with a fascinating autobiography, which to our regret never got published. We were, in short, a sort of gatehouse or preliminary point of comfort for those seeking refuge in America from the more and more bloody tyranny in Russia. It was a grotesque and subterranean kind of eminence, but we enjoyed it. These men who plunged through the hazard of death, the barriers of habit, and the false restraints of patriotism to tell us the first intimate truth about Stalin's "socialism," were of high caliber, penetrating, realistic, exciting to know and converse with.

Chapter 92

CONVALESCING FROM SOCIALISM

It is needless to say that these years of insane horror in Moscow and insane folly in New York sank me deep into my political self. I wrote brief lyrics from time to time, as always, but it was hard to devote my mind to literary and psychological problems when my hopes of socialism were undergoing a twofold torture. The companion-poems I had hoped to compose for "Lot's Wife"—"Vashti's Rebellion" I had even begun—got lost in my business of warfare against the religion of Russia-worship that was sweeping like an epidemic fever through some of the soberest minds in the country. It was a belated result, I could not help knowing, of imprudent enthusiasms that I had helped to propagate. I had now also the task of drawing, with a good deal of pain and labor, my own inferences from the miscarriage of revolution in Russia and this failure of political intelligence in America. Of the two, I think the latter had a stronger effect on my thinking about socialism. History had taught me that tyrants might arise anywhere; to both Plato and Aristotle they seemed the inevitable end term of democracy, and perhaps they are. But that modern minds, free from all pressure and educated in political and social science, should be the enthusiastic dupes of one of the cruelest and craziest tyrants in history, gave me a light on human nature that I had not seen before.

In 1937, I had written to Little, Brown asking them not to advertise *The End of Socialism in Russia* as though it were the end of my belief in socialism. "I am going to write about the socialist hypothesis in the light of the Russian experiment," I said, "but I do not want to prejudice the question in advance."

In 1938 and 1939, much of my time was spent wrestling with the question: How much remains of the socialist theory? The book which resulted I called *Stalin's Russia and the Crisis in Socialism*, describing it in a foreword as "the fruit of long and anxious study, first of Marx's theoretical philosophy, second of Lenin's impetuously practical application of it, third of the gradually developing results of the revolutionary experiment set going under Lenin's guidance." I now pointed out the fatal error in Lenin's conception of a party and his scheme of party rule, which I had described with so much enthusiasm—and yet even then with a grain of doubt—to the Foreign Policy Association in 1930. Indeed, in this book I put the principal blame for the failure of socialism in Russia on Lenin's methods rather than Stalin's character. I saw now that the brilliant device for engineering a seizure of power, invented by Lenin with a super-democratic purpose, was in fatal conflict with the purpose.

The book contained a chapter on "The Meaning of the Moscow Trials," in which I would make few alterations today. A chapter entitled, "Stalin Beats Hitler Twenty Ways" would have changed the history of the world if the authorities in Washington had read and believed it. This is not a personal boast, but a reminder of indubitable facts. No one of us who knew the truth about Russian communism and about Stalin was ever consulted by those in high office who controlled, throughout and after the Second World War, the essential political history of the world. We huddled in unnoticed corners, nursing our knowledge with an agony of pain, throughout the years when, through sheer ignorance in Washington, the positions of power, wrested with immeasurable sacrifice from one tyrant, were handed over to another. William C. Bullitt, one of us who knew, tried to talk Roosevelt out of his folly, but got the answer: "What you say seems logical, Bill, but I am going to follow my own hunch," or words to that effect.

Significant of a more theoretical trend in the book I am discussing was a chapter called "The Motive Patterns of Socialism." Here I pointed out that the socialist ideal appeals to three essentially contradictory types of people. First, the rebels against oppression, in whose motivation the concept of human freedom formed the axis; second, those yearning with a mixture of religious mysticism and animal gregariousness for human solidarity—the united brotherhood pattern; third, those anxious about efficiency and intelligent organization—a cerebral anxiety capable of rising in times of crisis to a veritable passion for a plan. This versatility of the socialist ideal, so advantageous in the days of propaganda, was the principal cause, I declared, of the confusion prevailing among socialists "now that they are confronted with results." But instead of rejecting the too versatile ideal, as with a little more mental boldness I might have done, I merely made my choice among the confused patterns. "The concept of human freedom . . ." I concluded, "forms the axis of the motive-pattern of all who can be called radical."

Stalin's Russia was published by Warder Norton early in 1940. Later in the same year he published *Marxism Is It Science*, my final criticism of the philosophy of dialectic materialism from the standpoint of scientific method. This book was a redoing in more mature and wiser form of the task I had tackled while in Russia, and published in 1925 with the title, *Marx and Lenin, the Science of Revolution*. It is a different book, and all the differences are in its favor. It contains my most studious contribution to a conflict which divides the world now, and I think will continue to divide it until the Western half wakes up to the necessity of meeting these metaphysical bigots of Marxism with intellectual and not only political artillery.

My ideological journey was approaching its inevitable end in the abandonment of the socialist hypothesis as disproven by two decades of experimentation. I had not been forgetful of the noble saying of Darwin: "I shall endeavor to keep my mind free so as to give up any hypothesis, however much beloved, once facts are shown to be opposed to it." But I had not been ready until then to give up my beloved hypothesis of class struggle as the method of progress toward liberty. Although I did reject, along with the Marxian metaphysics, the scheme of party control with which Lenin implemented it, I still hoped that by combining engineers and scientists with the working classes in a new party to be named "radical," a hard-headed yet not fanatical movement toward social ownership might be set going.

What I had still to realize was that social ownership—which means, and can only mean, state ownership—is incompatible with the goal of freedom or any approach to it. Even while my book was on the press, I was beginning to realize this. It is not often easy to say just when such a basic change of opinion arrives in one's mind. "Who can determine," says Cardinal Newman in his *Apologia*, "when it is that the scales in the balance of opinion begin to turn, and what was a greater probability in behalf of a belief becomes a positive doubt against it?" I can, however, describe the exact moment when in my mind the balance turned on this question of socialism. At a cocktail party given by Freda

Utley—I think for her friend Bertrand Russell—during a conversation about some counterrevolutionary news that had just come out of Russia, she suddenly asked me:

"Aside from these Russian developments, do you still believe in the socialist idea?"

I said, "No," and I could not have said it with more conviction if I had made the decision months before. My mind had made it, I suppose, but at that moment I threw off the constraining emotions, the conception of self, the position in society, the way of life—the *being a believer* as well as the belief.

Chapter 93

THE FINAL RECOVERY

Having thrown off these adventitious restraints, I found the door open to a few simple acts of good judgment which seemed to have been waiting just outside. I had believed, or hoped, that when people could no longer compete for private property they would compete for honorific attainments. Merit, instead of money, would be the object of endeavor and the basis of invidious distinction. It did not occur to me that the new goal might be power—still less that the new rulers by getting power would manage to get most of the money as well. I had to learn also that power directly exercised can be more hostile to freedom, more ruthless, more evil in its effect upon the character of the wielder, than power wielded indirectly through a preponderance of wealth. It is an old tale of folly, as old as Wat Tyler's rebellion.

"For when the great ones have been rooted up and cast away," said John Ball in those earlier days of hope and violence, "all will enjoy equal freedom, all will have common nobility, wealth, and power." That is the mistake revolutionists have always made. It doesn't work out that way.

Marx and Engels, with all their mighty show of intellectuality, made exactly the same mistake.

As soon as there is no longer any class of society to be held in subjection . . . there is nothing more to be repressed which would make a special repressive force, the state, necessary. The first act in which the state comes forward as the representative of society as a whole—the taking possession of the means of production in the name of society—is at the same time its last independent act as a state. Interference by a state power in social relations becomes superfluous, and then ceases of itself. The government of

633

persons is replaced by the administration of things and the directing of the processes of production. The state is not abolished, it
withers away.

I wonder if there is a more fanciful notion in the history of sober
thought than that "things" could be administered, and the "processes
of production" directed, without *telling people* what to do, and where
and when to do it. Is there, indeed, any meaning at all in the phrase
"administration of things"? * And yet this was the maturest formula-
tion of the goal, and justification of the gigantic travail, of the world
socialist revolution. It was written by Engels in 1878, read and
explicitly endorsed by Karl Marx, and cited as gospel by Lenin on the
eve of the seizure of power by his party in October 1917.†

For twenty-five years I had adhered, with whatever qualifications, to
this verbal fabrication of an earthly paradise. I had journeyed through
an epoch with my mind at rest in such thoughts. I hope the story of my
journey may suggest, at least in some general way, how I came
gradually to realize—what is so obvious to me now—that it contains no
exercise of practical judgment, not a sign of realistic reflection. In a
debate on the air with Harry Laidler, executive director of the League
for Industrial Democracy, I attempted a more down-to-earth prophecy of
the result of "a taking over of the means of production in the name of
society":

> The size and complexity of the administrative problem gives
> rise to an enormous bureaucracy, and the power and privilege in-
> volved in governmental status becomes so unique and so vital that
> this bureaucracy is impelled by the basic drives or tendencies in
> human nature to crystallize into a ruling class. It becomes a ruling
> class with a power over the lives of the masses that few, if any,
> ruling classes ever had before. Its power over the workers is par-
> ticularly despotic, because it combines in itself the characters of all
> three of the chief enemies of the labor struggle. It is at once em-
> ployer, strike-breaker, and police.‡

It was by ignoring those basic drives or tendencies in human nature
that Marx and Engels, and Lenin after them, had managed to give
belief to that abstract and unreal fabrication. "Ignore" is not exactly

* The German word is *Verwaltung*.
† The references are to Engel's *Anti-Dühring* and Lenin's *State and Revolu-
tion*.
‡ June 19, 1942.

the right word either; they were *ignorant* of them. The whole Marxian *schema* had been rigged up out of philosophical concepts before any study of human nature that could be called scientific had come into existence. Anthropology, sociology, psychology, as we knew them—these were all modern disciplines. Even biology, in its post-Darwinian form, was born twelve years after Marx and Engels finished off the theory which they called "scientific socialism." The science in it, so far as concerns human nature, is a hundred and fifty years out of date. Marx had no glimpse, for instance, of the truth that traits acquired during the life of an individual are not transmitted in heredity. He thought that man's instinctual nature would change with a change in the economic environment—or more exactly, he did not think about man's instinctual nature as opposed to his learned accomplishments at all. "Man," he said, "is a complex of social relations. The individual has no real existence outside the milieu in which he lives." By which he meant: change the social relations, change the milieu, and men will change to the extent necessary to produce the earthly paradise toward which, according to our credo, the dialectic universe is evolving. To the same effect he said: "All history is nothing but a continual transformation of human nature," although the opposite statement would be as true.

I set this forth in a scholarly essay which I called "Socialism and Human Nature," adding a few other traits of man that the behavioral sciences are pretty well agreed upon, but that socialists have ignored: among them a strong dose of belligerence, and those twin impulses toward dominance and submission which enable gregarious animals to gang up and fight. I did not pretend that we know more than we do about human nature, but asserted that a person ignorant of what we do know could not speak wisely about the building of an ideal human society. And I concluded, mildly enough, it seems to me: "Socialism was amateur—we must learn to be expert."

Chapter 94

MY SELF AND THE READER'S DIGEST

Eliena and I talked very seriously about what to do with my essay. I wanted to make it known; I wanted to make it widely known, but I did not want to publish it in any of the big-circulation magazines which my socialist and progressive friends regarded as inherently reactionary. It was not only a change of mind on my part, but a change of allegiance, a crossing-over into the enemy camp. People who never dwelt in the political homeland, the nation within a nation, constituted by those who confront the general assumptions of mankind with a notion like that of working-class revolution, will hardly understand what my feelings were. I was destined to be denounced as a renegade, to be subjected to "economic interpretation"—accused, that is, of selling out—no matter where my words might appear. But I did not intend to make this job easy by appearing under the auspices of class-conscious capitalism or what we called Wall Street. I was not well acquainted with the *Reader's Digest* then, but I knew that it was firm against tyranny, both communist and fascist, and understood that otherwise it offered a nonpartisan survey of opinions in general. We were wondering whether it might not be an auspicious place in which to make the distressing and yet necessary announcement that life and history had taught me a momentous lesson.

It happened just then that my gentle friend, George Bye, the literary agent, knowing that I was having money troubles, suggested that I write something for the department in *Reader's Digest* called "My Most Unforgettable Character."

"How can anything be *most* unforgettable?" I said rather testily. "Either you forget it or you don't."

But I had, in a memoir I was writing, a portrait of my mother, and with a few additions I did send it to the *Reader's Digest*. To my amazement, I received within two days a telephone call at Croton from the editor, DeWitt Wallace. He praised my portrait in breath-taking language, and asked me to come over and see him—right off. He was only ten miles away and I drove over with very little delay. It was the first hospitable message I had ever received from a magazine that paid big money. Mr. Wallace and I had hardly finished our greeting when he said: "Now I would like to have you, in the next two years, write about nine articles for us on the general subject of the Art of Life."

I said I was still a novice in that art, but perhaps I could try to pretend to know something about it. Meanwhile would he be interested, I wondered, in an essay I had in preparation explaining why I had ceased to believe in socialism?

"I should say I would," he exclaimed, in so delighted a tone that my heart sank a little. (The renegade complex makes cowards of us all.) But I braced myself and promised to deliver within two months an essay on "Socialism and Human Nature." The Art of Life we agreed to postpone for a subsequent conference.

I stipulated that I should see and revise the proofs of my essay the last thing before it went to press. "To you it is just another article," I said. "But in my life it is an event of momentous importance. I want every word in it to express my thought exactly."

He agreed. And he kept his word, telephoning me to come over to his office late one April afternoon. The proofs were lying on his desk and he left me alone with them. I found my thoughts, although somewhat compressed, carefully unaltered in the process. I fixed the proofs to my satisfaction, and went home to await, with what courage I could, the storm that would break over me from the Left.

I had seen every word that was to appear over my signature, but two things I had not seen. One was a brash new title invented by the editors: instead of "Socialism and Human Nature"—"Socialism Does Not Gibe with Human Nature." That would go off like a bomb in the minds of my astonished colleagues. And far worse than that: a "box" had been prepared with loving care to stand at the entrance to my article and give it prestige—a veritable shout of welcome from Wendell Willkie, ex-head of a capitalist corporation and rightwing candidate for President of the United States. Wendell Willkie! The Southern Light and Power Company! The Republican Party! That would prove I had "sold out," if my words did not.

I don't know whether DeWitt Wallace knew, or even suspected, what a blow that was to me, and what a boon to those who would assault me. I never spoke of my misery to him or to any of his editors, but I was sick for two weeks. The *Socialist Call* held a three-column funeral service: "*In Memoriam—Max Eastman.*" Dwight MacDonald, an editor of *Partisan Review*, wrote: "Max Eastman, hero of the old *Masses* trial . . . publishes an attack on socialism which Wendell Willkie implored every good American to read, and which is the low-water mark to date in such affairs for vulgarity and just plain foolishness." Even the *Progressive*, a liberal magazine, permitted my old friend Harry Elmer Barnes to denounce me as a "renegade." "What Has Happened to You, Max?" was his title, and in the next issue I tried to tell him. But that millstone, Wendell Willkie, around my neck had drowned me. There was no use explaining.

I was resuscitated at last by my friend, the late Sol Levitas, editor of the *New Leader*, a "labor liberal" paper, once party socialist but now boasting its independence. Sol republished my essay with its original title—uncondensed, and unendorsed by Wendell Willkie.* To further rehabilitate me, he followed it in twelve subsequent issues with a series of essays by his most distinguished contributors, both socialist and nonsocialist, debating my thesis with respectful attention. So I had a place in my own world after all. I became a regular contributor to the *New Leader*, and on one occasion—with Stanley High to help me—I went out and raised thirty thousand dollars from wealthy philanthropists to help it out of a hole. It was the only weekly in the country, we pointed out to them, that was understandingly fighting the Communists.

As to those "nine articles on the Art of Life,"—that too is a story with consequences. It's the story of how the roan member of my troika tried hard but not successfully to run away with the whole gig. I was at the time very anxiously concerned with that economic third of my life problem. I had used up the eight thousand dollars advanced on my autobiography but had not finished the book. My political books, *Stalin's Russia* and *Marxism Is It Science*, were both against the current of opinion. Though a modest edition of each was ultimately sold, and *Stalin's Russia* was translated into three languages, my royalties did not greatly exceed the thousand dollars which had been

* My essay appeared, side-by-side with the portrait of my mother, in the *Reader's Digest* for June 1941. It was republished, in a divided form, in my *Reflections on the Failure of Socialism* (Devin Adair, 1955; in paperback, *The Universal Library*, Grosset & Dunlap, 1962).

advanced on each. I had either to find a steady source of income or face the miserable life-end of a professional lecturer. Thus I grabbed eagerly at the idea that I might contribute my thoughts on the Art of Life to the *Reader's Digest.* I would have to think the thoughts first, of course, but that seemed a small obstacle. Hadn't I, in fact, begun my literary career with essays on the art of life? They had been slightly imitative of Charles Lamb or Robert Louis Stevenson perhaps, but what difference would that make to a popular magazine?

The first one had been called "Mastication and Morality," but that, it seemed obvious now, was out-of-date. It belonged in the days of "Fletcherism," when all progressive parents were holding up as an example to their children the aged Prime Minister, William Ewart Gladstone, who kept his health and held the British Empire together by giving thirty-two chews to every bite of his breakfast, dinner, and supper.

There was another one called "On the Folly of Growing Up" that seemed less dated. In fact it turned out, on re-examination, to be a timeless little essay, playful yet with a rewarding underflow of truth. Unfortunately it had already been published, having been found in my attic desk by my mother and sent to her friend, the editor of the *Christian Register.* But that was in the spring of 1908, and the *Reader's Digest* was a reprint magazine anyway, so what did it matter?

In due course then, "The Folly of Growing Up" was disinterred, fixed up a little, and sent over to Pleasantville. It must have pleased somebody over there, for they did not send it right back. They called me over and told me it was a good idea, but couldn't I make it more practical?

"What is there in your conclusion that would be helpful to a kindergarten teacher, or a mother who is rearing a young child?"

I said that I thought something of a more practical nature might be worked into it, and took it home with a feeling of dismay. I knew that I couldn't make it practical. I couldn't write essays on the Art of Life for the *Reader's Digest.* Writing for the *Reader's Digest* is commercial journalism, the very thing I had so brashly distinguished from literary art in the little square book that Knopf had published twenty-five years before. Although dedicated to the *Masses* artists, who published their work without remuneration, *Journalism Versus Art* had not been a wildly utopian book. It acknowledged that journalism has brought some benefit to the literary tradition. "It has elevated lucidity and human interest to the high place of esteem where in a democratic society they belong. It has made the laborious task of imitating library echoes in order to get into the *Atlantic Monthly* unnecessary. It has rendered book-fed and literarious writers as obscure as they are tiresome. But it is not literature, it is business." And as a business, its motive is "to please as many readers as possible and to offend none."

That, I asserted, is what the editor is hired by the stockholders to do, and that is what the editor hires the writer to do. "And the writer cannot do that by allowing *himself* to flow into his pen, for then, though he will captivate those who like that kind of a self, he will offend those who do not. In order to please everybody and offend none he must eliminate all those warm and spontaneous impulses that are his very own, whatever they be."

To illustrate this, I cited the example of a distinguished cover artist who in a moment of abandon painted a girl with a puppy in her arms. The editor sent it back and asked him to change the puppy, because they had tried a puppy before, and found that their readers "didn't like to see a girl's affections wasted on an animal."

"This courteous consideration of editors for their readers' feelings," I remarked, "comes as near to Christian charity as anything we have."

That was the mood and general drift of my book, but I was seriously thoughtful about it. "The desire to support oneself, and if possible one's family," I noted, "is a civilized expression of that instinct of self-preservation which lies at the heart of all animal and vegetable life. And this desire is so fundamental, so strong, and so accustomed to bend all other passions, whims, caprices, energies and ideas, to its service, that when it is once aroused and functioning, nothing else in us can withstand it. A man is either living or earning his living. He is never doing these two things, purely, at once. And the literature we love is the literature whose motive is pure living."

That was an oversimplification, to be sure, but it expressed the ideal with which I started out as a literary artist, and I had stuck to it pretty faithfully. It did not quite gibe with writing essays on the Art of Life for the *Reader's Digest*, a magazine which, it seemed, had pleased more readers and offended fewer than any other publication ever created. I felt like stuffing "The Folly of Growing Up" back in the dusty box in my attic, and saying a grateful good-bye to the *Reader's Digest*. But I was intrigued by the experiment: I wondered how much of my real self would get lost in the course of it. So I carried my little essay home and went to work trying to make it practical. The humiliating truth is that I resubmitted it, and took it back again, three different times. Each time it got a little less like Charles Lamb, or Robert Louis Stevenson, or me, or anybody with a taste for whimsical literature. In the end it turned out to be a very sensible treatise on modern education. And even then, to my dismay—and also my immense relief—it was rejected.

Thus I had failed as a traitor to my ideal. I was driven back, rather ignominiously, into the temple of my own austere religion of Literary Art against Journalism. I began looking around for a nonwriting job again, or trying to think one up. It occurred to me that my good friends Simon & Schuster might use me as an editor or something. It was a far chance, but I went down to their sumptuous office one morning to make the proposal. I had hardly finished describing my plight when Max Schuster said: "Why don't you go up to see DeWitt Wallace on the *Reader's Digest?* He's all pepped up over the idea of sending out what he calls roving editors. I think that kind of a life would suit you fine."

I was then still in touch with DeWitt Wallace. Indeed I had a date for a luncheon with him and a selection of his editors—a kind of obsequy, I imagined, or post-mortem, on my little essay, to see if I could understand what, from their standpoint, was the matter with it. I thought I understood only too well, but during that luncheon Mr. Wallace said something that rather put my thoughts to shame.

"You write so beautifully," he said, "that I'm sure you can write for us."

In answer I said something like this: "If anyone writes beautifully, Mr. Wallace, it is because he is writing straight out of his own head and heart. You can't do it at the bidding of an editor, or a tableful of editors, no matter how charming they are and how much you enjoy lunching with them."

There was a pause after I said this, a smiling pause, during which I summoned the courage to bring forth an idea I had thought up as a result of my conversation with Max Schuster.

"I think perhaps there is one thing I could do that would be pleasing to you and at the same time spontaneous with me. I could write a whole series of articles like the one you liked about my mother. It might be called 'Men with Ideas.' I would pick out people who stand for something and go and get acquainted with them—not just interview them, but get to know each one well enough to write a biographical portrait—and then weave into it an exposition of the thing he stands for."

Wallace's answer came so fast, and with so little motion of his lips, that I could barely hear it.

"I agree to that, and I propose that you become a roving editor of the *Reader's Digest*. We will pay you a living wage, and we won't tell you whom to write about. You pick your own subjects, write as you please"—he paused—"and send us your expense account."

I don't know what I said—I think I merely gasped. When I came into our apartment after the trip home, Eliena said: "Max, what's the matter with you, you look pale?"

"I'm a roving editor of the *Reader's Digest!*" I answered, and dropped into a chair.

The "Men of Ideas" series was forgotten, but not the promise to let me choose my own subjects and treat them as I pleased. No task of writing was ever assigned to me, and no change ever made without my consent in what I wrote.

A roving editor, I must explain, is not an editor; he has nothing to do with the contents or policy of the magazine. He is a contributor on salary, a man actually paid money to roam the earth, and the libraries, and his mind if he has one, in search of exciting facts and bright ideas. It is journalism all right—a craft and not an art in the immaculate sense in which I had revered it. There were many million people to please, many million not to displease very much. Their time, besides, was limited; they could not linger in the magazine as in an art gallery. I learned this from an American engineer in Athens on one of my rovings; he was working on the new harbor at the Piraeus. Hearing of my connection with the *Reader's Digest*, he said:

"Your magazine is slipping. I wish you'd tell your editor that in my opinion he's slipping."

"Why? What's the matter with it?" I asked.

"He used to print nothing over two or three pages long—now some of 'em go up to four or even five! I can't take it. I haven't the time."

It was a new audience for me to be addressing—and yet not different, after all, from those who filled my lecture halls. My lecturing had been writing. Indeed I made over two of my lectures into articles for the *Reader's Digest*. So where was the shrine in which I kept this sacred art of writing? And just why had I tried to hold my art so priggishly high above the conditions in which most artists throughout history have done their work—Dickens and Dostoyevsky, for example, who wrote great novels not only for pay, but chapter by chapter against a deadline? Was it perhaps an *increased*, or *increasing*, pressure of commercial competition on the style and thinking of literary artists against which I was protesting?

I have, I must say, found signs of this pressure on my own style—though not, I hasten to say, on my thoughts—in some of the articles I have written for the *Reader's Digest*. When you are addressing many millions of readers, it is hard to stick by your own arrogant judgment as to how a thing ought, on eternal principles of symmetry and beauty, to be said. Instead of either art or journalism, I have thought of it as *teaching* when writing for these millions. I *am* a teacher and I love to teach. And like all teaching, my work for the *Reader's Digest* has involved the steadier joy of learning. A visit to Guatemala, described in "Report On Paradise"; a month's residence in Haiti, "Where None o' God's Children Got Shoes"; two weeks in Athens, discovering that "The Greeks Are Still Greek"; a studious long stay in Switzerland, "The Oasis of Europe"; another in Germany, another in Norway—these were not only jobs, but life-enhancing experiences. I added a whole semester to my education in making an abstract of Friedrich Hayek's *The Road to Serfdom*. And when, defying the war-mad infatuation with our "noble ally," DeWitt Wallace gave me seventeen pages at the front of his magazine for an article, "To Collaborate Successfully We Must Face the Facts About Russia," and the letters and clippings applauding and denouncing me came home in bushel baskets, I saw another aspect of this problem about popular journalism. I might be, from the standpoint of pure aesthetics a "demi-prostitute," as Cummings once laughingly called me, but there are other standpoints. There are other passions in a man's heart. I at least am not only an artist. And everything else that I am was royally glad to have my most specialized political knowledge and understanding unburied from the recondite pages of the *Modern Monthly*, and issued like a trumpet blast to millions of people.

Those were my thoughts, and those are my thoughts, about this still living question of Journalism versus Art.

Chapter 95

CONCLUDING TWO STORIES

A fascinating book could be written about the varying reactions of radical idealists to the collapse of their hope of an ideal society in Soviet Russia. Most of them had committed their hearts and life-interests to that hope more completely than I had. My vow of unconsecration in *Colors of Life* was a blessing to me now. So also was my "revolutionary revision" of Marxism, my conception of the revolution as a large-scale scientific experiment. I could acknowledge that the experiment had failed with a tranquillity of spirit unattainable to those more religiously committed. Moreover my own religion, if I possess anything that can be called by that name, is a dedication to truth-telling, to "living real," rather than to any specific creed or consolation. Thus I experienced an emotion not far from devoutness, at least a feeling of standing firm rather than of betrayal, in making statements about the failure of socialism which to my consecrated colleagues seemed both treacherous and tinged with blasphemy.

I was sustained, too, by the fact that I had made, however belatedly, a more thoroughgoing study of Marxism than was customary among American radicals. My attempt to create out of Marx's theories and Lenin's application of them, a "science of revolution" had been foolhardy and foolish. But it had led to a proof, which I still think conclusive, that the Marxian system as a whole, notwithstanding incidental contributions to science, is in the most technical sense a religion—a welding of Universal Being with the particular aims of the believer. It is a grandiose enterprise in wishful thinking—begun, continued, and guided at every critical point by the determination to defend a faith, not by an interest in factual understanding. A full realization and demonstration of this truth is the important result of the long political journey I have been describing. Until it is learned by the

Communists, we cannot reasonably hope for an end of the cold war. For a conviction that this religious mystique is the last word of science on human life and history is what upholds these otherwise educated men in their relentless assault on a comparatively free and civilized world.

The attempt to dissuade them on the ground that their Marxian religion ignores God, only strengthens their conviction, for science also ignores God. The attempt of "democratic socialists" to prove that genuine Marxism differs from their Leninist interpretation of it, is equally futile, for there is as much in the Marxian scripture to support Lenin as to support them. Indeed the sole indubitable big political difference between Marx and Lenin is that Lenin had a revolution to practice on and Marx had not. But that is unimportant. The important thing is that both were believers in a faith. And faiths, whether overtly supernatural or read into nature by politically motivated philosophers, are a final roadblock on the path to civilization. We have to cultivate in their place the mood of free inquiry and the praise of factual knowledge. We have to accept life as it is, and learn to live steadfastly and nobly, as Confucius did, and Mark Twain, and millions of other strong men, without the support of beliefs that are wishes.

With that I conclude the political story contained in this book.

To conclude the love story, I will have to skip over another whole epoch as epochs go by these days—a second World War, a string of smaller wars, a dozen or so revolutions, a plenty of personal entanglements— and tell you about the winter of 1956. We spent that winter, Eliena and I, at the Huntington Hartford Foundation in California. I had received, while on a "roving" expedition in Norway, a letter announcing that we had been awarded a six-months' residence at the Foundation, "in recognition of my contributions to creative art." I had never heard of the Huntington Hartford Foundation—nor indeed of my contributions to creative art—but it was a fine feeling to receive an award, something that hadn't happened to me since my graduation from college. We hesitated a little at the idea of dining like monks or convicts in a refectory or common dining room, but we accepted the invitation at least for the winter months of 1956. I went ahead by train, and Eliena followed with Peggy Duhrssen in a car, hastening rather madly so that we might be together on my birthday, which is January 4th. They arrived on the third, and we *were* together on my birthday, but in the excitement caused by the beauty of the place, and the joyous welcome extended to us by those "monks" or "convicts" we forgot all about it.

Two days passed before Eliena remembered to give me the present she had so punctually brought. That beauty of the place you can hardly imagine unless you have lived in a leafy and flowery, fragrantly sunny valley up in the mountainous approaches to the Swiss Alps. And the good-natured mirth and joviality of those breakfasts and dinners in the "refectory," I cannot myself imagine without Eliena's spontaneous radiations to relieve me of the timors and responsibilities of social intercourse. We had a cottage to ourselves with every convenience, not only for gracious living, but for painting and writing. (We couldn't buy a paint brush or a typewriter ribbon with our own money.) And we had as happy and fruitful a three months as I can remember in my life.

Early in April Eliena began to feel a mysterious discomfort in her abdomen and we went home to a physician friend in New York, who, finding signs of malignant tissue, recommended a hysterectomy. She entered a hospital with a view to that operation, but the surgeon, on exploring the region, found cancerous tissue already spreading throughout her body so far that there was no use performing the operation, no point of application for x-ray treatment, no faintest hope of recovery. She was dying in the same rapid way in which she had done everything else that was to be done. She would not have pain, the doctors said, but she would live at most only a few months.

They insisted that I must not tell her this truth. It seems to be almost an established part of the treatment of cancer to deceive the patient about his condition—and especially, perhaps *her* condition, as though women were less brave than men. I collaborated in the deception unhesitatingly until she recovered from the exploratory operation, but after that it became very difficult, and began to seem an indignity to a person who had faced life's traps and terrors with the gallantry that Eliena had. She had marched with her head high toward death by a firing squad—why must she be protected by a shield of delusion from the approach of this less violent death? Why should we not face the advancing tragedy together? Would she not rather have it so? Would she want me, whom she had trusted so absolutely for thirty-five years, to turn hypocrite and surround her with a web of diplomacy, a constancy of disingenuous precautions, a task of withholding my true self, for the last months of her life? One of the doctors, to whom I confided my misery of doubt, said:

"We were discussing the question at home this morning, and my wife said she would want to know."

That was a relief, and the opening of a door to me, for the insistence of those specialists that in loyalty to Eliena I must join them in deceiving her, had been hard to resist. I decided finally that after the opening of an exhibition of her paintings to be held in New York in June, I would tell her the truth.

I had feared that the knowledge of it might change her aspect or destroy her pleasure in the gathering of her friends and the connoisseurs and art critics, of whom there were many who admired her pictures. I was wrong about that. To judge by the result when I did tell her that she was dying, it would have made no vital difference at all. She was standing by her bedside, and had opened the way for me by remarking:

"I don't feel as though I were recovering very fast from that operation."

"Darling, you are not recovering," I said. "I must tell you the truth. You have a cancer and the doctors hold out very little hope for us."

I did not see the hint or flicker of a change in her attitude or expression. I never from that day to the day of her death saw a look of dismay or woefulness cross her features. She merely said, as though satisfying an objective curiosity:

"Then they didn't perform the operation at all, did they?"

She took an earnest though not anxious interest in my frantic efforts to find a quack, or some self-deceiving expert, who would offer a remedy or hold out some promise. But she was ready to abandon, sooner than I was, that futile search. She asked only to go back to our home on the hilltop in Martha's Vineyard and die in the sunshine by the sea.

And in that place, out of some deep well of resolution in her heart, there poured up a feeling of elation—a feeling, perhaps, like that of a warrior winning his last battle. Late in September, two or three weeks before she died, she said to me—she said also to our neighbor, Virginia Berresford:

"These two months have been among the happiest in my life."

After she died, while I was groping toward the day when she would become a sustaining memory instead of an unbearable absence, I wrote two brief notes about our last days and hours. Like a number of things in this book, they were written only for my own reading. But now that Eliena has grown into a kind of hero of the latter parts of this book—for the word "heroine" hasn't enough valor in it—I feel that they belong here. It belongs here to say that she died as she had lived, glad of every day that remained, glad to have lived and not asking the consolation of any faith.

I. *Remembered from the Last Days*

Virginia says she was "amazed" at Eliena's statement about her happiness in the two last months, and I cannot pretend to explain it. We had given the little study over the hill to her very dear friend, Tom Filer, her "godson" as she called him. Our beloved Eula came from Ossining to cook and care for us and sit at the table with us. Our hilltop house was, as Cummings long ago called it, "a dwelling place of love." The dining table is in the large living room, and so now was her bed—over by the window looking across the lagoon to the Quitsa hills and the ocean beyond them. She could hear and enjoy our conversation even after she did not get up and come to the table. She could watch her adored little birds eating seeds and grain from the fountainlike platter we had prepared for them on the lawn. And I loved her as I had never loved before in my life. Her upholding to the very last moment, with death advancing, of that gay, laughter-loving zest for life which I adored, was truly, as the neighbors and visiting friends all said, heroic.

Katharine Cornell drove up from Tashmoo every day or two—"not for her sake," she told me, "but for what she gives me." Strong-hearted Dr. Nevin asked me if she believed in a future life, and when I said, "No," he murmured: "In all my practice I have never seen anything like it," and added, after a pause: "I love her—as a doctor may love his patient."

Something descended into me during those last months more good and generous than I am. Besides the lesser ways of loving, I loved her like a mother. From the day we came back from New York she could never get any food past her stomach. She was kept alive by intravenous injections, and she had to vomit from twelve to fourteen times a day the secretions that came into her stomach, or any tiny bits of food she ate to keep us company or satisfy a habit of hunger. We had only the one nurse, "Turk" Kingsbury—a congenial and most admirable person—and though Turk slept in the study just the other side of an open door from Eliena, she was not awakened by her retching. She awoke only when her name was called. But I, although I slept down the little hall with a door closed between us, awoke at the first sound as a mother does at the cry of her baby. Always, two or three, and sometimes four times in the night I would jump up and go in to help

Eliena, or at least be with her, during that distressing process, and empty the little pan she kept by her bed. To enable me to go to sleep again after these heart-breaking moments, I had to take sleeping powders every night, but they never slowed my reaction to the sound of her need. What astonishes me about this, and would astonish anybody who knows me, is that I did it without any resolution—without any effort over myself at all. I wanted to do it. This is what makes me dare to speak of a mother's love. Eliena said to me: "In these two months you have repaid all that I ever did for you."

But I am not sure that all these external things together account for that amazing happiness she spoke of. Toward the end of that period, she was having occasional shots of pantapon—a preparation of morphine. I suppose it is a privilege to take habit-forming drugs when the fear of a life habit is past. But that again is far from an explanation of what she said about those two months. I think the explanation lay within, in the unshakable force of her character. She believed in life; she loved it; she accepted the terms of it. And she had a power over herself that I have never seen equalled. She *decided* to live those months zestfully and without thought of the advancing shadow—above all without making them gloomy for me—and she did it right up to the end.

II. *The Last Hours*

The nurse was having her afternoon off and I sat with Eliena alone during her last hours of life. She felt more than the usual discomfort from the pressure under her stomach and I gave her an extra injection of pantapon and moved her to a chair nearer the window. I read to her from Rewald's *Post-Impressionism* the stories about Gauguin and Vincent Van Gogh. She sat forward in the chair, leaning to her right, and with her eyes closed all the time. When I commented on something I had read, she was not always quite clear what it had been, and I would tell it over again. Still she was listening, and said once that she knew certain pictures that I was reading about. Her face was terribly thin and haggard, but when I asked her how she was feeling, she looked up at me bright-eyed, smiled her unfailing but now imperfect smile, and said, "Fine!"

She knew that her death was approaching, for when Tom came in at dinnertime, she made some mischievous allusion to the latest of a series of vast boxes of flowers which had come from Morrice, the florist in Vineyard Haven. "Morrice himself should send us the final bunch free of charge," she said. It was Tuesday and Estlin and Marion Cummings, whom she loved dearly, had promised to come from New Hampshire on Saturday. On Monday she had still hoped to see them. "I think we must end this soon," she had said to me, "I am getting to be such a bother to you and Turk. But I do want to wait long enough to see the Cummings." But now, in the same hour that she was opening her eyes to give me that brave smile and saying, "Fine!" she murmured to Tom: "I guess I won't wait for the Cummings after all."

After dinner Tom drove down to Vineyard Haven to get the nurse, and I continued my reading. I helped her change her position once, just arranging a small towel that she had folded in a certain place behind her. She seemed to be listening a little more vividly and I felt more sure that we were together. Turk, the nurse, came in at about half-past nine with Tom and she greeted them gaily—a wonderful nurse and a most wonderful friend.

Was she ready for bed? the nurse asked, and she said yes. As the nurse slipped into the big bedroom to make some preparation, I got up and stood for a moment. I leaned down with my arm around Eliena and my lips against her cheek. "I love you so very much," I murmured, and she answered, "I am so very glad you do."

The nurse came back and I went to my own little "cubicle" opposite the bathroom to undress. I heard the nurse bringing her with those slow heavy steps to the bathroom. I heard her say just as she crossed the doorsill, "I feel very tired." Then the nurse called sharply, "Max! Max!" Eliena's swollen legs had collapsed, but I reached her in time to take her torso in my arms and help lower her to the floor. "Darling! Darling!" I cried, looking into her eyes. But there was no sight in them. She gasped for breath at irregular intervals for about two minutes, but the sight never came back into her eyes.

During the last weeks, sitting up in bed, Eliena wrote a letter of farewell to her fellow citizens of the little town of Gay Head, whose children she had taught to dance. Henry Hough published it in his paper, the *Vineyard Gazette*, after she died.

Once more I want to say a word of greeting and of best wishes to my dear friends and fellow-citizens of Gay Head—those whom I have known personally and those whom I knew only by sight. We have shared for fifteen years so many activities, so many gay or disastrous events: the war, the hurricanes, fires, weddings, wedding anniversaries, voting, square-dances (with Adrian calling), red-brown cranberry days, exhilarating mornings scalloping on the pond, and above all the happy hours you let me spend with your children dancing in the town hall.

It moved me deeply today to learn from Amos of your concern about me, which means that you accept me as part of your lives. I have felt happy and at peace ever since Max agreed that East Pasture is to be the place of my rest, and that he is not going to leave me and our home here. Now I can feel that I am just stepping aside on the shore, joining the others that landed ahead of me —dear Betty Ryan, and friendly Linus, and Vi, and gay and vibrant Adrian, his lovely wife, and the others we remember—to watch you go scalloping in the winter on a bright sunny day.

Another reason your concern makes me happy is that it tells me I am leaving Max among friends. Perhaps you and he, with the help of a few hurricanes, will be able to stave off the onrush of "progress" and preserve some of the simple and quiet beauty of this legendary land. I hope so.

And now my love to you all and good luck,

September, 1956

INDEX

ABOUT THE AUTHOR

MAX EASTMAN, whose mother and father were both Christian ministers, was born in Canandaigua, New York. He attended the Mercersburg Academy and Williams College, and taught logic and philosophy for four years at Columbia University.

His first book, Enjoyment of Poetry, *is generally regarded as a classic. In the year of its publication, 1913, Mr. Eastman became a socialist editor, and the tumultuous career of the two magazines he edited, the* Masses *and the* Liberator, *forms the core of the early chapters of* LOVE AND REVOLUTION. *He went to Russia in 1922, learned the language, and although not a Marxist, became personally involved in the feuds and disputations among the Bolshevik leaders following the death of Lenin. He is the author of six books dealing with Marxism and the development of the revolution in Russia. He has also published a novel, five volumes of poetry, studies of the psychology of literary art and humor,* Enjoyment of Laughter, *a bestseller, and in 1948* Enjoyment of Living. *Mr. Eastman is as well known for his oratorical as his literary gifts, and has lectured throughout the country on the subjects treated of in his books.*